the new

joys

of

yiddish

Revisions and Commentary by

Lawrence Bush

Illustrations by

R. O. Blechman

the new joys of yiddish

Completely Updated

LEO ROSTEN

ARROW

SHLEP

Published by Arrow Books in 2003

1 3 5 7 9 10 8 6 4 2

Copyright © 2001 by The Rosten Family LLC

The right of Leo Rosten to be identified as the author of this work has been
asserted under the Copyright, Designs and Patents Act, 1988

This revised edition first published in
the United Kingdom in 2003 by Arrow Books
Originally published by McGraw-Hill, Inc. in 1968. Copyright © 1968
and renewed 1996 by Leo Rosten

Arrow Books
The Random House Group Limited
20 Vauxhall Bridge Road, London SW1V 2SA

Random House Australia (Pty) Limited
20 Alfred Street, Milsons Point, Sydney,
New South Wales 2061, Australia

Random House New Zealand Limited
18 Poland Road, Glenfield,
Auckland 10, New Zealand

Random House (Pty) Limted
Endulini, 5A Jubilee Road, Parktown 2193, South Africa

The Random House Group Limited Reg. No. 954009

www.randomhouse.co.uk

A CIP catalogue record for this book is available from the British Library

Papers used by Random House are natural, recyclable products
made from wood grown in sustainable forests. The manufacturing processes
conform to the environmental regulations of the country of origin

ISBN 0 09 944694 4

Typeset by SX Composing DTP, Rayleigh, Essex
Printed and bound in Great Britain by
Cox & Wyman, Reading, Berkshire

contents

introduction

"Oy, a lebn af dayn kop!" "Life on your head!" This was my grandmother's favorite Yiddish blessing, which she showered on me whenever I did something appealing. A smile, a nod, an intelligent word—it didn't take much to earn "life on my head," neither as a boy nor as a grown man.

"Bobby," as we called her (a childish corruption of *bobe*, "grandmother"), lived to be ninety-seven and to embrace her great-grandchildren. They, too, experienced Yiddish as a kiss on the brow. The real vitality of the language, however—its laughter, its anger, its insurgent brilliance, its gummy accent—could not and would not be a part of my kids' future without Leo Rosten's *The Joys of Yiddish.*

True, Bobby's *mameloshn* (mother tongue) has echoes all over the place: in college classrooms, on the Internet, on the theater and concert stage, at festivals and retreats. Still, the generations for whom Yiddish was a voice and not an echo are going if not gone, and the generation gap created by the Nazis' crematoria has proved unbridgeable. As a result, Yiddish has just one viable survival strategy—and Leo Rosten is its champion.

Rosten recognized that *Yiddishkayt,* the pathways and spirit of the language, was finding a new homeland in American culture. Unlike many Yiddish scholars, he delighted in this fact and treasured every Yiddish word or phrase, intonation or sentence structure, that had entered into English usage. Each, to his mind, was a "carrier" of the complete genetic code of Yiddish. In writing *The Joys of Yiddish,* Rosten was mapping the Yiddish genome.

The map was incomplete, of course. Rosten left out the double helix of modern Yiddish literature and poetry. He avoided the recombinant material of Yiddish political rhetoric and social criticism. He ignored most of the non-American strains of Yiddish culture. He chose humor, anecdote, and breezy erudition as his best tools because, as he wrote in his preface, "a good story is exceedingly hard for anyone to forget." As a result, certain more sober Yiddishists were unhappy that Rosten, the *kibitzer*, won the commercial "patent" on Yiddish through the success of *Joys*. (A punch line from one of his many jokes might serve to express their attitude: "Eh! If I had his voice, I'd sing just as good!")

Patents do need periodic renewing, however. American life and Jewish life worldwide have all undergone tremendous transformations in the thirty-plus years since *The Joys of Yiddish* was published. My task has been to reflect some of these changes through a concise commentary on Rosten's text. For example:

*   When Rosten wrote, no women had been ordained as rabbis, nor had the nascent women's movement affected the organizational culture, ritual practice, or liturgy of the Jewish community. Today, women's representation—the adult *bas mitzva*, the creation of egalitarian prayer language, female inclusion in the *minyan*, the cantorate, the rabbinate—is probably the most dynamic force in American Jewish life.

*   When Rosten wrote, Israel was united by the victory of the Six-Day War, and Jewish identity was stirring to life worldwide, even in the heavily repressed Soviet Union. Today, Israel is divided by religious and political conflict, the Soviet Union is a memory, and nearly 20 percent of Israel's population consists of recent Russian immigrants.

* When Rosten wrote, Reform and even Conservative Judaism were widely satirized as "watered down" versions of Judaism. Today, the Reform and Conservative denominations are flush with spiritual renewal and a return to tradition, and a fourth denomination, Reconstructionism, has grown to one hundred congregations.

* When Rosten wrote, *cabala* and Jewish mysticism were the exclusive provinces of Chasidic sects and Jewish historians. Today, Jewish mystical traditions have made a major comeback, riding the wave of "spirituality" that has drenched the baby boom generation and its younger siblings.

* When Rosten wrote, Jewish identity suffered from boredom, ennui, the attractions of assimilation, and the repressed memory of the Holocaust. Today, a renaissance in Jewish literacy, text interpretation, ritual innovation, creative arts, and Holocaust commemoration has fostered a revitalization—and reinvention—of Jewish identity.

* When Rosten wrote, the final barriers to Jewish entry into the American mainstream—and America's most elite circles— were eroding, largely as a result of the civil rights movement. Today, that entry is so complete that some 50 percent of Jews are intermarrying, and Jews are self-conscious about being overrepresented in *Forbes* magazine's annual listing of the wealthiest Americans.

One other change has informed my work and leaves me in a state of apprehension. (*Dem Yidns simkhe,* says one Yiddish proverb, *iz mit a bisl shrek:* A Jew's joy comes with a little fear.) When Rosten wrote, the amount of Jewish information available in English to a general readership was fairly skimpy. Today, there is as much free-floating Jewish knowledge between book covers and on the Internet as you could want—which will make my errors, and especially my omissions, seem all the more blatant. Hopefully, I have enough of my *bobe*'s easy blessings stockpiled to endure the embarrassment, and enough scholarly sensibility to want my mistakes consigned to oblivion rather than made authoritative by the reputation of Rosten's book.

Very special thanks go to Gerald (Yankl) Stillman, upon whom I have relied heavily for commentary on Yiddish usage and derivations. I also would like to thank Madeline Lee and Margaret Muir, Leo Rosten's daughters, for entrusting me with their father's legacy.

The former president of the Reform synagogue movement, Rabbi Alexander M. Schindler, with whom I collaborated closely for the past sixteen years, died during the months when I was working on *The Joys of Yiddish*, and I would like to dedicate my portion of the book to his memory. Alex was the son of a Yiddish poet and led a life woven from incredibly diverse strands of Jewish experience. In *Gan Eden*, he and Leo Rosten are no doubt surrounded by the same flock of angels, eager for a tasty story.

—Lawrence Bush
Accord, New York

preface to the
british edition

At the end of the nineteenth century a wave of immigrants poured
out of Eastern Europe, fleeing its prejudice and poverty and making for the Statue of Liberty, and a better and freer life for themselves and, more importantly, for their children. ("Mummy,
mummy, I don't want to immigrate to America," cries a little
child. "Quiet, darling," says its mother compassionately. "Reserve
your energy. Just keep on swimming!") There were Poles and
White Russians and Lithuanians and Ukrainians and especially
there were Jews. After all, the words on that Statue, welcoming the
huddled masses longing to be free, were written by the Jewess
Emma Lazarus.

My grandparents who brought me up were just two droplets
in that wave. Not all of them made it. Some were tragically turned
back at Ellis Island and some, like my grandparents, only made it
half-way and settled near the London docks in England. Which is
why my childhood memories are in Yinglish, not Ameridish.
(Consult *New Joys* for the differences.)

The linguistic acrobatics of my grandparents perplexed me.
They addressed the Almighty formally in stately Hebrew. (Like the
way we would have addressed kings and queens and one-time
emperors if they had dropped in for a slice of Bubbe's strudel.)
Zayde could put on a wonderful turn of speed in Aramaic as well as
Hebrew. ("But did he understand it, I ask you?" "Don't ask!") They
swore in Slav. I once recited what I remembered to a Slav professor
at a conference. I promised him never to say such things again.
To our non-Jewish neighbours and friends, my grandparents

communicated in Yiddish-cockney. They tried to dance the Lambeth Walk, to strut "dahn the Old Kent Road" and sing out "'Ave a banana!"

But for their deepest feelings about love and life and why God let the righteous suffer and the wicked prosper they spoke the Yiddish of the little villages they had left, their *Heym*. They made love in it, they argued in it, they gossiped in it, they sang in it, they saw Shakespeare in it (even *The Merchant of Venice*). It was their *Mameloshn*, their mother tongue.

My parents didn't want me to learn it. I was the only grandchild and it was my duty to get them all out of London's poor Jewish East End and on to the refined heights of Hampstead and Highgate where Yiddishkeit gave way to Englishkeit. But I did learn it, though patchily, and even now though I think in English I feel in Yiddish and when relaxed revert to Yinglish.

Now, my grandparents were poor as I have said. Grandpa was a cobbler and he was bombed out three times during the London Blitz. So my inheritance was only a few photos and language. But that language was the door to a world, of piety and patience, of heartbreaking songs and some very irreverent ones too. Through it I returned to a *heym* I had never known.

"*Heym!* Home!" – a distinction without a difference, you might say. After all, the words are the same. *The New Joys of Yiddish* is a dictionary, you might say, but it isn't; it's much more. There's so much generosity, so much knowledge of what it is to be human, and even knowledge and pity of what it must be like to be God, in those Yiddish words that, as well as being among the most curious (and scholarly) of dictionaries, it is also

- a book of spirituality
- a therapy to help you smile through life's tears
- a comforter during the dark hours of the night

- a *heym* which is open to you when you are a long way from home
- the best introduction to the *comedie humaine*
- a book which helps you grow up and mature
- a book which teaches you kindness and mercy and what it is like to be at the other end of the stick
- a work of scholarship that wears its scholarship so lightly, you are not aware of what a profound education you receive as you browse through the stories and usages of those Yiddish words
- a way to recover your Jewish roots if you are Jewish and to feel yourself Jewish if you are not.

Now, my old copies of *The Joys of Yiddish* needed replacement. And *The New Joys of Yiddish* has just come in time. The old pages were dog-eared with over-use and stained with strudel and chicken soup. The covers had long disappeared. What New Joys could be added to something so complete? Well, one very important addition is the inclusion of English Yiddish which is subtly different from American Yiddish. East London is not just a colony or an extension of the East Side. Other very important additions are the user-friendly footnotes which help me to understand my cousins, the Jews of America, and also our Jewish past.

These footnotes also help me to understand the non-Jewish as well as the Jewish present in which most of me lives. That's because Yiddish adapts naturally to the cultures in which it settles. In Britain it was as much concerned with class as with wealth. After all, we had our aristocratic Rothschilds who were genuine Lords and Ladies, and the compliment I most remember from my childhood was the word "*Eydl*" which meant ladylike, gentlemanly, genteel, classy. My Bubbe was certainly *Eydl*. My Zayde could be too, but the pub he caroused in was definitely not. I looked up "*Eydl*" in *New Joys* and, lo, there was my sermon for the coming week. "Such *eydlkayt!*" people said. And yet a saying goes: "Too humble is too proud." How true! Not many dictionaries suggest your sermons to you.

On the other hand, I discovered the meanings of Yiddish words I never knew or wasn't allowed to know, like "*Tsatske*" – "a sexy, but brainless broad". We didn't even know what a "broad" meant. You had to go to New York for that.

Over the years, Yiddish gently flowed into the mainstream of English for Jew and non-Jew alike. "*Chutzpah*" was recognized by the august BBC. It was too good to leave out "being the quality enshrined in a man who, having killed his mother and father, throws himself on the mercy of the court because he is an orphan." *New Joys* also told me it had crossed the Channel, too, and was now ensconced in Paris!

Britain, or the U.K. or G.B. or whatever you like to call it, has never been a one-language country. Besides English there were Irish, Welsh, Gaelic, Cornish and Manx. This is in addition to the new immigrant languages such as Hindi, Urdu, Swahili and Cantonese, and there had been a revival in all of them. I was steered away from Yiddish as a child as I have said, but now it is the height of London chic to take lessons in it and speak it correctly, whatever that may mean. Bubbe would have laughed till her belly shook (like Sarah in the Bible) to peep into seminars of scholars and eydl upper-classniks conscientiously learning regular and irregular verbs in Mameloshn.

Jewish people have never tried to keep this treasure of a language to themselves. I remember in my childhood a cockney drayman who picked it up and even taught his beloved horses commands in Yiddish, such as "Geh!" and "Steh!", so that the Jewish children, who had been told stories of horses running down their parents in eastern Europe, should get to love them like him. On the other end of the social scale, at a royal lunch in a royal palace, a royal highness over a pre-prandial drink told me Yiddish jokes with a fair accent. The compassion and realism of Yiddish has also permeated the humour of our comedians, without the Yiddish vocabulary but with its spirit. In vicarages I have been told to "live till a hundred and twenty," that "I should live so long," that "genug is genug" and how to answer a question with another question.

After I wrote this heartfelt appreciation of *The New Joys of Yiddish*, I had to travel up to a college in and old and distinguished university, where I was giving seminars on Jewish literature and Jewish life. Both need explaining in these tense times.

I gave my students this guidance. "Get *The New Joys of Yiddish!*" I told them. "Keep it by your bed as well as on your desk and whenever you feel puzzled or upset by life pick it up and turn to any page. As you wander through it (reading it is addictive) then you will understand the Jewish life I was born into. There are more notes and more information than in the older editions, and the scholarship is so user-friendly you digest and learn without realizing how much you are absorbing. If you start to use it as I think you will, you will become part of the inner life of what you are studying. You will experience it. This is more than most other textbooks will ever give you."

Thank you once again, Leo Rosten. May your work be for a blessing!

—Rabbi Lionel Blue, London January 2003

preface

I wrote this book because there was no other way in which I could have it. For many years I had craved and sought and failed to find a lexicon of just this type.

What This Book Is Not

This is not a book about Yiddish. It is not a dictionary of Yiddish. It is not a guide to Yiddish. It is not written for experts in, or students of, Yiddish.

What This Book Is

This is a book about language—more particularly, the English language. It shows how our marvelously resilient tongue has been influenced by another parlance: Yiddish. It illustrates how beautifully a language reflects the variety and vitality of life itself; and how the special culture of the Jews, their distinctive style of thought, their subtleties of feeling, are reflected in Yiddish; and how this in turn has enhanced and enriched the English we use today.

So, this book explores a fascinating aspect of English: those words and phrases from Yiddish (some I call "Yinglish," some "Ameridish") that we today encounter in English books, magazines, newspapers; or hear on television or radio, in movies or nightclubs; or may overhear on the street or in a bus in many a large city in the United States.

By "Yinglish" I mean Yiddish words that are used in colloquial

English in both the United States and the United Kingdom: *kibitzer, mish-mash, bagel,* etc.

By "Ameridish" I mean words coined by, and indigenous to, Jews in the United States: *kochaleyn, utz, shmegegge,* etc.*

"Yiddish," "Hebrew," and "Jewish"

For the benefit of innocents, I hasten to add that Yiddish and Hebrew are entirely different languages. A knowledge of one will not give you even a rudimentary understanding of the other. True, Yiddish uses the letters of the Hebrew alphabet, employs a great many Hebrew words, and is written, like Hebrew, from right to left, thusly:

UOY EVOL I ACIREMA

—which should delight any reader under fourteen. But Yiddish and Hebrew are as different from each other as are English and French, which also use a common alphabet, share many words, and together proceed from left to right.

Nor is "Yiddish" a synonym for "Jewish." "Yiddish" is the name of a language. Technically speaking, there is no language called "Jewish." Jews do not speak "Jewish" any more than Canadians speak Canadian or Baptists read Baptist. But it would be foolish to deny that in popular English usage, "Jewish" is used as a

---

*Rosten also classifies as "Yinglish" words that are hybrid English-Yiddish contractions: *opstairsikeh* (upstairs neighbor), *singlemon* (bachelor), etc. These were used almost exclusively by Yiddish-speaking immigrants and their children and cannot really be said to have entered colloquial English. In such cases, the distinction between Yinglish and Ameridish can get fuzzy. In this edition, words with obvious English roots and Yiddish suffixes are generally classified as Yinglish; more "pure"-sounding Yiddish words that are nevertheless American Jewish inventions or adaptations are generally classified as Ameridish.

synonym for "Yiddish." After all, "Yiddish" comes from the German *Jüdisch,* meaning "Jewish," and in the Yiddish language itself *Yiddish* means "Jewish." We may as well accept reality.

The Scope of This Wordbook

This book, accordingly, is a lexicon of certain foreign-born words that

1. are already part of everyday English (*shmaltz, ganef, shlemiel*);
2. are rapidly becoming part of English (*chutzpa, megillah, shlep, yenta*);
3. should be part of our noble language, in my opinion, because no English words so exactly, subtly, pungently, or picturesquely convey their meaning (*shmooz, kvetch, shlimazl, tsatske,* etc.).

Were I writing all this in the style and with the impudent imagery so characteristic of Jewish humor, I would say: "This book is a collection of three kinds of simply *delicious* words: those that are naturalized citizens; those that have taken out their first papers; and those that should be drafted into our army just as soon as possible."

The Influence of Yiddish on English

It is a remarkable fact that never in its history has Yiddish been so influential—among Gentiles. (Among Jews, alas, the tongue is running dry.)* We are clearly witnessing a revolution in values

---

*Evidence of Yiddish's tenacity and small revival—in universities, theaters, on the concert stage, on the Internet, and in the state of Israel (where the language has long been shunned and neglected)—is scattered throughout my notes.

when a Pentagon officer, describing the air bombardment pattern used around Haiphong,* informs the press: "You might call it the bagel strategy" (*Newsweek*, Sept. 25, 1967). Or when the London *Economist* describes a fuss over mortgage rates as "Home Loan Hoo-ha" (Nov. 19, 1966). Or when *The Wall Street Journal* headlines a feature on student movements REVOLUTION, SHMEVOLUTION (Jan. 12, 1968). Or when England's illustrious *Times Literary Supplement*, discussing the modern novel, interjects this startling sentence: "Should, schmould, shouldn't, schmouldn't" (Feb. 3, 1966). Or when a musical play about the Jews in the Polish *shtetl* of fifty years ago, *Fiddler on the Roof*, scores so phenomenal a success.†

Yiddish phrasing and overtones are found in, say, the way an Irish whiskey advertises itself:

> Scotch is a fine beverage and deserves its popularity.
> But enough is enough already.

Or in an advertisement for a satirical English movie, *Agent 8 ¾*:

> By Papa he's a spy,
> By Mama he's a spy,

---

*Haiphong was a port city in North Vietnam that was damaged extensively by U.S. bombings during the Vietnam War.

† More contemporary, and equally telling, was President Jimmy Carter's citing of "an old Yiddish proverb" during his 1980 concession speech after losing the presidential election to Ronald Reagan: "God gives burdens," said Carter, "also shoulders." A born-again Christian who spoke openly about his religious commitments, Carter was at first distrusted by the Jewish community but proved a very staunch ally, particularly in his establishment of the President's Commission on the Holocaust (which led to the building of the U.S. Holocaust Memorial Museum on the Washington Mall) and his negotiating of the 1978 Camp David peace agreement between Israel and Egypt.

But from spies he's no spy!

(This ploy of deflation originally involved the playwright Samson Raphaelson and his mother. Mr. Raphaelson, having scored a considerable success on Broadway and in Hollywood, bought himself a yacht—and a nautical cap, on which "Captain" was embroidered. Old Mrs. Raphaelson studied the cap on her proud son's head and won immortality by saying, "By you you're a captain, and by me you're a captain, but tell me, Sammy, by a *captain* are you a captain?")

I can cite dozens of similar uses of Yiddish or Yinglish idiom.

Yiddish Words and Phrases in English

Every so often I run across the statement that *Webster's Unabridged Dictionary* contains five hundred Yiddish words. I do not know if this is true, and I certainly doubt that anyone actually counted them. For my part, I am surprised by the number of Yiddish words, thriving beautifully in everyday English, that are *not* in *Webster's*, or in other dictionaries of the English language—including the incomparable *Oxford English Dictionary*. You will find many of these lamentably unrecognized words in the volume you now hold in your hands.

Many a scholar has commented on the growing number of Yiddish words and idioms that "invade" English. But English, far from being a supine language, has zestfully borrowed a marvelous gallimaufry of foreign locutions, including many from Yiddish; and who will deny that such brigandage has vastly enriched our cherished tongue? (I have elsewhere pointed out [in *Look* magazine, December 26, 1967] that a sentence like "The pistol in our bungalow is stuffed with taffy" contains words from six languages [Slovak, Czech, Hindustani, Tagalog, Old French, English—via Old Frisian] and that an utterance such as "Oh, bosh! Some nitwit has put alcohol in the ketchup!" entails the uncopyrighted use of Turkish, Dutch, Arabic, French, Malay, Chinese, and pidgin Japanese.)

Take the popular usage of the suffix -*nik*, to convert a word into a label for an ardent practitioner or devotee of something: How could we manage without such priceless coinages as *beatnik* and *peacenik*? *The New York Times* recently dubbed Johann Sebastian's acolytes "Bachniks"; some homosexuals dismiss nonhomosexuals as "straightniks"; the comic strip *Mary Worth* has employed *no-goodnik*; and a *Times* advertisement even employed Yiddish-in-tandem to urge, NOSHNIKS OF THE WORLD, UNITE!

Many a student of contemporary mores has discovered the degree to which novelists, playwrights, joke writers, and comedians have poured Jewish wit and humor into the great, flowing river of English. This is also an indication of the extraordinary role of Jewish intellectuals, and their remarkable increase during the past forty years, in the United States and England.

Who has not heard or used phrases such as the following, which, whatever their origin, probably owe their presence in English to Jewish influence?

Get lost.	How come only five?
You should live so long.	Do him something.
My son, the physicist.	*This* I need yet?
I need it like a hole in the head.	A person could bust.
Who *needs* it?	He's a regular genius.
So why do you?	Go hit your head against the wall.
All *right* already.	You want it should sing, too?
It shouldn't happen to a dog.	Plain talk: He's crazy.
Okay by me.	Excuse the expression.
He knows from nothing.	With sense, he's loaded.
From that he makes a *living*?	Go fight City Hall.

I should have such luck.	On him it looks good.
It's a nothing of a dress.	It's time, it's time.
You should live to be a hundred and twenty.	Wear it in good health. Listen, *bubele* . . .

What other language is fraught with such exuberant fraughtage?

Colloquial Uses in English of Yiddish Linguistic Devices

But words and phrases are not the chief "invasionary" forces Yiddish has sent into the hallowed terrain of English. Much more significant, I think, is the adoption by English of linguistic *devices*, Yiddish in origin, to convey nuances of affection, compassion, displeasure, emphasis, disbelief, skepticism, ridicule, sarcasm, scorn. Examples abound:

1. Blithe dismissal via repetition with a *sh* play on the first sound: "Fat-shmat, as long as she's happy." (This is somewhat similar to the English "teeny-weeny," "razzle-dazzle," etc. This device is called, technically, "second-order reduplication.")
2. Mordant syntax: "Smart, he isn't."
3. Sarcasm via innocuous diction: "He only tried to shoot himself."
4. Scorn through reversed word order: "Already you're discouraged?"
5. Contempt via affirmation: "My *son*-in-law he wants to be."
6. Fearful curses sanctioned by nominal cancellation: "A fire should burn in his heart, God forbid!"
7. Politeness expedited by truncated verbs and eliminated prepositions: "You want a cup coffee?"

8. Derisive dismissal disguised as innocent interrogation: "I should pay him for such devoted service?"

9. The use of a question to answer a question to which the answer is so self-evident that the use of the first question (by you) constitutes an affront (to me) best erased either by a) repeating the original question, or b) retorting with a question of comparably asinine self-answeringness. Thus:

[A]

Q: "Did you write your mother?"

A: "Did I write my mother!" (Scornful, for "Of course I did!")

[B]

Q: "Have you visited your father in the hospital?"

A: "Have I visited my father in the *hospital?*" (Indignant, for "What kind of a monster do you think I am?")

[C]

Q: "Would you like some chicken soup?"

A: "Would I like some *chicken* soup?" (Emphatically concurring, for "What a stupid thing to ask.")

[D]

Q: "Will a hundred dollars be enough?"

A: "Will a hundred dollars be *enough?*" (Incredulously offended, for "Do you think I'm crazy enough to accept so ridiculous a sum?")

[E]

Q: "Will a thousand dollars be enough?"

A: "Will a *thousand* dollars be enough?" (Incredulously delighted, for "Man, will it!")

[F]

Q: "Will you marry me?"

A: "Will I *marry* you?" (On a note of overdue triumph, for "Yes, yes, right away!")

Or consider the growing effect on English of those exquisite shadings of meaning, and those priceless nuances of contempt, that are achieved in Yiddish simply by shifting the stress in a sentence from one word to another. "Him you *trust?*" is entirely different, and worlds removed, from "*Him* you trust?" The first merely questions your judgment; the second vilipends the character of the scoundrel anyone must be an idiot to repose faith in.

Or consider the Ashkenazic panoply in which insult and innuendo may be arrayed. Problem: Whether to attend a concert to be given by a neighbor, niece, or friend of your spouse. The same sentence may be put through maneuvers of matchless versatility:

1. "*Two* tickets for her concert I should buy?" (Meaning: "I'm having enough trouble deciding if it's worth one.")
2. "Two *tickets* for her concert I should buy?" ("You mean to say she isn't distributing free passes? The hall will be empty!")
3. "Two tickets for *her* concert I should buy?" ("Did she buy tickets to my daughter's recital?")
4. "Two tickets for her *concert* I should buy?" ("You mean to say they call what she does a 'concert'?!")
5. "Two tickets for her concert *I* should buy?" ("After what she did to me?")
6. "Two tickets for her concert I *should* buy?" ("Are you giving me lessons in ethics?")
7. "Two tickets for her concert I should *buy?*" ("I wouldn't go even if she gave me a complimentary!")

Each of the above formulations suggests a different prior history, offers the speaker a different catharsis, and lets fly different arrows of contumely. And if all emphasis is removed from the sentence, which is then uttered with mock neutrality, the very unstressed-ness becomes sardonic, and—if accompanied by a sigh, snort, cluck, or frown—lethal.

On the Yiddish Language

A word about Yiddish itself. It is older than the English we speak, although it did not come fully into its own, building a literature of its own, until the mid–nineteenth century—since which recent time it has produced an impressive body of stories, poems, novels, essays, and social criticism.

Yiddish is the Robin Hood of languages. It steals from the linguistically rich to give to the fledgling poor. It shows not the slightest hesitation in taking in houseguests—to whom it gives free room and board regardless of genealogy, faith, or exoticism. A memorable remark by a journalist, Charles Rappaport, runs: "I speak ten languages—all of them in Yiddish."

I think Yiddish is a language of exceptional charm. Like any street gamin who has survived unnamable adversities, it is bright, audacious, mischievous. It has displayed immense resourceful-ness, immenser resilience, and immensest determination not to die—properties whose absence has proved fatal to more genteel and languid languages. I think it a tongue that never takes its tongue out of its cheek.

Yiddish lends itself to an extraordinary range of observational nuances and psychological subtleties. Steeped in sentiment, it is sluiced with sarcasm. It loves the ruminative, because it rests on a rueful past; favors paradox, because it knows that only paradox can do justice to the injustices of life; adores irony, because the only way the Jews could retain their sanity was to view a dreadful world with sardonic, astringent eyes. In its innermost heart, Yiddish swings between *shmaltz* and derision.

I have always marveled at how fertile this lingua franca is in what may be called the vocabulary of insight. The Jews were forced to become self-conscious from the day Moses warned them to invest every act with piety in preparation for a strict heavenly accounting. Knowledge, among Jews, came to compensate for worldly rewards. Insight, I think, became a substitute for weapons: one way to block the bully's wrath is to know him better than he knows himself.

Jews *had* to become psychologists, and their preoccupation with human, no less than divine, behavior made Yiddish remarkably rich in names for the delineation of character types. Little miracles of discriminatory precision are contained in the distinctions between such simpletons as a *nebekh*, a *shlemiel*, a *shmendrik*, a *shnook*; or between such dolts as a *klutz*, a *yold*, a *Kuni Lemmel*, a *shlep*, a *Chaim Yankel*. All of them inhabit the kingdom of the ineffectual, but each is assigned a separate place in the roll call. The sense of differentiation is so acute in Yiddish that a word like, say, *paskudnyak* has no peer in any language I know for the vocal delineation of a nasty character. And Yiddish coins new names with ease for new personality types: a *nudnik* is a pest; a *phudnik* is a *nudnik* with a Ph.D.

Were I asked to characterize Yiddish—its style, its life story, its ambience—in one word, I would not hesitate: irrepressible.

Isaac Bashevis Singer reminds us that Yiddish may be the only language on earth that has never been spoken by men in power.* (In Israel, where Hebrew is the official parlance, they say that Prime Minister Levi Eshkol† often injected Yiddish into cabinet meetings—and was resented for it.) Few instruments of human speech have led so parlous a life, amid such inhospitable neighbors, against such fierce opposition. And I know of no tongue so beset by schisms and fevers and ambivalences from within the community that had given it birth: Jews themselves.

Purists derided Yiddish for its "bastard" origins, its "vulgar" idioms, its "hybrid" vocabulary. Hebraicists called it "uncivilized cant." Germans called it a "barbarous argot," a "piggish jargon." But English, French, Italian, German, all began as "vulgar" tongues, as jargon, as the vernacular of uneducated masses: the priests and intellectuals and noblemen (if educated) used Latin and Greek. And not too long ago, in Russia, Poland, Scandinavia, and the Balkans, the nabobs learned French, a "refined" language, but remained ignorant of the national, "the servants'," language.

English Words in Yiddish

Many English words are part of today's Yiddish. In the American

---

*Singer reiterated this in accepting the Nobel Prize for Literature in 1978: Yiddish, he said, was "a language of exile, without a land, without frontiers, not supported by any government, a language which possesses no words for weapons, ammunition, military exercises, war tactics. . . . There is a quiet humor in Yiddish and a gratitude for every day of life, every crumb of success, each encounter of love. The Yiddish mentality is not haughty. It does not take victory for granted. It does not demand and command, but it muddles through, sneaks by, smuggles itself amidst the powers of destruction, knowing somewhere that God's plan for Creation is still at the very beginning. . . . In a figurative way, Yiddish is the wise and humble language of us all, the idiom of frightened and hopeful Humanity."

†Eshkol was Israel's third prime minister, from 1963 until he died in office in 1969.

households of Jewish immigrants from eastern Europe, the parents spoke Yiddish to each other—and to the children. But the passionately eager-to-be-American children customarily replied in English. (Hence the witticism, as true for other immigrants as for Jews, "In America, it is the children who raise the parents.")

The vigorous Yiddish press, striving to make life in the boom and bewilderment of the New World easier for its readers, taught them many useful English words. (A study by Dr. J. H. Neumann of three New York Yiddish daily newspapers in 1938 showed that 20 percent of the words on the advertisement pages of the newspapers were English loanwords; in the smaller and more personal ads, the percentage ran 28 percent.) Since these words were spelled in Yiddish, their pronunciation was necessarily determined by the pronunciational aspects of Yiddish—and by the habituated reflexes of the Jewish tongue and larynx. And so proud new patriots swiftly enlarged their vocabularies with such useful, everyday words as

vindaw	window
stritt cah	street car
sobvay	subway
tex	tax
sax	sex

Let me point out that one reason for these aural transformations lay in the way many Jews pronounced *any* language—German, French, or Yiddish itself.

Such pronunciational shifts affect a whole range of vowels; the teaching of English to Jewish immigrants was an undertaking pregnant with surprises. For instance:

1. The short *a* becomes a short *e*: "cat" is pronounced *ket*, and "pat" becomes *pet*.

2. The short *e*, in turn, emerges as a short *a*: "pet" is

rendered as *pat*. I hate to think what must have occurred with "a bad bed."

3. The short *i* becomes a long *e*—and vice versa. This means that "pill" is pronounced *peel* and "peel" comes out as *pill*. An Ashkenazic dentist (his patients called him "dentnist") might well fall into this euphoric promise: "Rilex! I'll feel your cavity so you won't even fill it!"

4. The long *o* becomes *aw* or *u*, and the *aw* sound, in turn, becomes a long *o*: thus, "phone" becomes *fawn* or *fun*; "saw" becomes *so*.

5. The long English *oo* undergoes a transformation to a short *u*; a "pool" becomes a *pull*—and vice versa. To say that a dumbbell is drunk, a virtuoso might declaim, "That full is fool *shnaps!*"

6. The rounded *ow* becomes *ah*: "how" is rendered *hah*, "powder" as *podder*, and "louse" sounds exactly like the Spanish article *las*.

7. The *w* regularly becomes a *v*: "We went to Willie's wedding" is vivified into "Ve vent to Villie's vaddink."

8. The final *g* becomes a *k*; thus "walking the Muggs' pug dog" becomes "valkink the Mucks' puck duck"—a most unholy metamorphosis.

9. The *ng* and *ngg* sounds are often confused; thus "singer" rhymes with "linger," and in Brooklynese "Long Island" sounds like "Long Guyland."

10. Voiced final consonants tend to become unvoiced: in such a vagarious world, one eats corn on the *cop*, spreads butter on *brat*, and consumes potato chips by the *back*.

It should be noted that some of these vowel shifts are consistent and others are not, and that pronunciational variations appear in the speech of people who *can* conform to accepted sounds. In Yiddish itself, for instance, the word for "bread" is pronounced not *Broht*, as in German, but *broyt* or *breyt*. What accounts for the transposition of *a*'s for *e*'s, the interchangeability of the short *i* and the short *e*, or the use of *v*'s for *w*'s when—obviously—each can be enunciated with ease, is a mystery I cannot resolve.

Any reader who feels superior to such quaint English might remember that when the overwhelming majority of humankind was illiterate, it was hard to find a Jewish lad over six who could not read and write (Hebrew). Most adult male Jews could handle at least *three* languages: they used Hebrew in the synagogues and houses of study (see **Besmedresh**), Yiddish in the home, and—to Gentiles—the language of the land in which they lived. My father, a workingman denied the equivalent of a high school education in Poland, handled Yiddish, English, Hebrew, and Polish. Jews were linguists of necessity.

Mr. Harvey Swados reminds us (in *The New York Times Magazine*, September 18, 1966) that of all the public libraries in New York City, the largest circulation of the classics was found in the Seward Park branch on the Lower East Side; and the Metropolitan Museum of Art finally opened its doors on Sundays because of a persistent campaign born in, and championed by, residents of the Lower East Side. To me, one of the noblest images of human history is that described by Harry Golden:* the newly arrived immigrant mother, unable to speak a word of English, who hastened to her branch library and held up one, two, three fingers—the number signaling the number of children for whom she wanted library cards.

*Humorist Harry Golden, author of *Only in America* and *For Two Cents Plain*, died in 1981 at the age of seventy-nine.

Brief Note: The History of Yiddish

For the picaresque history of this spirited and gallant tongue, see the entry Yiddish. Here I need only say briefly: Around the tenth century, Jews from what is now northern France, who spoke Old French and, of course, Hebrew, migrated to towns along the Rhine, where they began to use the local German dialect. Hebrew remained untouched as the "sacred," the liturgical, language—for reading *Torah* and *Talmud,* for use in prayer and in scholarly or theological discourse.

In the Rhineland, Jews wrote German phonetically, using the letters of the Hebrew alphabet, just as Jewish sages in Spain wrote Spanish (and Arabic) with Hebrew letters.†

Yiddish really took root and flowered, as a vernacular, in the ghettos—which began in walled *juderías* in Spain in the thirteenth century. (The Lateran Councils of 1179 and 1215 forbade Jews to live close to Christians, and in 1555 Paul IV ordered segregated quarters for Jews in the Papal States.) This new parlance was a mélange of Middle High German, some Old German, remnants of Old French and Old Italian, Hebrew names and phrases, and local dialects. (Interestingly enough, some ancient German words, no longer used in German, survive in Yiddish.)

But Yiddish did not really settle down and raise its own young until after the fifteenth century, when the Jews went to eastern Europe—Poland, Galicia, Hungary, Romania, Russia. There the buoyant tongue picked up new locutions, adapting itself to the street and the marketplace. Yiddish became the Jews' tongue via

---

† A handwritten prayer book from 1272 from the city of Worms contains the earliest known written Yiddish sentence (according to the February 2001 issue of *Jewish Currents* magazine). For information about some other historical factors in the formation of Yiddish, see my notes to Rosten's entry for YIDDISH.

the Jewish mother, who, not being male, was denied a Hebrew education.

Professor Max Weinreich has given us an exhilarating epigram: "A language is a dialect that has an army and a navy." Yiddish, unlike Hebrew, the official language of Israel, has neither army, navy, police, nor governmental mandate. It has only ardent practitioners and sentimental protectors. In Israel, Yiddish was accorded short shrift by officials and populace alike, until quite recently. The official disfavor and unofficial scorn account for the joke I heard in Jerusalem:

> On a bus in Tel Aviv, a mother was talking animatedly, in Yiddish, to her little boy—who kept answering her in Hebrew. And each time the mother said, "No, no, talk Yiddish!"
>
> An impatient Israeli, overhearing this, exclaimed, "Lady, why do you insist the boy talk Yiddish instead of Hebrew?"
>
> Replied the mother, "I don't want him to forget he's a Jew."

That mother knew what Israel Zangwill meant when he said, in 1906: "Yiddish incorporates the essence of a life which is distinctive and unlike any other."

Perhaps the most eloquent statement of the case for Yiddish as the special language of the Jews was penned by the writer I. L. Peretz (as quoted in Joseph L. Baron's *A Treasury of Jewish Quotations*, A. S. Barnes and Co., 1965):

> Yiddish, the language which will ever bear witness to the violence and murder inflicted on us, bears the marks of our expulsions from land to land, the language which absorbed the wails of the fathers, the laments of the generations, the poison and bitterness of history, the language whose precious jewels are undried, uncongealed Jewish tears.

Do All Jews Understand Yiddish?

No. Rabbi Morris N. Kertzer makes the point vividly (in his *What Is a Jew?*, 1953):

> If an international conference were called today, bringing together Jews of a dozen different countries, no single language would be understood at all. This fact is a source of wonder to many Jews and non-Jews alike. . . . In Italy, France and North Africa, I frequently saw a look of amazement on the faces of American Jewish soldiers who addressed the elders of a synagogue in Yiddish and found no response. In Dijon, most Jews were at home only with their native French; in Algiers, Arabic and French were the languages in most Jewish homes; and in Naples, only a rare soul had ever heard a word of Yiddish.
>
> Hebrew, the language of prayer and the Bible, is spoken only by Israelis and a handful of scholars. . . . Yiddish . . . is today unintelligible to Jews of Italy, Turkey, Spain, North Africa, a goodly number of Americans, and many native-born Israelis. . . . Jews throughout the world today have as their first, and most often their only, language the tongue of the land in which they live.*

The Use of Stories, Humor, and Anecdotes

I have used a story, joke, or anecdote in the main body of this lexicon to illustrate the meaning of a word, wherever possible. Since

*The 1990 U.S. Census identified 213,064 Americans speaking Yiddish in the home. The 1993 UNESCO Red Book on Endangered Languages estimated there to be 200,000 Yiddish speakers in Israel and 153,385 in the former Soviet Union.

this is highly unorthodox in lexicography, a brief for the defense may be in order.

I consider the story, the anecdote, the joke, a teaching instrument of unique efficacy. A joke is a structured, compact narrative that makes a point with power, generally by surprise. A good story is exceedingly hard for anyone to forget. It is therefore an excellent pedagogic peg on which to hang a point. Those who do not use stories when they try to explain or communicate are either inept at telling them or blindly forfeit a tool of great utility.

The Jewish anecdote possesses a bouquet all its own. Since almost every Jew is raised to reverence learning, and encouraged to be a bit of a teacher, the Jewish story *(mayse)* is at its best when it points to a moral or moralizes a problem.

A very large part of Jewish humor is cerebral. It is, like Sholom Aleichem's, reason made mischievous, or, like Groucho Marx's, reason gone mad. Jewish jokes drape their laughter on logic—in despair.

In nothing is Jewish psychology so vividly revealed as in Jewish jokes. The style and stance of its humor reflect a culture, I think, no less than its patterns of shame, guilt, hostility, and approval.†

The first riddle I ever heard, one familiar to almost every Jewish child, was propounded to me by my father:

---

† William Novak and Moshe Waldoks describe Jewish humor (in their *The Big Book of Jewish Humor*, Harper & Row, 1981) as "optimistic in the long run, but pessimistic about the present and the immediate future," with "twin currents of anxiety and skepticism that can become so strong that even the ancient sources of Jewish optimism are swept up in them." In America, they note, "Jewish humor . . . has in some ways come to replace the standard sacred texts as a touchstone for the entire Jewish community. Not all Jews can read and understand a page of *Talmud*, but even the most assimilated tend to have a special affection for Jewish jokes."

"What is it that hangs on the wall, is green, wet—and whistles?"

I knit my brow and thought and thought, and in final perplexity gave up.

"A herring," said my father.

"A *herring?!*" I echoed. "A herring doesn't hang on a wall!"

"So hang it there."

"But a herring isn't green!" I protested.

"Paint it."

"But a herring isn't *wet!*"

"If it's just painted, it's still wet."

"But—," I sputtered, summoning all my outrage, *"a herring doesn't whistle!"*

"Right." My father smiled. "I just put that in to make it hard."*

> *In a common variation on the joke, the last response goes: "So it doesn't whistle!"

We need not be surprised to find countless Jewish jokes mocking the Jews themselves. Self-awareness, pushed into self-analysis, turns into self-criticism.

I once defined humor (in *The Return of H*Y*M*A*N K*A*P*L*A*N*, Harper, 1961) as "the affectionate communication of insight." Humor also serves the afflicted as compensation for suffering, a token victory of brain over fear. A Jewish aphorism goes: "When you're hungry, sing; when you're hurt, laugh." The barbed joke about the strong, the rich, the heartless powers-that-be, is the final citadel in which human pride can live. "All sorrows can be borne," said the Danish writer Isak Dinesen, "if you put them into a story."

But *writing* jokes proved far, far more difficult than I ever anticipated. (Think how much you are aided, in telling a joke, by tonal variations and strategic gestures; by artful pauses and inflections; by the deliberate camouflage of chuckles, dismay, smiles, murmurs.) And certain stories, gorgeous in the telling, just cannot be put into print without suffering more than a sea change. As good an example as I know is this classic:

> During a gigantic celebration in Red Square, after Trotsky had been sent into exile, Stalin, on Lenin's great tomb, suddenly and excitedly raised his hand to still the acclamations. "Comrades, comrades! A most historic event! A cablegram—of congratulations—from Trotsky!"
>
> The hordes cheered and chortled and cheered again, and Stalin read the historic cable aloud:
>
> JOSEPH STALIN
> KREMLIN
> MOSCOW
> YOU WERE RIGHT AND I WAS WRONG. YOU ARE THE TRUE
> HEIR OF LENIN. I SHOULD APOLOGIZE.
> > TROTSKY
>
> You can imagine what a roar, what an explosion of astonishment and triumph, erupted in Red Square now!
>
> But in the front row, below the podium, a little tailor called, "Pst! Pst! Comrade Stalin."
>
> Stalin leaned down.
>
> The tailor said, "Such a message, Comrade Stalin. For the ages! But you read it without the right *feeling!*"
>
> Whereupon Stalin raised his hand and stilled the throng once more. "Comrades! Here is a simple worker, a loyal Communist, who says I haven't read the message from Trotsky with enough feeling! Come, Comrade Worker! Up here! *You* read this historic communication!"
>
> So the little tailor went up to the reviewing stand and took the cablegram from Stalin and read:

JOSEPH STALIN
KREMLIN
MOSCOW

Then he cleared his throat and sang out:

YOU WERE RIGHT AND I WAS *WRONG?* *YOU* ARE THE
TRUE HEIR OF LENIN? *I* SHOULD APOLOGIZE??!!
TROTSKY

Finale

I am happy to acknowledge below the many kind people who helped me during the years it took to finish this opus.

As for the errors and lapses and shameless omissions that will be brought to my attention by irate grammarians, dissenting rabbis, philologists, historians, fervent Yiddishists, inflexible Hebraicists, or readers simply devoted, as I am, to their beloved *mameloshn,* I shall try to console myself with the words of Samuel Johnson, who sent his great dictionary out into the world with this marvelous admonition (quoted in *A Johnson Reader,* Pantheon, 1964):

> . . . a few wild blunders and risible absurdities, from which no work of such multiplicity was ever free, may for a time furnish folly with laughter. No dictionary of a living tongue can ever be perfect . . . a whole life cannot be spent upon syntax and etymology . . . What is obvious is not always known, and what is known is not always present. In this work, when it shall be found that much is omitted, let it not be forgotten that much likewise is performed.

—Leo Rosten
New York, New York

acknowledgements

It is a pleasure for me to thank the following persons for their expert advice, their sharp criticism, their helpful comments, and their consummate patience with an obsessive and impatient author: none of them should in any way be blamed for my final text.

Maurice Samuel, distinguished author and *mavin* par excellence on Sholom (or Sholem) Aleichem and Jewish life, greatly encouraged me throughout, and generously read and analyzed the entire manuscript. Dr. Shlomo Noble, secretary, the Commission on Research, YIVO Institute for Jewish Research, helped me on many troublesome points of etymology. Dr. Bernard Mandelbaum, dean, Jewish Theological Seminary, served as a persistent critic-theologian—and a treasure-house of Talmudic stories. Chancellor Louis Finkelstein and Rabbi Seymour Siegel, of the Jewish Theological Seminary, resolved many perplexing problems in the final stages. Dr. Gershon Winer, dean, Jewish Teachers Seminary and People's University, helped provide definitions and derivations during the very first stages of this undertaking. Rabbi Isaiah Rackowsky of Bridgeport, Connecticut, saved me from several important errors, as did Rabbi Solomon Goldfarb of Long Beach, New York. Mrs. Priscilla Fishman assisted me in research for a month.

I am especially grateful to my learned friend Felix Kaufmann, who conducted a most difficult and painstaking critique of the entire final manuscript, to which he brought his singular acquaintanceship with ancient history, Latin, Greek, German, Italian,

Hebrew, Aramaic, and Sanskrit. My rigorously analytic friend and counsel, Bruno Schachner, contributed several illuminating suggestions.

I would like to thank Alfred Hart, whose original germ of an idea grew into this opus—which I never would have undertaken had I realized how prolific and tormenting this germ would turn out to be.

My wife was unbelievably helpful—in letting me alone during those unconscionably long stretches of time, in New York and Westhampton Beach, when I absented myself mentally from her incomparable company and conversation.

For cooperation, skill, equanimity, and patience far beyond the call of salary or duty, I cite with gratitude my assisting angels, Edna Collins Reed, Susan Klein, and Maureen Lally.

guide to this lexicon

How to Pronounce Yiddish

Only two sounds in Yiddish or Yinglish present any problem to the laryngeally ungifted: the *r*, and the famous *kh* (which I spell ch,* for reasons explained below). Both sounds can be rendered without pain if the reader will heed the following hints:

*Many of Rosten's *ch* spellings have been rendered in this edition as *kh*, in accordance with the YIVO transliteration standards, as explained in a note on page xxviii.

How to Pronounce the R

There are two *r* sounds in Yiddish: the trilled *r* and the deep-throated or guttural *r*. So:

1. Place the tip of your tongue against the front edge of your upper gums and vibrate (your tongue, not your gums). This is the lingual or trilled *r*.
2. Gargle, which means vibrate your uvula. This is the small, fleshy appendage that hangs down, above the back of your tongue, from the middle of the soft palate. (The palate or roof of the mouth is hard and bony in front, soft and fleshy in back. The phrase "He has a good palate," anatomical nonsense, comes from the day when the sense of taste was incorrectly believed to reside in the palate.)

NOTE: The hard English *er* ending to a word is unknown to Yiddish; pronounce any Yiddish word that ends in *er* with the soft *air* sound: "fathe" is rendered as *fat-hair*, "dancer" as *dan-sair*, and so on.

How to Pronounce KH or CH

If you can pronounce the Scottish *loch* or the German *ach!*, you can pronounce the Yiddish *ch* (or *kh*). (The sound is designated in phonetics as *kh*. In technical language, this phonetic *kh* is "the unvoiced velar" or "the unvoiced uvular fricative.")

Here are five different, easy ways of producing this sound:

1. Prepare to say "yes." Now, instead of pronouncing the y, simply expel air, in a little spurt, blowing it through the passage between the roof of your mouth and your tongue.

OR

2. Set your tongue as if you are going to pronounce a *k*, but let the air out to pronounce an *h*. That's the *kh* sound.

OR

3. Pretend you have a fishbone stuck in the roof of your mouth. Now *cccchh* it out. That's the sound.

OR

4. Pretend you have a bread crumb stuck in your throat. Expel it by rattling wind and saliva around sonorously.

OR

5. Pronounce the *Yecch!* made famous by *Mad* magazine. Even a Cabot can do this.

If you use any of these five pronunciatory gambits, you may now delight yourself, and Semitic cynics, by pronouncing

> *cheder*
> *chutzpa*
> *yikhes*
> *Chasidim*

with careless aplomb. You should even be able to pronounce *khokhem,* thus becoming one.

Rules Followed for Listing and Cross-Referencing Words

1. All words are listed in alphabetical (English alphabet, that is) order.
2. I have tried to list every form I have encountered for the spellings (transliterations) of a word, but I *define* the word under the spelling I consider best.*

*Transliterations of Yiddish words have been updated in this edition to reflect both "standard" and "popular" or "folk" spellings. "Standard" means according to the orthography established by the YIVO Institute for Jewish Research, which has been adopted by increasing numbers of Jewish editors, writers, students, and scholars since the original publication of Leo Rosten's book. Many Yiddish words, however, have entered so solidly into English usage with "folk" transliterations and Anglicized pronunciations that their standardization might confuse the reader. In these instances (and there are quite a few), Rosten's original favored transliterations have been retained as first choice. The best example might be the one used by Rosten on page xxix: CHANUKAH. The YIVO spelling for this holiday, KHANIKE, would be unrecognizable and bewildering to most American readers.

Where more than one transliteration is listed, YIVO spellings are indicated with the symbol Y. Rosten's original preferred transliterations are indicated with the symbol R. Other commonly used transliterations may also be listed beneath these. In instances where Rosten's and YIVO's spellings coincide, no symbols are appended.

For "Yinglish" words (that is, Anglicized Yiddish or blended Yiddish-English words—usually an English root with a Yiddish suffix) and "Ameridish" words (that is, authentic-sounding Yiddish words that nevertheless are strictly American inventions or adaptations), Rosten's transliterations are retained, without YIVO alternatives. For words from German, Russian, Hebrew, Slavic, Polish, and other languages, Rosten's original spellings and transliterations have also been retained. Most Yiddish and Hebrew words and phrases associated with religious observance, including the names of classic prayers, are transliterated in accordance with popular usage.

(Continued on page xliv)

3. Each entry that is not defined is cross-referenced to the place where it is.

4. Where three or four spellings are listed together, in columnar order, the first entry is the one preferred. Thus:

CHANUKAH
KHANIKE
HANUKA, HANUKKAH, CHANNUKAH

5. I have listed some spellings I consider outlandish, because I did find them in English transliteration: for example, *schatchen* for *shadkhn*, *schlemiehl* for *shlemiel*, etc. Such entries are cross-referenced to the spelling under which they are defined.

6. I list no form of spelling that is not based on one that I have, in fact, seen in an English book or periodical.

7. Hebrew words are listed in both their Hebrew and Yiddish spelling, where such spellings differ; they are also cross-referenced; they are *defined* under their Yiddish spelling:

SHOLEM (Yiddish)
SHALOM (Hebrew)
or
BESMEDRESH *(Yiddish)*
BET MIDRASH *(Hebrew)*

(Continued from page xxxliii)

YIVO transliterations are strictly phonetic. In a nutshell, the vowel sounds are *a* as in *father*, *ay* as in *my*, *e* as in *bed* (*e* is never silent, even at the end of a word: *mame* would be pronounced as MA-MEH); *ey* as in *day*; *i* as in *fit* and *feet*; *o* as in *sort* and *hut*; *oy* as in *boy*; *u* as in *flute* and *put*. Most consonant sounds follow English consonants; exceptions include *kh* for the guttural sound; *tsh* as in *church*; *dzh* as in *judge*; *zh* as in *measure*.

Readers can rely on Rosten's creative pronunciation clues to make sense of all transliterations.

The Pronunciations Used in This Lexicon

Two dialects, broadly speaking, characterized and dominated the way Yiddish was spoken in eastern Europe: the northern, or *Litvak*, which centered in Lithuania; and the southern, or *Poylish*, followed by Jews from Poland to Romania and the Ukraine. Claims and counterclaims for each fly about like swallows in the spring.

In the United States, the southern dialect was preferred in the Yiddish theater. The northern pronunciation, preferred in literary discussions and on the lecture platform, was considered "standard" Yiddish. This did not in the slightest affect those who had spoken southern Yiddish as their first language, their *mameloshn*, their "mother tongue." (I have heard the simple word for "where" rendered as *voo, voe, vee*.)

I trust I will be forgiven for favoring the southern pronunciation, on which I was raised, in the case of many words. It is not simply bias on my part: an enormous number of Jews followed the Polish pronunciation and saw no reason to alter it, especially since it was used in the great Yiddish theater.

In general, I have tried to accommodate both the northern and southern camps as well as I could. I have followed these guiding rules for pronunciation:

1. The pronunciation of *vowels*, as in "standard" Yiddish, follows that used by Russian and Lithuanian Jews.

2. The pronunciation of a few *consonants* follows that used by Polish Jews. (This may seem confusing, but only because it is explained; you can be just as discombobulated by the technical preface of an English dictionary.)

3. Hebrew words are pronounced differently in Yiddish than they are in Hebrew. (The Hebrew *th* or *t* is pronounced *s*, for instance; and whereas Hebrew words are accented on

the last syllable, Yiddish words are not.) I use the Yiddish or Yinglish pronunciation throughout.

4. Whenever a Hebrew word, or a word derived from Hebrew, appears in Yiddish, I use the Ashkenazic (eastern European) pronunciation—not the Sephardic (Mediterranean) version.* Yiddish is, after all, the language of the *Ashkenazim*. (The distinctions between the two are explained in the respective entries in the lexicon.)

Rules Used for the Spelling of Yiddish Words

Is there a "standard" or official way of spelling Yiddish words in English? Not really. In 1937, the YIVO Institute of Jewish Research established governing rules for orthography, but they are widely ignored by editors and writers who use Yiddish words in English.†

In this lexicon, I have followed a few simple rules—choosing

---

*In his information about word derivations, however, Rosten often cites Hebrew words with Sephardic transliterations/pronunciations as sources of Yiddish. In most of these cases, the showcased Yiddish word should more simply be identified as the Hebrew word with Ashkenazic pronunciation. The entries have nevertheless been left standing so that contemporary readers familiar with modern Hebrew, which is spoken with Sephardic pronunciation, can readily recognize the relationship between Yiddish words and their Hebrew equivalents.

Rosten also preferred Hebrew to Yiddish for the names of holidays and other religious terms, such as *Shevuot* instead of *Shevuos*. This has been altered in the new edition: holidays and religious terms are now usually given in the Yiddish.

†The generations of Jews that have grown into adulthood since the publication of *The Joys of Yiddish* have experienced a small renaissance of Yiddish that has been shaped, in part, by academic influences, including Yiddish immersion programs at many universities. For these Jews, the YIVO standard of transliteration emphasized in this updated edition is familiar and widely accepted.

those forms of spelling that seem to me to offer the greatest help to readers who have not pronounced Yiddish words before.

1. I spell words phonetically, wherever possible. (In Yiddish itself, words are spelled quite simply, according to the way they are pronounced, and without the maddening malformations of English, say, that make it possible to write the *ee* sound in sixteen different ways; see my "Tiptoe thru Lingo," *Look*, Dec. 17, 1967.)

2. I use *ch* instead of *kh* wherever possible, greatly preferring *chutzpa* to *khutzpa* (which no one ever spelled that way), or *cheder* to *kheder* (which some do spell in that odd way).

    I am perfectly well aware that phonetic purists want the "uvular fricative" written *kh*, not *ch*. But since the reader of English will encounter the *ch* form far more often than the *kh* form, I think it best (and least misleading) to follow the most common practice.*

3. I try to use *sh*, not *sch*, to begin a word that is pronounced *sh*, not *sk*.†

    The *sch* is misleading to the Anglo-Saxon eye and tongue; it may misdirect the innocent into such barbari-

---

Kh or *ch*? This is one main "battlefront" between YIVO and Rosten, and as indicated in the note on page xxviii, my choice has been to go with YIVO *(kh)* except in cases where other transliterations have implanted themselves solidly in American culture. The two examples Rosten offers here are illustrative of established "popular" transliterations: both *chutzpa* (not *khutspe*, as YIVO spells it) and *cheder* (not *kheyder*, as YIVO spells it) are well established among English speakers and have therefore been retained as the favored spellings in the book.

† *Sh* or *sch*? Rosten's choice of *sh* conforms with YIVO standards.

ties as pronouncing *shlemiel,* if spelled *schlemiel,* as *sklemiel.*

But where a *sch* usage is so widely used and familiar as to have become "standardized," I bow to the weight of usage and conform.

4. Certain choices on my part are admittedly arbitrary:

   a. I prefer *meshugge* to *meshuge,* or *shmegegge* to *shmegege,* because the double *g* tells the English reader to use a hard *g* and avoids making the preceding vowel long, as in English.‡

   b. I select the Yiddish as against the German spelling of certain words: *gefilte* for *gefülte.*

   c. I use the opening *tch* instead of *ch,* in some cases, because I have tried to reserve the use of *ch* for the phonetic *kh* sound.§ (This is not always possible because of the way some spellings have caught on.)

5. Where authorities differ over the spelling of certain words, as indeed they do, I have chosen the spelling that provides the quickest, clearest visual guidance to the reader.

In general, I spell the Yiddish words phonetically. But the best-intentioned phoneticists run into the obdurate walls of demotic usage and custom: I found that I had to depart from consistency if I wanted to avoid outlandish, visual departures from the familiar.

---

‡ In this new edition, the simpler YIVO single *g* is often preferred, but both versions are offered. For Ameridish words such as *shmegegge,* Rosten's transliterations are used.

§ The YIVO system spells *tch* as *tsh.*

Pronunciation Aids

I have tried to help the reader manage unavoidable uncertainties, inconsistencies, and confusions by offering a pronunciation aid, or phonetic indicator, for every word; thus: "*Sephardic* . . . pronounced *seh-*FAR-*dick.*"

I have tried to provide a "rhymes with" device (*shtetl* rhymes with "kettle") for every word. This proved impossible for some words—and in some instances I was driven to extremes, as gruesome to me as they may seem to you. For this I can only beg your indulgence. The lot of phoneticists, like that of policemen, is not a happy one.

By and large, then, I have done my very best to give the swiftest, clearest, simplest assistance to the unpracticed or unwary tongue. Where my efforts have not proved successful, my intentions remain as pure as they were innocent.

The Jews are just like everyone else—only more so.
—ANON

What is lofty can be said in any language, and what is mean should be said in none.
—MAIMONIDES

When a Jewish farmer eats a chicken, one of them is sick.
—FOLK SAYING

When a father helps a son, both smile; but when a son must help his father, both cry.
—FOLK SAYING

If I am not for myself, who will be for me? And if I am only for myself, what am I . . . And if not now—when?
—HILLEL

Jewish dropout: a boy who didn't get his Ph.D.
—ANON

lexicon of yiddish-in-english

a

Adonai[R]
Adonoy[Y]

Pronounced *ah-doe-*NOY, to rhyme with "follow Roy."
Hebrew: "**My Lords.**"* (The singular form is *Adoni,* but
the plural is customarily used, perhaps to magnify God's
majesty and to distinguish the deity from earthly sovereigns.)

The sacred title of God, never pronounced by pious
Jews except during solemn prayer, and with head covered.

*The classic translation of YHVH/Adonai as "My Lords" or "Lord" was
rejected in the name of gender-neutrality by the Reconstructionist synagogue
movement when it published its new prayer book series, *Kol Haneshamah,* in
the 1990s. Wherever *Adonai* appears in the liturgy, these books translate it
into a variety of metaphorical names that reflect the spirit of each specific
prayer: Healer, Redeeming One, Intimate One, etc.

Leo Rosten might have asked: Never mind His aliases, what's His alibi?

Reconstructionism, by the way, is the fourth and newest denomination of
Judaism, founded by Rabbi Mordecai Kaplan (1881–1983), who taught at the
Conservative movement's Jewish Theological Seminary for more than half a
century. In his major work, *Judaism as a Civilization* (1934), Kaplan sought to
rid Jewish belief and practice of superstition. He posed a theology that envisioned God not as a being or spirit with whom humans can have a personal
relationship, but as a universal "power that makes for redemption"—a power
that human beings themselves actualize through love and good deeds. Kaplan also emphasized the need for a Judaism that would reflect the virtues of
Western civilization, including democracy, pluralism, and inclusiveness. His
movement became a denomination with the launching of the Reconstructionist Rabbinical College in 1968. Currently, some one hundred congregations are affiliated with the Jewish Reconstructionist Federation.

When God is mentioned in ordinary discourse, devout Jews say *"Adoshem."*

F our Hebrew letters, *YHVH*, form the Hebrew name for God. *Adonai* is a substitute for these "sacred" letters.

Adonai literally means "My Lord" in Hebrew; but, as Rabbi I. Rackovsky told me, when God, speaking, uses *Adonai* in the Bible, the word obviously cannot mean *"My Lord." Adonai* has come to assume an identity independent of its strict literal meaning.

We simply do not know how YHVH was pronounced by the ancients.* There are no vowel letters in Hebrew; vowel *sounds* are indicated by diacritical marks (dots, dashes). But the *Torah* scrolls are not so marked or "vocalized."

Only in the ancient Temple in Jerusalem was the utterance of *YHVH* permitted. And when the awesome appellation *was* pronounced by the high priest, the musical part of the service swelled up loud so that worshipers would not hear the Name.

In English, *YHVH* (which I read somewhere appears 6,823 times in the Old Testament†) is rendered vocally as "Yahweh" or "Yahveh." "Jehovah," which first appeared in Christian texts in 1516, is simply incorrect; it is based on a German papal scribe's reading of *YHVH* with the diacritical marks of *Adonai,* which had been added as a pronunciation aid.

---

*One creative Jewish theologian, Arthur Waskow, has interpreted the sacred name יהוה, YHVH or YHWH, to sound the way it reads, like an audible breath: YHHH . . . WHHH. This popular portrayal of God as the "Breath of Life" is typical of a variety of modern Jewish theologies, which have shaved off God's white beard and portrayed the deity more abstractly—and in a contingent relationship with the human heart.

†Rosten here uses the Christian term for the Five Books of Moses, known in Hebrew as the *Torah* and in Greek as the *Pentateuch.* (The term *Torah* also refers to the entirety of Jewish scripture and law; see Rosten's entry for **Torah.**) Some Jews have taken to referring to the "Old Testament" and "New Testament" as the "Old Testament" and "Young Testament"!

The King James Version of the Bible usually translates *YHVH* as "Lord."

Another substitute name, *Shaddai,* or *Shaday,* according to *midrash,* indicates God's contentment with the size of the world after He had created it and it had grown and grown. God said *"Dai!"* (Hebrew: "Enough!") and the universe stopped growing. . . . So *Shaddai,* for "the One Who Said 'Enough!,'" represents the divine attribute of Plenty. Modern cosmologists, torn between the "steady growth" and "big bang" hypotheses, will find the regal *"Dai!"* a delightful explanation of extremely complex matters.)‡

Other names for God among Jews are *Borey Olam* (the Creator of the World), *Kedosh Yisrael* (Holy One of Israel), *Ha-Makom* (the Omnipresent Place), *El Elyon* (Most High One), and *Ayn Sof* (Infinite One).

NOTE: When religious Jews refer to God, in speaking, they change even the substitute names: instead of *"Adonai,"* they say *"Adoshem";* when saying *"Elohim,"* they alter one sound to make it *"Elokhim."*

For an illuminating discussion of "God" (as an English word, as a concept with antecedents in prehistory, as one of the deity's names in the **Old Testament**), see James Hastings, ed., *Dictionary*

---

‡ The cabalistic tradition of Jewish mysticism portrays God as "shattering the vessel" of creation by pouring out too much divine energy. In a second, successful attempt to create the universe, God "contracts" to make room for material reality (a process called *tsimtsum*). The concept of *tikkun olam,* "repair of the world," which has become synonymous these days with "social action," was envisioned by mystics as the "gathering of divine sparks" left scattered by that first creation effort—to be achieved by human beings through the performance of *mitzvos,* ethical and spiritual deeds (see Rosten's entry, and my note, for **cabala**).

For an up-to-date religious discussion of physics, cosmology, and Judaism, see Daniel C. Matt's *God & the Big Bang* (Jewish Lights, 1998).

of the Bible, revised edition, by F. C. Grant and H. H. Rowley, Scribner's, 1963.*

"If God lived on earth," goes a sardonic Yiddish saying, "people would knock out all His windows."

A remarkable directness and intimacy characterize the attitude of even the most God-fearing Jews to the Almighty. They may offer personal orisons to God in free-wheeling recitatives that are richly garnished with complaints, irony, and critical questionings. Consider this lovely old story:

On the eve of *Yom Kippur,* that most solemn and sacred day, an old Jew looked up to heaven and sighed: "Dear God, listen: I, Hershel the tailor, put it to You! The butcher in our village, Shepsel, is a good man, an honorable man, who never cheats anyone, and always gives full weight, and never turns away the needy; yet Shepsel himself is so poor that he and his wife sometimes go without meat! . . . Or take Fishel, our shoemaker, a model of piety and kindness—yet his beloved mother is dying in terrible pain. . . . And Reb Label, our *melamed* [teacher], who loves all the lads he teaches and is loved by all who know him—lives hand to mouth, hasn't a decent suit to his name, and just developed an eye disease that may leave him blind! . . . So, on this most holy night, I ask ɪou dɪrectly, God. Is this faɪr? I ɪɪ ɪк ɑl. Is this fair? . . . So,

---

*Karen Armstrong's best-selling *A History of God: The 4,000-Year Quest of Judaism, Christianity and Islam* (Ballantine Books, 1994) is one of the most accessible contemporary narratives about these matters. Rabbi Sandy Eisenberg Sasso's children's book, *In God's Name* (Jewish Lights, 1994), offers insight into the humanistic meaning of God's many names: "The woman who cared for the sick called God *Healer.* The slave who was freed from bondage called God *Redeemer . . . .*"

tomorrow, O Lord, on our sacred *Yom Kippur*—if You forgive us, we will forgive You!"

"God, I know, will provide," sighed one disconsolate Jew. "I only wish He would provide until He provides."

Another story tells us of a legendary *zeyde* (grandfather) in "Shpolle," who was called "the Saint of Shpolle." He was said to have become so heartsick over the sufferings of the Jews and the injustices of the world that he decided to put God on trial. So he appointed nine friends as judges, himself being the tenth needed for a *minyan*, and summoned the Almighty to appear on the witness stand. (Since God is everywhere, the *zeyde* simply closed his door.)

For three days and nights this remarkable juridical body tried the Lord: they presented charges, devised defenses, pondered, prayed, fasted, consulted the *Torah* and the *Talmud*. Finally, in solemn consensus, they issued their verdict: God was guilty. In fact, they found Him guilty on two counts: (1) He had created the spirit of Evil, which He then let loose among innocent and pliable people; (2) He clearly failed to provide poor widows and orphans with decent food and shelter.

Adoshem

Pronounced *ah-doe-*SHEM, to rhyme with "follow them." From Hebrew: *Ha Shem,* "the Name."

A cryptonym for *Adonai,* the title of God. *Adoshem* is used when the name of God is uttered outside of formal religious service.

Much mystification and magic, down the centuries, attended the utterance of God's Name, and many substitutes for It abound in Hebrew. Here are a few: *Elohim*—(when the attribute of God's justice is cited); *Ha Shem*—when God's mercy is cited; *El Elyon*—God the Most High; *Hakodesh Barukh Hu*—the Holy One, blessed be He; *Robon Olam* —Ruler of the World; and *Yah* (which is never pronounced)—a word formed from two Hebrew letters, *yud* and *hei*, which are the first and last letters of *YHVH*, God's unutterable **Holy Name.***

See also **Adonai.**

aha!

Pronounced with a note of sudden comprehension, pleasure, or triumph.

The versatile expletive, widely used by old-fashioned Jews, to signify

1. COMPREHENSION. "You don't subtract, but multiply? *AhA!*"
2. ILLUMINATION. *"AhA! That's* why they called off the party!"
3. SURPRISE. "The *doctor* was wrong? *AHA!*"
4. SENTENTIOUS HINTING. "Just ask her—and watch her expression. *Aha!*"
5. DELIGHT. "*Ah-A!* Then *I* win the bet!"

*The reverence attached to names of God is expressed in writing by many observant American Jews through the use of a hyphen: "G-d." Within the small, mystically oriented Jewish Renewal movement, this hyphen has recently given way to an exclamation point ("G!d"). Nevertheless, what Rosten calls the "never pronounced" *Yah* (as in "Hallelujah") is now commonly used as a name for God in some non-Orthodox worship settings.

6. TRIUMPH. *"AhA!"* ("So now do you admit you're wrong?")

A*ha!* is not to be confused with *hoo-ha!*, its blood cousin. Perhaps the best way to illustrate the difference is with the following story:

For twenty years Mr. Sokoloff had been eating at the same restaurant on Second Avenue. On this night, as on every other, Mr. Sokoloff ordered chicken soup. The waiter set it down and started off. Mr. Sokoloff called, "Waiter!"

"Yeah?"

"Please taste this soup."

The waiter said, *"Hanh?* Twenty years you've been eating the chicken soup here, no? Have you ever had a bad plate—"

"Waiter," Sokoloff said firmly, "taste the soup."

"Sokoloff, what's the *matter* with you?"

"Taste the *soup!*"

"All right, all right," the waiter said, grimacing. "I'll taste— where's the spoon?"

"Aha*!*" cried Sokoloff.

ai-ai-ai
ai-yi-yi

Pronounced *ay-ay-*YI, or AY-*yay-yi,* to rhyme with "my my my."

This exquisite exclamation should not be confused with the classic *oy-oy-oy.* A folk saying goes, "To have money may not always be so *ai-yi-yi,* but not to have it, you may be sure, is *oy-oy-oy!*"

Ai-ai-ai is cried, crooned, or sung out in a juicy repertoire of shadings; it is sent forth forte or pianissimo; it can run up or down the tonal scale; it is counterpointed by a fruity variety of facial expressions—according to the vocalizer's intention and histrionic talent.

The three syllables should not be clipped, as Spaniards do in mouthing their stern Iberian *ay-ay;* nor should the syllables be barked out, as the Japanese do with their *"hai!"* ("yes"); nor should the syllables be murmured genteelly, as in the fine old British nauticism "aye, aye, sir."

The Yiddish *ai-ai-ai* is of another and altogether different genre: it ties the consonantal *y* right into the compliant *ai* in a liquid linkage that enhances both euphony and meaning thusly:

1. SUNG OUT HAPPILY, upscale (*ai-yi-*YI?!) with a beam or laugh, it expresses admiration, envy, surprise, all-other-words-fail-me enthusiasm.

2. UTTERED SADLY, with a dolorous expression, sheep eyes, a shake of the head, or in hollow *diminuendo* (AI-*yi-yi*), it emits monosyllabic pellets of dismay, pity, lamentation, regret, quite akin to *oy-oy-oy.*

3. UTTERED SARCASTICALLY, or garnished with a glare, a snicker, a sneer, *ai-ai-ai* is a scathing little package of scorn: "So he's on the committee for the annual picnic. *Ai-ai-ai.*"

These feeble ground rules are not to be interpreted rigidly. (My father, for instance, a virtuoso of the *ai-ai-ai,* could make it jump through hoops beyond the three delineated above.)

Many an accomplished complainer can trill an *ai-ai-ai* upscale as if it were a dirge, which is no small feat, and some can produce a downscale *ai-yi-yi* with so joyous and percussive a first syllable that the rest sounds like not depression but exhaustion from too much delight.

When Mr. Olinsky returned from Europe, his partner in Marlborough Men's Coats hung on his every reminiscence.

"And I even was in a group who went to the Vatican," beamed

Olinsky, "where we had an audience with the pope!"

"*Ai-ai-ai!* The pope! . . . What does he look like?"

"A fine man, thin, spiritual, I figure a size 38, short."*

---

*Rosten's description applies to Pope Paul VI, who headed the Roman Catholic Church from 1963 to 1978.

Pope jokes remain a fixture in Jewish life—a long-cultivated response to exile, Inquisition, auto-da-fés, and other sufferings imposed upon Jews by the Catholic Church over the centuries. The current pope, however, has very actively sought improvement in Catholic-Jewish relations. Pope John Paul II grew up in Poland, with Jewish friends, and witnessed firsthand the destruction of the Polish Jewish community by the Nazis. He is the first pope ever to have visited the ancient Jewish community in Rome; he was responsive to Jewish protests against the establishment of a Carmelite nunnery at the historical site of the Auschwitz death camp; he has helped to eliminate anti-Semitic passages from the Catholic liturgy and has broadly condemned anti-Semitism as a sin.

The pope's efforts to heal the wounds of history reached a crescendo during his spring 2000 visit to Israel in celebration of Christianity's second millennium. There he visited Yad Vashem, the Holocaust memorial site in Jerusalem, where he wept and prayed and declared that "the Catholic Church, moved by the Gospel law of truth and by no political considerations, is deeply saddened by the hatred, the acts of persecution and displays of anti-Semitism directed against Jews by Christians at any time and in any place."

Not all Jews or Jewish organizations have been satisfied, however, by the level of responsibility accepted by the church for the brutalities of the past. Ongoing controversies, such as the church's recent beatification of Pope Pius IX (1792–1878) despite his explicit anti-Semitism, reveal that Jewish-Catholic relations are far from healed.

Pope John Paul II's leadership on the Catholic-Jewish front recalls a discussion at an interfaith conference between a priest and a rabbi, both young men, about their career ambitions. The priest admits that he hopes to become a bishop one day.

"And then?" the rabbi asks encouragingly.

"Well," the priest says with a blush, "I suppose that I occasionally fantasize becoming a cardinal, although the chances are very, very slim."

"And then?" the rabbi coaxes him.

The priest laughs. "Pope! I guess I could, conceivably, become the pope!"

"And then?"

"Are you crazy?" cries the priest. "Higher than the pope? Are you suggesting that I aspire to become God Almighty?"

"Well," says the rabbi, "one of our boys made it."

alef-beys^Y
aleph-baiz^R
aleph-bez, aleph-baz, alef-beis

Pronounced OL-*lif* BAZE, in my Yiddish circles, to rhyme
with "Ma riff haze." Hebrew: the names of the Hebrew
letters *a, b.*

The alphabet, that is, the "ABCs." "He is learning
his *alef-beys.*"

A lef is the name of the first letter in the Hebrew alphabet; *beth*
is the name of the second letter (*beys* in Ashkenazic, or
Yiddish, pronunciation). The similarity of *alef-beth* to "alphabet" is
obvious.

The Hebrew alphabet, incidentally, came from the inhabi-
tants of Canaan, which was that part of Palestine the Greeks called
Phoenicia. Hebrew was most probably the language spoken by the
Phoenicians/Canaanites (Isaiah spoke of the "language of Canaan"),
who almost surely created those letters that formed a Semitic
alphabet and from which all the alphabets in Europe descended.
Hebrew was one of a cluster of related languages (Aramaic,
Ugaritic, Akkadian, Arabic, etc.) known as "Semitic."

One of the most endearing customs I know involved a Jewish
boy's first day in Hebrew school, or *cheder.* The teacher would
show the boy the alphabet, on a large chart, and before (or after)
he repeated the teacher's *"alef"* a drop of honey was placed on his
tongue. "How does that taste?" the boy would be asked.

"Sweet."

"The study of the Holy Law," was the answer, "is sweeter."

Sometimes the boy's mother would give him honey cakes,
shaped in the letters of the alphabet, before he went off to the

cheder on his first day, or when he returned, to make him know and remember that "learning is sweet."

And after the boy completed his first lesson, some parents would surreptitiously drop a coin before him. "Ah, an angel dropped that from heaven to show you how pleased God is that you learned your first lesson."

alevai
See halevay.

alev ha-sholem[R] (masculine)
olev ha-sholem[Y]
aleha ha-sholem[R] (feminine)
oleho ha-sholem[Y]

Pronounced *aw*-LUV *ha sha*-LOAM or AH-*luv ha* SHO-*lem* (the first pronunciation is Hebrew, and elegant; the second is Yiddish, and brisk). The two Hebrew words are often pronounced as if one: *alevasholem*. The feminine form is *aleha ha-sholem*, pronounced *ah-leh-ha ha*-SHO-*lem* or SHA-*loam*.

Literally: "On him [or her], peace."

The phrase is used, automatically, when referring to someone who is dead—as, in English, one says "of blessed memory" or "May he rest in peace."

When a man says, "My uncle Harry, *alevasholem*, once said . . . ," you can be sure that Uncle Harry is dead.

As a boy, I was fascinated by the obligatory *"alevasholem"* but puzzled to hear: "That man? A liar, a no-good, *alevasholem*." Thus realism, wrestling with ritual, resolves ambivalence. In fact, the primary purpose of ritual is to provide a routine for the management of emotion. Routine reduces anxiety by removing choices.

It also used to please me, as a boy, to hear a patriarch utter a fearsome oath thusly: "May beets grow in his belly! God forbid." It pleased me, I say, because "God forbid" took the edge off a malediction uttered in anger—*after* the anger had been healthily expressed.

Jews are at home with strong emotions. They express feelings with ease, to say nothing of eloquence, then politely dilute them— to be on the safe side of things.

It was at the great Café Royale, on Second Avenue in New York City, *alevasholem*, that I first heard this classic joke:

> *Waiter:* "Tea or coffee, gentlemen?"
> *First customer:* "I'll have tea."
> *Second customer:* "Me too—and be sure the glass is clean!"
> (WAITER EXITS, RETURNS)
> *Waiter:* "Two teas. Which one asked for the clean glass?"

almone^Y
almona^R
almoona, almoneh

Pronounced *oll*-MAW-*neh*, to rhyme with "Ah'll pawn a," or *oll*-MOO-*na*, to rhyme with "Altoona." Hebrew: "widow."
  Widow.

Though no more than descriptive, *almone* is pronounced with a hint of sadness, for widows, orphans, and even the grown motherless or fatherless are accorded conspicuous sympathy in

Jewish circles. And the reverent son or daughter of a departed virago, or a deceased wastrel, will refer to "my saintly mother" or "my sainted father." Such generous, not to say effusive, sentiments are sometimes applied to mothers-in-law, too.

When old Isadore Litvak, dealer in ribbons and buttons, died of a heart attack, he left, to everyone's surprise, insurance policies that totaled $100,000.

Did this, in some small measure, help console the widow? No. For what the *almone* wailed was: "My poor Isadore—all his life he worked, day and night, and we lived poor as mice, and just when God decides to drop a fortune in our lap, Izzy drops dead!"

alrightnik (masculine)
alrightnikeh, alrightnitseh (feminine)

From the English "all right," with the incomparable -*nik* added. Pure Yinglish.
1. One who has succeeded, done "all right," and shows it by boasting, ostentation, crude manners.
2. Nouveau riche, with trimmings.

As is true of many Yiddishisms, the pungent suffix -*nik* is enlisted in the service of scorn.

Alrightniks are materialists; they parade their money; they lack modest, sensitive, *edel* qualities. They talk loudly, dress garishly, show off.

Alrightniks may be envied but are not admired; for they have succeeded whether or not they have taste, breeding, or spiritual

values. Above all, they are not learned or devoted to learning—
hence cannot be really **respected.***

An *alrightnik*, drowning, was pulled out of the water, and an
excited crowd gathered, crying, "Stand back!" "Call a doctor!"
"Give him artificial respiration!"

"Never!" cried the *alrightnik*'s wife. "Real respiration or nothing!"

The rabbi came to a rich Jew and asked for a contribution to the
poor.

The *alrightnik* refused. "They are nothing but lazy loafers!
Their poverty is their own fault!"

The rabbi said, "Come to the window. Look out. What do you
see?"

"I see—people," said the *alrightnik*.

"Now look into that mirror," said the rabbi. "What do you see?"

"Why, myself."

"Isn't it astonishing," sighed the rabbi, "that when you cover a
clear glass with a little silver, you see only yourself?"

An attractive *alrightnikeh* was depressed by the suburb into which
she and her husband had recently moved. One day she hastened
to her neighbor's house and, embarrassed, said, "Shirley, you're
the only one I can ask. Would you give me some—confidential
advice?"

---

*Rosten emphasizes the materialism and philistinism of the *alrightnik* and
alrightnikeh, but it is their conformism that particularly makes them an object
of scorn. The *alrightnik* "is all too willing to accept the status quo," writes
Gene Bluestein in his *Anglish-Yinglish* (University of Georgia Press, 1989),
"thus, to say 'all right' even when one should resist." The term was especially
popularized by the left-wing Yiddish press during the radical infighting of the
early to mid–twentieth century.

"Gladly."

The *alrightnikeh* blushed. "How—do you go about having an affair?"

"I," beamed Shirley, "always start with 'The Star-Spangled Banner.'"

An *alrightnikeh* (or *alrightnitseh*) called a decorator to her new apartment. "I want you should fix up this place from top to bottom. Money is no object."

The decorator asked, "Would you like it to be modern?"

"Modrin? N-no."

"French?"

"French?" echoed the *alrightnikeh*. "How do *I* come to French?"

"Perhaps Italian provincial?"

"God forbid!"

The decorator sighed. "Madame, what period *do* you want?"

"What 'period'? I want my friends to walk in, take one look, and drop dead! Period."

alter kocker^R
alter kaker^Y
A.K.

Pronounced OLL-*ter* KOCK-*er*, to rhyme with "Sol the mocker." From the **German**:* *alter*, "old"; *Der Alter*, "the old man." What *kocker* means I had rather not tell you in street argot, but *kockn* means "to defecate."

Vulgarism: A crotchety, fussy, ineffectual old man.

A.K. is a testimonial to the ineradicable earthiness and vigor of Yiddish. (My mother *never* let me use such a phrase or employ such vulgarity.)

A.K. is as often used in mild, fond condescension as it is in derision: "Let him alone: he's just an *A.K.*" "He lies in bed all day, like an *alter kocker*."

I make no special plea for *alter kocker*, but I certainly prefer *A.K.* to its English equivalent, "old fart."

*Rosten writes "from the German" for many Yiddish words with Germanic roots, but it should be noted that Yiddish is a thousand-plus-year-old language with an evolutionary path that parted ways centuries ago from the path leading to modern German.

Two *A.K.*'s had sat in silence on their favorite park bench for hours, lost in thought. Finally, one gave a long and languid, *"Oy!"* The other replied, "You're telling *me*?" †

And perhaps it was the same two *A.K.*'s on the same park bench, observing the same prolonged, silent communion. At last one said, "How are things?"

"Eh!" The other shrugged. "How about you?"

"Mn-yey."

They rose. "Well, good-bye. It's always nice to have a heart-to-heart talk."

---

† This joke was popular among Soviet Jews during their emigration campaigns of the 1970s and 1980s, with a new punch line: "If you're going to talk politics, I'm leaving!"

Leave they did: from 1989 to 2000, after decades of being refused the right to emigrate, some 1.4 million Jews departed from the republics of the former Soviet Union (FSU) and went to live in Israel and the United States (with a small minority settling in Germany and other European states). As much as 20 percent of the Jews of Israel are now native Russian speakers.

Between 1 million and 1.5 million Jews remain in the FSU today, mostly in Russia, Belarus, and the Ukraine. Their lives include a fast-growing level of religious, educational, and cultural activity—including some vibrant Yiddish theater and publishing ventures.

The struggle for Soviet Jewish emigration and against Soviet anti-Semitism was a major unifying force in the American Jewish community during the two decades preceding the breakup of the USSR. The campaign brought the liberal majority of the community into harmony with the foreign policy of the American government and fine-tuned the lobbying capacity of American Jews—as revealed by the 1974 passage of the Jackson-Vanik Amendment to the Trade Act, which withheld trade favors from the Soviet Union unless it liberalized its emigration policies.

amen^R
omeyn^Y
amain, ameyn

Pronounced, according to regional variation, *aw*-MAIN, to rhyme with "raw lane"; *aw*-MINE, to rhyme with "jawline"; or even *oo*-MINE, to rhyme with "do fine." Hebrew: "So be it."
   Amen.

1. The word used during and at the end of prayer to signify affirmation. It is one of the most widely known words in all the world: Jews, Christians, and Muslims share its usage.

   When services were held in the Temple in Jerusalem, a longer formula was used as the response of affirmation made by the people during the liturgy recited by the priests and Levites. After the Temple was destroyed, *amen* was retained in Jewish liturgy.

   The *Talmud* ruled that *amen* was to be recited "with the full power" of the voice. (A forceful enunciation of *amen* was believed by the credulous to help open the doors of Paradise.) The loud, emphatic utterance of *amen* was connected with the expression of repentance, which is very strong in Judaism.

   The Great Synagogue of Alexandria was said to be so huge that worshipers in the rear, who could not hear the cantor, could not know when he had finished the prayer. To enable these unfortunates to participate in a mighty responsive *amen* at the right moment, an attendant signaled with a flag when it was time for all the faithful to thunder out in chorus: "*Amen!*"

2. An interjection used as a response to a good wish.

   "I hope you get well quickly."

"*Amen.*"

3. An expletive uttered in malediction, to co-wish misfortune upon someone disliked, or disaster upon someone hated. Thus:

"May a *kazarnya* [armory] collapse on him!"

"*Amen!*"

"May all his teeth fall out!"

"*Amen.*"

"Killed he should be before nightfall!"

"*Amen!*"

"Like a beet should he grow—with his head in the earth!"

"Ah, *amen!*"

am horets^Y
am ha-aretz^R

Pronounced *am-*HOR-*ets* in Yiddish, to rhyme with "Tom Boretz." From the Hebrew: "people of the soil" or, less literally, "an uneducated man."

1. An ignoramus.
2. A vulgar, boorish, ill-mannered man or woman.
3. A country bumpkin.

In the Jewish communities of Europe, learned but poor Jews were much, *much* more highly respected than rich but unlearned ones.

Am horets meant "uneducated" or "uncultured" (just as "villain," in English, originally designated a serf, and "boor," a peasant); after the Babylonian Exile, "none remained save the poorest sort of the people of the land" (II Kings 24:14). These unlearned farmers drifted away from Judaic practices and married into the surrounding populations. The rabbinical leaders stigmatized such backsliders as vulgarians and transgressors of the law.

The *Talmud* describes an *am horets* as one who does not respect the Law and the rabbis. Maimonides defined him as "a boor in whom is neither learning nor moral virtue." Rabbi Nathan ben Joseph called an *am horets* "one who has children and does not educate them. . . ."

An *am horets* may be shrewd, though ignorant. But not these two ignoramuses who were arguing: "Does a slice of bread fall with the buttered side up or down?"

Jacob said, "With the buttered side down!"

Max said, "With the buttered side *up!*"

So they made a bet.

Jacob buttered a slice of bread, raised it, and let it drop. It fell— buttered side up.

"I win!" cried Max.

"Only because I made a mistake," Jacob protested.

"What mistake?"

"I buttered the wrong side."

"How just is the Lord," said an *am horets* from Chelm, the mythical town inhabited by fools. "He gives the food to the rich—and the appetite to the poor!"

FOLK SAYING: "The luck of an *am horets* is this: He doesn't know that he doesn't know."

apikoyres^Y
apikoros^R
apikores, apicarus, epicoris

Pronounced *ah-peh*-KAY-*riss,* to rhyme with "Papa Bayliss," or *eh-peh*-KOY-*riss,* to rhyme with "Effie coy miss." From the Greek philosopher Epicurus, via rabbinical literature.

1. An unbeliever, a skeptic, an agnostic, an atheist. (*Apikorsus,* pronounced *ah-peh*-CORE-*suss,* means "skepticism" or "heresy.")
2. A Jew who does not observe religious practices. The *Mishnah* states: "All Israelites have a share in the future world [except] he who says there is no resurrection, he who says the Law has not been given by God, and an *apikoyres.*"

I have always loved the charming story about the brilliant young student who came to the old, learned rabbi and defiantly exclaimed, "I must tell you the truth! I have become an *apikoyres.* I no longer believe in God!"

"And how long," asked the elder, "have you been studying *Talmud?*"

"Five years," the student said.

"Only five years," sighed the rabbi, "and you have the nerve to call yourself an *apikoyres?! . . .*"

aroysgevorfn^Y
aroysgevorfen^R

Pronounced *ah-*ROYCE-*ge-vor-fen,* the *royce* rhyming with "choice," the *vorfen* with "orphan." From German.

Thrown out.

This simple adjective carries a cargo of regret, for it means "wasted," and Jews are not second to New Englanders in their disapproval of wastefulness; *aroysgevorfn* is applied not only to material things.

My mother would often end a lecture to me with the dour lament that her words were probably in vain: "*Aroysgevorfne verter*" (*ah-*ROYCE-*ge-vor-f'neh* VER-*ter,* meaning "Thrown out words"). Was ever a phrase more heartfelt?

Aroysgevorfne yorn ("years"), enunciated with a sigh deep from the diaphragm, or with bitterness, refers to the wasted years that can never be relived. Jewish women are, by tradition, prone to lament their lot with this phrase.

Aroysgevorfne gelt ("money") describes a useless purchase, an investment that did not prove fruitful, or (as in the story below) a gesture that went awry.

Benny and Moe wanted to give their mother a new and different birthday present. They went from shop to shop until, to their wonder and delight, they found—a parrot that spoke Yiddish! This astonishing bird cost $500, but the devoted sons decided it was worth it. Think of the hours and hours of pleasure their old-fashioned mother would derive from conversing with the extraordinary parrot; and think of the admiration the bird would elicit among Mama's friends in the sisterhood!

So the sons bought a beautiful gilded cage, placed the parrot inside, and had the singular birthday gift delivered to Mama.

Then, in great excitement, they telephoned: "Mama, Mama, how did you like your present?"

"Delicious!" said Mama.

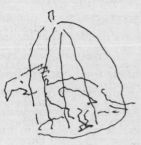

Ashkenazi
Ashkenazim (plural)
Ashkenazic* (adjective)

*"Ashkenazic" is an English adaptation of *Ashkenazi.*

Pronounced *osh-ken-NOZ-zee,* to rhyme with "Gosh Ben Ossie." Hebrew: *Ashkenaz,* "Germany." (Originally, *Ashkenaz* referred to a kingdom of sorts in ancient eastern Armenia.)

The name applied, since the sixteenth century, to the Jews of central and eastern Europe—ancestors of the vast majority of Jews in the United States.

Ashkenazim and *Sephardim* are the two main branches of Jewry. The Sephardic Jews live in, or come from, Portugal,

Spain, and **southern France.**† The *Ashkenazim* moved from northern France to Germanic cities along the Rhine, then to central and eastern **Europe,**‡ where they found settlements of Jews who had emigrated, long before, from Babylon and Palestine.

Medieval rabbis dubbed Germany *Ashkenaz,* after a passage in Jeremiah (51:27), and decided that after the Flood, one of Noah's great-grandsons, named Ashkenaz, had settled in Germany. I have no idea what inspired the rabbis.

Ashkenazic Jews are distinguished from Sephardic Jews in many ways: the Yiddish they speak, their style of thought, their pronunciation of Hebrew, aspects of their liturgy, many customs, food habits, ceremonials. This is not surprising, given the considerable differences in history and experience across a span of a thousand years.

Yiddish is an Ashkenazic invention—and universe. The vernacular of Sephardic Jews is Ladino.

From 1880 to 1910, about one-third of the *Ashkenazim* of eastern Europe migrated—over 90 percent of them to the United States. To the already established, prosperous, Americanized German Jews, the new immigrants looked like "medieval appari-

---

†As Rosten notes in his entry for **Sephardi**, Israeli Jews with roots in Arab and North African countries are also referred to nowadays as *Sephardim*—or, more correctly, as *Mizrachi* Jews (both are preferred to the outdated "Oriental Jews"). *Sephardi/Mizrachi* Jews are among the poorer and less educated inhabitants of the Jewish state, whereas the *Ashkenazim* comprise the Israeli middle class and elite. The Labor Party and its left-wing coalition partner, Meretz, have their political bases among the *Ashkenazim*; the Likud and Shas, the fastest-growing religious party, are *Mizrachi*-based. While some 30 percent of Jewish marriages in Israel today are "intermarriages" between the groups, their social and political tensions remain fierce.

Israeli has two chief rabbis, one Sephardic, one Ashkenazic. See Rosten's entry and my note for **mizrach**.

‡See my notes for Rosten's entry for **Yiddish** for a somewhat more complicated picture of the evolution of Ashkenazic culture.

tions." To the *Deutsche Yehudim* (German Jews), the new *Ashkenazim* were religious fanatics or—doubly puzzling—"agitators," union organizers, socialists, radicals. And the German Jews loathed Yiddish, which they thought a vulgar corruption of their own language.*

See Ladino, shtetl, Sephardi, Yiddish.

aveyre^Y
averah^R

Pronounced *ah-*VAY*-reh,* to rhyme with "Ah, say the." Hebrew: "sin."

1. Literally: A transgression against God's will.
2. More loosely: An unethical or undesirable act.
3. Colloquially: "Too bad," "what a pity." "It's an *averah* to discard that dress; I've only worn it twice."

---

*Notwithstanding these antagonisms, the German Jews ("uptown" Jews, as opposed to the immigrant masses on the Lower East Side) played a very benevolent role in establishing organizations designed to "uplift" and protect their Ashkenazic brethren. These institutions included the Educational Alliance, American Jewish Committee, Hebrew Orphan Asylum, Mt. Sinai Hospital, and United Hebrew Charities. Lillian Wald, born in Cincinnati in 1867 to German-Jewish parents, became a legendary "angel of mercy" on New York's Lower East Side through her work as a nurse and founder of the Henry Street Settlement House. In other cases, the charitable German Jews "held themselves aloof," according to their communal leader, Louis Marshall, ". . . bringing gifts to people who did not seek [them]. . . . The work was done in such a manner as not only to give offense, but to arouse suspicion of the motives" (quoted in Gerald Sorin, *A Time for Building*, vol. III of *The Jewish People in America*, Johns Hopkins University Press, 1992). The German-Jewish disdain for Yiddish played no small role in widening this gulf.

An *aveyre* is the direct opposite of a *mitzva,* as we shall see. The words are often contrasted, as in the saying "One *mitzva* leads to another; an *aveyre* leads to an *aveyre.*"

Mr. Popper was challenged to fight a duel with Weishaupt, a well-known anti-Semite. The time was set for six A.M., in a field beyond the city.

Promptly at six, Weishaupt appeared with his seconds.

They waited.

At six-twenty, a messenger came running toward them, with a telegram:

> UNAVOIDABLY DETAINED. IT WOULD BE AN *AVEYRE* TO
> DISAPPOINT YOU.
> SO DON'T WAIT FOR ME—SHOOT.
> POPPER

Centuries before Sigmund Freud published his *Interpretation of Dreams* (1900), the Jews had a saying: "In sleep, it is not the man who sins—but his dream."

No man sings for someone else.

—Baba Metziah *(Talmud)*

aynredenish[Y]
einredenish[R]

Pronounced INE-*red-e-nish,* to rhyme with "Fine bed of fish." From the German *aynreden:* "to make one believe"; literally, "to talk into." Yiddish adds the all-purpose *-ish* to convert the verb into a noun.

1. Something, usually wrong or unwarranted, that one has talked oneself into believing.
2. A delusion, an idée fixe. "She has an *aynredenish* that he hates tea."

Y ou can't have a true or correct *aynredenish*, please notice. If it's an *aynredenish*, it partakes of the unrealistic or the insupportable.

"An *aynredenish* is worse than a disease," goes a Yiddish apothegm. This anticipated Freud and expresses the impressive popular insight that physical diseases are more readily cured than psychological delusions.

The history of the human race would have been far less monstrous had God substituted diseases for delusions. Between psychosis and sciatica, I'll take (or give) sciatica any day.

Aynredenish might well be adopted in English to mean "the incorrect, foolish, or fantastic things people talk themselves into believing."

My *aynredenish* is that you can get Iowans to pronounce the *kh*'s in *khokhem* the way Jews do—and Scots can.

FOLK SAYING: "A man's worst enemies can't wish on him what he can think up himself."

At a mass meeting in Berlin, Adolf Hitler, in thrall to a most appalling *aynredenish*, shrieked, "And who is responsible for all our troubles?"

Ben Cohen shouted, "The bicycle riders and the Jews!"

Hitler looked up, astonished. "Why the bicycle riders?"

"Why the Jews?" replied Cohen.

Poor Mr. Gittelman could not sleep. No pills from his doctor, no advice from his friends, helped his tormenting insomnia. Mr. Gittelman began to look so haggard that his partner, Mr. Feigenbaum, said, "You'll end up in a loony ward!"

"So what can I *do*?" moaned Gittelman. "I drink hot milk. I take warm baths. I play soft music. I take every sleeping pill the doctor prescribes. . . ."

"What about the oldest trick of all: counting sheep?"

Gittelman smote his forehead. "Harvey, so help me, I forgot that one. You're a lifesaver. Tonight, I'll count sheep, and if I have to count up to ten thousand, I'll fall asleep at last!"

The next morning, the moment Gittelman entered the loft, Feigenbaum asked, "Did it work?"

"No," Gittelman groaned. "I counted sheep. Oh, how I counted sheep. I counted up to two thousand without getting tired. So I sheared the sheep—all two thousand—and still I was wide awake. So I had an idea, and I made up two thousand overcoats. Do you *know* how tiring it is to make two thousand overcoats?! I was exhausted and practically snoring—when it happened!"

"What happened?"

"All night I was up, worrying: Where could I get two thousand linings?"

bagel

Pronounced BAY-g'l, to rhyme with "Nagel." From German, *Beugel*, "a round **loaf of bread**."*

A hard doughnut-shaped roll, simmered in hot water for two minutes before baking, then glazed with egg white.

If you have never tasted a *bagel*, I feel sorry for you.

Bagels are known as doughnuts with a college education—and the college is probably *yeshiva*.

Because *bagels* were made of white flour, they were considered great delicacies in eastern Europe, where the poor Jews (and most Jews were very poor indeed) ate black bread except on the Sabbath, when the queen of breads, *challah*, was eaten.

A *bagel* was supposed to be lucky, because it is round. Don't laugh at the Jews: the wise Greeks thought a circle the "perfect"

---

*Yiddishist Gerald Stillman argues (in *Jewish Currents*, May 2000) that "*bagel* comes from the Yiddish word for 'to bend,' which is *beygn* if you're a *Litvak* and *baygn* if you're a *Galitsyaner*."

Be that as it may, the ubiquity of the *bagel* in American culture has become firmly established. Dunkin' Donuts and other food chains now offer their own varieties, and the *bagel* has undergone many innovations that purists might consider abominations: green *bagels* on St. Patrick's Day, orange *bagels* on Halloween, and jalapeño pepper *bagels*, oat bran *bagels*, chocolate chip *bagels*, etc., all year 'round. As a result, old-line *bagel* makers have taken to advertising their manufacturing process, "hand-rolled" and "water-boiled," to distinguish their "real" New York Jewish *bagels* from all-American varieties.

form because it had neither beginning nor end; therefore God, being perfect, chose the circle as the basic form in constructing the universe. The orbits of the stars and planets were assumed to be circular. Even Aristotle thought so, and so did Ptolemy, and so did Copernicus, who nearly drove himself crazy trying to rearrange Ptolemy's elaborate observations into a new set of circles with epicenters. (The mystical assumption about circles plagued and stymied astronomers until Kepler.)

Bagels and hard-boiled eggs were traditionally served in Jewish homes after a funeral, for they were thought to symbolize the unending "round" processes of life and the world. The custom may have developed from interpretations of the passage in Ecclesiastes: "One generation passeth away, and another generation cometh, but the earth abideth forever."

The first printed mention of *bagels,* by the way, is to be found in the Community Regulations of Cracow, Poland, for the year 1610—which stated that *bagels* would be given as a gift to any woman in childbirth.

I suppose that you, like most people, think that a *bagel* and lox (smoked salmon) is the traditional Sunday morning breakfast for Jews. It is certainly widespread, but not traditional: it is a triumph of cuisine invented by American Jews.

Slices of tender lox, topping a layer of sweet butter on which cream cheese has been **lathered**,* the whole enclosed by a toasted *bagel,* is so delicious that, to stop the watering in my mouth, I am going out to lunch.

*See my note to Rosten's entry for **lox** for comment on this high-cholesterol recipe.

INTERMISSION

A Yiddish expression, *"Er ligt in der erd un bakt bagel,"* is readily translated as "He lies in the ground and bakes *bagels.*" But what does that mean? "He's not doing so well, poor chap."

A man from Mars landed on Second Avenue and looked into a store window, fascinated. Finally, he entered the shop and asked the owner: "What are those little wheels in the window?"

"Wheels? What wheels?"

The Martian pointed.

"Those aren't wheels." The *balebos* smiled. "They're called *bagels*. We eat them. . . . Here, try one."

The Martian bit into a *bagel* and smacked his lips. "Man! This would go great with cream cheese and lox."

On St. Patrick's Day 1968, Macy's ran an advertisement in the New York papers such as I had never thought I'd see:

BAGELS,

BEGORRAH!

(green ones, yet)

The ad ended: "Cream cheese and lox . . . eighth floor."

Of such is the history of human culture compounded. Begorrah.

balebatim[Y]
balbatim[R]

Pronounced *bol*-(eh)-вот-*im*, to rhyme with "Moll got him."
From the Hebrew: *balei ha-bayet*, "masters of the house."

Persons of high standing, impeccable repute and responsibility; community leaders.

The board members of a synagogue or temple are *balebatim*.
The crude, the vulgar, the superficial, however successful, are not *balebatim* or *balebatish* (adjective).

See balebos.

Young Rabbi Shulman finally summoned up enough courage to say to Mr. Benenson, one of the *balebatim* of the community, "I trust you won't mind my mentioning it, but I can't help noticing that—you always fall asleep when I'm preaching."

"Why not?" replied Benenson. "Would I sleep if I didn't trust you?"

balebatish[Y]
balbatish[R]

Pronounced *bol*-(eh)-вот-*ish*, to rhyme with "doll tot-ish."

This is the adjective of *balebos*. *Balebatisher* is masculine; *balebatishe* is feminine.

1. Quiet, respectable, well mannered.
2. Responsible; of some consequence.

What nicer adjective is there? To call someone *balebatish* is to endow him or her with quiet, admirable traditional virtues. "What a *balebatish* child." "He is a *balebatisher* merchant." "She is a *balebatishe* woman."

"My little *balebatishkayt*" means "my few possessions."

A Texan, driving down the great flat desert near Beersheba in Israel, spied a tiny but *balebatish* house in the distance, and he drove up and stopped and knocked on the door.

An old Jew came to the door. "Good morning."

"My throat is so dry it's on fire," said the Texan. "I wonder if you would be good enough to give me a glass of water."

"Certainly; come in, make yourself at home."

The Texan entered and drank the water and thanked his host, then said, "Do you own this little house?"

"Yes."

"What do you do way out here?"

"I raise chickens."

"How large is your property?"

"Well," said the Jew, "in front, it's a good sixty feet—and in back, it must be a hundred, a hundred and ten, feet at *least*."

The Texan smiled. "Back home, on my ranch, I get up and get in my car around nine A.M. and I start to drive, and I drive and drive and drive—and I don't reach the end of my property until six o'clock that night!"

"*Tchk!*" sighed the Jew. "I once owned a car like that."

balebos^Y (masculine)
baleboss^R
baleboste^Y (feminine)
baleboosteh^R

The masculine form is pronounced either *bol-eh-*BAWSS, to rhyme with "Walla hoss," or *bol-eh-*BOOSS, to rhyme with

"Walla puss." The feminine form is pronounced either *bol-eh*-BAWSS-*teh*, to rhyme with "Walla costa," or *bol-eh*-BOOS-*teh*, to rhyme with "Walla puss ta." From the Hebrew, *bal ha-bayit*, "master of the house"; but the female, *baleboste*, is entirely and delightfully Yiddish.

A *balebos* is

1. the head of the household, the man of the house.
2. the owner of a store, shop, establishment.
3. the manager or superintendent.
4. one who assumes authority.

A *baleboste* is the wife of 1, 2, or 3, or

5. an excellent and praiseworthy homemaker.
6. a female owner.
7. a female manager.
8. a bossy woman.

Number 5 is the most common usage today, given the notable decline in the number of Jewish women who (a) work behind the counter in the shop owned or managed by their husbands, or (b) are themselves owners and/or operators of businesses.*

When one Jewish housekeeper calls another a *baleboste*, it is usually with an appreciative "Pssh!," raising eyebrows, pursed lips, or with an admiring "*Tchk!*"

To call a woman "a real *baleboste*" is to bestow high praise

---

*As of 1999, there were 9.1 million women-owned businesses in the United States, 38 percent of all firms, and it is fair to estimate that Jewish women are as involved in this ownership trend as any other minority group. The decline to which Rosten refers is in the realm of retail shops owned by Jewish couples, which in most cases were sold or went out of business a generation ago. While 16 percent of today's Jews in the workforce are self-employed, fewer than 3 percent work in the classic "family business." More typically, today's Jewish working couple has two incomes, often from white-collar jobs.

indeed: it means the honoree is a splendid cook, baker, and laundress and, above all, keeps so immaculate a home that "you can eat off the floor." No one I knew ever did, in fact, eat off anyone else's floor, but I cannot count the number of times I heard the phrase—or the number of times that symbolic riband of the Légion d'honneur was pinned upon my mother's apron.

I was greatly impressed, as a child, by the obsession with cleanliness in our household and the scorn with which untidiness was castigated. Cleanliness was not second to godliness; it was second to nothing.

In Hebrew, *baal* means master and *bayit* means house, and *baaleboss* originally meant a man who owned a business, a house, or a piece of land. It was extended to mean "master of the house," lord of his domain. Jewish men did traditionally dominate the home and were respectfully obeyed by wife and children in all those domains considered man's high and exclusive responsibility.

There is a charming Yiddish expression for a Jewish girl's fond hope: "*A tishele, a benkele, a baleboste bey zikh zu zayn!*" "A little table, a little bench—oh, to be a *baleboste* of one's own!"

A newly arrived Jewish immigrant entered a kosher restaurant on Delancey Street. The waiter who poured his water was— *Gottenyu!*—Chinese! And the Chinese servitor proceeded to rattle off the menu in fluent Yiddish, even unto the idiomatic grunts, sighs and *nu*'s.

When the Jew was paying his bill, he asked the cashier, "Are you the *balebos* [owner]?"

"Who else?"

"Well, I certainly enjoyed my dinner—and even more, the fact that your waiter speaks such excellent Yiddish!"

"Sha!" hissed the proprietor. "He thinks we're teaching him English!"*

balmelokhe^Y
balmalocha^R
balmalucha, balmelokheh

Pronounced *bahl-m'*LUH-*kheh,* or *bahl-m'*LAW-*kha;* make the *kh* Scottish and uvular, as in *loch;* rhymes with "Moll m'cooka." From Hebrew: "craftsman."
1. An expert. "Where pants are concerned, he is a real *balmelokhe.*"
2. In a derisive sense: Maladroit, inexpert, "*some* crafts-man"—that is, no craftsman at all. "His son-in-law? Oh, there's a *balmelokhe!*"

In a small *shtetl* notices appeared that, at five o'clock on the first day of June, "The Great Isadore Bloomgarten, World-Famous Trapeze Artist," would walk across the river on a tightrope. Admission: 25 kopecks.

The whole town turned out.

They saw a rope tied to a tree, stretched tight across the river, anchored to a tree on the other side. Out came the Great

---

*Given the upscale occupational demographics of the American Jewish community, it is no longer so unusual to be served by non-Jewish employees in kosher-style, if not *glatt* kosher, eateries. Israel's multicomplected Jewish population and large number of *yordim* (Jews who have emigrated from the Jewish state) have also made the sight of a Yiddish-speaking Chinese waiter in America a bit less likely to evoke a "*Gottenyu!*" In the *bagels*-and-appetizing trade, even the *balebos* may not be Jewish any longer: Koreans, Pakistanis, Latin Americans, and other shopkeeping immigrants have entered the business in major cities.

Bloomgarten—but in an old suit and frayed shoes. He climbed up the tree, set one foot warily on the rope, and turned to address the audience: "Ladies and gentlemen, good Jews—I have a confession to make. I am not a trapeze artist. I'm just a poor man trying to earn a living. If I try anything as crazy as starting across the river on this rope, I'll fall, break my neck, and drown right before your eyes. Now, if it's all right with you that for a miserable twenty-five kopecks a poor Jew should have that happen to him, I'll proceed. . . . So let's vote. How many want me to go on?"

As a tightrope walker, Bloomgarten was no *balmelokhe*, but as a salesman—!

Bal Shem[Y]
Baal Shem[R]

Pronounced *bol*-SHEM, to rhyme with "doll hem." Hebrew: "the master of the [good] Name."

The name given to saintly men who were believed to be endowed with mystical and healing powers, which they attained (it was claimed) through manipulations of God's Name.

*B*al Shems practiced folk medicine, employed amulets to ward off the evil eye, and dispelled spirits. They also dispensed psychiatric advice. They were believed, or claimed, to be chosen by the Deity, as spiritually superior souls, for the performance of divine interventions.

The *Bal Shem,* or *Bal Shem Tov* ("good"), was the most famous of these holy men. Born Israel ben Eliezer (c. 1700–1760), the *Baal Shem* was an itinerant evangelist, a mystic, an ecstatic, a poet. He preached in simple language: "My teaching rests on three kinds of love: love of God, love of the *Torah*, love of humanity." He told his followers to laugh, to sing, to dance in adoration of the Holy One—which scandalized the traditionalists. What distinguished him from other *Bal Shems* was that whereas they dabbled in spiritualism and were steeped in mysticism, numerology, the abracadabra of endless, abstruse rearrangements of one or another of the Names of God, the *Bal Shem Tov* preached a down-to-earth, untormented gospel: He was a gentle visionary who extolled the expression of joy and the enjoyment of life.

The *Bal Shem Tov* derided the learned Talmudists, branding them sterile pedants who "through sheer study of the Law have no time to think about God." One serves God through deeds, he said, through living out the precepts of the *Torah*, not just studying them.

The rabbis Galicia and Poland branded Israel ben Eliezer a heretic, but thousands of simple people venerated him as a true saint and miracle worker.

He became known to his followers as the *Besht* (an acronym formed from the first letters of *Bal Shem Tov*), and his influence spread rapidly. He brought the excitement of hope into the lives of Polish Jewry, who had been decimated during a decade of savage Cossack pogroms.

The *Besht* said to the poor and the ignorant: God is in everything, including human beings. Everyone, therefore, is good, and even a sinner can approach God with devotion. It does not matter that a simple Jew is unlearned—honest prayer is as important as erudition. Unity with God is achieved not through suffering, weeping, and asceticism, but through emotion, through rapture in spontaneous song and dance, in rejoicing and ecstasy. People must enjoy human passions, not repress or run from them.

This extraordinary gospel became the basis of the Chasidic movement. Although the illustrious and revered Gaon of Vilna excommunicated the *Besht* and banned his teachings, the Chasidic movement swept with singular speed and fervor through Poland, Galicia, Bohemia, and Hungary. An entire culture within the culture of the *shtetl* grew up around the liberating visions of the *Bal Shem Tov*—and ended, as movements begun by simple men often do, in a cult.

The *Bal Shem* "rejuvenated" Jewry, says Rabbi Abraham Joshua Heschel, for Jews "fell in love with the Lord and felt such yearning for God that it was unbearable. . . . In the days of Moses, Israel had a revelation of God, in the days of the *Bal Shem,* God had a revelation of Israel" (*The Earth Is the Lord's,* Abelard-Schuman, 1964).

FOLK SAYING: "Some scholars are like donkeys: they merely carry a lot of books."

bandit^Y
bonditt^R
banditt

Pronounced *bon*-DEET, to rhyme with "Ron's feet." From German: *Bandit:* "rogue," "bandit."*

1. A clever, resourceful, beguiling fellow.
2. Someone with a delightful sense of mischief.
3. A bandit.

"Oh, what a *bandit!*" is uttered with a grin, or an appreciative cluck, the way Westerners say, "That son of a gun!"

*Yiddishist Gerald Stillman notes (in private correspondence) that "the Yiddish *bandit* is probably derived from Russian *bandit* or Polish *bandyta;* the German *bandit* is too recent."

To ring a change on the immortal precedent of *The Virginian:* "When you call me *bandit*—smile."

Parents may say of a boisterous, bright child, "Oh, what a *bandit!*" ("Oh, what a little devil.")

I used to think that *bandit* was an adaptation from the English "bandit" by way of the villains in early westerns, who were called "bandits" more often than "robbers." But *bandit* was widely used by Jews in Russia, Poland, and Romania long before they saw a movie.

See also ganef, mamzer, mazik.

Two lawyers met in the lobby of the Empire State Building.

"Abe Epstein!" cried the first. "What a surprise! I haven't seen you since we both lived on Eldridge Street, on the Lower East Side. How are things?"

"You want to see something?" Epstein led his friend proudly to the large directory in the lobby and pointed. "'Eldridge, C. R.' That's me."

"*Eldridge!* You *bandit!*"

Epstein said, "Don't think I'm ashamed of my origins! The initials stand for 'Corner Rivington.'"

bar mitzva^R
bar mitsve^Y
bar mitzvah

Pronounced *bar-*MITZ*-vah,* to rhyme with "car hits ya."* From Aramaic/Hebrew: "son of the commandment"; more broadly, "man of duty."

---

*This is an Anglicized pronunciation. Yiddish purists would say *bar-*MITS*-veh.*

The ceremony, held in a synagogue, in which the thirteen-year-old Jewish boy reaches the status, and assumes the duties, of a "man." It is usually held on the Saturday closest to the boy's thirteenth birthday.

For the equivalent ceremony for girls, see bas mitzva.

The *bar mitzva* ceremony is not an ancient institution; it did not even exist until the fourteenth century. It is not a sacrament or a sacramental ritual. It simply signalizes the arrival of a Jewish boy at the age when, presumably, adult reason and responsibility commence. (The thirteenth year, in many cultures, is considered the beginning of puberty and is celebrated with initiation rites.)

Ancient rabbinical sources contain the alarming notification that after his thirteenth birthday a Jewish boy is responsible for observing 613 (!) holy commandments. I must record my very grave doubt that a careful accounting of this is kept, even in heaven.

Please note that in traditional Jewish life the *bar mitzva* is a ceremony, a celebration, not a confirmation. In Reform Judaism there arose, in addition to the *bar mitzva*, a ceremony of confirmation; at age fifteen or sixteen, the boy (*or girl*) confirms his faith and responsibility. Confirmation services en masse are held during the festival of *Shevuos*. Some Conservative synagogues have also embraced this practice as a way of keeping teens involved in Jewish life. Nevertheless, Jews regard Jewishness as something that does not require confirmation: a Jew is a Jew;†

---

† "A Jew is a Jew" is no longer so easy a formulation in Jewish life, and the question of "who is a Jew" now plagues Jewish communities worldwide. Orthodox disdain for the legitimacy of Conservative, Reform, and Reconstructionist rabbis (who lack legal status in Israel yet form the great majority of the rabbinic corps in the United States) has long been an interdenominational sore point, but the contention spilled over to the general Jewish population when the Reform movement, in 1978, adopted a policy of "patrilineal descent" in determining who is to be considered Jewish. Traditionally, the

(continued on page 44)

Jewish life is one long, unbroken continuity; one only celebrates the arrival at the age of thirteen.

The *bar mitzva* signifies that a young male, now a "man of duty," is committed to lifelong religious and ethical obligations. In earlier days, the "*bar mitzva* boy" was obliged to deliver a scholarly address on some aspect of Talmudic law. He did not deliver a speech. In America, the custom arose of delivering a *bar mitzva* speech, which began, "Today, I am a man." (When a rosy-cheeked thirteen-year-old announced this in a piping tenor, broad smiles, of both pride and polite dubiety, danced through the congregation.)

Today, the boy usually delivers a prayer, in Hebrew or English, pledging himself to live up to the ideals of Judaism, dedicating himself to the *Torah*, and thanking his father and mother for all they have done for him. (At this point, parental and grandparental eyes well up.) The boy is called to the altar to read the week's section from the *Torah* and the attached section (the *Haftorah*) from later parts of the Bible.

After the *bar mitzva*, the boy is, technically, required to wear phylacteries (*tefillin*) during morning prayer. He can now be counted as an adult in the *minyan* of ten males required before public prayers can begin and can be called to the pulpit to recite a passage from the *Torah*.

(continued from p 43)

children of Jewish women are seen as Jewish ("matrilineal descent"), even if the fathers are non-Jews; the Reform (and Reconstructionist) policy extends recognition to the children of Jewish fathers, even if the mothers are non-Jews, as long as the children are raised in no other religious tradition. People are therefore being embraced as Jews under terms that neither the Conservative nor Orthodox communities accept. The patrilineal policy has opened up liberal Jewish life to intermarried couples and their children—and has further weakened Jewish unity on matters of marriage, divorce, and Israeli citizenship.

To Jewish parents, the *bar mitzva* is a proud landmark of high symbolic meaning: that is, their son's dedication to the lofty precepts of an ancient people and tradition. Papa, Mama, sisters, brothers, grandparents, in-laws, friends, friends of friends, business associates, neighbors—all are present at a *bar mitzva*. The parents and grandparents beam and kvell to the bursting point.

It is customary to give gifts to the young man—who at one time was sure to receive at least six **fountain pens,*** with chagrin. The parents give the boy a *tallis* (prayer shawl) of his own. A *bar mitzva* feast follows the service.

If you want to know more about *bar mitzvas,* go to one. They're charming and innocent and always put a **lump in my throat.**†

At the last *bar mitzva* I attended, I heard this story:

*Rabbi Jeffrey Salkin observes (in *Searching for My Brothers,* Putnam, 1999), "Two generations ago, the fountain pen symbolized American corporate masculine privilege—the ability to endorse checks and sign contracts." Salkin infers from this that "boys are socialized to look at incipient manhood as a time of privilege," while girls "have a deeper sense of what it really means to become a woman, because there is a far deeper discussion among girls of the physical aspects of maturity." Salkin is author of *Putting God on the Guest List* (Jewish Lights, 1996), a popular guide to preserving spirituality in the modern *bar* or *bas mitzva.*

† In *MAD* magazine's 1973 lampoon of the Broadway hit *Fiddler on the Roof,* Tevye sang not about "Tradition!" but about "Possessions!"—a friendly slap at conspicuous consumption that seems particularly deserved when it comes to today's *bar* (and *bat*) *mitzva* parties. Outrageous expenditures, exotic locales, fatuous party themes, and sheer glitz have turned many celebrations into something between an Academy Award presentation and a Roman bacchanale. In response, the Reform synagogue movement passed a resolution in 1992 calling on Jews to have celebrations characterized by "family cohesion, authentic friendship, acts of *tzedakah* and parties suitable for children." Whether the majority of Jewish families will quit trying to "keep up with the Cohnses" remains to be seen.

Two Martians who had landed in America happened to run into each other.

"What's your name?" asked the first.

"4286. And yours?"

"3359."

"That's funny; you don't look Jewish."

bas mitzva^R
bas mitsve^Y
bas mitzvah

Pronounced *bahs*-MITZ-*vah*, to rhyme with "Joss pits ya."* Hebrew: "daughter of the commandment."

The ceremony for girls, akin to the *bar mitzva* for boys.

In recent years, some Reform, Conservative, and even Orthodox congregations have introduced a *bas mitzva* ceremony, which is a *bar mitzva* open to girls when they reach the age of twelve. (The ancients realized that girls mature earlier than boys.)

Many an Orthodox Jew still shudders at the idea of a *bas mitzva*, and others give a girl a *bas mitzva* at home, but not in the synagogue.

Bas mitzva services are sometimes held en masse, for girls from twelve to eighteen **years of age.**†

---

*An un-Anglicized pronunciation would be *bas*-MITS-*veh*.

†In all American streams of Judaism but the Orthodox, the *bas mitzva* has become as much a part of Jewish life for girls as the *bar mitzva* is for boys. At its best, *bas mitzva* training provides a rich alternative to the media messages that pressure adolescent girls to be sexy, stylish, and conformist. *Philadelphia Inquirer* columnist Jane R. Eisner calls the process of becoming a *bas mitzva* "the antidote to everything negative and frightening about modern girls."

batkhn^Y
badchen^R
batkhonim (plural)

Pronounced BOD-*kh'n*, and *bod*-KHAW-*nim*, with the uvular Scottish/German *kh*. Hebrew.

A professional funmaker, jester, entertainer.

M errymakers, masquers, clowns, improvisers of doggerel, traveling players, and musicians—all these were common figures in Europe during the Middle Ages. And the Jewish populace loved their own professional *batkhonim*, who attended weddings, anniversaries, *bar mitzvas*, to enliven the festivities.

The *batkhn* would offer a serious poem to bride and groom, would orate on the glory and sanctity of marriage, would extol the ancestors, the parents, the guests—and then would lampoon everything, teasing the nuptial couple, spoofing the ceremony itself, extemporizing poems, perhaps donning a mask, ad-libbing jokes, dancing, leading songs.

The rabbis urged Jews to "make merry" at weddings—even proclaiming it one's duty to be sportive. Perhaps the singularly perceptive sages sensed how important it was for Jews, condemned to so much suffering and fear, to enjoy periodic catharsis.

The *bas mitzva* has also become a very popular way for adult Jewish women, denied a Jewish education and a place at the *bema* (pulpit) during their girlhoods, to assert their rights within Judaism and their leadership within the synagogue. These days, therefore, the en masse services that Rosten describes more typically involve baby boom adults than teenagers.

Judith Kaplan Eisenstein (1910–1996) became the first *bas mitzva* in modern times when she came to read from the *Torah* in 1922 at the Society for the Advancement of Judaism in New York. Her father was Rabbi Mordecai Kaplan, the founder of Reconstructionist Judaism (see my note to Rosten's entry for **Adonai**). Eisenstein herself became a leading Jewish musicologist, music educator, and composer.

The *batkhn,* incidentally, often composed his own verses and music—much of it extempore—and the *batkhonim* left a legacy of folk songs that have come down the centuries and form a cherished part of Jewish life and lore.

One of the most renowned of *batkhonim* was Eliakim Zunser, a poet of considerable talent.

The *batkhn* has all but disappeared from Jewish life (in the United States, at least) but surely left his mark and example: the *batkhn* is the direct lineal progenitor of the tum*ler,* which entry you ought to read.

See also klezmer.

batlen^Y
batlan^R
batlonim^Y (plural)
batlanim^R

Pronounced BOT-*l'n,* to rhyme with "totlin"; *bot*-LON-*im.* Hebrew: "A man who does nothing."

1. Someone without a trade or regular means of livelihood.
2. An unemployed or lazy man.
3. A misfit, such as a *Talmud* student of no promise.
4. Someone with intellectual pretensions and half-baked ideas.

Men who lived on the fringes, as it were, often spent most of their time inside the *besmedresh,* the house of study, there seeking a way of picking up a few pennies—for making up the tenth (plus ninth or eighth, too, sometimes) man for a *minyan.* For this service, some congregations paid, out of a special fund.

A *batlen* might be given a small fee to join a group studying the *Talmud* in honor and memory of a deceased relative. When a bereaved family had no males, a *batlen* might be retained, in an emergency, to recite the prayer for the dead, the *Kaddish,* twice daily.

The *Talmud* says that every Jewish community must contain ten *batlonim*—that is, ten men who, since they do no work, can devote all their time to prayer and study.

___

The phone rang at the nurses' desk in ward four.

"Nurse, can you tell me how Hershel Resnick is getting along?"

The nurse consulted her charts. "Just fine. The doctor says he can go home on Thursday. . . . Whom shall I say called him?"

"No one. *I'm* Resnick. That doctor treats me like a *batlen* and won't tell me a thing!"

beheyme[Y]
behayma[R]
behama, behayme

Pronounced *b'*HAY-*muh,* to rhyme with "the Dana." From Hebrew: *behama,* "animal (domesticated)."

1. Literally: Animal—especially **used for a cow.***

---

*Beheyme became embroiled in a college speech codes controversy in 1993 when a Jewish freshman at the University of Pennsylvania hollered, "Water buffalo!" at a rowdy group of black female students. The women charged him with "racial harassment," which prompted the student to explain that "water buffalo" was simply his translation of *beheyme,* a word that he'd often heard used as a harmless put-down in his days as a *yeshiva* student. The explanation didn't satisfy either Yiddishists or the students he'd insulted—and the controversy took on national proportions when UP president Sheldon Hackney was nominated to head the National Endowment for the Humanities (he was confirmed by the Senate, 76–23).

2. A stupid man or woman; a dumbbell; an ignoramus. "Don't ask that *beheyme* for an opinion." "She looks like an angel but thinks like a *beheyme*."

3. A drudge; a stolid, hardworking, uncomplaining, unimaginative sort. "That *beheyme* works ten hours a day." "A worker is a man, not a *beheyme*."

An old man was walking down a country road carrying an enormous load of wood on his shoulders. He struggled up a long hill, muttering and cursing, "I'm not more than a *beheyme*!" when the bundle slipped off his shoulders and he cried out, "I can't go on! Let the Angel of Death come and take me!"

At once the Angel of Death appeared. "You called?"

Said the old man quickly: "To help me get that load back on my shoulders!"

Moral: Men prefer misery to death.

ben

There is no way to mispronounce this, unless you *try*.
Hebrew: "Son."

Son.

Before family names were common, a Jew was known by his
given name plus the name of his father: such as Yochanan
ben (son of) Zakkai.

Sometimes the form used was *bar,* which is Aramaic; thus
Shimon bar Kochba.

For a girl one said *bas*: Rivka *bas* Bethuel.

The old form—for instance, Yitzkhok *ben* Shmuel—is still used
on many wedding certificates and in the synagogue when people are
called up to read a passage from the *Torah.*

Both *ben* and *bar* are widely used in Hebrew to form compound
nouns: *ben Torah* (an educated person); *bar mitzva* (one who has
reached the age of responsibility); *bar mazel* (a lucky person).

A Jew is considered a *ben bris,* or "son of the covenant."

For more information about Jewish naming practices, see bris.

bentsh
bentshn (infinitive verb)

Pronounced BENCH. From the Romanic *benedicere:* "to
bless."

1. To bless. "May God *bentsh* you."
2. To recite a blessing.
3. To recite the Grace after Meals.
4. To recite a particular blessing; thus to *bentsh licht* is to
   recite the blessing over Sabbath or holiday candles;
   to *bentsh gomel* is to recite the blessing after having

recovered from a serious illness, escaped an accident, etc. The Grace after Meals appears to have been instituted during the period of the Second Temple. It begins with four benedictions: thanking God, who provides food; blessing the land that produces it; expressing hope for the rebuilding of *Zion;* attesting to God's love and kindness. These are followed by a series of petitions varied to suit the occasion (for one's guests, relatives, visitors), plus verses from Psalms, and—always—ending with a prayer for peace.

gebentsht (verb)

>Blessed.

>>"He is *gebentsht* with patience."

gebentshte^Y (adjective feminine)
gebentshteh^R
gebentshter (adjective masculine)

>Talented, blessed—such as, blessed with exceptional gifts.

>>"He has a *gebentshte* mouth" means "He is an eloquent speaker, a superlative orator." Of a surgeon, one might say, "He has *gebentshte* hands." And in irony, "With brains, he wasn't exactly *gebentsht.*"

An angry man is unfit to pray.

—Nachman of Bratslav

berye^Y
berrieh^R

Pronounced BERR-*yeh*, to rhyme with "dare ya." From Hebrew: *briah*, "creature."

A woman of remarkable energy, talent, competence; a female live wire; one who gets a lot done, does it swiftly, does it well; a real *baleboste*.

This term of approbation is nearly always exclamatory: "My, is she a *berye!*" "To do a thing like that, you have to be a regular *berye!*"

The cardinal importance of the woman in the home has always been stressed within Jewish culture. (Jews never held with the "I'm just a housewife" nonsense.) The Jews knew that the wife and mother was the homemaker and found many ways of complimenting her. (See Shabbes.)

The doctor examined the eighty-three-year-old woman and said, "Some things not even modern medicine can cure. . . . I can't make you any younger, you know."

"Who asked you to make me younger?" retorted the *berye*. "I want you to make me older."

bes din^R
bezdn^Y

Pronounced, in Yiddish, *"base* (or *bez*) *din"* to rhyme with "case (or Pez) tin." Hebrew: "House of Judgment." Plural: *batte din.*

A rabbinical court.

Jewish communities in Europe usually had their own civil courts, presided over by a chief rabbi or a *dayen*. These courts dealt with religious and local (Jewish community) problems and with those domestic and commercial disputes (marriage, divorce, inheritance, debts, etc.) in which the disputants sought advice or arbitration.

When a dispute involved litigation, at least three rabbi judges sat.

In the Middle Ages, there were special "guild" *batte din* for different trades and occupations.

In the United States, many observing Jews preferred to bring their troubles to their rabbi, or to a *bes din* of three rabbis, instead of going into the public courts. (*"Er past nit,"* a commonly heard phrase, means "It's not nice" or, as the English would say, "It isn't done.")

These *batte din* had no legal authority: the Jews who came to them came voluntarily. Such courts are still found in religious communities.

In Israel, the *batte din* are official, operate in the office of the central rabbinate, and have exclusive jurisdiction over certain areas of status, marriage, **inheritance, and so on.***

See Sanhedrin, dayen.

---

*Orthodox rabbinic control over these civil functions in Israel, where non-Orthodox rabbis have no legal standing, has engendered much political controversy. Orthodox *batte din* have called into question the Jewish legitimacy of immigrants from the states of the former Soviet Union and have denied Jewish burials to families of uncertain status. Orthodox representatives in the Knesset (Israel's legislature) have also made repeated efforts to amend the historic Law of Return, which guarantees Israeli citizenship to all Jews, in order to exclude those converted to Judaism by non-Orthodox *batte din* in other lands. Meanwhile, the plight of *agunot*—"chained" women, divorced from their husbands but unable to remarry for want of a *get*, a religious divorce document—has become one of the focal points of the Israeli feminist movement in recent years. All in all, the deal struck during Israel's founding,

besmedresh[Y]
bes midrash[R]
bet midrash, beth hamidrash,
beysmedresh

Pronounced *bess*-MED-*rish*, to rhyme with "less red fish."
Hebrew: *bet hamidrash*, "house of study."

Sometimes used as another name for synagogue. (See shul.)

The synagogue, from its inception, was a place for both prayer and study, and in Jewish life the distinction between the two is exceedingly difficult to draw. The *besmedresh* was, originally, the place where male Jews met to study.* And since prayers were frequent there, the name came to be used for synagogue, too.

which left matters of civil law in the hands of rabbinic courts, has fostered a kind of hybrid identity for Israel as half-theocratic, half-secular state. (See Rosten's entry, and my note, for **get**.)

In America, ultra-Orthodox *batte din* periodically excommunicate prominent Jewish innovators and activists for their "sins" against conservative Jewish sensibilities. The most recent move was taken in October 2000 by a *bes din* in Brooklyn against Joseph Lieberman, running on the Democratic ticket as the first Jewish nominee for the American vice presidency. The excommunication (*herem*) order stated that Lieberman caused "grave scandal . . . by the fact that, while claiming to be an observant Jew, Lieberman has been misrepresenting and falsifying to the American people the teachings of the *Torah* against partial birth infanticide, against special privileges and preferential treatment for flaunting homosexuals, and against religious intermarriage of Jews." While such condemnations are essentially propagandistic, they can sometimes incite aggression against their targets. The assassination of Israeli prime minister Yitzhak Rabin in 1996, for example, was foreshadowed by violent rhetoric against his peacemaking efforts by ultra-Orthodox rabbinic authorities in Israel.

*Barbra Streisand's 1983 film, *Yentl,* based on a short story by Isaac Bashevis Singer, tells the story of a girl so determined to break the bonds of illiteracy, which traditional Jewish life imposed on women, that she disguises herself as a male, a *yeshiva bokher,* and takes her place in the *besmedresh.*

Study and prayer, or (better) study-prayer, was the most potent mortar in Jewish life and history. It was the linchpin in a Jew's self-esteem. It lent meaning and purpose to the most difficult and desperate of existences. It illuminated life. It ennobled, inspired, redeemed. It admitted even the humblest Jew to the company of sages, prophets, scholars, saints.

Virtually all of male Jewry participated in a perpetual seminar on the *Torah* and the *Talmud*. Even the cobblers. Even the tailors. The drovers and diggers, farmhands and carpenters. The peddlers and beggars and shopkeepers. Should a merchant have to miss his daily lesson, he would "repay" his debt on his return home. There were also some who would learn a certain section of the *Talmud* by heart and repeat it on the road, lest they violate the commandment to study, even when they had no books with them.

Collective study was also very popular. The Talmudic sentence "Learning is achieved only in company" (*Berakhot* 63) was always highly thought of, and it was not particularly difficult to find friends with whom to study in the cities and towns of eastern Europe. Most Jews past the age of six (except for mental deficients) could read and write. They were all arguers, dialecticians, amateur theologians—albeit their poverty was great, their living precarious, their security at the mercy of local fanatics. When studying *Talmud*, every Jew felt elevated, a participant in an eternal dialogue on divinity, truth, the purpose and obligations of life.

Part of this singular obsession with "reading *Torah*" (or *Talmud*) rested in the notion that a man could actually earn a "portion of bliss" in the hereafter by performing certain acts—among which reading his "portion" ranked high. Some Jews were eager to read aloud from the pulpit in the synagogue, not simply as an honor, which it was, but as a means of winning extra merit in the heavenly record. Whatever the motives, however naive the reasoning, an entire culture was structured around reading, study, a reverence for words.

Jewish communities all over Europe automatically established formal study groups, communally supported. Abraham Menes points out that in 1887, in the small town of Kroz, no fewer than nine separate study societies thrived. Kroz had only two hundred Jewish families but supported twelve teachers (two women, to teach girls) and two bookbinders!

"In almost every Jewish home in Eastern Europe," writes Rabbi Abraham Joshua Heschel, in his lyrical *The Earth Is the Lord's* (Abelard-Schuman, 1964), "even in the humblest and poorest, stood a bookcase full of volumes. . . . Almost every Jew gave of his time to learning, either in private learning or by joining one of the societies [for] studying the *Talmud*. . . . At nightfall, almost everyone would leave the tumult and bustle of everyday life to study in the *bet ha-midrash*."

And in the house of study every Jew sat "like [an] intellectual magnate. . . . When a problem came up, there was immediately a host of people pouring out opinions, arguments, quotations. . . . The stomachs were empty, the homes barren, but the minds were crammed with the riches of the *Torah*."*

Heschel also quotes from a Christian scholar who visited the city of Warsaw during the First World War: "Once I noticed a great many coaches on a parking place but with no drivers in sight. In my own country I would have known where to look for them. A

---

*The passion for study could often lead to neglect of family responsibilities. The *Talmud* (*Ketubot* 62b) tells the story of Rav Rechumi, who returned home from the *besmedresh* only once a year. (Adding insult to injury, he returned on the eve of *Yom Kippur*, when marital relations with his wife were forbidden!) One year, Rechumi became so absorbed in his studies that he forgot to make the trip. His disheartened wife wept—and as soon as a tear fell, the *Talmud* reports, the roof of the *besmedresh* collapsed, killing her recalcitrant husband.

Latter-day versions of workaholism still afflict many Jews, despite extensive Jewish teachings about *Shabbes* (the Sabbath) and the need for a life that balances work, pleasure, and spirituality.

young Jewish boy showed me the way: in a courtyard, on the second floor, was the *shtibl* of the Jewish drivers. It consisted of two rooms: one filled with *Talmud*-volumes, the other a room for prayer. All the drivers were engaged in fervent study and religious discussion . . . It was then that I found out . . . that all professions, the bakers, the butchers, the shoemakers, etc., have their own *shtibl* [room] in the Jewish district; and every free moment which can be taken off from their work is given to the study of the Torah. And when they get together in intimate groups, one urges the other: *'Zog mir a shtikl Torah'*—'Tell me a little *Torah.*'"

Many, many Yiddish words are related to study and scholarship: see melamed, yeshiva, talmid khokhem.

An eleventh-century poet sang:

> He who has toiled and bought for himself books,
> But his heart is empty of what they contain—
> Is like a lame man, who engraved on a wall
> The figure of a foot, and tried to stand in vain.

> —Samuel Ha-Nagid, 993–1005, *Granada*

Someone once asked a scholar, "Why is it that you study so slowly—but pray so fast?"

"Because," sighed the sage, "when I pray, I am talking to God; but when I study, God is talking to me."

bialy

Pronounced *bee-*OLL-*lee*, to rhyme with "fee dolly." Colloquial abbreviation of "Bialystocker."

A flat breakfast roll, shaped like a round wading pool,

sometimes sprinkled with onion.

I choose the wading pool as a model because, like it, the *bialy* has a bottom—it is not empty in the center, like a tire or a *bagel*.

The *bialy* roll, a growing packaged favorite in food stores across the country, is second only to the *bagel* as a base for cream cheese and lox.

The name is taken from the bakers from Bialystok, a city in Poland, where this exquisite product was presumably perfected.

"Forty cents a dozen for *bialies*?" protested Mrs. Becker. "The baker across the street is asking only twenty!"

"So buy them across the street."

"Today, he happens to be sold out."

"When I'm out of *bialies*, I charge only twenty cents a dozen, too."

blintz
blintzes (plural)
blintse[Y]
blintzeh[R]

Rhymes with *chintz* and *chintzes*. From Ukrainian: "pancake." *Blintz* is actually Yinglish; in Yiddish, the singular is *blintzeh*.

A pancake, rolled around a filling, most often of cottage cheese.

I list *blintz* and *blintzes* together, because I never heard of anybody eating only one. *Blintzes* are traditional delicacies for the festival of *Shevuos*.

Blintzes today may contain jam: strawberry, cherry, blackberry; potatoes; fish concoctions; apples; peaches; etc. Hence the need to say "cheese blintzes," which once would have sounded as redundant as "wet water."

Blintzes, as eaten by Jews, are ordinarily smothered under thick sour cream. Jet-set Jews, aspiring to crêpes suzettes, have taken to smothering *blintzes* with honey or jam instead of sour cream. There is no accounting for tastes.

Blintzes have become as much a part of Jewish summer cuisine as *borsht* or *shtchav* (sorrel soup).

bluffer (masculine)
blufferkeh (feminine)

Pronounced BLUFF-*er* and BLUFF-*er-keh,* to rhyme with "duffer" and "duffer-keh." Yinglish.

One who bluffs, deceives, exaggerates, vaingloriously, mixes hyperbole with hot air.

A *bluffer* may bluff because he is boastful, foolish, or vain or because, as in poker, he is trying to mislead or deceive you. "He is nothing but *bluff"* means "He's full of hot air." "Watch out, he's a *bluffer"* was not an injunction to call a bluff but urged caution in the acceptance of representations.

Among certain Jewish groups, *bluffer* is often associated with the adjective "Americaner," just as various characteristics were attributed to other groups: "Polish *yakhne,"* "Romanian *ganef,"* "German *yekke* (pedant)."

A farmer asked his neighbor if he could borrow his horse for a few minutes. The neighbor said, "I would, gladly, but my helper took the horse to the vet, and they'll be gone all day."

At this point, the neigh of the horse was heard in the stable.

"So whom do you believe?" cried the *bluffer*. "Me or a horse—and a horse who's a notorious liar to boot?!"

B'nai Brith

Pronounced *b'*-NAY BRITH, to rhyme with "René Smith." Hebrew: "sons of the covenant." (The *th* ending never appeared in classical Hebrew. See bris.)

A Jewish society, organized in 1843, that devotes itself to philanthropic and community activists. It supports the Hillel Foundations on college campuses, engages in youth and vocational services, adult education, etc. The organization founded the superb nonsectarian National Jewish Hospital in Denver. Perhaps its best-known division is the Anti-Defamation League (ADL), which has long studied and fought discrimination and anti-Semitism.

B'nai Brith has branches in **fifty-five countries.***

*While the ADL "division" established budgetary independence from *B'nai Brith* in the 1990s, the organizations remain intertwined in a relationship of mutual support. *B'nai Brith's* women's division, however, split off in 1995, after much legal squabbling, to become Jewish Women International.

American Jews are represented by several hundred national organizations, from the Jewish Peace Lobby to the Jewish War Veterans, from Agudath Israel to the Zionist Organization of America. These groups compete for the loyalty of fewer than 5.5 million Jews—a majority of whom are unaffiliated with any Jewish organization!

boarderkeh

Pronounced BORD-*er-keh*, to rhyme with "for Decca." Yinglish.

A female boarder (obviously) who pays for room and board.

Purists, of both English and Yiddish, greatly disdain and openly deplore such "loanwords" as *boarderkeh*. I find them delightful.

The blithe adoption of English words, to which Hebrew or Yiddish endings were tacked on, rapidly enlarged an immigrant's vocabulary and served as a lingua franca, equally comprehensible to American and Jew. Who, for instance, could fail to understand the meaning of *optsairsikeh? donstairsikeh? nexdoorikeh?*

As for *boarderkeh:* When the immigration waves brought so many newcomers to America, rare was the flat in a poor neighborhood that did not rent out at least one room. The foreign enclaves in every large American city were crammed with ROOM AND BOARD signs in German, Italian, Polish, Norwegian, Russian, Hungarian—and Yiddish.

Poor people had to help finance their rent by taking in a roomer or a boarder, who usually ate with the family. Greenhorns, for their part, could not afford a flat of their own. Except for immigrants from the British Isles, the language problem was staggering—hence the wisdom of living for a while amid *landslayt* (people from your old country) whom you could understand, who understood you, and whose longer residence in the golden land made it possible for you to pick up the basic words, phrases, practices, and mores of the bustling new world.

The kind of English that immigrants of, say, six months' standing confidently passed on to newer greenhorns created a rich argot of its own: it can be dubbed Yinglish or Ameridish. It is an extremely descriptive, functional, picturesque, and vigorous vernacular.

SCENE: *Classroom, Lower East Side, 1926.*

Teacher: "Who can tell us where the Romanian border is?"

Student: "In the park with my aunt, and my mother doesn't trust him!"

The galloping difficulties of a foreign tongue are suggested in this anecdote:

A Mr. Goldberg, from Pinsk, coming to America, shared a table in the ship's dining room with a Frenchman. Mr. Goldberg could speak neither French nor English; the Frenchman could speak neither Russian nor Yiddish.

The first day out, the Frenchman approached the table, bowed, and said, *"Bon appétit!"*

Goldberg, puzzled for a moment, bowed back and replied, "Goldberg."

Every day, at every meal, the same routine occurred.

On the fifth day, another passenger took Goldberg aside. "Listen, the Frenchman isn't telling you his name. He's saying, 'Good appetite.' That's what *'Bon appétit'* means."

At the next meal, Mr. Goldberg, beaming, bowed to the Frenchman and said, *"Bon appétit!"*

And the Frenchman, beaming, replied: "Goldberg!"

At his wife's graveside, Mr. Berman wept copiously.

The Bermans' boarder, Mr. Kipnis, wept even more—and, indeed, carried on so hysterically that Mr. Berman said, "Kipnis, don't take it so hard! I'll get married again."

(I have heard this story as typically French, too.)

bobe-mayse[Y]
bubbe mayseh[R]
bubbe maiseh, bobbe-mayseh,
boobe-myseh

Pronounced BOB-*eh* by Lithuanian Jews and BAW-*beh* or
BUB-*beh* (using the *u* as in "put") by Polish Jews; MY-*seh*
rhymes with "Rye, suh." *Bobe* (or *boobeh* or *baba*) is the
affectionate name for grandmother; *mayse* means tale,
story, from the Hebrew *ma'aseh*.

Old wives' tale; nonsense; something patently silly
and untrue. "Did she try to sell me a *bobe-mayse!*" "She
believes every *bobe-mayse.*"

*B*obe-mayse is a most effective compound noun for the sarcastic dismissal of something. I know an erudite professor at
Cambridge (England) who often vents his ire on pretentious social
sciencing with this epithet. It puzzles Cantabrigians.

Now that you know all this, it is my duty to inform you that
bobe-mayse may derive from a Yiddish adaptation of *The Story of
Buvo* or *Buovo*, a romantic fifteenth-century tale that was, in turn,
an Italian reincarnation of the Bevis of Hampton cycle of
romances. The stories, originally written in English, were translated into Italian and from Italian were turned into Yiddish! In this
vernacular they became popular among Jewish women.

If you are interested, Bevis of Hampton is a fictional figure who
appeared in a fourteenth-century Anglo-Norman metrical
romance, then in a French chanson de geste, *Beauve d'Hanstone.*
Italian-poem versions called the protagonist *Bovo d'Antona;*
Germanic versions called him *Boeve de Haumtone.*

Elijah Bochur (1468?–1549) wrote two novels in Italian ottava rima stanzas: *Bova Bukh* and *Paris un Viene;* both are Yiddish adaptations of Italian romances. (See Yudel Mark's "Yiddish Literature," in *The Jews: Their History, Culture and Religion,* vol. II, Louis Finkelstein, ed., Harper, 1960.)

bobkes^Y
bubkes^R
bopkes, bupkes

Pronounced BOP-*kess*, to rhyme with "mop kiss," or BUB-*kiss*, to rhyme with "put this," or BAWP-*kess*, to rhyme with "stalk mess," or BUB-*kess*, to rhyme with "pub mess." Russian: "beans." But Jews say *"Bobkes!"* not to designate beans (*beblakh* does that), but to describe, with considerable scorn,

1. something trivial, worthless, insultingly disproportionate to expectations. "I worked on it three hours—and what did he give me? *Bobkes!"* (I think *"Bobkes!"* more eloquent, because more harsh, than "Peanuts!")

2. something absurd, foolish, nonsensical. "I'll sum up his idea in one word: *bobkes!"**

> *Rosten may be too polite to note that *bobkes* also means goat or rabbit droppings —which adds to its scornful power.

*B*obkes must be uttered with either scorn, sarcasm, indignation, or contempt. The expletive takes over where "Nonsense!," "Baloney!," or "Bushwa!" stops for a rest.

I know of no English word that carries quite that deflating, even bitter, aroma.

The man who exclaims, *"Bobkes!"* is a man who understands the place of pride in the protocol of humiliation.

Only the proud say, *"Bobkes!"*

_____

SCENE: *A pushcart on the Lower East Side.*
A woman customer picks up a broken fork. "How much?"
"One cent," says the proprietor.
"One cent? That's too much!"
"So make me an offer."

P.S. This bit of sociology may not illustrate *bobkes* (although that was what the argument was about), but it establishes the penurious universe in which so much of Jewish life was lived and in which so much compensatory humor was born.

boo-boo
See bulbe.

bopkes
See bobkes.

borsht
borscht

Pronounced BOAR*scht*; from the Slavonic, where it is pronounced *bor-sh-tch*. (I see no reason to suggest an *sk* sound by spelling it *borscht* instead of *borsht*.)
Beet soup, served hot or cold (delicious!), often with a dab of sour cream (superb!), sometimes with tiny new potatoes bobbing in it or cucumber slices floating on it (a *mekhaye!*).

*B*orsht was a great staple among Jews, because beets were so cheap. "You don't need teeth to eat *borsht*." Another saying goes, *"Bilik vi borsht,"* "Cheap as *borsht."*

In recent years, a group of language manglers have gone around altering restaurant menus and removing the *t* from the end of *borsht*. I do not approve of this. The Russian/Polish/Ukrainian word is spelled with a *t*, to be sure, so I suppose restaurants of those persuasions have the right to protect the linguistic purity of their menus. But I see no reason for Jewish restaurants to drop the *t*. In Yiddish, it is spelled and pronounced *borsht*.

The *"Borsht Belt"* refers to that sizable suzerainty, in the Catskill Mountains, of summer (and now winter) resorts that cater to, and were once **patronized almost exclusively by, Jews.***

See tumler, kochaleyn.

———

SCENE: *A restaurant.*

First Customer: "Give me the *borscht."*

Waiter: "Take my advice: Have the chicken soup."

Second Customer: "I'll have the pea soup."

Waiter: "Don't take the pea soup—take the barley."

THE SOUP IS BROUGHT, THE CUSTOMERS SERVED.

First Customer: "This chicken soup is marvelous! The best I ever tasted!"

Second Customer: "Waiter! Why didn't you recommend me the chicken soup?"

---

*Laboratory and launching pad for many nationally known comics and entertainers, the Borsht Belt fell on hard times in the 1970s and 1980s, and into permanent eclipse in the 1990s, as the flagship resorts of Grossinger's and the Concord declared bankruptcy. The vibrancy of this Jewish vacation "culchah" has been conveyed in such contemporary movies as *Dirty Dancing, Mr. Saturday Night, Enemies: A Love Story,* and *A Walk on the Moon.* Reunions of Borsht Belt comics have also been mounted successfully on Broadway, where ticket prices are anything but "cheap as *borsht."*

Waiter: "You didn't ask for the *borsht!*"

SCENE: *A dance hall in the Borscht Belt.*
   Young Man: "Are you dancing?"
   Young Lady: "Are you asking?"
   Young Man: "I'm asking."
   Young Lady: "I'm dancing."

boychik
boychikel (diminutive)
boychiklech (plural)
boychikl, boychiklakh

Pronounced BOY-*chik,* rhymes with "Roy chick." Plural: BOY-*chik-lekh* (the final *"kh"* is guttural). An affectionate, more diminutive neologism is *boychikel.* Yinglish, pure and simple, though it uses the common Slavic suffix *tchik.*
   1. Diminutive of "boy."

*B*oychik or *boychikel* is used with affection, even admiration, the way some people say, "That's my boy," or the way an earlier generation said, "Oh, you kid!"

"Hello, *boychik*" or "How are you, *boychikel?*" may be uttered to males long past their boyhood; generally, when used to or about an aging man, *boychik* carries a tinge of sarcasm—but it can be used fondly:
   Affectionate: "That Sam"—sigh—"he has the spirit of a *boychik.*"
   Sarcastic: "At his age to go after young girls . . . ! Some *boychik!*"

   2. Critically: A sharp operator; one who cuts corners. "He's some *boychik*" can mean anything from "He's a tricky fellow" to "Watch your pocket."

bren

Pronounced BREN, to rhyme with "wren." German: *bre-nen,* "to burn."

Someone of great energy, vivacity, competence, and optimism; a "fireball."

"She is a real *bren.*" "Don't worry about him; he was born a *bren.*"

On his first day as a bus driver, Maxey Eckstein handed in receipts of $65. The next day his take was $67. The third day's income was $62. But on the fourth day, Eckstein, a *bren,* emptied no less than $283 on the desk before the cashier.

"Eckstein!" exclaimed the cashier. "This is fantastic. That route never brought in money like this! What happened?"

"Well, after three days on that *cockamamy* route, I figured business would never improve, so I drove over to Fourteenth Street and worked there. I tell you, that street is a gold mine!"

bris
briss, brit, brith

Pronounced BRISS by most Jews in America; pronounced BRIT by Israeli Jews. NOTE: The *th* ending (as in B'nai Brith—see entry) was unknown in Hebrew; Gentile scholars (of Hebrew and the Bible) decided upon it a few hundred years ago. Yemenite Jews differentiate between the *t* and *th* sound.

Bris means "covenant" but usually refers to the circumcision and naming ceremony: in Hebrew, *Brit Milah.*

The *Brit Milah* is observed on a boy's eighth day of life, even if that day falls on *Yom Kippur*.

The circumcision is usually performed by a *moyl,* who is not a rabbi but an expert in this sharply circumscribed (no pun) surgical area. Tradition-observing Jews insist on a *moyl;* others may ask an M.D. to do the cutting.

The **baby boy**** to be circumcised is carried into the room where the circumcision is to be performed. One of the waiting men (the *sandek,* or godfather) seats himself on a chair known as the "Chair of Elijah." The baby is placed on the knees of the *sandek,* and a service begins. Prayers—before, during, and after the circumcision—are pronounced.

After the circumcision, the *moyl* or a rabbi utters this prayer: "May the lad grow in vigor—of mind and of body—to a love of *Torah,* to the marriage canopy, and to a life of good works." A name is given to the baby. Then a blessing is offered over wine, a drop of which is placed on the baby's lips.

A celebration follows, favoring wine and sponge cake, which I think well named.

Circumcision is described as "the seal of God"—a seal in the flesh,

**Jewish boys receive their Hebrew names as part of the *brit milah* ceremony. Baby girls are traditionally named by fathers in synagogue during an *aliyah* to the *Torah* approximately one month after their birth. Jewish families seeking an egalitarian model of Jewish practice have in recent years made the arrival of daughters more special and notable through *brit ha-bat* ceremonies—naming rituals on a par with the *brit milah.* There is no physical cutting or alteration involved; "female circumcision" is unknown in Judaism.

During the 1970s and 1980s, there were some efforts by Jewish activists to portray the *bris* as a barbaric act of child abuse and to devise a ritual substitute. The hold of this fundamental *mitzva* upon the Jewish imagination is very powerful, however, so even among nonreligious Jews, the overwhelming majority obey the commandment to circumcise their sons. ("The sign of circumcision," wrote the heretical Baruch Spinoza, "is . . . so important, that . . . it alone would preserve the nation forever.")

as it were. (In the early days of Christianity, baptism was called "seal-ing.") In Genesis 17:10, you may remember, the Lord says: "This is my covenant ... every man child among you shall be circumcised." And Abraham, who was a very great man, circumcised himself.

The circumcision is held to signalize an obligation—to observe the covenant between God and Israel, to live and exemplify the life of virtue, to obey, teach, and transmit God's law. In a wider sense, circumcision imprints onto a man's body a lifelong sign that Israel will be perpetuated through him—that his seed, passing through the circumcised portal, will create children who will in turn be pledged to the Jews.

Down the ages, circumcision met with vicious repression: Antiochus Epiphanes made it punishable by death; Hadrian for-bade circumcision (an edict contributing to the rebellion led by Bar Kochba); and a Visigoth monarch named Sisebut, which is a peculiar name for a king, ordered Jews to baptize, instead of cir-cumcise, their sons. But circumcision remained one of the most unalterable practices among Jews everywhere.

Jewish Hellenists, eager to Grecianize themselves (and to pass muster in a gymnasium), used to undergo an operation to remove all signs of circumcision. The rabbis countered this ploy by emphasizing that the glans be laid bare through a firm pushing back of the skin during circumcision.

The Jews did not invent circumcision. Herodotus mentions the custom among ancient Egyptians, whose hieroglyphic sign for a phallus is a circumcised specimen. The Syrians, Phoenicians, and Ethiopians practiced circumcision—as did (and do) many tribes around the world, in India, Africa, Oceania, Indonesia, the Philippines, and Australia.

Among Moslems, of course, circumcision is universal: it is called "purification." (In Lahore, India, the ceremony is known as "wedding.")

In some cultures, the women refuse sexual congress with an uncircumcised man.

But few peoples circumcise as early (the eighth day) as Jews do. In Africa, the rite usually occurs at puberty or just before marriage. With other peoples, circumcision may be performed at the fourth, fifth, or even sixth or seventh year. Often it is performed en masse, as part of an annual ritual or seasonal festival.

Genesis 17:25 tells us that Ishmael was circumcised at the age of thirteen. This led some (who apparently had not read Genesis 17:12) to conclude erroneously that to the Hebrews circumcision was a puberty rite.

The medical and hygienic advantages of circumcision are so widely known today that I need not expatiate upon them. And circumcision has become so widespread in the United States that it is no longer possible to distinguish Jews from non-Jews in a **locker room.***

At a *bris,* the proud father raised his glass of wine for a toast, sipped, and beamed. "Lovely wine. Good year: 5721."**

*The proportion of non-Jewish American men who were circumcised increased from about 30 percent in the 1930s to 80 percent in the early 1970s. That rate declined to 65 percent by 1995, after the American Academy of Pediatrics and other medical authorities repeatedly dismissed the alleged health advantages of circumcision as negligible. Today the choice, for non-Jews, seems mostly aesthetic. As "Elaine" of television's *Seinfeld* said of an uncircumcised boyfriend (in an episode entitled "The Bris"): "It had no face, no personality. It was like a Martian."

Recent medical research, however, has indicated that there may be an important public health benefit to widespread circumcision: it seems to lessen heterosexual transmission of the HIV virus, which causes AIDS.

**The Hebrew calendrical equivalent to 1960–61.

Sephardic Jews often name a child after a living relative, but the *Ashkenazim* have a distinct and abiding dread of doing so. A certain trepidation is felt by old-fashioned parents even when a young man or woman selects a mate who bears the same given name as a living parent. (In some cases of this sort, the bride- or groom-to-be will adopt a second name or nickname.)

Anxiety about names and naming is, of course, not limited to Jews. Many Native American peoples considered their names an integral part of themselves and were convinced that if anyone pronounced a name balefully or malevolently, their very bodies would suffer. In some Australian tribes, every man has two names, the secret one being known only to the ceremonially initiated. The Kirghiz in Asia forbid a woman to utter her husband's name or any word like it. In Hungary, centuries ago, men tried to outwit ghoulish spirits, who were all around searching for human prey, by using horrid, magically protective names for their children. The idea seemed to be that an incubus would give a wide berth to a child who is loudly called, say, "Death." The Chinese had a similar custom.

Ashkenazic Jews generally named a child after a deceased relative. This was, however, only a custom and in an increasing number of cases is being ignored. Even where the custom is still honored, the "naming after," in recent decades, may be as nominal as it is farfetched: Mervyn for Moshe; Barton for Benjamin; Natalie ("Christmas Child"!) for Nechama.†

† A revival of traditional Jewish names is noted by Julie Hilton Danan in *The Jewish Parents' Almanac* (Jason Aronson, 1993): "My grandparents Anglicized their own Yiddish names (Feigel to Fanny), then gave their children 'apple-pie' American names, Betty and Charles. Our 'All American' generation got appellations suitable to our future careers in Hollywood: Julie, Missy, and Ali, tenuously referring to our Yiddish-named antecedents Gitel, Michle, and Elke. . . .

(continued on page 74)

Every Jewish child was once given a Hebrew name at birth. (Some parents gave the child a Yiddish name, unaware of the difference between the languages.) Some parents sought a name that "sounded like" Hebrew.

First-generation Jews in America took Yitzchak (Hebrew for Isaac) or Itzik (Yiddish) and Anglicized it to Isadore, Irwin, Irving; similarly, Avraham (Hebrew) or Avrum (Yiddish) became Alan, Allen, Allan, Albert, Alvin, Arnold; Chaim became Hyman, Herman, Herbert, even Charles.

Jews adjusted biblical names to the orthography of the language in their country of residence: Yosef (Joseph) appears as Yussuf, Giuseppe, Beppo, Peppo, José, Pepe, Pepito, Josko, Joska, Joey.

Yaakov (Jacob) has the following variations: Jacques, Giacomo, Giacobbi, Jacobus, Jakob, Jaime, James, Jake, Jack.

Despite the feeling among religious Jews that Mary and John are "Christian" names, both are Hebrew, of biblical origin: Miriam and Jochanan.

Many common Yiddish names are of biblical or Talmudic origin:

Avrum (Abraham)	*Dovid* (David)
Yankel (Jacob)	*Dvora* (Deborah)
Yisroel (Israel)	*Mayer* (Meir)
Itzik (Isaac)	*Leib* (Levi)
Yussel (Joseph)	*Yudel* (Judah)

(continued from page 73)

When the time came to name my children, the pendulum had long since swung back. Now Great-Grandma Rose's (née Ruchel) namesake is known as Shira Rachel. . . . Anglo-biblical names, with their Jewish yet American-Colonial sound, have enjoyed a renaissance: plenty of Benjamins, Rebeccas, Sarahs, Joshuas, and Hannahs in Hebrew school these days. And . . . whoever expected that American Jewish children would once again be named Sadie and Rosie and Max?"

Rivke (Rebecca)	*Shmuel* (Samuel)
Ruchel (Rachel)	*Michel* (Michael)
Moishe (Moses)	*Chana* (Hannah)

Names like Sarah, Leah, etc. are identical in both Bible usage and Yiddish.

Other Jewish names have their origin in other languages, mainly German: *Freda, Freida, Freyde* (Joy), *Raizel* (Rose), *Fruma* (Grace—pious), *Sheine* (Grace—pretty), *Feigel* (Birdie).

In biblical times, children seem never to have been named after relatives—not even in the royal family. Scholars hold that not one of the twenty-one kings of Judah was named after a predecessory.

After the Exile, Jews began to use foreign, rather than Hebrew, names—such as Abba (Aramaic), Alexander (Greek), and Philo (Greek). During the Hellenistic period, Jews began to name a boy after his grandfather.

The use of surnames first became common among Arabic-speaking Jews; Arabs form family names by adding *Abu* (Abudarham), *Ibn* (Ibn Ezra), and *Al* (Alharizi).

During the Middle Ages, the Jews often took names from the languages of the countries in which they lived, although they kept Hebrew names for "sacred" purposes (*bris, bar mitzva,* marriage, blessings attendant to reading from the *Torah,* etc.).

Surnames were not unknown among Jews (they were common among *Sephardim*) but came into general usage among the *Ashkenazim* only in the eighteenth century. The Austrian empire compelled the Jews to adopt surnames in 1787; Napoleon followed suit in 1808. Part of the reason, at least, was the difficulty presented to the authorities in collecting taxes in communities where individuals were known as Shmuel the Red-Haired, Harry the Cobbler, Isadore the Lame, etc.

The names *Alte* (fem.) and *Alter* (masc.) have a double origin, from the Latin ("other") and from German ("old"). These names, often given a child born after someone in the family had died, were designed to confuse the Angel of Death—should that malevolent worthy come looking for the newly born baby; for he would find "another" or "an old one"! A boy who was precocious was sometimes called *Alter.*

brokhe[Y]
broche[R]
brokheh, brocha, brucha

Pronounced BRAW-*kheh,* making that *kh* a throat-clearing sound as in *Mad* magazine's "*Yecch!*" Hebrew: "benediction." Plural: *brokhes.*

1. Blessing; a prayer of thanksgiving and praise.
2. To "make a *brokhe*" is to offer a blessing.
3. A Jewish girl's name.

The ceremonial demands on very religious Jews are very heavy, however much the faithful rejoice in the repetition.

Brokhes are recited during prayers (three times daily, plus special *brokhes* on *Shabbes* and in festival services). The silent prayer that precedes and follows communal praying contains nineteen *brokhes.* In the morning prayer, there are three *brokhes* associated with the *Shema;* in the evening prayer, four *brokhes* are associated.

The formula for a benediction must include "*Shem U'Malkhus,*" the name of God affirmed as **King.***

*Some liberal-minded Jews have sought alternatives to the classic Hebrew *Melekh Ha'Olam*—"King of the Universe" or "King of all the Worlds"—to whom *brokhes* are typically addressed. Other formulations include *Shekhinah* (the Divine Spirit or Light; see Rosten's entry and my note for **Shekhinah**), *Ruakh Ha'Olam* (Soul or Breath of all the Worlds), *Khey Ha'Olamim* (Life of all the Worlds), and the feminine *Berukhah aht Yah* (Blessed are you Yah).

To a tradition-observing Jew, the occasions that call for a *brokhe* include

> the first act upon arising
> the last act before retiring
> before and after every meal
> before eating and/or drinking at any time (even between meals; there are separate *brokhes* for different foods and drinks)
> upon washing one's hands—which is strictly enjoined (this must be done as soon as one gets out of bed in the morning, before praying, before eating)
> upon returning from a hazardous journey
> upon recovering from a grave illness
> upon performing any religious ritual
> upon the arrival of a new season
> upon seeing the new moon
> upon donning a new garment
> upon smelling a fragrant odor
> upon seeing such natural phenomena as lightning, majestic mountains, a magnificent sunset, etc.
> upon seeing a beautiful person or animal
> upon seeing a strangely shaped person or animal
> upon receiving bad news
> upon seeing a scholar or sage
> upon seeing a king
> Et cetera.

The *Talmud* gives the exact form to be followed in "making a *brokhe*." Tradition holds that the texts were formulated during the time of Ezra (2,500 years ago) by the sages of the time, called the Men of the Great Synagogue. In the second century, Rabbi Meir declared it to be the duty of everyone to say no fewer than one hundred *brokhes* daily!

About a hundred *brokhes* are reserved for the Sabbath.

One of the best known *brokhes* is *Shehecheyanu,* which thanks God for having enabled one to live and reach whatever auspicious occasion.

For a delightful insight into the range and psychological functions of *brokhes,* see chapter 11 of Maurice Samuel's classic, *The World of Sholem Aleichem.*

See also daven.

When S. Y. Agnon was named Nobel Prize Laureate for Literature, in 1966, he was told he would have to go all the way to Sweden, where he would receive the award from the king.

"Good," said Mr. Agnon, who observes Orthodox religious rites, "I have never had the opportunity to say the *brokhe* one makes upon seeing a king."

Mrs. Gidwitz told her benevolent old Orthodox rabbi, "My grandchildren are driving me crazy this year: they want to have a Christmas tree. Rabbi, could you maybe make some dispensation, a special *brokhe* over such a tree . . . ?"

"Never!" said the rabbi. "Impossible."

So Mrs. Gidwitz consulted a more lenient rabbi, a Conservative. "No," he said. "I'm sorry."

So poor Mrs. Gidwitz went to the young new Reform rabbi. "I'll be glad to," he said. "Only tell me: What's a *'brokhe'*?"*

---

*Stereotypes die hard, but the reality of Reform Judaism for the past twenty years or more has been one of deepening Jewish literacy and spirituality, especially in the higher echelons of the movement. This trend culminated in the May 1999 adoption by the Central Conference of American Rabbis of a new "Statement of Principles for Reform Judaism," which seeks to revitalize many traditional Jewish practices, including the use of *brokhes*. The old joke about the Reform temple being "closed for the Jewish holidays" is truly anachronistic in the twenty-first century.

bubbe
See bubeleh.

bubee
bubby

Pronounced BU-*bee*, to rhyme with "goody." Ameridish. Cf. bubeleh.

Affectionate term of endearment, the diminutive of *bubeleh*, used between a husband and wife, a parent and child, between siblings—and among members of the theatrical profession surprisingly soon after they begin to work together.*
See bubeleh.

> *Bubee* (or *Bubby*) is also used as an Americanized nickname for Grandma, in which cases it is usually pronounced to rhyme with "tubby."

bubeleh^R
bobele^Y
bubele, bubbele, bubbala, bobeleh

Pronounced BUB-*eh-leh,* using the *u* of "put," not of "tub"; rhymes with "hood a la." From Russian/Hebrew. In Hebrew, *buba* means "little doll." But the Yiddish *bubbe* and *bubeleh* seem independent of the Hebrew, say the experts.

Grandmother; the affectionate diminutive, really: "little grandma." (*Baba*, which means midwife or grandmother in Russian or other Slavic tongues, was often used in addressing any old woman, whether one's grandmother or not.)

Bubeleh, a term of endearment, is widely used for "darling," "dear child," "honey," "sweetheart."

A husband and wife may call each other *bubeleh*.

Jewish mothers call both female and male babies *bubeleh*. This carries the expectation that the child in the crib will one day be a grandparent. It also honors the memory of the mother's mother: in calling a baby "little grandmother," a mother is addressing the child in the way the child will in time address *its* grandmother—and its child.

Bubeleh has come into vast popularity in recent years—via television. On all the night "talk" shows, the garrulous comedians, actors, and actresses try to display warm, outgoing, loving natures, in fact all the obligatory coziness of show business, by greeting each other with kisses, embraces, cheek pattings—and generous doses of *"bubeleh."* Thus: "How *are* you, *bubeleh?*" or "I just loved your last picture, *bubeleh!*" or even, "*Bubeleh*, baby, where have you *been?*"

What struck me during the birth and vehement barrage of *bubelehs* among emphatically Anglo-Saxon, Italian, Greek, and African American entertainers was the fact that no one seemed to think it necessary to explain what *bubeleh* meant. I often wonder what residents of Idaho or Mississippi think those crazy people in New York or Hollywood are talking about.

A Jewish mother sent her son off to his first day in school with the customary pride and precautionary advice: "So, *bubeleh*, you'll be a good boy and obey the teacher? And you won't make noise, *bubeleh*, and you'll be very polite and play nice with the other children. And when it's time to come home, you'll button up warm, so you won't catch cold, *bubeleh*. And you'll be careful crossing the street and come right home . . ." etc. etc.

Off went the little boy.

When he returned that afternoon, his mother hugged him and kissed him and exclaimed, "So did you like school, *bubeleh?* You made new friends? You *learned* something?"

"Yeah," said the boy. "I learned that my name is Irving."

bulbe^Y
bulba^R

Pronounced BULL'*y-beh*, with a liquid *l* (as in "million"); or BULL-*ba*, to rhyme with "full, ma." From Polish: "potato."

1. Literally: A potato.
2. An error, a boner, a faux pas.

The second usage is the most frequent—and amusing. "Oh, did she make a *bulbe!*" "He is famous for his outlandish *bulbes.*"

This is not literary Yiddish, mind you, or pure, or even high-toned, but *bulbe* is used most expressively in colloquial Yiddish.

It has been suggested to me that boo-boo, that recently coined synonym for a gaffe, descended from *bulbe;* but it seems more likely that boo-boo is pure onomatopoeia to describe the sort of faux pas that is made by a child and is followed by tears.

As far as I can discover, boo-boo came out of show business— probably Hollywood. I first heard it in a skit by Dean Martin and Jerry Lewis.

For more colorful denotations of *bulbe,* see bulbenik.

bulbenik

Pronounced BULL-*beh-nik*, to rhyme with "pull the pick." Strictly Ameridish.

1. One who is inept, clumsy, all thumbs, who fouls things up.
2. An actor "who talks as though he has a potato in his mouth"—that is, an actor who "blows" his lines, mixes them up, commits embarrassing spoonerisms; a malaprop.

I once wrote an article about New York's Café Royale (alas, now defunct), the favorite congregating place for the stars and devotees of the Second Avenue (that is, Yiddish) theater. (See my collection, *The Strangest Places,* Harcourt, Brace & Co., 1939.)

The Café Royale was the Sardi's, Lindy's, and 21 of the Lower East Side, all in one. The air in the Café Royale was as thick with theatrical lore, with stories, jokes, sagas, and memories, as the blintzes were thick with sour cream. And there I heard heart-rending tales of a famous *bulbenik*.

In one play, this earnest thespian strode front center, held forth his hands in tragic appeal, and (all through rehearsal, at least) faultlessly delivered this line: "Oh, God, I have five children—dear, sweet children—" etc. (The Yiddish for children is *kinder*, pronounced KINN-*der*.) But on opening night, the *bulbenik* strode front center, extended his hands, and said, "Oh, God, I have five *finger* [fingers]..." Understandably, he brought the house down.

In another play (*The Dybbuk*), a white-garbed maiden is possessed by a demon or *dybbuk;* she writhes, cries out in terror, falls, loses consciousness. The maiden lies there, alone on the stage. Then villagers, each holding a candle, enter; they see the maiden's lifeless form, draw back in horror. Their leader, stepping closer, exclaims, "A *dybbuk!* A *dybbuk* has entered the maiden!" Cries, screams, swoons, etc.

All went well through rehearsals. Came opening night. The maiden, possessed by the awful spirit, writhed and cried and fell stricken. The column of villagers appeared, drew back. Their leader stepped forward, raised his candle, and cried, "A candle! A candle has entered the maiden!"

He was a *bulbenik*.

bulvon^R
bolvan^Y
bulvan

Pronounced *bull*-VON, to rhyme with "full on." Slavic: "dolt," "blockhead."

A gross, thickheaded, thick-skinned oaf.

No English word carries quite the sneer of *bulvon* or quite the implicit devaluation of brute strength. "Any *bulvon* could do that." A *bulvon* has no sensitivity, no insight, no spiritual graces.

A *bulvon*, about to go on a date with a girl he had never taken out before, begged a friend to advise him: "Girls just don't like me," said the *bulvon*. "But you—you have your pick. How do you do it? What's the real way to talk to a dame?"

"I'll tell you the secret," said the Lothario. "Jewish girls love three topics of conversation: food, family, philosophy. That's all you need to remember. To inquire about a girl's likes in food is to make her feel important. To inquire about her family shows that your intentions are honorable. And to discuss philosophy with her shows you respect her intelligence."

The *bulvon* was delighted. "Food, family, philosophy!"

He met the girl and blurted, "Hello. Do you like noodles?"

"N-no," said the startled girl.

"Do you have a brother?"

"No."

The *bulvon* hesitated but a moment: "Well, *if* you had a brother, would he like noodles?" That was philosophy.

bummerkeh

Pronounced BUM-*er-keh*. Yinglish.

A female bum; one who "bums aron'"—lives loosely; a disreputable lady.

Old Mr. Trabish, sitting near the pool of a Catskill resort, could not help noticing the white-haired man at the next table: there he sat, with two beautiful *bummerkehs*, as he had every day during the week, drinking and laughing and eating. Every day he went off the high diving board and swam seven lusty laps without stopping. And every night he was in the nightclub, dancing with different *tsatskes* until the wee hours.

After two weeks of observing this strenuous schedule, Mr. Trabish leaned over and said, "Mister, it's amazing the condition you're in, the way you live!"

"Thank you," said the white-haired man.

"Excuse me for asking, but how *old* are you?"

The roué shrugged. "Twenty-seven."

burtshen^Y
burtchen^R

Pronounced BOOR-*chen*, to rhyme with "poor gin." Slavic: "to mumble."

1. To grumble, to growl, as (a) a stomach, or (b) a person.
2. To complain.

"What's he *burtshing* about?" is a reasonable facsimile of "What's he griping about?"—in spades.

See also kvetch, krekhts.

cabala^R
kabole^Y
kabbalah, kabbala, cabbalah, cabballa

Pronounced *ka*-BAH-*la*, to rhyme with "a dolla(r)."
Hebrew: "Tradition," from the verb meaning "to receive."

1. The Jewish mystical movement; the complex and esoteric body of Jewish mystical tradition, literature, and
   thought.
2. A receipt, as for a purchase.

C abalism was a movement of profound mystical faith fused to,
and steeped in, the superstitions and occult preoccupations
of pre–Middle Ages. It was a minor but meaningful stream of
thought and experience, a pious attempt to fathom the awesome,
fearful mysteries of God and creation. Originally, cabalism meant
the Oral Tradition; in the twelfth century, Jewish mystics adopted
this term, claiming an unbroken link between their ideas and
those of ancient days.

Cabalists claimed that their revelation was part and parcel of
Scripture. But cabalism's divinations and abracadabra, its intricate
numerology (see gematria), remained in a shadowland until the
eighth century C.E., when *The Book of Formation* appeared in Italy.

Not until *The Book of Splendor* (the *Zohar*) appeared in Spain in
the thirteenth century did a formidable metaphysical text on
cabalism appear. Two hundred years later the great Renaissance

humanist Pico della Mirandola translated the *Zohar* into Latin. And not until the seventeenth century did cabalism become a movement of consequence.

The cabalists held that reason alone could never penetrate the exalted mystical experiences involved in their perception of God and His mysteries. Esoteric formulas, numerological acrobatics, and theological mumbo jumbo went into the cabalists' efforts to apprehend God's will. And many a cabalistic omen or prophecy excitedly hailed the imminent appearance of the messiah and the Day of Judgment. The fearful and the faithful found sustenance in a bizarre succession of self-proclaimed holy men and putative messiahs. (See my entry for meshiekh.)

God was known to the cabalists as *En Sof* (Infinite One); His existence was made known through ten *sefiros,* or "divine radiations": Crown, Wisdom, Intelligence, Mercy, Judgment or Strength, Beauty, Victory, Glory, Foundation, and Kingdom.

Some cabalists followed the example of Christian flagellants and mortified the flesh; others set themselves prodigious tasks of fasting, penitence, prayer, and fearsome ordeals of suffering—all to atone for evil, purge the soul of sin, redeem the spirit, or break the dread Devil's awful hold.*

The center of cabalistic teaching was Safed, in Palestine, which in the sixteenth century was the seat of a sizable community of mystics. Isaac Lurie, the outstanding cabalist (he was known as the Ari—"the Lion"), a visionary who claimed to speak with the Prophet Elijah, presided over a circle of fervent disciples to whom he expounded arcane formulas and invocations; their prayers

---

*An actual Christian version of *cabala* emerged in the eighteenth century and influenced Madame Helena Blavatsky, who founded the Theosophical movement and was a leading figure in the occult spiritualism craze of late-nineteenth-century America.

contained many secret, hidden Names of God, upon which the faithful were exhorted to meditate. Esoteric and minatory rituals were ordained. Elaborate number manipulations and abracadabras attended every conceivable interpretation of passages from the *Torah* and the names of prophets.

It is not so hard to understand why such supernatural and mystical doctrines attracted so many Jews for so many years. Given the wretchedness, the poverty, the abiding terror under which Jews lived, many devout souls became convinced that they would be delivered from the terrible tribulations of the *galut* (exile) only by the messiah, who would come down to earth to usher in the Day of Judgment. One may ask: What else except the miraculous was there to place hope in? Heaven is the poor man's last hope—and reward.†

†The involvement in the late 1990s of pop idol Madonna in the study of *cabala* marked its revival as a hot commodity among Jews and non-Jews alike and made clear that its appeal is not limited to times of poverty and tribulation. At this writing, on-line bookseller Amazon.com offers 439 books with *"Cabala"* or *"Kabbalah"* in their titles. Spiritual retreat centers devoted to cabalistic meditation and study have full enrollments in Jewish population centers from New York to California. Cabalistic mysticism has also become the subject of serious study by scholars, preeminent among them Gershom Scholem (1897–1982) of Jerusalem's Hebrew University, whose 1941 *Major Trends in Jewish Mysticism* remains the most comprehensive work on the subject.

In contemporary synagogue life, the arcane cabalistic concept of *tikkun olam* (repair of the world) has been elevated into a major Jewish *mitzva* (commandment). The concept is based on a cabalistic legend about God's first "failed" effort at creation, which resulted in a scattering of "sparks" of holiness that can now be "redeemed" by human action. In essence, *tikkun olam* now means "social action" in the synagogue lexicon.

Other aspects of the Jewish tradition have also been enlivened by the revival of *cabala*. The ritual of "counting the *omer*" (marking the days from Passover to *Shevuos*) is made far more colorful through applied cabalistic teachings about the *sefiros* (faces of divinity), mentioned by Rosten in his entry above, and their associated emotional, psychological, and aesthetic features. The practice of joyously "welcoming the Sabbath Bride" with the song *"Lecha Dodi,"* which dates back to the sixteenth-century cabalists of Safed, is observed on Friday evenings in many Jewish congregations. In short, the cabalistic revival has brought much creativity and spirituality—and gullibility—back into Jewish life. (See Rosten's entries and my notes for **gematria** and **Sefirah**.)

canary
See keyn eynhore.

Chaim Yankel[R]
Khayim Yankl[Y]

Pronounced as one word, *khym-*YONK-*l* (not "chime," but with the throat-clearing *kh* of *ecch!*); rhymes with "dime jonquil."

Two masculine names, in common usage among Jews, pronounced as if one and used to describe

1. a nonentity, a nobody, any "poor Joe."
2. a colloquial, somewhat condescending way of addressing a Jew whose name you do not know—just as "Joe" or "Mac" is sometimes used in English. "Hey, Mac, you dropped something." "Eh, Reb Yankel, look where you're going."

Yankel is the familiar form of Yaacov (Jacob): *Chaim* (Hebrew for "life"), a common boy's name, was sometimes hastily acquired during a serious illness—as a talisman against death. It was actually believed that a changed name might confuse the Angel of Death, who would be looking for the victim under his original handle. It is doubtful that this had any effect upon the vital statistics.

See also nebekh, shlemiel, Kuni Leml.

A *Chaim Yankel,* visiting a cemetery, beheld a magnificent marble mausoleum, on the portal of which was incised ROTHSCHILD.

"Ai-ai-ai!" exclaimed the *Chaim Yankel.* "Now that's what I call living!"

chairlady

Pronounced as spelled. Yinglish.
A female chairman.

My mother was a prime mover in organizing one or another "group" of women to send clothing to Poland and to raise funds to be sent there for shoes, milk, and hot lunches for infants and schoolchildren. And it was at an "organizing meeting" of such ladies, held in our "front room," that I first heard the neologism *chairlady*. It was twenty years before I learned that un-Jews address a *chairlady* as "Madame Chairman," which is surely a contradiction in terms. I still think "chairlady" more sensible, to say nothing of **sexually unconfusing.****

As a child in Chicago, I was often taken by my parents to meetings of the Workmen's Circle (Lodzer Branch) and to endless "benefits," concerts, recitals, choral groups, Yiddish-theater parties. It was at the last that I first saw live theater and first realized what passionate lovers of theater and recitals (of poetry no less than music) Jews are—and what enthusiastic and energetic audiences they constitute.

In an old theater on Blue Island Avenue I saw admirable performances by New York companies of the Yiddish theater, appearing in Chicago in such classics as *Yoshe Kalb, The Dybbuk,* and *The Golem.* It was theater in the grand style and European tradition, with

---

*"Mira was hiding in the ladies' room. She called it that, even though someone had scratched out the word ladies' in the sign on the door. . . ." This is the opening scene of Marilyn French's 1977 best-seller, *The Women's Room,* which became standard college reading. Ever since, "lady" has been used far less as a synonym for "woman," except when specifying class status ("English lady" or "She's a real lady"). *Chairlady* has thus faded with the Yiddish accent, giving way to the nothing-funny-about-it "chairwoman" or the simple, ungendered "chair."

full-bodied performances of exceptional power by artists of the rank of Boris Thomashevsky, Jacob Adler, Bertha Kalish, Maurice Schwartz, the sensitive Jacob Ben-Ami, and young Muni Weisenfreund (later Paul Muni). Little did I know that such orotund voices and grandiose gestures, such full-bodied tears and laughter, such outbursts of passion and fierce orchestrations of feeling— all, all were rigorously muted and repressed on the English stage.

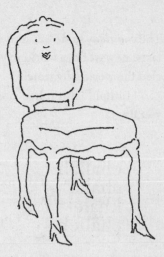

I learned to love the baroque, unabashed expressionism in those marvelously eloquent matinees. I could also gain an advance sense of the nature of the play we were to attend by the sartorial preparations my mother made: a bright frock and only one handkerchief signaled a comedy; a somber dress and several handkerchiefs clearly foreshadowed a heartrending, "true to life" tragedy or tearjerker. Years later, in Hollywood, I heard blasé friends characterize plays as "three handkerchief" or "four handkerchief" **productions.**†

---

† Asked years ago about the future of Yiddish theater, Isaac Bashevis Singer quipped: "The Yiddish theater has been dying for a thousand years." Its seeming immortality is today best demonstrated by New York's *Folksbiene* theater (founded in 1905), which receives major support from the Workmen's Circle. The *Folksbiene* consistently performs for sell-out audiences (many of whom wear headphones giving simultaneous English and Russian translation). The company weathered a crisis in 1999 when the historic Central Synagogue, which had been its home for fifteen years, was devastated by fire; shortly after, a new Yiddish musical, written by company co-director Eleanor Reissa, was successfully mounted in a new location. With audiences galvanized by the *klezmer* music revival (see Rosten's entry and my notes for **klezmer**), Yiddish theater is far from waving a white handkerchief of surrender!

The *chairlady* said, ". . . and we must all learn to adjust to this fantastic new world, a world in which, only last week, an astronaut circled the world fifty times!"

"Humph!" humphed one of the ladies. "If you have money, you travel."

challah
challa^R
khale^Y
challeh

Pronounced KHAHL-*leh,* with the rattling *kh.* Rhymes with "dolla." Hebrew: *challah.*

A braided loaf of white bread, glazed with egg white, very soft, delicate in flavor.

I for one, consider *challah* a Jewish contribution to distinguished cuisine (there are not many), a bread to rank with the most exquisite productions of the baker's art.

Challah is a Sabbath and holiday delicacy. For *Shabbes* it is always made in a braided form. On holidays it may be kneaded into other shapes: circular, ladderlike, etc.

Children especially adore *challah*—for its almost-like-cake texture, its braided top, its crisp crust and ever-so-soft inside.

Two *challahs,* uncut, are on the table of observing Jews on Sabbath eve; they are not cut until after the *brokhe* (blessing). This practice perpetuates the memory of the wilderness, where God dropped a double portion of manna on Friday (and none on the Sabbath); or, say some, it recalls the Temple, where two rows of bread were lined up before the altar. The home, which is of limitless importance in Jewish life, is in fact called in Hebrew *migdash mehad*—"a small temple."

When a *challah* (or any Sabbath bread) is baked, a small piece of dough is, by tradition, tossed into the oven or fire—as a token of sacrifice. Why? Because *challah* is a Hebrew term used in Numbers 15:20 and Ezekiel 44:30, where it means "the priest's share" of the baking dough.

If you have never tasted *challah*, stop reading and repair to a Jewish bakery.

Some American Jews pronounce *challah* "holly," the younger ones not being able to manage the uvular *kh*, the rest thinking "holly" more genteel, more Americanized. This is deplorable.

How can one recognize a Reform Jew in a bakery on Friday? He orders a *challah* and says, **"Slice it."***

chaloshes
See khaloshes.

chalutz
See khalutz.

*Enough with the Reform Jewish jokes, already! (See my footnote to **brokhe**.)

There are two competing schools of *challah* "cutting" in contemporary Jewish life. In one, the *challah* is torn by hand immediately after the *brokhe*. Anyone who can't reach the loaf touches the shoulder or arm of someone who can, and people often feed chunks of bread to one another. In the second, more dignified school of *challah fressing* (see Rosten's entry for **fress**), the bread is sliced by knife after the *brokhe*—and a most delicious French toast can be made from the leftovers, if you're fortunate enough to have any.

Chanukah^R
Khanike^Y
Hanuka, Hanukkah, Channukah

Pronounced KHON-*eh-keh* or KHON-*ee-keh*, with a Hebrew
or Scottish *kh*, not an English *ch;* rhymes with "Monica."
Hebrew: "Dedication."

"The Feast of Dedication," more colloquially known
as "the Feast of Lights." One of the less solemn Jewish
festivities.

This eight-day holiday usually falls in December. Unlike the
festivals of *Succos, Shevuos, Pesach,* and *Rosh Hashanah,*
Chanukah does not have its origin in the Bible. It commemorates
the victory of the Jewish Maccabees over Syrian despots (167
B.C.E.) in a fight for religious freedom that rescued Judaism, as a
culture, from annihilation. The Apocrypha tell the story
(Maccabees I and II).

The rebellion was led by a priest, Mattathias of the Hasmonean
family, and his son, Judah the Maccabee (the Hammer). It continued for three years of guerrilla warfare against the armies of
Antiochus IV, who was known to his minions as Epiphanes: "the
Risen God." Antiochus planned to convert the Jews by force to
Greek polytheism, and he ordered them to build altars and shrines
for idols, to stop circumcising male babies, etc. In 168 B.C.E., the
great Temple was desecrated by a huge statue of Zeus, and Jewish
courts were used for orgies. Thousands of Jews fled to caves; thousands wandered about in disguise.

The Maccabean uprising seemed hopeless. Guerrilla groups of
Jews, unaccustomed to fighting and equipped with primitive
weapons, fought the well-armed Seleucid soldiers—and won out at
Emmaus. They returned to Jerusalem to find a sacked, burned

Temple, and they set about restoring it. On the twenty-fifth day of the Hebrew month of Kislev, in 165 B.C.E., Judah Maccabee solemnly rededicated *Zion*'s **temple***—lighting the lamps of a great menorah—and celebrated the beginning of a week-long festival.

To this day, each *Chanukah,* Jews light candles for eight days—one the first evening, adding one light each night on the nine-branched menorah. A special ninth candle, called the *shammes* (servant), stands taller than the rest in the menorah and is used to light the others. This is interpreted to show that one can give love and light to others without losing any part of one's own radiance.

Chanukah is the only Jewish festival connected with a warring event, and it is a secular, not a religious, **celebration.†** (So deeply ingrained is Jewish distaste for violence that King David himself was not permitted to build the Temple, because he had been

---

*Judah Maccabee was eventually killed in battle. The struggle had many aspects of civil war, between the class of Jews that embraced the Hellenistic culture of the Syrian conquerors and the Maccabean rebels who were religious nationalists. Ultimately, the Hasmonean dynasty established by the Maccabean victory pursued its own policies of conquest and forced religious conversion until the ascendant power of Rome took over Judea.

A statue of Judah Maccabee stands in administration building 600 at the U.S. military academy at West Point, New York.

† *Chanukah* was raised to prominence late in the nineteenth century precisely because of its militaristic emphasis, as eastern European Zionists held *Chanukah* celebrations to mobilize Jewish self-defense against pogroms and to raise up the banner of national rejuvenation. Modern Israelis later embraced the holiday to celebrate their military prowess and ongoing "miracle" of survival. It is in the United States, however, that *Chanukah* has most achieved "major holiday" status as the Jewish equivalent of Christmas. Menorah lighting is now a close second to the Passover *Seder* as the most widely observed American Jewish ritual among both all-Jewish and intermarried families. Nevertheless, the proper transliteration of this festival's name remains one of the great mysteries of modern Jewish life!

"stained" by the blood of war.) Each *Chanukah*, the prophecy of Zechariah is read: "Not by strength, not by power, but by My spirit, sayeth the Lord of Hosts."

Chanukah is observed with parties, games, and gifts to the children. *Chanukah gelt*, a small gift of cash, is often distributed.‡ A favorite food is *latkes*, potato pancakes.

A delightful *Chanukah* game is a put-and-take game played with a four-sided top (a *dreydl* or *trendel*), using nuts for the betting. The four sides of the *dreydl* were originally initialed *N*, *G*, *H*, *S*—for German-Yiddish words *Nichts* (nothing), *Ganz* (all), *Halb* (half), and *Stell* (put). In time, the *N*, *G*, *H*, *S* were reinterpreted to be *nun*, *giml*, *hey*, and *shin*—the first letters of the Hebrew "*Nes Gadol Heya Sham*," meaning "a great miracle happened there."§ The miracle referred both to the Maccabean victory and to a one-day supply of oil that somehow burned for eight days when the Temple was rededicated. The letters also stand for the Yiddish words *nem* (take), *gib* (give), *halb* (half), and *shtel* (put)—which provide all the instructions needed.

I have it on indisputable authority that in Scarsdale, during a school celebration of Christmas, one of the children sang the carol as "God rest ye, Jerry Mandelbaum."

‡In some Jewish families, the tradition that Rosten describes of giving *Chanukah gelt* has been augmented by a "new" tradition of *Chanukah tzedakah*, charitable giving. (In eastern Europe, *tzedakah* was a traditional part of *Chanukah* observance, and the *melamed*, the teacher of young children, often depended upon this *gelt* for his livelihood.)

§In Israel, the letter *shin* is replaced on the *dreydl* with a *peh*, for the word *poh*—"A great miracle happened *here*."

Chasid[R]
Khosed[Y]
Chasidim (plural)
Chassid, Hassid, Hasid

Pronounced KWAH-*sid,* to rhyme with "saw mid"; *Khah-*SEED-*em;* begin with the rattling in the back of the throat for a uvular *kh.* Hebrew: "pious," "pious one."

1. A most pious man; a disciple of a great rabbi.
2. A follower of the Chasidic philosophy and way of life.

The extraordinary Chasidic movement, opposed by many rabbis and pietists, raced through the Jewish communities of eastern and central Europe in the eighteenth century. It was founded by a simple man, a mystic, named Israel ben Eliezer (1700–1760—see **Bal Shem**), who loved to wander about the open country, where he felt he could best commune with God. He preached a folk gospel that had enormous appeal to small-town Jews because it opposed the rabbinical emphasis on formal learning and derogated the endless Talmudic casuistry of the wise men.

Criticizing the pedantic reiterations of scholars, and the doom-ridden visions of the Orthodox, Israel ben Eliezer sang the praises of simple faith, joyous worship, everyday pleasures. God can be worshiped anywhere, said the *Baal Shem Tov,* directly and simply: God requires no synagogues, except "in the heart." Prayers should be spontaneous, personal, happy—not the formalized, automatic rote of the *shul.* (The parallel to Martin Luther's gospel of faith and anticlericalism is striking.)

The *Chasidim* preferred gay songs to magisterial invocations. They danced and clapped hands while singing out the Lord's praises, and they invited group expressions of religious rapture.

The Chasidic celebration of God offered poor Jews a new kind of communion—warm, intimate, personal—with a hitherto somber God; it also gave them precious catharsis. The *Chasidim* preached and evangelized with homely stories and delightful parables, charming anecdotes and folk sayings anyone could understand. Their ecstatic songs and "frivolous" dances angered many of Jewry's elders. The rabbis denounced Israel ben Eliezer as ignorant and irreverent. Nonetheless, the Chasidic movement spread through eastern Europe with gusto—except in Lithuania, where the great Gaon of Vilna (the head of the rabbinical academy), Rabbi Elijah ben Solomon (1720–1797), publicly anathematized the *Baal Shem Tov*.

A Chasidic *rebbe* (rabbi) was treated by his followers with greater awe than Jews customarily gave a rabbi. Disciples repeated a *rebbe's* every phrase, imitated his every gesture. As is not unusual in religious movements that begin with simple affirmations and oppose priestly protocol, the *rebbes* were soon elevated by their followers into holy men.

Chasidim's leaders became known as *tzaddikim*—seers, near saints, prophets believed to possess supernatural powers. Ironically enough, the *tzaddik* became an ecclesiastical bridge between man and God such as rabbis had never been. The title *tzaddik* even became hereditary.

The *tzaddik* was often asked by his worshipful believers to intervene with God during an illness or crisis, to speak directly to the Almighty. Some *tzaddikim* used talismans and amulets to ward off the evil eye. The faithful hung on a *tzaddik's* every breath; every comment was invested with supernatural meaning.

Chasidism still has its passionate adherents, in small but lively enclaves in New York, Chicago, Boston, and even some suburbs.*

---

*While the various Yiddish-speaking Chasidic movements of eastern Europe were decimated by the Nazis, a few that managed to transport their leaders to America and Israel have endured. Among these, the Lubavitch

Chasidic tales and parables run into thousands. Many are recounted in *The Hasidic Anthology*, by Louis I. Newman, and, more portentously, in two volumes by Martin Buber, *Tales of the Hasidim: Early Masters* and *Later Masters.*†

See also tzaddik.

FROM CHASIDIC STORIES AND SOURCES: Why do the wicked always form groups, whereas the righteous do not? Because the wicked, walking in darkness, need company, but the righteous, who live in the light, do not fear being alone.

When a poor coach driver apologized to a *Chasid* because his work kept him from going to the synagogue, the *Chasid* asked: "And do you ever give free rides to the poor?"

"Often."

"Then you are already serving the Lord."

Chasidim (Chabad) are most prominent and best funded, with estimated contributions of up to $250 million annually. The Brooklyn-based Lubavitchers do worldwide outreach work, which has included underground work among Soviet Jews and conservative political organizing in Jerusalem. Messianic fervor took hold of the Lubavitchers throughout the 1980s and 1990s, as they began to regard their *rebbe*, Rabbi Menachem Schneerson, as the *meshiakh* (messiah; see Rosten's entry for **meshiakh**). Speculation died down following Schneerson's death in 1994, and the movement has been relatively subdued since.

A second surviving Chasidic sect, the Satmarers, regularly burn the Israeli flag at street demonstrations. The Satmarers consider the establishment of a Jewish state prior to messianic redemption to be a blasphemy.

Two charismatic Lubavitcher rabbis, the late Shlomo Carlebach and Zalman Schachter-Shalomi, strayed far from their origins during the past three decades to create a blend of Chasidic philosophy and song, cabalistic mysticism, self-actualization therapy, and New Age spirituality described as "Jewish Renewal."

† Eli Wiesel's *Souls on Fire: Portraits and Legends of Hasidic Masters* (Simon & Schuster, 1982) is probably the best-known nonscholarly work on Chasidic folklore published since Rosten wrote.

A king, visiting a prison, began to interview the inmates. Prisoner after prisoner insisted that he was innocent, that he had been framed, that a terrible injustice had been done.

The king asked the last prisoner, "And are you, too, as innocent as a lamb?"

"No, Your Majesty. I'm a thief. I was caught, fairly tried, sentenced."

"You admit you're a thief?" asked the king in surprise.

"Yes, Your Majesty."

The king said, "Throw this crook out of here!"

The thief was promptly ejected.

The other prisoners raised a fearful clamor. "Your Majesty, how can you do such a thing? How can you free a confessed criminal while we—"

"I was afraid," the king said, smiling, "that that wicked scoundrel would corrupt all you innocent souls."

chassen
See khosn.

chasseneh
See khasene.

chaver^R
khaver^Y
haver

Pronounced KHAH-*ver*, with a strong, throat-clearing Germanic *kh* sound, as in *"Ach!" Khaver* rhymes with JOB-*ber*. From Hebrew: *khaver*, "comrade, friend." Plural: *chaverim*, pronounced *khah*-VAY-*rim*. The feminine form is *chaverta*, pronounced KHAH-*ver-ta*.

1. Friend, comrade, pal. "He's my closest *chaver*."
2. The form of address used instead of "Mister" in many Jewish fraternal, trade union, or **political organizations**.* "The chair now recognizes Chaver Falstein."

I hear that some years ago, the presiding officer at a meeting of officials from several trade unions called upon "the head of the Steamfitters, *Chaver* O'Malley."

chazzen^R
khazn^Y
hazzan

Pronounced KHAZ'*n*, with the *kh* functioning like the *ch* in the Scottish *loch*. *Khazzen* rhymes with "rosin." The plural

---

*Chaver or *chaverta* was an especially popular form of address in Jewish Communist and Socialist-Zionist circles. It faded from common usage just as the *chavurah* movement (same Hebrew word root) was developing during the 1970s and 1980s. These were small Jewish communities, usually without rabbinic leadership, that creatively experimented with Judaism to shape it to their feminist, democratic, and environmentally conscious mores. *Chavurot* (plural) are today represented by the National Havurah Institute, which holds an annual retreat in the Northeast.

is *chazzonim,* pronounced *khah-*ZAW-*nim.* From Hebrew: "a seer."

A cantor—that is, the trained professional singer who assists the rabbi in religious services.

The *chazzen* sings long passages of the liturgy. His† recitation is not chant or singsong, as is that of ordinary Jews in prayer: it is virtuoso singing, especially in the falsettos, which are singularly sweet and soft.

The melodies that cantors trill out are not written down, but they are standardized; anyone familiar with the liturgy can enter a synagogue and know from the cantor's melodic line whether it is an ordinary service, Sabbath, Passover, or *Rosh Hashanah.*

The cantor (who can be any member of the congregation) sings out the opening words of a prayer, which the congregation takes up. The cantor sings the final verse and starts a new prayer by intoning its initial phrases. There were times when a cantor's bravura passages in a synagogue would be greeted by outbursts of applause.

Much Semitic music seems born in a wail and swathed in suffering; Jewish *chazzanut* (cantorial art) emphasizes the mournful and the lamentative. Emotion is expressed with intensity, because the cantor speaks for the congregation, as it were (he is known as the *sheliakh tzibur,* or "emissary of the congregation"), in intoning the emotions embedded in Hebrew texts: suffering, contrition, compassion, despair—and always gratitude to a benevolent (!) God.

---

†The Reform movement graduated its first woman cantor in 1975. The Conservative Jewish Theological Seminary waited until 1988, though a number of Conservative pulpits had non-ordained women cantors during the decade before. Among the issues of Jewish law that continue to block women from taking the pulpit in Orthodox communities is that of *kol isha* (woman's voice), which is traditionally considered too sensual and alluring to lead men in prayer. In the United States there is now a Women Cantors Network, with a sister group called Kol Nashim in Canada.

For more than ten centuries, no device or instrument for the making of music was heard in any Jewish synagogue. The use of instruments in synagogues was discontinued after the destruction of the Temple (where harp, cymbal, and horn had been used to accompany the worshipers). Today, some Conservative congregations use an organ—but only Reform and Reconstructionist synagogues permit the use of other instruments.

As Catholic and Protestant religious services grew more and more melodious, to say nothing of opulent, Jewish worshipers, too, sought musical enrichment, and toward the end of the Renaissance, in a quite radical departure from tradition, congregations began to employ professional cantors, men with singing talent. (Few congregations could afford to pay them very much, so cantors also taught Hebrew to the young; some even served as sextons.)

In Italy, where Jewish musicians headed important music schools, the traditional singsong of the Middle East was embroidered with the lush melodic interplay of Baroque Italian music.

One famous *chazzen*, Salomone Rossi of Mantua, advocated the introduction of a choir and soloists and an organ into synagogue services. This simply scandalized the Orthodox. (Rossi wrote many lovely hymns for religious services.)

By the middle of the eighteenth century you could hear music (a choir, an organ) in the synagogues of well-to-do congregations across Europe—in England, France, Germany, and Italy, but not in eastern Europe, where the idea was anathema to the pietists.

In time, a special bravura style of rendering the prayers, with remarkable falsetto effects, won over even the fundamentalists of Poland.

The cantors, of course, loved long, solo recitatives and were important in altering the monotonous singsong of services that were part praying, part mumbling, part keening, and much wailing, rather than singing. Nathan Ausubel notes, in his article in

The Book of Jewish Knowledge (Crown, 1964), that after Franz Liszt went to hear a famous cantor sing in Vienna, he wrote: "Seldom were we so deeply stirred by emotion as on that evening, so shaken that our soul entirely surrendered to . . . participation in the service."

The cantors also served to spearhead a remarkable rebirth of music among east European Jews. Music offered one nearly magical way to "break out of the ghetto"—to have a career, to win fame and fortune, to travel, to become renowned and honored in an otherwise inhospitable Gentile world. Soon Russia, Poland, Germany, Hungary, Austria, Lithuania, Galicia, and Romania produced an amazingly large and remarkably gifted stream of Jewish violinists, pianists, cellists, composers, and conductors. In this century, of course, Jewish musicians have scored spectacular successes around the world. And in America, rare was the Jewish boy who was not hounded to play the fiddle, or the girl not *mutched* to play the piano.

Chazzonim were once widely admired for their art (for example, Yossele Rosenblatt), but today they are not accorded the respect given a rabbi or the deference given any learned man. The intellectual status of *chazzonim* is, indeed, derided. "He has the brain of a *chazzen*" is not a compliment.

The *chazzen* is, by tradition, regarded as a simple man—even a simpleton. Away from the panoply of the pulpit, he is viewed as a gifted larynx. "Any Jew can be a *chazzen*," goes the saying, "except it just happens that at this moment, he's hoarse." Another folk saying is even more unkind: "All cantors are fools, but not all fools are cantors." It is even libeled that *chazzen* is an acronym, formed from the first letters of *"Chazzonim zenen naronim,"* a hallowed apothegm: "Cantors are fools." Poor chaps.

A familiar sideswipe, in Reform congregations, is found in the wisecrack "When the *chazzen* knows no Hebrew, he is called a cantor."

Joseph Zabara, a thirteenth-century physician-poet of Barcelona, wrote that a cantor is a fool because "standing on a platform, he thinks he is on a pedestal." And it is said that "the song of fools" in Ecclesiastes 7:5 referred to cantors who, singing, interrupt the solemn ritual of prayer—so that the congregation may have a chance for some pleasant gossip.*

Modern *chazzonim* are often university graduates and hold teaching certificates, combining *chazzanut* with Hebrew school teaching in smaller congregations.

It is said that when you inform a *chazzen* of a calamity, he whips a tuning fork out of his pocket, taps it, gets the right key, then cries, *"Gevaaaaalt!"*

"Our new *chazzen!*" said one Jew. "What beautiful singing, no?"

"Eh," the other scoffed. "If I had his voice, I'd sing just as good."

At the time of the creation, it is said, every living creature was told what his duties would be and was asked by the angels to suggest the length of its life span.

The horse, told that men would ride on his back, said, "In that case, please—twenty years of life will be enough for me!"

The donkey, told he would bear heavy burdens and hear many curses, said, "I'll be satisfied with twenty years, too."

The cantor, told he would do nothing but sing hymns, asked

---

*Many of Rosten's remarks about disrespect for *chazzonim* seem anachronistic, perhaps because of the increase of Jewish musical illiteracy among synagogue-affiliated Jews (resulting in dependence upon, and less competition with, the cantor), in combination with the increased professionalism and academic certification of the cantorate. In many synagogues today, cantors also serve as educational directors.

for sixty years. The angels felt that was too much and suggested forty. The cantor protested, "I think I ought to get sixty years!"

So the angels took ten years from the life of the horse and ten from the life of the donkey and added them to the forty of the cantor.

That's why, say the Jews, a cantor sings beautifully for the first forty years of his life, for the next ten sounds like a horse, and for the ten after that brays like a donkey.

Bahya, a second-century Spanish moralist (born Joseph ibn Pakuda), tells us of a king who dismissed the dramatics of a *chazzen* thusly: "He prays to impress me, not God."

"A *chazzen* without a voice is like a sheep without wool." Note "sheep"—no one would dream of comparing *chazzonim* to lions, say, or tigers.

cheder^R
kheyder^Y
heder, cheyder

Pronounced KHEY-*der*, with a throat-clearing *kh;* rhymes with "raider." Hebrew for "room." Plural: *chedarim*, pronounced *kheh*-DAW-*rim* in Yiddish.

The room or school where Hebrew is taught.

Jewish boys would begin studying as early as age three (!) and rarely remain illiterate past six. They would study six to ten hours a day, six days a week. Many Jewish boys received their early Hebrew education in a room (*cheder*) in the home of a paid *melamed* (teacher). In the larger *Talmud Torah* schools there were several rooms and more than one teacher. These schools customarily were supported by the synagogue and charged no tuition.

The emphasis Jews give to education seems to be as old as the Jewish people. (See the book of Joshua.) Jews held that the Jewish community must provide an education to every boy, no matter who or how poor. Virtually universal, democratic, elementary education (for males) existed among the Jews to a degree unknown, I think, among other people. Rabbinical authority even forbade a Jew to remain in any place that had no Hebrew teacher for the young.*

To be sure, the *cheder* curriculum was narrowly limited, the pedagogical methods primitive: drill, repetition, and cracks across the knuckles with a pointer or ruler. But at a time when the overwhelming majority of humanity was illiterate, there was hardly a Jewish male over the age of five who could not read and write. The cultural impact and importance of this are for historians, sociologists, and educators to appraise.

The *Torah* (the Five Books of Moses) was the only elementary *cheder* text. Students would recite en masse, in a high singsong, swaying back and forth in a traditional rhythm, the tempo set by the teacher, the pace hastened or slowed by his appraisal of the students' comprehension of the passage they were droning out. (Advanced students learned the musical notations for the cantillation of religious texts.)

*Jewish *cheder* education for both boys and girls is expanding beyond Orthodox circles in contemporary Jewish life in the form of the "Jewish day school" movement. The Conservative Solomon Schechter Day School network in 2000 has more than seventy institutions in the United States, Canada, and Israel, and the Reform movement counts more than twenty schools that are either Reform or interdenominational. All of these schools teach both Jewish and secular subjects and are fully accredited in accordance with state educational standards. According to the 1999 *American Jewish Yearbook*, there are now approximately 180,000 American Jewish children in Jewish day schools, a 300 percent increase since the early 1960s.

In the old country, before a boy entered a *cheder* he was carried into the synagogue by his father or *melamed* and placed in front of the *bema* (pulpit) to face the entire congregation; then the Scroll of the *Torah* (*Sefer Torah*) was unrolled and the Ten Commandments were read aloud, addressed to the little boy directly, reenacting the scene on Mount Sinai.

On his first day in *cheder*, the boy's mother and father would stand over him as the teacher pointed to the letters of the *alef-bet* (alphabet). The lad repeated the names of the Hebrew letters: *alef* . . . *beyt* . . . *giml* . . . *daled* . . . And for each name, his mother would give him a little honey cake or cookie, shaped in the form of that letter, or would put honey into his mouth, to eat with the cake—to show how sweet learning is.

At the end of this first lesson, the mother would enfold the boy and pray that her son fulfill his life with years of *Torah* study, marriage, and good deeds.

The Jews are so often referred to as "the children of Israel" that a *cheder* boy once asked, "Didn't the grown-ups ever do anything?"

Two *cheder* students were discussing how hard and tiring their studies had become, and impulsively one blurted: "Let's run away!"

"Run away? . . . Our fathers would catch up with us and give us a sound thrashing."

"So we'll hit them back!"

"*What?* Hit your *father?!* You must be mad. Have you forgotten the Commandment—always to honor your father and mother?"

"Mmh. . . . So you hit my father and I'll hit yours."

Chelm^R
Khelm^Y

Pronounced KHELM, with the guttural *kh*.

The name of a "legendary" town inhabited by befuddled, stupid, foolish, but endearing people.

Chelm is used as the name of a mythical place, but there is and was a real Chelm, some forty miles east of Lublin, with a population of around four thousand, the majority of whom were Jews. Another Chelm exists just east of Tarnow. How Chelm achieved its reputation for hilarious non sequiturs I do not know.

Chelm would enjoy no special name or fame, and surely no place in this lexicon, were it not that in Jewish folklore it has become the archetypical home of simpletons, an incubator of amiable fools, the Jewish equivalent of that Gotham from which "the wise men" came, Holland's Kampen, Italy's Cuneo, and Germany's Schildburg—all famous for fools.

There must be a thousand tall tales about Chelm and the unbelievable Chelmites; I'll give you but a handful.

The rabbi of Chelm visited the prison, and there he heard all but one of the inmates insist on their innocence. So he came back, held a council of wise men, and recommended that Chelm have *two* prisons: one for the guilty and another for the innocent.

The sages of Chelm began to argue about which was more important to the world: the moon or the sun. The community divided into two passionate camps. The reigning wise man then ruled: "The moon *must* be more important than the sun, because without the light of the moon our nights would be so dark we could not see anything. The sun, however, shines only by day—which is when we don't need it!"

A wise man of Chelm said, "What a crazy world this is. The rich, who have lots of money, buy on credit, but the poor, who don't have a cent, must pay cash. It should be the other way around: the rich, having money, should pay cash; and the poor, having none, should get credit."

"But if a storekeeper gives credit to the poor," objected another, "he can become poor himself."

"So fine!" said the idiot savant. "Then *he'll* be able to buy on credit, too!"

A farmer, riding home in his wagon, picked up a peddler from Chelm who was carrying a heavy bundle on his shoulder. The peddler sat down beside the farmer but kept his bundle on his shoulders.

"Why don't you put your bundle down?" asked the farmer.

"It's nice enough your horse is *shlepping* me," said the peddler. "Do I have to add my bundle to his burden?"

cheppeh
See tshepe.

chevra^R
khevre^Y

Pronounced KHEV-*ra*, with a German *kh* sound. From Hebrew: *khevara*, "comradeship."

A group of friends; one's pals or "gang." "He plays poker every Thursday night with his *chevra*."

I n Israel, where the very religious rail against the modern dress and freer ways of the young people, a bitter joke goes: "She came back from the *kibbutz* pregnant, gave birth to a boy, and should name him after the father: *Chevra*."

chillul hashem^R
khilel hashem^Y
hillul hashem, chillul ha-shem

Pronounced KHILL-*el ha*-SHEM, to rhyme with "l'il o' them." Hebrew: "profaning God's Name."

A deed that leads or encourages others to disbelieve in, or withdraw from, God. A publicly performed transgression. The opposite is *kiddush hashem*.

A transgression against God's law is a desecration of God's Name, hold the faithful, for every person is created in God's image, and humanity is only slightly less holy than the angels. Moreover, an act of immorality discredits all of Israel. God entered into a covenant with Israel: "Neither shall ye profane my holy name; but I will be hallowed among the children of Israel: I the Lord who hallow you" (Leviticus 22:32).

The more learned or influential a religious Jew is, the greater is the responsibility to serve as an example of honor. The concept of noblesse oblige is strong in Jewish life, but the aristocracy of Jews is one of knowledge plus morality in practice.

When the great Rab, who founded the Talmudic academy of Sura in Babylonia (two hundred years before the Christian era), was asked to give an example of what would be an act of *chillul hashem*, he replied, "In my case, if I bought meat and did not at once pay the butcher."

chloppeh
See khlyape.

chmallyeh
See khmalye.

choleria
See kholyere.

chometzdik^R
khometsdik^Y
hometzdik, chametzdik

Pronounced KHAW-*metz-dick,* with a fishbone-stuck-in-the-roof-of-your-mouth *kh,* like a MacTavish's *ch;* rhymes with "Paw gets sick." From the Hebrew: *chametz:* "sour," "leavened," "fermented."

Unfit to eat during **Passover.***

*Removing *chometz* before Passover traditionally involves a thorough spring cleaning of the home. All cereals and grains, including corn and rice (for Ashkenazic Jews), as well as millet, peas, beans, and peanuts, are collected and "sold" to a non-Jew, to be returned after the holiday. (In some communities, *chometz* is donated to hunger relief programs.) Also considered *chometzdik* are grain-based liquors (which means nearly all alcoholic beverages but kosher wine), canned foods with cornstarch or corn syrup, vinegar made from grain, and various toothpastes, cosmetics, etc. On the eve of *Pesach,* the family "hunts" in every nook for *chometz* with a candle, and a symbolic sweeping is performed to declare the household *chometz*-free. *Chometz* that has been gathered during this final sweep is burned outside the next morning. This ritual has been variously adapted by Jews of every denomination to immerse families in a feeling of spiritual renewal: whatever ferments and sours the soul is cleaned away.

North African Jews hold a huge *chometz* party immediately following Passover, in celebration of the *yortsayt* (death anniversary) of Maimon ben Joseph, an honored rabbinic commentator who was the father of Maimonides and a leader of Moroccan Jewry during the twelfth century. In North America, *chometz* parties are also popular after Passover, featuring pizza, beer, ice cream, and other *chometzdik* foods.

"*A chometzdike Yidene*"—KHAW-*metz-dick-eh* YEED-*en-eh* (a Jewish woman)—means a sour old biddy, an unpleasant old nag.

See Pesach.

chotchke
chotchkele

Pronounced T-CHOTCH-*keh*, to rhyme with "botch the," and TCHOTCH-*keh-leh*, to rhyme with "notch fella."

I prize these words, which are Americanized forms of *tsatske* and *tsatskeleh*, which I urge you to savor.

See tsatske.

A fur salesman, asked by a pretty young *chotchke* if the mink coat would be damaged if she were caught in the rain, replied, "Lady, did you ever see a mink carrying an **umbrella?**"*

chozzer^R
khazer^Y
chazzer

Pronounced KHAHZ-*zer*, with the emphatic Yiddish-German-Scottish *kh* sound: rhymes with "Roz her." Plural: *khazerim*, pronounced *khahz*-ZAY-*rim*, rhymes with "Pa's day dim." Hebrew: "pig."

*Calling a young woman a *chotchke* (or *tsatske*) these days has gone the route of calling her a "pretty young thing"—a usage that feminism has made into a "thing of the past."

1. Pig, hog, or the meat thereof.
2. One who acts in an ungrateful way.
3. One who is uncouth.
4. One who is cheap, venal, selfish.
5. One who is stingy.
6. One who is greedy.
7. One who takes advantage of you or tricks you through sharp practices.

In Yiddish, oddly enough, one rarely says *chozzer* ("pig!") to describe someone dirty—as in English. *Chozzer* is used for the ungrateful, the cheap, the selfish, greedy, stingy, or flagrantly unfair.

Observing Jews do not eat ham, bacon, or pork, which are forbidden to them by the Bible. (See kosher.)

The seemingly contradictory phrase *kosher chozzer fisl* ("kosher pig's feet") is used to describe someone who tries to be holier-than-thou but has conspicuous defects.

Chozzerish (piglike) is used in an exuberant way to describe abandon, indulgence, pleasure. Thus, the phrase of good wishes: "Go, live a *chozzerish tog*," which means "Go, have yourself a ball—live it up."

The greenhorn in the Automat fed nickel after nickel into the apple pie slot.

His friend exclaimed, "Are you crazy, you *chozzer*? You have already fifteen pies!"

Said the greenhorn: "Why should it bother you if I keep winning?"

chozzerai^R
khazeray^Y

Pronounced *khoz-zair-*EYE to rhyme with "Roz her eye." A Yiddish derivation from the Hebrew *khazir,* "pig."

1. Food that is awful. "Who can eat such *chozzerai?*"
2. Junk, trash. "That movie was nothing but *chozzerai.*"
3. Anything disgusting, even loathsome. "A good deal of contemporary theater strikes me as *chozzerai.*" "I wish he would learn the difference between art and *chozzerai.*"

*C*hozzerai could do us all a great service, I think, if it replaced the now popular "in" word, "crap."

This may be a gross libel on the innocent pig, I realize, since the pig, contrary to popular belief, is a quite tidy creature; he wallows in mud because he likes to stay cool; mud is often the best barnyard medium for reducing body temperature. Mud looks filthy, but in fashionable spas the rich pay to bathe in it.

chuppa^R
khupe^Y
chuppah, huppa, chuppeh

Pronounced KHU-*peh,* to rhyme with "book-eh"; make the *kh* a guttural *kh.* Hebrew: Originally, "chamber" or "covering."

Wedding canopy.

*T*he *chuppa* is used in all Orthodox and Conservative, and in some Reform, marriage ceremonies.

It is a fine canopy, usually made of white silk or satin, under which the bride and groom take their vows, and is held aloft by male relatives of the couple—one holding each of the wooden poles at the corners.* The *chuppa* is often embroidered with some biblical quotation, such as the one from Jeremiah: "The voice of mirth, and the voice of gladness, the voice of the bridegroom, and the voice of the bride" (16:9).

The *chuppa* suggests a royal canopy; the bride and groom are indeed considered "king and queen of this day."

It used to be that the bride left her father's house to go to her new husband's domain—which was symbolized by the *chuppa.* (One custom was to cut the poles from wood taken from trees that had been planted at the time of birth of the groom and bride.)†

In some areas, Jews called the veil that covers the bride a *chuppa;* in others, the *chuppa* was the cloth or shawl that covered the heads of the marriage couple; in still others, bride and groom were wrapped in a large prayer shawl. In Poland, the *chuppa* became the canopy top used today. It was set up inside the synagogue, or in a courtyard, or out of doors.

In American synagogues, the *chuppa* is often a canopy of greens and flowers.

Of the *chuppa,* Sholem Aleichem once wrote: "You enter it living and come out a corpse."

Nuptial canopies are, of course, found in many cultures. The

---

*Egalitarianism has caught on in wedding ceremonies, too, and *chuppa* pole holders (in non-Orthodox circles) may include both male and female relatives and friends.

†The Talmudic tradition that Rosten describes is making a small comeback in our environmentally conscious age, though the traditional trees—a cypress for a girl, a cedar for a boy—do not necessarily grow well in all climates.

Greeks use a *thalamos,* or bridal bower; the Brahmans use a twelve-pole canopy; in Spain and Scotland, newlyweds pass under a bower of leaves or boughs. In Sweden, bridesmaids hold a covering of shawls over the bride, to ward off the evil eye. (In many cultures, the wedding couple is protected from the evil eye by covers, cloths, or enclosures.) In Tahiti, the couple is surrounded by, or rolled into, a mat.

The *chuppa,* in short, is not unique to Jews, nor was it invented by the Israelites. But it symbolizes the home and its very special, central meaning in Jewish life—as life's hub, life's refuge, life's temple.

The rabbis held the first positive commandment of the Bible to be the one that enjoins, "Be fruitful, and multiply" (Genesis 1:28), and looked favorably upon early marriage. The *Talmud* sets eighteen as the proper age for marriage; some rabbis encouraged marriage as early as fourteen.

A man who remained unmarried after twenty was considered cursed by God Himself, living without joy and without blessing.

Legend has it that forty days before a child is born, its *khosn* (bridegroom) or *kale* (bride) is determined in heaven.

Elaborate premarriage "arrangements" or "conditions" (*tena'im*) were once required. A dowry (*nadan*) was, of course, part of every Orthodox nuptial contract. Presents of value were exchanged between bride- and groom-to-be. The latter usually gave his betrothed a prayer book (*siddur*), a veil, a fine comb, a sash, and a ring. The bride-to-be gave her "intended" a prayer shawl (*tallis*) and a gold or silver chain or watch, or both.

Jewish wedding ceremonials vary greatly throughout the world. In ancient times, a Jewish bride and groom followed the Greek custom of wearing garlands and wreaths, like crowns. In Roman days,

Jews used lighted torches. In some Arab countries, fireworks were set off. In the Middle Ages, the Jews in Germany married only during a full moon, the Jews in Spain only under a new moon.

The breaking of the glass, after the rabbi has pronounced his benediction over one glass, and after both bride and groom have sipped from another glass, has many interpretations. Some maintain that the breaking of the glass reminds the wedding party of the destruction of the Temple. The *Talmud* often counsels Jews to remember that happiness is transient and that Jews must never forget the sufferings of Israel; it records the example of a fourth-century wise man who was so disturbed by the high jinks at his son's wedding that he broke "a very fine glass . . . and they became sad."

Many people other than Jews follow a similar custom. Some nationalities break a dish or a jar, or the glass from which all the guests have drunk, or old crockery. Egyptians smashed clay pots on which they had entered the names of their enemies. It may even be that breaking objects was a form of magic to frighten away evil spirits.

Orthodox Jews celebrate a wedding for seven days running, for that is the Bible's account of the festivities after Jacob married Leah; and each wedding added to Israel's estate—and children.

It was customary for teachers to adjourn their classes and join a wedding party with their students: it was a *mitzva* to participate in the happiness of a bride and groom.

Under the old laws, groom and bride fasted on their wedding day, to atone for past sins and start connubial life with a clean slate. (In the synagogue, the groom would recite the *Yom Kippur* confession before the congregation.)

Most *shtetl* weddings occurred on Fridays. This gave everyone a chance to celebrate on the Sabbath.

At one time, a procession of lighted torches and gay musicians preceded the groom, his *mishpokhe* (family), and the rabbi; then the procession hurried off to provide the same triumphant parade to the bride.

Guests would shower the couple with barley grains or kernels of wheat—as explicit a hope for fertility as rice, it seems. Further to enhance fertility, a hen and rooster once preceded the couple.

A fertility "fish dance" was the custom of Sephardic Jews in the Balkans, because fish were considered exceptionally fecund; a bride and groom often made their posthymeneal dinner one of fish.

The Orthodox bride was customarily shorn of her hair and given a wig (*sheytl*) while seated before her girlfriends who, holding lighted candles, bade a ceremonial farewell to her maidenhood.

The dance at weddings was spirited (see *klezmer*), and the dances at weddings were many: the *mazel tov* dance, the dance for the parents of the bride and groom, etc. A *badkhn* often enlivened the proceedings with mock songs and laments, traditional jokes and freewheeling badinage.

At some Orthodox ceremonies, the bride, her parents, her "sponsors," circled the groom seven times, each holding a lighted candle. (This may derive from a cabalistic practice of making a mystic circle to shut out the dastardly demons who resent happiness.)

chutzpa[R] (noun)
khutspe[Y]
chutzpadik (adjective)
chutzpah, hutzpa

Pronounced кHOOTS-*pah;* rattle that *kh* around with fervor; rhymes with "Foot spa."* Pronounce the

*The YIVO transliteration indicates a pronunciation as кHOOTS-*peh,* to rhyme with "foots feh."

ch not as in "choo-choo" or "Chippewa," but as the German *ch* in *Ach!* or the Scottish in *loch.* Hebrew: "insolence," "audacity."

Gall, brazen nerve, effrontery, incredible "guts"; presumption plus arrogance such as no other word, and no other language, can do justice to.

The classic definition of *chutzpa* is, of course, this:

Chutzpa is that quality enshrined in a man who, having killed his mother and father, throws himself on the mercy of the court because he is an orphan.

A *chutzpanik* may be defined as the man who shouts, "Help! Help!" while beating you up.

In Paris, a plump Brooklyn *touristke* entered a fine linen shop and, fingering a lace tablecloth, asked the proprietress the price thusly: "*Combien pour cette tishtokh* [tablecloth]?"

"*Cinquante francs, madame.*"

"*Cinquante francs?*" echoed the American. "*Mais, c'est une shmatte* [rag]!"

The *baleboosteh* drew herself up in high dudgeon. "*Une shmatte, madame? Quelle chutzpa!*"

A woman, feeling sorry for a beggar who had come to her door, invited him in and offered him food. On the table was a pile of dark bread—and a few slices of *challah*. The *shnorrer* (beggar) promptly fell upon the *challah*.

"There's black bread, too," the woman hinted.

"I prefer *challah*."

"But *challah* is much more expensive!"

"Lady," said the beggar, "it's worth it."

That, I think, is *chutzpa*.

And if you need one more example, *regardez* this:

A *chutzpanik*, having dined well in a restaurant, summoned the proprietor, to whom he said as follows: "My friend, I enjoyed your food, but to tell you the truth, I haven't a penny to my name. Wait: Don't be angry! Hear me out. I am, by profession, a beggar. I happen to be an extremely talented *shnorrer*. I can go out and within an hour *shnorr* the entire amount I owe you. But naturally, you can't trust me to come back. I understand. You'd be well advised to come with me and not let me out of your sight for a minute, right? But can a man like you, a well-known restaurateur, be seen in the company of a man who is *shnorring*? Certainly not! So, I have the perfect solution. I'll wait here—and you go out and *shnorr* until you have the cost of this dinner!"

That, certainly, is *chutzpa*.

"The bashful go to Paradise," said Judah ha-Nasi, twenty centuries ago, "and the brazen go to Purgatory."

A friend of mine swears that in a Jewish restaurant he once asked a passing waiter, "What time is it?"

Icily, the waiter said, "You aren't my table."

cockamamy
cockamamie

Pronounced COCK-*a-may-me*, to rhyme with "lock a Mamie." Derivation: Ameridish, or children's argot.

1. Mixed up, muddled; ridiculous, implausible; not credible, foolishly complicated. "Did you ever hear such a *cockamamy* story?" "Of all the *cockamamy* excuses I ever heard."

This is not Hebrew and not Yiddish, but indigenous argot. H. L. Mencken's *Dictionary of American English,* surprisingly, does not list *cockamamy.* Neither does Eric Partridge's *Dictionary of Slang.* Nor, to my chagrin, does the comprehensive Berrey and Van den Bark *American Thesaurus of Slang* (Crowell, 1943).

I never heard *cockamamy* used in Chicago but have often encountered it in New York. It is a pungent adjective of disesteem.

2. Decalcomania: that is, a picture or design left on the skin as a "transfer," from specially prepared paper that is wetted and rubbed.

I am informed by veterans of the Lower East Side that decalcomania pictures were called "cockamamies" because no one knew how to spell "decalcomania." That's not as *cockamamy* a feat of etymology as you might think. I have found none better.

In the movie *Teacher's Pet,* Clark Gable used *cockamamy* with scornful relish to dismiss an idea as totally absurd, desperately invented.*

cohen
See Kohen.

---

*Former Beatle George Harrison gave this word an international flair with his 1989 song "Cockamamie Business"—"Didn't want to be a star— wanted just to play guitar / In this cockamamie business."

darshn^Y
darshan^R

See maggid.

An agnostic smiled and said, "But Darwin has proved that man is only another animal."

The *darshn* replied, "Then why has not a single breed of animal ever produced a Darwin?"

daven^R
davn^Y
davven

Pronounced DAH-*ven*, to rhyme with "robin." The origin of *daven* is unknown; it may be descended (remotely) from the French: *l'office divin*, "divine service." The word *daven*, incidentally, is used only by east European Jews and those descended from them.

To pray.

A traditional Jew *davens* three times a day (*shachris, mincha,* and *mairev*) and adds supplementary prayers on the Sabbath and festivals. The main part of any prayer is the silent or whispered part, called *shemona esrey*, always uttered while standing. The *shemona esrey* originally contained eighteen benedictions; a nineteenth was added in the second century, but the name *she-mona esrey* (eighteen) was retained.

The cardinal role that *davening* has played in the life of the Jews will be seen in dozens of entries in this lexicon.

One of the most touching prayers is the one offered after rising: it thanks God for having "returned to me my soul, which was in Your keeping."

In the West, Jews face east when *davening*, for that is where Israel—nay, *Eretz Yisroel!*—is.

The Bible lists many examples of individual prayers of thanks (Moses after crossing the Red Sea, in Exodus; Deborah after her victory over Sisera, in Judges) or prayers in petition for help (Abraham requesting leniency for Sodom, in Genesis).

Most of the Psalms originated as religious-philosophical-poetic affirmations, composed by individuals for use in public prayer. Communal prayer accompanied the bringing of sacrifices to the ancient Temple. When the Temple was destroyed, congregational prayers took the place of the Temple offerings.

A devout Jew will not read from the *Torah*, or recite the *Shema*, or pronounce the sacred Hebrew Name of God, unless his head is covered; and the Orthodox never leave their heads uncovered by hat or *yarmulke*.

No law in the Bible, or among the writings of the rabbis, seems to cover the custom of covering the head. This practice was, of course, not limited to the Jews: the use of a turban, fez, or other head covering is considered a sign of respect in many parts of the Orient and the Middle East.

Why do Christians bare their heads in church and while praying? The practice originated with Paul (original name: Saul), who wrote (I Corinthians) that any who covered his head while "praying or prophesying . . . dishonoureth his head." I can only assume that Paul was overreacting against his early training.

See brokhe.

The extraordinary place and power of prayer among religious Jews is described by Maurice Samuel in his sensitive and enchanting classic, *The World of Sholem Aleichem* (Knopf, 1943):

> The God in whom he [Tevyeh, the dairyman] believes with all his heart, whom he loves and prays to at least three times daily . . . he addresses . . . with affection, irony, sympathy, reverence, impudence, and indestructible hope. . . .
>
> . . . every morning, at sunrise or shortly before, Tevyeh has to say his long morning prayers, the *Shachris,* and he has to say them, on weekdays, with the prayer-shawl over his head, and the phylacteries on brow and arm. It's no good arguing with Tevyeh on this point. It is worse than useless to talk to him of superstition, mummery, and the opiate of the masses. He will only have one answer, delivered in a Talmudic singsong: "If all the persecutions of the ages, and all the bitterness of exploitation, could not prevent me from repeating the prayers of my fathers, shall I be made to fall away from them in a world of freedom?"
>
> But *Shachris* is only a beginning. During the day Tevyeh must take time out—and he does it . . . under the most discouraging circumstances—for other prayers. Do what you like with Tevyeh, chain him to a galley, yoke him to a chariot, starve him, break him, he is going to say his three prayers daily.

An observing Jew will recite the *Shema* four times daily. The *Shema* is today what it was over 2,500 years ago. (See Shema.) The Silent Devotion, an extraordinary prayer of eighteen (really nineteen) benedictions, is also offered four times daily. Recited or chanted while standing, it involves three thoughts: wisdom, learning, immortality. It extols God's glory; it offers a hope for the welfare of the pray-er, the family, and the community at large; and it thanks God for His blessings.

Reciting the Ten Commandments is no longer customary among Jews, as it was long ago. One school of thought holds that the practice ended when rabbis astutely observed that the incessant recitation of the Commandments tended to overglorify them as against God and tended to fortify the impression that the Commandments are "all there is" to Judaism.

A large part of Jewish praying entails reciting the Psalms.

For centuries, Jews have had the sense of being part of one flowing, continuous, uninterrupted prayer to (and dialogue with) God.

Consider the psychological importance of that moment when the weekly readings from the *Torah* have reached the final paragraph of all Moses' five Books, on the holy day *Simchas Torah:* instantly, the entire congregation declaims with excitement, "*Chazak, chazak, venit chazak!*" "Be strong, be strong, and let us gather new strength!"

And at once, all over again, the cycle of reading-praying begins, from the first words in Genesis.

dayen^Y
dayan^R
dayenim (plural)
dayyan

Pronounced DY-*en*, to rhyme with "Zion," or *die*-ON, to rhyme with "lie on;" pronounce the plural *die*-AW-*nim*. Hebrew: "Judge."

A rabbinical judge.

I n the rabbinic literature, *dayen* meant "sage," a student of the Law, a rabbi of the community. (God is called *Dayen Emes,* "the True Judge.")

The responsibilities of the rabbi and the *dayen* were often distinct and separate. Every *dayen* was a rabbi, trained in interpreting the *Torah* and *Talmud,* but not every rabbi was a *dayen.* In many communities, the *dayen* was more respected than the rabbi. His decision was known as a *Din Torah* (a verdict of the *Torah*).

The *Talmud* is full of instructions for the administration of justice: the judge may not listen to the arguments of one litigant in the absence of the other; equality before the law is underscored— no preference should be shown even to the learned; the first question put to litigants is, "Do you wish law or arbitration?"

In countries where Jewish communities were forced to live apart from the general population, the governments often granted judicial authority (in cases involving only Jews) to the *dayenim.* The general tendency was to submit to the law of the land except in matters affecting and within the confines of the Jewish community. Yitzhak Baer wrote of the Jewish community in Spain: "In matters of jurisprudence, the laws of the Torah prevailed. The decisions of the Jewish judges were recognized, confirmed and executed by the Christian kings and their officials. . . . The *dayen* wielded the same decisive authority in the *aljama* [Jewish community] as the *ukulde* did in the municipality." (*A History of the Jews in Christian Spain,* vol. I, Jewish Publication Society, 1961.)

My maternal grandfather was a *dayen* in Lodz, Poland, and to his home Jews came with a multitude of problems. He held himself quite superior to rabbis, who came to him with their problems. He also preferred to conduct services in his home, regarding the synagogue as a place for less illustrious worshipers—hence, his followers would make up a *minyan,* over which he presided.

For sensitive and haunting recollections of how a *dayen* lived and worked, see Isaac Bashevis Singer's stories about his father, *In My Father's Court* (Farrar, Straus, Giroux, 1966).

See bes din.

The old *dayen* called before him the newest rabbi in town and, sighing heavily, said, "My heart is heavy. My words are like lead: for I have heard a rumor about you—"

"It's not true!" cried the young rabbi. "I know the rumor, *Rebbe;* there's not a word of truth in it!"

The *dayen* drew himself up in horror. "*True* it should be yet? Isn't it bad enough there is a *rumor?!*"

A husband and wife came to the learned *dayen*, wrangling and fuming. The *dayen* first asked the woman into his study, where he plunged into a recitation of her husband's unkindnesses and inconsiderateness.

"—and I can't *stand* it anymore, Rabbi! I want to leave him! I want a divorce!"

The *dayen* nodded gravely. "You're right," he said, and sent her out.

Now her husband entered, ranting: "She probably told you such a *megillah* of lies I wouldn't recognize them! The truth is she's a lazy, no-good *yenta*, a terrible *baleboste*, she's mean to me and my friends, I should throw her out of the house! I want a divorce!"

"You're right," said the *dayen*.

The man left.

One of the *dayen's* students, who had observed all this with a puzzled air, inquired: "But *Rebbe:* you told her *she* was right, and you told him *he* was right; I don't see how both of them can be—"

"You're *right!*" said the *dayen*.

Diaspora
See galus.

donstairsike (feminine)
donstairsiker (masculine)

Pronounced *don*-STARE-*zi-keh*. Yinglish.

The neighbor who lives downstairs. "My *donstairsike* is an angel."

A *donstairsike* is doppelgänger to an *opstairsike*.

dopes[Y]
doppess[R]

Pronounced DOP-*pess*, to rhyme with "mop-less."

Useless but commiserating bystander; ineffectual observer who is of little help.

This word thrived in the garment trade—possibly as a more scornful version of dope, *shlemiel, shmegegge*. It may come from *arum-tapn*, "to grope about, to fumble in the dark." Dutch and German Jews who heard no Yiddish used *dopes* for a clumsy groper.

Dopes served a need for those who wanted a word to convey, with both precision and subtlety, a character type known in all cultures: the useless observer who, in a crisis, does nothing more than offer obligatory sympathy.

My erudite friend Professor Daniel Bell tells me that a 37th Street

Webster once defined *dopes* for him with picturesque precision: "The *shlemiel* is the pants presser who always drops the hot iron off the ironing board. The *shlimazl* is the *shmo* on whose foot the iron always falls. And the *dopes* is the one who says, 'Tsk, tsk!'"

The man who habitually clicks, "Tsk, tsk!" is also called a *tsitser*.

FOLK SAYING: "One man chops the wood, the other does all the grunting."

drek^Y
dreck^R

Rhymes with "fleck." From the German *Dreck:* "dirt," "filth."

1. Excrement.
2. Trash, junk, garbage.
3. Cheap or worthless things.
4. Plays, movies, or performances, in any of the arts, of grossly inferior quality.

Drek is forceful, but vulgar—like its English equivalent, "crap." If you want to say "dirt," don't use *drek,* use *shmutz* (rhymes with "puts").

I would not recommend your using *drek* in front of my mother, much less yours, any more than I would approve of using the sibilant four-letter English word for excrement.

Drek is used for a wide variety of judgments of disapproval— from the condition of the streets to the caliber of a poem. I do not approve of careless usage: both English and Yiddish have a rich enough vocabulary of disparagement. To say *drek,* save in extreme cases, is *drekish.* Better stick with *chozzerai.*

dresske

Pronounced DRESS-*keh;* rhymes with "press the." Yinglish.
Diminutive for "dress."

But stop! A *dresske* is not just a small dress, or a little dress, or even a bikini. *Those* would be called, in either fondness or ridicule, a *dresskeleh*—which is a diminutive, like "teeny-weeny."

A *dresske,* in classic Yinglish, means the kind of dress women dismiss as "a little nothing," or a garment for which the owner paid little.

Dresskes come from bargain basements, off racks labeled "Marked Down Drastically," and from certain emporia of notable values on 14th Street. I do not think anyone ever found a *dresske* at Bergdorf's or Neiman Marcus.

My favorite way of suggesting the true flavor of *dresske* involves the lady who, complimented on her new frock, replied with disdain: "This little *dresske?* It's nothing: I just use it for streetwalking."

dreykop[Y]
draykopf[R]

Pronounced DREY-*kup,* to rhyme with "gray pup," or DREY-*kawp,* to rhyme with "gray hawk." German: *drehen:* "to turn" or "twist"; *kopf:* "head."

1. A finagler who talks you into something, who "turns your head," who befuddles your good sense.
2. Someone who confuses you, bothers you, "talks off an arm and a leg."

3. An addlepate; one who is confused, whose head was turned.

The following involves two *dreykops*, as far as I'm concerned:
   The phone rang in the law offices. A voice answered, "Zucker, Zucker, Zucker, and Zucker."
   "Hello, may I please speak to Mr. Zucker?"
   "I'm sorry, but Mr. Zucker is in court."
   "Well, then, can I speak to Mr. *Zucker?*"
   "Sorry, Mr. Zucker is in Washington."
   "Well, how about connecting me with Mr. *Zucker?*"
   "Mr. Zucker won't be in until two."
   Sigh. "Okay, then, I'll speak to Mr. Zucker."
   "Speaking."

dybbuk ᴿ
dibek ʸ

Pronounced DIB-*book*, to rhyme with "rib hook." Hebrew: "evil spirit," "incubus."
1. An evil spirit—usually the soul of a dead person that enters a living person on whom the dead one had some claim.
2. A demon who takes possession of someone and renders the mortal mad, irrational, vicious, sinful, corrupt.

When someone went mad, became hysterical, or suffered an epileptic seizure, Jews would cry, "A *dybbuk* has entered into him [or her]!"
The idea of the *dybbuk* is as old as demonology itself, and demonology is as old as humanity.
A prominent demon in Jewish lore, particularly associated

with King Solomon (whom he dethroned for several years, according to legend), is Ashmedai, or Asmodeus.

Jews do not have a very vivid sense of the Devil, in the medieval Christian sense, as the incarnation of evil, the supreme, cunning tempter.

A *dybbuk* is the closest thing in Jewish folklore to a ghoul, vampire, or incubus—a migrating spirit who has to find a living body to inhabit. To protect women in childbirth from such demons, superstitious Jews used odd amulets and fervent incantations.

Dybbuks, of course, can be exorcised. The approved method is offered here as a special service to my readers:

Get a holy man or wonder worker, a *tzaddik* or even a *Bal Shem*, who will preside over a *minyan*. He reads the Ninety-first Psalm aloud, then, in a fearful voice, orders the damned *dybbuk* to vacate the body of the possessed person and, in God's name, go off to "eternal rest." This closely resembles the official rites recommended by the Roman Catholic Church. (See the manual: *De Ordinatione Exorcistarum*.)

If the *dybbuk* is stubborn and refuses to behave, as may be the case with such perverse critters, the *Bal Shem* orders a ram's horn *(shofar)* blown at once. That ought to do it.

One of the more charming details in the lore alleges that when a *dybbuk* flees a man or woman, a tiny, bloody spot, the size of a pinhead, appears on the pinky of the right foot. Either that, or a window develops a little crack.

S. Ansky (pen name of S. Z. Rapoport, 1863–1920) wrote a remarkable and compelling play, a classic of the Yiddish theater, called *The Dybbuk*, that has been performed around the world in many languages.*

I own a little book written by Jacques-Albin-Simon Collin de Plancy (1793–1887), *A Dictionary of Demonology*, that has long beguiled me. It catalogs all sorts of spooky spirits, from a Neopolitan pig with the head of a man to Adram-melech, "grand chancellor of hell," whom the Assyrians worshiped with infant sacrifices and who, learned rabbis said, took the shape of either a mule or a peacock, which runs a gamut of pretty versatile disguises. Amduscias, a grand duke of hell, is shaped like a unicorn—and gives concerts.

My favorite in the bogeyman league is Tanchelin, a heretic who lived in the twelfth century. Tanchelin had such awesome powers that husbands begged him to sleep with their wives. I am not sure that Tanchelin was a demon so much as a *dreykop*—which please see.

Dybbuks continue to haunt the culture through the work of creative artists. In 1974, Ansky's play was transformed into a ballet by Jerome Robbins, with music by Leonard Bernstein. Later that decade, the play received an avant-garde treatment by Joseph Chaiken at the Public Theater in New York and was most recently adapted by Tony Kushner, author of the Pulitzer Prize–winning play *Angels in America*. A handful of modern films have joined the original 1939 Yiddish masterpiece in treating the *dybbuk* theme—which has also inspired comic book artists and science fiction writers.

A splendid compendium to consult on matters concerning angels, demons, spirits, spooks, and allied suprahuman powers and beings, both good and evil, is Gustav Davidson's *A Dictionary of Angels* (Free Press, 1967).*

dzhlob
See zhlob.

*An excellent latter-day anthology of the Jewish supernatural is *Lilith's Cave: Jewish Tales of the Supernatural,* edited by Howard Schwartz and illustrated by Uri Shulewitz (Oxford University Press, 1991). The figure of Lilith, "Adam's first wife," who became a demon baby killer in Jewish folklore, has been appropriated by Jewish feminists as a symbol of independence and rebellion. Lilith emerged from rabbinic attempts to reconcile two contradictory passages in Genesis: first, man and woman are created simultaneously (1:27), then the woman is shaped from the man's rib (2:21–22). Lilith came to be identified as that first woman, who fled Adam's effort to husband and dominate her. Eve was then created as "a fitting helper for him" (2:18).

Lilith, a Jewish feminist quarterly magazine, has been publishing in New York since 1980.

Elohim
See Adonai, Jehovah.

Epicoris
See apikoyres.

epes^Y
eppes^R

Pronounced EP-*pis,* to rhyme with "hep miss." From Middle High German.

1. Something, a little.
2. A somebody.
3. Quite; perhaps; maybe; for some inexplicable reason.
4. Debatable, unsatisfactory.

This delightful, resilient word has chameleon properties of a high order and a surprising number of subtly shaded, shrewdly freighted connotations.

a. "Eat *epes.*" ("Eat something.")
b. "*Epes* I'm not hungry." ("For some reason, I am not hungry.")
c. "She served *epes* a meal!" ("She served quite some meal!" But see i. below; the tone is critical.)
d. "Is that *epes* a beauty!" (If uttered with enthusiasm: "Wow, is she a beauty!" Note the exclamation mark.) *But note:*

e. "That is *epes* a beauty?" (Uttered as a question, a hypothesis, with a frown or arched eyebrow, in hesitancy or oozing irony, this means: "You call *that* a beauty . . . ?" Note the absence of an exclamation mark.)

f. "He thinks he's an *epes*." ("He thinks he's a somebody.")

g. "There is *epes* a painter!" ("There, by God, is a painter!" Here *epes* is kin to the French *formidable*.)

h. "Who has *epes* an idea?" ("Who has any kind of an idea, *please?*")

i. "This is *epes* some explanation!" (Sarcastic: "This is a most unsatisfactory explanation.")

An official brought the chief rabbi of a town before the Court of the Inquisition and told him, "We will leave the fate of your people to God. I'm putting two slips of paper in this box. On one is written 'Guilty.' On the other is written 'Innocent.' Draw."

Now this inquisitor was known to seek the slaughter of all the Jews, and he had written "Guilty" on both pieces of paper.

The rabbi put his hand inside the box, withdrew a slip of paper—and swallowed it.

"What are you doing?" cried the inquisitor. "How will the court know—"

"That's simple," said the rabbi. "Examine the slip that's in the box. If it reads 'Innocent,' then the paper I swallowed obviously must have read 'Guilty.' But if the paper in the box reads 'Guilty,' then the one I swallowed must have read 'Innocent.'"

That was *epes* brilliant!

There is no truth in the allegation that on Halloween Jewish children ring doorbells and ask, *"Epes for yontif?"*

Eretz Yisroel^R
Erets Yisroel^Y
Eretz Israel, Eretz Yisrael

Pronounced EH-*retz yis*-ROY-*el*, to rhyme with "ferrets this toy El," or EH-*retz yis-roe*-AIL, to rhyme with "merits this tow rail." Hebrew: "The land of Israel."

The land of Israel.

*E*retz Yisroel has been the focus of Jewish dreams since the year 70 C.E., when the Second Temple was destroyed and the Jews were scattered throughout the world (see galus).

Eretz Yisroel is the believing Jew's "Promised Land," promised by God to Abraham and his descendants, the land of the kingdom of David and Solomon, the land in which the holy city of Jerusalem was built, the land where all Jews buried in the Diaspora will come to life again and where, in the very end of days, the Messiah will appear. Some Jewish prayers end, ". . . and next year, in Jerusalem."

During the long, long centuries of the Dispersion, *Eretz Yisroel* became to observing Jews more than a piece of land or a place on the map: it became the Promised Land, El Dorado, a vision of a society free from prejudice, a utopia where Jews could live, study, and worship freely. It was literally the Holy Land; as such, it became the inspiration for a great body of Hebrew literature. (Under rabbinical law, if a man asked his wife to go with him to Israel to live and she refused, without some overriding reason, such as health, it was grounds for divorce.)

eydem^Y
aydem^R

Pronounced AID'*m*, to rhyme with "raid 'em." From German (archaic): *eidam*.
Son-in-law.

The Jews' extraordinary emphasis on education was expressed not only in the most extreme effort to educate one's sons, but in the longing and search for a son-in-law who would be a student, a scholar, a *talmid khokhem*. It was quite common for a family, as part of a girl's dowry, to pledge support of the young couple for a number of years. The son-in-law would move into his in-laws' home, there to receive free room **and board*** and devote himself solely to Talmudic studies.

Eydem oif kest: a son-in-law who boards.

Mr. Baum was showing his friend Kipnis through his new apartment, and Kipnis, greatly impressed, was clucking and marveling in the most de rigueur fashion.

"But you've seen nothing yet!" said Baum. "You should see how my *eydem* lives! Come!"

He hurried Kipnis up the stairs, to an apartment on the floor above, and flung open the door.

"*Ai-ai-ai!*" Kipnis exclaimed. "It's beautiful! It's magnificent! A palace—and for such a young man. . . . Tell me, what does your *eydem* do?"

---

*Eydem lore received an update recently in this item, circulated on the Internet as "Authentic Personals from Israeli Newspapers":
> Jewish male, 34, very successful, smart,
> independent, self-made. Looking for a girl
> whose father will hire me. POB 53.

"Four As and a B plus!" said proud Baum.

Janowitz was complaining to a friend that a disaster had befallen him. "My *eydem*—I tell you, I am cursed, cursed!"

"What's wrong with him?"

"What's *wrong* with him?" Janowitz moaned. "That boy doesn't know how to drink and he doesn't know how to play cards!"

"*That* you call a curse? That's a blessing. Why are you complaining?"

"Because he does drink and he does play cards!"

eydl^Y
edel^R
eydel

Pronounced AID-*d'l*, to rhyme with "cradle." German: *edel:* "noble," "refined."

1. Gentle, sensitive, refined.
2. Shy, modest, humble.

"He is *eydl*" is a compliment of the highest order.

eydlkayt^Y
edelkeit^R
eydelkayt, edelkayt

1. Gentleness, sensitivity.
2. Modesty, sweetness of character.

We had a butcher on the West Side of Chicago who was revered by one and all because of the singular sweetness of his character. "Such *eydlkayt!*" people said.

And yet, a saying goes: "Too humble is half-proud."

f

farbisn[Y]
farbissen[R]
farbisener[Y] (masculine)
farbissener[R]
farbisene[Y] (feminine)
farbisseneh[R]

Pronounced *far*-BIS-*sen*, to rhyme with "car listen." From German *verbissen:* "obstinate," "sullen."

Embittered.

A *farbisner* is dour, mean, unpleasant, unlikable. So is a *farbisene*.

Farbisn carries the implication of psychologically distorted, crippled.

A *farbisener* doctor was called to the hut of a shoemaker whose wife was seriously ill.

"Please, doctor. Save her!" cried the husband. "I'll pay anything, even if I have to sell everything I own."

"But what if I can't cure her?" the doctor said shrewdly.

"I'll pay you whether you cure her or kill her!" cried the desperate husband.

A week later, the woman died. The doctor sent the shoemaker a huge bill. And now the poor man suggested they both go to the rabbi to discuss the fee.

The rabbi, who knew the doctor's reputation, said, "What was your agreement with this man?"

"He agreed to pay me for treating his wife," said the doctor, "whether I cured her or killed her."

"And did you cure her?"

"No."

"Did you kill her?"

"Certainly not!"

"Then," said the rabbi, "under what contract are you claiming your fee?"

farblondzhet^Y
farblondjet^R

Pronounced *far*-BLAWN-*jit*, to rhyme with "car lawn kit." Slavic: "wander," "roam."

Lost (but *really lost*), mixed up, wandering about without any idea where you are.

I include *farblondzhet* not because English lacks adequate words for what *farblondzhet* describes, but because *farblondzhet*'s euphony exudes an aroma all its own. It refers not simply to being lost, but to having-gotten-way-the-*hell*-and-gone-off-the-track.

You can describe a meandering statement, a fouled-up presentation, a galloping non sequitur, a thoroughly confused contretemps, as one in which someone got really *farblondzhet*. "He drove toward New Rochelle but got so *farblondzhet* that he ended up in White Plains." "His appeal to the jury? Man, was he *farblondzhet!*"

Professor Prescott asked a colleague in the Philosophy Department, Professor Minkus, "What does *farblondzhet* mean?"

"Wandered way off course, lost, gone far astray," said Professor Minkus. "When I started my career, for instance, I was really *farblondzhet:* I was a Reform rabbi for six years."

"Really?" said Professor Prescott. "Were you—unfrocked?"

"No," sighed Minkus, "just unsuited."

farpatshket^Y
farpotshket^R*

Pronounced *far-*POTCH*-ket,* to rhyme with "car NOTCH let."

*Farblondjet, farchadat, farpatshket—*Saturday Night Live* alumnus Mike Myers introduced America to another Yiddish word with the *"far"* prefix: *farklemt,* meaning "choked up" or "anxious." In his role on *SNL* as "Linda Richman," hostess of "Coffee Talk," Myers would periodically halt the conversation (which often focused on the talents and charms of Barbra Streisand) and fan himself frantically while gasping, "I'm getting a little *farklemt!*"

From the German: *Patsche,* "slap."

1. Messed up, sloppy, crossed-out-and-erased-and-written-over-again.
2. Anything bollixed up, from a painting to a cause.

*F*arpatshket has an onomatopoetic splash to it I greatly enjoy. "His painting was certainly *farpatshket.*" "Their statement to the press was really *farpatshket.*" "He's famous for his *farpatshket* logic."

See patsh.

farshtinkener†

Pronounced *far*-SHTINK-*ener* or *far*-SHTUNK-*ener*. From the German: *verstinken,* "to stink up."

Stinking, all stunk up.

*T*his uncouth word may be shunned by keepers of the flame, but it expresses feeling forcefully.

"What a *farshtinkener* business!" has the edge on "What a stinking business" in my opinion, because the *sh* is more elo-

---

† *Farshtinkener* found its way (as *farshtunkener*) into early editions of MAD magazine, along with *Hoo-ha* and several other Yiddish gems. A strip in the premiere issue (1952) was titled *Ganefs* (thieves), while in a spoof of *King Kong,* Western explorers try to communicate with the Ookabalaponga natives by asking, "*Vos machst du?*" ("How you doin'?"). MAD thus became a major source of exposure for American youth to what Rosten describes in his preface as the "bright, audacious, mischievous properties" of Yiddish. For some in the mainstream, this audacity was too much: a storm of censorship broke when MAD's wittiest artist, Bill Elder, created an illustrated spoof of the classic "A Visit from Saint Nicholas" ("'Twas the night before Christmas . . .") for *Panic,* one of MAD's sister publications. The hooplah that followed led to Senate investigations of the comic book industry and establishment in 1954 of the *farshtinkener* "Comics Code," which blunted the creativity of comic book art for years.

quent than the *s* in the communication of obloquious nuances. It is also more chic to enlist a foreign word when driven to coarse utterance.

———

At a dinner party, a *farshtinkener* anti-Semite, recounting his trip to central Africa, said, "It was wonderful. I didn't run into a single pig or Jew."

A hush fell over the table.

Then the voice of a Jewish guest was heard. "What a pity. The two of us could have corrected that so easily."

"Oh? How?"

"We could have gone there together."

fartshadet[Y]
farchadat[R]

Pronounced *far-CHAH-det*, to rhyme with "car got it." Slavic: *chad:* "smoke," "daze."

1. Dizzy, confused, dopey, "punchy." "That guy walks around all *fartshadet*."
2. Having a headache. "My head is really *fartshadet*."
3. Smitten, charmed, beguiled. "He is *fartshadet* by the girls."
4. Surprised, stunned, shocked. "When she heard the outrageous prices they were asking, she was positively *fartshadet!*"

It's a good and useful word; it actually sounds *fartshadet*. One says of a mixed-up person, "He has a *fartshadetn kop* [head]."

Misha and Grisha were discussing the wonderful life they would live come "the Revolution."

"Comes the Revolution," said Misha, "we'll all eat strawberries and cream!"

"But I don't like strawberries and cream," said Grisha.

"Comes the Revolution, you'll *have* to eat strawberries and cream!"

Was he *fartshadet!*

fartutst[Y] (adjective)
fartootst[R]
fartutster[Y] (masculine)
fartootster[R]
fartutste[Y] (feminine)
fartootsteh[R]

Pronounced *far*-TUTST, to rhyme with "bar footst;" *far*-TUTS-*ter*, to rhyme with "car suits her," and *far*-TUTS-*teh*, to rhyme with "bar foots eh." From the German: *verdutzt:* "confused," "mixed up."

The state of being bewildered, disoriented, discombobulated; slightly more intense than *tsedreyt*. "He's all *fartutst*."

When used as a modifier or as a noun, *fartutst* becomes *fartutster* (masculine) and *fartutste* (feminine). "She's a *fartutste* hostess." "He's a *fartutster*."

Mr. Chamish called Mr. Nudelman indignantly: "Your bill is two months overdue already!"

"What?" said Nudelman. "Didn't you receive my check?"

"No."

"I'll put it in the mail immediately!"
(He was not *fartutst*.)

fayfer^Y
fifer^R

Pronounced FIE-*fer* to rhyme with "lifer." German: "whistler."

1. A whistler, a piper.
2. A loud, shrill, noisy, aggressive, or ill-mannered fellow.
3. A braggart.

A *fayfer* is not quite infra dig enough to be a *grobyon;* he may *fayf* without intending to mislead or misrepresent, the way a *fonfer* does.

4. A type who sets your teeth on edge. "She married a real fayfer."

The phrase "I *fayf* on you!" means "The heck with you!" or "Who cares about your opinion?"

Mr. Rubin, who had just returned from his first trip to Europe, was regaling his friends with stories.

"And did you get to Rome?" one asked him.

"Naturally! Who doesn't go to Rome?"

"How did you like the Colosseum?"

Mr. Rubin made a regal gesture. "Very nice—if you like modern."

feh!

Pronounced always with feeling, as FEH! Possibly from the German: *pfui*.

This juicy expletive cannot be enlisted without its exclamation point.

"Feh!" is the Yiddish replacement for exclamatory expressions of disgust such as "Phew!," "Pee-oo!," "Ugh!," "Phooey!," "Ecch!," and "Pfrr!" It strikes me as a crisp and exact delineation of distaste. In saying *"Feh!,"* you may bare the teeth and wrinkle the nose, in visible reinforcement of the meaning.

Here are some circumstances in which *"Feh!"* may serve as the perfect utterance:

a. Smelling a rotten egg.
b. Passing an open sewer.
c. Inhaling Los Angeles smog.
d. Driving past the sulfur pits that fringe New York in New Jersey.
e. Whiffing a rotten fish.
f. Depicting a beatnik with mare's-nest hair.
g. Summarizing a political position you detest.
h. Appraising the honor or benevolence of an enemy.
i. Contemplating an operation for hemorrhoids.
j. Responding to an invitation to a bullfight (although there was a Jewish matador from Brooklyn who fought in Spain as Sidney Franklin).
k. Reporting (the next day, to your loved ones) how the over-ripe grouse or pheasant smelled at the dinner last night, which, excuse the expression, was plain *khaloshes*.
l. Delineating the character of the *paskudnyak* or *paskudnika* who ran off with your mate.

m. Anticipating the *shlump, shmendrik, kolyike,* or *shlemiel* of a relative whom you had to take into the business because your partner insisted on "giving at least a *chance*" to her own flesh and blood.

n. Describing the *chutzpanik* who thinks he's going to marry your daughter.

o. Reporting a *klutz's* performance of Mozart.

p. Recounting how a soprano murdered an aria.

q. Depicting a hangover.

r. Portraying strongly negative feelings about any sight, event, person, crisis, experience, or emotion.

Feh!, I salute you!

I once wrote an entire story to illustrate the puissance of this incomparable expletive: "Mr. K*A*P*L*A*N and the Unforgivable 'Feh!'" (in *The Return of H*Y*M*A*N K*A*P*L*A*N,* Harper, 1959).

feygele^Y
faygeleh^R

Pronounced FEY-*geh-leh,* to rhyme with "May bella." Diminutive of the German *Vogel:* "bird." The German *Vögele* is pronounced FEY-*geh-leh,* too.

1. Little bird.
2. A girl's name.
3. A dear little, sweet little, tiny, helpless, innocent child. CAUTION: Use *feygele* for a little girl, not for a little boy, because *feygele* also means:

4. Homosexual. Quite common (the word, not the libidi-
nal arrangement) in the American-Jewish vernacular. A
synonym for the English "fairy" or "fag."

Jews use *feygele* as a discreet way of describing a homosexual—
especially where they might be *overheard.**

fin
finf ^Y
finif ^R
finiff, finnif

Pronounced to rhyme, respectively, with "tin," "lymph,"
"sin if." Yinglish. From German: *fünf,* "five."
1. Five.
2. A five-dollar bill; a five-pound note.

---

*During the past two decades, gay and lesbian visibility emerged as a major
issue in Jewish life. Synagogues with mostly homosexual constituencies were
established in New York, San Francisco, Los Angeles, Atlanta, and other
cities. The World Congress of Gay and Lesbian Jewish Organizations convened international conferences in Jerusalem, Amsterdam, and several
American cities. The Reform and Reconstructionist movements embraced the
ordination of openly gay men and women as rabbis and cantors. And in the
spring of 2000, the rabbinic association of the Reform movement resolved
that Reform rabbis should feel free to officiate at and bless the holiness of
same-sex unions.

Speaking about the AIDS crisis in 1998, Rabbi Alexander M. Schindler,
then president of the Reform synagogue movement, observed, "There is a
new interpretation we must attach to the Star of David . . . an interpretation
that the Nazis, in their persecution of gays in the concentration camps,
clearly recognized . . . that the Star of David contains, within it, the triangle"
(that is, the "pink triangle," symbol of gay liberation).

Trembling Before God, a documentary film by Sandi DuBowski about gay
Orthodox Jews and their identity contradictions, premiered at the Sundance
Film Festival in January 2001.

3. A five-year jail sentence.

"Fin" is the Anglicized and contracted form of *finf*, the Yiddish word for "five," and is widely used in colloquial English, especially by sports fans, gamblers, Broadway types, nightclub habitués, and newspaper columnists who memorialize these gaudy provinces of diversion. "Fin" is so much a part of American vernacular that I do not italicize it.

"Fin" and *finf* were used with his customary felicity by Damon Runyon, in his stories about that after-twilight world in which lived his "more than somewhat" unforgettable guys and dolls. "Fin" appears in John O'Hara's emphatically non-Jewish dialogue, going back to the early 1930s. It is standard argot among connoisseurs of boxing, racing, dice, poker, et alia.

H. L. Mencken attributes "fin" to German, not Yiddish (in *The American Language*, Knopf, 1962, p. 578). I think this is wrong. The word *fünf* is indubitably German; but the pronunciation *finif* in two syllables, or *finf* (not *fünf*) in one, is just as indubitably Yiddish.

Wentworth and Flexner's excellent *Dictionary of American Slang* (Crowell, 1967) attributes "fin" flatly to Yiddish, as do I.

fleyshik[Y]
flayshig[R]
fleyshedik[Y]
flayshedig[R]

Pronounced FLEY-*shik*, to rhyme with "say Dick," or FLEY-*sheh-dik*, to rhyme with "pay the sick." From the German *fleischig*: "meaty, fleshy."

Meats, poultry, or foods prepared with animal fats,

which, according to the dietary rules *(kashrut)*, may not be eaten with dairy foods.

See kosher.

folks-mentsh[Y]
folks-mensh[R]
folks-mentsch, folksmentsh

Pronounced FOKES-*mentch*, to rhyme with "Folks bench." German: *Volksmensch*, "man of the people."

Jews are likely to harbor strong feelings about their "folk," meaning the Jewish people; in Yiddish, *folks-mentsh* has come to mean more than a man of the people. Hence:

1. One who identifies with the masses, not the elite. You don't have to be Jewish to be a *folks-mentsh*.
2. An honest, simple, unpretentious man or woman.

3. One who could, by virtue of achievement or wealth, be a snob—but is not. The opposite of a Brahman. Franklin D. Roosevelt, my mother says, was at heart a *folks-mentsh*.
4. One who is interested in Jewish life, values, and experience and wants to carry on the tradition.
5. A man or woman with a strong interest in popular culture, in the folk arts—whether Jewish or not.
6. One who displays a strong social conscience.

Jews refer to the collective body of Jews as "the *Yiddishe folk*," or people. Hence, a *folks-mentsh* originally meant a man or woman interested in, and working for, Jewish causes.

I know a *folks-mentsh* who wants the cabin notices in all El Al aircraft to read:

FASTEN YOUR SEAT BELTS

NO SMOKING

EAT FRUIT

fonfer
fonfen (infinitive verb)

Pronounced FUN-*fer*, to rhyme with "bun fur." Slavic: "to nazalize."

1. Someone who *fonfes*—that is, talks through his nose, unclearly, or as if he has a bad cold. One of Sholem Aleichem's characters always pronounces "I am" as "I ab" and "You may" as "You bay." He was a *fonfer*.
2. A double-talker. "That *fonfer* can drive you out of your mind."

3. One who is lazy, slow, "goofs off." "Don't be a *fonfer*—work!"

4. One who does not deliver what he promises: thus, he *fonfes* promises.

5. A shady, petty deceiver. "That *fonfer* will make you think black is white."

6. One who cheats. "He's a *fonfer;* watch his addition." "Don't let him *fonfe* on the amount."

7. One who goes through the motions of a thing without intending to perform to his capacity or your proper expectations. "It took him three hours to walk from here to Fourteenth Street to deliver that package. Did you ever hear of such a *fonfer?*"

8. A boaster, full of bravado. "He talks like a hero but acts like a *fonfer.*"

9. A specialist in hot air, baloney—a trumpeter of hollow promises. "He should be selling lots on the moon, that *fonfer.*"

A friend tells me that his mother accompanied a neighbor to her citizenship hearing, years ago. The judge asked the neighbor, "Who was the first president of the United States?"

The poor soul's mind went blank.

"Do you know what she answered?" my friend exclaimed. "She turned to my mother for help, and after my mother *fonfes* aid into her ear, the neighbor said, 'Columbus.'"

frask^Y
frosk ^R

Pronounced to sound like "mosque."
  A slap.

The beauty of its euphony, *frask,* beguiles me—as I hope it will you.
  "I gave him a *frask in pisk"* is a splendid, sibilant way of saying, "I gave him a slap in the puss."

"My father was so mad yesterday," said little Morris, "that five separate times he wanted to give me a *frask.*"
  "How do you know it was exactly five times?"
  "Because I counted."
  "What did you count?"
  "The number of times he hit me."
  "I thought you said he *wanted* to hit you."
  "I did. Would he have hit me if he hadn't wanted to?"

fress^R
fres^Y
fresser ^R (noun)
fresn^Y (infinitive verb)

Rhymes with "DRESS-*in.*" From German: *fress,* "to devour."
  1. To eat a great deal. "Did you ever see anyone *fress* like that?"
  2. To eat quickly, noisily. "Don't act like a *fresser.*" "Slow down; don't *fress.*"

G erry Blumenfeld writes that she once saw a restaurant in Mexico City whose menu, under "Sandwiches," read:

Pastrami por Fressers .... 10 pesos
Pastrami (Double Decker) por Grandes Fressers ... 15 pesos
Pastrami (Triple Decker) por Grandísimo Fressers . 20 pesos

frum
frumer[Y] (masculine)
frummer[R]
frume[Y] (feminine)
frummeh[R]

Pronounced with the short "u" or "oo" of "good," *not* to rhyme with "crumb" or "broom." German: *fromm*, "pious."

Religious, observant, Orthodox. "He is *frum*." "He is a *frumer* Jew." "She is a *frume*."

I t is said that when pious Jews left the old country, they would address God thusly: "And now, good-bye, O Lord; I am going to America."

Galitzianer

Pronounced *goll-itz-ee-*ON*-er*, to rhyme with "doll itsy on her."

A Jew from Galicia, a province of Poland/Austria. (When Poland was partitioned in 1772, Austria grabbed Galicia.)

G alicia, heavily populated by Jews (in the early twentieth century, they constituted over 10 percent of the population), was a seat of Talmudic learning; it had several important *yeshivas* that produced prominent rabbis and scholars. The Jewish population of Galicia benefited from Emperor Joseph II's decree of 1780, making education compulsory for his subjects.

The *Galitzianer* and the *Litvak* were often at odds, each claiming superiority over, and looking with a certain disdain upon, the other. The respective chauvinists viewed a marriage between a *Litvak* and a *Galitzianer* as almost exogamous, and wedding guests were fond of predicting that no good could come of such a strange misalliance.

My parents spoke with a certain prissiness about both *Galitzianers* and *Litvaks*. We were *Poylish* (Polish)—and were no doubt regarded, in turn, as infra dig by such *Galitzianers* and *Litvaks* as put on airs.

And Russian Jews, especially of the intelligentsia, looked down with cool impartiality upon all the rest. Among *Galitzianers*, a *Deutsch* (German) Jew was regarded as modernized, probably unreligious, and certainly one who wore no beard, *payess,* hat, *sheytl* (the wig worn by Orthodox women), or other trappings of piety. As for German Jews—! A self-appointed elite, they clearly disliked, snubbed, or despised non-German *Jehudim*; and they were (if one must generalize) heartily disliked—and envied—by the poorer, less assimilated, much more religious kin to their east.

The *familiengefil* (family feeling) of a common heritage, shared values, common problems, common threats, misfortunes, and persecutions was nevertheless exceedingly strong among European Jewry.

In the United States, the social prestige scale was sensitive and exact: first-generation Jews envied second-generation Jews; and German Jewish families—Kuhns, Warburgs, Seligmans, Kahns,

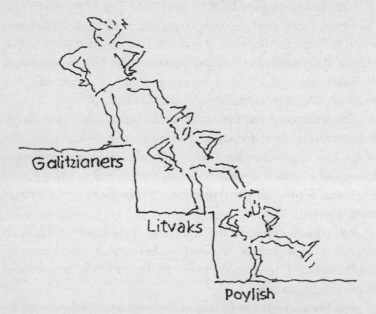

Galitzianers

Litvaks

Poylish

Schiffs, Lehmanns, Loebs, Ochses—became an elite of remarkable influence and social cohesiveness. The "pecking order" of this establishment, its pride, philanthropy, snobbery, and Pecksniffian patronage of Russian and Polish Jews—all this is described by Stephen Birmingham in *Our Crowd: The Great Jewish Families of New York* (Harper & Row, 1967). San Francisco's Jews became a distinguished, conspicuously civic-minded group of descendants of settlers dating back to the Gold Rush.

For an illuminating inquiry into the identification patterns, social hierarchy, practices, values, and conflicts within the conglomerate Jewish communities in America, see Nathan Glazer's excellent *American Judaism* in the Chicago History of American Civilization series, Daniel Boorstin, ed. (University of Chicago Press, 1957); also Moses Rischin's *The Promised City: New York's Jews: 1870–1914* (Corinth Books, 1964); also the articles by Nathan Glazer, Simon Kuznets, and Jacob Lestchinsky in *The Jews: Their History, Culture and Religion*, vol. II, third ed., Louis Finkelstein, ed. (Harper, 1960); and *The Jews: Social Patterns of an American Group*, Marshall Sklare, ed. (Free Press, 1960).*

See Litvak.

Up to 1825, there were only about six thousand Jews in the United States—and only five hundred in New York City. Then, as waves of immigration from Germany began, New York's Jewish population grew.

It was heavy German immigration that, by 1848, made New York's Jewish population the largest in the United States (nearly thirteen thousand); after that, the Jewish population of New York

*More recently published sociological studies include Charles Silberman's *A Certain People: American Jews and Their Lives Today* (Summit Books, 1985); Leonard Fein's *Where We Are: The Inner Life of American Jews* (Harper & Row, 1987); Marshall Sklare's *Observing America's Jews* (Brandeis University Press, 1993); and Arthur Hertzberg's *The Jews in America* (Columbia University Press, 1998).

grew pretty much in proportion to the growth of the Jewish population in the United States. By 1880, sixty thousand Jews were living in New York City—about 25 percent of the number in the United States.

The first census of American Jews, conducted by the Union of American Hebrew Congregations (Reform) in 1877–1879, disclosed some surprising data:

There were Jews in every state in the Union and in every new territory except Oklahoma. And the Jews in the West represented a higher percentage of the population than those in and around New York: 1.6 percent in the West and only 0.6 percent in the Northeast. Of course, the population was exceedingly sparse in the far West, as compared with the Northeast.

In some thirty years after 1880, about one-third (!) of the entire Jewish population of eastern Europe emigrated—and 90 percent of them came to the United States. Here is a vivid and memorable account by Moses Rischin (in *The Promised City: New York's Jews, 1870–1914*, Corinth Books, 1964):

These immigrants packed their few household belongings, pots and pans, samovar, pillows and bedding, much of which would be lost or pilfered on the way, and forsook their native towns and villages to embark on the greatest journey of their lives. They parted with loved ones, seemingly forever, and made their way by foot, coach, and train to the bewildering port cities of Western Europe. There they sailed direct from Hamburg or Bremen at a cost of thirty-four dollars, some for a saving of nine dollars traveling by way of Liverpool. Crammed into steerage for as long as three weeks, Jewish immigrants were confined to herring, black bread, and tea by their loyalty to dietary laws, until the water journey's end. It was "a kind of hell that cleanses a man of his sins before coming to Columbus' island," insisted a popular immigrant guidebook that attempted to minimize the torments of the ocean voyage. Whatever the spiritually therapeutic values of that epic crossing, few immigrants would ever forget its terrors.

galus^R
goles^Y
galut

Pronounced by *Sephardim* as *ga*-LOOT, to rhyme with "a boot," and by *Ashkenazim* as GOLL-*us*, to rhyme with "call us." Hebrew: "exile."

1. Exile; the Diaspora; the dispersion of the Jews among the lands outside of Israel.
2. A state of alienation.
3. Residence among others and insubordinate status.

This is the Hebrew word for "exile"—especially *the* exile of Jews from the Holy Land.

Gan Eydn^Y
Gan Eden^R

Pronounced *gon* EY-*din*, to rhyme with "wan maiden." Hebrew: "Garden of Eden."
The Garden of Eden.

"God planted a garden eastward, in Eden," says Genesis, and there Adam and Eve dwelt in innocent bliss—until their curiosity got the better of them, and all of us. This story was almost certainly borrowed from Babylonian mythology.

Where was Eden? Popular theory placed it between the Tigris and Euphrates Rivers.

Now, the Talmudists and cabalists are persuaded that there were *two* Gardens of Eden: the luxuriant garden on earth; and one in the heavens, the eternal abode of all the righteous after death. This celestial *Gan Eydn* was (and is) synonymous with Paradise.

When people die, their good deeds are weighed against their bad deeds. The tipping scales indicate their fate—*Gan Eydn* or *Gehenna.*

Humanity's early images of Paradise were singularly simple—and naive. The celebrated Talmudic savant Rab said: "In *Gan Eydn* there is no eating, no drinking, no cohabitation, no business, no envy, no hatred or ambition; but the righteous sit with crowned heads and enjoy the luster of the *Shekhinah* [Divine Presence]." But Maimonides remarked, "To believe so is to be a schoolboy who expects nuts and sweetmeats as compensation for his studies. Celestial pleasures can neither be measured nor comprehended by a mortal being, any more than the blind man can distinguish colors or the deaf appreciate music."

See Gehenna.

A rabbi once dreamed that he was in *Gan Eydn*. There he saw all the sages, sitting and studying *Talmud*.

"Is this all there is to Paradise?" he exclaimed. "Why, we do this on earth!"

An angel answered, "Ah, you think the scholars are in *Gan Eydn*, but you are wrong. It is the other way around: *Gan Eydn* is in the scholars."

The Mezeritzer *Maggid* said: "A man's good deeds are used by the Lord as seeds for the planting of trees in the Garden of Eden. Thus each man creates his own Paradise. . . ."

ganef^ᵧ
gonif^ᴿ
ganif, gonef, goniff, ganov

Pronounced GON-*iff*, to rhyme with "Don if." Hebrew: *ganov*, "thief."
1. Thief, crook.
2. A clever person.
3. An ingenious child.
4. A dishonest businessman.
5. A shady, tricky character it would be wise (a) not to trust, and (b) to watch every minute he's in the store.
6. A mischievous, fun-loving prankster.

The particular meaning depends, of course, on context, tone of voice, inflection, and accompanying gestures.

* If uttered with a beam, a grin, an accompanying *"Tchk! Tchk!,"* or an admiring raise of the hands, *ganef* is clearly laudatory. Thus, a proud grandparent will say of a child, metaphorically, "Oh, is that a *ganef!*" (God forbid you should think a grandparent is lauding a child's criminal characteristics.)

* If uttered with pulled-down mouth, in a lugubrious tone, or with heartfelt dismay ("A *ganef* like that shouldn't be allowed among respectable citizens"), the meaning is derogatory.

* Uttered in steely detachment ("That one is, plain and simple, a *ganef*"), the word describes a crook, thief, purloiner, trickster.

* Said in admiration, with a wink, cluck, or shake of the head ("I tell you, there is a *ganef!*"), the phrasing is equivalent to "What a man!" or "There's a clever cookie."

* The usage I find most interesting is the one I often heard as a child and sorely puzzled over: "America *ganef!*" In that phrase was (and is) wrapped admiration, awe, gratitude, and a declaration of possibilities beyond belief and without limit. To say "America *ganef*" was to say "Anything is possible in this wonderful land." "America is a miracle!" "America? Inventiveness, resourcefulness, ingenuity—and that's what it rewards." "Where but in America could such **a thing happen?**"*

If you wish to express some of these sentiments vis-à-vis a

*Notwithstanding Rosten's patriotism, the phrase "America *ganef*" could also betray a certain ambivalence. Yiddish-speaking immigrants who still carried the moral yoke of Jewish tradition on their shoulders were often stunned by the moral license of their new country. They were especially likely to cry "America *ganef*" in response to the more risqué, shrewd, *chutzpadik* aspects of American culture.

Today it might be the pop star who dresses like a hooker and makes that look fashionable who would evoke the cry "America *ganef!*" The Jewish comedian who creates a television show "about nothing" and makes mil-

person, try *geneyvish* (pronounced ge-NAY-*vish*), which is simply *ganef* turned into an adjective. Thus: "He has a *geneyvish* [clever, diabolic] mind." "That lad has *geneyvish* [remarkable] ingenuity." "Take my advice, stay away from those *geneyvish* [clever, but tricky] ideas."

You can also say *geneyvisher*, which prolongs the descriptive titillation.

See gazlen.

Eric Partridge, in *A Dictionary of Slang and Unconventional English* (Macmillan, 1961), avers that *ganef* has been used in England since 1835.

H. L. Mencken, in *The American Language* (Knopf, 1962), spells *ganef* as *ganov* and *gonov* and attributes *gun* (to mean a gunman) and other peculiar derivatives to it. Absurd. A *ganef* is hardly a gunman.

"Carny" (carnival) folk use *gonov* to mean a fool, says Mencken, not a smart, sharp fellow. David Maurer's *American Speech* (1931) cites a similar meaning. I am surprised.

In *The American Thesaurus of Slang* (Crowell, 1943), compiled by Berrey and Van den Bark, *ganef* is cited with these variant spellings: *gonef, gonof, gonoph*. All I can say to such improvisations is that only a *ganef* would dream up such orthography.

The first day home from school, little Milton was met by his mother, who ran out eagerly to greet him.

lions: America *ganef!* The candidate who weathers a scandal and wins the election: America *ganef!*

Ganefs was the title of a comic strip by Harvey Kurtzman and Bill Elder in the premiere issue of *MAD* (1952)—see my note to Rosten's entry for **farshtinkener**.

"So what did you learn?"

"I learned to write," said Milton.

"On the first day already you learned to *write*? America *ganef!* So what do you write?"

"How should I know?" said Milton. "I can't read."

FOLK SAYING: "A man is not honest simply because he never had a chance to steal."

gaon^R
goen^Y

Pronounced GUY-*awn*, or *guy*-AWN, to rhyme with "high lawn"; or GA-*own*. Hebrew: "genius," "learned." Plural: *geonim, guy*-AW-*nim*.

1. The head of a Talmudic academy (especially in Babylonia).
2. A rabbi whose learning was so great that he was given the honorary title of *gaon*.
3. A genius.

The title *gaon* was held by the heads of the Talmudic academies of Babylonia from 589 to 1040. Then the title fell into disuse; it was later revived and again applied to a rabbi of exceptional learning.

The *geonim* judged religious questions. Questions were sent them from all parts of the Diaspora, and they provided the responsa.

Saadiah *Gaon* (892–942) translated the Bible into Arabic, wrote a biblical commentary, defended the *Talmud* against the

Karaite sect, and wrote a book that argues that Judaism rests on reason.

The *Gaon* of Vilna (1720–1797), *Talmud* genius and implacable opponent of Chasidism, was one of the outstanding Jewish figures of eastern Europe. Aside from his extraordinary Talmudic studies, he recognized the need for secular learning; he wrote a book on mathematics and a Hebrew grammar.

The famous Dubner *maggid*, a *gaon*, was asked by an admiring student: "How is it that you always have the perfect parable for the topic under discussion?"

The *gaon* smiled. "I'll answer with a parable." And he told the following story:

A lieutenant of the Tsar's cavalry, riding through a small *shtetl*, drew his horse up in astonishment, for on the side of a barn he saw a hundred chalked circles—and in the center of each was a bullet hole! The lieutenant excitedly stopped the first passerby, crying, "Who is the astonishing marksman in this place? Look at all those bull's-eyes!"

The passerby sighed. "That's Shepsel, the shoemaker's son, who is a little peculiar."

"I don't care what he is," said the lieutenant. "Any man who can shoot that well—"

"Ah," the pedestrian said, "you don't understand. You see, first Shepsel shoots—*then* he draws the circle."

The *gaon* smiled. "That's the way it is with me. I don't search for a parable to fit the subject. I introduce the subject for which I have a perfect parable."

gazlen^Y
gozlin^R
gozlen

Pronounced GOZ-*lin,* to rhyme with "Roslyn." Hebrew: *gozlon,* "one who deprives others of their rightful possessions by force."

1. A thief—but not a professional; a professional is a *ganef.*
2. A swindler, one who outwits others.
3. A merciless, rapacious, unethical person. "Who would have believed that he would turn into such a *gazlen?*"

FOLK SAYING: "Not only did he break the Commandment not to steal, he also stole the Bible."

gefilte fish
gefulte fish

Pronounced *ge-*FILL-*teh.* From the German: "stuffed."

Fish cakes or fish loaf, made of various fishes that are chopped or ground and mixed with eggs, salt, and lots of onions and pepper (sometimes with sugar). The traditional Friday night fish, served at the Sabbath dinner.* I find *gefilte fish* delicious, hot or

---

*While Sabbath dinner *gefilte fish,* like the Sabbath dinner itself, is customary only for a decreasing minority of American Jews, *gefilte fish* and its accompanying "bitter herb," horseradish, is the appetizer of choice at the Passover *Seders* of many Ashkenazic Jews.

Joan Nathan, author of *Jewish Cooking in America* (Knopf, 1998) observes that **Galitzianers** (see Rosten's entry) tend to add sugar to their *gefilte*

cold, and recommend that red or white *khreyn* (horseradish) be
handy, to dip the fish into, or suit your palate.

Recipes for *gefilte fish* can be found in many cookbooks.

A waiter brought a smoked fish to a customer, who studied it,
sniffed at it, then leaned down and began to talk to the fish in a
confidential whisper.

"Mister," asked the startled waiter, "what are you doing?"

"I'm talking to this fish."

"Talking to a *fish?*"

"Certainly. I happen to know seven fish languages."

"But what did you tell him?"

"I asked him where he was from, and he answered, 'From
Peconic Bay.' So I asked him how things are in Peconic Bay, and
he answered, 'How should I know? It's *years* since I was there!'"

Gehenna^R
Gehenem^Y

Pronounced g'-HEN-*a* or gay-HEN-*a*, to rhyme with "say
when a." Hebrew: *Gehinom,* "Hell." Literally: the Valley
(gay) of Hinnom. Veteran Yiddish speakers add an *m* to

fish recipes ("the farther south in Poland, the more sugar would be added"),
while *Litvaks* pass on the sugar but might add beets to the cooking stock.
Freshwater species such as carp and pike are the fish customarily used.

Perhaps because of the attraction/revulsion ambivalence provoked by
the bottled variety, *gefilte fish* seems to promote kibitzing of all kinds. Posted
at the Web site of the Society for Developmental Biology (http://sdb.bio.
purdue.edu/SDBEduca/Gefilte.html) is a photograph of the "long-sought
gefilte fish embryo." And the weekly *Forward* of April 7, 2000, ran a mock ad,
designed by this commentator, of a "Mr. Gefilte Head" toy (a lampoon of the
classic "Mr. Potato Head")—"Now with extra redi-jelled broth!"

the end of the word; this has fallen away in American usage.

Hell.

In the "valley of the sons of Hinnom" south of Jerusalem, says the Bible, children were sacrificed to the idol Moloch. For this reason, the valley was said to be accursed: *Gay-Hinnom*, or *Gehenna*, became synonymous with Hell. But Hell, according to early but "apocryphal" texts, is located not in the netherworld, but in "the third heaven!" (Lubricious angels who consort with human females are allocated to the second heaven and are flogged each day.) The *Midrash Tannaim* locates Hell as "side by side" with Paradise. (See Gustav Davidson, *A Dictionary of Angels*, Free Press, 1967.)

The *Talmud* pictures *Gehenna* as a dark place, filled with everlasting fire and sulfurous flames. (The hot springs and sulfuric smells of the medicinal waters of Tiberias were said to have their origin in *Gehenna*.)

Gehenna is the abode of the wicked after death. Some of the sins that lead to it are unchastity, adultery, idolatry, pride, mockery, and hypocrisy.

Gehenna may also exist on earth: "His life with her is a *Gehenna*." Conversely, it may be a *Gan Eden*.

Purgatory, incidentally, is nowhere named in the Bible but was made official by the Roman Church councils from the thirteenth century on. (Back in the third century, the celebrated scholar Origen had said that souls wait in a fearful place to be "purged of evil" so they may enter the Kingdom of Heaven "undefiled.") The Church of England scorned Purgatory as "grounded upon no warranty of Scripture, but rather repugnant to the Word of God" (Gustav Davidson, ibid.).

Folk saying: "Better to be in *Gehenna* with a wise man than in *Gan Eden* [Paradise] with a fool."

Jack Wishnograd was reading the obituaries in the morning paper when, to his astonishment, he read his own name! As his eyes raced down the column, his stupefaction rose: the entire obituary was his—every date, place, fact of his life! Wishnograd dashed to the phone and called his lawyer.

"Hello, Irwin? Did you read this morning's paper?"

"Sure. Who is this?"

"What do you mean, 'Who is this?' It's me, Jack! I want you to sue—"

"*Jack?*" cried the lawyer.

"Certainly! I want you to—"

"Where are you calling from?"

gelt

Rhymes with "felt." From German: *Geld*, "money."
Money.

Gelt, like *shekels* or *mazuma*, has long been a part of American slang. (See shekel, mazuma.) "Where did he stash the *gelt*?" "He'll do anything for *gelt*."

George S. Kaufman, a prince of wit, once remarked that he liked to write with his collaborator, Moss Hart, because Hart was so lucky. "In my case," said Kaufman, "it's *gelt* by association."

Gemara[R]
Gemore[Y]
See Mishnah and Talmud.

gematria

Pronounced *ge-MOT-ree-a,* to rhyme with "the spot Rea."
From the Greek: *geometria.*
The use of letters as numerals; numerology.

In Hebrew, the letters of the alphabet also served the ancients as numbers. Each letter, hence each word or phrase, possessed a numerical "value." Mystics converted the numerical values into supposed keys to the meanings of passages in the holy texts and "equated" different words and phrases according to the total values of their letters: this naturally yielded startling coincidences. Where neither statistics nor probability theory existed, abracadabra could flourish uncontested.*

The letters of the Hebrew alphabet represented the following numerical values: *alef* 1; *beys* 2, etc., through *yud,* which is 10; *knof* is 20, *lamed* 30, etc., through *tsadik,* which is 90; *koof* is 100, *reysh* 200, *shin* 300, and *tof* 400. Thousands are indicated by a letter with an apostrophe after it.

---

*Even in our "enlightened" age of statistics and probability theory, *gematria* has made a powerful comeback. Since the mid-1990s, for example, more than one hundred thousand people in the United States have attended the "Discovery" seminars of the Aish HaTorah (Fire of *Torah*) yeshiva, which teach about numerology-based "Bible Codes" that allegedly reveal the hidden messages and divine nature of the *Torah.* Steven Spielberg, Kirk Douglas, Tom Cruise, and Nicole Kidman are among the celebrities quoted in testimonials for these seminars, even while mathematicians and professional skeptics (Orthodox rabbis among them) have demolished the "Bible Codes" by reveal-

Gematria starts with the premise, not uncommon to true believers, that the words in a holy text contain hidden and apocalyptic messages. (God, for reasons I have never understood, is often credited by His faithful with vast, calculated obscurity.) When one finds different phrases with the same numerical value, this presumably indicates a relationship in thought—which should reveal a new meaning or resolve an old ambiguity.

Here is a pretty example of *gematria:* The Hebrew word for pregnancy, *herayon,* turns out to have the numerical value of 270, which is also 30 times 9—"the number of days a woman carries a child." *Voilà!*

Here are four other examples:

Genesis 14:14 says: "And when Abraham heard that his kinsman was taken captive, he armed his trained servants, born in his own house, 318, and pursued them into Dan." Why is the number 318 mentioned—a specific number, not really a "round number" like 300 or 350? Ah: this number "really" refers to "Eliezer," which also has the value of 318, and he was the only servant of Abraham's known to us by name!

Simon the Just used to say: "Upon three things the world is based: upon the Torah, upon worship, and upon the practice of loving kindness." (*Sayings of the Fathers* 1:2). So: *Torah,* numerical value of 611; *avodah* (worship), value of 87; *gemilus chasadim* (deeds of loving-kindness), value of 611.

ing how their numerological methods produce similar hidden messages when applied to secular literature. As usual with pseudoscience, it is the testimonials rather than the contradictions that make headlines.

Theistic "proofs" aside, *gematria* can also simply spark the religious imagination and add playfulness to the sometimes arduous process of Jewish education. The most common expression of modern *gematria* is found in Jewish charitable giving, which often involves multiples of 18 ($18, $36, $180, etc.), the numerical value of *chai* (life). See Rosten's entry for **l'chayim**.

From this we are supposed to learn the coequality of *Torah* and practicing loving-kindness! Moreover, if Israel observes the obligations it assumed when it accepted the Lord "to be your God" (value, 611), then "His Kingdom will come" (611).

The place of *avodah* (worship), between *Torah* and the practice of loving-kindness, is held to be highly significant: worship is central to the other qualities, because it inspires us to fulfill them. Why do we worship? Because we accept God: "I am the Lord," which adds up to 87. Moreover, 87 emphasizes the Jew's responsibility for his brethren: "Where is Abel thy brother?" (87). Et cetera.

Hillel's Golden Rule has the numerical value of 1021; here we must realize, said the rabbis, that we and our neighbors are different kinds of people, with variant characters, just as are the branches and fruits we use at the Feast of *Succos* (which are said to represent the diverse types that make up the Jews). Now, "The boughs of goodly trees, branches of palm trees, and willows of the brook" (Leviticus 23:40) have the numerical equivalent of 3063, which is 1021—three times! (For the material on 611, 87, and 1021, we are indebted to Harold Roland Shapiro, who published these and other interpretations in *The Light,* February 1963 and February–May, 1964.)

The manipulation of numbers for arcane purposes proliferated in the Middle Ages, when it became a popular mode of biblical and Talmudic interpretation. Many scholars played with *gematria* in the hope of discovering the exact date the messiah was scheduled to arrive. Many extravagant hopes were raised and affixed to dates that were interpreted as foretelling when the heavenly messiah would rescue the Jews from a no longer endurable suffering and despair. Professor Hugh Trevor-Roper observes that "when popes and kings allied themselves with the blind prejudices of the church and the mob . . . whither then were the persecuted remnant to turn for relief . . . but to that stock refuge of the oppressed: mysticism, the messiah, the millennium?"* (Hugh Trevor-Roper, *Historical Essays,* Macmillan, 1963.)

Nor were Jews alone in their preoccupation with miraculous deliverance. The Muslims, too, dreamed of supernatural salvation: seventeenth-century Anabaptists made their own mathematical hocus-pocus out of Holy Scripture to help along the Apocalypse; and otherwise sober English, the Millenarians, claimed to have found the exact date of the Second Coming.

The misterioso approach to biblical exegesis was extensively followed in cabalistic literature, of course. Many ingenious, albeit ludicrous, rules were developed to govern the permutation of letters, words, and phrases in the quest for God's secrets.

*Millennial numerology reached a feverish pitch during the worldwide Y2K scare, which led Jews to comment that while the rest of the world was facing Armageddon, the Jewish world was merely entering the sixties (the Hebrew calendrical equivalent to the turning of the year 2000 was 5760).

geshmat
geshmott

Pronounced ge-SHMOTT, to rhyme with "the hot." From the Hebrew root *shemad*, from which are derived words meaning "destruction," "annihilation," and "apostasy." The connection between the two meanings is rooted in history.

1. Converted from one faith to another. *Geshmat* generally describes a Jew who is converted to the Christian faith, rather than a Gentile who converts to Judaism.
2. A marked change in belief or conduct. (This usage is less common than the first.)

Jews are not **proselytizers.*** Rabbis are required to make three separate efforts to discourage a would-be convert.

A Bulgarian proverb goes: "When you baptize a Jew, hold him underwater for five minutes."

. . . in converting Jews to Christians you raise the price of pork.
— *The Merchant of Venice*, act III, scene v

---

*Responding to the high rate of Jewish-Christian intermarriage—estimated by 1990 to exceed 50 percent of marriages involving Jews in the United States—the Reform synagogue movement inaugurated a Jewish Outreach program in 1978. Outreach orients primarily toward intermarried couples and their children but includes in its purview adult children of intermarriages as well as the "unchurched"—that is, non-Jews seeking a spiritual home who are unaffiliated with any other religion. Programming ranges from brief "Taste of Judaism" offerings to more intensive courses designed to encourage conversion to Judaism.

This open-door policy has been a great improvement over the traditional Jewish response to intermarriage and apostasy, which was to declare the person "dead." According to the late Rabbi Alexander M. Schindler, who launched the program during his presidency of the Reform movement (1974–

Daniel Abramovich Chwolson (1819–1910), a Jewish professor under the Tsars, had been converted to the Greek Orthodox faith. When asked if he had done this out of conviction or expedience, he replied dryly, "I accepted baptism entirely out of conviction— the conviction that it is better to be a professor in the Imperial Academy in St. Petersburg than a teacher in a *cheder* in Vilna." (Another version goes ". . . than a *melamed* in Eyshishok.")

Daniel Abramovich Chwolson is an extraordinary figure, a noted scholar who, after his conversion, courageously defended the Jews during the odious Saratov trial, in which the ghastly canard that Jews drink Christian blood in religious services was once again dragged out. Chwolson taught Hebrew in a Roman Catholic seminary from 1858 to 1884 and often delivered lectures denouncing the heinous "blood accusation." He wrote several scholarly volumes about these libels and even persuaded the Tsar's brother to change his mind about "ritual murders." (See David Gunzberg's brief "Daniel Chwolson; a Christian Jew," in

1997): "Outreach has mitigated the most damaging effects of intermarriage: the alienated Jews, the spiritually rootless children, the stressed marriages, the bruised grandparents . . . the healing has been profound."

One result of Outreach is the bulging presence of non-Jews in synagogues and Jewish schools, which has led to many debates and rulings about the rights of non-Jews to serve on synagogue boards and committees, to participate in services and *Torah* readings, and so on.

While the American Jewish community is far more aware of and concerned about Christian baptisms than other forms of apostasy, Buddhist influences are also having a large impact on contemporary Jewish life. Estimates hold some 30 percent of American Buddhist practitioners to have Jewish backgrounds. Many of these "Bujews" have not formally left their Judaism behind through Buddhist conversion or formal initiation. Certain synagogues and Jewish retreat centers (notably Elat Chayyim, the Woodstock Center for Jewish Healing and Renewal in Accord, New York) now offer Jewish meditation workshops and are actively exploring the Jewish mystical tradition to uncover Jewish analogies to Buddhist spiritual practices.

the excellent anthology *The Golden Tradition*, Lucy S. Dawidowicz, ed., Holt, Rinehart and Winston, 1967.)

Heine dryly called a baptism certificate "the passport to European civilization."

Berele, the pickpocket, was brought before a judge who had been converted to Christianity.

"Your Honor," cried Berele, "I am confused!"

"Confused? Why?"

"I don't know whether to appeal to the quality of mercy that lives on in your Jewish heart, or to the Christian forgiveness you have recently adopted."

On a bitterly cold, snowy, dreadful night in a Polish town, old Salkowitz, feeling his time had come, called to his wife: "Shurele, please, send someone to the priest and tell him to come right away—I am dying!"

"The priest? You must have a fever! You mean the rabbi."

"I mean the priest!" snapped Salkowitz.

"May God protect us! Are you secretly *geshmat?*"

"No, no; but why disturb the rabbi on a night like this?"

When Messrs. Ginsberg and Grabow, both *geshmat*, opened their new store, they decided, for tactical reasons, to call it "O'Neill and O'Neill."

On their very first day, a customer said to one of the salesmen, "I want to see Mr. O'Neill."

"Which Mr. O'Neill do you want?" replied the salesman. "Ginsberg or Grabow?"

get

Pronounced as in English. Hebrew: "divorce."
Divorce.

Rabbinical laws considered and ruled on divorces of every conceivable type, arising from almost every conceivable cause. The process and ritual entailed in a religious divorce was, and is, complex; only a small number of scholars, specially trained,* can undertake the task.

A religious (as distinguished from a civil) divorce terminates a marriage among Orthodox Jews only if both husband and wife agree to it and if the civil courts have already granted a **civil divorce.**†

---

*Rabbis trained to write and deliver a *get* are known as *mesadderei gittin.* The *get* is also known as a *sefer k'ritut* ("scroll of cutting off").

†Initiating a *get* is strictly a "man's job" in the Jewish tradition—which means that a husband can exercise an enormous amount of power over his wife during the divorce process. If he abandons the marriage without delivering a *get*, she becomes an *agunah*—a chained, or anchored, woman—and will be unable to remarry under Jewish law. If she then remarries under civil law, any children of her new marriage will be considered *mamzerim*, children of adultery, which may seriously affect their own status in Jewish life, since a *mamzer* is halachically forbidden to marry a Jew. The *get* therefore becomes a weapon for an embittered husband. He can use the threat of withholding a *get* to gain custody of children or possessions—or he can simply "punish" his wife by abandoning her without a *get*.

In Israel, recalcitrant husbands can be held in contempt for refusing to deliver a *get*—and women's organizations have been pressuring the courts to do just that. In North America, obviously, civil courts can grant a divorce but have no power to enforce religious observance. It is up to the religious community, therefore, to bring social and even economic pressures upon the offending men.

Women in the Orthodox community have been organizing over the past several years to confront the *agunah* problem. *Nissan*, the month of Passover,

(Continued on page 182)

Reform rabbis do not, on the whole, ask for a religious divorce in addition to a civil divorce before husband or wife may remarry.

FOLK SAYING: "To a wedding, walk; to a divorce, run."

gevalt!ᴿ
gvald!ʸ
gevald!

Pronounced *ge*-VOLLT!, the exclamation point being, at least psychologically, an inseparable part of the spelling. German: *Gewalt*, "powers," "force" (*höhere gewalt* is an "act of providence").

(Continued from page 181)

was declared "Freedom for *Agunot* Month" in 2000 by a broad coalition of Orthodox groupings; a conference held at that time was keynoted by Rabbi Eliyahu Ben-Dahan, general director of the Rabbinic Courts of the State of Israel, and received sponsorship from most of the central Orthodox Jewish organizations in North America.

Conservative Judaism's approach to these issues has been to respect the traditional divorce process, to train Conservative rabbis to serve as *mesadderei gittin* (see my previous note), and to issue annullments of some dissolved marriages in which the *get* has been withheld. Annulments, which have grounding in the *Talmud*, do not produce *mamzer* status for the children of the marriage, since their mothers are then technically unmarried (children born to unwed mothers have no tainted status under Jewish law).

The Reconstructionist movement has created an egalitarian *get* that it encourages Jews to use in dissolving marriages. This *get* can be inaugurated by wives as well as husbands. The *agunah* problem is therefore nonexistent in Reconstructionist communities. Since this alternative *get* is not respected by Orthodox or Conservative authorities, Reconstructionist divorces include a document that husbands must sign, agreeing to grant a second, traditional *get* should the need arise in the future.

The Reform movement, as Rosten notes, has abandoned the *get* and treats divorce as a civil matter, though various healing rituals for people divorcing have been created by Reform liturgists.

1. A cry of fear, astonishment, amazement. *"Gevalt!* What happened?"
2. A cry for help. *"Gevalt!* Help! Burglars!"
3. A desperate expression of protest: *"Gevalt,* Lord, enough already!"

Gevalt is a versatile, all-purpose word—used as both an expletive and a noun. "She opened the door and cried, *'Gevalt!'"* "He took one look at her and let out a *gevalt!* you could hear in New Jersey." "Now take it easy, don't make a *gevalt.*"

PROVERB: "Man comes into the world with an *oy!*—and leaves with a *gevalt!"*

The special flavor of *gevalt!* is expressed in the story of the apocryphal Countess Misette de Rothschild, half French, half English, who lay in childbirth in the magnificent bedroom of her mansion off the Champs-Élysées, moaning and wailing. Downstairs, her husband, the count, wrung his hands anxiously.

"Come, come," said the obstetrician. "She's not ready to deliver. Let's play cards. There's plenty of time."

They played cards for a while.

From above came the shrill cry of the countess: *"Mon Dieu! Mon Dieu!"*

The husband leaped up.

"No, no," said the doctor. "Not yet. Plenty of time. Play."

They played on.

Soon the countess screamed: "Oh, God. Oh, *God!"*

Up leaped the haggard husband.

"No," said the doctor. "Not yet. Deal."

The husband dealt. They played on.

Came a resonant *"Ge-valt!"*

Up rose the obstetrician. "Now."

gezundheit
gesundheit, gesundhayt, gezundhayt

Pronounced *ge-ZUND-hite*, to rhyme with "the Bund kite." German: "health."*

1. Health.

> *Gezundheit* is actually a full-fledged German, not Yiddish, expression, although many Jews use it. Yiddish speakers might say to a person who sneezed, "*Tsu gezunt*," "To your health."

Someone once said you can tell if people are Jewish by how they answer the question "How are you?" If they say, "Fine!" or, "Couldn't be better," they're not Jews. For Jews, by tradition, fear that boasting (of good health or good luck) may attract some jealous and punishing evil spirit. The typical Jewish reply to "How do you feel?" is "Not bad" or "So-so."

2. The verbal amenity uttered when someone sneezes, "Kerchoo!" "*Gezundheit!*"

"*Gezundheit!*" is as obligatory a response to a heard sneeze as "*Aleichem sholem*" is to the greeting "*Sholem aleichem*." (See entry for sholem aleichem.)

FOLK SAYING: "Your health comes first; you can always hang yourself later."

Apocryphal, but not less amusing:

When an El Al plane leaves New York, the pilot greets the passengers with these words: "*Sholem aleichem*, ladies and gentlemen, and welcome to El Al airlines. This is your pilot, Itzchak Levin, wishing you a happy, restful trip, which we certainly expect to have, God willing. And if by some remote chance we do run into trouble—God forbid!—do not panic, keep calm. Your life belt is under your seat. And if you must put it on, wear it in the best of health!"

gilgul ᴿ
gilgl ʸ

Pronounced GILL-g'l, to rhyme with "sill pull." From Hebrew: *gilgul*, "rolling" (as of a wheel) or "turning" (as of a wheel). Plural: *gilgulim*, pronounced *gill-GOO-lim*.

1. Literally: A turning or rolling, as of a wheel.
2. More important: A reincarnation; someone with a reincarnated soul.
3. Sarcastically: A person whose behavior, irrationality, stupidity, tactlessness, can only be explained by assuming that he is a *gilgul*. "That man is a *gilgul* of a horse!" "Such stubbornness you find only in the *gilgul* of a jackass." "Such crazy behavior comes only from a *gilgul* of a hyena."

D o not confuse a *gilgul* with a *dybbuk*, a demon. The idea of the *gilgul*, of the reincarnation of souls, of metempsychosis, plays an important role in Jewish cabalism and the writings of the *Chasidim*.*

---

*The influence of Buddhism and New Age spirituality upon the baby boom generation (see my note to Rosten's entry for **geshmat**) has led to a renewal of interest in Jewish reincarnation beliefs. This is particularly so within the Chasidic and Jewish Renewal communities, where cabalistic traditions are most influential. According to Dr. Louis Jacobs, "Hardly any Orthodox Jew today will positively denounce the doctrine" of past lives and the transmigration of souls (*The Jewish Religion, a Companion*, Oxford, 1995).

In the Jewish tradition, reincarnation is said to occur within four basic situations:

1. *Gilgul*, in which the souls of the demised return within new bodies; *tzaddikim*, enlightened Jews, are supposedly able to recall their past lives and predict their future ones.
2. *Ibbur*, "impregnation," in which a departed soul seeks to help a living soul—and/or to seek rest for itself.

(Continued on page 186)

The idea of the transmigration of souls after death into the body of another mortal or animal is of course found in many "mystery religions" of the East. It was found among the Egyptians, in India and Persia, in certain Greek cults, among the Pythagoreans, and in the Mithraic and Zoroastrian creeds.

The history of medicine, and especially of efforts made to understand and alleviate mental disorders, is replete with the problems presented by evil demons who "possess" the unfortunate: spirits, devils, incubi, et alia.

See dybbuk, cabala, Chasid, Zohar.

(Continued from page 185)

3. The transmigration of souls into plants, animals, and even inanimate objects—often as punishment for sin. Adultery, for example, may be punished with reincarnation as a dog, or pride with reincarnation as a worm. This motif receives particular attention in Chasidic folklore.

4. Possession of the living by a guilty or angry soul—see Rosten's note for **dybbuk**.

Rabbi Jacobs believes that the mystical faith in *gilgul* took root "because of the theological difficulties in God allowing little children to suffer. That they do, it was argued, is because of sins they had committed in a previous existence." The death of well over a million Jewish children in the Holocaust, however, makes this theological "solution" to the problem of evil intolerable. Nevertheless, there are some voices in the Chasidic and mystical Jewish worlds who interpret even the Holocaust through the lens of reincarnation.

In a far more mainstream use of the concept of *gilgul*, Nathan Englander wrote "The Gilgul of Park Avenue," in his 1999 short-story collection, *For the Relief of Unbearable Urges*, in which a nonbelieving Christian man acquires a Jewish soul, and a compulsion to fulfill Orthodox *mitzvas*, while riding in a New York taxicab. Readers who have ridden in New York taxis should empathize with this sudden need for faith.

glitch^R
glitsh^Y

Pronounced GLITCH, to rhyme with "pitch." German: *glitschen,* "to slip."*

1. A slide; to slide or skid on a slippery surface. "Be careful not to *glitch.*"
2. A risky undertaking or enterprise. "Be careful. It could be a *glitch.*"
3. A shady, not *kosher* or reputable affair.

The adjective is *glitchidik,* pronounced GLITCH-*i-dik*. To warn your child that the pavement is *glitchidik* seems to me delightful. Not, mind you, that "slippery" is any slouch as a word. *Glitchidik* just takes longer and lingers in the ear.

goldene medine^Y
goldeneh medina^R

Pronounced GOLD-*en-eh* m'–DEE-*neh. Goldene* is from German for "golden"; *medina* is Hebrew for "country," "land," "province."

1. Literally: "Golden country."

Goldene medine meant America: land of freedom, justice, opportunity—and protection against pogroms. Rarely did I

---

*This word has entered the English language forcefully during the past decade to describe inadvertent errors, especially in scientific work, most especially those computer program problems that cause headaches in Silicon Valley: "There was a *glitch* in the program and my computer crashed" has become the new standard excuse (unfortunately true!) for missed deadlines.

hear such overtones of gratitude as went into the utterance of this compound noun.

That America's streets were "paved with gold" was more than a metaphor to the millions in Europe who dreamed of coming here.

> 2. A fool's paradise.

In irony or sarcasm, *goldene medine* is used to mean a miraculous hope that ends in disappointment.

A poor tailor who lived in a cellar and slaved for a pittance once voiced his bitterness by describing New York as "some *goldene medine!*"

A lady from Brooklyn was watching a parade on fifth Avenue.

"Look!" someone cried. "There goes the mayor of Dublin—and he's a Jew!"

"*Ai-ai-ai,*" clucked the matron. "Where could such a thing happen? Only in this *goldene medine!*"

golem^R
goylem^Y

Pronounced GO-*lem*, to rhyme with "dole 'em," or GOY-*lem*, to rhyme with "boil 'em." From Hebrew: "matter without shape," "a yet unformed thing" (Psalm 139:16).

1. A robot; a lifeless figure.
2. A simpleton; a fool.
3. A clumsy man or woman; a clod; someone who is all thumbs, poorly coordinated.
4. A slow-moving man or woman.
5. A graceless, tactless type.

6. Someone who is subnormal.

Typical phrases: "He looks like a *golem*." "He walks like a *golem*." "He is as slow-witted as a *golem*." "He barely gets around, poor *golem*."

The *Talmud* poetically speculates: "How was Adam created? In the first hour, his dust was collected; in the second hour, his form was fashioned; in the third, he became a shapeless mass *[golem]*; . . . in the sixth he received a soul; in the seventh hour, he rose and stood on his feet. . . ."

A *golem* can be virtuous, kind, just, said Maimonides, but his intellectual capacities are arrested.

The most famous of these imaginary creatures was the *Golem* of Prague. In the seventeenth century, a legend grew around Rabbi Judah Lowe (or Löw) of Prague, a renowned scholar who was supposed to have created a *golem* to help protect the Jews from many calamities the anti-Semites attempted. The *golem* helped Rabbi Lowe bring criminals to justice; he exposed spreaders of anti-Semitic canards; he saved an innocent girl from apostasy by force; he even discovered in the nick of time that the Passover *matzos* had been poisoned! Rabbi Lowe, the story went, removed all life from the *golem* every Friday night, for he would not allow the creature any mobility that might desecrate the Sabbath.

A well-known play, *Der Goylem* (1921), modeled on *Faust* and sensitively written in Yiddish by the Jewish poet Leivick Halpern (1888–1962), who wrote as H. Leivick, was performed for years all over Europe and America. The story of the *golem* was made into a movie several times: in French, German, and Yiddish.*

---

*A comic book series, *Mendy and the Golem,* by Leib Estrin (writer) and David Sears (artist), appeared for about twenty issues during the 1980s. Published by a Lubavitcher businessman and reflecting Chasidic ideology, it was infused *(Continued on page 190)*

Perhaps the most famous literary treatment of a *golem* is Meyrink's, in German, translated by Pemberton.

Mary Shelley, who wrote *Frankenstein,* may have gotten the idea from the *golem* legends.

(Continued from page 189)

with a surprisingly hip cultural sensibility: Sholem the Golem—so named because he brings "peace to the Jewish people" (*sholem* meaning "peace") and "because he doesn't know if he's coming or going" (*sholem aleichem* being the phrase for both good-bye and hello)—lived with the Klein family and battled such evil characters as "Oy Vayder" (Darth Vader) in such locales as "Yankel's Stadium" (Yankee Stadium). Rabbi Klein was regularly portrayed doing kitchen chores, while his wife fixed the car or did the plumbing.

Current uses of the *golem* name and legend include Golem Software, which manufactures programs for handheld computers; the Golem Web server, an Internet search engine; the Golem Lunch Club, a "virtual restaurant" (food delivery and catering); and Golem, a popular fantasy card game.

When the scientists at the great Weizmann Institute in Rehovoth, Israel, built their first large electronic computer, they dubbed it "Golem I."†

Gott^R
Got^Y

Pronounced GAWT, to rhyme with "taught." From German: *Gott*, God.

God.

(But see Adonai, Adoshem, Gottenyu.)

Gottenyu^R
Gotenyu^Y

Pronounced GAWT-*en-yew!* (*Gott* rhymes with "caught," not "cot.") From German: *Gott*, "God."

"Dear God," "Oh, dear God," or "How else can I describe my feelings!"

Gottenyu! is an exclamation that is uttered with affection, despair, or irony, to lend force to a sentence by adding fervor to sentiment.

It is a warm, informal, personal way of enlisting God's attention, *not* invoking His aid. Nor does it describe the Lord in any way.

---

†Golem I was built in 1964, Golem II in 1972. These were preceded by WEIZAC, one of the world's first computers, built in 1954. The Weizmann Institute has also innovated in the fields of cancer research, science education, technological entrepreneurship, and atomic research.

It is a colloquial epithet used, for the most part, without really meaning God per se (I guess I must capitalize Se here). "Were we happy! *Gottenyu!*" "*Gottenyu!*—you never saw such a mess!" "Was I scared? Miserable? Oh, *Gottenyu!*" A common phrase is *"Zise Gottenyu,"* "Sweet God."

A charming dictum has it that, under stress, Jews exclaim, "*Oy, Mamenyu!*" When stress becomes fear, they cry, *"Oy, Tatenyu!"* (*tate* being "father"). And when things *really* get tough, Jews cry, "*Gottenyu!*"

goy
goyish (adjective)
goyim (plural)

Rhymes with "boy," "boyish," "doyen." The plural is pro-nounced GOY-*im*. The adjective is *goyish* (neuter), *goyisher* (masculine), or *goyishe* (feminine). From the Hebrew: *goy,* "nation."

1. A Gentile—that is, anyone who is not a Jew. (This covers an enormous amount of ground.) A young male Gentile is a *sheygets,* the female a *shikse.*
   a. It is important to note that the idea of respect for others and the values of a pluralistic society form an old, integral part of Judaism and Jewish tradi-tion. The rabbis taught that all people are equal in the eyes of God if they do the will of God: "Whether Jew or Gentile, man or woman, rich or poor—according to a man's deeds does God's presence rest on him."
   b. Mormons call any non-Mormon a Gentile; Jews are therefore Gentiles to Mormons; I have never

met a Jew who quite knows how to adjust to this
startling idea. I once spent three happy days in
Utah without observing any noticeable **change in
my disposition.***
2. Someone who is dull, insensitive, heartless.

Just as some Gentiles use "Jew" as a contemptuous synonym
for too shrewd, sly bargaining ("He tried to jew the price down"
is about as unappetizing an idiom as I know), so some Jews use
goy in **a pejorative sense.**†

Relentless persecution of Jews, century after century, in nation
after nation, left a legacy of bitter sayings: *"Dos ken nor a goy"*
("That, only a *goy* is capable of doing"); *"A goy blaybt a goy"* ("A
Gentile remains a Gentile," or, less literally, "What did you expect?
Once an anti-Semite, always an anti-Semite").

Experience made many Jews feel that Gentiles are not gentle.

---

*Mormon-Jewish relations hit a very peculiar bump when it was revealed in
1994 that the Mormon Church (the Church of Jesus Christ of Latter-day
Saints) was posthumously baptizing hundreds of thousands of Jews, including many, many victims of the Holocaust, before including their names in the
church's vast *International Genealogical Index (IGI)*. For example, all 128,000
German-Jewish names listed in the *Gedenkbuch* (*Memorial Book,* a register of
those who died under the Nazis) had been subjected to the surrogate baptisms. These names were then listed in the *IGI* with the circumstances and
place of death—usually concentration camps—replaced by the word *baptized*.
Offended by this bizarre and presumptuous practice, Jewish leaders
expressed fear that the *IGI* entries would be misinterpreted by future historians as evidence that massive numbers of Jews had forsaken Judaism—or be
used to fuel the propaganda of those who deny the reality or the scope of the
Holocaust.

†The liveliest contemporary enunciation of the Jewish-goyish difference was
the following *shtik* by Lenny Bruce: "Dig . . . If you live in New York or any
other big city, you are Jewish. It doesn't matter even if you're Catholic, if
you live in New York, you're Jewish. If you live in Butte, Montana, you're
(continued on page 194)

(Continued from page 193)

going to be goyish even if you're Jewish. Kool-Aid is goyish. Evaporated milk is goyish, even if the Jews invented it. Chocolate is Jewish and fudge is goyish. . . . Mouths are very Jewish. And bosoms. Baton-twirling is very goyish. . . . 'Celebrate' is a goyish word. 'Observe' is a Jewish word. Mr. and Mrs. Walsh are celebrating Christmas with Major Thomas Moreland, USAF (Ret.), while Mr. and Mrs. Bromberg observed Chanukah with Goldie and Arthur Schindler from Kiamesha, New York." (From *The Essential Lenny Bruce*, Ballantine Books, 1967.)

High rates of Jewish-Christian intermarriage and ongoing Jewish assimilation into the American mainstream have begun to erode much of the shared Jewish cultural sensibility that gave rise to Lenny Bruce's insightful *shpritz*. Many converts are now participating in synagogues and Jewish organizations—Jews by choice who nevertheless retain a *goyisher kop*, for they cannot possibly "convert" to the irreverencies and neuroses bred by growing up in a Jewish household. There are also many outright *goyim* participating in Jewish life, who are partnered with Jews but have not taken the conversionary plunge. (See my note to **geshmat** for a discussion of Jewish intermarriage and conversionary outreach.) Large numbers of Jews have also abandoned the cities and neighborhoods in which they were raised to make homes in "Butte, Montana"–type outposts—smaller cities of the American landscape. In combination, these forces of dilution and dispersion have somewhat subdued the brash clubbiness that Lenny Bruce identified as Jewish.

On the other hand, "Jewish" as Bruce defined it has already been infused into the American mainstream through the involvement of many Jews in the entertainment industry. Once upon a time it was the Marx Brothers, Sid Caesar, Benny Goodman, and other obviously but unexplicitly Jewish Jews who exported Jewish humor, music, and soul into the American mainstream. Today, Jewish artists with *explicitly* Jewish characters and themes have taken over. In 1986, for example, Art Spiegelman emerged from the world of underground adult comics to achieve best-seller status with *Maus*, an adult comic-book history of Holocaust trauma that won the Pulitzer Prize. Comics for kiddies, meanwhile, now include Jewish superheroes such as Seraph, Rambam, Golem, Judith, Sabra, Ragman, and numerous others. Apparently, the "secret identity" is a thing of the past. If Superman (created by "nice Jewish boys" Joe Schuster and Jerry Siegel) were reborn today, he'd probably keep his Hebraic-sounding name, Kal-El.

In the 1990s, Matt Stone of *South Park*, Arlene Klasky of the *Rugrats*, and other Jewish animators tore open the boundaries of what can be shown and said on television—and among the taboos they shattered is that of *not* portraying overtly Jewish characters and themes. Jewish holidays, characters, accents, and even stereotypes abound in these new cartoon series; one *South Park* episode featured a mystical war for world domination between Moses

"Goyisher kop" means "Gentile brains" or "Gentile ways." It is not, alas, **complimentary**.*

When endurance is exhausted, kindliness depleted, the effort to understand useless, the epithet "A *goy!*" is used—just as, I suppose, Armenians say "Turk!" or Mexicans say *"Gringo!"* or Frenchmen *"Boche!"* or—but there is no end to the catalog of xenophobic depreciation.

The rabbis long tried to moderate the bitterness of their flock: "A Gentile who observes the Torah is as good as a High Priest," wrote a fourth-century sage.

The *Sefer Hasidim,* a thirteenth-century work, says: "If a Jew attempts to kill a non-Jew, help the non-Jew."

The great Rashi, eleventh-century French rabbi, reminded Jews that Gentiles "of the present age are not heathens."

And in *Tosefta Baba Kamma* it is solemnly noted that to rob a non-Jew is more heinous than to rob a Jew—because such robbery

and Haman (the villain of the *Purim* holiday), with the setting a Jewish summer camp. Numerous non-animated Jewish characters have also appeared as major players on screen, ranging from Goldie Hawn's "Private Benjamin" to Jenna Elfman's "Dharma Finkelstein" on television's *Dharma and Greg.* Such characters are not limited to Jewish milieux, nor are Jewish milieux excluded from the plots. Instead, Jewish life is readily incorporated into the portrait of America now being created by the entertainment media.

Completing the cycle of Jewish-goyish exchange, many young Jews who are "returning to tradition" are smuggling in idioms from the non-Jewish world—as witnessed by the rise of heavy metal–Chasidic rock, Jewish rap music, etc. This "cool Judaism," writes Jonathan Schorsch in *Tikkun* magazine (March/April 2000), "has enabled young Jews to express ethnic pride in themselves and in Judaism, now that they've discovered that the 'true' Judaism repressed by their bourgeois parents is ethnic, oppressed and Other."

*A favorite joke tells of a Jew forced to convert to Christianity, who nevertheless starts in on his morning prayers the following day until his wife interrupts to remind him that he is no longer Jewish. *"Ai-ai-ai!"* the man cries, smacking himself on the forehead. *"Goyisher kop!"*

"involves the desecration of the Name."

FOLK SAYING: "Gentiles are not used to Jewish problems."

A London Jew became so prosperous that he changed his name from Nate Greenberg to Noel Greenhill, bought a fine home on Park Lane, and proceeded to acquire various objets d'art—including a beautiful painting by Rubens.

The following year, his affluence having increased, he exchanged the Rubens—for a Goya. . . .

On Houston Street, a young priest saw a large sign over a hardware store: PINCUS AND O'TOOLE.

The priest went in, to be greeted by a man with a beard and *yarmulke*.

The priest smiled. "I just wanted to come in to tell you how wonderful it is to see that your people and mine have become such good friends—even partners. That's a surprise!"

"I've got a bigger surprise," sighed the old man. "I'm O'Toole."

Mr. O'Neill and Mr. Pinsky were chatting. O'Neill said, "Did you hear about the fight between Cooley and McGraw?"

"How could I miss it?" said Pinsky. "Wasn't it in front of my eyes?"

"I didn't know you were there."

"What then? I was maybe in the White House?"

"Whose fault was it: Cooley's?"

"Who else?"

O'Neill sighed. "Pinsky, *why* do Jews answer every question with another question?"

Pinsky pondered. "Why not?"

grizhen^Y
gridzhen^R

Pronounced GRI-*zh'n*, to rhyme with "pigeon," or (in a Yinglish adaptation) GRID-*zhen*, to rhyme with "Ridge-yen." Slavic: "to gnaw."

Literally, to chew or to gnaw, the way an animal does, with slobby, slobbering sounds; to grind one's teeth.

As used, *grizhen* conveys the idea of carping, beefing, complaining, nagging. The grating sound of the word is itself unpleasant. "Stop *grizhing*." "All she does is *grizhe*." "*Es grizhet mir*" means "It gripes me."

See also nudzhn, tshepen.

grob^Y
graub^R
grober ^Y
grauber ^R
grobyon^Y
graubyon^R

Pronounced GRUB or GRAWB, to rhyme with "daub," and GRAW-*ber*. From the German: *grob*, "coarse, uncouth, rough."

1. Coarse, crude, uncouth, vulgar; ill-mannered.
2. Ignorant; insensitive.

"A *grober yung*" (exactly as "Jung") means a coarse young man, a crude fellow, an uneducated poltroon. Jews tend to equate education with gentleness, knowledge with considerateness.

In our house, *grob* was used as an expletive of forceful

contempt: "He's a *grob!*" meant the mortal under discussion was a goon, a vulgarian, one of low sensibility. "What a *grob* thing to do!" conveyed an ocean of scorn and dismay.

A *grobyon* (derived from Russian) is a person who is a *grob*.

A rabbi came to the notoriously brutal governor of a province in Poland and pleaded for help for the many who were starving.

The *grober* governor struck the rabbi across the face. "Jew, take that!"

The rabbi nodded. "That, sir, is for me. Now what will you give to my people?"

h

Hadassah

Pronounced *ha-DAH-sah,* to rhyme with *"La casa."*
Hebrew: "myrtle." *Hadassah* is the Hebrew and Yiddish
form of the biblical **Esther.***
1. Esther.
2. The Women's Zionist Organization of America.

Founded in 1912 by the remarkable Henrietta Szold, the
Hadassah organization today has over three hundred thousand members in some 1,200 chapters. It was originally organized to raise the standards of health, hygiene, and public
medicine in Palestine, which was ridden by diseases; and to widen

---

Hadassah (Esther) is the heroine of the springtime *Purim* holiday. She saved
her people from slaughter in the fifth century B.C.E. at the hands of Haman, a
Persian minister (see Rosten's entry, and my note, for **Purim**). Hadassah
courageously revealed her Jewish identity and appealed to the mercy of her
husband, King Ahasuerus, who authorized Jewish defense, punished Haman
with a public hanging, and appointed Hadassah's uncle, Mordecai, in his
stead. While none of these figures has been granted historicity by archaeologists or scholars, the holiday has been observed since the first or second century C.E., and the *Megillah Hadassah* (the book of Esther; see Rosten's entry
for **megillah**) was canonized as part of the *Torah.*

America became acquainted with *Hadassah* as a personal, as opposed to
organizational, name when Vice President Al Gore chose Senator Joseph
Lieberman of Connecticut as his running mate in the 2000 presidential election. Lieberman's wife, Hadassah, is the daughter of Holocaust survivors.

and deepen the awareness, among Jews in America, of Jewish traditions and ideals.

In Israel, *Hadassah*'s hospitals and services have made striking contributions to medicine. The Hadassah Medical School, the only one in Israel,† is part of Hebrew University.

Haftorah^R
Haftoyre^Y
Haftarah

Pronounced *haff*-TOE-*reh*, to rhyme with "doff Mona," or *hoff*-TOY-*reh*, to rhyme with "doff Moira." Hebrew: "end," "conclusion."

A chapter from the Prophets, read in the synagogue (after the portion from the Pentateuch) on Sabbaths and festivals.

The practice of reading a passage from the Prophets, after the *Torah* reading, has been observed since the first century. Each portion of the *Torah* has a specific *Haftorah* of its own.

The *Haftorah* is chanted with a specific system of cantillation. Jewish children learn this cantillation and on their *bar* or *bat mitzva* day chant the *Haftorah* assigned to that Sabbath.

---

† Israel now also trains medical personnel at the Sackler School of Medicine of Tel Aviv University and at Haifa's Technion-Israel Institute of Technology, where the Rappaport Faculty of Medicine admitted its first class in 1973. Hadassah remains the driving force behind many of Israel's medical achievements. Organizational milestones during the past three decades include the founding in 1973 of Kibbutz Ketura in the Negev by graduates of Hadassah's Young Judaea program; the creation in 1977 of Israel's first neonatal medical unit, and in 1986 of Israel's only Jewish hospice for the terminally ill; and the creation in 1998 of Israel's first completely handicapped-accessible park, in Jerusalem.

Haggadah^R
Hagode^Y
Hagada
Agada^R *
Agode^Y
Aggada, Aggadah

*Rosten's first spelling, *Haggadah*,
is most commonly used with his
second definition (the Passover
Haggadah), while the latter
spellings, *Agada* or *Aggada* or
Aggadah, are commonly associated
with his first definition (Talmudic
Agada)—and if you understood that
on first reading, you may be a
natural for Talmudic study!

Pronounced *ha-*GOD-*da,* to
rhyme with the way an English-
man pronounces "Nevada."† Hebrew: "tale" or "telling."

1. The enormous respository of Jewish allegorical material,
   including historical episodes, theology, folklore, fable,
   prayers, parables, witticisms, anecdotes, ruminations,
   sermons, etc., etc., found in the *Talmud.* Scholars classify the material as exegetical and nonexegetical; history; religion, and ethics; mysticism; eschatology—and
   even superstition.‡

The *Haggadah* appealed to the common people, for it contains
a wealth of enchanting episodes and marvelous stories about
scholars and saints and martyrs. Four qualities distinguish it, says

† Most Yiddish speakers would say *ha-*GAW-*deh.*

‡ The most enduring modern compendium of *Agada* (rabbinic storytelling, as
opposed to *Halakha*, the system of rabbinic law) was published in 1908–11 by
the outstanding Hebrew poet H. N. Bialik and editor/journalist Y. H. Rav-
nitzky. Over the century, their *Sefer Ha-Aggadah (Book of Legends)* was published eighteen times, most recently in 1992 (Shocken Books). The book
organizes by topic materials from the *Talmud* and *Midrash* (collections of biblical exegesis and folklore—see Rosten's entry for **midrash**) and offers tremendous accessibility to the casual reader. Bialik described the project as
"fragments of stones . . . joined into layers, layers into walls, and walls into a
complete fortress" that enables readers to "grasp finally that worldview and
perspective on life in whose spirit the *Agada* was originally created, an entity
unique to the Jewish people."

Professor Judah Goldin: charm, extraordinary piety, ethical fervor, and affirmations of God's love for the children of Israel (*The Jews: Their History, Culture and Religion*, vol. I, Harper, 1960). See Talmud.

2. The narrative that is read aloud at the Passover *seder*, piecing together, from many sources, the story of Israel's bondage in, and flight from, Egypt.

The *Haggadah* draws material from the book of Exodus and from the *Talmud*. It contains psalms, prayers, hymns—even several amusing jingles at the end to hold the interest of the children, who must sit through a very long ceremony and feast. When the youngest child asks the "Four Questions" on Passover, the adult reader responds from the *Haggadah:* "Slaves were we unto Pharaoh in Egypt."

The *Haggadah* has **grown down the centuries.*** Some of its contents trace back to ancient liturgy, but most of it is a creation of laypeople throughout the centuries. The basic form seems to have been set in the second century; the first *Haggadah,* as a sepa-

---

*"In every generation," the Passover *Haggadah* says, "each person should feel personally redeemed from Egypt." In fulfillment of this commandment, there has been an explosion in contemporary rewrites of the *Haggadah* over the past thirty years, ranging from lavishly illustrated best-sellers to photocopied booklets, with themes of vegetarianism, feminism, Arab-Jewish reconciliation, and more. The Passover *seder* is far and away the most widely observed Jewish ritual among American Jews, and the hunger for alternatives to the traditional, long-winded, Hebrew and Aramaic *Haggadah* has fostered tremendous creativity—and creative license. Rabbi Susan Schnur of *Lilith* magazine, for example, augmented "Elijah's Cup" (filled with wine and set out in hope that Elijah the Prophet will appear to herald the Messiah) with "Miriam's Cup," filled with spring water, to represent the central role played by Moses' sister in the Passover story (saving Moses from Pharaoh's decree, helping to lead the Hebrew people into the wilderness, and providing them with water). See my note to Rosten's entry for **Pesach.**

rate collection of prayers, appeared around the thirteenth century.

Prior to Guttenberg, the *Haggadahs* were, obviously, written out by copyists and calligraphers; some are as magnificent as only medieval illuminated manuscripts can be—with exquisitely ornamented Hebrew letters and lavish illustrations of biblical events, the coming of the Messiah, the restoration of *Zion*. The library of the Jewish Theological Seminary in New York contains some marvelous old *Haggadahs*.

See Pesach.

hak a tshaynik[Y]
hok a chainik[R]

Pronounced HOCK *a* TCHY-*nik,* to rhyme with "Sock a guy Nick" (with the *tsh* sounding like the *ch* in "church"). *Hak* is "strike," *tshaynik* is "teapot," "teakettle," from the Russian and Polish.

I would not dream of burdening your mind with *hak a tshaynik,* "knock a kettle" or "beat a teakettle," if that's all it meant. To "knock a teapot" means

1. to talk a great deal; to yammer, to yak.
2. to talk nonsense or "bushwa."

This is a widely used phrase in the conversational badminton of Jews. "Please, *hak nit kayn tshaynik!*" ("Please, stop talking so much," "Stop spouting all that nonsense," "Stop talking my ear off.")

The expression may have come from the meaningless rattling of a cover of a boiling pot or from the noisy whistling of steam in a kettle. Or it may have come from the improvised toys of children at play. Since toys were a rarity among the poor in the *shtetl,* children made use of ordinary objects. To simulate a drummer or a band, it was easy enough to bang away on a pot or kettle.

In any case, "knocking a teapot" has become a picturesque phrase for constant chatter.

Halakha^R
Halokhe^Y
Halakhah, Halakah

Pronounced *ha*-LOKH-*eh*, with the guttural *kh* sound of "Loch Lomond." Hebrew: "law."

1. Jewish law—*and* accumulated jurisprudence: that is, the decisions of the sages, but without biblical citations, notes, references. The *Halakha* simply states the laws crisply, as in a code.
2. The part of the *Talmud* that is not *Agada*—that is, the part that deals with laws.

The great rabbis did not "create" *Halakha:* what the rabbis did was to codify and clarify the legal teachings, adapting them to changing social conditions. "The Rabbinic *Halakha*," writes Judah Goldin, "protected legislation from inflexibility and society from fundamentalism"* (*The Jews: Their History, Culture and Religion,*

---

*One interesting example of this, relevant to contemporary times, is the *Halakha* on capital punishment. The *Torah*, like other ancient law codes, assigns the death penalty to many proscribed behaviors besides murder—including adultery, rape of a betrothed woman, giving insult or injury to one's parents, witchcraft, male homosexuality, and public profanation of the Sabbath. By the second century c.e., however, the Talmudic rabbis, whose debates and rulings constitute the main body of *Halakha*, had virtually nullified the death penalty. The *Mishnah* (the codification of law that forms the core text of the *Talmud*) states, "A *Sanhedrin* [governing council] that puts

vol. I, Louis Finkelstein, ed., Harper, 1960). The *Talmud* is composed of *Halakha* and *Agada*.

halava
halavah
See halvah.

halevay^Y
halevai^R
alevai

Pronounced *hah-liv-*EYE, to rhyme with "dollify." An Aramaic word, found quite frequently in the *Talmud*.

"Would that," "Oh, that . . ." meaning "I hope," "I wish," "I hope so," "I wish I had," "If only I had," etc.

Jewish women sprinkle *halevay* around generously in conversation: "*Halevay* [if only] she should meet a nice boy!" "Sick? He's dying, the poor man—*halevay* [I hope] I am wrong." "Next year could be better, *halevay*." "He has a chance of getting into Harvard. *Halevay!*" "They warned me a hundred times. I should have listened. *Halevay*."

a man to death once in seven years is called destructive. Rabbi Eliezer ben Azariah says: even once in seventy years. Rabbi Akiba and Rabbi Tarfon say: had we been in the *Sanhedrin* none would ever have been put to death" (*Makkot* 7A). Even in murder cases, the *Torah*'s requirement of two eyewitnesses for a sentence of death was interpreted by the Talmudic rabbis to make capital punishment highly unlikely: the murderer's own confession could not be accepted as evidence, and the two eyewitnesses were required also to have warned the criminal beforehand that he would be executed! Justice tempered by mercy thus became the Jewish ideal.

He sat there, sighing and moaning and ruminating thusly: "Oh, if only the Holy One, blessed be His name, would give me ten thousand dollars, I promise I would give a thousand to the poor. *Halevay!* . . . And if the Holy One doesn't trust me, He can deduct the thousand in advance and just give me the balance."

"*Halevay* you should live a hundred and twenty years, plus three months!"

"Thank you. But why 'plus three months'?"

"I wouldn't want you to die suddenly."

As a child, and probably according to one of the principles of Piaget concerning the development of reason in the young, I went into stitches over this one:

"Let's go to a movie Sunday—if, *halevay,* we're alive. And if not, we'll go Tuesday."

halla
See challah.

halvah
halva, halava, halavah

Pronounced *holl*-VAH, to rhyme with "solve uh," or *holl-a-*VAH, to rhyme with "doll of uh," or *khal*-VAH, with the German *kh*. From Turkish: *helva,* and Arabic: *halva.*

A very sweet, flaky confection of distinctive texture made of honey and ground-up sesame seeds; chocolate is sometimes swirled through it.

Halvah, which crumbles into sticky flakes in the mouth, is a "treat," a *nosh* or dessert prized by those with a more-than-average sweet tooth. It is found in Turkish, Syrian, and Armenian food stores and in many delicatessans in Jewish neighborhoods in the United States. *Halvah* is a particular favorite of children.

The confection is made up in oblong blocks, about twelve inches by three inches, from which a portion is sliced off according to the size requested by the customer.

Contrary to demotic mythology, *halvah* is not a "Jewish" goody and is not typical of Jewish comestibles. Most Jews first encountered it in New York, where it was sold by Turkish, Syrian, and Armenian vendors. Its popularity spread swiftly, because it was sweet and cheap, but today it seems to have lost a good deal of its appeal. It is almost impossible to eat very much of it.

hamantash^R
homentash^Y

Pronounced HAW-*men-tosh*, to rhyme with "Jaw men bosh." Presumably named after Haman (see below); *Tasche* is German for "pocket."

A special cake: a triangular "pocket" of dough filled with poppy seed or prune jelly. The plural is *hamantashn*, and children love them.

Hamantashn are the triangular little cakes that are special treats during the Feast of *Purim*, a happy day that celebrates the foiling of the plot of Haman, first minister to King Ahasuerus, who wanted to destroy all the Jews in Persia. The story is told in the bible's Book of Esther.

See megillah and Purim.

Hanuka
Hannuka
Hanukkah
See Chanukah.

haseneh
hasene
See khasene.

Hashem

Pronounced *ha*-SHEM, to rhyme with "bosh hem."
Hebrew: "The Name."
    One of the words used in referring to God.
See Adoshem.

Hasid
Hasidim
Hassid
Hassidic
See Chasid.

Haskala[R]
Haskole[Y]
Haskalah

Pronounced *has*-KOL-*leh*, to rhyme with "La Scala."
Hebrew: "knowledge," "education, "erudition."

The movement of enlightenment, intellectual emancipation, and libertarian and secular education among Jews, like the European Enlightenment of the eighteenth century.

*H*askala was bitterly denounced and resisted by many rabbis, by Orthodox Jews, by *Chasidim*, and by fundamentalists—all of whom recognized the grave threat that secular education, and Western rationalism and philosophy, posed to traditional faith and orthodoxy.

Those who followed and furthered the *Haskala* called themselves "enlightened ones," or *Maskilim* (singular: *Maskil*).

The founder of the *Haskala* was the philosopher Moses Mendelssohn (1729–1786; he was the model for Gotthold Lessing's *Nathan the Wise*), who was determined to end the superstition, the intellectual conformity, the poverty and social backwardness, of ghetto and *shtetl* life. He attracted collaborators and students from all over Europe. Mendelssohn inveighed against Judaism's "narrow labyrinth of ritual—theological casuistry." He opened the first school of Jews to include courses in German, French, geography, and mathematics. Mendelssohn's disciples published a Hebrew magazine *(Ha-Me'assef)* that served to channel to Jewry the whole ferment of ideas, literature, and political liberalism that swept Europe after the French Revolution. The *Haskala* transformed Hebrew itself into a living, changing language—a Hebrew that came to be used by poets, novelists, journalists, and the man in the street.

The *Haskala* laid the groundwork for the strong socialdemocratic movement that captured the imagination of young Jews; it served to encourage the entry of Jews into politics; it spurred interest in agriculture and manual labor. It also aroused strong nationalism among some Jews, just as the Napoleonic era galvanized nationalist feelings among Germans, Italians, and Poles. The *Haskala* was the forerunner of Reform Judaism in religion and socialism and Zionism in politics.

Hatikvah

Pronounced *ha*-TICK-*vuh,* to rhyme with "a kick huh." Hebrew: "the hope."
The national anthem of Israel.

The song "Hatikvah" was written in 1878 by Naftali Herz Imber and set to music by Samuel Cohen. It was adopted as the Jewish national anthem at the first Zionist Congress in Basel, Switzerland, 1897.

When the state of Israel was established in 1948, "Hatikvah," with a slight change in its wording, became the national anthem.

Havdala[R]
Havdole[Y]
Havdalah, Habdala, Habdalah

Pronounced, in Yiddish, *hahv*-DOL-*leh,* to rhyme with "Bob Dole-leh." Hebrew: "separation."
The ceremony that signalizes the ending of the Sabbath.

The sweet-sad rite that each week says farewell to "Queen Sabbath" is traditionally performed by the male head of the family when he comes home from the evening service (*mairev*) in the synagogue. He lights a braided candle and a saucer of alcohol, by which he warms his hands with certain traditional gestures, and, his family close to and around him, over a wineglass he recites this solemn benediction: "Blessed art Thou, O Lord our God, King of the Universe, who makes a distinction between holy and profane, between light and darkness, between Israel and the nations, between the seventh day and the six days of work." It is customary to sing a melody, to either Hebrew or Yiddish words, asking God's grace for the week ahead.

Then an ornamental box, in which spices are kept, is raised and its sweet aroma sniffed—to revive the spirit saddened by Sabbath's end.*

The *Chasidim* used to celebrate the *Havdala* with rhapsodic dances in a circle, to which cabalistic significances were assigned.

hazzen
See chazzen.

---

*While the number of Jewish families who regularly observe *Havdala* as a home ritual is small, the ceremony remains a Saturday-evening staple of Jewish conventions and gatherings—and the range of ritual practice goes beyond Rosten's portrait. *Havdala* blends several sensual experiences: the glow of the double-wicked candles, the scent of the *besamim* (spices, usually clove, but any fragrant spice or flower can be used), the sharp taste of the wine (or grape juice), the passing of these ritual objects from one person to another. Since *Havdala* symbolizes a moment of transition, from the peace and non-doing of the Sabbath to the action-oriented days of the week, blessings offered over the candle can include personal, improvisational words about transitions that people are facing.

The *Havdala* ceremony also includes the extinguishing of the candle by dipping it into a saucer containing a little ritual wine. Warmed brandy used for this purpose will flame up like fireworks as the candle goes out.

heymish^Y
haimish^R
heymisher ^R (masculine)
haimisher
heymishe^Y (feminine)
haimisher ^R

Pronounced HAME-*ish*, to rhyme with "Danish" or "Jame-ish." From German: *Heim,* "home."

1. Informal, cozy, warm.
2. Having the friendly characteristics, or kind of rapport, that exist inside a happy home.
3. Without "side," unpretentious; putting on no airs; unspoiled by office or honors.

The last usage is the most frequent. President Truman was ever so *heymish.* No one in his right mind would call Generals de Gaulle and MacArthur *heymish.*

Heymish is the opposite of snobbish, supercilious, or, to get fancy about it, charismatic.

"A *heymisher mentsh*" means someone with whom you can take your shoes off or let your hair down.

Jews put a high value on being *heymish.*

Hillul Hashem
Hillul ha-Shem
See chillul hashem.

holdupnik
holdupnick

Pronounced *hold-*UP*-nick*. Yinglish.

One with a penchant for robbing—holding up—people.

hoo-ha!

Pronounced WHO HAH!, to rhyme with "poo bah."

An immensely impressive Yiddishism for the expression of

1. admiration. "His new house? *Hoo-ha!*"
2. astonishment. "*She* ran away? *Hoo-ha!*"
3. envy. "Did he marry a pretty girl? *Hoo-ha!*"
4. skepticism. "I can't lose? *Hoo-ha?!*"
5. deflation. "He calls himself a singer—*hoo-ha!*"
6. scorn. "Some friend. *Hoo-ha!*"

Also used, depending on vocal emphasis and accompanying facial expression, to convey the essence of

1. "Imagine that!" ("Left his wife? *Hoo-ha!*")
2. "You don't mean it!" ("Her, *hoo-ha?!*")
3. "Well, whaddaya know!" or "I'll be damned." ("Right in the middle of the lecture, *hoo-ha!*, he stood up and left!")
4. "Wow!" ("What a party! *Hoo-ha!*")

5. "Who do you think you're fooling?" ("Sure, I believe every word, *hoo-ha!*")
6. "That'll be the day!" ("He wants to be president, *hoo-ha!*")
7. "Like hell!" ("I'll give him a present, *hoo-ha!*").*

Hotseplots^Y
Hotzeplotz^R
Hatzeplatz

Pronounced HOTS-*eh-plotz*, to rhyme with "lots o' cots."
1. A mythical, remote town.
2. "Way to hell and gone," "way out in the sticks," "God only knows where." "I went from here to *Hotseplots* looking for you!" "They've sent him to a new post all the way in *Hotseplots* . . . ." "Lost? We could have been in *Hotseplots!*"

*H*otseplots is recommended as a ploy, for use with hitchhikers, drunks, obnoxious colleagues, or people who latch on to you during a taxi strike and ask could you just drop them off, it's only forty-three blocks out of your way. Thus: "Sorry, but we're going to *Hotseplots*" or "Where do I live? In *Hotseplots*."
See also Shnippishok.

hozzer
See chozzer.

---

*The early *MAD* magazine added "Help!" to the list of meanings for *hoo-ha!* by using it as the distress call of "Melvin of the Apes," a parody of Tarzan.

huppe
See chuppa.

hutspa
hutzpah
See chutzpa.

in mitn drinen[Y]
in mitn derinnen[R]

Pronounced *in* MIT-*ten d'*RIN-*en.* German: "in the middle of the thing."

Out of the blue; all of a sudden; for no reason.

I happen to be fond of this phrase. Tossed into an English sentence, it underlines the inexplicable, stresses the illogic of an act, or calls attention to the insufficiency of a cause.

"We were discussing the concert when, *in mitn drinen,* he starts to criticize the president!"

"She was telling me about their trip to Europe when, *in mitn drinen,* her husband brought up his cavities!"

"What makes you say that, *in mitn drinen?*"

in mitske drinen[Y]
in mitske derinnen[R]

A popular and potent variation of *in mitn drinen.*

Little Benny was watching his mother bake cookies. He stood there for a long time, then said, "Mama, why don't you ask me something?"

"What should I ask you, *in mitske drinen?*"

"You could ask me, 'You want a cookie, Benny?'"

j

Jehovah

Pronounced (in English) *Jee-*HO*-vah*. Not a Yiddish word. It is not a Hebrew word. It is some scribe's Latin transliteration of YHVH, to which the vowel marks for *Adonai* were added. The word appeared for the first time in an English text in 1530.

God.

Yahveh, which was mistransliterated into *Jehovah*, is the word formed by adding vowel sounds to the Tetragrammaton, the four Hebrew letters that stand for the Mystical and Ineffable Name of God. The English equivalents of the Hebrew letters are *YHVH* (called *yud, hay, vav, hay*).

These letters were the Unutterable Name, so the Mazoretes (who observed the tradition of *Masorah,* interpretive notes for the "correct" spelling and meaning of ancient Hebrew texts) added vowel marks to *YHVH* as a signal to readers to say *"Adonai"* instead; and this *combination* was mistakenly transliterated into Latin as JeHoVa(H)—or Jehova(h)—so used for the first time in the year 1516, says *The Oxford English Dictionary.* This is as clear as I can make it.

See Adonai.

An aging Jew, crossing the street in front of a church, was knocked down by a hit-and-run driver. As he lay there, half-conscious, a priest hurried out, knelt, and prepared to administer the last rites.

"Do you believe in God the Father, God the Son, and God the Holy Ghost?"

Cried the old man, "I'm dying and he asks me riddles!"

Judezmo
See Ladino.

kabbala
kabbalah

See cabala.

Kaddish^R
Kadish^Y

Pronounced KOD-*dish* or "cod dish." Aramaic: *kadosh,* "holy."

1. A prayer glorifying God's name, recited at the close of synagogue prayers; this is the most solemn and one of the most ancient of all Jewish prayers.
2. The mourner's prayer.
3. A son is sometimes called, affectionately, *"Kaddishel," "Kaddishnik,"* or *"my Kaddish."*

The *Kaddish* (originally recited after completing a reading from the Bible, a religious discourse, or a lesson) is a doxology that glorifies God's name, affirms faith in the establishment of God's kingdom, and expresses hope for peace within Israel. The language of the prayer is not Hebrew but Aramaic, which was the vernacular spoken by the Jews in their Babylonian Exile and during the days of the Second Temple.

In time, a belief arose among the Jews that the praises of God in the *Kaddish* would help the souls of the dead find lasting peace—and the prayer became known as the Mourner's Prayer, even though it contains not one reference to death or resurrection.

The *Kaddish* is recited at the grave, for eleven months after a death, by the children of the deceased, and each year on the anniversary of the death. (See yortsayt.)

Couples who had no son would sometimes adopt an orphan (a relative, if possible) and raise him as their own. He was called their *Kaddish* and guaranteed there would be someone to recite the prayer for them after their death.

Judaic law forbids any form of display or ostentation at a funeral. The rabbis of yore instituted simple burial rites, and this served to enforce a "democracy in death" in which no family, however poor, would be shamed by the simplicity of coffin or shroud.*

Cremation, incidentally, is expressly forbidden to Jews; the Bible says, "Dust returneth unto dust," and Jews have always felt a profound obligation to, and respect for, the body—which God created.†

---

*The *chevra kadishe*, or Jewish burial society, a fixture in most Jewish communities of past generations, has been making a comeback in synagogues across the denominational board as Jews seek meaningful alternatives to the high-glitz, high-expense practices of the funeral industry. In Washington, D.C., for example, a consortium of thirty-five synagogues of every denomination has developed a Jewish Funeral Practices Committee Contract that assures a low-cost Jewish funeral to members of participating congregations, including *takhara* (ritual washing of the body), a plain wooden casket, prompt burial, and other procedures in keeping with Judaism's very wise and respectful manner of caring for the dead and for their mourners. Rabbi Linda Holtzman, active in *chevra kadishe* work in Philadelphia, observes that Jewish burial rituals "have two primary values: equality in death and acceptance of death."

†Cremation is traditionally viewed as a denial of the doctrine of resurrection at the time of messianic redemption. In the *Talmud* (*Gittin* 56b), the Roman emperor Titus is said to have ordered cremation of his corpse and the scattering of the ashes so that he might escape God's judgment. Louis Jacobs notes, however (in *The Jewish Religion, A Companion*, Oxford University Press, 1995), that this is "the weakest of the arguments against cremation. For one thing, many believing Jews do not [embrace] the doctrine of the resurrection in a crude literal sense, and even those who do can hardly believe that it is beyond God's power to reconstitute a body that has been cremated, just as it

Mr. Morton Wishengrad wrote a television program for the admirable *Eternal Light* series, in which he imagined a genesis for the *Kaddish* (as a mourner's prayer) that deserves to be repeated:

A great scholar died, deeply mourned by the community and his disciples, one of whom mused: "When we end our reading of a chapter from *Torah,* we pronounce a *Kaddish* in praise of the Lord. Why not then utter a *Kaddish* when a chapter of a man's life is ended?"

Sholem Aleichem has left us this delightful memory of the *Kaddish* that he and his five brothers recited in mourning for their mother (translated by Maurice Samuel):

You should have heard us deliver that *Kaddish!* A pleasure! All our relatives beamed with pride, and strangers envied us. One of our relatives . . . exclaimed, When a woman has six sons like that to say *Kaddish* after her, she will surely go straight to paradise. Either that or the world is coming to an end!

is in His power to reconstitute a body that has become decomposed in the grave." Nevertheless, in Israel there are squads of ultra-Orthodox Jewish men who rush to terrorist bombing scenes in order to recover every scrap of flesh from Jewish victims in order to assure their proper burial and prospects for resurrection.

Reform Judaism abandoned the resurrection doctrine in the nineteenth century, and Reconstructionist Judaism rejects it as well. However, the burning of corpses in crematoria in Nazi concentration camps has added a contemporary sense of horror to the notion of cremation for Jews, and most remain committed to burial in the earth.

kale^Y
kalleh^R
kolleh

Pronounced KOLL-*eh,* the way a Southerner might pronounce "collar," or to rhyme with either Walla in "Walla Walla."

Hebrew: "bride."

1. A bride; a recently married female.
2. A young married woman.
3. Your daughter-in-law (when you want to tease her).

A girl who is not yet married, or is ready to be married, is called a *kale moyd*—a "bride girl."

It is interesting to note that in old Babylonia, where *kale* meant "months of study," scholars would withdraw from the world for a "*kale* month"—that is, a month in which they would "remarry" the *Torah.*

See also khasene.

A follower of the great Hillel wrote: "Every bride is beautiful and graceful." (That's in the *Talmud.*)

"A bride with beautiful eyes need not worry about her figure." Hoshaia Zeera (died 350 C.E.) said that.

When something is exceptionally fortunate or felicitous, too good to be true, or when someone can't believe a stroke of great luck, a delightful comment is to be found in the saying "What's wrong? The *kale is tsu sheyn?*" ("Is the bride too beautiful?")

PROVERB: "A wise man, looking for a bride, should take an ignoramus along to advise him."

kalike^Y
kalikeh^R
kolyika

Pronounced KOL-*li-keh* or KOLL-*yi-keh,* to rhyme with "doll yucca." Russian and Polish: "cripple."

1. A cripple.
2. Someone who is sickly.
3. A clumsy person.
4. A stupid, ignorant man.
5. An inept performer: a singer off-key, a pianist who hits wrong notes, a waiter who spills the soup. "As a dancer (skater, laundress, barber, baritone, etc.), is he [she] a *kalike!*" *

*"Spaz" is a contemporary English equivalent to *kalike*—and just about as tasteful.

A *kalike* is often blood brother to a *shlemiel.*

Mrs. Rabinowitz was walking along 57th Street with six-year-old Genevieve. At the corner of Fifth Avenue, Genevieve sneezed.

"*Gezundheit,*" said her mother.

At the corner of Madison Avenue, Genevieve sneezed again.

"God bless you, sweetheart," said Mrs. Rabinowitz.

At the corner of Park Avenue, Genevieve sneezed twice.

Wham! went Mrs. Rabinowitz's palm against Genevieve's rear. "With all my other troubles, a *kalike* I've got!"

Mr. Katz fitted on the made-to-order suit and cried in dismay: "Look at this sleeve! It's two inches too long!"

"So stick out your elbow," said the tailor, "which bends your arm—and the sleeve is just right!"

"The collar! It's halfway up my head!"

"So raise your head up and back—and the collar goes down."

"But the left shoulder is two inches wider than the right!"

"So *bend*, this way, and it'll even out."

Mr. Katz left the tailor in this fantastic posture: right elbow stuck out wide, head far up and back, left shoulder tilted. A stranger accosted him. "Excuse me, but would you mind giving me the name of your tailor?"

"*My* tailor?" Katz cried. "Are you mad? Why would anyone want my tailor?"

"Because any man who can fit a *kalike* like you is a genius!"

kapore^Y
kaporeh^R
kapora

Pronounced *ka-POOR-eh*, to rhyme with "La Moora." Hebrew: "atonement," "expiatory sacrifice."

1. No good. "It is *oyf kapores*" means "It's good for nothing" or "It's a mess."
2. In a parlous state; in difficulties; sick. "He is *oyf kapores*" means "He is in trouble" or "He faces grave trouble."
3. "The devil with . . ." "The hell with . . ." "*A kapore* on the car; just so no one was hurt!"

4. Atonement by vicarious methods (the original meaning in Hebrew).

Very Orthodox Jews practice a ceremony known as *shlogn* (beating) *kapores* on the day before *Yom Kippur*. A fowl or (more often these days) a sum of money is offered to the poor, as a symbolic form of redemption for the life of the individual, and this prayer is said three times: "This be my substitute, my vicarious offering, my atonement. This [cock, hen] shall meet death, but I shall find a long and pleasant life of peace."

I have never seen the ceremony of *shlogn kapores,* which involves waving a rooster (!) over the head of someone whose sins are presumably passed on to the "scapegoat" fowl. My parents sighed and shook their heads over such "superstitious nonsense," such clearly "medieval *mishegas.*"

Rabbinical authorities in the Middle Ages opposed the practice, calling it pagan and foolish, but they were unsuccessful in their disapproval—for the frightened and the superstitious prevailed, as they, alas, so often do.*

---

*A second "superstitious" High Holy Day practice that rabbinic authorities frowned upon but failed to squelch is *tashlikh*, the "casting of sins" (represented by bread crumbs) onto flowing waters on the first day of *Rosh Hashanah*. Unlike the ceremony of *shlogn kapores,* which involves the very visceral killing of a rooster, *tashlikh* has made a notable comeback among Jews in recent years. Communal walks to the edges of rivers or streams have a feeling of a solemn parade, and the ceremony itself evokes a connection to nature that seems very relevant and affirming in this environmentally anxious age.

Tashlikh can also be adapted as a ceremony for renewing relationships. In my own family, we observe it by speaking praises of one another and enunciating hopes for growth in the coming year (each person, child or adult, takes a turn at speaking). We then make our "new year's resolutions" while throwing bread crumbs into the river.

Less idiosyncratic *tashlikh* practices include the recitation of scriptural verses (from Micah, Isaiah, and Psalms) and, in some communities, of readings from cabalistic texts.

Kapoyr
See Moyshe Kapoyr.

kaptsn[Y]
kabtzen[R]
kaptsonim (plural)

Pronounced KOP-*ts'n,* to rhyme with "Hopson." Hebrew: *kabotz,* "to collect." The plural is *kabtsonim (kop-*TSO-*nim),* and they will always be among us.

1. A pauper (literally; but the word is used as much for disdain as for **description**).*
2. One who does not amount to anything and never will.

"*Kaptsn!*" is often uttered with a sneer and is clearly a judgment about someone inferior or ineffectual. "Him pick up a check? He's a *kabtsn.*" "God forbid you should even think of marrying such a *kaptsn!*"

FOLK SAYING: "Poverty is no disgrace—which is the only good thing you can say about it."

---

*Rosten emphasizes the disdainful use of this word, but *kaptsn* translates to "pauper," not "bum," and the poignancy of "pauper" informs *kaptsn,* too. *Shnorrer* (beggar) might better be used to express scorn and condescension, as it expresses as much about attitude ("the world owes me a living") as livelihood. (See Rosten's entry for **shnorrer**.)

All words identifying people with their poverty can be used scornfully, of course, but the Jewish tradition strongly emphasizes the human dignity of all, regardless of economic status, and views wealth as a blessing from God, not as a personal achievement or status symbol. (See my comments on Rosten's entry for **pushke**.)

An ebullient *shadkhn* (matchmaker) brought his young male prospect to the home of a potential bride.

When they started homeward, the *shadkhn* said, "Well, was I exaggerating? Isn't that a doll of a girl? And can you imagine what a dowry she'll bring you? Did you see the furnishings in that house? The fine hangings? That collection of fine silver?!"

"But the father seemed awfully eager . . . ," said the young man uneasily.

"She has a dozen suitors!"

"The mother kept pushing, hinting . . ."

"She *likes* you!"

"For all I know, they even borrowed all that silver just to impress me!"

"*Borrowed* it?" cried the *shadkhn*. "Who would lend a nickel to such *kaptsonim?*"

Mendele Moykher Seforim ("Mendele the Bookseller"), pen name of Sholom Yankev Abramovitch (1836–1917), whom Sholom Aleichem dubbed *der zeyde* (the grandfather), of modern Yiddish literature, called one of his imaginary towns "Kabtsansk," or Pauperville.

FOLK SAYING: "A poor man has few enemies, but a rich one fewer friends."

"It's no disgrace to be poor, but it's no honor either."

"A full purse is not half as good as an empty one is bad."

A poor man found a wallet with ninety rubles in it. In the wallet was a name and address and this notice: "If found, return. Ten rubles reward."

The poor man rushed to the address, a fine home, where the *balebos* thanked him, counted the money, and said, "I see you have already removed ten rubles for your reward."

"I? No! Never! I swear it!"

The rich man sneered. "There were one hundred rubles in that wallet."

"I swear to you, on my mother's grave . . ."

At this point a rabbi entered. The poor man appealed to him, telling his tale. The rich man then told his and, slyly, ended: "So whom will you believe, *Rebbe*, that *kabtsn* or me?"

"You, of course." And the rabbi took the wallet from the rich man and gave it to the *kabtsn*.

"Rabbi, what are you doing?" cried the rich man.

"I'm taking you at your word," said the rabbi. "You said your wallet contained one hundred rubles. This man says the wallet he found contained only ninety. Therefore, this wallet can't be yours."

"But I—what of my money?"

"We must wait," said the rabbi with a smile, "until someone finds a wallet with one hundred rubles in it."

kashe^Y
kasheh^R
kasha

Pronounced KOSH-*eh*, to rhyme with "pasha." This word has two distinct derivations and two distinct families of meanings.

1. From Russian: *kasha*, "porridge."

In Yiddish, *kashe* (commonly spelled *kasha*) can mean buckwheat groats or a cooked **cereal;** * but it also means a mixed-up, difficult, irksome confusion—a "rhubarb" (in sports lingo). Anyone who causes confusion is said to have "cooked up a *kashe*."

2. From Hebrew: *kasheh*, "difficult."

This has come to mean, by extension, a question.

A person may come to a rabbi with a *kashe* about some aspect of keeping a *kosher* kitchen.

A child in the "why" stage will ask *kashes* until parents lose their minds.

A young Talmudist may try to stump his teacher with a casuistic challenge to an argument. "That's quite a *kashe*," might be his reply; or, "What kind of *kashe* is that?" (not so good-humored).

On *Pesach* (Passover), the youngest child at the *seder* asks the *Fir* (pronounced "fear") *Kashes*, the "Four Questions."

Weinstein and his son were taking a walk.

"Papa," asked the boy, "what's the highest mountain on earth?"

---

*Kashe varnishkes, a concoction of roasted buckwheat groats and bow tie pasta, often served with mushroom sauce, is a favorite lunch or dinner dish in Jewish and Ukrainian restaurants.

"I don't know."

A little later, the boy asked, "Who was the king who followed Napoleon?"

Weinstein scratched his head. "I don't know."

And a little later, the boy asked, "Why does the moon always have the same side facing us?"

"*Oy,*" sighed Weinstein. "I don't know . . ." Then, seeing the expression on the boy's face, he quickly added, "Ask, ask *kashes!* How else will you learn?"

kashrut
See kosher.

keyn eynhore[Y]
kayn aynhoreh[R]
kineahora, keinahora

Pronounced *kane-ane-*HAW*-reh,* or *kine-ine-*HAW*-reh,* or, more quickly, *kine-a-*HAW*-reh,* rhyming respectively with "lame Dame Dora,""fine line Laura," "Dinah Cora." From German: *kein,* "no," "not one"; and Hebrew: *ayin ha-rah,* "the evil eye." The *kein* and *ayin* have blended into one Yiddish word, *keyn* or *kayn.*

1. The magical phrase "No evil eye," uttered to ward off ill fortune—a reflex of mumbo jumbo employed to protect a child or loved one.

2. The phrase uttered to show that one's praises are genuine and not contaminated by envy—"That man is an angel, *keyn eynhore* [or *kineahora*]."

Our ancestors, Jew and *goy* alike, were constantly fearful of tempting the gods to anger; man's hubris, his boastings, his very successes, ran the risk of offending some god and boomeranging into disaster. An envious, jealous mortal could cast an evil spell on another's luck—or health. *Keyn eynhore* or *kineahora* was articulated to thwart such demons.

Jewish women, especially, employed the rubric *keyn eynhore* in contexts such as these: "My child? In perfect health, *keyn eynhore*." ["Thank God."] "We should only live, *kineahora*, to see that day." "My son? First in his class, *keyn eynhore*."

Virtually all people, and all religions, hold uneasy ideas about the cacodemons who operate through the "evil eye." Demonic spirits, diabolic ghosts, and evil sprites abound everywhere—and are thought to "come out" through the eye. So mothers would drop a little salt and a crumb into a child's pocket, to protect it— presumably to feed any goblins who came along. Little girls sometimes wore beads, as a necklace or bracelet, to ward off evil spirits.

Not all evil eyers were malevolent, incidentally; some were believed to be virtuous mortals to whom the powers of the supernatural had been given. (Simeon bar Yochai was believed to have the awesome power of reducing evil people to instant bones with one mordant look. Other learned men were credited with incendiary—"blazing"—eyesight.)

Back in the fourth century, a Catholic ecclesiastical council in Spain issued a canon announcing that no Jew would be allowed to stand in a field that belonged to a Christian—because a Jew's mere glance was so fiendish that it could wither an entire crop. Of such madness is the story of the human race compounded. (For an analysis of medieval conceptions of the Jew, and their influences on later anti-Semitism, see Joshua Trachtenberg's *The Devil and the Jews,* 1966.)

Envy and the evil eye are closely linked in popular mythology. The malignant forces of darkness are believed especially to covet any beautiful, bright, talented child; hence, elaborate magical methods were enlisted by mothers in the effort to protect their beloved young. From this came the swift and automatic formula *keyn eynhore*, uttered by a Jewish mother immediately after anyone chanced to comment on her child's graces or virtues.

The Chinese, incidentally, seek to outwit the demons by loudly announcing that a pretty girl is ugly or a bright lad stupid. And a well-educated Greek friend of mine periodically stuffs garlic into his pockets to ward off the *kalikantzaroi*, certain cloven-footed demons who are said to inhabit certain islands, on one of which he was born.

In the Bronx, if you overpraise someone or call attention to his good fortune, the recipient may blurt: "Don't give me a canary!"

Originally this ran, "Don't put the *keyn eynhore* [evil eye] on me."

A Jewish patriarch was on the witness stand.

"How old are you?" asked the district attorney.

"I am, *keyn eynhore*, eighty-one."

"What was that?"

"I said, 'I am, *keyn eynhore*, eighty-one.'"

"Just answer the question!" said the DA sharply. "Nothing else. Now, how old are you?"

"*Keyn eynhore*, eighty-one," said the old man.

Now the judge said, "The witness will answer the question and *only* the question, without additional comment, or be held in contempt of court."

Up rose the counsel for the defense. "Your Honor, may I ask the question? ...." He turned to the old man. "*Keyn eynhore*, how old are you?"

Said the old man, "Eighty-one."

khaloshes[Y]
chaloshes[R]

Pronounced *khol-*LAW*-shess* by *Litvaks,* to rhyme with "a cautious," and *kha-*LOO*-shess* by *Poles,* to rhyme with "achoo, sis." From the Hebrew: *holosh,* "weak." Used in Yiddish to mean "faint" (*faln in khaloshes,* to fall in a faint).

A revolting, disgusting, or loathsome thing—whether in food, drink, or conduct, whether visible or ethical.

" A *khaloshes!*" is an eloquent way of describing revulsion, disgust, or powerful umbrage. "The meal was a *khaloshes* to eat." "The movie? Sheer *khaloshes!*" "The speech he made? It was a *khaloshes* to listen to such tripe."

Mrs. Fleischman was checking out of Rosenbaum's Riviera Spa, in the Catskills.

"Did you enjoy your stay?" asked the owner.

"Well, to tell the truth, the food you serve here—it's terrible. A *khaloshes!* . . . And such small portions!"

khalutz[Y]
chalutz[R]
halutz
khalutzim (plural)

Pronounced KHA*-lootz* (with the guttural *kh*), to rhyme with "ma loots," or KHU*-lootz,* to rhyme with "the foots"; *kha-*LOOTZ*-im.* Hebrew: "pioneer."

1. Pioneer; a pioneer in any sphere of endeavor.

2. More particularly: A young man or woman who went to Palestine (today, Israel) to settle the land.

The *khalutzim* lived under the most primitive conditions, built roads, drained swamps, planted trees, reclaimed soil and desert that had been uncultivated for centuries. Many of them lived cooperatively in *kibbutzim*.

Many *khalutzim* were well-educated Europeans who gave up professional careers in order to "live their ideal: to build *Zion*" with the sweat of their brow and the toil of their hands. In the early years of the twentieth century they were considered the elite of Palestine, and from their ranks came many of the leaders of the new state of Israel. Today, they enjoy a status equivalent to that of our Pilgrims, "came over on the *Mayflower*," DAR (Daughters of the American Revolution).

See kibbutz.

khasene^Y
chasseneh^R
chaussen, chossen, hassen

Pronounced KHOSS-*se-neh,* with the Yiddish or MacGregor *kh,* not the *ch* of "chocolate." Hebrew: "wedding."
  Wedding.

This is not the place to describe, discuss, and analyze all of the ceremonies of a Jewish wedding, but a few aspects that please or impress me may interest you:*

*For an egalitarian blending of Jewish tradition and contemporary Jewish practice, see Anita Diamant's very popular guidebook, *The New Jewish Wedding* (Fireside, 2001).

It is obligatory for wedding guests to praise the bride and extol her beauties to the groom: to avoid hypocrisy (and pain, to plain or homely girls), the *Talmud* rabbis decreed, with peerless sagacity: "Every bride is beautiful—and graceful."

Every Jewish bride, however poor, wore a wedding gown and had a trousseau: a collection in the community insured that.

During the marriage ceremony, the groom consecrates the bride with these words: "Thou art consecrated to me according to the law of Moses and Israel." Traditionally, the bride has nothing at all to say during the ceremony! (Is she speechless with joy, or panic?)

It is traditional for the groom to give the bride a simple ring, unadorned with stones and decorations; the rabbis wanted to minimize the differences between the wealthy and the poor.

For a *khasene*, a rabbi and a formal religious service may be waived, by Talmudic dictum, under certain conditions: I have always loved the story of the Jew on a desert isle who wed himself to a woman and made Heaven and Earth his witnesses: "I call upon Heaven and Earth to witness that I consecrated you as my wife, according to the laws of Moses and of Israel."

FOLK SAYINGS:

"An old maid who gets married becomes a young wife."

"Parents can give a dowry, but not good luck."

"A groom and a bride have glass eyes." (They can see no faults in each other.)

"Early to rise and early to wed does no harm."

"One can't dance with one behind at two weddings."

"Dance at every wedding and you'll cry at every funeral."

khas vesholem^Y
chas vesholem^R
has vesholem

Pronounced KHAHS *ve-*SHO-*lem,* to rhyme with "joss the
tow men." Please clear your throat with that *kh.* Hebrew:
"God forbid." Literally: pity and peace.
"God forbid."

This phrase is used as a magical invocation to ward off any evil
spirit or undesired happenstance. "Be careful or you'll break
a leg, *khas vesholem.*"

The phrase also appears as *khas vekholila* (KHAHSS *ve-kho-*LEE-
la); literally: "pity" and "far be it from coming to pass."

The simple *kholile* is a short synonym.

khaver
See chaver.

khazer
See chozzer.

khazeray
See chozzerai.

kheyder
See cheder.

khlyape^Y
chloppeh^R
khlyapen^Y (infinitive verb)

Pronounced KHLYOP-*peh*, with the *ly* sound as in "million"—that is, a Castilian *ll*. From the Russian: "knock," "bang," "clap."

To rain in torrents; to pour down "in buckets." "It's *khlyapping* like a tropical storm." "She did not cry—she *khlyapped.*"

khmalye^Y
chmallyeh^R

Pronounced with a strong opening Scottish *kh* sound: KHMOLL-*yeh*, to rhyme with "Kh-doll ya." From Slavic.

A severe blow; a clout with the hand. "Did he give me a *khmalye!*"

Khmalye usually conveys the idea that the force of the blow was excessive or unjust.

khokhem^Y
chachem^R
haham, chacham

Pronounced KHAW-*khem* with two reverberating Scottish *kh*'s. The use of *two* uvular fricatives need not intimidate you: no word will more swiftly establish you as one who knows Yiddish. The plural is *khakhomim,* pronounced *kha*-KHUM-*im.*

Hebrew: "wise."

1. A clever, wise, or learned man or woman.

A *khokhem* is one who possesses or displays *khokhme,* wisdom. A *khokhem* is a savant, an expert, a brilliant mind, a person of learning and profundity. This person need *not* be an intellectual: many a cobbler or butcher, barber or vendor, was known as a *khokhem.* Some *khakhomim* were artisans *and* intellectuals. (Even many of the Talmudic sages toiled in humble occupations.)

A top the Jewish pyramid of respect stands the scholar—not, be it noted, the ruler, the conqueror, the prince, the millionaire, or even the rabbi, but the scholar. (A rabbi can, of course, be a great scholar, but scholars were loftier than rabbis.) Power, wealth, honors, prizes, social status—none of these was as respected as learning, which meant learning in *Talmud.*

Jewish mothers sang a lullaby of hope that the little son in the cradle might become that most glorious of men: wise, learned, a— mirabile dictu!—*khokhem.*

The first bright sayings of a child are hailed by ecstatic grandparents as *khokhmes.* It is promptly forecast that the babe will grow up to be a real *khokhem*—that is, profound, learned, virtuous.

The *Zohar,* a mystical thirteenth-century work, part of the cabalistic *Book of Creation*, defines the *khokhem* this way: "What does a fool see? A man's clothes. What does the *khokhem* see? A man's spirit."

The *Talmud*'s Pirkey Avos, or "Ethics of the Fathers," says: "In whom wisdom is—in him is everything. In whom wisdom is not—what has he? And he who has acquired wisdom—what can he lack?"

A *khokhem* is not the highest of *khakhomim*, please notice. That paragon is a *talmid khokhem*.

2. Used sarcastically: A fool, a wise guy; one who tries to be clever but suffers a downfall.

K*hokhem* is also used sarcastically, to indicate one who, pretending astuteness, does something absurd, foolish, disastrous.

"Some *khokhem!*" drips irony: it may be loosely rendered as "What a jerk."

A young *khokhem* told his grandmother that he was going to become a doctor of philosophy. The *bubbe* smiled proudly: "Wonderful. But what kind of disease is 'philosophy'?"

Kessler was awakened from a deep sleep by his wife, who nudged him again and again, saying, "Get *up*, Max. I'm freezing, close the window. It's cold outside!"

"*Khokhem!*" sighed Max. "And if I close the window, will it be warm outside?"

A Jewish merchant was returning to his small town, after having spent a week in the big city. Opposite him, in the train, sat a young stranger. The merchant, a gregarious soul, promptly introduced himself: "My name is Mandelbaum."

"My name," said the young man, "is Horowitz."

They shook hands.

"And where are you going, Mr. Horowitz?"

"To Glens Falls."

"Glens Falls? Well, what do you know? That's where I'm going. That's where I live!" Mandelbaum eyed the young man carefully. "Tell me, are you—married?"

"No," said Horowitz.

"Maybe—a salesman?"

"No."

"Are you going on business?"

"No," said Horowitz. "It's a social visit."

"Er—you have maybe relatives in Glens Falls?"

"No," said Horowitz.

Aha! thought Mandelbaum, every inch the *khokhem,* and proceeded to reason thuswise: He's going to Glens Falls, he's not married, he's not a salesman, and he has no relatives there. So why is he going? Obviously, to meet a girl—to meet her family, maybe to confirm an engagement. But who is the girl? To the Rabinowitzes this young man can't be going, because the Rabinowitzes have only one daughter, who was married six years ago. To the Plotniks? Nonsense! The Plotniks have two sons and no daughter. Perhaps the Arkins? But the Arkin girl is only seventeen; too young to get married, her father would never let her. Aha! The Mishnicks! No, because the Mishnick girl is already engaged to the son (the good-looking one) of Melnick, the tailor. Perhaps to the Bubricks? *Nya!* The Bubrick girl is at least thirty, has given up hopes of getting married, and anyway is visiting her aunt in Providence. The Shulmans! But the Shulmans' unmarried daughter is at college and doesn't come home until Passover, so she wouldn't be in Glens Falls now. The Feiffers? No, the Feiffers are rich and stuck-up; they would never let their daughter marry anyone but a rich young man—and this one, though very nice, is wearing an inexpensive suit and riding in the coach car, so he's not well-off, so the Feiffers are out. . . . The Hollanders? The Hollander girl is getting married next week to that *shlemiel* of a dentist from White Plains. The Pincuses? Sure! The Pincuses have *three* girls, all marriageable: Shirley, Ruth, and Helen. . . . But Shirley is a good twenty pounds overweight and this young man is good-looking enough to be able to pick and choose. Ruth? Ruth is a widow—young, pretty, but still a widow, and with a two-year-old child! Helen? Helen! There's a gay young thing, with mischief in her eyes, and only last week she went to the city for a weekend—

With a broad grin, Mandelbaum stuck his hand out: "Horowitz, let me be the first to congratulate you!"

"Congratulate me?" Horowitz blinked.

"On your forthcoming marriage to Miss Helen Pincus!"

As Mandelbaum pumped his hand, the young man stammered, "But—we have told no one, not even her parents. How did you find out?"

"How did I find out?" echoed Mandelbaum. "It's obvious!"

khokhme^Y
chachma^R
hachma, hochma, hochme, chochma

Pronounced KHAWKH-*meh*, rattling those two *kh*'s with uvular abandon, the way an Edinburghian would. Hebrew: "wisdom."

1. The divine spirit of Wisdom, which, according to the *Midrash*, existed long before the creation of the world and was the blueprint and ground plan for the creation.

(This resembles the Christian mystical use of *Logos*, the word, as in John I: "In the beginning was the Word, and the Word was with God, and the Word was God.")

2. A wise, profound, or astute saying.

3. The reservoir of erudite, wise, philosophical knowledge. And, since Jews are fond of paradox, knowing life to be full of it.

4. A jocular or clever remark.

5. A tricky, wily, cleverly concealed ruse, tactic, or arrangement.

6. Derisive: A foolish move or performance.

A *khokhme* is the product of a *khokhem*, obviously—though occasionally even an unlearned and unbrilliant man can come up with something so illuminating that one can call it a *khokhme*.

In Jewish thought, wisdom is not the fruit of intellect or knowledge alone; wisdom involves basic moral and character attributes: the highest *khokhme* lies in being righteous and spreading lovingkindness. Knowledge makes it possible for man to enter a state of grace in which true virtue, "doing good," can be practiced.

"Money can buy anything—except sense."

To the Jews, wisdom without love of man was a contradiction in terms. "The highest form of wisdom is kindness," goes an old proverb quoted by Jews.

Occasionally, *khokhme* is used to describe tricks, subterfuges, clever evasions, unrevealed meanings, or wily, casuistic hocus-pocus. If you want to cut through legalisms and double-talk, if you want something said plainly, say, "Now let's have it without *khokhme*."

Just as "wise" in English became the root for "wise guy," so *khokhme* became a scathing name for a gaffe, a faux pas, a bit of folly or stupidity.

During a frightful storm at sea, the captain asked one of the passengers, a professional magician, to distract the frightened passengers. The magician gave a dazzling performance: made cards disappear and scarves turn into flags and, for a desperate finale, presented a parrot who, he announced, "will now perform the greatest feat of magic in the history of prestidigitation!"

All eyes turned to the parrot. Drums rolled, trumpets blew— and suddenly a tremendous wave smashed the ship in two. The passengers found themselves thrashing in the water—including an old Jew who, hanging on to a plank for dear life, saw the parrot floating by. And to the parrot, the old man bitterly said, with a *"hoo-ha!"* inflection: *"Khokhme!"*

A Jew runs frantically into a railway station. Just as he gets to the track, the train pulls out. The Jew stops, looks after it, and sneers, *"Khokhme!"*

kholile[Y]
cholilleh[R]
chalileh, kholileh

Pronounced *kholl-ILL-eh*, to rhyme with "Moll Willa." From the Hebrew: "May it not come to pass" or "God forbid." Literally, it means "Far be it . . ." and appears in Genesis 18:25, when Abraham was enjoining God not to destroy Sodom.

1. A common magical expression for "God forbid that should happen," uttered promptly before and after some dire prediction, fear, or possibility; an automatic incantation, descended from varieties of hocus-pocus, enlisted to circumvent the wrath of the gods, the

malevolence of spooks, or the ubiquitous evil eye. "Be careful crossing the street you shouldn't *kholile* be hit by a car." "If a lunatic should *kholile* be elected president . . ." (My mother seemed to think "I hope he doesn't *kholile* get sick" was more efficacious, as a calamity preventer, than "I hope he doesn't get sick *kholile*"— apparently because the *kholile* precedes the naming of the calamity; there's no accounting for abracadabra.)

2. A tongue-in-cheek expression affecting dismay over a possible and desired happenstance: "If I should *kholile* become a millionaire . . ." "If my daughter *kholile* marries that wonderful boy . . ."

When the English and French governments opened the bidding for the digging of the great tunnel under the English Channel, engineering firms from all over the world placed their bids. And the lowest bid was from the firm of Marantz and Son.

Friends congratulated Marantz. "That's wonderful. How are you going to build the tunnel?"

"It's easy," said Marantz. "I'll start digging on the English side, and my son will start on the French side. And we'll dig and dig until we meet."

"But Marantz," an engineer protested, "don't you realize that one of the hardest problems in all of engineering—one that has stumped some of our finest scientists—is the problem of getting two tunnels to meet!"

"What do you mean, 'meet'?"

"I mean that the tunnel you start in England, and the tunnel your son starts in France—they start miles and miles apart, and they must come together exactly! What if *kholile* they don't?"

Marantz shrugged. "So the client will get two tunnels for the price of one."

Two Jews decided to kill Hitler. They bought revolvers and concealed themselves in the doorway of a building they knew Hitler was due to visit. Hour after hour, with beating hearts, they waited. Finally, one assassin turned to the other and whispered, "I hope nothing happened to him, *kholile.*"

kholyere^Y
choleria^R
kholerye

Pronounced *kho*-LYEH-*reh,* with a rattling uvular *kho* to lead off; rhymes with "Salieri." From Latin, into Slavic: "plague," "cholera."

1. A curse: "To hell with . . ."

One of the juicy curses, a *kholyere* meant "a plague upon you" and whatever additional disasters the wisher could conjure up. "A *kholyere* should possess him!" "A man like that—a *kholyere* on him!"

2. A hellcat of a woman, a termagant, a hellion, a virago, a nag of a woman who is exceptionally mean. "He is married to a *kholyere.*" "That *kholyere* will drive him to either suicide or murder."

khosn^Y
chassen^R

Pronounced KHAW-*sen*, to rhyme with "Lawson," or KHU-*sen*, to rhyme with "you, son." From the Hebrew; originally, "celebrant," "bridegroom"; also, "son-in-law."

1. Bridegroom.
2. The groom-to-be.
3. Occasionally: guest of honor; man of the hour.

G reat pressure is exerted, in a religious Jewish community, for every young man to get married (in the old country, before the age of eighteen). An unmarried man is looked upon askance: such a one is selfish, insensitive to his duty, perhaps a bit *meshuge*, indubitably antisocial. He is even something of a sinner, for he is evading the responsibility to "multiply," as God commanded; he is failing to perpetuate life itself; he fails to honor the solemn debt that attends the gift of having been born; he misses the chance to provide himself with a *Kaddish* who will mourn his death and honor his name.

An unmarried man is also regarded as derelict in his duty to Jewry—for who knows what learned sons, what marvelous *talmid khokhemim*, he might have sired?

In so emphatic, consistent, and homogeneous a consensus was born the useful, if quixotic, institution of the professional matchmaker. (See shadkhn.)

Long, long before Freud, the Jews had this saying: "When a son gets married, he divorces his mother."

khupe
See chuppa.

kibbutz
kibbutzim (plural)

Pronounced *kib*-BUTZ, with the *u* as in "puts," not "cuts." Hebrew: "collective," "group." Plural: *kibbutzim* (*kibbutz-IM*).

A coooperative settlement of farmers in Israel. (Do not confuse *kibbutz* with *kibitz*, even though every *kibbutz* probably has its *kibitzers*.)

Under the leadership of Edmond de Rothschild and Maurice de Hirsch, a Jewish Colonization Association was organized in 1899 to establish *kvutzot* in Palestine—the predecessors of the *kibbutzim*.

The *kibbutzim* of Israel have won international respect for the courage, idealism, and perseverance of their members, Jews from all parts of the world, who elected to live the extremely hard and dangerous life of settlers, in pioneer conditions, in Palestine. The *kibbutzim* played a central part in Israel's defenses, for many were established near the frontiers of the surrounding Arab states.

Kibbutzim are farm collectives* based on the ideals of Zionism, mutual aid, individual labor, and socialism. They vary greatly in size, degree of mechanization, details of authority, ownership,

*Kibbutzim have greatly diversified their economies during the past thirty years while enduring hard times. Current enterprises include the manufacture of electrochemical tools (Kibbutz Nahal Oz), cutlery (Kibbutz Nir Am), educational games (Kibbutz Regavim), textiles and jewelry (Kibbutz Urim), spices (Kibbutz Sde Eliyahu), electronic parts (Kibbutz Ein Hashofet), and much more. Other *kibbutz* undertakings include tourism, forestry, fisheries, and education. *Kibbutzim* are also no longer confined to the countryside: at least three urban *kibbutzim* have been launched successfully in Israel since the 1980s. As a whole, however, the *kibbutz* movement has been devastated in recent years by debt, attrition, deregulation, and the loss of both markets and idealism.

profit sharing. They have been studied intensively by economists, agronomists, social psychologists, and educators from **all over the world;**† their structure has been adopted in many of the underdeveloped countries of Africa and (less often) Asia. There is a Japanese Kibbutz Association, and some eighty Japanese students have worked in *kibbutzim* in Israel.

The pioneers who live on the *kibbutz* are called *khalutzim.*

Kibbutzim are no longer increasing in number. As living standards in Israel rise, there has been a decline of enthusiasm for the extremely hard and simple life of the *kibbutzim.* There is also an increasing desire on the part of young Israelis to leave the *kibbutz* for cities, superior schools, and broader opportunities.

kibitz^R
kibits^Y
kibbitz

Pronounced KIB-*its,* to rhyme with "Tibbets." From German: *Kiebitz,* "lapwing" and "spectator at card game." (Do not confuse with *kibbutz.*)

1. To comment while watching a game. "I was *kibitzing,* not playing."
2. To joke, fool around, wisecrack; to socialize aimlessly. "We were *kibitzing* around."
3. To tease, needle, gibe, second-guess. "Don't *kibitz;* he's sensitive" (Don't needle, tease, or "ride" him).
4. To carry on a running commentary while another is

---

† *Kibbutzim* are still being actively studied at the University of Haifa's Institute for Research on the Kibbutz and the Cooperative Idea, which serves also as a clearinghouse for *kibbutz*-related publications.

working. "He was *kibitzing* us all the way" (advising, second-guessing, criticizing). "He's not employed there, he just *kibitzes*."

See kibitzer.

It has been said that when you tell a joke to a German, he laughs. When you tell it to an Englishman, he laughs twice: when he hears it and when he understands it. When you tell it to a Frenchman, he laughs three times: when you tell it, when he recalls it, and when he repeats it.

But when you tell a joke to a Jew, he interrupts to say he's heard it before—then he tells it to you in an "improved" (i.e., his) version.

It has also been said that in this sense, at least, every Jew likes to *kibitz*.

kibitzer ᴿ
kibitser ʸ
kibbitzer

Pronounced KIB-*itz-er,* to rhyme with "Lib hits 'er." From the German name for a bird, the *Kiebitz* (Latin name: *vanellus*), a lapwing or peewit, reputed to be especially noisy and inquisitive, and called, colloquially, *Kibitzer*. Staunch Yiddishists seem to forget that in German *kieb-itzen* means to look over the shoulder of a card player.

1. Someone who *kibitzes*—that is, gives unasked-for advice or suggestions, especially as a bystander-observer at a game (bridge, poker, checkers, chess).
2. Someone who butts into the affairs of others, sticks in his nose or his "two cents."
3. Someone who joshes or teases.
4. Someone who flatters.
5. Someone who humors one along.

*K*ibitzers are rarely knowledgeable or respected; if they were, they would be advisers, not *kibitzers*. "What are you—a *kibitzer*?" (a wise guy who doesn't participate but offers easy advice). "As a poker player, he's a good *kibitzer*" (second-guesses better than he plays; better as a cocky bystander than as a player). "As a worker, he's a fine *kibitzer*" (talks more than he works; puts on airs). "I'm afraid it's a slipped disk, and that *kibitzer* tells me one good cha-cha will get me back in shape." "Oh, stop your *kibitzing!*" (He has carried flattery beyond credibility.)

Jablonsky sent up a cry of rapture when he won first prize at a lottery.

A *kibitzer* asked him, "What made you pick a number like sixty-three, anyway?"

"It came to me in a dream!" cried Jablonsky. "I dreamed I was in a theater, and on the stage was a chorus of sevens—each dancer a number seven, in a line, exactly eight sevens long! So I chose sixty-three."

"But eight times seven is fifty-six, not sixty-three!"

Jablonsky chortled, "So okay, *you* be the mathematician!"

The play *The Kibitzer*, by Jo Swerling (1929), made both the title and its star, Edward G. Robinson, famous overnight.

The sign on the door read:

DR. JOSEPH KIPNIS——PSYCHIATRIST

DR. ELI LOWITZ——PROCTOLOGIST

Under this, a *kibitzer* had written:

"Specialists in Odds and Ends."

With great pride, Benjamin Bernstein painted himself a sign to hang over his store:

FRESH FISH

SOLD HERE

DAILY

As Bernstein placed the ladder to hang up the sign, a *kibitzer* sang out, "What kind of *cockamamy* sign is that?"

"Why? What's wrong with it?"

"'*Fresh* fish,' Bernstein? It would never occur to your customers that you sell fish that *aren't* fresh—unless you advertise it!"

"You're right." Bernstein took his brush and painted out "Fresh."

"Wait!" said the *kibitzer*. "What about 'Sold'? Obviously you sell fish; you don't give them away free."

Mr. Bernstein painted out "Sold" and said, "Okay?"

"No, why 'Here'? Obviously, you don't sell fish over *there*. . . ."

"You're right!" And Bernstein painted out "Here."

"That leaves 'Daily,'" said the *kibitzer*. "I ask you, is that smart? If fish are fresh, they *must* come in and go out daily. Right?"

"Absolutely!" Bernstein crossed out "Daily," leaving a sign that read only:

FISH

"Perfect," said the *kibitzer*.

Now Bernstein started up the ladder, when along came another *kibitzer*.

"Why are you putting up that ridiculous sign?"

"What's wrong with it?"

"You don't have to put up any sign, Bernstein. *Your* fish everyone smells a mile away!"

So Bernstein put up no sign at all, thinking how lucky he was to have friends of such uncommon acumen.

kibosh

Pronounced KY-*bosh*, to rhyme with "my gosh." **Derivation: mysterious.***

1. Nonsense, "bosh" (when used as a noun; this was the nineteenth-century usage).
2. "To put the *kibosh* on," which is the way the word is used today, means to arrange things so that something will not occur; to put an end to something; to "jinx" something so that it will fail or not take place; to spoil, impair, squelch, or veto. "His decision put the *kibosh* on all our hopes and plans."

Is *kibosh* of Yiddish extraction? Good question.

• *The Oxford Dictionary of English Etymology*, edited by C. T.

---

*The origins of *kibosh* remain mysterious, while its popularity in usage persists. On the Internet, over two thousand Web sites currently use the word, some speculating about its origins (often referencing Leo Rosten). The 1997 film for children, *Casper: A Spirited Beginning*, featured the voice of James Earl Jones as Kibosh, the dictatorial director of Ghost Central Station.

Onions (1966), says *kibosh* is of uncertain origin. Dickens used *kibosh* back in 1856, the word at that time meaning "nonsense" or "bosh."

- *Webster's Unabridged Dictionary*, third edition (1966), says that *kibosh's* ancestry is unknown.
- *The Oxford English Dictionary* laconically says that *kibosh* is of "heraldic" origin—which is no help.
- Eric Partridge, in his *Dictionary of Slang and Unconventional English* (1961), agrees with the *OED* (above) but says that "to put the *kibosh* on," meaning to seal the doom of, comes from Yiddish. Why, I don't know; he offers no evidence.
- Padraic Colum, the Irish poet, asserts that *kibosh* comes from Irish Gaelic *cie báis*, meaning "cap of death." (*Báis* is pronounced "bawsh" in Gaelic.)
- In *Phrase and Word Origins*, Alfred H. Holt says that a "Mr. Loewe, who ought to know," traces *kibosh* to a Yiddish word "formed from four consonants, representing eighteen-pence. When, at a small auction, an eager bidder jumped his offer to eighteen-pence, he was said to have 'put the *kibosh*' on his fellow-bidders."

But I have not the faintest notion what those "four consonants" could be or why they represented "eighteen-pence."

(One suggestion is that *kibosh* is an acronym composed of the initial letters of three Yiddish words for "18 British coins." In Hebrew, *chai* was often used to signify 18; the *sh* might be the initial sound of the word *shekel*; but this linguistic reconstruction falls down on the "b" sound. It might stand for "British," but would not the acronym then be "ki*b*rosh?" The number 18 possessed magical properties, since the letter equivalents formed the word *life*. Thus, by extension, its use could presumably put the "hex" on an opponent.)

• *Webster's New World Dictionary of the American Language* says of *kibosh:* "earlier . . . *kybosh,* prob. Yid.?," which puts it indecisively and proceeds to cite Germanic possibilities I find no more impressive. (Why should *kiebe,* which means "carrion" in Middle High German, lead to *kibosh?*)

• H. L. Mencken records the fact that *kibosh* was included in a glossary of about 125 Americanisms that were added to Sinclair Lewis's *Babbitt* when it was published in England in 1922. But Mencken did not stick his neck out anent *kibosh*'s parentage (see *The American Language,* Knopf, 1962).

• William and Mary Morris, in their *Dictionary of Word and Phrase Origins* (1962), repeat the Yiddish-origin and Gaelic-origin attributions of this tantalizing word and conclude that *kibosh* has "according to H. L. Mencken, been widely used in America for more than a century."

• The admirably comprehensive *American Thesaurus of Slang,* by Berry and Van den Bark (1943), includes several uses of *kibosh* and even gives us a noun I never heard of, *kiboshery,* meaning "nonsense."

• Julian Franklyn, author of *A Dictionary of Rhyming Slang* (1960), suggests that *kibosh* originated in the heraldic *caboshed* or *caboched.*

Now, why do I bother you with this *megillah,* for a word that may not come from Yiddish at all?

- Because I always assumed that *kibosh* had a Jewish mother or father: it sounds mighty close to the name of a Hungarian or Romanian card game, *Kalabariasz* (mispronounced *Klabiotch* by Jews) I used to see old men play when I was a boy.
- I want to give you one little example of the prolonged, irksome, frustrating, and unbelievable *tsores* to which a writer subjects himself when he rashly undertakes to write a book such as this.

kichel ^R
kikhl ^Y

Pronounced KIKH-*el,* with a Germanic *kh.* The German root is probably *kochen,* "to cook."

A small, plain cookie.

This unpretentious little biscuit has been present at Jewish celebrations for hundreds of years. The current style of elaborate *bar mitzvas* and weddings has upstaged the *kichel,* but at less pretentious festivities guests still wish the hosts well with a glass of wine or *shnaps* and a *kichel.*

Kichelekh are made of unsweetened dough with a high egg content that makes the little cookies puff up. They may be baked plain or with a **sprinkling of sugar.***

*Bakeries that still produce *kichel* usually twist the dough into a bow tie shape (some varieties have a thin crust of apricot or other-flavored jam) or create a large, flat *kichel* pancake, about a foot in diameter.

Kiddush

Pronounced KID-*ish,* to rhyme with "Yiddish." Hebrew: "sanctification." (Do not confuse with *Kaddish.*)

The prayer and ceremony that sanctifies the Sabbath and Jewish holy days.

The *Kiddush* is recited before the Friday night Sabbath dinner begins, over a goblet or cup of wine. It begins with a recitation of Genesis 2:1–3, which tells how God rested on the seventh day of creation and made it holy. Two *brokhes* (blessings) follow: the first praising God for having created wine; the second thanking the Lord for having created the holy Sabbath "as an inheritance, a memorial of the Creation" and "in remembrance of the **departure from Egypt.**"†

†The traditional *Kiddush* blessing includes the Jewish doctrine of the "Chosen People"—"For You have chosen us," says the blessing, "and hallowed us above all nations. . . ." This biblically rooted concept of Jewish "election" by God has been broadly interpreted through the ages. In some strands of the Jewish tradition (Chasidic, medieval, cabalistic, Orthodox), "chosenness" is fundamentally qualitative: the Jews are seen as specially gifted, holy, soulful, and key to the fate of humankind. (The folk version of this interpretation simply *kvells* over the disproportionate number of Jewish Nobel laureates and world-historic intellectuals.) People of any race or ethnicity can convert to Judaism and gain this special status; nevertheless, given the prevalence of racialist thinking during the past three centuries (during which time the Jews themselves were widely viewed and persecuted as a "race"), the "Chosen People" doctrine has often smacked of racism to an unsophisticated world.

In more liberal and universalistic strands of the Jewish tradition, "chosenness" has been interpreted more as an ideal, a role model identity to which Jews should aspire—or simply as an honorific that the Jews have earned by expediting the religious evolution of humankind.

The Reconstructionist movement is unique among Jewish denominations in excising the "Chosen People" doctrine from the *Kiddush* and all other prayers.

Writing after the Holocaust had destroyed a third of the world's Jews, Yiddish poet Kadia Molodowsky (1894–1975) addressed the "Chosen People" doctrine most poignantly: "O God of Mercy," she wrote, "For the time being / Choose another people."

All those at the table share in the *Kiddush* wine.

Some Jews recite the *Kiddush* without wine, using the *challah* loaf instead—for the rabbis long ago realized that thousands of Jews were too poor to afford wine, albeit a sip, each Friday.

The *Kiddush* ceremony predates the Christian Communion and Eucharist. The first Christians were Jews and adapted and adopted the ritual of a communion (or "love feast") that was used among the sect of Jews called *Essenes*.

Kiddush Hashem
Kiddush ha-Shem

Pronounced KID-*dish ha*-SHEM, to rhyme with "Yiddish posh hen." Hebrew: "sanctification of God's name."

The concept that God needs mortal humans to hallow the Divine Name and that people become sanctified by following God's Commandments.

The book of Leviticus (22:32) has God say: "I will be hallowed among the children of Israel; I am the Lord which hallows you."

The opposite of *Kiddush Hashem* is *Chillul Hashem*—or "the profanation of God's Name."

It is important to note that *Kiddush Hashem* involves any generous, noble, altruistic, considerate deed *that honors all Jews*. This comes from the old idea that the Jews are "a kingdom of priests" and that each Jew therefore bears perpetual responsibility to act to all other people in such a way as to honor all Jewry. The *Talmud* cites as a case of true *Kiddush Hashem* a Jew's returning to an Arab, from whom he had purchased a camel, a jewel that he had found around the camel's neck: "I bought a camel, not a precious gem." And the Arab cried, "Blessed be [your] God; blessed be the God of Israel."

Being a martyr is the highest form of *Kiddush Hashem*—that is, enduring torture and accepting death because of faith in God or to prevent a profanation or desecration of God's name. (The idea of martyrdom as the ultimate testimonial to God arose during the Jewish wars against the Romans.)

The extraordinary importance, even magic, Orthodox Jews associated with the Name of God fascinated and puzzled me when I was a boy.

kike

Vulgarism pronounced to rhyme with "like." Yinglish.
From Yiddish: *kikel*, "circle."*
    A thoroughly offensive, obnoxious way of referring to a Jew.

*K*ike is meant to be contemptuous and to suggest a cheap, low-class, ill-mannered, or ugly Jew.

Eric Partridge (in *A Dictionary of Slang and Unconventional English*, 1961) cites 1935 as the probable date of *kike*'s "adoption" into English, but that date is much too late. *Kike* was used in New York as early as 1914 and is included in H. L. Mencken's *American Language* (1919) as one common term of disparagement, akin to "sheeny"—or to "dago" or "wop" for an Italian.

*Uriel Weinrich, in his authoritative *Modern English-Yiddish Yiddish-English Dictionary* (1968), does not include *kikel* (or *kaykl*) in his definitions for "circle" (*krayz* or *rod*). *Kikelen*, or *kayklen*, means "to roll." Rosten's conclusions about the derivation of *kike* seem doubtful.

The Oxford English Dictionary includes *kike* in its supplement volume, no. XIII (1961). In earlier editions, *kike* does not appear except as an obsolete form of *kick* or *keek*, a Scottish/north England dialect word, also spelled *kyke, keke, kike*, that means "to peep, to glance." The German *kieken* means "to peep"; the Yiddish version, *kick*, means "look."

Why, in the United States, was *kike* coined as an epithet for "Jew"? Assimilated German Jews, in the later decades of the nineteenth century, referred to the poorer, "pushy" immmigrants from eastern Europe as "kikey" or *kikes*. One reason today advanced for this is that many Ashkenazic names ended in *-sky* or *-ski;* presumably the taunt "ki-kis" led to *kikes*. (See Stephen Birmingham's *Our Crowd: The Great Jewish Families of New York,* 1967.) I find this quite unconvincing: the letters *ski* or *sky* were always pronounced *skee*, and repetition play would surely have given the neologism "kee-kees" or "keeks," not *kikes*.

My researches have led me to the following conclusions:

- The word *kike* was born on Ellis Island, when Jewish immigrants who were illiterate (or could not use Roman-English letters), when asked to sign the entry forms with the customary "X," refused—and instead made a circle. The Yiddish word for "circle" is *kikel* (pronounced KY-*kel*) and for "little circle," *kikeleh*.* Before long, the immigration inspectors were calling anyone who signed with an "O" instead of an "X" a *kikel* or *kikeleh* or *kikee* or, finally and succinctly, *kike*. (I obtained this information through the courtesy of Stephen Birmingham, who shared with me a letter sent to him by Mr. Sidney Berry. Mr. Berry's authority for his illuminating observation was the late Philip Cowen, "dean of immigration inspectors" at Ellis Island, later the founder and first editor of *The American Hebrew*.)

*See my note on page 258.

- Jewish storekeepers on the Lower East Side, and peddlers who went far out into the hinterlands with their wares, conducted much of their trade on credit; and these early merchants, many of whom could not read or write English, would check off a payment from a customer, in their own or the customer's account book, with a circle ("I'll make you a *kikeleh*")—never an "X" or a cross.

Why did Jews make an "O," never an "X"? Because of the profound fear, not to say revulsion, felt for the symbol of the cross—which to them represented not only a barbaric form of execution, but the very sign under which they had themselves been persecuted and their ancestors brutalized and slaughtered.

So those who drew *kikelehs,* whether on Ellis Island or Avenue B, in Ohio or Kansas, or wherever the hardy peddlers traveled into the Midwest and far West,* came to be known as "*kike* men" or "*kikes.*" Dr. Shlomo Noble informs me that the miners of northeastern Pennsylvania would say, "I bought it from the *kike* man," or, "The *kike* man will be coming around soon."

*Jewish peddlers also actively penetrated the American South, dating back to Revolutionary times, with some establishing businesses that became critical to southern towns such as Mobile, Alabama, or Natchez, Mississippi. "Before the railroad made possible modern techniques of distributing consumer goods," writes Morris U. Schappes (*The Jews in the United States,* 1958), "the peddler was a necessary link between expanding manufacture and the otherwise inaccessible consumer in the rural areas in which the vast majority of the people lived." Schappes estimates that the majority of more than 16,500 peddlers listed in the 1860 census were Jews. Hasia R. Diner notes (in vol. 2 of *The Jewish People in America,* Johns Hopkins, 1992) that peddling also "bridged Jewish life between American Jewish communities. Charles Wessolowsky, a peddler in the South from Gollub, Poznan, served as a circuit rabbi, simultaneously selling his wares and burying, marrying and consecrating synagogues and cemeteries in the pockets of Jewish settlement in George and elsewhere below the Mason-Dixon Line," while the "first Jewish institution in Woodville, Mississippi . . . was a cemetery that came into being in 1849 when two Jewish peddlers had to bury a third."

Some say that the word *sheeny* began, in a similar way, as a strictly descriptive, nonpejorative word.

See sheeny.

kinder

Pronounced KIN-*der*, to rhyme with "tinder." German: "children."

Children.

B ut how little does "children" convey that bursting sentiment, *naches*, and pride with which Jews say *"kinder."*

Sometimes this parental feeling is carried to startling extremes. My wife remembers a neighbor who was so fierce in her maternal affections that when her *no-goodnik* son was arrested for some petty infraction of the law, she returned from visiting him in jail to announce, "You never *saw* such a beautiful jail as my Morris is in!"

kinderlakh[Y] (diminutive)
kinderlach[R]

Pronounced KIN-*der-lakh*, with a Scottish *kh*.

Little children.

T o express special affection to friends, a gathering, a dinner party, a committee, one may say, "Well, *kinderlakh* . . ."

kineahora
kine-ahora
See keyn eynhore.

kishke^Y
kishka^R

Pronounced KISH-*keh,* to rhyme with "shishke" as in "shish kebab." Russian: "intestines," "entrails."

1. Intestines.
2. Stuffed derma: a sausagelike comestible of meat, flour, and spices stuffed into intestine casing and baked.
3. A water hose (colloquial, and vivid enough).

*K*ishke is a delicacy of Jewish cuisine (which, to tell the truth, is not noted for range). It is made according to the cook's ancestry, palate, spices, and patience.

Aside from food, the words *kishke* and *kishkes* are used to mean intestine, "innards," belly. Genteel Jews hesitate to do so. My father and mother never would use, or approve of, the following: "His accusation hit me right in the *kishke.*" "I laughed until my *kishkes* were sore." "Oh, my full *kishkes!*" (I think this is less offensive, in postprandial praisings, than "Oh, my stuffed stomach.")

4. Plural: *kishkes*—even though the same intestine is being described. To hit people "in the *kishkes*" means to hit them in the stomach or, in indelicate parlance, "in the guts."

A person with an undiscriminating palate is said to possess a *"treyfene kishke"*—an un-*kosher* intestine. To say "a *Yiddishe kishke*" or "You can't describe a *Yiddishe kishke*" is to say that no one can gauge the prodigious appetite of a hungry Jew.

Mrs. Gershenbaum, in Moscow, sent a telegram to her husband, in Kiev: SAYS TO OPERATE OPERATE.

Mr. Gershenbaum replied: SAYS TO OPERATE OPERATE.

The police promptly arrested Gershenbaum: "What secret code are you using?"

"No code," said Gershenbaum.

"Do you take us for fools? Just read these telegrams!"

"Well, my wife is sick in the *kishkes*. So she went to Moscow to see a famous surgeon, and she wired me: 'SAYS TO OPERATE! OPERATE?' So I replied, 'SAYS TO OPERATE? OPERATE!'"

kitl[Y]
kittel[R]

Pronounced KIT-*t'l*, to rhyme with "little." German: *Kittel*, "smock," "overall."

The white robe worn by the cantor (and some others) at services on High Holy Days and at major festivals.

A mong the Jews of eastern Europe, most men wore a linen *kittel* during the High Holy Days: the simple, spotless white robe signified purity and simplicity.*

---

*The *kitl* is actually a burial shroud, which some (Ashkenazic) Jews wear as a reminder of death on the solemn days of *Rosh Hashanah* and *Yom Kippur*. Rabbi Edward Greenstein (in Michael Strassfeld's *The Jewish Holidays: A Guide and Commentary*, Harper & Row, 1985) observes that the *kitl* is worn "to symbolize a new beginning," which is why a new father may wear it at an

(Continued on page 264)

klap
klop

Rhymes with "slop." From German: *Klaps,* "blow," "hit."

1. A blow; to strike a blow; to hit. "Give him a *klap;* you're closer."
2. More colorfully, to *klap* is to yammer, to yak, to blab on at great length and without mercy. "He *klapped* me in *kop*" means either "He knocked me in the head" or, better, "He talked my ears off." "All day long, he *klaps* about his troubles." *"Klap dir kop in vant"* means "beat your head against the wall."

   See khmalye.

(Continued from page 263)

infant son's *bris,* a bridegroom at his wedding, and others at the Passover *seder*—each marking a passage into new possibility.

The *kitl* dates back to the first or second century, when Rabban Gamaliel, leader of the Jewish community in Palestine, left instructions for his students to bury him in simple shrouds. This custom, the *Talmud* relates, was adopted to protect people from being impoverished by heavy funeral expenses.

Rosten's failure to identify the *kitl* as a burial shroud may be indicative of the assimilative tendencies of his generation, which, in Rabbi Greenstein's words, "instead of wearing the traditional *kitl* or white robe, don the sort of dress they would wear to attend the opera" to attend High Holy Day services. During the past two decades, however, with the revival of interest among the baby boomers in Jewish ritual practice, use of the traditional *kitl* has made a comeback.

See Rosten's entries for **Kaddish** and **levaye**.

klezmer

Pronounced KLEZ-*mer* or KLETS-*mer*, to rhyme with "Mesmer" or "gets her." Plural: *klezmorim* (klez-MOR-*im*). From the Hebrew: *klei-zemer*, "musical instruments."

An informal group of musicians; many were itinerants who went from village to village, in eastern Europe, playing traditional music, folk songs, folk dances, solemn hymns before prayer.

These musicians rarely knew how to read music (what Jews could afford music lessons, and who in the *shtetl* would teach them?) and passed their skill down from father to son. They earned very little and had to keep moving, seeking out country fairs, weddings, synagogue dedications, *Purim* festivities, etc.

As characters, the shabby *klezmorim* were familiar to all Ashkenazic Jews; they were regarded as drifters, odd types, itinerant minstrels. They are a recurrent theme in the paintings of Marc Chagall and Chaim Gross.

Klezmer music was played on trumpets, bugles, flutes, clarinets, fifes, violins, cellos, and drums. A typical group would contain three to six members.

In some ways *klezmer* music was like the music of jazz "combos" in that it grew out of improvisation, ingenious harmonizations, solo innovations. It reflected the patchwork quilt of national cultures in which Jewish life was lived. Hebraic themes were embroidered with motifs from the folk music of Russians, Poles, Czechs, Germans, Hungarians, Romanians, Slovenes, Greeks, and Arabs.

During the Middle Ages, the making of music was a recognized profession among both Oriental and European Jews. In many places, Jewish musicians played at Christian religious ceremonies. They were, indeed, often preferred to other minstrels because of their reputation for "modesty and sobriety"—and once they came into demand, punitive taxes were imposed to discourage them. (See Abraham Z. Idelsohn, *Jewish Music*, 1944.)*

*Better yet, see Henry Sapoznik's *Klezmer! Jewish Music from Old World to Our World* (Macmillan, 1999). Sapoznik is one of the pioneers of the *klezmer* revival that has swept the Jewish world during the past three decades, bringing the sounds of Yiddish and the rhythms and melodies of eastern Europe to hundreds of thousands of listeners. His own band, Kapelye, was one of the earliest to reintroduce *klezmer* tunes and styles of play to the listening and dancing public, and his earlier book, *The Compleat Klezmer* (Tara Productions), has become the standard introduction for musicians wanting to play *klezmer* music.

Today, dozens of *klezmer* bands are recording, and hundreds are performing at weddings, *bar* and *bas mitzvas*, and concert halls. Among the most successful are the Klezmatics, who toured and recorded with Israeli diva Chava Alberstein in 1998–99. Other outstanding *klezmorim* include fiddler Michael Alpert's avant-garde *klezmer*/jazz band Brave Old World; Andy Statman, mandolinist and clarinetist extraordinaire; and the eleven-member (including four women) Klezmer Conservatory Band, directed by Hankus Netsky. (For an astoundingly broad listing of *klezmer* bands active in North America, visit www.klezmershack.com.)

Klezmer music has also graced numerous film sound tracks, and a few *klezmer* maestros from the early to mid–twentieth century, most notably clarinetist Dave Tarras, have been filmed, interviewed, and recorded by younger musicians and scholars (Tarras died in 1989, shortly after working with Henry Sapoznik to produce *Dave Tarras, Yiddish-American Music, 1925–1956*, on Yazoo Records). Many Jewish jazz and classical musicians are today finding their way into the *klezmer* idiom. The result has been not merely a revival, but a reinvention.

klutz^R
klots^Y

Rhymes with "butts." From German: "log," or "block of wood."

1. A clod; a clumsy, slow-witted, graceless person; an inept blockhead.
2. A congenital bungler.
3. A block of wood.

The word even sounds **klutz-like.***
    A *klutz-kashe* is a silly question that brings up irrelevant problems or rests upon foolish premises.

To Mr. Meyers, in the hospital, came Mr. Glotz, secretary of the synagogue, who said: "I bring you the good wishes of our board of trustees, that you should get well and live to be a hundred and ten years old! That's an official resolution, passed by a vote of fourteen to seven!"
    Glotz was a *klutz*.

The men sat sipping their tea in silence. After a while the *klutz* said, "Life is like a bowl of sour cream."

---

*A publishing company named Klutz was incorporated in 1977 in Palo Alto, California, by three Stanford University students, who began with a book about juggling. Klutz books are packaged along with balls, yo-yos, dice, and other necessary accoutrements, so that each book is actually a "multi-sensory" kit capable of training the *klutz* right out of you.

"Like a bowl of sour cream?" asked the other. "Why?"
"How should I know? What am I, a philosopher?"

Two *klutzes* were discussing their wives. "My wife drives me crazy: every night she dreams she married a millionaire!"
"That drives you crazy? You're lucky. *My* wife dreams she's married to a millionaire in the daytime."

kneydl ^Y
knaydl ^R

Pronounced K-NAY-*dl*, to rhyme with "ladle." The plural, *kneydlekh*, is pronounced K-NAY-*dlekh*. From German: *knetn*, "to knead."

A dumpling—usually made of *matzo* meal, usually served in chicken soup, usually on Friday night, generally at the Passover *seder*.

*K*neydl is used affectionately for a child, as we say "my little dumpling," or to describe a round, fat, or chubby woman.

knipl ^Y
knippl ^R
knippel

Pronounced KNIP-*p'l*, to rhyme with "**ripple**."*
See pushke.

---

*Knipl itself means a "knot"—often referring to a knotted handkerchief in which money is stored. Gene Bluestein notes (in his *Anglish-Yinglish Dictionary*, University of Georgia Press, 1989) that it's also a way of choosing lots:

knish
knishes (plural)

Pronounce the *k* as well as the *n*. From Ukrainian.

1. Little dumplings filled with groats, grated potatoes, onions, chopped liver, or cheese. The *knish* has become an American *nosh* through the efforts of celebrated *knish* makers on the Lower East Side. In particular, Yonah Shimmel, a famed *knish* bakery, was established on Houston Street in 1910. It has flourished ever since.
2. A term of abuse. "He has the brains of a *knish*."
3. When you say you hit someone "with a *knish*," you mean you reward, instead of punish, him. Don't ask me why.
4. Vulgarism: Vagina.

k'nocker ^R
knacker ^Y

Pronounced not "nocker," but ᴋ'ɴᴏᴄᴋ-*er*, with the *k* a separate sound, as in "Canute." (I make the apostrophe part of the spelling to make sure you pro-

---

"You make a knot in one end and then show only the tips. Whoever gets the *knipl* is chosen."

The sound if not the meaning of *knipl* has become familiar to New York Jews and a broader swath of Americans through the innovative cartooning of Ben Katchor, whose strip *Julius Knipl, Real Estate Photographer*, has been running for years in the weekly *Forward*. Katchor's character wanders New York observing the peculiar activities of Jews involved in all sorts of obscure businesses and concerns. Both *Julius Knipl* and Katchor's historical strip, *The Jew of New York*, have been published as books. In 1999, Katchor received the MacArthur Foundation's "genius" award.

nounce both the *k* and the *n*.) From German: *knacken*, "to crack or snap." A *knacker* meant someone who cracked a whip, was a doer, a big shot. In Yiddish, *k'nocker* is derisive.

1. A big shot—who knows it and acts that way.
2. A boastful, cocky, self-advertising fellow; a "show-off."

The braggadocio aspect is important: a successful but modest man is ordinarily not called a *k'nocker*.

A *k'nocker* is someone who works crossword puzzles—with a pen (especially if someone is watching).

During the *Yom Kippur* services, a *k'nocker* was beating his breast, praying loudly; and, carried away, he cried out, "I am the lowliest of men, Lord, unworthy of Your goodness! I am a *no-goodnick*, a nobody, a nothing."

Next to the *k'nocker*, the poor *shammes* (sexton), too, was beating his breast and chanting his deficiencies. "Forgive me, O Lord, I'm a nothing."

The *k'nocker* promptly protested: "Look who claims he's a nothing!"

Two Jewish *k'nockers*, approaching Honolulu, got into an argument about the correct pronunciation of Hawaii: one was sure it was "Hawaii," the other positive it was "Havaii." They made a bet.

When they got off the plane, they hurried over to the first native they saw and said, "Aloha! How do you pronounce the name of this island: Hawaii or Havaii?"

"Havaii," said the native.

"Thank you."

"You're velcome," said the native.

kobtzen
See kaptsn.

kochaleyn
kokhaleyn, koch alayn, kochalayn, kochalein

Pronounced кокн-*a-lane* or кокн-*a-line;* be sure to make the uvular *kh* as bonnie as a Scot's. Strictly Ameridish. From German: *kochen,* "to cook"; *allein,* "alone."

A room or bungalow, in a summer colony, with cooking facilities.

This gorgeous specimen of Ameridish comes to us from the language crucible of the Catskill Mountains, the hallowed center and El Dorado of Jewish summer resorts.*

The culture of the Catskills distinguishes hotels, which are for *alrightniks,* from *kochaleyns,* which are for *balbatish* "singles," couples, or families.

*For a discussion of the fate of the Catskill Mountain variety of Jewish culture, see my note to Rosten's entry for **borsht**.

I first heard this indispensable word used thusly: "Who can *affoder* [afford] a fancy hotel? I take a *kochaleyn.*"

In the Catskills, it is claimed that an ingenious gentleman crossbred a Guernsey with a Holstein—to get a Goldstein.

This cow does not moan "Moo," but *"Nu?"*

Kohen
Cohen

Pronounced co-*en*, to rhyme with "go when" or CANE to rhyme with "Dane." Hebrew: *kohen*, "priest." Plural: *kohanim*, pronounced ko-HA-*nim*.

Priest—that is, a Hebrew priest of yore.

F amily names such as Cohen, Cohn, Cahn, Kahn, Kagen, Cahana, and even Echt and Katz (formed from the initials of *kohen tzedek*, "a priest of justice") often claim descent from the priests of ancient Israel—as do some Germans named Köhne, Schiff (a pun on *Kahn*: "boat"), and even Bloch.

Aaron, brother of Moses, was the first high priest, the ancestor of all Hebrew priests, the *kohanim*, who conducted sacrifices and services in the desert sanctuary and later in the great Temple in Jerusalem.

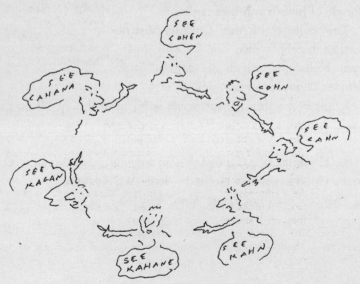

After the Jews went into exile, the title of *kohen* was passed down, even though the priestly prerogatives and responsibilities no longer existed.

Many proscriptive laws circumscribed the actions of a *kohen;* a few are still followed by traditional Jews:

A *kohen* may not marry a divorcée.

A *kohen* may enter a cemetery only for the funeral of a member of his immediate family.

A kohen is the first one called to the Torah reading in the synagogue.

I know of no sound historical evidence that links the Cohanes of Ireland to the **Cohens of Tel Aviv.***

The firm of Farnsworth, Sullivan, and Cohen was one of the largest and finest in the city. A friend of Cohen's asked, "Why is your name last? Everyone knows that Farnsworth spends all of his

---

*Based on surveys of Jewish gravestones, about 5 percent of the seven million Jewish males around the world are *kohanim*—more than one hundred thousand in Israel alone.

Genetic researchers in Israel say they have established a clear genetic link among Jews of the *kohanim* tribe, both Ashkenazic and Sephardic, based on a variation of the Y-chromosome, which is paternally inherited and does not recombine. Writing in the January 2, 1997, issue of *Nature,* a team of scientists headed by Prof. Karl Skorecki of the Rambam Hospital in Haifa asserted that their research with 188 subjects who were self-identified as *kohanim* "define a set of Y-chromosomes of recent common origin" that constitute a genetic marker not found in the rest of the Jewish population. This same marker has also been discovered among a black South African people called the Lemba, who have long claimed to be Jews; the Lemba have a remarkably high frequency of the Y-chromosome marker among their Buba clan, which is the Lemba's equivalent of the *kohanim*. Such research is the first indication of a possible dispersion of ancient Jews into sub-Saharan Africa.

Most such conclusions from genetic research remain controversial and contested. The recent completion of the human genome mapping project, however, promises the resolution of many such controversies in years to come.

time in the country and Sullivan most of it at the racetrack. Your name should be first!"

"Well," smiled Cohen, "*my* clients read from right to left."

There is no truth in the observation that after Robert Briscoe, a Jew, was elected Lord Mayor of Dublin, the Irish began to see leprecohens.

kokhlefl^Y
kochleffl^R

Pronounced KOKH-*lef-fl*, with a Glaswegian *kh*, as in "loch." From German: *kochen*, "to cook"; *löffel*, "spoon."

1. A cooking spoon. The *kokhlefl* was the long wooden spoon used for stirring a pot.
2. A busybody; a gadabout. What word is better than *kokhlefl* to describe someone who butts into everyone else's business?
3. A live wire, go-getter, organizer, activist, promoter; someone who stirs things and people up.
4. A bright, inquisitive, energetic toddler. "That little girl—a regular *kokhlefl!*"

Kol Nidre

Pronounced *Cawl* NID-*reh*, to rhyme with "Paul Sidra." Hebrew: "all vows."

The plaintive prayer that ushers in *Yom Kippur*. The words are not Hebrew, but Aramaic.

In synagogues and temples all around the globe, the cantor chants the *Kol Nidre* just before sunset, on the

*For information about women cantors, see my note to **chazzen**.

eve of *Yom Kippur*. He* sings it three times, first softly, then louder, then fortissimo—and the congregation responds antiphonally, reciting the prayer as a recitative. Throughout this, the *Torah* scrolls are held aloft by **three worshipers.**†

The *Kol Nidre* is chanted very solemnly, with more anguish than any other prayer, for it seems to recapitulate, in each worshiper's memory, the long history of violence and humiliation to which Jews have been subjected. The melody, as sung by the cantor in the falling twilight, is immensely moving. (Beethoven included a piece of it in his Quartet in C-sharp Minor. Tolstoy said it "echoes the story of the martyrdom of a grief-stricken nation.")

But the text of the *Kol Nidre*, surprisingly, is that of a legal document, not a paean to God.

Kol Nidre (all vows), obligations, oaths, anathemas, be they called *konam* or *knoas* or by any other name, which we may vow or swear or pledge . . . from this Day of Atonement until the next . . . do we repent. May they be deemed to be forgiven, absolved, annulled or void—and made of no effect. They shall not bind us nor have power over us [and] the vows shall not be considered vows nor the obligations obligatory, nor the oaths oaths.

Kol Nidre was originally *opposed* by the rabbis, because it suggested that vows could be taken not too seriously, since they could

†While the number of *Torah* scrolls held at the start of *Kol Nidre* varies among communities, it is most commonly two *Torah* holders who flank the prayer leader (who may or may not be a cantor), so that the three together represent a *bes din*, a Jewish court of justice.

be negated on *Yom Kippur*. But the chant/prayer became popular nevertheless—I think for three basic reasons:

1. Jews attach singular importance to a promise. Judaic law demands that every vow be fulfilled even, according to Rabbi Louis Finkelstein, if the fulfillment entails severe sacrifices (*The Jews: Their History, Culture and Religion,* vol. II, pp. 1,739–1,802).

2. Charlemagne forbade the Jews, when in a court, to swear by their own religious oath; instead, Jews were forced to use the repellent *More Judaico*. Oaths were "administered" to Jews in brutal ways: a Jewish witness had to kneel or was forced to don a wreath of thorns; he was made to stand in water (since he had declined baptism) or on a pigskin; he was instructed to repeat the oath while teetering on a low stool from which one leg had been removed. . . . It is no wonder to me that Jews asked God to exempt them from the performance of vows undertaken under such circumstances.*

3. Many Jews were forcibly converted during the Inquisition.† One can understand why these hapless "renegades" to their

---

*The *More Judaica* was imposed upon Jews because of *Kol Nidre* and not the other way around. "Because it was falsely assumed that *Kol Nidre* does apply to oaths taken in court," writes Dr. Louis Jacobs (*The Jewish Religion, a Companion,* 1995), "Jews were suspected of unreliability in this matter and in a number of countries the infamous *More Judaica* . . . was introduced."

†Rabbi Leila Gal Berner reports a Jewish folkloric interpretation of the *Kol Nidre*'s word for "transgressors," (עבריינים) *avaryanim,* to be a code word for "Iberians"—a reference to the multitude of Spanish-Jewish converts to Christianity who lived in terror of the Inquisition. "According to the legend," Berner writes, "in embracing these crypto-Jews within the community of believers and sinners, the *Kol Nidre* chant reminds us that we all wear masks, we all hide our true essence—and we all enjoy the possibility of God's forgiveness" (*Kol Haneshamah: Prayerbook for the Days of Awe,* Jewish Reconstructionist Federation, 1999).

faith would want God to absolve them from guilt in having taken vows they were forced to take, and to remit in advance any sin occasioned by vows they might have to take in the year ahead.

The rabbis taught that the dispensation allowed in *Kol Nidre* applies only to those vows that involve the vower alone—not any that entailed the interests of another. So a person might be absolved of responsibility for a vow of conscience to God, but not of a promise made to another person. *That* had to be fulfilled.

kopdreyenish

Pronounced KAWP-*drey-eh-nish,* to rhyme with "hawk bray a fish." German: *Kopf,* "head," *drehen,* "to turn."
1. Something that makes one's head spin with its difficulty.
2. Something that confuses one because of its noise; a tumult.
3. Something that turns one's head; flattery, a compliment.

"Who needs a *kopdreyenish* like that?" "He had so much *kopdreyenish,* he didn't now what he was doing." "Stop *dreying* me a *kop.*" "That's enough *kopdreyenish.*"

See also tsedreyt, tsedudlt.

kosher

Pronounced KO-*sher,* to rhyme with "no sir." From the Hebrew: *kasher,* "fit," "proper," "appropriate," "permissible."

Kosher is probably the Hebrew word most widely encountered in English. (Its multifarious meanings in American slang, and as a form of Yinglish, will be explored below.)

As a Hebrew-Yiddish word, *kosher* generally means only

1. fit to eat, because ritually clean according to the dietary laws.

Many a meat store in a Jewish neighborhood carries two Hebrew words on the window; they look alike but are not. They read, from right to left: *boser kasher* (pronounced, in Yiddish, BAW-*ser* KO-*sher*). *Bosar* means "meat."

A *kosher* meat store or restaurant serves no un-*kosher* meats.

Eating and drinking, to the ancient Jews, involved grave religious obligations and strongly reinforced the idea of the Jews as a people "set apart," chosen by the Lord as "Mine . . . ," "holy unto Me" (Leviticus). The strict observance of dietary rules was believed to strengthen the dedication of a Jew to his role as one of God's instruments for the redemption of humankind. (Some scholars think *kosher* practices were designed as acts of moral self-discipline, to resist the influence of the Greeks and Romans, who were given to prodigious self-indulgence and sensuality.) The strict observance of *kosher* laws has declined drastically among Western Jews.*

*Due to the baby boom generation's widespread concern with the purity, quality, and social implications of food, *kosher* practice has made something of a comeback in Jewish life during the past three decades—though with far more interpretive license and less strict observance than Orthodox law permits. Contemporary forms of *kashrut* (*kosher* observance) include "*kosher* vegetarian," which moots many of Judaism's traditional concerns about slaughtering animals, separating meat from dairy, etc., and "eco-*kosher*," which takes into consideration the manner in which food is grown, harvested, and packaged in determining whether it is acceptable for use. The eco-*kosher* concept is only slowly being elaborated as activists in the field evaluate the

In Yiddish, *kosher* is used to describe anything

2. pertaining to Orthodox Jewry. "He is a *kosher* Jew" means he observes the dietary laws.
3. pious, devout. "He is a *kosherer Yid*" means he is very pious; a female would be "a *koshere Yidene.*"
4. sympathetic. "He is a *kosher* kind of man" means he is kind, understanding.
5. dear, sweet, lovable. "She has a *koshere neshome*," a kosher soul.

In American slang, *kosher* comes in a gorgeous array of flavors.

6. Authentic; the real McCoy. "That's *kosher?*" can mean fourteen-karat gold, sterling silver, genuine antique.
7. Trustworthy, reliable. "Is he *kosher?*," which once meant "Is he Jewish?," is now taken to mean "Can I trust him?" or "Is he part of the group?" or even (as I heard it used in the Pentagon) "Has he been cleared for classified information?"
8. Legitimate, legal, lawful. "Is this deal *kosher?*" means "Is this deal on the up-and-up?" "Everything is *kosher*" means "Everything is proper."
9. Approved by a higher source; bearing the stamp of approval. "It's *kosher*," uttered by a company VP, can mean that the president has approved it; uttered by a lieutenant, it means it has the sanction of a superior.
10. Fair, fair and square, ethical. Eric Partridge says this

social responsibility of the food industry in light of various Jewish teachings about the environment, the treatment of workers, the treatment of the body as sacred, compassion for animals, and other concerns. For more information, see Rabbi Arthur Waskow's *Down-to-Earth Judaism: Food, Money, Sex and the Rest of Life* (William Morrow, 1995).

usage came into English from London's East End, around 1860.

All in all, *kosher* is, I suppose, the most resourceful Yiddish word in the English language.

Kosher: Dietary Data (in Brief)

Meat and milk may not be eaten simultaneously. (Orthodox Jews allow six hours to pass between a meat and a dairy meal, but less if vice versa.) Separate cooking utensils and vessels for the service and storage of foods are used for dairy and meat products—viz., Moses' thrice uttered warning (Exodus, Deuteronomy) not to seethe a kid in its mother's milk.

"Clean" and "unclean" animals are listed in Leviticus 11 and Deuteronomy 14. Precisely forty-two animals are named as taboo.

Only those four-footed animals that chew their cud *and* possess a cloven hoof are *kosher*. (This includes goat, gazelle, pygarg, and antelope, though I have yet to hear of a Jew going that far.) An animal that chews its cud but is not cloven-hoofed is *treyf* (non-*kosher*)—for instance, the camel, the rabbit. It grieves me to inform the pious reader that the camel, Bible notwithstanding, is cloven-hoofed and that the rabbit does not chew the cud. Creatures that crawl, like lizards and snakes, are forbidden. So is the mouse. So is the weasel. Only fish having both scales and fins are *kosher*. Shellfish are taboo. (What a pity.) Birds of prey (vultures, owls, hawks, eagles) are taboo, as are nearly all wild fowl. Any animal that has not been slaughtered according to ritual— even a chicken or a cow—is unclean and verboten.

The *shokhet*, a religious slaughterer, must examine each individual animal for signs of infection, disease, or abnormality. He must dispatch an animal by slashing the throat with one stroke. If the knife binds or sticks, even for an instant, the animal is no longer *kosher*. *Kosher* meat must be stamped or sealed by a *mash-giakh* (supervisor).

Any textbook in anthropology can testify to the ancient origin of, and universal human preoccupation with, food taboos: totemism, animal sacrifices, magical rites of propitiation, symbolic accretions of strength via ingestion, etc.

The Babylonian laws of Mani forbade the eating of birds of prey. In Egypt, priests were forbidden to eat birds that eat fish. Egyptians would not, of course, eat "deities": cats, cows, bulls. Romans would not offer the gods scaleless or finless fish in their sacrifices. (Iranians still will not eat them.) Many South Sea Islanders will not eat eel. Natives of Borneo, Guiana Indians, Laplanders, Navajo Indians, and the Yakuts of Turkey eschew (no pun) pork.

Muhammad forbade his followers to eat of the pig.

Genesis 9:4 forbade animal blood to all the seed of Noah. Moses himself, in Leviticus and Deuteronomy, forbade Jews to consume animal blood, internal fat or suet, carrion, or the carcass of an animal that has died instead of having been slain in the ritual manner.

In the *Talmud* it is written that forbidden foods "pollute the body and the soul."

The *Midrash* says that God is just as compassionate to beasts and birds as He is to people; hence Jews are told to be "kind and compassionate to all the creatures [God] created in this world. Never beat or inflict pain on any animal, beast, bird, or insect" (from the medieval *Book of the Pious*).

Eating and drinking, said the rabbis, are *religious* acts, for during them we partake of God's bounty. Even in eating, the mind should dwell on God: any meal, therefore, should begin with a benediction of thanks and end with **grace**.* This praying of the Jews before and after eating was carried into Christian practice. Paul also asked Christians to avoid the blood of meat and the meat of strangled animals (Apostles 21:25).

For over two thousand years, rabbis developed and refined an elaborate code of regulations concerning food. The ritualistic details became so minute that a major part of the rabbis' expertise lay in their mastery of the elaborate rules: what is proscribed and what permitted; the occasions when one food or another is allowed; the order in which one food or another may be consumed; how food must be prepared, how it must be cooked, etc.

The Orthodox Jews' horror of eating pork was (and is) indescribable. When Antiochus, the Seleucid king, conquered Judea, he ordered Jews to sacrifice pigs on their holy altars; the Jews simply rose in fury (the Maccabean revolt, 168 B.C.E., which is celebrated at *Chanukah*).

The persecution of Jews down the centuries often involved one or another mob's forcing a God-fearing Israelite to pollute his soul by eating pork.

Whatever it was that originally prompted the Jews to taboo pork, it was a fortunate decision for them. As is now well known, pork is the commonest carrier of the parasites of the dangerous disease trichinosis. Similarly, hepatitis has in some cases been

---

*"Whoever enjoys the goods of this world without reciting a blessing is like a thief," says the *Talmud* (*Tosefta Berakhot* 35a). Yet the bounty of life is to be enjoyed—or else! "A person will have to give reckoning and accounting," says the Jerusalem *Talmud* (*Kiddushin* 4:12), "for everything the eye saw that was not eaten. . . . Throughout the year . . . taste every kind of food at least once."

traced to contaminated clams, which are also taboo for observing Jews.†

The jokes Jews tell about matters *kosher* are endless. Here is one of the briefest:

Late one rainy afternoon, when he saw no other customers inside, Mr. Finkelstein walked into an elegant but not *kosher* delicatessen. He bought some tomatoes and, with elaborate insouciance, asked (for the first time in his life), "By the way, eh, how much costs that—bacon?"

Came a terrific flash of lightning and clap of thunder. Finkelstein looked up to the heavens. "I was only *asking!*"

koved
kovid

Pronounced KAW-*vid*, to rhyme with "law lid." Hebrew: "honor."

Honor, glory.

A man who pursues *koved,* from him glory runs away.

—Talmud

---

† Health-related arguments on behalf of *kosher* law generally overreach, as in the case of this trichinosis discussion. Cooking the flesh of the pig at reasonably high heat destroys the trichinosis parasite, and cultures that permit the consumption of pork have proved no more liable to lower life expectancy than the cultures that forbid it. If there is a discernible principle that binds together the dietary rules of Judaism, perhaps it is one of restraint, of eating in a "civilized" manner without overly inflamed appetite. Shellfish, for example (which is forbidden), cannot be consumed without a good deal of shlurping and sloppiness; likewise, it is the blood of meat (likewise forbidden) that causes meat eaters to salivate and "lust" for the meal.

And I have heard a clause tacked on: "But he who does good
and does not pursue *koved*, him *koved* overtakes."

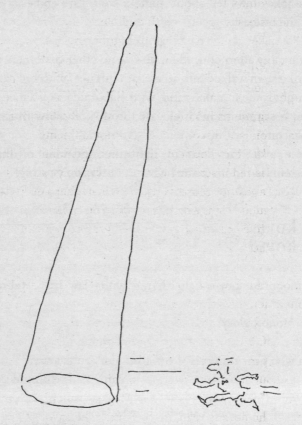

krekhts[Y]
krechtz [R]
krekhtsn[Y] (infinitive verb)

Pronounced KHREKHTZ, to rhyme with "Brecht's." German:
krächzen, "to croak," "to caw."

As a Verb

1. To grunt, groan, croak, moan, or wheeze in minor pain or discomfort.
2. To fuss or complain—with audible sound effects.
3. To make cranky, gasping, ambiguous noises.

As a Noun

4. A sound of complaint, discontent, or minor sadness.

*K*rekhtsing (which is Yinglish; in Yiddish, *krekhtsn*) is reserved for secondary discontents or minor ailments. You would never say *krekhts* for a sound of real pain or genuine tragedy.

A *krekhts* is not a scream, which is a *kvitsh,* or a full-throated cry, which is a *geshray.* Moreover, *krekhts* is neither a deep-throated moan nor a subtle sigh, which is a *zifts.* You moan a bit and sigh quite often while *krekhtsing.* A confined gasp-sigh-moan is best.

People who are hypochondriacs *krekhts* a good deal; so do middle-aged women in menopause—and Jewish men losing at pinochle; so do chronic gripers. Old people *krekhts* a good deal, especially when their children are around.

Note that *krekhts* describes the sounds one makes, not the cause thereof. You may *krekhts* about something, never *at* someone. And it is much more common to use *krekhts* about someone else than about one's self. "Are you in pain? You've been *krekhtsing* for an hour." "Why are you *krekhtsing* so much? Is the stock down?" "All he does is read and *krekhts.*" The savor of *krekhtsing* can be enhanced by liberal doses of "*Oy!*" In fact, "*Oy!*" is itself a *krekhts.*

Two men met on the street. Said the first: "How's business?"

Krekhtsed the second, "Eh."

"Well, for this time of year, that's not bad!"

In the old days, when trains welcomed customers, when there were few bedrooms and one slept in an upper or a lower berth, a Mr. Fortescue, tossing and turning in an upper, could not get to sleep because, from the berth below, came a woman's constant, mournful *krekhtsing:* "*Oy* . . . am I toisty . . . *Oy* . . . am I toisty!"

On and on went the murmurous lament, until Mr. Fortescue got out, crawled down the ladder, padded the length of the car, filled two paper cups with water, brought them back, and handed them in through the curtains to the passenger in the lower berth.

"Madame, here. Water!"

"God bless you, gentleman; thank you."

Fortescue crawled up into his berth, and he was on the very edge of sweet somnolence when, from below, came the suspiration: "*Oy* . . . vas I toisty. . . ."

krenk

Pronounced exactly as it is spelled, with the *e* as in "bent."
From German: *krank*, "sick."

1. An illness. To be *kronk* (sick) is to have some *krenk*.

I would not include so pedestrian a noun, except that *krenk* adorns some dire curses old Jews used to resort to: "He should only come down with a *krenk!*"

2. Nothing. Used ironically: "He asked me for ten dollars; a *krenk* [nothing] I'll give him!"

Mrs. Kaminsky telephoned a well-known psychiatrist. "Are you the crazy-doctor?"

"Well—I'm a psychiatrist."

"I want to come see you. I think maybe I have a psychological *krenk*. But first, how much do you charge?"

"A hundred dollars an hour."

"A hundred dollars an *hour*?" gasped Mrs. Kaminsky. "Good-bye. That crazy, I'm not."

kreplekh^Y
kreplach^R
kreplech

Pronounced KREP-*lokh* or KREP-*lekh,* as a German would render the *kh*. From German: *krepp* (diminutive: *kreppel*), derived from French, *crepe.*

A triangular or square dumpling, not unlike Italian ravioli, that contains chopped meat or cheese, etc. Usually served in soup.

K*replekh* are traditionally eaten on *Purim* and *Rosh Hashanah* and the day before *Yom Kippur.*

Mrs. Kushner was so upset about her little Sidney that she went to the school psychiatrist. "All of a sudden, my Sidney developed this thing: he just won't eat *kreplekh*. The minute he sees them, he throws a temper tantrum!"

"When did this start?" asked the psychiatrist. When she finished, he said, "Show your little boy exactly what *kreplekh* are, make him familiar with each ingredient, the entire process by which you cook them. And if you explain each step gently, patiently, whatever is causing his anxiety will disappear."

So Mrs. Kushner took little Sidney into the kitchen with many soothing sounds, and set him on a high stool, and smiled reassuringly. "So look, Sidneleh darling, here on the table I put a little square piece of dough. Dough. Right? Like I use in making the bread you love. Good? And in the middle of this tasty little square of dough I put some nice, chopped-up meat. *Oh*, such delicious meat! . . . Then I fold over one corner of the little square of dough—like this, nice, easy—then I fold the second corner over, just like the first—and then the third corner—my! Isn't that pretty? Just like a little hat. And now, the last thing I do is fold over the last corner and you see—"

"*Kreplekh!*" screamed Sidney. "*Kreplekh! Kreplekh! Kreplekh!*"

krikh arayn in di beyner ^Y
krich arein in di bayner ^R

Pronounced KRICKH (Scottish *kh* sound) *ah*-RINE *in dee* BAY-*nair*. German: *kriechen*, "to crawl," *Bein*, "bone."

Literally: "Crawl into one's bones"; to get under one's skin. To trespass on one's innermost and sensitive areas.

> "*Er krikht arayn in di beyner.*" "He crawls into your very bones."
>
> "*Krikh nit arayn in di beyner!*" "Don't crawl into my very bones."
>
> "*Zi krikht arayn in di beyner.*" "She worms her way into your most private affairs."

kugel ^R
kugl ^Y

Rhymes with "good'l." Also pronounced KIGL, to rhyme with "eagle." German: *Kugel*, "sphere" or "ball."

Pudding of noodles or potatoes, often round.

The name comes from the pan in which the pudding was baked and kept over the Sabbath.

A *kugel* is traditionally found on the Sabbath table because it can be prepared before *Shabbes* begins and be kept in the warm oven. (Injunctions against working on the Sabbath prohibit cooking or even lighting a fire.)

I feel obliged to tell you of an old saying: "If a woman can't make a *kugel*—divorce her." I disapprove of this.

Kuni Leml[Y]
Kuni Lemmel[R]

Pronounced koo-*ni* lem-*mel*, the first word rhyming with "oony." From German: *Lümmel*, "bumpkin," "lout."

A yokel, a simpleton, a simple Simon. (In Yiddish, *leml* means "lamb.")

Avrom Goldfaden (1840–1908), Yiddish playwright, producer, director, and composer, wrote a well-known operetta, *Di Tsvey Kuni-Leml*, with a confusion-of-identities plot that became popular.

See Chaim Yankel, shlemiel.

A *Kuni Leml* may be defined according to an old folk saying: "He is the kind who looks for a notch in the saw."

kurve^Y
kurveh^R

Pronounced KUR-*veh*, to rhyme with "purdah."
  Prostitute.

Around our house, *kurve* was absolutely, unequivocally taboo. I never heard my father or mother use the word when I was a boy; not until I was twenty did my father—apologetically—utter it.

When some news story, some discussion of an event, simply demanded that a prostitute be mentioned, my parents would say "a bad woman" or "an *oysvorf* of a woman."

See nafke.

kvell^R
kvel^Y
kveln (infinitive verb)

Pronounced exactly as it's spelled. From German: *quellen*, "to gush," "to swell."

1. To beam with immense pride and pleasure, most commonly over an achievement of a child or grandchild; to be so proudly happy that "your buttons can bust"; doting—with a grin, conspicuous pride, uncontainable delight. "At their boy's *bar mitzva*, naturally, they *kvelled*." "Watch her *kvell* when she reads his report card." "Let me *kvell* with you over such an honor."

Jewish parents are most energetic in *kvelling* over their children's endowments (real or illusory), achievements (major or minor), or praise from others (sincere or obligatory).

One authority I consulted put it this way: "Only from your children can anyone *shep* [derive] such *naches* [prideful pleasure] as makes you *kvell*—know what I mean?"

2. To enjoy, gloat, or crow over someone's defeat or humiliation. "All right, be charitable, don't *kvell* over his mistake." "Every decent man will *kvell* when that sadist goes to jail."

The ladies met on the Grand Concourse, Mrs. Blumenfeld carrying her groceries, Mrs. Kovarsky pushing a pram with two little boys in it.

"Good morning, Mrs. Kovarsky. Such darling boys! So how old are they?"

"The doctor," said Mrs. Kovarsky, "is three, and the lawyer is two."

kvetch[R]
kvetsh[Y]
kvetchen[R] (infinitive verb)
kvetshn[Y]
kvetcher[R] (masculine)
kvetsher[Y]
kvetcherkeh[R] (feminine)
kvetsherke[Y]

Pronounced KVETCH, to rhyme with "fetch"; KVETCH-*er*, to rhyme with "stretcher"; KVETCH-*er-eh*, to rhyme with "fetch 'er a." (Do not confuse with *kvitch* or *krekhts*.) From German: *quetschen*, "to squeeze," "to press." *Kvetcher* is a man who *kvetches*; *kvetcherkeh* is a female complainer.

As a Verb: *Kvetch*

1. To squeeze, pinch, eke out. "Don't *kvetch* the peaches." "He manages to *kvetch* out a living." "He'll *kvetch* the deal out to its last decimal point." "No one knows how someone else's shoe *kvetches*."
2. To fuss around, to be ineffectual. "She *kvetches* all day long."
3. To fret, complain, gripe, grunt, sigh. "What's she *kvetching* about now?" (An excellent companion to *kvetch*, in this usage, is *krekhts*. "All she does is *kvetch* and *krekhts!*" can hardly be improved upon for descriptive precision and power.)
4. To delay, stall, show reluctance. "He's still *kvetching* around."
5. To shrug. "He *kvetches* his shoulders."

As a Reflexive Verb: *Kvetchen zikh*
1. To exert or push oneself.

This can be used to describe a soprano straining to hit a high note, a stammerer bulling through a sound barrier, a woman in labor trying to hasten birth by squeezing, grunting, forcing.

As a Noun: *Kvetch, Kvetcher,* or *Kvetcherkeh*
1. Anyone, male or female, who complains, frets, gripes. A "sad sack" who magnifies minor aches and pains. A chronic complainer. "What a congenital *kvetcher!*"

To be strictly grammatical, a female *kvetcher* should certainly be called a *kvetcherkeh*, which, through the lilt of euphony, enhances the characterization.
2. One who works slowly, inefficiently, or pedantically. "It will take forever, he's such a *kvetch*."
3. One who constantly alibis for poor or lazy performance. "That *kvetch* comes up with a different excuse every

Monday and Thursday." (The phrase "Mondays and Thursdays" is Yiddish for constantly, repetitively. It derives from the fact that a small portion of the *Torah* is read in the synagogue on Monday and Thursday mornings, every week, every year, and has been repeated as a ritual for generations.)

4. A "wet blanket," one who diminishes the pleasures of others. "Don't invite him to the party; he's a *kvetch*."

There is a prized lapel button that reads:

FRANZ KAFKA

IS A

KVETCH.

kvitsh^Y
kvitch^R
kvitshen (infinitive verb)

Rhymes with "snitch." (Yiddishists might pronounce it to rhyme with "beach.") From German: *quietschen*, "to squeal."

Do not confuse *kvitsh* with *kvetch*. Do not confuse *kvitsh* with *krekhts*. *Kvitch*, *kvetch*, and *krekhts* often work beautifully in tandem but are not synonyms.

As a Verb
To scream—but not a scream of real terror. It is, rather, a yelp. A woman will *kvitsh* or "give a *kvitsh*" on sighting a mouse, scalding a finger, or meeting a long-lost friend. (In a moment of real fear or tragedy, Jewish women do not *kvitsh*, but give a *geshray*, which rhymes with "fresh fry.")

I think it correct to state that 95 percent of all the *kvit-shing* in the world is done by women. "Don't *kvitsh* when you see the bill." "When she stuck herself with the needle, she *kvitshed*" (or, better, "gave a *kvitsh*"). "*Kvitsh* day, *kvitsh* night, he won't change his ways!" "Please, no more or I'll *kvitsh!*"

As a Noun

A scream—but a special, not-to-be-taken-too-seriously exclamation.

A *kvitsh* is in no way a *geshray*; nor is it a substitute for *gevalt*. A *kvitsh* is midway between a squeal and a scream. It is not prolonged or cacophonous; it is a small, unpretentious, often obligatory exclamation of dismay, surprise, or not excessive alarm.

Approved or standard forms of *kvitshing*:

SURPRISE: "When I walked in, she gave a *kvitsh* you
    could hear in Canarsie."

DISTASTE: "When she saw the wound, she let out a
    kvitsh."

PLEASURE: "When they called her to the platform, she
    gave out with a *kvitsh*."

MINOR PAIN: "She stubbed her toe and gave a *kvitsh*."

DISCOMBOBULATION: "Everyone was running around;
    the *kvitshing* could drive you crazy."

DISAPPROVAL: "Please, no more *kvitshing* or you'll dis-
    turb the neighbors."

NOTE: To help you distinguish *kvitsh* from *kvetch* from *krekhts* (a salubrious set of niceties), I offer these observations:

You can always *kvitsh* sedately, charmingly, out of happiness; to *kvetch* is always negative, bilious, complaining; and to *krekhts* is to utter grating noises of physical discomfort or spiritual woe—possibly spurious.

Kvitshing may be hard on the ears, but *kvetching* is hard on the nerves. As for *krekhtsing*, it should be reserved for a hospital room.

Some families produce personality types that are adept, even effusive, in their *kvitshing;* other families specialize in *kvetching*—communal grousings drenched in self-pity; and some *krekhts* so loudly and so often that they sound like a convention of hypochondriacs.

If you take the trouble to familiarize yourself with the nuances of *kvitshing, kvetching,* and *krekhtsing,* you may zestfully add them to your arsenal of exclamatory locutions. Connoisseurs should enlist them for the relief of English words that are becoming exhausted from overwork.

To the widow, who was shrieking and wailing over her dear departed's body, a friend said, "Please, restrain yourself, enough *kvitshing.*"

To which the widow retorted, "This you call 'enough'? Wait until we get to the cemetery! *Then* you'll hear *kvitshing!*"

1

Ladino

Pronounced *lah-*DEE-*no,* to rhyme with "casino." Spanish: "familiar with **several languages.**"*

The vernacular used by Sephardic ("Spanioli") Jews, in Spain, Portugal, Turkey, the Balkans, Morocco; and by Spanish- and Portuguese-speaking Jews in Central and South America.

*L*adino is a form of fifteenth-century Castilian Spanish, profusely sprinkled with Talmudic expressions and Hebrew words, and with borrowed Arabic, Turkish, and Greek words and phrases. It is also called *Judesmo,* or Judeo-Spanish.

In *Ladino,* Spanish words are often given Hebrew prefixes or suffixes; Hebrew words are "Spaniolized" by using them as roots

---

*According to Dr. Jay Levinson (*Jewish World Review,* Oct. 20, 1998), *Ladino* was the term used in the Balkans and Turkey and is "a corruption of the word 'Latin,' used to distinguish it from Turkish. In Tangier and Tetuan in Spanish Morocco, it was called *Haquitiya.*"

Italian, French, and Serbo-Croatian words are also part of *Ladino*'s borrowings. The language originated through word-for-word translating of Hebrew into Spanish, dating back to the thirteenth century or earlier. With the exile of some two hundred thousand Jews from Spain on March 31, 1492 (all Jews who refused conversion to Catholicism were expelled by the Spanish monarchs Ferdinand and Isabella), Judeo-Spanish began to follow a different evolutionary course from mainstream Spanish. The classic work of *Ladino* is *Me-am Lo'ez,* a work of biblical and Talmudic commentary written by several authors over the course of more than 150 years.

and forming Spanish verb conjugations from them. Some such words have become part of modern Spanish and Portuguese: *malsin,* for example, meaning "slanderer" or "informer" (from Hebrew *malshin*), which dates back to the Inquisition.

Ladino is often called by Spaniards *idioma castellano* or *lengua vulgar.* Wry *Ashkenazim* called it "a Sephardic substitute for Yiddish."

Ladino can be written in either Hebrew or Roman characters. It is generally printed in what is called Rabbinical Hebrew letters or in Latin characters. In writing *Ladino,* the cursive Hebrew letters are used—just as in writing Yiddish.

The first book to be printed in *Ladino* appeared in 1510, in Constantinople, but some *Ladino* texts date back to the Middle Ages.

Ladino is spoken along the southeastern littoral of the Mediterranean—notably in Turkey, North Africa, and, of course, Israel—and in Brazil and in other parts of South America.*

As in Old Spanish, *Ladino* uses *f* or *g* instead of the *h* (*fablar* instead of *hablar*); often omits the *h* at the beginning of a word (*ermano* instead of *hermano*); replaces *n* with *m* (*muestros* for *nuestros*); uses *s* instead of *z* and *c*; and never uses a double *r.* And it changes the *ll* of Spanish to a *y* (*caballero* becomes *cabayero*).

---

*Although the United Nations listed *Ladino* as "seriously endangered" in 1993, cultural activists in Israel and elsewhere are intent on preserving the language. In Jerusalem, Moshe Shaul edits *Aki Yerushalayim,* a one-hundred-page biannual written in *Ladino* (www.trendline.co.il/judeospa/), and Avner Peretz of the Institute of Ladino has a large library of *Ladino* books, newspapers, and manuscripts. Universities in France and Brussels have teaching posts for *Ladino,* and institutions of higher learning in numerous other European countries teach it in conjunction with Hispanic linguistic courses. Musicians interested in Sephardic music have also contributed to the effort to keep the language alive, as have contemporary Sephardic poets. Estimates for *Ladino* speakers in today's world range from sixty thousand to four hundred thousand—virtually all of them adults.

lag baomer
See Sefirah.

landsman

Pronounced LONTS-*mon*, to rhyme with "nonce don." The plural is *landslayt*, to rhyme with "Don's height." German: *Landsmann*, "a fellow countryman."

Someone who comes from the same hometown—i.e., in Europe.

This usage was borrowed from the German immigrants in America, who quickly organized clubs, societies, and "circles" of acquaintances from their native areas.

Though *landsman* is purely descriptive, and describes one you do not necessarily like or admire, it did acquire warm, friendly overtones.

"He is a *landsman*" often means "He is our kind of person" or "He is Jewish."

A newly arrived immigrant could expect to find a bed and a bowl of soup in the home of a *landsman* and might be passed along from one home to another until gaining a start in the New World. A person who had established a toehold in America would often help a *landsman* find a job.*

---

*The role of *landsmanshaftn*—societies of mutual support among *landslayt* —in the American Jewish "success story" has been widely underestimated. According to Dr. Henry Feingold (*The Jewish People in America*, vol. IV, Johns

"My friend," said the owner of the men's clothing shop, "you are my *landsman*—and to a *landsman* I offer special bargain prices! Here is the best suit in the house. Will I ask you the one hundred dollars which, as you can see, is clearly marked on the label? No! A hundred I ask an ordinary customer, not a *landsman*. I also don't ask you ninety dollars. I don't even ask eighty! I ask seventy-five dollars, and not a penny more!"

"Ah," said the customer, "why should you lose money on me, just because we happen to come from the same place? You are my *landsman* no less than I yours. So what should I offer for this suit? Thirty dollars? Never. Thirty I would offer a stranger, not a *landsman*. Forty? That would be an insult. To you, my *landsman*, I offer fifty dollars, and not a cent less!"

"It's a deal."

Hopkins University Press, 1992), during the pre-Depression years, when Jews faced serious discrimination from the banking industry, several thousand *landsmanshaftn* and other self-help groups enabled Jews to withstand the rigors of the sweatshop economy through low-interest and no-interest loans. This, says Feingold, constituted "the most important Jewish asset . . . credit lines that permitted capital to be transferred from one generation to another and from one group to another within the community." Women played a notable role in the *landsmanshaft* movement: the Seattle Hebrew Free Loan Society, for example, was founded by a Jewish women's whist and sewing club. *Landsmanshaftn* also provided burial services, social and business opportunities, and other fundamental touchstones of community in the rough-and-tumble of immigrant life.

The example of the *landsmanshaft* is today being emulated in poor urban and rural communities, where community development banks, credit unions, and loan funds are helping to create desperately needed housing and business opportunities by providing affordable credit and technical assistance. These activist financial institutions now manage several billion dollars in capital and boast an overall loan-loss rate equal to or lower than that of commercial banks. One Jewish foundation, the Shefa Fund in Philadelphia, has for several years been organizing Jewish federations, family foundations, and synagogues to give support to the community development movement by investing part of their considerable pension and endowment funds in community development financial institutions.

Two *landslayt* met in Brooklyn. "So how goes it with you, Glickman?"

"Not so good," *krekhtsed* Glickman. "Last month I spent on doctors and medicines—forty-five dollars!"

"Forty-five dollars?! In one month! Back in the old country, you could have been sick two *years* on that kind of money!"

latke

Pronounced LOT-*keh*, like "vodka." Russian: "a patch."

A potato pancake.

*L*atkes were traditionally served at *Chanukah* but now are served anytime. I love them.

Jewish cooks pride themselves on their *latkes*, which vary in taste and texture.

Long before medical research caught up with her, my mother decreed that anything fried is bad for the digestion and discouraged my craving for the golden brown, crisp *latkes* she would, from time to time, make.

A common phrase is *"flakh vi a latke,"* "flat as a pancake."

l'chayim^R
l'khayim^Y
l'chaim, l'chayyim

Pronounced *l*-KHY-*im*, with a resounding German *kh*, to rhyme with "to fry 'em." Hebrew: "To life."

The toast offered, with raised glass, before sipping wine or liquor: "To your health."

Some innocents confuse *l'chayim* with *mazel tov,* using one when the other would be appropriate. There is no reason to err. *L'chayim* is used whenever one would say, "Your health," "Cheers!," or (I shudder to say) "Here's mud in your eye."

Mazel tov is used as "congratulations."

See mazel tov for a surprising number of variations on this theme.

An interesting practice grew up in connection with the Hebrew word *chai* (life). Each letter of the Hebrew alphabet also serves as a number. (This alphabet predated the Arabic numeral system.) Thus, the first letter of the Hebrew alphabet, *alef,* serves as a one; *bet,* as two, and so on through *yud,* which is ten. The next letter, *kaf,* is twenty; *lamed* is thirty; through *tsadeh,* which is ninety. *Kuf* is one hundred; *resh* is two hundred; *shin* is three hundred; and the last letter of the alphabet, *taf,* is **four hundred.*** Combinations of letters form the intermediate numbers, just as they do in the Roman numeral system.

> *Rosten here presents Sephardic pronunciation of the Hebrew letters. The Ashkenazic (Yiddish) variants would include *beys, khof,* and *tsadik.*

A favorite pastime of the rabbis was to read meaning into words or phrases in the *Torah* or Prophets, by adding the numerical value of their letters, totaling them, and then breaking down that total into other combinations of letters. Another game equated the letters of a word with a date and thus predicted the coming of the Messiah—or, ex post facto, discovered that a catastrophe had been "predicted" in the holy books.

Since the Hebrew letters forming the word *chai* (life) add up to the number eighteen (*khes* serves as eight; *yud* as ten), this number became charged with special attributes. Traditional-observing Jews give money to charity in amounts that are multiples of eighteen—in gratitude for a relative's recovery from illness, in honor of a child's birth, *bar* or *bas mitza,* or graduation, or as a gentle reminder to the heavenly tribunal when someone is sick.

In time of either stress or rejoicing, the Jew had one automatic response: Give to charity.

lendler

Pronounced LEND-*ler*. Yinglish.

The Jewish immigrants' pronunciation of the word for that repository of heartlessness and indifference to human suffering: the landlord. (Landlords suffer unpopularity in all cultures.)

*L**endler*** has come down through the decades to enjoy a place of its own in the distinctive argot of Manhattan, Brooklyn, the Bronx, and Queens.

When you rented rooms from a *lendler*, you became his *tenor*. Singing had nothing to do with it.

I once worked for a *lendler* who owned an apartment house that contained thirty *tenors*. The superintendent was called Mr. Janitor. (In Chicago we had janitors, not "supers.") The janitor complained that the *tenors* were insufficiently appreciative of his stellar "soivices." The tenants considered the janitor a "Mister Loafer-who-is-so-lazy-a-person-can-bust-from-aggravation-before-he-answers-a-polite 'Please-attend-to-the-radiator'!"

It was a full, rich life.

lets^Y
letz^R

Pronounced LETS, to rhyme with "gets"; plural LAY-*tsim,* to rhyme with "baits 'im." Hebrew: *letz,* "a cynic," "a scoffer."
A wit; a teasing, scornful jokester.

In the Middle Ages, *leytsim* referred to spirits who imitate and mock humans in order to torment them. Later, *lets* was used to describe any witty tease, a fun maker with a strain of scorn in his humor, a tart "card," the "life of the party."

Dr. M. J. Kornblum and Dr. Albert Steinhoff, both obstetricians, share an office. On the door, under their office hours, some *lets* printed:

24-HOUR SERVICE . . . WE DELIVER

levaye

Pronounced *le-*VY-*eh,* to rhyme with "deny ya." Hebrew: "funeral." Literally, "accompanying" or "escort."
Funeral.

Jewish law requires that burial take place as soon as possible after death and forbids any display or ostentation at a funeral. The rabbis insisted on simple burial rites, which served to enforce the egalitarianism of death. By tradition, a Jew is buried in a plain white shroud and an unadorned pine box. (Cremation is foreign to the Jewish tradition; Judaism stresses respect for the holiness of the body, God's creation.)

It is considered both a *mitzva* and a duty to attend a funeral, a mark of respect to the deceased and to the mourners. Since Jews have always taken this injunction seriously, a Jewish funeral is generally well attended. In the small communities of the "old country," everyone was expected to attend—except the teacher (*melamed*), who must not interrupt instructing the children!

Pious Jews sometimes have a little bag of soil from the Holy Land placed in their coffin.

It is not uncommon to hear a mourner, just returned from a funeral, comment on the size of the turnout, the beauty of the rabbi's eulogy, the attractive appearance of the cemetery. "Oh, a *sheyne levaye!*" ("A beautiful funeral.")

At Orthodox funerals, collectors for charity pass among the mourners, rattling their little boxes as they chant, "*Tzedakah tatsl mimoves*" ("Charity saves from death"). This minatory message to the living must surely strike some as a reflection (albeit unconscious) on the deceased.

How perceptive is the old folk saying "All things grow with time—except grief."

The mourners filed past his coffin, some sobbing, some sighing, and Mrs. Mittleman murmured, "**Look at him.*** How peaceful he looks . . . how relaxed . . . so tan . . . so healthy!"

"Why not?" replied Mittleman. "He just spent three weeks in Miami."

---

*The joke that Rosten tells involves an open coffin, which is not traditional at Jewish funerals. Though some Jews do choose nontraditional practices such as cremation, open coffins, elaborate burial sites, etc., there has been a strong return to the traditional Jewish burial and mourning practices in many communities during the past two decades. See my notes to Rosten's entry for **chevra** and **Kaddish**.

l'havdil ^R
lehavdl ^Y

Pronounced *l'*HOV-*d'l*, to rhyme with "m'cobble." Hebrew: "to separate."

1. The expression used to distinguish sacred from nonsacred discourse.
2. An expression of modesty, to show one's respect for, and inferiority to, another, as in, "Forgive the comparison." "I'm only starting in business, but *l'havdil*, at some point Rockefeller was only 'starting in business.'"
3. An ironic expression to indicate one's patent superiority over another. "Rabbi, you speak as beautifully as that rabbi over on Thirteenth Street." *"L'havdil."*
   See Shabbes and Havdala, to which *l'havdil* is linguistically related.

Litvak

Pronounced LIT-*vok*, to rhyme with "bit lock."

1. A Jew from Lithuania or neighboring regions.
2. An erudite but pedantic type—thin, dry, humorless.
3. A learned but skeptical sort. A *Litvak* is sometimes called a *tseylm kop* (a *tseylm* is a cross, but in this case the phrase means "death's head") because of the reputation for learning plus skepticism* enjoyed (in the eyes of the *Chasidim*) by Jews from Lithuania.

---

*In one of Yiddish literature's best-known and most moving stories—"If Not Higher," by I. L. Peretz—it is a *Litvak* skeptic who investigates the doings of a

(Continued on page 306)

4. A shrewd, clever fellow.
5. Derogatorily, by *Galitzianer* Jews: A sharp trader, a corner-cutting type—and one whose piety is shallow.

In some circles, *Litvak* is used not only to describe, but to deride. "What can you expect from a *Litvak?*" "He's as clever as a *Litvak.*"

(I have no doubt that a *Litvak* would refer to me as "a *Poylisher ganef.*")

Sholem Aleichem once said, "A *Litvak* is so clever that he repents before he sins."

See Galitzianer.

lokh in kop^Y
loch in kop^R

Pronounced LAWKH-*in-kawp* or *-kup,* with a Scottish or German *kh* sound; rhymes with "hawk in taut" or "talk in pup." German: "hole in the head."
Literally: Hole in the head.

This delectable phrase is used to characterize anything you definitely do not need. "That I need like a *lokh in kop!*"
For a related and splendid phrase, see ". . . toytn bankes."

(Continued from page 306)

"miracle-making" rabbi who supposedly ascends to Heaven during the High Holy Days. The *Litvak* discovers that the rabbi actually spends the holiday disguised as a peasant, chopping wood in the forest and delivering it to a sickly, impoverished Jewish woman. As a result of what he witnesses, the skeptic becomes a devoted follower of the rabbi, and when he hears the other *Chasidim* affirming that the rabbi ascends to Heaven, he says, "If not higher."

loksh
lokshn (plural)

Pronounced LUCK-*sh* (yes, I know I'm breaking up one syllable), to rhyme with the way a drunkard would pronounce "ducks."

1. A noodle.
2. A thin person.
3. A tall, thin person.
4. A dollar (don't ask me why).
5. An Italian. Why an Italian? Because Italians eat spaghetti, noodles, i.e., *lokshn*.

The phrase "*a langer* [LAHNG-*er*] *loksh*" is like "a long drink of water," to describe a very tall person.

A beggar came to Mrs. Gimpel's back door. "Lady, I'm starved. You have maybe something to eat?"

"Much, I haven't got," sighed Mrs. Gimpel. "Would you like some *lokshn* left over from last night?"

"Certainly!"

"Then come back tomorrow."

lox

You can't mispronounce this; it rhymes with "box." German: *Lachs,* and Scandinavian: *lax,* "salmon."

Smoked salmon.

Lox is highly salted; "Nova Scotia" salmon is more delicate, more bland, and more costly. *Lox* has become a Sundaybrunch delicacy. I have had it served me from Bel Air to Park Avenue, by bohemian cartoonists and investment bankers.

Usually, *lox* is served on a *bagel* (plain or toasted) that is coated with butter and lathered with **cream cheese**.*

It may startle you to know that the luxurious practice of eating *lox*, thought to be so typical of eastern European Jews, actually began for them in New York. *Lox* was almost unknown among European Jews and is rare to this day there—and in Israel.

Lox, incidentally, is a distant cousin to leax, the Anglo-Saxon for "salmon." And, though I hate to admit this, the finest salmon in the world is Scottish salmon; the most exquisite *lox* I ever tasted was at the Prince Connaught Hotel, London.

A beggar mooched half a dollar and raced into a delicatessen for a *bagel* and *lox*.

The donor followed him in angrily. "I didn't give you money to throw away on luxuries!"

To which the beggar replied: "When I'm broke, I can't afford *lox*. When I *have* money, you tell me not to spend it on *lox*. So tell me, Mr. Philosopher, *when* can I eat *lox*?"

luftmentsh[Y]
luftmensh[R]
luftmentsch, luftmensch

Pronounced LOOFT-*mensh*. German: *Luft*, "air," *Mensch*, "man."

---

*The butter–cream cheese combo that Rosten prescribes for *bagels* reflects a European culinary taste. In the United States, the "cheese stands alone"— although the wild proliferation of *bagels* as a mainstream food during the past two decades (see my note under **bagel**) has also brought about a range of adulterated cream cheeses: with chives, vegetables, *lox* bits, walnuts, etc.

1. Someone with his head in the clouds.
2. An impractical fellow, but optimistic.
3. A dreamy, sensitive, poetic type.
4. One without an occupation, who lives or works *ad libitum*.†

The prototype of the *luftmentsh* was one Leone da Modena, a sixteenth-century Venetian Jew, who listed his skills and cited no fewer than twenty-six **professions**.* His talents ranged from preaching to composing epitaphs. Why would so accomplished a man be classified as a *luftmentsh?* Because out of all

---

†The phrase "no visible means of support" dovetails nicely with the literal meaning of *luftmentsh* as "air man." "Kramer," the highly eccentric and surprisingly resourceful neighbor on television's *Seinfeld*, is a classic *luftmentsh.*

*Occupational versatility was very much a Jewish survival trait in Europe, where anti-Semitic restrictions and arbitrary persecutions made Jewish "career building" a risky business. Yet the very qualities of skills diversification and innovativeness that enabled European Jews to survive the chaos of Europe became the basis, in America, for tremendous entrepreneurial innovation. The combination of economic opportunity, a stable political system, and legal protections unleashed Jewish creativity—resulting in the "democratization" of the American economy. Art became mass entertainment under Sam Goldwyn, Cecil B. De Mille, David Sarnoff, and others in the radio, film, and television industries. Julius Rosenwald invented mail-order shopping through Sears, Roebuck, while A. Alfred Taubman almost single-handedly created the shopping mall. Felix Warburg and Jacob Schiff were two of a handful of financiers backing mass transportation (railroads) and communications (AT&T) early in the twentieth century. Louis Blaustein and his son Jacob responded to the growing automobile industry by inventing high-octane gasoline and founding Amoco. William Levitt's mass-housing construction techniques opened the suburbs to thousands of working families after World War II. Muriel Siebert became the first woman member of the New York Stock Exchange (1967) and promptly expanded popular access to stock ownership by launching one of the first discount brokerage houses. Ben Cohen and Jerry Greenfield of Ben & Jerry's Ice Cream have created innovative forms of corporate ownership and worker compensation. Thus do the sons and daughters of *luftmentshn* become millionaires!

twenty-six professions (plus assiduous alchemy on the side), he barely made a living.

Israel Zangwill wrote an amusing story, "The Luftmentsh," about a gentleman whose business cards read "Dentist and Restaurateur."

Perhaps the best-known *luftmentsh* in Yiddish literature is Sholom Aleichem's Menachem Mendel—a luckless dreamer, a meek *shlimazl*, fate's perpetual patsy.

lump

Pronounced so that the *u* rhymes with the *oo* in "oomph" and not with the *oo* in "loom." From German: *Lump*, "scoundrel."

1. A no-good.
2. A lowlife, a bum.
3. A man who makes unpleasant advances to a woman.
4. A coarse, unrefined, boorish fellow.
5. A scoundrel.

"He's a *lump*" is also used the way we say in English, "He's a bastard."

m

maarev

See mairev.

maggid^R
magid^Y

Pronounced MA-*gid,* to rhyme with "Pa did." Hebrew: "preacher." The plural is *maggidim (ma-*GID*-im.)*

A teacher-preacher, usually itinerant.

The *maggid* played a significant role in holding together the religious and cultural strands of life in the Jewish communities in eastern Europe. A humble, often untidy, shabbily clothed "country preacher," he wandered about on foot, by cart, by wagon, from *shtetl* to *shtetl*—teaching, preaching, comforting, an evangelist concerned with the poorest among the tribes of Israel.

Please remember that rabbis were not expected to preach sermons; they were much more occupied with advanced study, with teaching, with interpreting the law, with stimulating study and discussion of the *Torah.* The *darshn* was the one paid to deliver sermons in the synagogue on *Shabbes* afternoons. The *darshn* was a learned man, a Talmudist, a rabbi himself, whose preachings were erudite, technical, and often pedantic.

And because of the rabbis' aloofness from the pains and problems of ordinary people, which was akin to the remoteness of professors from peasants, intellectuals from housewives, the *maggidim* came to play a cherished role among the laity.

The *maggid* was much more of a *folks-mentsh* than either the rabbi or the *darshn*. With no set base, no home pulpit, no official status, he lived off the contributions made to him by his usually poor, unsophisticated listeners.

To be sure, some *maggidim* were messianic, fulminating orators of the fire-and-brimstone school, fundamentalists who hammered away at sin and its fearful punishment, like the revivalists of the American "Bible belt." But the most beloved *maggidim* were the homey philosopher types—good-natured, humane, tolerant of human frailty, skillful in mixing jokes, stories, and parables into their sermons.

The lore of Jews from eastern Europe was vastly enriched by the *maggidim* and by the delightful fables and moralistic tales they circulated.

See also tzaddik, Chasid, rebbe.

A most learned *maggid* used to ride from town to town to preach, and he loved to invite questions—questions of any sort—from the groups to whom he held forth.

Now the *maggid*'s driver always listened to the sermons, and to the questions and the answers, observing and admiring his *maggid*.

This went on for many years, until one day the driver said, "*Rebbe*, I have listened to you deliver sermons and answer questions for twenty years. I can recite them in my sleep. . . . Just once, before I die, I'd like to have the experience of being a *maggid,* as revered as you are. Tomorrow—forgive me—we're going to a village neither of us has ever seen before. Why can't we—just this once—change places? I'll wear your broad hat and caftan, and they'll ask *me* the questions, and I'll answer every one—exactly the way you would!"

The *maggid* thought this so interesting an idea that he agreed.

And so the *maggid* and the driver changed clothes, and the driver delivered a fine sermon, and then the congregation began to ask him questions, all of which he answered with the greatest of ease. But the last question was asked by a *yeshiva bokher* and was so new, so technical, so profound, that the poor driver had not the faintest notion how to answer it. So he drew himself up and thundered, "I am amazed anyone should ask me a question as simple as that! Why, even my driver back there, a poor, hardworking Jew who never set foot in a *yeshiva*, can answer it. Driver!" he sang out to the *maggid*. "Stand up so all can see you! You heard the question. Answer it!"

mah nishtana[R]
ma nishtane[Y]
mah nishtannah, mah nishtanu

Pronounced *ma nish-*TAH*-neh* or *ma nish-*TAH*-noo*, to rhyme respectively with "polish Donna" and "polish Baloo." Hebrew: *mah*, "what," and *nishtana*, "distinguishes."

The words that begin the Four Questions asked at the Passover *seder*. The full text is *"Mah nishtana ha-layla ha-zeh mikol ha-leylos?,"* meaning "What makes this night different from all other nights?"

A Jew may exclaim, *"Mah nishtana!"* to mean "How on earth can you explain that?" or "Who would have anticipated that?" See seder, Haggadah.

mairev ^R
mayrev ^Y
maarev, maariv

Pronounced MY-*rev,* to rhyme with "tire of." Hebrew: *maariv,* "the evening prayer" and "west."

1. The daily evening religious service.
2. The western direction.

The first Jewish **astronaut*** returned from a one-hundred-orbit voyage around the earth. When reporters asked him how he felt, he said, "Exhausted! Do you know how many times I had to say *shachris, mincha,* and *mairev?*"

Mairev (usually transliterated as *Maarev*) is the name of an evening newspaper in Israel.

---

*The first Jewish astronaut turned out to be a woman, Judith Resnick, who went into space for the first time in 1984 on the shuttle *Discovery.* She was not a religious Jew and would not have been concerned with saying the morning, afternoon, and evening prayers in space. Prior to her first flight, Israeli chief rabbi Shlomo Goren determined that she would not be "required" to light Sabbath candles, either, since Jewish earth time is calculated according to the sun and moon and cannot apply to people in orbit. On January 29, 1986, Resnick was killed in the tragic explosion of the *Challenger* space shuttle during liftoff.

makes^Y
makkes^R

Pronounced MOCK-*ess*, to rhyme with "Ho(tch)kiss." From Hebrew: *makot*, "plagues, blows, visitations . . ."

Nothing. (I mean that's what *makes* means: "nothing.") "You'll get *makes*" means you'll get nothing or worse than nothing.

*M*akes and *bobkes* are distantly related in meaning, *makes* being "nothing" and *bobkes* being a paltry, ludicrous, unworthy amount—almost **nothing**.*

I once coined the phrase "from *bobkes* to *makes*" (out of the frying pan into the fire; from bad to worse; from little to nothing), but it never caught on. I'd like to try once more.

> *Makes* is used as a curse, to mean "plagues." In the Passover *seder*, the Ten Plagues are called *makes*.

makher^Y
macher^R

Pronounced MOKH-*er;* be sure to use the German *kh,* as in "Ach!" From the German: *machen,* "to make," "to do."

1. Someone who arranges, fixes, has connections; a big wheel; an "operator."
2. Someone who is active in an organization, like the zealous president of the Sisterhood or the PTA; at college, a "BMOC" (Big Man on Campus).

*T*he man who could miraculously produce a visa, or provide immigration papers, or get an exit permit for a Jew, was known as a *makher.*

A *gantser makher* means a real operator, a real big shot.

Makhers can be *k'nockers* if they boast about their exploits (real *makhers* don't).

Most *k'nockers* are tenth-rate *makhers*—if, indeed, *makhers* at all.

See also k'nocker.

During a conversation in Miami, two female delegates, *makhers*, met in the lobby. Sadelle fell upon Shirley's neck, and they embraced and chattered away.

"Darling, you look wonderful," said Sadelle. "A regular new woman! Tell me, what do you do to look so good?"

"Shh. I'll tell you a secret. I'm having an affair!"

"Really? That's marvelous! Who's catering?"

mameloshn^Y
mama-loshen^R

Pronounced *ma-meh* LAW-*shen*, to rhyme with "Mama Caution." Hebrew: *loshn*, "tongue," "language."

1. Mother tongue.
2. Yiddish itself.

"Can I talk *mameloshn*?" means "Will you understand if I speak Yiddish?"

To say "Let's talk *mameloshn*" means "Let's cut out the formal talk [or double talk]," "Get to the heart of it," "Let's talk heart-to-heart," "Lay it on the line."

"Mama language" has an interesting background: Hebrew was the language of the synagogue, of the holy books, of prayer and study, which only Jewish males were taught to read. Yiddish became known as "the mother tongue," the language of the home.*

The most widely read book in all Yiddish literature was the *Tseno-Ureno (Go Out and See)* by Jacob ben Isaac Ashkenazi (1550–1628), a Polish Jew. Yudel Mark describes it thus (in Louis Finkelstein's *The Jews: Their History, Culture and Relgion,* Harper, 1960):

> Ostensibly a translation of the Pentateuch, the *Haftoros* and the Five Scrolls, it is actually a unique mosaic of commentary, legend, allegory, epigram and ethical observation. The author drew upon the entire popular literary heritage from the canonization of the Bible to his own day, choosing those stories which related to the passages of the Pentateuch he was paraphrasing. Directed to the feminine reader, the work became a kind of woman's Bible which has been the source of Jewish knowledge for generations of mothers, who, Sabbath after Sabbath, have absorbed its cabala-flavored philosophy of life.
>
> The *Tseno-Ureno,* reflecting the triumph of individual interpretation over literal translation, the prominence of the woman's role in everyday Jewish life and the paramount

---

*Hebrew was known as the *loshn kodesh,* the holy language. Gene Bluestein notes (in his *Anglish-Yinglish Dictionary,* University of Georgia Press, 1989): "As in many cultures, 'mother tongue' is a sexist notion, which relegates the feminine to a lesser role; notwithstanding, there is a certain sympathy and love" transmitted in the phrase. Several feminist scholars have written on the role that the sexist apprehension of language has played in the relegation of Yiddish to second-class status in modern Jewish life, most particularly in Israel.

A literature of devotional prayers written in Yiddish, called *tkhinas* (with a guttural *kh* sound, to rhyme with "to mean us"), was created for women from the seventeenth to the nineteenth centuries in eastern Europe. The best-known authors were Leah Horowitz and Sara bas Tovim. In some instances, men wrote *tkhinas* using female pseudonyms. See Chava Weissler's *Matriarchs: Listening to the Prayers of Early Modern Jewish Women* (Beacon Press, 1998).

influence of Polish ritual over the more worldly Germanic, overshadowed all previous works in Yiddish and affected the life of the general population more deeply and more lastingly than any other.

See Yiddish.

mamzer[Y]
momzer[R]
mamzarim (plural)

Pronounced MOM-*zer*; rhymes with "bombs her." Hebrew: "bastard." Plural pronounced *mom*-ZAY-*rim*.

1. A bastard, illegitimate. "She left home and gave birth to a *mamzer*."
2. An untrustworthy person. "I wouldn't trust that *mamzer*." "He may swindle you, that *mamzer*."
3. A stubborn, difficult man. "She married a real *mamzer*." "How can you get anywhere with such a bullheaded *mamzer*?"
4. A clever, quick, skillful fellow (said admiringly). "Oh, is he a *mamzer!*" "He has the wit of a *mamzer*."
5. An impudent sort. "Imagine such nerve! what a *mamzer!*"
6. An irreverent (but not offensive) character; a scalawag.
7. A detestable man, like the colloquial English "He's a bastard."

Mamzer is often used with affection and admiration to describe a very bright child, a clever or ingenious person, a resourceful, gets-things-done, corner-cutting type.

"Most bastards are bright," said Abba Saul. And the *Midrash* observes that no one is as bold as a bastard.

A proud grandfather may say, beaming, "My grandson, smart? A little *mamzer!*"

Mothers are less likely to employ the word—at least about their own—and consider *mamzer* a vulgar word, not to be used in "mixed company" or without blushing. Perhaps they remember the criticism "When a mother calls her child a *mamzer,* you can believe her."

CAUTION: Don't call anyone a *mamzer* to his face unless you are on friendly terms; and don't call a child a *mamzer* unless you're sure Papa or Mama will not be offended.

The biblical meaning of *mamzer* is not merely "a child born out of wedlock," but a child born of a man and a woman between whom there could be no lawful marriage (that is, the child of an incestuous relationship, or a married woman and a man not her husband). This was the *mamzer* who could not "enter into the congregation of the Lord" (Deuteronomy 23:3). The rabbis considered this law harsh and sought to limit the definition.

Under Jewish law, the illegitimate child of Jewish parents inherits from his natural father.

The Jews' reverence for learning is seen in the *Mishnah*'s judgment: "A learned bastard stands higher than an ignorant high priest" (*Horayot,* 3.8).

*See also my note to Ros- ten's entry for **get**.

See oysvorf.*

He kept trying to persuade her to come to his apartment. She kept refusing.

"Why *not?*" he persisted.

"Well, I just know I'd—hate myself in the morning."

"So sleep late," he said. (He was a *mamzer.*)

Marrano

Pronounced *m'*RAH-*no* to rhyme with "Milano." Spanish: "pig." Plural: *marranos*. (Derivations other than Spanish are sometimes suggested.)†

† *Marrano* is a Yinglish innovation; Yiddish purists would say *Maran* (plural *Maranen*).

The contemptuous name used by Spanish and Portuguese Catholics, five hundred years ago, for converted Jews—such conversions being by force and en masse—who remained "secret Jews."

It was said that the tears of the Jews blended with the waters of the baptism they were forced to undergo.

Conversions were effected, in the name of a sweet and gentle Savior, on the rack, in the pyre, on a torture wheel; via hot lead poured into bodily orifices, branding irons, blinding rods; during a process of detonguing, denailing, skin stripping, limb separation through literal horsepower.

Several popes, in different periods—Clement VI, Boniface IX, Nicholas V—were horrified by such persecutions and expressly forbade conversions by force; but the church in Spain, Portugal, France, Mexico, and Peru managed to carry on an effective Inquisition. Most of the forcibly made Christians practiced their Judaism in secret.

The story of the *Marranos*—from Portugal and England to Turkey and Persia—is unfailingly fascinating.

In Spain, before the expulsion of the Jews in 1492, many *Marrano* families, probably known to be pro forma converts, rose to positions of great influence and enjoyed high status. Many *Marranos* merged into the rarefied ranks of Spanish aristocracy. "It was not long before the majority [!] of distinguished Spanish families married into newly converted Christian families," writes Paul Borchsenius in *History of the Jews,* 1966. He cites the record of one family alone, the Caballerios of Saragossa, which came to include in its *mishpokhe* a minister of finance in the kingdom of Navarre, a vice chancellor of the kingdom of Aragon, the Speaker of the Cortes (Parliament), a bishop, a vice rector at the University of Saragossa, a judge of the high court—and a fanatical anti-Semite. "The example is by no means unique."

In the fifteenth century, Spain became a vast bonfire in which the unholy auto-da-fe (how ironically titled) burned "new Christians" by the hundreds and pious fanatics devised ever more hideous tortures. Torquemada, the chief inquisitor, persuaded Isabella and Ferdinand to expel all Jews. Between one hundred and fifty thousand and five hundred thousand human beings, including men at the very heart and mind center of Spanish life and culture, were driven out. About one hundred thousand found their first sanctuary in Portugal (whence they were soon expelled). A few thousand went to Italy, a like number to North African cities, and some went as far as Poland and Turkey, which accepted refugees in those days. And many *Marrano* families wandered, wretched and harassed, around the world, seeking shelter. To them, Pope Alexander VI, a Borgia, father of Cesare and Lucrezia, who flaunted his venality and licentiousness, hardly seemed Christ's vicar—for he gave Ferdinand and Isabella the title of "Catholic sovereigns" and cited, among their most appreciated services to the church and civilization, their **expulsion of the Jews.*** Spain never recovered from the disastrous excision.

---

*Spanish Jews who refused to convert were forced out of the country by the 1492 royal expulsion edict, but many *conversos* (or *Marranos*) also opted for exile, with Holland a favored destination. The tens of thousands who went to neighboring Portugal were converted or slaughtered within five years; as a

(Continued on page 322)

Marrano Jews founded the modern Jewish communities in Amsterdam and London. Other "crypto-Jews" existed in Majorca (the *chuetas*), in Persia (the *Jedid-al-Islam*), in south Italy (the *Neofiti*), and in Salonica (the *Donmeh*).

Mashiach
Moshiach
See meshiekh.

maskilim
See Haskala.

masmid
See yeshiva.

matzo[R]
matse[Y]
matzoh, matza, matzah

Pronounced MOTT-*seh* (not MOTT-*su*), to rhyme with "lotsa." Hebrew: The plural in Hebrew is *matzot,* pronounced

(Continued from page 321)

result, according to Rabbi Joseph Telushkin (*Jewish Literacy,* William Morrow, 1991), "only eight Portuguese Jews were actually expelled." As for the Inquisition, its persecutions and tortures were directed principally at *Marranos,* Jews who had converted to Christianity, usually under duress, and were suspected of heresy. Amazingly, the Inquisition remained active in Spain until the beginning of the nineteenth century.

MOTT-*sez* in Yiddish.

Unleavened bread (it comes in thin, flat, ridgy oblongs and is semiperforated to facilitate neat breaking).

During Passover, no bread, yeast, or leavened products are eaten. *Matzo* commemorates the kind of unleavened bread the Jews, fleeing from Egypt in the thirteenth century B.C.E., ate because they could not pause in their perilous flight long enough to wait for the dough to rise. Exodus 12:15: "Seven days shall ye eat unleavened bread. . . ." The passage is very severe about those who eat bread during the holiday: "that soul shall be cut off from Israel."

Today, *matzo* is enjoyed all year round and is served in many restaurants.*

*Which caused at least one unsuspecting blind diner, the story goes, to mistake a sheet of *matzo* for a menu and exclaim, "Who wrote this *chozzerai?*"

The following story has nothing to do with *matzo* but may give you an irreverent slant on Exodus. It is Hollywood's version of the flight from Egypt:

Moses, racing his harassed people across the desert, came up to the Red Sea and, snapping his fingers, called: "Manny!"

Up, breathless, ran Manny, publicity man. "Yes, sir?"

"The boats!"

"What?"

"The *boats*," said Moses. "Where are the boats—to get us across the Red Sea?!"

"Oh, my God! Moses, what with all the news items and human-interest stories—I forgot!"

"You *what?*"

"I forgot!"

"You forgot the *boats?!*" cried Moses. "You idiot! You moron! The Egyptians will be here any minute! What do you expect me to do—talk to God, ask Him to part the waters, let all of us Jews across, and drown the pursuing Egyptians? Is *that* what you think—"

"Boss," said Manny, "you do that and I'll get you two pages in the Old Testament!"

maven^R
meyvn^Y
mavin

Pronounced MAY-*vin*, to rhyme with "raven." Hebrew: "understanding."

An expert; a really knowledgeable person; a good judge of quality; a connoisseur. "He's a *maven* on Mozart." "Are you a real *maven*?" "Don't buy it until you get the advice of a *maven*."

*M*aven was recently given considerable publicity in a series of newspaper advertisements for herring tidbits. "The Herring *Maven* Strikes Again!" proclaimed the caption. The picture showed an empty jar.

A real advertising *maven* must have **thought that up.***

PROVERB: "Don't ask the doctor, ask the patient."

---

*In 1998, a Wesleyan University student named Matt Kelley founded an on-line magazine called *Mavin*, dedicated to celebrating the "mixed race experience." *Mavin*, says Kelley, "recognizes that mixed-race and transracially adopted people represent every community. . . . The growing ranks of self-identified racially mixed celebrities like Tiger Woods and Mariah Carey point to the growing role of mixed-race Americans in our country's future." The 2000 U.S. Census acknowledged this reality by allowing respondents to check "all that apply" on questions regarding race and ethnicity. "Jewish," however, is defined only as a religious identification.

mazel ᴿ
mazl ʸ

Pronounced MOZ-z'l, to rhyme with "nozzle." Hebrew: "luck"; "a constellation"; "a planet."

Luck; good luck.

See also mazel tov.

PROVERB: "When a man has *mazel,* even his ox calves."

One Jew said to another, "They say a poor man has no *mazel.* Do you believe that?"

"Absolutely! If he had *mazel,* would he be poor?"

mazel tov!ᴿ
mazl tov!ʸ

Pronounced MOZ-z'l, to rhyme with "schnozzle"; *tov* is pronounced TUV, TUFF, or TAWF. Hebrew: *mazel,* "luck," *tov,* "good."

"Congratulations!" or "Thank God!" rather than its literal meaning: "Good luck." The distinction is as important as it is subtle.

Don't *"mazel tov!"* a man going into the hospital; say *"mazel tov!"* when he comes out.

Do not say *"mazel tov!"* to a fighter entering a ring (it suggests you are congratulating him for having made it to the arena) or a girl about to have her nose bobbed (which would mean "and about time, too!").

Say *"mazel tov!"* to an Israeli ship captain when he first takes command: this congratulates him on his promotion; don't say *"mazel tov!"* when the ship reaches port—this suggests you're surprised he got you there.

At all Jewish celebrations—a *bris,* wedding, graduation, *bar mitzva*—you will hear *"Mazel tov!"* resounding like buckshot in a tin shed.

The ancient Hebrews, like the ancient Babylonians, Egyptians, and Greeks, fiddled around with astrology. In the Bible, *mazel* referred to a planet or a constellation of the zodiac, and the word was invoked when "fate" was involved. Later, Talmudic sages sternly warned the Jews to eschew soothsaying and diviners. (Poor believing Jews had a hard time knowing what to think: the Bible, after all, talks of the "signs of heaven"—Jeremiah, for instance, and Isaiah. But the *Midrash* teaches: "The Holy One forbade astrology in Israel"; and it is said that God made Abraham "a prophet, not an astrologer." The great Maimonides called astrology "a disease, not a science.") Nonetheless, Jews continued to utter *"mazel tov!"* Soon the supernatural or divinational aspects were forgotten (just as "God be with you" became "good-bye"), and *mazel* became simply "luck," and *"mazel tov!,"* "congratulations."

Mournfully, Mr. Lefkowitz entered the offices of his burial society. "I've come to make the funeral arrangements for my dear wife."

"Your wife?" asked the astonished secretary. "But we buried her last year!"

"That was my first wife," sighed the lugubrious Lefkowitz. "I'm talking about my second."

"Second? I didn't know you remarried. *Mazel tov!"*

"How am I doing?" the writer answered his friend. "You have no idea how popular my writing has become. Why, since I last saw you, my readers have doubled!"

"Well, *mazel tov!* I didn't know you got married."

Mr. Grossman entered the third-class compartment, found every seat occupied, and saw an old woman sprawled out over two seats, ready to doze off.

"Mazel tov!" said Grossman.

"Thank you," said the old woman, sitting up and moving over. "But—what's the occasion?"

"This is the first time I've seen you since your wedding," said Grossman, sitting down.

mazik

Pronounced MOZZ-*ik*, to rhyme with "Fosdick." Hebrew: "one who causes injury." The plural is *mazikim*, pronounced *mozz*-IK-*im*.

1. A bright, swift, mischievous, clever, or ingenious child. *Mazik* is used most frequently in this admiring or doting way. And in this usage *mazik* and *mamzer* have much in common. But *mazik* treads on no sensitive ground, where *mamzer* does. "He's a little *mamzer*" can mean "He's a clever little rogue" or "He's a little bastard." "He's a *mazik*" describes a little devil, not a diabolic child.
2. A quick, able, skillful person.
3. Someone ready to gamble and take a risk.
4. A mischievous fellow, a prankster.
5. A restless, happy-go-lucky type.

Used about an adult, *mazik* usually means "a hell of a fellow, happy-go-lucky, a live wire"—*not* a sinister or malevolent *mazik*. (See below.)

When used about an adult, *mazik* often has slightly ironic over-tones; it suggests achievement "no one dreamed that *mazik* capable of."

By now you have probably guessed that shadings of sarcasm and condescension are exceptionally subtle (and ubiquitous) in Yiddish.

6. A destructive person (rarely used today).
7. A demon or devil (rare).

The last two uses, which are much older than the first five, are infrequently employed today. And the user should offer sample indications in the context that he means the sinister type of *mazik*, not the pleasant kind.

Sidney and his little sister were visiting their grandmother, who placed two apples on the table—one large and red, the other small and withered.

"Now, darlings," she said, "I want to see which of you has the better manners."

"She does," said Sidney, taking the bigger apple.

He was a *mazik*.

mazuma[R]
mezuma
mezumn[Y]*

*Mezumn is the Yiddish word, not particularly slangy, for "cash."
Mazuma is an Ameridish version of the word and is listed in Webster's.

Pronounced *m'*-ZOOM-*a*, to rhyme with "bazooka." From the Hebrew, originally meaning "prepared" or "ready."

Slang: Money, particularly ready cash.

I always heard *mazuma,* clearly a vulgarism, used to mean money *(gelt). Mazuma* was used rather than *gelt* when a lingering, amusing effect was desired. Just as we say, "Man, is he loaded!" (to mean rich, not drunk), some say, "Has he got *mazuma!*"

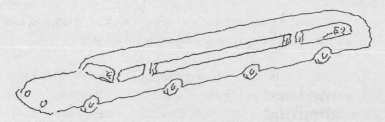

Mazuma and/or *mezuma* do not appear in the Bible or the *Talmud,* authorities aver, but *mezumn,* meaning term loan, appears in legal discussions.

This synonym for money ("scratch," "wampum," "the green") may come from the Chaldean *m'zumon,* according to H. Hishin (*American Speech,* 1926).

Eric Partridge says *mazuma* came into Canadian parlance around 1914, and it is cited in Brophy and Partridge's *Songs and Slang of the British Soldier.*

FOLK SAYING: "It's not that money makes everything good; it's that no money makes everything bad."

It is said of a couple in Chelm that the parsimonious husband always made his wife tell him exactly how she had spent the household *gelt.* One day, after she returned from shopping, he said, "I gave you five rubles when you left. How did you spend them?"

"Well," said his wife, "I bought a little this and a little that."

"That's two rubles," said the husband.

"Then I spent a ruble here—"

"That's three."

"—and a ruble there."

"Four," said the husband.

"Four?" His wife frowned. "Now what did I do with that fifth ruble?"

"See!" cried the husband. "You send a woman shopping and she wastes your money without knowing on what."

medine^Y
medina^R

Pronounced *m'*-DEE-*na;* rhymes with "farina." Hebrew: "country," "state," "land."

Province, area, country, land. In Yiddish it means, as well:

1. Domain.
2. Area of involvement. "That's his *medine*" means "That's his problem, his headache."

The United States was known as the *goldene medine*—El Dorado—to the Jews who came here.

A poor, undernourished tailor, working in a basement, once said ironically, "Observe the glory and the grandeur of my *medine*."

But one of his sons became a professor, another became an editor, his daughter a concert pianist.

His children became, as with millions of immigrants, his *goldene medine.*

megillah^R
megile ^Y

Pronounced *meh-*GILL-*eh,* to rhyme with "guerrilla."
Hebrew: "scroll."

1. *Megillah* usually describes the book of Esther, which is
   read in the synagogue during the *Purim* holiday; also
   the book of Ruth. (There are five *megillahs* in all.)*
2. Anything very long, prolix; a rigmarole. The book of
   Esther wanders through a crushing concatenation of de-
   tail, and the devout sit through the long, long reading
   after a day of fasting.
3. In popular parlance: Anything complicated, boring,
   overly extended, fouled up. "He'll put you to sleep with
   that *megillah.*" "Don't give me a *megillah*" means
   "Spare me the full, dull details."

In show business, *megillah* has become a much-favored word,
and I have heard it, not without surprise, on many a television
program: the *Tonight* show's chitchat; dramas in which shady
characters employ their special argot, not criminal but certainly
infra dig; scenes between lawyers; in comedy routines, by Jewish
and non-Jewish entertainers alike, instead of "all that jazz" or "all
that malarkey." Thus: "Cut the *megillah.*" "He gave me a real
megillah." "Who needs a *megillah* like that?"

Nightclub habitués and jet-set jokers, in Hollywood, New York,
and Miami, use *megillah* as matter-of-factly as if they were in the
synagogue during *Purim,* just as many Italians say *"una Iliade"*
who have never read the *Iliad.*

---

*The five *megillahs* are Ecclesiastes, Esther, Lamentations, Ruth, and the
Song of Songs. The *Talmud* also has a tractate known as *Megillah,* which
deals with the laws of *Purim.* See Rosten's entry and my note for **Purim.**

A *gantse megillah,* meaning "a whole *megillah,*" is a common phrase; it simply adds a note of dismissal via emphasis.

Two men sat opposite each other in the train. After a while, the first man said, "Uh—where are you from?"

"Newark," said the second, "and I'm going to Philadelphia. My business is insurance. My name is Boris Mishkin, I'm not rich, I have a daughter at Rutgers and a son who's married. My wife's maiden name was Kowalsky and she comes from Paterson. I'm a Democrat. I don't fish or play golf. I spend my summers in the Catskills and go to Miami for two weeks every December, where I stay in a motel. I go to a Reform temple and contribute to the UJA, B'nai B'rith, and the Community Chest. I don't have a brother of the same name because I don't have a brother, and my sister you couldn't possibly have known because she died thirty years ago in Cracow. Now, if I've forgotten anything in this *megillah,* please ask me right now, because I want to take a nap until we reach Philadelphia!"

mekhaye^Y
mechiaeh^R
mechaye, mechayeh

Pronounced *m'*KHY-*eh,* to rhyme with "Messiah." The *kh* sound is, of course, the way a MacTavish would roll it out. Hebrew.

Pleasure, great enjoyment, a real joy.

Mekhaye is invariably uttered with a smile, a grin, a patting of the stomach, a pleased cluck or shake of the head.

When you take off your shoes and stretch out in front of a fire, that's a *mekhaye*.

When you hear a great virtuoso sing, it's a *mekhaye*.

I suggest you preface *mekhaye* with a blissful "Oh!," "*Oy!,*" or "Ah": "Oh, this is a *mekhaye!*" *Oy* adds flavor to the utterance, but "Ah" is not to be sneezed at in this connection.

Mekhaye comes from the Hebrew *chai*, meaning "life." Technically, a *mekhaye* is one who gives life. (*Mekhaye* also meant God.)

Yiddish-speaking Jews converted the word to mean something that "puts life into" or "gives pleasure." That in itself was a *mekhaye*.

Finsterwald stumbled along the street, limping, moaning, groaning, leaving a trail of "*Oy vay!*" in his wake. A stranger stopped him. "What is the matter?"

"What's the *matter*? My shoes are absolutely killing me!"

"So why do you wear them?"

"I'll tell you. My business couldn't be worse. I owe the butcher, the baker, the grocer, the landlord. I have two daughters so ugly who knows if I'll ever be able to get them married. My son is a *zhlob*, and my wife nags, nags, nags until I can go crazy. I come home each night from a fruitless day's work, and I look at the bills and at my family, and at that point I could kill myself. So I take off my shoes—and mister, the minute these shoes are off my feet, it's such a *mekhaye* it's the only thing that makes life worth living!"

mekhule^Y
mechuleh^R

Pronounced *m'–*KHOOL-*eh,* to rhyme with "a pull a."
Hebrew: "finished," "destroyed."

Finished unsuccessfully, ended unhappily. "He went
mekhule" means he went bankrupt. "That marriage?
Mekhule!" means they're not living together anymore—at
least.

*M*ekhule is like *fini!* in French or phfft! in **Winchell-ese,*** if
that's any help to you.

In the Bible, *mekhule* was used to mean "to end" or "to exter-
minate." Later, the word came to mean "spoiled" or "damaged."
That's all I know about *mekhule.*
Mekhule.

mekhuteneste^Y
machetayneste ^R
makheteyneste

Pronounced *mekh-oo-*TEN-*es-teh,* or *mekh-oo-*TANE-*es-teh,* or
*mokh-oo-*TEN-*es-teh* (or TANE-*es-teh*); be sure to rattle the *kh*
in the back of your throat. Hebrew: *mechutan, mechutenet:*
"relative (m. and f.) by marriage."

Female relative by marriage. "My *makhuteneste*"
means my daughter's or my son's mother-in-law.

---

*Walter Winchell (1897–1972), radio gossip columnist and shaper of public
opinion, spoke in a tommy-gun staccato style. Winchell, who was Jewish,
began broadcasting in 1933 and eventually gained the wide world as his
audience.

Mekheneste describes a relationship for which there is no word at all in English.

See mekhutn.

One of the oldest of Jewish stories concerns the poor man who came to his rabbi and complained that he was living in one room with his wife and four children and *mekhuteneste*—and the congestion was impossible to bear any longer.

"Do you have a goat?" asked the rabbi.

"Yes."

"Take it into the room."

"What?"

"Do as I say."

So the poor man went home and brought the goat into his house.

A week later he hurried to the rabbi, sputtering: "I did what you asked. I took the goat in, and things are even worse than before! Rabbi, what shall I *do*?"

"Do you have any chickens?" asked the rabbi.

"Yes. Three—"

"Bring them into your house."

"Rabbi!"

"Do as I say."

So the poor man brought the three chickens into the house, and a week later he returned to the rabbi, wringing his hands.

"It's terrible! I can't stand it anymore!"

"Put out the goat," said the rabbi.

The poor man did as he was told and came back. "It's a little better, Rabbi, but three chickens in a room with seven people . . ."

"Throw out the chickens," said the rabbi.

And finally the man stood before the rabbi, overjoyed: "Rabbi, there's no one as wise as you! My house now is a paradise!"

mekhutn^Y
machuten^R
machutin

Pronounced *m'khoot-n,* to rhyme with "m'tootin." Note the larynx-seated *kh.* Derives from the Hebrew: *hatan,* "bridegroom." The masculine of *mekhuteneste.*

My son's or daughter's father-in-law.

English could heave a great sigh of relief if it adopted *mekhutn* and *mekhuteneste.**

> *Both *mekhuteneste* and *mekhutn* can be used sarcastically, to belittle a person's claim of closeness or connection: "She wants a key to the apartment? What kind of *mekhuteneste* is she to us?"

mekhutonim^Y
machetunim^R

Pronounced *mekh-eh-*TUN-*im,* with a crumb-expelling *kh,* or *mokh-oo-*TUNE-*im,* to rhyme with "Bach attune him." Yiddish variation and transformation of Hebrew *mechutan:* "relative by marriage."

The members of one's wife's or husband's extended family. "His wife comes from a large family; she must have fifty *mekhutonim.*" "I like her husband, but not all her *mekhutonim.*"

The definitive explication of *mekhutonim* is to be found in this sardonic conundrum:

Q: Why did Adam and Eve live so long?
A: Because their lives were not shortened by *mekhutonim.*

See mishpokhe.

melamed

Pronounced *m*-LAH-*med*, to rhyme with "Muhammed."
Plural: *melamdim*, pronounced *m*-LAHM-*dim*. Hebrew:
"teacher."

1. A teacher—of elementary Hebrew, more exactly.
   Hebrew teachers were not rabbis or sages, but an
   unworldly, impecunious lot whose social status was
   respectable, but not enviable. The *melamed*'s work was
   teaching by rote. (My father used to say, "If they were
   smarter, they'd be rabbis.")
2. An incompetent. To call someone a *melamed* who does
   not earn his living as a *melamed* is to speak with condescension. ("Those who can, do," said Shaw. "Those
   who can't, teach.")
3. A *shlemiel*, a well-meaning, innocuous drip.
4. An unworldly, unsophisticated, impractical type. There
   is a saying: "A *melamed* remains a *melamed*." It means
   "He'll never get anywhere" or "What did you expect?"

It always puzzled me that the Jews, who so revere learning,
should speak patronizingly of a teacher. The reason, I suppose,
is that the *melamed* is the teacher of elementary Hebrew of young
boys—teaching by sheer repetition—and every Jewish community seemed to contain a great many elders, perambulating repos-
itories of lore and wisdom, compared to whom the *melamed*
lacked luster.* Besides, *melamdim* were considered rather poor

---

*The sheer boredom of Hebrew school instruction, and the continued use of
underpaid, uninspiring teachers throughout the 1950s and 1960s, contributed mightily to the problem of alienation and non-affiliation in Jewish
life. In his book, *Jewish Renewal* (Grosset/Putnam, 1994), Rabbi Michael Lerner

(Continued on page 338)

teachers, and a Jew who had no way of making a living, or who had failed in what he had undertaken, could become a *melamed* as a last resort.

Among the *melamdim* were many deeply pious men, dedicated to teaching—but their teaching could not help becoming repetitious and boring.

A Jewish saying goes: "He has no luck—like a *melamed*."

Pitying, even derogatory, tales about *melamdim* abound among Jews. In all of them, the *melamed* is not the hero but the goat—hapless, unlucky, unresourceful.

Sholom Aleichem defined a *melamed* as "a Jew who deals with *goyim*"—meaning that a *melamed*'s students, being little boys, know about as much Hebrew as do Gentiles.

"Ah," sighed a *melamed*, "if I were a Rockefeller, I'd be *richer* than Rockefeller."

"How could that be?"

"I would do a little teaching on the side."

A *melamed* was given to taking a little nip while his pupils droned on. And when this became known, parents began to withdraw their boys from his class.

(Continued from page 337)

reports that of the "125 of us who graduated Hebrew school the year of my bar mitzva . . . only five of us continued through Hebrew high school. . . . Very few of the original 125 felt any particular connection to Jewish tradition by the time they reached their twenties. Most of them looked back on Hebrew school as an ordeal that they went through to please their parents, and once they were free to make choices of their own, they ran from the Jewish world as fast as they could." Efforts to professionalize the corps of Hebrew teachers have somewhat improved the situation during the past three decades.

His wife pleaded with him to change his ways. "Give up drinking and you'll get the pupils back."

Sighed the *melamed*, "You tell me to stop drinking so I should be able to teach, but I have been teaching so I should be able to drink."

The *melamed* asked one of his young students, "Yussele, do you say your prayers before each meal?"

"No, *melamed*."

"*What?* You don't pray before each meal?!"

"I don't have to. My mother's a good cook."

menorah

Pronounced *men-AW-ra*, to rhyme with "aurora." Hebrew: "candelabrum."

The *menorah* most commonly referred to is the eight-branched candelabrum lit on *Chanukah*, the Feast of Lights.

The word first occurs in Exodus 37, where you can find a detailed description of the seven-branched gold candelabrum made by Bezalel, the artisan, for the Tabernacle in the wilderness. The *menorah* was later placed in the Temple in Jerusalem.

The Arch of Titus in Rome, which commemorates the conquest of Judea by the **Romans**,* has a *menorah* depicted on it.

---

*By the time the Arch of Titus was built, Rome had been the controlling power in Judea for more than a century. The Arch honored the Roman suppression of the Jewish uprising of 66–70 C.E., which ended with the destruction of Jerusalem and the Temple. Titus, son of the emperor Vespasian, led the bloody military campaign, assisted by the Jewish renegade-turned-

(Continued on page 340)

Originally, it was an oil lamp that was lighted on Sabbath eve, with a flax wick soaked in eight or nine separate spouts arranged in a line or in a circle. Oil lamps gave way to brass or silver candlesticks in the eighteenth century.

mentsh[Y]
mensh[R]
mensch, mentsch

Rhymes with "bench." From German: *Mensch,* "person." Plural: *mentshn.*
1. A human being. "After all, he is a *mentsh,* not an animal."
2. An upright, honorable, decent person. "Come on, act like a *mentsh.*"
3. Someone of consequence; someone to admire and emulate; someone of noble character. "Now, there is a real *mentsh!*"

It is hard to convey the special sense of respect, dignity, and approbation that can be conveyed by calling someone "a real *mentsh.*"

As a child, I often heard it said: "The finest thing you can say about a man is that he is a *mentsh!*" Jewish children often heard

(Continued from page 339)

historian Josephus. It was during the siege of Jerusalem that Yochanan Ben Zakkai had himself smuggled out of the city and was permitted by the Romans to establish a Jewish center of learning in Yavneh—which proved critical to the future of Judaism once the Bar Kochba Jewish revolt against Rome was put down in 135 and Jewish sovereignty in Israel was destroyed until the modern era.

this admonition: "Behave like a *mentsh!*" or, "Be a *mentsh!*" This use of the word is uniquely Yiddish in its overtones.

The most withering comment one might make on someone's character or conduct is "He is not [did not act like] a *mentsh.*"

To be a *mentsh* has nothing to do with success, wealth, or status. A judge can be a *zhlob*, a millionaire can be a *mamzer*, a professor can be a *shlemiel*, a doctor a *klutz*, a lawyer a *bulvon*. The key to being "a real *mentsh*" is nothing less than character: rectitude, dignity, a sense of what is right, responsible, decorous. Many a poor person, many an ignorant person, is a *mentsh.*

See also balebatish.

PROVERB: "Ten lands are more easily known than one man."

meshiekh^Y
meshiach^R
mashiach, mashiakh, moshiakh

Pronounced *m'*SHEE-*ech,* with a rattling *kh* sound at the end; rhyme it with "Marie, *ech!*" Hebrew: *mashiah,* "the anointed." The Hebrew *mashiah* became, in Greek, *messias,* or, in translation, *christos;* hence, *messias* = messiah; *christos* = Christ—and both denote "the anointed one."

Messiah.

1. Originally, in the Old Testament, *meshiekh* was the title for kings ("God's anointed") and priests, who were initiated into sacerdotal status by being anointed with sacred oil. The Jews made a distinction between ordinary cosmetic anointment of the body *(sukh)* and the pouring of sacred oil as a consecration rite *(mashah)* on the head of a priest or king. A guest was often

honored by anointing his head—or feet. Except for one phrase in the book of Esther, where "oil of myrrh" is mentioned, all (over two hundred) scriptural references to anointing seem to mean olive oil.

2. Later, *meshiekh* meant a prophet or anyone with a special mission from God.
3. Then, *meshiekh* came to mean the awaited Deliverer of the Jews from their bondage and oppression, the one who will restore the kingdom of Israel.
4. Finally, *meshiekh* means the Savior who will make the world acknowledge God's sovereignty, thus ushering in the Day of Judgment.

English translations of the Bible tend to separate the idea of "the anointed" from the "messiah"—the first used for the living, the second for the expected. The Jewish concept needs to be understood historically. The Old Testament uses the term *meshiekh*, anointed king, for Saul, David, Zedekiah, and Cyrus of Persia (no Jew). David, "the anointed of Yahweh," establishes the dynastic principle among the Jews.

From this seems to have developed, across many years, the idea that some man, blessed by God with superior virtues, would come from the House of David to end Israel's tribulations and torment, to enforce justice and establish peace. A spiritual leader, a messiah, would establish that new messianic age—on earth, be it noted—that the great prophets Isaiah and Micah foretold. And in the new Age of Righteousness *all* of humankind would be redeemed.

Jews distinguished the earthly messiah from the heavenly messiah: the earthly messiah, a dreamed-of deliverer of the Jews, was to be a man born of the line of David; but the heavenly messiah lives in Heaven "under the wings of the Lord" (Enoch 39) and existed before the sun and the stars were made. And his mystical Name existed before the sun. The idea of a divine Son of Man was not understood by Jews in the later messianic sense.

The doctrine of the messiah has been one of the most powerful elements in the history of Judaism—and, of course, Christianity. Whenever epidemics, starvation, pogroms, wars, expulsions, or any of the thousand torments visited upon the Jews seemed unendurable, the faithful and desperate looked once more into their holy books for some hidden sign, some new revelation, some miraculous harbinger of hope; pious mystics, numerologists, astrologers, cabalists, and, later, *Chasidim* predicted the exact time when the glorious messiah would usher in the Kingdom of God.

The Romans, who could make no sense out of the Jews' concept of a messiah, feared messianic claims and predictions for political reasons, because they considered them a camouflage for rebellion against Rome's rule. And messianic hopes often did lead to political militancy; messianic ideas buttressed protests against a sense of resignation, an utterly passive acceptance of Israel's lot that, some Jews felt, was encouraged by Jewish law.

Around 60 c.e., and especially after the destruction of the Second Temple in 70 c.e., messianic fevers raged among Jewry. Daniel's book of prophecies was seized upon and quoted to prove the imminence of the messiah's arrival. And when, in the year 132, the Jews, led by the remarkable Bar Kochba, rose in armed rebellion against Rome, and for over three years held off superior forces, Bar Kochba was acclaimed "the messiah."

The revered scholar-saint Rabbi Akiba (also spelled Akiva) supported Bar Kochba—whom most rabbis and the *Sanhedrin* regarded with some distaste. Rabbinical sources called him Bar Coziba, which means "son of deceit"! (Bar Kochba was so irreverent as once to have cried, "O Lord, don't help us—and don't spoil it for us!") And the great Akiba, head teacher of a rabbinical academy where he is said to have had some twenty-four thousand pupils, supported Bar Kochba's claim to being the messiah, descended from **King David.*** Both Akiba and Bar Kochba called the Jews to arms against Rome. Akiba acted as Bar Kochba's sword-bearer. (Trajan had already crushed a rebellion in 113 C.E., in a three-year war.)

It took Emperor Hadrian and his ablest general, Julius Severus, three long, brutal, bloody years to defeat the Jews— 580,000 of whom were casualties, to say nothing of thousands more, men, women, children, who starved or died of one or another disease brought on by the revolution. Bar Kochba was slain at Bethar in the year 135. (In 1953 and 1960, letters written by Bar Kochba were discovered by archaeologists in Israel.) Akiba was captured, flayed alive with a cruelty exceptional even for those dreadful times, and died with singular composure. Louis Finkelstein writes (in *Akiba,* Jewish Publication Society, 1962): "The association of the *Shema* with the great martyr's death made its recitation a death-bed affirmation of the faith, instead of a repetition of select verses: and to this day the pious Jew hopes that when his time comes he may be sufficiently conscious to declare the Unity of his God, echoing with his last breath the words which found their supreme illustration in Akiba's martyrdom."

It is hardly surprising that the history of the Jews is studded with pseudoprophets and false messiahs, all self-proclaimed:

*Rabbi Yochanan ben Torata replied to Akiba's proclamation (in the Jerusalem *Talmud,* *Ta'anit* 4:5): "Akiba, grass will grow from your cheeks before the Son of David will come."

The *Talmud* includes a range of messianic speculation and some very strong preachments against it. These discussions took place with the wholesale destruction of Israel by Rome still a fresh memory, and the rabbis were generally reluctant to stoke the kind of feverish messianism that might lead to conflict with Rome once again.

mystagogues, adventurers, some sincere but paranoidal visionaries, some charlatans—each claiming to be fulfilling a divine mission, or claiming to have received a revelation directly from God. They fanned the fires of hope for miraculous deliverance in hundreds of thousands of desperate hearts. These mountebank messiahs were as colorful and brazen a company of crackpots and *saltimbanques* as ever paraded across the pages of history.

I admire the passage in *Antiquities of the Jews* in which Josephus writes: ". . . they were deceivers and deluders of the people, and under [the] pretense of divine illumination . . . prevailed upon the multitude to act like madmen."

One man's *meshiekh* may be another's *meshugener.*

Josephus cites the case of a Jew called "Judas of Galilee" who, in the year 6 c.e., led a rebellion against the Romans, claiming to be a messiah come to deliver the Jews.

In 44 c.e., a gaudy character named Theudas led his bedazzled followers to the Jordan, where he promised to part the waters, as had his predecessor, Moses, at the Red Sea. There is no record that the ambitious Theudas parted a single liquid yard of that river, which is considerably narrower than the Red Sea. The iconoclastic Roman authorities terminated the post-Mosaic mission of Theudas, first by crucifying, then by beheading, him.

Around 58 or 59 c.e., one "Benjamin the Egyptian" managed to assemble twenty-five thousand or more followers, with whom he marched up to the Mount of Olives. Benjamin announced that he would now make the walls of Jerusalem tumble down, à la Joshua before Jericho, but an unimaginative Roman procurator broke up the historic meeting. Of Benjamin, "the Lord's anointed" (so he said), no more was ever heard.

Around 66 or 67 c.e., the inventive grandson of the "Judas of Galilee" cited above, one Menachem, announced that *he* was the *meshiekh* and, with men armed from and by a raid on the fortress of Masada, marched upon holy Jerusalem—before reaching which he was stopped by superior Roman forces and disappeared from history's pages, at least those possible to believe.

In 431 C.E. there appeared on the island of Crete a new messiah, called Moses, who told his followers that he would lead them to the Holy Land—right across the water from Crete. Moses seems to have disappeared (not under or over the waters) after many of his gullible disciples were drowned, in both their faith and the Mediterranean.

In the eighth century, pseudomessiahs sprouted in many places; examples are the brazen Abu Issa al-Isfahani, in Persia; one Severus, or Serene, which I do not doubt, in Syria; and an obscure *Yudghan* in Hamadan, a city in western Persia.

In the ninth century, an enthusiastic Eldad Ha-Dani announced that the lost ten tribes of Israel had been discovered: the glorious messianic age would now commence. Exit Eldad Ha-Dani.

The Crusades, which spelled repeated horrors to thousands of powerless and innocent Jews, saw a predictable uprise in the market for messiahs: the singular David Alroy of Mesopotamia (about 1160 C.E.) and *meshiekhs* of a lesser luminosity who flourished in Persia, Morocco, Spain, and France. Alroy, whose real name was Menahim ben Solomon, was a leader of considerable intellectual stature. He was killed by assassins sometime between 1135 and 1160.

In 1295, a *meshiekh* appeared in Avila, Spain. Born Nissim ben Abraham, he announced he would inaugurate the redemption on the last day of the month of Tammuz. Mass fastings promptly began, worldly possessions were given away, prayers and ecstasies accompanied the impatient wait for the commencement of the Kingdom of God. Alas, poor Jews. . . .

A Spanish Jew named Avrum (Abraham) Abulafia (1240–1291), who had steeped himself in cabalistic writings and assorted abracadabra, went on a trip to the Holy Land, where he had a vision: a voice told him to hasten home and announce himself to be a prophet. Later, the voice told him to convert no less than Pope Nicholas III! This, believe it or not, he set about attempting. Abulafia actually obtained an audience with the pope, who, discovering what the astounding Spanish Jew was up to, promptly condemned him to be burned at the stake. Abulafia escaped this incendiary fate because Nicholas III died a few days after issuing his awesome order. So Abulafia went on to Sicily, where the voice now told him he was the messiah long promised to the Jews. So he said, so he said. . . . Farewell, **Abulafia.***

A most remarkable, brave (or presumptuous) genius of a charlatan was one David Reuveni, or Reubeni, a dwarf, who in the year 1524 announced in Venice that he was the brother of the king of one of the Lost Tribes, the tribe of Reuben. Reuveni sought to win the pope's support for a joint crusade against the Turks, who were marching into Europe, by disclosing that his "brother" commanded thousands of splendid Jewish soldiers *behind* the Turkish lines, a most happy place to be. Pope Clement VII did grant little Reuveni an audience, and the papal astrologers not only approved the dwarf's credentials, whatever they could be, but even certified his prophecies of a fraternal military victory.

The pope then communicated with the king of Portugal—and David Reuveni sailed for Portugal, under a Jewish flag! . . . The *Marranos* in Portugal hailed Reuveni as the messiah—and one

---

*An interesting comparison of Abulafia and Swami Muktananda (1908–1982), who gained fame as a yoga teacher in America, can be found in *The Fifty-eighth Century: A Jewish Renewal Sourcebook*, Shohama Wiener, ed. (Jason Aronson, 1996). Diane M. Sharon writes that Abulafia "is among the most prolific of Jewish kabbalists. He wrote numerous manuals of mystical technique which serve as instructions for achieving ecstatic mystical experiences. . . . Many of these works still exist today, and . . . Gershom Scholem and Moshe Idel have published many lengthy segments which are available for study."

Diego Pires (1500–1532) became so entranced by Reuveni that he underwent circumcision and changed his name to Solomon Molko or Molcho, under which sobriquet you may encounter him in encyclopedias. Molko joined Reuveni in Italy, then fled to the Holy Land to escape the Italian Inquisition and in time returned to announce the happy tidings that *he* was the messiah. The pope exempted him from the mounting umbrage of the Holy Inquisition.

Reuveni and Molko together went to Charles V, emperor of the Holy Roman Empire, to ask for support for the apocryphal Jewish legions in Arabia. Charles turned both of them over to the Inquisition. Molko refused a chance to recant and, apparently thinking his sacrifice would redeem humanity, was burned at the stake in Mantua. The year was 1532. Reuveni was shipped off to Spain and ended in an auto-da-fé. (His travel diary is in the Bodleian Library at Oxford.)

At the beginning of the sixteenth century, one Asher Lammlein (or Lemmlin) proclaimed himself Elijah, herald of the *meshiekh*. . . . Some Jews thought that Lemmlin was actually the messiah himself, and not merely Elijah, but was too noble to admit it. Many Jews were "baptized" in purification ceremonies to hasten the messiah's arrival. Exit Lammlein or Lemmlin.

The most spectacular of fake messiahs, of course, was Sabbatai or Shabbatai Zvi (1626–1676). In Yiddish, he is also known as "Shabtsai Zvi," pronounced "sHOP-*tsay-tzvy*."

Repeated and terrible pogroms in the mid–seventeenth century (Cossack bloodbaths slaughtered some three hundred thousand souls, about half the Jews in the Ukraine) led many pious Jews to think that the messiah was about to appear—for an ancient tradition held that when the misery of Israel reached the point of utter unendurability, God would end it by sending a messiah down to earth.

In Salonika, in the year 1648, a twenty-one-year-old Turkish Jew announced that he was the messiah. His name was Sabbatai Zvi. Zvi was born in 1626, in Smyrna (Izmir). He was of Spanish descent, apparently. His father was the local agent for an English firm. Sabbatai, who sang psalms very sweetly and was much loved by children, was engrossed in the mystical teachings of Rabbi Isaac Luria, a famous cabalist known as the *Ari* (the Lion).

Zvi seems to have been able to induce prolonged ecstastic states in himself, and he came to believe that he was destined to fulfill the prediction of certain Christians in England who had set 1666 as the year in which the millennium would begin. (Jewish cabalists, by elaborate numerical mumbo jumbo, had concluded that 1648 was the year of salvation.)

Sabbatai Zvi went to Jerusalem in 1662, after Safed had been sacked by the Turks and Tiberias had been laid waste by the Druse. There he prayed fervently at the tombs of the patriarchs of old; he fasted and mortified his flesh—and won followers by the score.

Sent to Egypt by his zealous believers, Zvi was received with great honors. In Cairo, he married a prostitute named Sarah, a rather remarkable lady who had been raised in a Polish convent (her parents had been slain in a pogrom). She had traveled to Amsterdam, where she experienced a vision, she later claimed, that told her of the miracle worker Sabbatai Zvi, who would become her husband. One legend indeed held that the messiah would take an unchaste woman for his bride.

Sabbatai returned to the Holy Land, his visionary pronounce-ments greatly aided by one Nathan of Gaza, who took it upon him-self to act as "Elijah," the prophet and pathbreaker for "Our Messiah, Sabbatai Zvi."

The rabbis of Jerusalem, furious, threatened to anathematize Sabbatai Zvi, who went back to Smyrna, where he was received with fantastic enthusiasm. And the Sabbatean movement began to spread through the Jewish centers of Asia Minor.

The ecstasy and hysteria produced by Zvi's mystical evangelism is difficult to describe. A messianic fever spread from Turkey to Venice, on to Hamburg, to Amsterdam, even to London. Sabbatai became the "King of the Jews" to many, on whom the earlier parallel of Jesus was not lost. Thousands of Jews actually prepared for the end of the world, sold all their possessions, settled their affairs, prayed for the Day of Judgment, left their homes, covered themselves with ashes and sackcloth, and started prolonged fasting and praying.*

In 1666, Zvi went to Constantinople, where he was arrested by the Turkish authorities. Accounts of his miraculous doings continued to spread, nevertheless. Zvi was brought before the sultan and given the choice of having his head chopped off or embracing the faith of Islam. Zvi kept his head on his shoulders.... He and his wife became, respectively, Mehemet Effendi and Fatima Radini.

Many ardent, if embarrassed, followers found a way to explain Sabbatai Zvi's apostasy, and a small sect of Muhammadans in Turkey are still **Sabbatean.**†

---

*Gershom Scholem maintains that more than half of the Jewish world, including populations throughout Europe, believed the messianic claims of Sabbatai Zvi, who was more than likely a manic-depressive personality. Nathan of Gaza was a cabalist of substantial reputation before becoming Zvi's prophet. It should be noted that cabalistic beliefs were very widespread in Jewish life, including among scholars and rabbis, during this period of history. See Scholem's authoritative work, *Sabbatai Zevi, The Mystical Messiah* (Princeton University Press, 1976).

†In Turkey, the Sabbatean vestiges are known as the *Donmeh*. According to Yakov Leib HaKohain, who maintains a Web site (www.kheper.auz.com) dedicated to Sabbatean history and thought, "To this day, pockets of radical cabalists throughout the world, but particularly in Asia Minor, covertly worship Sabbatai as the Promised Messiah and an incarnation of the Godhead. However, to my knowledge, and in my experience of Sabbateanism (which

Sabbatai Zvi died a Muslim, obscurely, it is reported, in Albania, in 1676.

A member of a surviving Sabbatean sect, the flamboyant and thoroughly detestable Jacob Frank (1726–1791), attacked rabbis and Talmudists and deplored the Jews' devotion to holy books and book learning; Jews should become warriors, he cried, and Israel a military nation. "The Resurrection will be by the sword," said Frank. So far, so good. But the odious Frank, a traveling salesman by trade, was a sensualist by inclination. He became a member of a Sabbatean sect, then issued a novel ukase: Redemption was to be achieved through *im*purity. The road to Heaven ran through the boudoir. It is said that his religious sessions were small saturnalia and featured quite orgiastic rites.

In Poland, Frank claimed to be Sabbatai Zvi—reincarnated. Indeed, he altered the personnel of the Trinity to include himself. The audacious Frank lived in great splendor off the donations of his gullible followers and soon ennobled himself—or at least called himself "Baron."

The rabbis anathematized Frank for licentious behavior, to say nothing of blasphemy and heresy; and the church in time jailed Frank (who had been converted, along with many of his followers) because of his startling and sacrilegious alteration of the doctrine of the Trinity. After thirteen years in prison, Frank was freed (by the Russians).

He now journeyed to Vienna, where he became a great society favorite. He was known as "the Man with the Gospel" and favorably regarded by the empress herself, Maria Theresa. Frank's followers again showered funds on him, and they paraded around in

spans over forty years), Donmeh-L is the only collective of Sabbatian/Frankist 'fellow travelers' west of Turkey, and certainly the only one on the Internet."

Uhlan uniforms, on splendid steeds, and carried lances and pennants adorned with various mystic symbols.

After Jacob Frank's unmessianic death in 1791, his energetic daughter Eve carried on Daddy's fakery. She was known as "the Holy Lady." Apparently as lustful as her father had been, little Eve, like the Byzantine empress Theodosia, joined venery with hocus-pocus—a combination certain to appeal to many mortals.

Messianic hopes, like hallucinatory visions, may be directly correlated to adversity, hunger, suffering, despair, and the obsessional-paranoidal quotient of any population at any time. Maimonides set down rules for the judging of allegations, prophecies, and "miracles" purporting to be messianic.

A group of ultra-Orthodox zealots called *Neturei Karta*, who today live in Israel, refuse to recognize Israel as an independent state because, they maintain, such a holy sovereignty could have been established only by the *meshiekh*—and the *meshiekh* has, clearly, not yet arrived.*

*For mention of the modern Lubavitcher Chasidic movement's campaign to gain recognition for their *rebbe* as *meshiekh*, see my note to Rosten's entry on **Chasid**.

meshuge^Y
meshugge^R

Pronounced *m'*SHU-*geh*, to rhyme with "Paducah." Hebrew: "crazy."

Is there anyone who does not know that *meshuge* means crazy? Crazy, nuts, wildly extravagant, absurd.

The potent *sh* and muscular *ug* unite to give *meshuge* a ripe combination of sounds that may account for the word's increasing popularity in English.

A crazy man is a *meshugener*.

A crazy woman is a *meshugene*.

NOTE: "That's *meshuge*," but "that's a *meshugene* idea."

Also see mishegas.

FOLK SAYING: "Every man has his own *mishegas*."

Old Mr. Yonklowitz could not sleep. For nights on end, week after week, the old man complained of insomnia. His children had brought in doctors; they had given the old man pills, syrups, tranquilizers—all to no avail.

The frantic children finally decided to call in a hypnotist. They did not decide that lightly, mind you, but in desperation. And to find a reliable hypnotist, they consulted a psychiatrist.

When the hypnotist arrived, the children introduced him to the old man. "Papa, a wonderful doctor, a man who works miracles, a *specialist* who makes people sleep!"

The hypnotist said, "Mr. Yonklowitz, if you'll have just a little faith in me, you'll fall asleep like a child." He held up a watch and said, "Keep your eyes here. That's right. . . . Good." The hypnotist now swung the watch back and forth, slowly intoning: "Left . . . right . . . Your eyes are getting tired . . . tired . . . Your eyelids are heavy . . . heavy . . . sleep . . . sleep . . . sleep."

The old man's head hung low, his eyes were shut, his breathing was as rhythmic as a babe's. The hypnotist placed his finger on his lips, cautioning the children to remain silent, and stole out.

Whereupon the old man opened one eye. "That *meshugener*! Has he gone yet?"

meshumed^Y
meshumad^R

Pronounced *m'sHU-med*, to rhyme with "diluted." Hebrew: "apostate." Plural: *meshumedim*.

    A willing convert from Judaism; an apostate.

Note the word *willing*. Jewish history is full of so many mass conversions, by hair-raising tortures and threats of death, that Jews distinguished forced converts, or *anusim*, from those who joined another faith of their own volition, **meshumedim**.*

    The most famous and important of Jewish *anusim*, of course, were the *Marranos* of Spain.

    See Marrano.

metsieh^R
metsie^Y

Pronounced *meh-TSEE-eh*, to rhyme with "Let's see a." Hebrew: "find."

1. A bargain, a lucky break. "Believe me, that's a *metsieh*."
2. No bargain (used bitterly), nothing to brag about. "He married some *metsieh*." "Oh, thank you for such a *metsieh!*"

Today, *metsieh* is used mostly in this dry, disillusioned, sarcastic way.

---

*The 1990 National Jewish Population Study of the Council of Jewish Federations showed rough parity in numbers between *meshumedim*, Jews voluntarily converting out of Judaism, the majority of whom are the offspring of intermarriages, and adults converting into Judaism, two-thirds of whom are women.

Metsieh originally meant something valuable that was found. The *Talmud* expresses this lovely thought: "God found the Jews as one finds grapes in the desert."

I know of no English word with quite the bouquet of *metsieh* and commend it to you. It's a *metsieh* in itself.

The *Baba Metsieh* ("Middle Gate") is a tractate of the *Talmud* that deals with laws of possession, obligations of guardianship, and so on.

Meylekh Hamlokhim^Y
Melech Ham'lochim^R

Pronounced MEY-*lekh ham*-LAW-*khim*, to rhyme with "derrick papa saw him," using the guttural *kh* twice. Hebrew: "King of kings."

One of the titles used to avoid uttering the Name of God (see Adonai, Adoshem).

$\mathbb{S}$ ince God is the King of kings, all men, whether princes or paupers, are His servants. Hence, the rabbis taught that no man should serve another,* for all are servants of God alone.

---

*Rosten is offering a loose interpretation of the word *service*. Judaism forbids the deification of earthly rulers, but it does encourage obedience to the civil laws of the ruling power (assuming these laws do not force Jews into murder, fornication, or idolatry). Both the Bible and rabbinic literature, moreover, permitted human slavery (or "servitude")—although under distinctly more humane conditions than prevailed in most ancient cultures. Jews participated in the ownership of human beings right up through to the nineteenth century, and biblical texts were quoted by some Civil War–era American rabbis to justify the South's "peculiar institution." At the same time, some Jews were prominently active in the abolitionist movement: the outspoken Rabbi David Einhorn was driven from his pulpit by pro-slavery mobs in Baltimore, and John Brown's abolitionist band in "Bloody Kansas" included August Bondi,

(Continued on page 356)

A sign in a café in Jerusalem reads: "Self-service. 'For you are servants unto Me,' saith the Lord."

mezuzah[R]
mezuze[Y]
mezzuza, mezzuzah

Pronounced *meh-zu-zeh,* with a short "u" as in "put." Rhyme it with "kazoo's a." In Hebrew, *mezuzah* means "doorpost," but don't use it that way, unless you're in Israel.

The little oblong container (about the size of two

(Continued from page 355)

Jacob Benjamin, and Theodore Weiner, all recent Jewish immigrants to America.

Attacks against the Jews for allegedly playing a disproportionate role in the American slave trade have been leveled in recent years by the Nation of Islam, led by Minister Louis Farrakhan, and have required active refutation by scholars and Jewish defense organizations. The charges are rooted in the fact that numerous *conversos* (see Rosten's entry and my note on **Marrano**) were prominent within the ranks of Spanish and Portuguese slavers, as they were in all Spanish and Portuguese mercantile trades. Hugh Thomas, author of *The Slave Trade* (Simon & Schuster, 1997), notes that "one would be hard put to find more than one or two Jewish slave traders in the Anglo-Saxon traffic," yet "much of the [West African] slave trade in the sixteenth and seventeenth centuries in Lisbon was financed by converted Jews." Thomas also sheds revealing light on the Muslim Arab slavers who dominated the East African trade, the African rulers who facilitated and profited from the denuding of their continent, and the European monarchs and Catholic leaders who exported the slave trade to the New World. "[H]istorians should not look for villains," Thomas concludes. "All were caught up in a vast scheme of things which seemed normal at least till 1780."

Thomas also offers an interesting Jewish footnote to the history of servitude: the uninhabited African island of Sao Tomé in the Gulf of Guinea, settled by the Portuguese in 1486, became the home to two thousand *conversos* children, whose parents had been enslaved by the king of Portugal.

cigarettes) that is affixed to the right of the front doorjamb of the home, in a slanting position, by a Jew who believes in putting up a *mezuzah.*

A n Orthodox Jew touches his fingers to his lips, then to the *mezuzah,* each time he enters or leaves the home.

Inside the *mezuzah* is a tiny, rolled-up paper or parchment on which are printed verses from Deuteronomy 6:4–9, 11:13–21. The first sentence is Israel's great, resounding watchword: "Hear, O Israel, the Lord our God, the Lord is one." The inscribed passages contain the command to "love the Lord your God, and to serve Him with all your heart and with all your soul"; they end up with an inscription reminding the faithful that God's laws are to be observed away from, as well as at, home, and that children must have a respect for God's laws instilled in them. (The enclosed material also includes the injunction to inscribe these words "upon the doorposts of your house.")

The *mezuzah* consecrates the home, which is so very important in the life and the ethos of Jews; the home is, in fact, a temple; it is known, in Hebrew, as *migdash mehad.*

Some scholars say that the *mezuzah* carries on the Egyptian practice of writing "lucky" sentences over the entrances to their houses. Muslims inscribe "Allah" and verses from the Koran over their doors and windows.

An old Brooklyn Jew, after much cajoling from his children, took the train to Florida for the winter. His children had arranged for him to stay in one of the nicest hotels on the ocean. The hotel, they assured Grampa a hundred times, was strictly *kosher.* That was, indeed, the only kind of hotel the old man could be coaxed into entering.

The manager took the old man up to his room while

expatiating on the hotel's features: "Pinochle every afternoon; movies twice a week; a TV set in every room . . ."

"But your kitchen," asked the *zeyde*. "Is it strictly *kosher?*"

"Absolutely!" said the manager. "We serve only *kosher* meat; everything is cooked in a strictly *kosher* manner."

At the door of his new room, the *zeyde* reached up automatically to touch the *mezuzah*. There was no *mezuzah*.

"Don't get excited," said the manager, smiling. "On the roof, we have a master *mezuzah!*"

midrash

Pronounced MID-*rash*, to rhyme with "bid posh." Hebrew: "commentary," "interpretation." From the root verb meaning "to study," "to investigate." Plural: *midrashim*.

The very highly developed analysis, exposition, and exegesis of the Holy Scriptures.

The scholars of the period of the Second Temple (fifth century B.C.E. to 70 C.E.), convinced that the words of the Bible lent themselves to many interpretations and could be applied to all ages, to varied social conditions, and to all types of human beings, initiated complex midrashic interpretations of the Bible. These savants read involved ideas into simple verses and found esoteric meaning in every jot and tittle of the holy texts.

After the dispersion of the Jews, the rabbis, their leaders, carried on the hermeneutic tradition; their sermons, based on biblical texts, included a great deal of homiletic material—parables, allegories, illustrative stories, inspirational and edifying interpretations, that spoke directly to the common people. And beginning in the fourth century, many of these curious sermons were written down and collected. There are over one hundred books of *midrashim* extant.

What is the difference between a *midrash* and any other analysis of, say, a verse? The *Midrash* purports to penetrate the "spirit" of the verse and derive an interpretation that is not obvious. (It is often also not persuasive.) In *midrash* there is total amnesty for non sequiturs, and poetic license—greatly inflated—becomes philosophy or, at least, theology.*

---

*Rosten's scorn for the midrashic tradition may obscure the fact that it was a major tool used by the Talmudic rabbis to expand and liberalize biblical teachings and keep scripture relevant to the evolving Jewish civilization. The harsh justice of the Bible, for example—prescribing the death penalty for crimes ranging from murder to idolatry to insulting one's parents!—was ameliorated by the rabbis through interpretations that left execution in the hands of God. Many of the most enduring Jewish concepts and practices are rooted in midrashic "inquiries" into biblical texts. In essence, *midrash* was the primary hermeneutical method by which Judaism was established and rooted in biblical sources.

Midrash refers both to the method of inquiry and to classic books of *midrashim,* collectively known as the *Midrash.* These include the *Midrash Rabbah* (the "Great Midrash"), the *Midrash of Rabbi Tanhuma, Mekhilta* ("Measure") to Exodus, *Sifra* ("Book") to Leviticus, and *Sifre* ("Books") to Numbers and Deuteronomy.

In recent decades, midrashic interpretation of Jewish texts has undergone a notable revival in liberal Jewish circles. Rabbi Arthur Green describes this revival (in *These Are the Words, A Vocabulary of Jewish Spiritual Life,* Jewish Lights, 1999) as "colored by deep psychological insight into the biblical narrative. . . . Creative *midrash* also characterizes much of the writing and teaching that takes place within Jewish feminist circles," where it is "sometimes viewed as the restoration of a 'lost' portion of the tradition, a women's understanding that had never been recorded in writing." This "burst of creative energy," Green writes, "is only beginning to find written (and more often electronic) expression."

mikveʸ
mikvaᴿ
mikveh, mikvah

Pronounced MICK-*veh*, to rhyme with "pick the." Hebrew: "a pool of water."*

The bath, prescribed by ritual, that a Jewish bride took before her wedding, and which religious Jewish women took (1) at the end of their menstrual period, and (2) after bearing a child.

Under rabbinical law, a husband and wife were not permitted to come into close physical contact, much less cohabit, throughout the time of her menstruation or for seven days afterward. On the seventh day, the wife was required to bathe in running water or in a bath built expressly for that purpose: a *mikve*.

A community of Jews was obligated to have and maintain a community *mikve*.

The rules and regulations governing the *mikve* are quite detailed; in fact, a whole section of the *Mishnah* explores this recondite subject. The woman recites a benediction while in the water.

Today, only very religious Jewish women observe the *mikve* custom†—or attend a bathhouse for *mikves* such as were found in Europe and on the Lower East Side.

---

*More elegantly, *mikve* translates to mean a "gathering of waters." The word appears in Genesis 1:10, when God "called the dry land Earth, and the gathering of waters He called Seas." The *mikve* must contain at least eighty gallons of naturally gathered waters—flowing from an undammed river or lake or gathered from rainwater using only the natural force of gravity.

†The *mikve* has made something of a comeback among non-Orthodox observant Jews interested in exploring all aspects of the tradition. Contributing to this revival has been the increase of interest in Jewish women's rituals as part

Gentiles sometimes remarked on the unusual emphasis Jews placed upon cleanliness and hygiene; some said this amounted to a veritable "cult of purity." Such a "cult" was of immense value in keeping Jewish women cleaner, and the Jewish family healthier, than might otherwise have been the case. Bathing frequently must also have created and intensified a sense of self-respect.

See also shvitsbod.

milkhik ^Y
milchik ^R
milkhedik ^Y
milkhedig ^R

Pronounced MILL-*kheh-dik*, to rhyme with "bill the sick," with a throat-clearing *kh*, or MILL-*khik*, to rhyme with "fill Dick." From German: *Milch*, "milk," *milchig*, "milky."

1. Dairy foods, which, according to the dietary laws *(kashrut)*, may not be eaten with or immediately after meat. Such foods as those that contain milk, butter, cream, cheese.

of a general upsurge of a feminist presence in Jewish life and the increasing number of converts to Judaism, whose conversionary process includes immersion in the *mikve*.

The *mikve* is closely associated with marital sexuality and concepts of ritual purity (as opposed to personal hygiene). The period of abstinence prescribed by Judaism is designed, according to the *Talmud*, so that a wife "will be as beloved to her husband as she was when she entered the *chuppa*,"—that is, on their wedding day. Men also utilize the *mikve* on Sabbath eves, on the eves of important holidays, or at other times when a "purification" is desired. For a wide-ranging discussion of the *mikve* in contemporary Jewish life, see Rivkah Slonim's *Total Immersion: A Mikvah Anthology* (Jason Aronson, 1997).

2. Pale, sickly looking. "She's been sick for a week and looks *milkhedik*."
3. A colorless, ineffectual personality, a Caspar Milquetoast. "She's married a real *milkhediker*."

mincha^R
minkhe^Y
minhah

Pronounced MIN-*kha*, with a Caledonian *kh*. Hebrew: "an offering."
    The daily late afternoon religious services.

By tradition, pious Jews pray at least thrice a day: *shachris* in the morning; *mincha* in the afternoon; *mairev* in the evening.

minyan^R
minyen^Y

Pronounced MIN-*yon;* rhyme it with "Binyon." Hebrew: "number," or "counting."
1. Quorum. (Sometimes used in a jocular way.)
2. The ten **male Jews*** required for religious services. No congregational prayers or rites can begin "until we have a *minyan*."

To have ten men is to have a "synagogue." Children do not count, because children are not mature enough to under-

---

*In the decades since Rosten wrote, Jewish women have begun to be counted to constitute a *minyan* in the great majority of non-Orthodox communities.

stand the prayers. Since one cannot always find ten adult male Jews, exceptions to the *minyan* are permitted for a wedding, for instance, or a **circumcision**.†

Solitary prayer is laudable, but a *minyan* possesses special merit to the observant, who have held from antiquity that when ten male Jews assemble, for either study or worship, God's Presence, or *Shekhinah*, dwells among them.

You will remember that Abraham asked the Lord to save the righteous in Sodom, and God said He would spare Sodom if at least ten truly righteous men could be discovered in that sink of corruption. The *Mishnah* says that since God exempted Caleb and Joshua from his denunciation of the spies returned from Canaan (in Numbers), a congregation is twelve minus two—or ten.

It is worth remarking on the number of times the magical number ten (which is the normal number of fingers we are allotted on hands and feet) appears in Judaic law, lore, and history:

- the Ten Commandments
- the ten plagues visited on Pharaoh
- the ten days of penitence (from *Rosh Hashanah* to *Yom Kippur*)
- the ten generations cited in the Bible from Adam to Noah, and from Noah to Abraham
- the ten tests of faith God gave Abraham
- the unit of ten, in the clan structure, established by Moses (Exodus 18:25)

---

†Activities that are *not* permitted without a *minyan* include the *Barechu* (call to worship), the *Kaddish* (mourner's prayer), and the *Torah*-reading service in its entirety.

Minyan is often used in a jocular way, to mean "Do we have a quorum [or a majority]?" or "Have most of those we expected arrived?"

FOLK SAYINGS: "Nine wise men don't make a *minyan,* but ten cobblers do."

"Nine saints do not make a *minyan,* but one ordinary man can by joining them."

mise meshune^Y
miessa meshina^R
mise meshine

Pronounced ME-*sa* m'-SHE-*na,* to rhyme with "Lisa Farina," or m'-SHOO-*neh,* to rhyme with "spoon neh." Hebrew: *meshuna,* "unusual, abnormal," *m'ess,* "death."
    An ugly or unfortunate fate or death.

The phrase is widely used by Jews either as a lament ("What a *mise meshune* befell him!") or as a curse ("May he suffer a *mise meshune!*").

mishegas^Y
mishegoss^R
meshugaas

Pronounced *mish-eh-*GOSS, to rhyme with "dish o' Joss." Hebrew: *meshuga,* "insane."
    Literally: insanity, madness.

But *mishegas* is more often used in a lighter vein to describe not mental disease, but

- a wacky, irrational, absurd belief; nonsense; hallucinations. "Did you ever hear such a piece of *mishegas?*"
- a state of affairs so silly or unreal that it defies explanation. "No one can figure it out; it's plain *mishegas.*" "How can you cope with such a *mishegas?*"
- a piece of tomfoolery, clowning, "horsing around." "He's the life of the party with his jokes and *mishegas.*" "Please, cut out all the *mishegas.*"
- a fixation, an idée fixe. "She has a new *mishegas*—that the neighbors are trying to ruin her."
- an idiosyncrasy.

Note that *meshuge* can be used both seriously ("The psychiatrists declared him *meshuge*") and playfully ("Oh, he's hilarious, he acts *meshuge*"), but *mishegas* is nearly always used in an amused, indulgent way.

See meshuge.

Mr. Samuel Goldwyn once remarked, during a dinner table argument about psychiatry: "Anyone who goes to a psychiatrist ought to have his head examined."

The office of three psychoanalysts is alleged, by a malicious wit, to carry this shingle:

S. M. Spero, M.D.

J. Melnick, M.D.

R. Gabrilowitz, M.D.

6 couches—no waiting

And since we're on the subject, you may be interested in this definition of a psychoanalyst: "A Jewish doctor who hates the sight of blood."

When Mr. Klein returned from a visit to his friend Teitelbaum, in the psychiatric ward, Mrs. Klein bombarded him with questions.

"Poor Teitelbaum," sighed Mr. Kline. "Sick in the head. He rants, he raves, he talks *mishegas*."

"So how could you even talk to him?"

"I tried to bring him down to earth. I talked of simple, every-day things: the weather; did he need warm clothes; the ten dollars he owes us . . ."

"Aha! Did he remember?"

"That *meshuge* he isn't," said Klein.

mish-mosh
mish-mash

Pronounced MISH-MOSH, to rhyme with "pish-posh." I pre-fer to spell this delicious word *mish-mosh,* as it is pro-nounced, but the thirteen-volume *Oxford English Dictionary* spells it *mish-mash* and traces it to the German *mischmasch* and the Danish (!) *misk-mask.* It is unnerving to learn that *Junius' Nomenclator* called it mishmash as far back as 1585.

1. A mix-up, a mess, a hodgepodge, a fouled-up state of things.
2. Confusion galore. "What a *mish-mosh!* " "You never heard such a *mish-mosh* of ideas."

No Jew pronounces this "mish-mash." In fact, when a con-gressman on one of Groucho Marx's *You Bet Your Life* television shows did say "mish-mash," Groucho gave him a startled stare and remarked: "You'll never get votes in the Bronx if you go on saying 'mish-mash' instead of *mish-mosh*." (Mr. Marx later wrote the same advice to Governor Scranton of Pennsylvania.)

I consider *mish-mosh* a triumph of onomatopoeia—and a word unlike any I know to suggest flagrant disorder.

Mishnah[R]
Mishne[Y]
Mishna

Pronounced MISH-*neh,* to rhyme with "wish the." Hebrew: literally, "to repeat one's learning," "review."

One of the two basic parts of the *Talmud;* the other (and much later) part is the *Gemara.* The *Mishnah* is the codified core of the Oral Law—that vast body of analysis and interpretations that was originally not written down for fear of affecting the sanctity of the *Torah.*

The *Mishnah,* which is written in Hebrew (the *Gemara* was written in Aramaic), is divided into six "orders" (*sedarim*) and, in turn, into sixty-three *massekhtot,* or tractates. (Only thirty-six and one-half of these, incidentally, have a *Gemara* appended.) Each tractate or treatise is divided into *perakim,* or "chapters," and each chapter into paragraphs. There are 523 "chapters."

The *Mishnah*'s six "orders":

1. *Seeds,* which discusses agricultural problems and laws, the products of orchards and fields, the rituals attending each.
2. *Festivals,* which sets forth the *halakha* (law, rules) for fast days, festivals, the Sabbath.
3. *Women,* which covers relations between men and women,

betrothals, nuptials—and divorce (the Jews very early on reconciled themselves to human incompatibilities).

4. *Damages,* a detailed code of civil and criminal law, with cases.

5. *Sacred things,* rituals, offerings, sacrifices, services.

6. *Purities* or *Purifications,* matters of personal hygiene, clean and unclean foods, etc.*

*Rosten here conflates issues of personal hygiene with the complex issues of ritual purity. Judaism has a mass of laws, most of them established in Leviticus, concerning the religious status of people who have come into contact with a corpse, have a skin affliction, unwittingly transgress a religious law, menstruate, ejaculate, give birth, etc. Most of these laws prescribe a period of quarantine or separateness and a procedure of "cleansing" that often involves bathing, fresh clothes, and so on. However, according to Rabbi Adin Steinsaltz—the English (and Hebrew) translator and leading contemporary authority on the *Talmud*—"purity and impurity are not concepts related to the sphere of cleanliness or hygiene. Observance of the laws of purity may in some ways serve as an aid to hygiene, but this is neither the reason nor the explanation for their issue." Rather, Steinsaltz says, "purity" is associated with life and sanctity, while "impurity increases as an object comes closer to death. Thus the most impure thing . . . is a corpse." (For a compact discussion of the history and content of the *Mishnah* and other fundamental Jewish texts, see Steinsaltz's *The Essential Talmud,* Jason Aronson, 1992.)

Many contemporary women nevertheless view Judaism's purity laws, particularly those concerning menstruation and childbirth, as expressing revulsion over women's bodily functions—a perspective that is well borne out by some of the language of the Talmudic tractate *Niddah.* Rachel Adler, a leading Jewish feminist theologian, urges the acknowledgment of both the traditional and feminist perspectives. "*Tumah/taharah* [impurity/purity] remains one of the few major Jewish symbolisms," she writes, "in which women had a place. . . . Is it worthwhile to reject . . . because later generations of men have projected their repugnance for women upon it? Ought we not, rather, to urge men to recognize the process of death and renewal in their own bodies, not simply by joining us in our immersions [*mikve*], but by reappropriating immersion after the loss of semen, as the tradition offers precedent for them to do?" (*The Jewish Woman, New Perspectives,* Elizabeth Koltun, ed., Schocken, 1976.)

See also my note under **timtum**.

The *Mishnah* had its origin after the return of the Jews to Judea from their Babylonian Exile (537 B.C.E.), when the scholars of the Great Assembly (*Sanhedrin*), the Jews' religious and legislative body, established basic rules for the interpretation of Jewish law. The Great Assembly produced a group of scribes (*soferim*) who were the official copyists and teachers of the Bible. They were followed by the *tannaim*, sages who continued to interpret biblical laws and apply them to changing historical circumstances. Their discussions, ordinances, and interpretations were, by tradition, transmitted orally, lest they diminish the sanctity of the Bible (the Written Law). Finally, their sheer accumulated bulk and breadth impelled some scholars to codify and transcribe them.

Hillel (c. 30 B.C.E.–20 C.E.), the greatest Pharisee, a tower of wisdom, a model of humility and benevolence (Jesus of Nazareth was clearly influenced by Hillel's teachings), made one of the earliest attempts to codify the vast, tangled body of oral teachings. No one knows what happened to his effort.

The illustrious Rabbi Akiba initiated the pioneer work of collecting and classifying the oral traditions, legal decisions, and precedents into a *mishnah,* or "review," and Akiba's work was continued by Judah ha-Nasi, "the Prince." (He was said to have been born on the day Rabbi Akiba suffered a martyr's death in 135 C.E.) Rabbi Judah, known also simply as "Rabbi," was head of the *Sanhedrin,* the high court that compiled, edited, and codified the accumulated body of Oral Law, and around 200 C.E. declared the canonical labor closed. (It was Judah ha-Nasi who said, "Much have I learned from my teachers, more from my colleagues, but most from my students.") Fearing that *Mishnah* would depart too far from *Torah* and might even create heretical departures from the true faith, Judah ha-Nasi declared *Mishnah* to be closed (as Ezra and Nehemiah had "closed" the *Torah*). "Oral Law" was to be frozen.

But such fundamentalist constraints succeeded no more in Judaism than in other religions. For in the *yeshivas* of Babylonia there soon arose (indeed, from the efforts of several of Judah ha-Nasi's disciples) a continuation of *Torah* interpretation called *Gemara* ("Supplement"). This *Gemara* observed the solemn restrictions governing Oral Law, used Aramaic instead of Hebrew as its language, and appeared to be, at first, simply an extension of *Mishnah* itself. Like *midrash*, like *Mishnah*, so *Gemara* was strictly oral for centuries, and the academies of Babylonia reigned as authority, in Judaic thought and discussion, from 200 to 600 C.E.

The historic shift to a *written* form was born of a political crisis in the sixth century. Zoroastrian fanatics, rebelling against the influence of both Judaism and Christianity, came to power and launched severe repressive programs against Jews and Christians in the Persian realm. Jews fled, dispersed, were killed, and the rabbis realized that the collective "memory" of *Mishnah* and *Gemara* was in peril of extinction. A group of scholars, the *Saboraim*, who were at home in both Hebrew and Aramaic (not too hard, given the similarities of the two languages), were now set the task of writing down the precious interpretative materials. These are to be found in the Babylonian *Talmud*.

The work went on for over two hundred years (!). And the new interpreters, being only human, often resolved points of unclarity or ambiguity by becoming high courts themselves—adding, interpreting, interpolating, ingeniously revising—until a *Gemara* of their own grew up around the *Gemara* they were reducing to written form.

See my entry for Talmud.

mishpokhe^Y
mishpocheh^R
meshpocheh, mishpocha

Pronounced *mish*-PAW-*kheh*, to rhyme with "fish locheh."
Hebrew: "family."

1. Family, including relatives, far, near, remote, and numerous.
2. Ancestors, lineage.

The closest thing in English to *mishpokhe* is "clan."

Parents, grandparents, siblings, uncles, aunts, and cousins (first, second, once removed) all form part of that extended family Jews call *mishpokhe*.

Nothing is more flattering than to say someone comes from a fine or distinguished *mishpokhe*.

"All Jews are *mishpokhe*" means that all Israel is one family. This intense feeling of a common heritage, common obligations, common values, has led the state of Israel to accept, without exception, Jewish immigrants of the widest, sharpest cultural differences.*

The Chase Manhattan Bank's memorable advertising campaign is built around the slogan "You have a friend at Chase Manhattan."

---

*Not all Jewish immigrant groups in Israel have been treated to family-style hospitality, however. Moroccan, Yemenite, and other *Mizrachi* or Sephardi Jews who came to Israel in the 1950s, as well as the Ethiopian Jews (*Falashas*) who were airlifted en masse to Israel between 1985 and 1995, have complained of discrimination, insult, condescension, substandard housing and employment, questioning of their Jewish identities, forced assimilation of their children, and worse. During his 1999 electoral campaign to become prime minister of Israel, Ehud Barak offered an official apology to *Mizrachi* Jews "in the name of the Labor Party over the generations."

'Tis said that a sign in the window of the Bank of Israel reads:

"—But here you have Mishpokhe!"

Here is a glossary of Yiddish terms for family members, by blood and by marriage:

father .... *tate* or *tata* (TAH-teh)
mother .... *mame* or *mama* (MAH-meh)
husband .... *man* (MON)
wife .... *vayb, froy* (VIBE, FROY OR FRO)
son .... *zun* (ZUHN)
daughter .... *tokhter* (TAWKH-ter)
brother .... *bruder* (BROO-der or BREE-der)
sister .... *shvester* (SHVES-ter)
uncle .... *feter* (FEH-ter)
.... *onkl* (AWN-kel)
aunt .... *tante* (TAHN-teh)
.... *mume* (MOO-meh or ME-meh)
nephew .... *plimenik* (pleh-MEN-ik)
niece .... *plimenitse* (pleh-MEN-it-zeh)
cousin .... *kuzin* (m.) (koo-ZIN)
.... *kuzine* (f.) (koo-ZEE-neh)

.... *shvesterkind* (SHVES-ter-kind)

grandchild .... *eynikl* (ANE-ek-el)

grandchildren .... *eyniklekh* (ANE-ek-lekh)

grandfather .... *zeyde* (ZAY-deh)

grandmother .... *bobe* (BAW-beh or BUB-beh)

great-grandfather .... *elter zeyde* (EHL-ter ZAY-deh)

great-grandmother ...... *elte bobe* (EHL-teh BAW-beh)

great-grandchild .... *ur-eynikl* (oor-ANE-ek-el)

great-grandchildren ..... *ur-eyniklekh* (oor-ANE-ek-lekh)

father-in-law .... *shver* (SHVAIR)

mother-in-law .... *shviger* (shvi-ger)

brother-in-law .... *shvoger* (SHVAW-ger)

sister-in-law .... *shvegerin* (SHVEH-geh-rin)

son-in-law .... *eydem* (AID'm)

daughter-in-law .... *shnur* (SHNOOR or SHNEE-air)

mitzva^R
mitsve^Y
mitzvah

Pronounced MITZ-*veh*, to rhyme with "fits a." Hebrew: "commandment."

1. Commandment; divine commandment.
2. A meritorious act, one that expresses God's will; a "good work," a truly virtuous, kind, considerate, ethical deed.

*M*itzva is second only to *Torah* in the vocabulary of Judaism. The *Talmud* elaborates the concept in many places. *Mitzvas* are of various kinds: those of positive performance (caring for the widow and orphan) and those of negative resolve (not accepting a

bribe); those between man and God (fasting on *Yom Kippur*) and those between man and man (paying a worker promptly); those that specify the duties required of rabbis and those that state the special sympathy for suffering required of any Jew.

Mitzvas are regarded as profound obligations, as inescapable burdens, yet they must be performed not from a sense of duty, but with "a joyous heart."

There are 613 (!) separate *mitzvas* listed in the third-century *Sefer Mitzvas Gadel*, of which 248 are positive (the first being "Be fruitful and multiply") and 365 negative. Maimonides, who listed all the *mitzvas* in his *Book of the Mitzvas* (written in Arabic, incidentally), remarked that a person who performed in accordance with only 1 of the 613 deserved salvation—if it was done so not out of self-interest, or to win credit, but entirely out of love and for its own sake.

The rabbis often used the phrase *simcha shel mitzva* ("the joy of fulfilling a pious act, a commandment") to hammer home the notion that good deeds performed out of a sense of requirement are not as meaningful as those performed out of desire and with enjoyment.*

---

*Yet the *Talmud* also says, in the name of Rabbi Chanina: "Someone who is commanded to do something, and does it, is greater than someone who is not commanded to do something, and does it." The sense of covenantal obligation is heavily stressed in Judaism. Chasidic spirituality further emphasized that *every* human activity offers the opportunity for people to find God's presence—a perspective that brings us closer to the commonplace use of the word *mitzva* to mean a good deed, whether or not it is commanded by religious law.

It has been said that the basic principle of Jewish ethics lies in the idea of mandatory *mitzvas*. Said Eleazar ben Simeon: "The world is judged by the majority of its people [and] an individual by the majority of his deeds. Happy is he who performs a good deed: *that may tip the scale for him and the world* [italics mine]."

Israel Zangwill called the *mitzvas* the Jews' "sacred sociology."

If you do something honorable, especially kind, or considerate, a Jew may say, beaming, "Oh, that was a *mitzva!*" or, "You performed a real *mitzva!*"

FOLK SAYINGS: "One *mitzva* leads to another."

"The reward of a *mitzva*? Another *mitzva.*"

At the end of a pier in Tel Aviv, a man was about to jump into the sea when a policeman came running up to him. "No, no!" he cried. "How can a man like you, in the prime of life, think of jumping into that water?"

"Because I can't stand it anymore! I don't want to live!"

"But listen, mister, *please*. If you jump in the water, I'll have to jump in after you, to save you. Right? Well, it so happens *I* can't swim. Do you know what that means? I have a wife and four children, and in the line of duty I would drown! Would you want to have such a terrible thing on your conscience? No, I'm sure. So be a good Jew, and do a real *mitzva*. Go home. And in the privacy and comfort of your own home, hang yourself."

Mr. Berkowitz stood before the angels in Heaven anxiously, as they examined the record of his deeds on earth. And the Chief Admitting Angel exclaimed, "But this is fantastic! This is unprecedented! In your entire lifetime did you not commit even *one* little sin?"

"I d-did try to live in virtue," stammered Mr. Berkowitz, "as a good Jew and a God-fearing man. . . ."

"But not one little *aveyre* in a whole lifetime!" sputtered the Admitting Angel. "You performed nothing but *mitzvas?!* . . . We can't let you into Heaven: you are practically an angel. No, no, you must be like other men—fallible, subject to temptation, prone to transgress . . . at least *once*. So, I will send you back to earth for twenty-four hours, during which time you must commit a sin— *one little sin*. Then appear before us again, at least *human!*"

The sinless and bewildered Mr. Berkowitz found himself back on earth, unhappy and uneasy, determined to try to take one step off the impeccable path of his righteousness. An hour passed, then two, then three; poor Mr. Berkowitz had found no opportunity to commit an *aveyre*. And then a buxom woman gave him a wink. . . . Mr. Berkowitz responded with alacrity. The woman was neither young nor beautiful—but she was willing! And when she blushingly hinted that he might indeed spend the night with her, Mr. Berkowitz was in sixth heaven (the seventh was yet to come).

In the dark, wee hours, Mr. Berkowitz looked at his watch: only one more hour before he would be whisked back to Heaven . . . Only half an hour . . . And as he quickly put on his clothes, preparing for his return to the celestial region, his blood froze as the woman in the bed sighed, "Oh, Mr. Berkowitz, what a *mitzva* you performed this night!"

mizrach^R
mizrakh^Y
mizrachi

Pronounced MIZZ-*rokh*, with the Germanic *kh* sound as in *Ach*; rhymes with "Fizz loch." *Mizrach:* Hebrew, "east," "sunrise." (For *Mizrachi*, see below.)

A framed picture hung on the wall of every house of study (or *besmedresh*) and in front of the synagogue lectern from which the readings are made.

The *mizrach*, which is often beautifully appliquéd and embroidered, is intended to show the congregation in which direction to face while praying—the direction always being where Jerusalem is. Thus, Jews in Persia or China or India turn to the west when praying.

Fifty years ago, a *mizrach* adorned many a Jewish home; not so today.*

Mizrachi is the name of an organization of Orthodox Jews, staunch Zionists, who conduct much fund-raising for Israel; the *Mizrachi* were important in Hebrew education in America and very important in working for the creation of an independent Jewish state in Palestine.†

Mogen David^R
Mogn Dovid^Y
Magen David

Pronounced MAW-*ghen* DU-*vid* in Yiddish, to rhyme with "fog in tumid." Hebrew: "Shield of David."

---

* A contemporary revival of Jewish crafts has restored the *mizrach* to many observing Jewish homes. Examples of modern *mizrach* themes can be found in Mae Rockland Tupa's *The New Work of Our Hands: Contemporary Jewish Needlework and Quilts* (Chilton Books, 1994).

† As noted in my comments on Rosten's entries for **Ashkenazi** and **mishpokhe**, Israeli Jews of Middle Eastern origin (Iraq, Morocco, Yemen, etc.) are now also referred to as *Mizrachi*.

Star of David; the six-pointed star that is the national
symbol of Israel.‡

No one is sure how and when the Star of David first came into
use as a symbol of Jewry. The first Zionist Congress adopted
it in 1897.

No reference to the *Mogen David* is found in rabbinical writings
until the thirteenth century, and the first explicitly Jewish association did not occur, it seems, until the seventeenth century. More,
I cannot tell you.§

motzi

Pronounced MOE-*tzee*, to rhyme with "goat sea." Hebrew:
"provide," "bring forth."

The blessing over bread, recited before each meal.

This benediction goes: "Blessed art Thou, O Lord our God,
King of the universe, who brings forth [*hamotzi*] bread from
the earth."

This brief blessing is one of the most common in Jewish
observance.

See brokhe, daven.

‡The official symbol of the Jewish state is the *menorah*, but the *Mogen David*
appears on the national flag and is widely used in Israeli and Jewish iconog-
raphy.

§A synagogue from the third or fourth century dug up in Capernaum, Israel,
has the six-pointed *Mogen David* as part of its design. The symbol was also used
widely on Christian churches and cathedrals throughout the Middle Ages. The
Nazis, of course, appropriated the symbol to mark their Jewish victims for
degradation, ghettoization, and death.

In modern Israel, the first-aid and disaster-relief organization analogous to
the Red Cross is the Mogen David Adom (Red Shield of David), founded in 1930.

moykhl ^Y
moichel ^R

Pronounced MOY-*khel*, to rhyme with "joyful." Hebrew: *mochel*, "pardoner," "forgiver."
1. Forgive. Literally: "I forgive you."
2. Ironically: "No thanks."

"*Ich bin dir* [or *ihm*] *moykhl*," an exquisitely dry, ironic phrase, is used to mean "Thanks a *lot;* you [or he] can keep it"; "Don't do me any favors"; "Oh, *dandy!*"

moyl ^Y
mohel ^R

Pronounced MOY-*l*, to rhyme with "Doyle" (though I never heard of a *moyl* named Doyle), or "goil" (though that would be a startling combination, given *moyl*'s meaning).* The English pronunciation is *mole.* Hebrew: a circumciser.

The person who circumcises the male baby in the ritual of *Brit Milah* eight days after birth.

See bris.

Circumcision is performed mostly by physicians today, but historically the *moyl* was a specialist in this quite unique, not to say narrow, field.

The knife a *moyl* uses must be double-edged—not for symbolic

---

*At least twenty-six women are now included on the list of available *moyls* trained by the movement for Reform Judaism, which has been certifying rabbis, doctors, and midwives since 1984 (www.rj.org/beritmila/wwwavail.html).

reasons, but to make sure the baby gets a swift, clean cut. If the knife were not double-edged, reasoned the rabbis, the blunt side might be used by mistake and the baby hurt. (That always struck me as a good example of how closely those old sages reasoned.) The *moyl* usually comes prepared with two knives, each double-edged, in case one turns out to be dull.

In Europe and the United States, the circumcision is conducted in the home—or in the hospital, if the child is still **there.***
Mizrachi Jews perform circumcisions in the synagogue.

The *moyl* holds no hallowed spot in the Jewish hierarchy of respect. He is regarded as a technician; God forbid he should perform any other type of surgery.

Like *chazzonim, moyls* are often the butt of jokes.

One of the first puns I ever heard was this: "The rabbi gets the fees, but it's the *moyl* who gets all the tips." I puzzled over that one for years.

A man passed a store window with nothing in it but a clock, stepped inside, and asked, "How long would it take to fix my watch?"

"How should I know?" shrugged the *balebos.* "I don't fix watches. I'm a *moyl.*"

"But—in your window—you have a clock!"

"So what would *you* put in the window?"

---

*Babies still hospitalized eight days after birth might not be subjected to circumcision, as the operation is traditionally delayed if the infant is too sickly or frail.

Moyshe Kapoyr
Moishe Kapoyr

Pronounced MOY-*sheh ka*-POYR. *Moyshe* is the Yiddish pronunciation of "Moses"; *kapoyr* means "backward," "reverse,"
"the other way around," possibly from Russian *kubaryom,*
"head over heels."

Anyone who persists in being contrary, opposing, con-
tradicting, putting things exactly opposite to what others
do. "He has a streak of *Moyshe Kapoyr* in him." "Don't
argue; don't be a *Moyshe Kapoyr.*" "He gets things so balled
up, so topsy-turvy, his name could be *Moyshe Kapoyr.*"

A *Moyshe Kapoyr* must have a strong streak of perversity in
him. With little effort he can be a *nudnik.*

In the 1920s, the *Jewish Daily Forward* ran a continuing series of single-frame cartoons about a contumacious character named *Moyshe Kapoyr,* who delighted a nationwide public with his comic absurdities and "upside-down" comments.*

mutshen[Y]
mutchen[R]

Pronounced MU-*chen;* rhymes with "putsch-hen." Russian: *mutchit,* "to torture," "to torment."

1. To nag. "She *mutshes* him day and night about his appearance."
2. To harass.
3. To struggle along, barely making ends meet. "How are things?" "Oh, I *mutshe* [he *mutshes*] along."

The most common usage is the last: "One *mutshes* oneself to make a living."

This is so common that a typical conversation in Yiddish will run:

"*Sholem aleichem* [Hello]. How are things?"

"Eh! One *mutshes* oneself. And with you?"

"Likewise."

"*Nu,* stay healthy. I'll see you soon."

A most pious old Jew had prayed in the synagogue thrice every day of his adult life. His worldly business partner had not once set foot

---

*The *Forward,* launched as an English-language weekly in 1990, has contin-ued the tradition of including cartoons full of creative energy. Art Spiegel-man's Pulitzer Prize–winning *Maus* first appeared in the paper as a weekly strip. See also my note to Rosten's entry for **knipl**.

therein. And in his seventieth year the old Jew addressed the Lord thusly: "O, God, Blessed be Thy Name, have I not every day since my *bar mitzva* celebrated Your Glory? Have I ever made a move, named a child, taken a trip, without consulting You first? Is there a more devout, humble, observing soul in all Your fold? . . . And now I'm old, I can't sleep, I'm poor. . . . But my partner! That no-good! That *apikoyres!* Not *once* has he even made a prayer! Not a penny has he given to the synagogue! He drinks, he gambles, he runs around with loose women—and he's worth a *fortune!* . . . Dear God, King of all the universe, I am not asking You to punish him, but please tell me: Why, why, *why* have You treated me this way?"

The synagogue rumbled as the Voice intoned: "Because all you do, day after day, is *mutshe* me!"

n

naches^R
nakhes^Y

Pronounced NOKH-*ess*, to rhyme with "Loch Ness"—with the *kh* sound a Scot would use in pronouncing "loch." Hebrew: *nakhat*, "contentment."

1. Proud pleasure, special joy—particularly from the achievements of a child. Jews use *naches* to describe the glow of pleasure plus pride that only a child can give to its parents: "I have such *naches*: my son was voted president of his play group." "Are you *shepping* [getting] *naches* from your daughter's career?"

2. Psychological reward or gratification. I am getting *naches* from writing this book, since a new book is indeed a brainchild.

   See also kvell.

A very proud woman said to her friend, "My son, the doctor, is such a marvelous doctor—you *must* go to him."

"But why? There's nothing wrong with me."

"Believe me, with my son, go only once and he's sure to find *some*thing!"

Two old friends meet (in Jewish anecdotes, old friends are always meeting).

"I haven't seen you in twenty-five years. Tell me, how is your boy Harry?"

"Harry? *There's* a son! He's a doctor, with a wonderful office, with patients from all over the United States!"

"Marvelous. And what about Benny?"

"Benny? A lawyer. A *big* lawyer. He takes cases all the way up to the Supreme Court!"

"My! And your third boy, Izzy?"

"Izzy's still Izzy. Still a tailor," sighed his father. "And I tell you, if not for Izzy, we'd all be starving!"

nadn^Y
nadan^R

Pronounced NOD-'n, to rhyme with "sodden." Hebrew: *nadan,* "dowry."

Dowry.

In the *shtetl,* even the poorest of brides had a dowry—collected by the community.

"Sell even the Holy Scrolls," goes an old saying of the Jews, "to make sure a poor girl has a dowry."

nafke^Y
nafka^R

Pronounced NOFF-*keh.* Aramaic: *nafka,* "streetwalker."

Prostitute.

See kurve.

nar^Y
narr ^R
naar

Pronounced NAHR, to rhyme with "far." German: *Narr,*
"fool," "buffoon."

1. Fool.
2. Clown, buffoon. "He acts like a *nar.*" "Don't be a *nar!*"

Two Israeli spies, caught in Cairo, were put up against the wall.
The firing squad marched in. The Egyptian captain asked the first
spy, "Do you have any last wish?"

"A cigarette."

The captain gave him a cigarette, lighted it, and asked the second spy, "Do you have a last request?"

Without a word, the second spy spat in the captain's face.

"Harry!" cried the first spy. "Please! Don't make trouble."

He was a real *nar.*

A *nar* said, "We have a rabbi, he gets paid so little, I don't know
how he keeps alive. In fact, he would starve to death except for one
thing: every Monday and Thursday—he fasts."

narishkayt ^Y
narrishkeit ^R
naarishkeit

Pronounced NAHR-*ish-kite,* to rhyme with "Carr is right."
German: *Närrischkeit,* "foolishness."

1. Foolishness.
2. A triviality; trivia. "The movie? A piece of *narishkayt.*"

nebekh^Y
nebbech^R
nebech, nebish, nebbish

Pronounced NEB-*ekh* or NEB-*ikh,* with the *kh* as sounded by Scots or Germans. Probably from Russian: *nebawg,* "not God"; or from the Czech: *neboky.*

In recent years, no doubt to help the laryngeally unagile, the pronunciation NEB-*ish* (note the *sh*) has gained currency. The word is even spelled *nebbish.* My feeling is that *nebbish* should be used only by people unable to clear their throats.

As an Interjection
1. Alas, too bad, unfortunately, "the poor thing." "He went to the doctor, *nebekh.*" "She, *nebekh,* didn't have a dime."

   In this usage, *nebekh* expresses
   a. sympathy. "He lost his job, *nebekh.*"
   b. regret. "They asked me, *nebekh,* to break the sad news."
   c. dismay. "He looked, *nebekh,* like a ghost!"
   d. "Poor thing." "His wife, *nebekh,* has to put up with him."

Never say *nebekh* about something you welcome, enjoy, are happy to report, or are glad happened. Hence the irony of this: "What would make me the happiest man in the world? To be sitting on a park bench in the sun, saying to my best friend, 'Look! There, *nebekh,* goes Hitler.'"

As a Noun
2. An innocuous, ineffectual, weak, helpless, or hapless unfortunate. A Sad Sack. A "loser." First cousin to a

shlemiel. "He's a *nebekh*." "Once a *nebekh*, always a *nebekh*." "Whom did she marry? A real *nebekh!*"

3. A nonentity; "a nothing of a person."

To define a *nebekh* simply as an unlucky man is to miss the many nuances, from pity to contempt, the word affords.

Nebekh is one of the most distinctive Yiddish words; it describes a universal character type.

A *nebekh* is sometimes defined as the kind of person who always picks up what a *shlemiel* knocks over.

A *nebekh* is more to be pitied than a *shlemiel.* You feel sorry for a *nebekh;* you *can* dislike a *shlemiel.*

There is a well-known wisecrack: "When a *nebekh* leaves the room, you feel as if someone came in."

Stories, jokes, and wisecracks about the *nebekh* are, by careful count, countless.

As the apothegm has it: "A man is, *nebekh*, only a man."

A *nebekh* went into a store to buy a little hand fan for his wife, who liked to fan herself while rocking on the porch. He examined a hundred fans, unable to make up his mind. The *balebos*, disgusted, exclaimed, "What's so hard?"

"I can't decide between the fans that cost a nickel and the fans that cost a dime. . . . What's the difference?"

"The difference is this," said the owner. "With a ten-cent fan, you make like this." He waved a fan vigorously in front of his face; then he lifted a five-cent fan. "And with the five-cent model, you do like this." He held the fan still—and waved his head.

This mordant reprimand went for naught.

Said the *nebekh:* "I wonder if my wife will think it's worth it."

PROVERB: "Better ten enemies than one *nebekh*."

A *nebekh* pulled into a parking lot on a busy street in Tel Aviv. Along came a policeman.

"Is it all right to park here?" asked the *nebekh*.

"No," said the cop.

"*No?* But look at all those other parked cars! How come?"

"They didn't ask."

A seventh-grader was so late coming home from his suburban school that his mother was frantic.

"What happened to you?" she cried.

"I was made traffic guard today, Mama, and all the kids have to wait for my signal, after I stop a car, before they cross the street."

"But you were due home two *hours* ago!"

"Mama, you'd be surprised how long I had to wait before a car came along I could stop!"

He had the makings of a *nebekh*—maybe even a *shlemiel*.

nebekhl^Y
nebechel^R
nebechl

The Jewish love of affectionate (or disdainful) diminutives is seen in this variant, which means an even more pitiful specimen or *shmatte* of a *nebekh*.

nefesh^Y
nayfish^R
nafish, nefish

Pronounced NEH-*fesh*, to rhyme with "less flesh," or NAY-*fish*, to rhyme with "bay dish." From Hebrew: "a being," "person," "soul."

1. An innocent.
2. A person of no consequence—weak, ineffectual, pathetic.
3. A contemptible or cowardly sort.
4. A person, a soul.

In most cases, a *nefesh* is clearly related to a *shlemiel*.

A *nefesh* handed the druggist a prescription. The druggist gave him three little bottles of pills.

"All these?" asked the *nefesh*. "What are they for?"

"The red ones calm your nerves; the white ones relieve your headaches; the blue ones are for asthma."

"Amazing. Such little pills, and each one knows exactly what to do."

nekhtiker tog, a^Y
nechtiger tog, a^R

Pronounced *a* NEKH-*tik-er* TAWG, to rhyme with "a Brecht bigger dog." Yiddish: *nekhtn*, "yesterday." German: *Tag*, "day."

1. Literally: "A yesterday's day," hence an impossibility, an absurdity, a self-contradiction; unfounded.

    A *nekhtiker tog* is also used as a sarcastic exclamation of denial.

2. Don't believe it. "Did he return the book? *A nekhtiker tog.*"

3. Not on your life. "Would I go on such a mission? *A nekhtiker tog!*"

4. Whom is he trying to kid? "He said they netted ten percent. *A nekhtiker tog!*"

5. Like hell, or "Tell it to Sweeney." "It will be finished by Thursday? *A nekhtiker tog!*"

neshome^Y
neshoma^R
neshuma

Pronounced *ne*-SHAW-*ma*, to rhyme with "the fauna," or *ne*-SHU-*ma*, to rhyme with "Petluma." Hebrew: *neshamah*, "soul."

1. Soul.
2. The source and breath of life.
3. A "soul" in the sense of a man, a mortal being. "He is a tortured *neshome.*"

    See nefesh.

No precise distinction existed between body and soul until rabbinical times (postbiblical days), when the Hebrew *neshamah* came to mean that aspect of man that is spirit, spiritual, noncorporeal—and immortal. Jews were probably influenced in these theological and metaphysical niceties by Greek thought.

In the *Talmud* it is said that God created individual souls when He created the world; empirically, when a child is born, his or her preassigned *neshome* joins the body. Evidence for this is lacking.

In Orthodox Judaism, the idea of resurrection plays an important part—and the concept of bodily resurrection is often closely linked to the immortality of the soul, or *neshome*.

Judaism has no serious problems about the "evil," "impurity," or carnality of the body. The human body is holy, being God's creation, God's gift, God's design. How, then, can natural human needs and functions—if moderately, properly, not harmfully expressed—be immoral? Sex is treated with surprising ease and "modernity" in rabbinical thinking.*

Jews never made "vile bodies" the culprit in that lamentable

*Judaism's laws of *onah* (sexual intimacy) are meant to cultivate marital bonding and lift up the sexual relationship to a holy plane. At their best, these laws might help men transform lust-driven sexuality into a striving for emotional connection. Calling these laws "modern," however, ignores the fact that women's voices are not heard at all when it comes to Judaism's sexual coaching. While the rabbis emphasized the husband's obligation to respond to and satisfy the wife's sexual desires, the texts essentially speak only to men. As Rabbi Jane Litman complains (in *Lifecycles, Vol. 2,* Jewish Lights, 1997): "Jewish tradition provides extensive guidelines in a wide variety of areas. We are told how and what to eat; how to allocate money; how to fulfill our duties toward our children, families, communities. Why then does it give so little advice to women about how to have a satisfying sexual life?" Gay and lesbian relationships are similarly ignored or proscribed. In general, only a narrow band of the sexual spectrum, even within a monogamous, heterosexual couple's life, seemed admissible or visible to the rabbinic sages.

carnival of life called Sin. Body and soul form a unity; neither is purer or more wicked than the other; when a mortal commits a sin, the soul is as responsible as the body.

nexdoorekeh (feminine)
nexdooreker (masculine)

Pronounced *neks*-DOOR-*eh-keh*. Pure Yinglish.

The female neighbor who lives next door. "My *nex-doorekeh* is very friendly." The masculine form, for a male neighbor, is *nexdooreker*.

Maurice Samuel tells me he never heard the masculine form used, "because the man next door was never at home: he was working."

But I once had a *nexdooreker* who told me this memorable story:

Two *shlemiels* were discussing the meaning of life and death. Finally, one sighed: "Considering how many heartaches life holds, death is really no misfortune. In fact, I think sometimes it's better for a man not to have been born at all!"

"True." The other nodded. "But how many men are that lucky? Maybe one in ten thousand!"

-nik
-nick

Pronounced NICK. A suffix, from Slavic languages.

This multipurpose syllable converts a verb, noun, or adjective into a word for an ardent practitioner, believer, lover, cultist, or devotee of something.

Thus, a *nudnik* is someone who *nudzhes* or pesters. An *alright-nik* is someone who has done so well that he is prosperous.

We are familiar, of course, with "beatnik" and "peacenik." *The New York Times* has referred to "Bachniks," and a friend of mine, dieting, wailed that it was especially hard for her because at heart she was a *noshnik*.

-Nik lends itself to delightful ad hoc inventions: A "sicknik" would be one who fancies "sick" or "black" humor. A "Freudnik" would be an uncritical acolyte of the father of psychoanalysis. And recently homosexuals began to refer to heterosexuals, with some amusement, as "straightniks."

no-goodnik

Pronounced *no-GOOD-nik*, to rhyme this with "so good, Nick." Yinglish. This mutation borrows the phrase "no-good" and adds the stalwart suffix *-nik*.

1. Someone who is "no good"—unethical, irresponsible, undependable. A man who does not keep his word or honor his obligations.
2. One who does not earn an honest living; a wastrel; a drifter.
3. A shady character, a bum, a lowlife, a be-careful-you-shouldn't-get-involved-with-that-type type.
4. A petty lawbreaker, a trickster, a cheat.

"Remember Mrs. Plotnick, she had three sons? *Nu*, the oldest became an *alrightnik*, he lives in Scarsdale; the second went to Columbia, he became a Ph.D.; but the *boychik*, who does who knows *what* for a living, turned out a *no-goodnik!* From him, be sure, Mrs. Plotnik will never get *naches*."

nokh^Y
noch^R

Pronounced NAWKH; rhyme this with the Glasgow rendition of *loch.* German: *noch,* "another."

1. Another. "Give me *nokh* an example."
2. Else, more. "What *nokh* did he tell you?" "I'll give him *nokh* a chance."
3. Yet—but a "yet" of surprise. "Did you tell him more, *nokh?*" "You expected praise, *nokh?*" "For such cowardly conduct did you think he'd get a medal, *nokh?*"

The last is the most subtle and distinctive usage, emphatically and characteristically Yiddish.

An elderly Jew, riding in the subway, saw a black man reading the *Jewish Daily Forward.*

The Jew watched, spellbound, as the man read sedately on. Finally, unable to contain himself, the old man asked, "Excuse me, mister. I don't want to be rude—but I have to ask it: Are you Jewish?"

The black man lowered the paper in disgust. "That's all I need, *nokh!*"

nokhshleper^Y
nuchshlepper^R

Pronounced NUKH-*shlep-per,* with the *kh* guttural and far back in the throat, as if trying to clear out a crumb; to rhyme with a Berliner's rendition of "Hoch leper." German: *Nachshlepper,* "a straggler."

1. One who drags along after someone; a toady, a fawner;

a tolerated supernumerary. "A Hollywood actor can't take a walk without at least one *nokhshleper*." "She got in on someone else's ticket, the *nokhshleper*." (She was also a *trombenik*.) "He doesn't work for us; he's just a *nokhshleper*."

2. A dependent. "A successful man's family always provides him with at least one *nokhshleper*."

See also tsutshepenish.

nosh[R]
nash[Y]
nosher
noshn (infinitive verb)

Rhymes respectively with "gosh," "josher," "joshin'."

Nosh

1. A snack, a tidbit, a "bite," a small portion.
2. Anything eaten between meals and, presumably, in small quantity: fruit, a cookie, "a piece cake," a candy.

Jews loved to *nosh* long before they ever went to a cocktail party or tasted tidbits.

Nosher

1. One who eats between meals.
2. One who has a sweet tooth.
3. One who is weak-willed about food and dieting.

Noshn

To *nosh* is to "have a little bite to eat before dinner is ready" or to

"have a little something between meals." "I came in to find her *noshing*." "He's used to *noshing* after midnight."

Many delicatessen counters display plates with small slices of salami, or pieces of *halvah*, with a legend affixed to a toothpick: "Have a *nosh*." The *nosh* is not free, but it is cheap. In some Jewish delicatessens a lucky customer sees a little "flag" stuck into an open plate of goodies: "*Nem* [take] a *nosh* a nickel."

New York is full of the most extraordinary items and opportunities for *noshing*.

nu
nu?
nu!
nu-nu?
noo-ooo . . .

All pronounced NOO, to rhyme with "coo," but with various intonations and meanings. From Russian: *nu*, "well," "well now," etc.; cognates are common in Indo-European languages.

Nu is a remarkably versatile interjection, interrogation, expletive.

Nu is the word most frequently used (aside from *oy* and the articles) in speaking Yiddish. And with good reason: *nu* is the verbal equivalent of a sigh, a frown, a grin, a grunt, a sneer. It is an expression of amusement or recognition or uncertainty or disapproval. It can be used fondly, acidly, tritely, belligerently.

Nu is a qualification, an emphasizer, an interrogation, a caster of doubt, an arrow of ire. It can convey pride, deliver scorn, demand response. When used in tandem, as *nu-nu*, it carries another cargo of nuances.

Here are a near score of shadings of this two-lettered miracle:

1. *"Nu?"* (Well?)
2. "I saw you come out of her apartment." *"Noo-oo?"* (So-o?)
3. *"Nu*, after such a plea, what could I do?" (Well, then.)
4. *"Nu?"* (How are things with you?)
5. *"Nu?"* (What's new?)
6. "I need the money. . . . *Nu?"* (How about it?)
7. "— and he walked right out. *Nu?!"* (How do you like that!! Imagine!)
8. "I'm going to the dentist." *"Nu?"* (What's the hurry?)
9. *"Nu*, I guess that's all." (I'll be finishing or going along now.)
10. "— and you're supposed to be there by noon. *Nu?"* (What are you waiting for?)
11. "— and signed the contract. *Nu!"* (That's that!)
12. *"Nu-nu?"* (Come on, open up, tell me.)
13. "My wife was wondering what happened to the coffeepot she lent you. . . . *Nu?"* (I hate to mention it, but—)
14. "They doubled the rent! *Nu?"* (What can one do?)
15. "Did you or didn't you tell him? *Nu?"* (I challenge you.)
16. *"Nu-nu*, my friend?" (One must resign oneself.)
17. "They all agreed with him. But I—*nu?"* (I, for one, am dubious.)
18. "They waited and waited. *Nu*, he finally showed up." (And so, in the course of time.)
19. "She accused him, he blamed her. *Nu*, it ended in court." (One thing led to another, and . . .)

Nu is so very Yiddish an interjection that it has become the one word that can identify a Jew. In fact, it is sometimes used just that way—instead of asking, "Are you Jewish?" one can say, *"Nu?"* (The answer is likely to be, *"Nu-nu."*)

nudnik
nudnick

Pronounced NUD-*nick*, to rhyme with "could pick." From the Russian: *nudnyi*, "boring," or "tedious." *Nudnik* has become as uniquely Yiddish a word as there is. It is sometimes pronounced NUD-*nyik* by those who wish to add a vocal prolongation of distaste.

A pest, a nag, an annoyer, a monumental bore.

A *nudnik* is not just a nuisance; to merit the status of *nudnik*, a nuisance must be a most persistent, talkative, obnoxious, indomitable, and indefatigable nag. I regard *nudnik* as a peerless word for the characterization of a universal type.

A mother often says to a child, "Stop bothering me. Don't be a *nudnik*."

Morris Rosenfeld, the poet, wrote an entire essay on the *nudnik*, whom he defined as someone "whose purpose in life is to bore the rest of humanity."

See nudzh.

A derivative of *nudnik*, recently coined, covers the special category of pedantic or pedagogical bores: *phudnik*. What is a *phudnik*? A *nudnik* with a Ph.D.

Mr. Polanski complained to his doctor: "Something terrible has happened to me. I try to stop it, but I can't. . . . Morning, noon, and night—I keep talking to myself!"

"Now, now," the doctor crooned, "that isn't such a bad habit. Why, thousands of people do it."

"But doctor," protested Polanski, "you don't know what a *nudnik* I am!"

nudzh (noun)
nudzhn (infinitive verb)
nudzhedik (adjective)
nudzhik (adjective)

Nudzh is pronounced NUD-*jeh*, to rhyme with "could ya," NUDJ-*eh-dik* to rhyme with "would ya dig," and NUDJ-*ik* to rhyme with "could ya" plus a wisp of a hiccup. From the Slavic: *nudnyi*, "boring," or "tedious."

As a Verb
Nudzhn means to bore, to pester, to nag. A person who *nudzhes* you is a *nudnik*. If he annoys you long enough, you can say, "Stop *nudzhing* me!"

As a Noun
Nudzh is a Yinglish word, descended from "nudge." But where a nudge is open, a *nudzh* is surreptitious, a kick under the table, a widening of the-eyes-accompanied-by-a-slight-tilt-of-the-head to indicate that the recipient of the *nudzh* is being reminded: of a job to be done, or a nicety that has been overlooked, or a gaucherie committed by a third party, or the impossibility of swallowing what was just said.

A *nudzh* is also a Yinglish synonym for *nudnik.*

As an Adjective

Nudzhedik and *nudzhik* are Yinglish adjectives and mean unsettled, queasy, upset, nauseated. "I can't settle down today; I feel so *nudzhedik*." "Whenever I take a bus, I get *nudzhedik*." The Yiddish word is *nudne*.

See mutshen.

O

ongepatshket ^Y
ongepotchket ^R

Pronounced AWN-*ge-potch-ket*, to rhyme with "Fonda Lodge kit." From Russian: *pachkat*, "to soil, to sully."

1. Slapped together or assembled without form or sense.
2. Messed up; excessively and unaesthetically decorated; overly baroque. "She wore her new diamond earrings, a necklace, bracelet, two rings, and a brooch. *Oy*, was she *ongepatshket.*"

A suggested connection between the German *Patsch* and the Yiddish *ongepatshket* derives from the fact that overhandling spoils an article. In cooking, the less it has been handled, the lighter the pastry; hamburgers will be more tender if *patshed* less.

Mr. Fleishman, a new art collector, bought a painting that was much admired by his friend Meyerson, a self-proclaimed expert. The painting was one large square of black, with a dot of white in the center.

A year later, Mr. Fleishman bought another painting by the same modernist genius: a large square with *two* white dots.

Proudly, Fleishman hung the picture over his fireplace and telephoned his *maven* friend Meyerson to come right over. Meyerson took one look at the picture and wrinkled his nose: "I don't like it. Too *ongepatshket.*"

opstairsikeh (feminine)
opstairsiker (masculine)

Pronounced *op-*STARE-*zi-keh.* The male who lives upstairs is an *op-*STARE-*zi-kair.* Pure Yinglish.

The neighbor who lives upstairs. "My *opstairsikeh* is a music teacher." "My *opstairsiker*—a man, an angel—is moving out."

oy
oy!
oy oy!
oy-oy-oy!

Pronounced—well, how else can you pronounce it? The exclamation point is part of the spelling when *"oy!"* has a full head of steam. From the Slavic: *oy,* "oh!"

*O*y is not a word; it is a vocabulary. It is uttered in as many ways as the utterer's histrionic ability permits. It is a lament, a protest, a cry of dismay, a reflex of delight. But however sighed, cried, howled, or moaned, *oy!* is the most expressive and ubiquitous exclamation in Yiddish.

Oy is an expletive, an ejaculation, a threnody, a monologue. It may be employed to express anything from ecstasy to horror, depending on (1) the catharsis desired by the utterer, (2) the effect intended on the listener, (3) the protocol of affect that governs the intensity and duration of emotion required (by tradition) for the given occasion or crisis.

Oy is often used as lead-off for "*oy vey!,*" which means, literally, "oh, pain!" but is used as an all-purpose ejaculation to express anything from trivial delight to abysmal woe. *Oy vey!* is the short form of "*oy vey iz mir!*" (pronounced *oy* VAY *iz meer*), an omnibus phrase for everything from personal pain to emphatic condolences. (*Vey* comes from the German *weh*, meaning "woe.")

Oy is also used in duet form, *oy-oy!,* or in a resourceful trio: *oy-oy-oy!* The individual *oy!* can play varying solo roles, to embellish subtleties of feeling: thus *OY!-oy-oy* or *oy, oy, OY! OY-yo!*** can mean "And how!"

---

*Bob Marley gave a reggae flavor to *oy-oy-oy* when he chanted it in his "Buffalo Soldier" (released posthumously in 1983), a mournful historical song about African American cavalrymen, products of slavery, who fought in the Indian Wars of the 1870s. Notwithstanding the Rastafarian religion's many "borrowings" from Judaism (the concept of *Zion*, the name "Jah" for God, "Babylon" as a symbol of exile, the Lion of Judah symbol representing Haile Selassie, emperor of Ethiopia), this seems to be its first borrowing from Yiddish!

Rastafarianism has roots in Ethiopia, which in turn has a dynamic Jewish element in its history. This became more widely known during Israel's heroic ten-year airlift of more than thirty-six thousand Ethiopian Jews, who call themselves Beta Israel, the House of Israel, but are called *Falashas*, "alien ones, invaders," by their Moslem neighbors. Four main theories exist about

It is worth noting that *oy!* is not *ai!* and runs a decidedly different gamut of sensibilities. *Ai!* is used in tandem (*ai-ai!*) and *à trois,* as the French, no novitiates in the *ai-ai-ai!* league, would put it.

As for the difference between *oy!* and ah!, there is (naturally) a saying to illustrate the distinction:

"When you jump into cold water you cry, '*Oy!*' and then, enjoying it, say, 'A-aah.' When you commit a sin, you revel in the pleasure, 'A-aah'; then, realizing what you've done, you cry, '*Oy!*'" *Oy,* accordingly, can be used to express

1. SIMPLE SURPRISE. "When she saw me there, she said, '*Oy,* I didn't expect you!'"

2. STARTLEDNESS. "She heard a noise and exclaimed, '*Oy!* Who's there?'"

3. SMALL FEAR. "*Oy!* It could be a mouse!"

4. MINOR SADNESS (SIGHED). "When I think of what she went through, all I can say is *o-oy!*" (Note the *oy* prolonged, to indicate how sensitive one is to the troubles of others.)

the origins of Beta Israel: (1) They may be the lost Israelite tribe of Dan; (2) They may be descendants of King Solomon and the queen of Sheba (herself from Ethiopia), whose son Menelik is held by legend to have brought the Ark of the Covenant to the city of Axum in Ethiopia; (3) They may be descendants of Ethiopian converts to Judaism from centuries ago; (4) They may be descendants of Jews who fled Israel after the destruction of the First Temple by the Babylonians in 586 B.C.E.

In the sixteenth century, Egypt's chief rabbi declared the Beta Israel to be authentic Jews. By the early 1900s, the chief rabbis of forty-five countries had officially affirmed this recognition. In 1972, Israel's chief Sephardic rabbi, Ovadia Yossef, urged the immigration of Ethiopian Jews to Israel, and in 1975, Ashkenazic chief rabbi Shlomo Goren wrote to them as "our blood and our flesh. You are true Jews." Later that year, Israel officially recognized the Beta Israel as Jews under Israel's Law of Return. Cold War politics and persecutions in Ethiopia, however, delayed their immigration, which was eventually brought about through two whirlwind airlifts. For more on their mixed reception in Israel, see my note to Rosten's entry for **mishpokhe.**

5. CONTENTMENT. "*Oy*, was that a delicious dinner!"
6. JOY. "*Oy*, what a party!"
7. EUPHORIA. "Was I *happy*? *Oy!* I was dancing on air!"
8. RELIEF; REASSURANCE. "*Oy*, now I can sleep."
9. UNCERTAINTY. "What should I do? *Oy*, I wish I knew."
10. APPREHENSION. "Maybe he's sick? *Oy!*"
11. AWE. "He came back alive yet? *Oy!*"
12. ASTONISHMENT. "*Oy gevalt*, how he had changed."
13. INDIGNATION. "Take it away from me. *Oy!*"
14. IRRITATION. "*Oy*, is that some *metsieh!*"
15. IRONY. "*Oy*, have you got the wrong party!"
16. PAIN (MODERATE). "*Oy*, it hurts."
17. PAIN (SERIOUS). "*Oy, Gottenyu!*"
18. REVULSION. "*Feh!* Who could eat that? *O-oy!*"
19. ANGUISH. "I beg you, *tell* me! *Oy!*"
20. DISMAY. "*Oy*, I gained ten pounds!"
21. DESPAIR. "It's hopeless, I tell you! *Oy!*"
22. REGRET. "*Him* we have to invite? *Oy!*"
23. LAMENTATION. "*Oy*, we cried our eyes out."
24. SHOCK. "What? Her? Here? *Oy!*"
25. OUTRAGE. "That man will never set foot in this house so long as I live. *Oy!*"
26. HORROR. "Married a murderer? *Oy gevalt!*"
27. STUPEFACTION. "My own partner . . . *o-o-oy*."
28. FLABBERGASTATION. "Who ever *heard* of such a thing? *Oy!* I could *plotz!*"
29. AT-THE-END-OF-ONE'S-WITTEDNESS, OR I-CAN'T-*STAND*-ANY-MORE. "Get out! Leave me alone! *O-O-O-o-o-oy!*"

Mrs. Fishbein's phone rang.

"Hul-lo," a cultivated voice intoned, "I'm telephoning to ask whether you and your husband can come to a tea for Lady

Windermere—"

"*Oy*," cut in Mrs. Fishbein, "have *you* got a wrong number!"

oyrekh^Y
oyrech^R

Pronounced oy-*rekh* (note the guttural *kh*); rhymes with nothing I can think of. Hebrew: *orekh*, "guest."

Guest.

The word is used mostly in the phrase *un oyrekh oif Shabbes*, "a guest for the Sabbath."

It was a *mitzva* for the head of a Jewish household to try to bring a stranger home, usually from the synagogue, to share the Sabbath dinner. A Jewish stranger in any *shtetl* or community on a Friday night was fairly certain to receive an invitation to "come home and make *Shabbes* with us."

Jews placed great emphasis on such hospitality; to be alone, far from the bosom of one's own, on a Friday night—that was just too sad to contemplate or permit.

An *oyrekh* for *Shabbes* was not simply welcome; he supplied others with the coveted opportunity of doing a good deed.

One of the outstanding *mitzvas* and virtues, among Jews, is hospitality. It was drilled into me, as a child, how wonderful it is to be a host and how alert and attentive one must be to the needs and "good time" of anyone who enters one's home. The food offered a guest must be as abundant and as costly as one can possibly make it—even if (as was often true) a family had to "go without" for many a day to come. *Hakhnoses orkhim*, an important, recurrent Hebrew phrase for hospitality, was Abraham's salient virtue.

The wildest story I ever heard about hospitality deals with a Mr. Ostrovsky, let us say, a traveling salesman, who found himself in the synagogue in a little *shtetl* in Galicia one Friday night. After the prayers, as the Jews turned right, turned left, in the traditional manner, smiling, shaking hands, uttering the *"Gut Shabbes!"* greeting, Mr. Ostrovsky, sighing and melancholy, set off in search of a place to sleep.

"Where are you going?" exclaimed a man. "A Jew, alone, on *Shabbes?* Come, man. Come home with me! Have dinner in my house, spend the night with us. No, no; no excuses! My name is Glantz. Come along. My wife is a marvelous cook, and you'll have a dinner you'll never forget!"

Off went the grateful Ostrovsky with his exuberant host.

Mr. Glantz's promises were not empty: no host and hostess could have been warmer, kinder, more considerate. Ostrovsky was given a fine bedroom, urged to soak in a hot tub, given fluffy towels and scented soap—and fed a superlative dinner. He slept that night between fine linen sheets and next morning ate a sumptuous breakfast.

As he made his heartfelt farewells to his host, Ostrovsky said, "How can I ever thank you?"

Said his host, "Just attend to this." And Glantz handed Ostrovsky a piece of paper. The incredulous Ostrovsky read:

1 Bath hot water	10	kopecks
1 Cake scented soap	20	kopecks
1 Large towel	10	kopecks
1 Sabbath dinner (complete)	2.50	rubles
2 Fresh sheets	20	kopecks
1 Fresh pillowcase	10	kopecks
1 Breakfast	75	kopecks
TOTAL	3.95	rubles

"But—what's this?" asked Ostrovsky.

"Your bill," said Glantz.

"You expect me to *pay* this?"

"Certainly," said Glantz. "Are you denying that you bathed here, slept here, ate like a king—"

"Deny it? I'm flabbergasted!" Ostrovsky exclaimed. "You *invited* me here! You *asked* me to be your *Shabbes oyrekh!* I've never heard a more outrageous—"

"Stop!" Glantz held up his hand peremptorily. "Let's not argue, my friend. Will you agree to come to our rabbi and tell him everything, and abide by his decision?"

"Will I?" cried Ostrovsky. "I can't *wait* to hear what the rabbi tells you about such disgusting behavior!"

Off went the two men to the rabbi, who, seeing their expressions, said, "Well, my friends, what happened so to spoil your Sabbath?"

Ostrovsky told his tale to the rabbi, pouring the words out with fervor.

The rabbi turned to Glantz. "And what do you, the host, have to say?"

"Nothing," said Glantz. "Everything he said is accurate, just as it happened."

"There you are, Rabbi!" cried Ostrovsky. "You see?"

The rabbi nodded. "After hearing you both, and considering all the delicate ethical problems involved, and based on the wisdom—on just such problems—I have studied for years in the *Talmud*, my decision is clear: Ostrovsky, pay the bill."

Ostrovsky could hardly believe his ears. He was speechless. He was shocked. He was discombobulated. And yet . . . a rabbi had pondered; a rabbi had spoken. . . .

With a heavy heart, Ostrovsky sighed. "Very well."

Ostrovsky and his host left the rabbi's house, and Ostrovsky started to count out money.

"What are you doing?" asked Glantz.

"Paying your bill," Ostrovsky said.

"*Paying* me? For my hospitality? You must be crazy. Do you think I would accept money from you, my honored guest, my *oyrekh oif Shabbes?*"

Ostrovsky sputtered: "*You* gave me the bill! You *asked* for money! *You* made me come here! *You*—"

"Oh, that," scoffed Glantz. "I just wanted you to see what a dope we have here for a rabbi."

oysgematert

Pronounced *oyss-ge-*MOT-*tert*, to rhyme with "Royce besotted." From German: *matt*, "exhausted."

To be utterly exhausted, worn out. "I'm *oysgematert!*" "After what she went through, who can blame her for being *oysgematert?*"

oysvorf

Pronounced OYSS-*voorf*, to rhyme with "Royce woof," or -*vawrf*, to rhyme with "wharf." From German: *Auswurf*, "trash," "outcast."

1. A dissolute person, a scoundrel, a bum.
2. An outcast, an antisocial type. "Sure he's a Bohemian; even as a child, he was an *oysvorf.*"
3. A mean, meddlesome, ungrateful person. "I can't understand an *oysvorf* like that one!" "One *oysvorf* can paralyze the work of a whole committee."
   See parkh, no-goodnik.

oytser

Pronounced OY-*tser*, to rhyme with "Roy, sir." From
Hebrew: *o-tsar*, "treasure."

1. TREASURE. "My child? An angel, an *oytser* to us both."
"Our maid is an *oytser*." But again, as with so many Yiddish words, *oytser* can be employed to mean exactly its
opposite.

2. IRONICALLY: By no stretch of the imagination a treasure. "Her son? God save you from such an *oytser!*"
"He almost ruined me, that *oytser!*" "Such an *oytser* I
wish my worst enemies."

The ironic meaning is heard as often as the straight one.

Spitzer, who sold hot dogs, was accosted by a friend. "How's business?"

"Not bad," said Spitzer. "I've already put away a thousand dollars in the bank."

"In that case," said the friend, "maybe you can lend me five dollars."

"I'm not allowed to."

"What do you mean, you're not *allowed* to?"

"I made an agreement with the bank. They agreed not to sell
hot dogs if I promised not to make loans."

Spitzer was some *oytser*.

pareve^Y
pareveh^R
parev (masculine)

Pronounced PAAR-*eh-va,* to rhyme with "jar of a," or (more often) PAAR-*va,* to rhyme with "larva." The origin of *pareve* is **unknown.***

Neutral **dietetically.**†

*Macy Nulman writes (in *The Encyclopedia of the Sayings of the Jewish People,* Jason Aronson, 1997) that *pareve* is derived from *parbar,* a Talmudic word pertaining to a small passageway in the Temple that "helped to make the whole Temple court fit for the consumption of most holy sacrifices and the slaughter of minor sacrifices."

Foods, to be *pareve,* include neither animal nor dairy products and can therefore be eaten with either. (Jewish dietary laws require that meat and dairy foods not be consumed at the same meal. See kosher.) To be *pareve,* a cake, for instance, can be made with coffee or fruit juice instead of milk and with vegetable fat or oil substituted for butter.

The marvels of modern technology have expanded the roster of *pareve* foods to include margarine made without milk solids or butter fat (often sold as "diet" margarine), as well as *pareve* milk, cream, and even ice cream, which is made with hydrogenated soybean oil.

† Just as *kosher* is used as slang for "legitimate" or "a-okay," *pareve* has slang connotations, too. A *pareve* person is wishy-washy and vague; a *pareve* deed or decision is "neither fish nor fowl," of no great consequence, middle-of-the-roadish.

parkh^Y
parech^R
parekh

Pronounced PARR-*ekh*, with a Germanic *kh*. Hebrew: *parach*, "sprout."

1. An unpleasant, sly, low-grade person.
2. Someone unreliable and to be avoided. "Don't confide in that *parkh*."
3. Someone ungrateful and presumptuous, who takes advantage of the probity of others.

I n the Bible, *parkh* means to sprout—referring especially to scabs in the scalp, which were considered contagious. In time, *parkh* came to mean a scabrous person.

paskudne
paskudneh

Pronounced *poss*-KOOD-*neh*, to rhyme with "Joss would na"; or *poss*-KOOD-*nyeh*, with the *ny* as rippling as in "canyon," to rhyme with "Joss could knee a." From the Polish/Ukrainian word for "nasty," "dirty," "sloppy."

1. Nasty, dirty, sloppy. "What a *paskudne* experience!" "The weather? *Paskudne!*" "He is cursed with that *paskudne* mouth of his." "They served us a *paskudne* dinner."

2. Mean, unkind, disgusting. "Such *paskudne* treatment I never got anywhere else." "She is a *paskudne* type."
3. Contemptible, odious, the opposite of simpático (which, in Yiddish, is *sympatish*). "That whole family is *epes paskudne*." "What drives a man to such *paskudne* conduct?"

paskudnyak
paskudnak

Pronounced with full fruitiness: *poss-kood*-NYOK, slurring the *n* into the *y* as in "canyon"; to rhyme with "Joss would 'nyok.'" From Polish/Ukrainian. Spelled with or without a *y*, the use of which adds to the effect of acute distaste.

A man or woman who is *paskudnye*, hence nasty, mean, odious, contemptible, rotten, vulgar, insensitive, petty, and—in general—opprobrious. "I wouldn't say 'Hello' to a *paskudnyak* like that!" "Did you ever hear of such a *paskudnyak*?" "That whole family is a collection of *paskudnyaks*."

This word is one of the most greasily graphic, I think, in Yiddish. It offers the connoisseur three nice, long syllables, starting with a sibilant of reprehension and ending with a nasality of scorn. It adds cadence to contempt.

A Jew, crossing the street, bumped into an anti-Semite.

"Swine!" bellowed the *paskudnyak*.

"Goldberg," said the Jew, bowing.

paskustve^Y
paskustva^R

Pronounced *poss*-ĸooss-*tva*, to rhyme with "Las puss tva."
1. A female *paskudnyak*.
2. A *paskudne* act. "That was a piece of *paskustve*" means "That was a disgusting thing to do."

Passover
See Pesach.

patsh^Y
potch^R
patch

Rhymes with "botch." Both noun and verb. From German, *patsch*, a "smack," a "blow."
1. A slap, a smack. "Man, did she give him a *patsh!*" "Don't be fresh or I'll *patsh* you!"
2. An insult, a blow to one's pride. "To me, his words were a terrible *patsh*." "When I read it, it was like a *patsh*."
3. A reverse or setback to one's hopes. "Last season gave me a *patsh*."

There is a saying, "*A patsh fargeyt, a vort bashteyt*"—"A slap passes, but a word [that is, an insult] remains."

patshke^Y
potchkeh^R
potshkee (Ameridish)

Pronounced POTCH-*keh*, to rhyme with "notch k'"; or rendered as POTCH-*kee*, to rhyme with "watch me," for playful phonetic effect. From Russian: *patshkat,* "to soil" or "to smear."

1. To fuss or "mess around" inefficiently and inexpertly. "He *patshkes* around with paint and they call him a painter." "When you *patshke* around, your work is *ongepatshket.*" "I spent all day in the kitchen *patshkeeing* around."
2. To dawdle, to waste time. "Let's go; don't *patshke.*" See ongepatshket.

payess^R
peyes^Y

Pronounced PAY-*ess.* Hebrew: *pe'ah* (singular) and *pe'ot* (plural), "side earlocks," "curls."

The long, unshorn ear-ringlet hair and sideburn locks worn by very Orthodox Jewish males.

The custom among Orthodox Jews of letting their ear curls grow, and wearing a full beard, comes from an instruction in Leviticus 19:27: "Ye shall not round the corners of your heads, neither shalt thou mar the corners of thy beard."* (A learned friend

---

*The verse was interpreted by the Talmudic rabbis as an injunction not against a clean-shaven face, but against the use of a razor. Jewish law permits the use of scissors for cutting facial hair, and some Orthodox Jews have extended this permission to include electric razors, which use two blades.

informs me that *payess* are regarded as symbolizing the uncut corners of the field at harvesttime, which were by tradition left to be gleaned by the widow, the orphan, and the stranger.)

In the Middle Ages, church and secular powers often *forbade* Jews to trim their beards in any way. Why? To be certain that a Jew could be identified.

Payess were savagely resented, in many Gentile areas, and were forbidden by law for a time in Tsarist Russia.

To wear or to cut the *payess* became an important question among Jews—especially where an exit from the *shtetl* was possible: for example, in the United States after 1880, during the great immigration movements from eastern Europe. To cut the *payess* was an open and defiant sign of departure from Orthodoxy, a desire to become Americanized as soon as possible. Families were split asunder over *payess*.

The bearded beatnik confronted his girl's father arrogantly: "Man, how come you treat me so nasty—when *your* old man always gives me the big hello?"

"My 'old man,'" the father said with a scowl, "thinks you're studying at the *yeshiva!*"

pekl
pekel, peckel

Pronounced PECK-*l*, to rhyme with "freckle." From the Bavarian dialect of German: *Päckl*, "little package."

1. Bundle, parcel, little package.
2. A knapsack or bundle carried on the back or shoulders (see below).

3. "To send a *pekl*": to send food and gifts, for a holiday or (with clothing) to relatives overseas.

4. "To have a *pekl*" means to be in trouble, to have a "passel" of problems.*

> *In more modern lingo, to have "baggage."

5. "He left her a *pekl*" is an idiomatic expression for "He got her pregnant."

6. "He always carries his *pekl* with him" is a way of describing a hunchback.

*P*ekl evokes special and warm associations among Jews, for it was from the little *peklekh* of wares—containing ribbons, needles, threads, pins, buttons, hooks-and-eyes, laces, scissors, etc.—that many Jews made their living, in Europe no less than in the New World to which they came. (The first peddlers in America, incidentally, were not Jews, but "Connecticut Yankees.") From the *pekl* of the Jewish peddler and itinerant merchant in America came a wagon of wares, then a little store, then an "emporium," then a department store, and in future generations a retail chain . . . .*

The adventures and adversities of the peddler who set off on foot, crossing strange new land and hills and even mountains, bringing his commodities to farmers' and miners' wives; the dietary difficulties he endured; the prejudices and popularity he encountered (in New England and the South, Jews were welcomed by many pious folk as "people of the Book," "living witnesses" of the Word, authorities on Hebrew and the Old Testament)—all this forms one of the sagas of the aliens who made America what it is.

Pesach^R
Peysakh^Y
Pesakh

Pronounced PAY-*sokh*, with a guttural *kh*, to rhyme with "bays loch." Hebrew: "to pass over," "to spare."

The Passover holiday and **celebration.**†

This is the most cherished of Jewish holidays, the Festival of Freedom. It lasts eight days. The first two and last two days are full holidays; the intermediate days are semiholidays, known as *chol hamo'ed* (rhymes with "ol' man NOAH'd").

In Israel, *Pesach* is observed for seven days. The three major festivals of the Jewish year, Passover (*Pesach*), Pentecost (*Shevuos*), and the Feast of Booths (*Succos*), were originally marked by pilgrimages to the Temple in Jerusalem. The dates for these

in the American credit union movement. Under his leadership, credit unions in America multiplied from forty-eight to over one thousand in just fifteen years, 1915–1930, freeing thousands of American workers from usury.

† For information on contemporary innovations in Passover observance, see my note on the next page and my note to Rosten's entry for **Haggadah**.

festivals were determined by the authorities after observing the previous new moon. They then sent messengers to the distant communities where Jews dwelled, establishing the date of the festival. In order to allow for a possible delay in receiving the message, or for any inaccuracy in the report, an additional day of observance for these festivals was added in the communities outside of Israel.

Pesach commemorates Israel's dramatic deliverance from enslavement in Egypt over 3,200 years ago, as recounted in Exodus.*

On the evenings preceding the first and second nights of Passover, a great family *seder* (SAY-*der*) is held. (*Seder* means order of procedure.) This combination banquet and religious service is

---

*There is no convincing archaeological evidence that the Jewish people were enslaved en masse in ancient Egypt. As Chaim Potok notes, however, "We see three thousand years of Egyptian civilization through the dubious optic of tattered scribal documents, damaged art, and chance discovery" (*Wanderings: Chaim Potok's History of the Jews*, Knopf, 1978). Some scholars believe the story of Joseph in Egypt to have occurred during the period of rule in Egypt by the Hyksos—Semitic foreigners who occupied the seat of power in the seventeenth century B.C.E. The Egyptian kings who drove out the Hyksos— Amenhotep I, Thutmose I, and Thutmose II—would constitute the "pharaoh who knew not Joseph" (Exodus 1:8). Their dynastic descendants are known to have invaded Canaan, during which time the word *Hapiru* appears for the first time in Egyptian records. But the relationship between the words *Hapiru* and *Hebrew* remains uncertain.

Jewish tradition dates the liberation from Egypt at about 1300 B.C.E. About all of this, including the plagues sent by God to terrorize the Pharaoh, "the land of the Nile is silent," writes Potok.

Rather than discrediting the tradition of Passover, however, the lack of positive historical evidence makes the holiday's ongoing commemoration for centuries even more impressive. What other peoples have embraced as their role model for national and ethical identity that of a ragtag army of degraded slaves? The God of the Bible repeatedly roots demands for social justice in the fact that "you were slaves in Egypt." Because of this memory—mythic or otherwise!—Jewish tradition demands that kindness and charity be shown to the stranger, and that human pride be tempered with gratitude.

the highlight of the holiday—and, to many, of the year. Since nothing containing leavening, or which has come in contact with a leavening agent, may be used during the festival, special china and utensils are set aside for the Passover week.

On the table are symbolic foods commemorating events connected with Passover: the *matzo,* or unleavened bread, a reminder of the haste in which the Israelites left Egypt, without waiting for their bread to rise; bitter herbs, marking the bitterness of slavery; a roasted egg and bone, symbolic of the offerings brought to the Temple on this festival; and *charoses* (kha-RO-ses), a mixture of chopped nuts, apples, cinnamon, and wine, representing the clay from which the Israelites made bricks while in slavery. Each setting has a wineglass.

The leader of the *seder* half reclines at the head of the table, propped up on pillows or on a sofa; this dramatizes freedom and ease (perhaps in imitation of Roman patricians at a banquet).

By custom, guests are sought for a family *seder:* friends, a student living away from home, a traveler, a neighbor, a soldier.

Traditionally, the grandfather, father, or oldest son is the leader of the service.† He opens the *seder* with an Aramaic prayer.

---

† As reflected in Rosten's choice of words, the Passover *seder,* like many rituals of Judaism, is traditionally a male-dominated and male-led event, and the language of the *Haggadah* tends to render women and girls invisible. Feminist reactions to this over the past thirty years have brought about several innovations in both custom and liturgy. Many families now share the reading of the *Haggadah* among all literate members. The role of Shifrah and Puah, the Hebrew midwives who defy Pharaoh's order to kill all newborn Hebrew sons, is given greater emphasis, as is the role of Moses' sister and mother, Miriam and Yocheved. The miraculous "parting of waters" has been interpreted as a form of midwifery by God, by which the slave people are "birthed" or "delivered" from *Mitzrayim* (Egypt, literally, the "narrow places").

These and many other text-based interpretations have enlarged the meaning of the Passover *seder* and revitalized the interest of many Jewish women and men. At Ma'yan, the Jewish Women's Project of the Jewish Community Center of the Upper West Side in New York, an annual feminist *seder* attracts more than 1,500 attendees each year.

(Aramaic was the vernacular of the post-Exilic Jews from the sixth century B.C.E.) He raises a tray with three *matzos* on it, displays them to the company, and intones the ancient litany:

> This is the bread of affliction that our fathers ate in the land of Egypt. All who are hungry, let them come and eat—all who are needy, let them come and celebrate Passover with us. Now we are here: next year may we be in Israel. Now we are slaves: in the year ahead may we be free men.

The prayer was probably composed shortly after 70 C.E., when the Romans crushed Judea and the Jews went into *galut*—exile. The use of the present tense stresses the underlying significance of the *seder* as the re-creation of a living experience. The rabbis of old taught that "every man in every generation must look upon himself as if he personally had come forth out of Egypt. It was not our fathers alone that the Holy One redeemed, but ourselves also did He redeem with them." Every generation can know slavery in one form or another; and every generation can be redeemed.

The leader then raises his wine goblet: "Not only once have they risen to destroy us, but in every generation. . . . But the Holy One, blessed be He, always delivers us from **their hands.**"*

---

*The Passover season has historically been one of terrible violence and woe for the Jews. Concurrent with Easter, it became a season for pogroms against the "Christ-killers." The Nazis, too, launched their liquidation of the Warsaw ghetto during Passover in 1943, only to be met with a shocking Jewish resistance that lasted for more than two months.

David Mamet's brief novella, *Passover* (St. Martin's Press, 1995), provides a chilling picture of a Jewish woman saving herself from rape and possible death by faking a bloody scene in her house that convinces *pogromchiks* that the place has already been ransacked. The story resonates powerfully with Exodus 12:21–28, the text in which the Israelites mark their doorposts and lintels with the blood of sacrificed lambs to alert the Angel of Death to "pass over" their homes.

A favorite moment of the *seder* arrives when the youngest child at the table asks why this night is different from all other nights of the year and poses "Four Questions" (the *Fir Kashes*) to the father: Why do we eat unleavened bread? Why do we use bitter herbs? Why do we dip the herbs in salt water? Why do we recline at the table?

The father replies with the phrase "Slaves were we unto Pharaoh in Egypt" and continues retelling the ancient story of Pharaoh's refusal to let the children of Israel go, the plagues visited upon the Egyptians, the miraculous salvation at the Red Sea, and the arrival at Mount Sinai, where the *Torah* was given to the children of Israel. (The name of Moses occurs but once, oddly enough.)

The *Haggadah*, the narrative read at the *seder*, also includes many rabbinic comments, hymns, prayers, and stylized questions and answers—the whole constituting a ceremony of celebration and praise to the Lord.

When the *Haggadah* reaches the story of the ten plagues that afflicted the Egyptians, everyone at the table spills a little wine from his or her glass as each plague is named. Why? So that their cup of joy, even when celebrating a moment of deliverance, should not be full. The sages taught the Jews not to rejoice over another's misfortune. "Rejoice not when thine enemy falleth" (Proverbs 24:17).

(I must confess that *I* have always enjoyed gloating over the comeuppance suffered by the detestable, regardless of race, color, or creed.)

A story in the *Talmud* relates that after the Israelites had safely crossed the **Red Sea**,* they sang a song of praise to God, but when the angels sought to join the triumphant paean, God thundered: "You shall not sing while my other children [the Egyptians] are drowning."

Late in the *seder* ritual, a large goblet of wine is poured for the

---

*Nowadays more usually called the Sea of Reeds.

Prophet Elijah, and the front door is opened, while all sing a hymn welcoming him in. Elijah plays a leading and greatly beloved role in Jewish lore; it is Elijah who will blow his ram's horn to signal the Redemption and prepare the way for the Messiah.

According to the Bible, you may remember, Elijah never died: he was transported directly to Heaven—in a chariot of fire, within a whirlwind.

Elijah became the most popular of seraphim among Jews: he was thought to be a special protector of the sick, the poor, and the harassed and was credited with all sorts of miracle-working powers and wondrous disguises.

But some hold that opening the door during the *seder* is connected to the terrible "Blood Accusation" against Jews (the charge that Jews drank Christian blood at Passover), used to justify both terror and murder. The door was opened during the holiday feast, they say, to allay any suspicion on the part of Gentile neighbors that secret or dastardly practices were being followed inside.

The repeated, fanatical slaughter of Jews during Passover finally led some rabbis to ban the use of red wine at the *seder*. Until a hundred years or so ago, white wine, raisin wine, was used sacramentally on the Sabbath and holidays alike.

Sholom Aleichem dryly remarks somewhere that even though *Pesach* comes along once a year, Jews insist on asking questions all year long.†

See also **Haggadah**.

---

† Sholom Aleichem (pen name for Shalom Rabinowitz) had at least four well-known short stories on Passover themes: one about Fishel the *melamed*'s much-detoured journey home for the holidays; one about a "revolutionary expropriation" of the resources of a wealthy Jew by Jewish socialists; another about another "expropriation" of family wealth by a Jewish con artist; and a fourth about a Jewish boy, sleepy with ritual wine, who faces kidnapping by the Prophet Elijah! See Rosten's entry, and my note, for **sholem**.

pilpul

Pronounced PILL-*pull*, to rhyme with "fill full." Hebrew: "debate," "dialectics."

1. A form of analysis and debate used in Talmudic study.
2. Unproductive hairsplitting that is employed not so much to advance clarity or reveal meaning as to display one's own cleverness.
3. Colloquially: Any hairsplitting or logic chopping that leaves the main boulevard of a problem to bog down in the side streets.

FOLK SAYINGS: "If you insist long enough that you're right, you'll be wrong."

"'For instance' is not proof."

pisha paysha[R]
pishe peyshe[Y]

Pronounced PISH-*eh* PEY-*sheh* (or PEH-*sheh*), to rhyme with "dish acacia." Yinglish.

A card game, played by two—one of whom is usually a child.

It is a very simple game, often one of the first taught to children, and particularly useful in whiling away the hours of convalescence after an illness. It was a good game to play with a child because a child could easily win; only luck is involved. (Jewish parents preferred to say that *pisha paysha* is "educational" because it helps teach the young the sequence of numbers.)

The game is played this way: The deck is placed facedown; one card is placed face upward; the players draw from the deck, in turn, and seek to build upward or downward upon the open card; for instance, if a five is exposed, you may place upon it either a four or a six. The player with the fewest cards in his hand when the deck is exhausted **wins**.*

I was taught to play *pisha paysha* by my father, when I was six or seven. I have spent many an idle moment since then wondering what on earth *pisha paysha* means and where on earth it originated. By a feat of uncanny bookmanship (happening to open a published-in-England book on games), I am at last able to dispel the world's ignorance: *Pisha paysha* is some Jew's corruption of the name of a card game known in England as "pitch and patience." Some call it "peace and patience." In my memory, it will remain imperishably inscribed as *pisha paysha*.

---

*No wonder Rosten scorns the educational value of *pisha paysha*—he didn't play by my *bobe*'s rules!

In her version of the game, each player draws from the central deck to build a face-up stack of cards in his or her place. The players can then "hit" the other person's stack with a sequential card (if she had a five exposed, I could place on her stack either a four or a six). Both players also jointly build stacks based on suits off to the side of the table, starting with the aces. Eventually, as those stacks build sequentially, the personal stacks diminish, until one player runs out of cards and is declared winner.

If a player fails to take a chance that is available, the opposing player can slap a palm to the deck and cry, "*Pisha paysha!*"—in which case the neglectful player loses that turn. The game therefore develops children's powers of observation and attention, as well as numerical skills, and is pretty fast-moving!

In my household, *pisha paysha* was pronounced as if spelled *peesha peysha* (PEE-sha PEY-sha).

pisher
pisherke (feminine)
pishn (infinitive verb)

Rhymes with "fisher." From German: *pissen,* "to urinate."

Vulgarism
1. A bed wetter.
2. A young, inexperienced person, a "young squirt."
3. An insignificant or inconsequential person, a "nobody."

Literally, a *pisher* is one who urinates; but that is a far cry from present and popular usage. "He's a mere *pisher*" means "He's very young" or "He's still wet behind the ears" (excuse the misleading metaphor). "You can't let him decide; he's only a *pisher!*" means he's too young and inexperienced to be given such responsibility. "He's just a *pisher*" means "He's a nobody," has no influence.

A common saying (common in both senses) is "So call me *pisher*" or "So let him call me *pisher,*" which means "I don't care," "What does that matter?," or "Sticks and stones may break my bones, but names can never harm me."

In France, an elderly Jew, tired of hearing a young man boast of his ancestry, finally said, "Listen, La Fontaine: I knew your grandfather, who changed his name to La Fontaine from Schpritzwasser [Squirtwater]. And he told me that *his* father changed his name to Schpritzwasser from what everyone called him, which was Moishe the *Pisher!* So please, don't put on airs, 'La Fontaine.'"

pishke
pishkeh
See pushkeh.

pisk

Pronounced PISK, to rhyme with "risk." Polish or Russian: "to squeak" or "to screech."

1. The mouth of an animal or a human.
2. Colloquialism: An eloquent or garrulous speaker.
3. A brusque slang word for "mouth," used in expressions such as "Shut your trap."

To say that someone has a *pisk* can mean that he speaks eloquently, brilliantly—or without decorum or restraint. "I heard him lecture. There is a *pisk!*" "She had to open her big fat *pisk!*"

The diminutive, *piskel* or *piskeleh,* is often applied admiringly to a child who speaks precociously. "Does he have a *piskeleh.*"

A meaningless folk saw goes: "A fox runs from Brisk to Trisk carrying a rifle in his *pisk.*"

pitsl [Y]
pitsel [R]
pitsle [Y] (diminutive)
pitseleh [R]

Pronounced PITS'*l* and PIT-*seh-leh,* to rhyme with "Fritzl" and "Fit Sulla." From German: *Bissel,* "a little piece."

1. A small piece, a morsel, a bit of something.
2. A baby; an infant. "And how is your darling *pitsle?*" "I think she's carrying a *pitsle.*" ("I think she's pregnant.")

platke-makher ^Y
platke-macher ^R

Pronounced PLAWT-*keh* MA-*kher*, to rhyme with "Maude k'Bach'er," or PLYOT-*keh* MA-*kher*. Polish: *plyotka*, "gossip"; and German: *Makher*, "maker."

1. A malicious, troublemaking carrier of rumors or animadversions, who enjoys creating suspicion or animosity among friends. "The minute you tell that *platke-makher* something personal, he can't wait to tell it to your friends."
2. A gossipy intriguer, who deliberately repeats confidences and spreads unpleasant tales. "God spare me from the wiles of that *platke-makher.*"
See also yenta, yakhne.

pletsl

Pronounced PLETS'*l*, to rhyme with "Edsel."

A thin, flat, crisp roll, often garnished with poppy seeds or **onion**.*

---

*The onion *pletsl* is variously called an onion *zeml*, onion *pampalik*, or onion board.

Pletsl, as a diminutive of *plats* (place), describes a marketplace in Polish towns where Jewish vendors set up stalls. The city of Paris also has a *Pletsl*, a
(Continued on page 430)

plosher

Pronounced PLOE-*sh'r*, to rhyme with "*kosher*." From German: *Plauschen,* "chat" (dialect).

1. A braggart, a blowhard, a "hot air" artist.
2. An indiscreet and unreliable gossip.
3. One who inflates and exaggerates his own talents or resources.

See fonfer, trombenik.

The nouveau riche Nathansons had gone to Europe and visited Israel and were now home, boasting about their trip to friends.

"And in Rome we had an audience with the pope!" said Mr. Nathanson.

"With the *pope?*" echoed an astonished friend. "So how did you like him?"

"*He* was marvelous. Her, I didn't care for."

What a *plosher!* †

In the plane headed for Arizona, two of Abraham's progeny were chatting.

"I can't wait to get to the hotel," said the first, "and change and rush out to the golf course! . . . Are you a golfer?"

The other replied, "Me? Golf is practically my whole life! I'd

---

(Continued from page 429)

predominantly Jewish neighborhood in the Fourth Arrondissement that centers on the rue des Rosiers. In the thirteenth century, this neighborhood was known as *La Juiverie* (the Jewry). During the Nazi era, Jews were deported to concentration camps from this and other neighborhoods.

† For comment about pope jokes, see my note to Rosten's entry for **ai-ai-ai**.

rather play than eat! I belong to the finest country club in Cleveland! I play every chance I can!"

"Really? . . . Well, I play in the low seventies. . . ."

"So do I," exclaimed the *plosher,* "but if it gets one degree colder, I go right back to the hotel!"

plotz ᴿ
plats ʸ
plotsenᴿ (infinitive verb)
platsnʸ
platst, plotzed

Pronounced PLOTZ, to rhyme with "Watts." From the German: *Platz,* "place," *platzen,* "to burst."

As a Noun

A place, a seat. "Save my *plotz.*" (But this is not why I include *plotz,* a word with another ambience, one all its own.)

As a Verb

1. To split, to burst, to explode. "From so much pleasure, one could *plotz!*" "What they went through would make a person *plotz.*" "I can't laugh any more or I'll *plotz!*"

2. To be aggravated beyond bearing; to be infuriated; to be outraged. "His heart will *plotz* from such suffering." "He makes me so angry I could *plotz.*" "From such conduct, one can *plotz.*" "I wish he would *plotz* from frustration!"

Plotzed (or *platst*) is the Yinglish past tense of the Yiddish *platsn.* "He laughed so hard, he practically

plotzed." "What did he do? He *plotzed!*" "Is he a comedian? Why, the whole theater *plotzed!*"

Pincus and Bernstein were walking down a street in Berlin when
they saw an SS cop approaching. Only Pincus had an identity card.
Bernstein said, "Quick, run! He'll chase *you*, and I'll get away."

So Pincus broke into a run, and he ran and he ran until he
thought his heart would *plotz*.

"Stop! Stop!" cried the policeman, who finally caught up.
"Jew!" he roared. "Show me your papers."

The gasping Pincus produced his papers.

The Nazi examined them and saw they were in order. "But why
did you run away?"

"Eh—my doctor told me to run half a mile after each meal!"

"But you saw me chasing after you and yelling! Why didn't you
stop?"

"I—thought maybe you go to the same doctor!"

prost

Pronounced PRAWST, to rhyme with "lost," or PRUST, to
rhyme with "crust." From Russian: *prostoy*, "plain" or
"common."

1. Common, vulgar.
2. Unlearned.
3. Ill-mannered, boorish.
4. Simple.

No more cutting or scornful adjective existed, in my home,
than *prost*. To call someone "*proster Yid*" or "*a proster mentsh*"
was to dismiss him as hopelessly deserving of disrespect. Money,

success, influence, had nothing to do with it: "*Prost* is *prost!*"

A *proster* Jew can redeem himself by applying himself to learning and good deeds and by adopting the gentle, modest demeanor that distinguishes "a man of *yikhes.*"

See yikhes, grob.

pupik

Pronounced PU (the *u* of "put") *–pik*, to rhyme with "look it." From Russian: *pupok*, "navel."

Navel.

Pupik is used in a variety of broad, colorful expressions—ironic, maledictory, and ribald.

A *sheynm dank in pupik* ("a pretty thanks in the navel") means "Thanks for nothing."

"*Zol vaksn tsibeles in zayn pupik!*"—"Onions should grow in his navel!"

"What does he do? He sits around all day looking at his *pupik.*"

A classic definition of an unrealistic, impractical type is this: "He's the kind who worries whether a flea has a *pupik.*"

Purim

Pronounced POOR-*im* (not PURE-*im*); rhymes with "tour 'em." Hebrew: *pur*, "lot."

The Feast of Lots, commemorating the rescue of the Jews of Persia from Haman's plot to exterminate every Jewish man, woman, and child.

Lots had been drawn or cast by Haman, first minister of King Ahasuerus (possibly Artaxerxes II), to determine the date on which the Jews of Persia would be slaughtered. A miraculous deliverance was effected by the heroism of beautiful Queen Esther, who was Jewish, and the sagacity of Mordecai, her uncle and guardian. Haman ended up being executed on the gallows he had erected to dispatch Mordecai. The story is told in the book of Esther.

Purim is a day that Jews regard fondly, because it tells them that tyrants and fanatics *can* be defeated. In a larger sense, it signifies that evil cannot prevail forever. Since the Middle Ages, an enemy of the Jewish people has been known as a "Haman." Deliverances from other calamitous events have been celebrated and called *Purim Katan* (Little Purim) by Jewish communities in Saragossa, Frankfurt, Egypt, and Tiberias. There is a saying, of rueful sagacity: "There are so many Hamans, but only one *Purim*."*

In synagogues, the *Megillah* (Scroll of Esther) is read on the eve and morning of *Purim*. Whenever the name of Haman is uttered, the children set up a racket of boos and jeers and spin ratchety noisemakers *(groggers)* around and around. In some communities, Haman's name is written upon the soles of one's shoes, so that his name may literally be wiped out.

Among the customs associated with *Purim* are the sending of gifts (food and money) to the poor and the exchanging of gifts of

---

*Rabbi Michael Strassfeld notes (in *The Jewish Holidays: A Guide and Commentary*, Harper & Row, 1985) that there are "over a hundred such special Purims," including some "special Purims observed by a family because an ancestor was saved from death. One of the better-known is that of the Heller family of Prague who to this day still gather on the first of Adar to read a scroll describing how Yom Tov Lippman Heller, rabbi of Prague, was saved from a death sentence in 1629."

food with friends. Feasts, dances, and masquerades are held. *Purim* is the closest thing to the carnival in Jewish life; in Israel, it is celebrated with public processions, complete with floats and costumes, and private **masquerade parties**.†

The symbolic food of *Purim* is the *hamantash,* a three-cornered sweet pastry with prunes or **poppy seeds**.‡

Scholars have long questioned the authenticity of the colorful and dramatic Esther-Mordecai-Haman story. One theory holds that the *Purim* festival is a carryover from an old pagan carnival that used to take place on the Babylonian New Year—a festival that Persians and Jews alike loved because of its masks, dances, and Mardi Gras shenanigans; the Jews could not be persuaded by their rabbis to reject such unseemly disportment, so (it seems) the wise men finally decided to use the Esther-Haman drama as the

† Despite the joviality of *Purim,* the holiday has not really caught on in a big way in America, for three probable causes: (1) the widespread popularity of Halloween seems to exhaust people's energies for masquerading and partying; (2) the tongue-in-cheek quality of *Purim* seems to mystify many Jews, who are accustomed to associating their faith with sobriety, introspection, and historical suffering—anything but hilarity; and (3) the holiday is synagogue centered and community centered; *Purim* has no significant home rituals (unlike American Jews' two most popular Jewish holidays, Passover and *Chanukah*)—yet only a plurality of American Jews, approximately 40 percent, are synagogue members, and most Jews no longer live in all-Jewish neighborhoods. In Orthodox and Chasidic neighborhoods, by contrast, the level of *Purim* festivity on the streets is riotous.

‡ *Hamantash* means "Haman's pocket." According to *The Encyclopedia of Jewish Symbols,* by Ellen Frankel and Betsy Platkin Teutsch (Jason Aronson, 1992), the pastry represents "the bribes stuffing this corrupt villain's pockets." In Israel, the pastry is called *ozney Haman*—"Haman's ears"—supposedly based on an old custom of cutting off a criminal's ears before hanging him. The triangular shape of *hamantashn* (plural) also reflects medieval depictions of Haman that typically (and anachronistically) portray him in a three-cornered European hat.

purported reason for carnival celebrations they could neither ignore nor condone.

There are close resemblances between *Purim* and non-Jewish holidays such as Shrovetide, and ordinary carnivals descended from pagan festivities. The burning of Haman in effigy, the choosing of a special "*Purim* rabbi," the masks and dances and mummeries—all these are related to celebrations that burn "the spirit of the preceding year," or burn evil and malevolent demons, or appoint a "Bishop of Fools" just for the holidays, or stage masques and miracle plays.

pushke
pishke

Pronounced PUSH-*keh*, PUSH-*key*, or PISH-*key*. From the Polish or Russian: *puszka*, "can" or "cannon."

1. Any can.
2. The little container kept in the home, often in the kitchen, in which money to be donated to charity is accumulated.

E ach charitable organization would provide its own *pushke*. (Jewish housewives customarily put a few coins in the *pushke* every Friday night, before lighting the Sabbath candles.) Collectors for the various charities would come around at regular intervals, and the *baleboste* (housewife) would empty her *pushke*.*

---

*Tzedakah maven (expert) Danny Siegel, who runs a highly personalized Jewish charitable organization, Ziv Tzedakah Fund, tells about Sylvia Orzoff, who "in 23 years of collecting money in a blue-and-white tin can in front of Canter's Deli on Fairfax Avenue [Los Angeles] has netted more than $2 million for the Jewish National Fund" (*Gym Shoes and Irises: Personalized Tzedakah*, Town House Press, 1988).

The *pushke,* set out on a shelf or the kitchen windowsill, carried labels that read like a catalog of human misery—and benevolence:

For Orphans

For Widows

For the Anshe _____ Synagogue

For Trees to Be Planted in Palestine

For Victims of Persecution

For the Blind

For the Lame

For the Hebrew Home for the Aged

For a Rabbinical Trip to the Holy Land

For Milk for Jewish Children in Hospitals in the Old
Country

For a Library Wing for the Yeshiva

For the Importation of a Noted Cantor from Poland for
Rosh Hashanah Services

For Meetings to Protest Pogroms in the Ukraine

For Men Maimed While Returning from Religious
Services

For the Romanian Brotherhood
For the Galician Brotherhood
For the Hungarian Brotherhood
For the Lithuanian Brotherhood
For the Training of Newly Arrived Immigrants
For Resettlement of Jewish Refugees from Turkey in the
    Land of Israel
For Machinery and Farm Equipment to Be Sent
    to Jewish Farmers in Indiana
For the Jewish Chicken Raisers in Kankakee
    Recently Bankrupted by the Ravages of Red
    Tick among Rhode Island Roosters

I can't, offhand, remember *all* the titles.

The word for charity is *tsedakah,* which means justice. Charity was, and is, considered a duty, an obligation, a necessity, a God-forbid-you-should-ever-forget-to-give-to-the-poor-and-orphaned-and-needy-or-any-other-worthy-cause.*

*The *mitzva* of *tzedakah,* says the *Talmud* (*Baba Batra* 9a), "equals all the other commandments." Among the rules governing this Jewish form of wealth redistribution are these: Jews are expected to give 10 percent of their income for *tzedakah;* they should not give so generously that they impoverish themselves; even the poor who are kept alive by *tzedakah* must give *tzedakah;* neither poverty nor wealth should be considered measures of the human being—all people should be treated with dignity; anonymous giving is preferred to minimize power relationships; means testing is generally discouraged; distribution of *tzedakah* funds should be exercised by no fewer than three people; the highest form of *tzedakah* is considered to be partnership with the poor by offering loans or going into business so that their poverty can be permanently overcome.

These Jewish teachings about poverty and poverty relief contrast sharply with our modern society's tendency to stigmatize the poor. The *Midrash* (see Rosten's note on **midrash**) even teaches that "the poor person does more for the householder than the householder does for the poor person" (*Leviticus Rabbah* 34:8). *Tzedakah* is designed to uplift both the recipient *and* the giver.

3. The money saved up by a married woman, out of the household funds her husband gave her; a nest egg. In this usage, a *pushke* is often known as a *knipl.*†

Women fiercely guarded as earnings the small amounts their careful management of the household made possible for them to divert to personal, undisclosed causes. The woman would spend her "little *pushke*" as she saw fit: for a charity, a treat for the children, a special holiday delicacy, a small luxury for herself. Often the *pushke* was the family's only emergency fund for doctor bills, operations, etc.‡

My wife claims that when I married her she had already saved up her own little *pushke,* which I was *not* to consider "divvies," which is not Yiddish but Chicagoese for anything to be divided up. (When we saw a pal pick up a coin or other object, we would scream, "Fen dibs!," "Fen dibby!," or "Fen divvies!" That established, the finder had to cut in the caller for half the spoils. I have no idea where this custom originated, but it always gave me

It helps establish a covenantal community despite inevitable differences in ability, power, wealth, and privilege among people. For more on Jewish economic teachings, see my book *Jews, Money and Social Responsibility: Developing a "Torah of Money" for Contemporary Life* (Shefa Fund, 1993), coauthored with Jeffrey Dekro, as well as Rabbi Meir Tamari's *"With All Your Possessions"—Jewish Ethics and Economic Life* (Free Press, 1987).

† See my note to Rosten's entry for **knipl**.

‡ The American Jewish community created its own communal *pushke* in 1893 with the establishment, in New York, of the Hebrew Free Loan Society (originally the Hebrew Gemilath Chassadim Association), founded with $95 in capital. Within a century, it had distributed $108 million in interest-free loans to over one million families, for both emergency use and business investments. The story is told eloquently in Jenna Wiessman Joselit's *Lending Dignity* (Hebrew Free Loan Society, 1992). See also my note to Rosten's entry for **landsman**.

romantic images of the Klondike, where bearded, desperate miners hoarsely croaked, "Fen dibs!" to establish their claim to a stake in the Cornucopia Lode. . . . I have wandered pretty far from *pushke,* but I'm entitled to some fun, too.)

putz^R
pots^Y

Rhymes with "nuts." From the German: *putzen,* "to decorate."

Literally, *putz* is vulgar slang for "penis." But the vulgarism is rarely used to designate the member; the word *shmuck* does that.

As used, *putz* is a term of contempt for

1. a fool, an ass, a jerk.
2. a simpleton or yokel; an easy mark.

CAUTION: *Putz* is not to be used lightly or when women or children are around. It is more offensive than *shmuck;* the latter may be used in a teasing and affectionate way, vulgar though it is, but *putz* has a pejorative ambience.*

See shmuck.

---

*When New York's Republican senator Alfonse D'Amato referred to his political rival, Charles Schumer, as a "putzhead" during their 1998 electoral race for the Senate, *The New York Times* cited Rosten's entry for *putz* in *The Joys of Yiddish* to establish that D'Amato's remark was a serious slur and did not merely mean "fool," as the senator insisted. The incident helped create Jewish voter disenchantment with D'Amato—who had been a strong advocate on Jewish issues such as Holocaust reparations—and Schumer won the election.

rabbi
See rebbe.

rakhmones ^Y
rachmones ^R

Pronounced *rokh-MAW-ness*, to rhyme with "loch [as a Scot pronounces it] lawless." Hebrew: "compassion," "pity."
Pity, compassion.

This quintessential word lies at the heart of Jewish thought and feeling. All of Judaism's philosophy, ethics, ethos, learning, education, and hierarchy of values are saturated with a sense of, and heightened sensitivity to, *rakhmones.*

God is often called the God of Mercy and Compassion: *Adonai El Rakhum Ve-Khanum.*

The writings of the prophets are permeated with appeals for *rakhmones,* a divine attribute. (So, too, are the words of Jesus and the books of the New Testament.)

Note that the Hebrew root *rekhem,* from which *rakhmones* is derived, means "a mother's womb." The rabbis taught that a Jew should look upon others with the same love and feeling that a mother feels for the issue of her womb. "He is in such straits one can only have *rakhmones* on him." "The least one can show is *rakhmones.*"

reb
Reb
See rebbe.

rebbe

Pronounced REB-*ba*, to rhyme with "jeb-a," or REB-*beh*, to rhyme with "web beh," or REB-*bee* (Yinglish), to rhyme with "Debby." From the Hebrew: *rabi*, pronounced *rah*-BEE, meaning "my teacher."

1. **Rabbi.***

The title "rabbi" does not have the same connotation as does "priest" or "minister." A rabbi is not an intermediary between God and people, as is, say, a Catholic priest. A rabbi is not even or always a spiritual arbiter, as is a Protestant minister. A rabbi is—a rabbi. His position traditionally gives him no power, no hierarchical status. This may be hard to believe, but it is so. The authority of a rabbi rests on his learning, his character, his personal qualities: ordination, although it has ancient roots, did not become institutionalized until **modern times.**†

*Outside of the Chasidic community, the use of *rebbe* to mean "rabbi" is an Ameridish adaptation. In classical Yiddish, *rov* is used for "rabbi," and *rebbe* is a title either for a Chasidic rabbi or a *melamed* (an elementary school teacher).

†The institutionalization of rabbinic ordination has led to the ordination of women as rabbis in all three non-Orthodox movements: beginning in 1972 by the Reform Hebrew Union College—Jewish Institute of Religion, in 1973 by the Reconstructionist Rabbinical College (which accepted women as students from the time it opened its doors in 1968), and in 1985 by the Conservative movement's Jewish Theological Seminary. Women now make up more than 16 percent of 1,700-plus Reform rabbis, about 40 percent of 180-plus Recon-

Even now a rabbi may be ordained by another rabbi.‡

A rabbi enjoys no priestly privileges. In Orthodox worship, in fact, the rabbi rarely leads the services: the *chazzen* (cantor) usually does, but any respected, learned layman may take the pulpit to lead the prayers. (Only in modern times, incidentally, did rabbis become Sabbath preachers. See maggid.)

The title "rabbi" was given to those men learned in Jewish law who taught in the academies, large and small. The title was not used until the beginning of the Christian era. To Jews, Moses is

structionist rabbis, and 8 percent of 1,500-plus Conservative rabbis.

The presence of women in the rabbinate has been quite transformative to Judaism and Jewish institutions. Women rabbis have created rituals for divorce, for menarche and menopause, for a child's departure for college, and for other life transitions that had previously been ignored by Jewish custom. They have helped to change the language of prayer books to make them gender-neutral; they have brought women's voices and women's interpretations to Judaism's texts and to the study of Jewish history; they have inspired many women to wear prayer clothes that were previously reserved for men—particularly the *yarmulke* (skullcap) and *tallis* (prayer shawl)—and they have changed Jewish perceptions, particularly among young people, of what Jewish leadership looks like.

Problems of sexism nevertheless still afflict the rabbinate. *Moment* magazine reported in 1993 that 70 percent of women rabbis had experienced some sort of workplace sexual harassment—25 percent on a recurring basis. Only a small percentage of senior posts in large congregations are held by women. Salary inequities between male and female rabbis persist. Efforts at pan-denominational rabbinic cooperation frequently founder on Orthodox insistence on excluding women rabbis. These issues are likely to fade, however, as more and more Jews grow up used to the sight of a woman on the *bema* (pulpit).

‡Ordination used to involve the laying on of hands, called *smikhe*, by the ordaining rabbi, who has found the candidate worthy of the title "rabbi" (teacher). This practice is based on Numbers 27:18–23, in which God instructs Moses, "Single out Joshua son of Nun, an inspired man, and lay your hand upon him." *Smikhe* remains the term used for rabbinic ordination, though the physical gesture is no longer used (it apparently came to an end, after long suppression by the Romans, in 425 c.e.). In Orthodox life, many small, individual yeshivas ordain rabbis; in the other movements, ordination is performed only by the large seminaries.

the exemplar of a rabbi, for he was the most important teacher of all. Pious Jews call Moses *Moishe Rabbenu* (MOY-*sheh* rab-BAY-*noo*), which means "Our Teacher, Moses."

Beginning with Ezra, Jewish scholars established the precept that no man should use the *Torah* as a "spade" with which to dig for wealth. The great names of the *Talmud* were mostly the names of workmen-scholars: Hillel was a woodchopper; Shammai, a surveyor; Ishmael, a tanner; Abba Hoshaiah, a launderer.

The extreme sense of humility among rabbis, which extended to their walking always with lowered eyes, is seen in the case of the famous and learned Rabbi Shalom Shakna of Lublin, to whose *yeshiva* came scholars from all Europe. The rabbi never wrote a single tract or book, though students and colleagues pleaded with him to leave a written record of his brilliant Talmudic inquiries, his juridical decisions, and the reasons for them. Rabbi Shakna said it would be wrong for him to do this, because he could not bear the thought that future scholars and students and laypeople might attribute too much and too great importance to his writing or might be influenced too strongly in their own thinking and judgment!

Rabbi Shakna's renowned teacher, Rabbi Jacob Polak of Cracow, wrote no book, either. Neither of these good and learned men, said Shakna's son, made "any copies of their responses to be sent abroad, for the same reason."

The secular and the scholarly can only mourn the disappearance of the cerebrations of such *khokhemim*.

Traditionally, a rabbi is a teacher of the *Torah* (in the broad sense, the Bible, *Talmud*, and later rabbinic works), and seeks to apply it to daily life.

Down the centuries, the sages stressed that scholars must share their knowledge with the less learned, and their insights with the less spiritually sensitive; hence, rabbis were enjoined to spread instruction and enlightenment, to uplift the moral, ethical, and religious life of their congregations. One of the loveliest of Yiddish songs, "Oyfn Pripetchok" ("On the Hearth"), mentions how the *rebbe* teaches little children their ABCs.

What does a rabbi do? Today, pretty much what any clergy does: performs the ceremonials that attend birth, confirmation, marriage, death; interprets the tenets of Judaism; is responsible for teaching and overseeing religious instruction in the synagogue school; preaches sermons; offers comfort and consolation; visits hospitals; counsels families; tries to "guide the perplexed"; advises members of the congregation about problems ranging from the connubial to the collegiate; comments on the social scene; ventures into psychotherapy. A rabbi today combines the functions of minister, lecturer, counselor, social worker, and psychiatrist. He is also the representative of the Jewish community vis-à-vis the public.

Rabbis are graduates of a *yeshiva* or seminary. In addition, Reform, Reconstructionist, Conservative, and a growing number of Orthdox rabbis hold degrees (often more than one) from secular universities.

The rabbi is not imposed upon the congregation by an ecclesiastical hierarchy, but is freely engaged—and disengaged—by members of the community.

2. The spiritual leader of a Chasidic group or sect, not necessarily ordained.

A Chasidic *rebbe*, though well grounded in Jewish learning, does not necessarily have formal ordination from a seminary or *yeshiva*. He may have inherited his position from his father, or he may have been invited to assume the leadership of a group of *Chasidim* because of his personal qualities.*

*In the case of the Chasidic and Orthodox rabbinate, Rosten's use of the masculine pronoun is correct: there are no female *rebbes* among them, and the separation of women and men is strongly enforced.

The relationship of the Chasidic *rebbe* to his followers is very close. He is often the object of a veneration that gives rise to stories of mystical abilities.

See Chasid.

It was hard for Satan alone to mislead the whole world, so he appointed prominent rabbis in different localities.

—A Chasidic saying attributed to Nachman of Bratzlav,
early nineteenth century

Three women were discussing their sons, with the customary pride and *naches*.

"*My* boy," said the first, "is a famous surgeon, and president of his medical association!"

"*My* son," said the second, "is a professor in the law school!"

"*My* son," said the third, "is a rabbi."

"A *rabbi*? What kind of career is that for a Jewish boy?"

A rabbi whose congregation does not want to drive him out of town isn't a rabbi; and a rabbi they do drive out isn't a man.

—Folk saying, based on a saying in the *Talmud*

Unless you can play baseball, you'll never get to be a rabbi in America.

—Solomon Schechter (former head of the Jewish Theological
Seminary of America), to Louis Finkelstein (then chancellor),
quoted in *Time*, October 15, 1951

Glickman came to a rabbi to confess his sins but he was so shamestricken that he said, "I'm not here for myself, Rabbi, but—for a friend."

"What sins did he commit?"

"Oh, my friend often takes the name of the Lord in vain; and he has cast envying eyes on his neighbor's wife; and he—"

"Stop," sighed the rabbi. "Your friend is foolish: why did he not come here himself? He could have told me that *he* had come for a friend, and saved you this embarrassment."

rebbitsin^R
rebetsn^Y
rebbetsen, rebbitsin

Pronounced REB-*bit-tzin*, to rhyme with "debits in."
The wife of a rabbi.

The *rebbitsin* played an important role in the Jewish community of yesteryear. She often served as mother surrogate to her husband's students. Like Caesar's wife, she was supposed to be a model of probity, and as a *rebbitsin* she was expected to be a strong right arm to the rabbi and a ministering angel to the community.

There is a saying (*naturally*, there's a saying): "Better close to the *rebbitsin* than to the rabbi."

The modern *rebbitsin* often teaches in the congregational school, lectures on Jewish customs to women's organizations, helps guide the Sisterhood, visits the sick, comforts the bereaved, and serves as hostess for many occasions. And like the wife of a college president, or any modern corporation executive, she is carefully "looked over" by the board of a new congregation before her husband is engaged as spiritual cicerone.

"All *rebbetsins* are magicians, for how else can they raise a family on a rabbi's salary?"*

There was a rabbi who was known for his absolute fairness.

One day, his *rebbitsin* accused their maid of having stolen a candlestick. The wretched maid wailed that she was innocent.

"Very well," said the *rebbitsin*, "let us go to the rabbinical court and let them decide!"

The rabbi said, "I'll come along."

"You don't need to go," said his wife. "I can plead the case against this wretched girl."

"I'm sure you can," said the rabbi. "But who will plead her defense?"

Reboyne Shel Oylem[Y]
Riboyne Shel O'lem[R]

Pronounced *ri-BOY-neh shel OY-lem,* to rhyme with "Lemoyna shall boil 'em." Hebrew: *Ribono Shel Olam,* "Master of the World."

---

*Rabbis' salaries have grown to respectable professional levels. A typical starting salary for congregational work is $50,000–$60,000, and veterans in large congregations can earn well into six figures. Health, pension, vacation and sabbatical benefits are generally included in compensation packages.

The salaried rabbi was unknown until the fourteenth century, when European anti-Semitic persecutions and expulsions expanded the rabbi's role from teacher and interpreter of *Torah* to spiritual and political leader of the Jewish community—and often cut off rabbis (and many other Jews) from outside means of earning a living. Since Jewish law forbids profiting from teaching *Torah*, rabbinic salaries are halakhically justified as *sekhar battalah,* compensation for the loss of time associated with their duties.

1. Oh, God in Heaven! A ringing, rhetorical ejaculation that appeals to God to witness
   a. some remarkable thing. *"Reboyne Shel Oylem,* just look at that rain come down!"
   b. some unexpected development. "We were finishing when—*Reboyne Shel Oylem,* in walked their lawyer!"
   c. something disgraceful, unfair, brazen. "It was a scandal, *Reboyne Shel Oylem!"*
   d. anything that leaves one speechless, from the sublime to the unforgivable. *"Reboyne Shel Oylem,* what could I say?"

      Although God is being addressed directly, the phrase is not religious, strictly speaking. It is a synonym for "Oh, God!," "God in Heaven!," "This you have to see for yourself!," "I don't *believe* it!," "Holy Moses!," and so on.

2. God willing; if only God will help me; if only God will do it; dear God, *please.* "If only she would recover, *Reboyne Shel Oylem!"* "The day he comes home—*Reboyne Shel Oylem*—will we celebrate!" "I just want to get through these next weeks, *Reboyne Shel Oylem."*

Mr. Abraham, driven to desperation by the endless delays of the tailor who was making him a pair of trousers, finally cried, "Tailor, in the name of Heaven, it has already taken you six *weeks!"*

"So?"

"*So,* you ask? Six weeks for a pair of pants? *Reboyne Shel Oylem!* It took God only six days to create the *universe!"*

"*Nu,*" shrugged the tailor, "look at it. . . ."

PARIS, 1939

Three weary German refugees stood in line, in the offices of a relocation committee.

"Where would you like to go?" an official asked the first refugee.

"London."

"And you?" the official asked the second.

"Switzerland."

"And you?" he asked the third.

"Australia."

"Australia?" echoed the official. "Why so far?"

The refugee said, "Far from where?"

Reboyne Shel Oylem!

Rosh Hashanah
Rosh Hashonah, Rosh Hashona,
Rosh Hoshanah,
Rosh Hashana

Pronounced *rawsh ha-*SHAW*-neh* (rhyme with "cautious fauna"); or *rosh ha-*SHO*-na* (rhyme with "cautious Mona"); or *rawsh ha-*SHAH*-na* (rhyme with "cautious Donna"). Hebrew: "beginning (of the) year."

Rosh Hashanah commemorates the birthday of—the world.

So said the rabbis, in the *Talmud* and the *Midrash*, who held that *Rosh Hashanah* celebrates the anniversary of creation itself.

Rosh Hashanah begins the Ten Days of Penitence (also known as the Days of Awe), which end with the most solemn of religious days in the Jewish calendar, *Yom Kippur*. During these days of penitence and prayer, all humankind presumably passes before the Heavenly Throne, and God looks into their deeds and hearts. Judgment will be passed on *Yom Kippur*, the devout aver, but "prayer, penitence, and charity may avert the stern decree."

The dominant and recurring theme throughout *Rosh Hashanah* services is the sovereignty of God. The *shofar* (ram's horn) is blown several times, in a prescribed pattern of notes, the first to celebrate God's kinship, the second to stress the role of the individual, the third to remind the congregation of all the events associated with the blowing of the ram's horn. (In ancient Judea, the ram's horn was used as a communications device to send signals from one mountain peak to another.) In the *Talmud*, it is ventured that the *shofar* helps confuse Satan and his hosts, those cunning spirits of perdition who try to influence God when He judges us sinners.

Rosh Hashanah is a solemn yet very happy time; entire families gather from everywhere for the holiday and for the feast; bread or apple is dipped in honey to symbolize a hoped-for sweetness in the year ahead. A blessing (the *Shehecheyanu*) thanks the Lord for having "sustained us to this day."*

The traditional *Rosh Hashanah* greeting is "*Leshana tova tiko-sevu,*" *le-*SHAH-*nah* TOE-*vah tee-kah-*SAY-*vu*—"May you be inscribed for a good year."

Rosh Hashanah, like all Jewish holidays, is determined by the lunar calendar and falls in late September or early October at the time of the new moon.

Johanan ben Nappaha said that on *Rosh Hashanah* three ledgers are opened in Heaven: the Book of Life, in which the names of the truly righteous are inscribed; the Book of Death, in which the names of the unredeemably wicked are entered; and a sort of in-between ledger, where the rest of humanity is found. The fate of the in-betweeners is held in abeyance for ten days, until *Yom Kippur.* Between *Rosh Hashanah* and *Yom Kippur,* those who gain merit, by penitence and deeds, are written into the Book of Life; the rest are marked for Death.

"On Rosh Hashanah and Yom Kippur," says a passage in the *Yerushalmi* (Jerusalem) *Talmud,* "Jews should not appear depressed and in somber clothes, as suppliants before a human judge, but joyous, dressed in festive white, betokening a cheerful and confident spirit."

Rosh Hashanah used to be called *Yom ha-Zikaron,* "the Day of

---

*According to the 1990 National Jewish Population Survey of the Council of Jewish Federations, close to 60 percent of American Jews attend synagogue during the Days of Awe (compared with only 10 percent or less who attend synagogue on a weekly basis).

Remembrance," *Yom ha-Din*, "the Day of Judgment," or *Yom Teruah*, "the Day of Blowing of the Horn."

The earliest mention of *Rosh Hashanah* appears to be in a second-century passage in the *Mishnah*.

The first month of the Hebrew calendar is *Nisan*, which comes in March–April and commemorates the Exodus. Yet the Jewish New Year is the first day of *Tishri*, the seventh month. This suggests a close relationship to the same timing for the Babylonian "Day of Judgment," the New Year's day when, the Babylonians believed, all their gods assembled in the temple of Marduk, their chief deity, to pass judgment on mortals and record each individual's fate for the next year.

rov

Pronounced RUV, to rhyme with "dove," or RAWV, to rhyme with "mauve." Hebrew: "rabbi."

Rabbi.

See rebbe.

A great king, grown old and eccentric, called before him the chief rabbi of his realm. "Before I die, there's something I want you to do, Rabbi. Teach my pet monkey how to talk!"

"*What?*"

"That's a command: Teach my monkey how to talk, within one year, or your head will be chopped off!"

"But Your Majesty, to carry out a request like that, I need more than a year—I need at least ten."

"I'll allow you five and not a day more!"

The rabbi returned to his flock and told them what had

happened. And they all cried out in sympathy. "But what will you *do, Rov?*"

"Well," said the *rov*, "in five years, many things can happen. For instance, the king could die. Or, I could die. Or—the monkey could die. And besides, in five years, who knows—maybe I can teach that monkey how to talk!"

S

Sabbatai Zvi
Shabtsi Tsvi
Shabbatsi Zui, Shabtsi Zvi
See meshiekh.

Sabbath
See Shabbes.

Sanhedrin

Pronounced *san*-HED-*rin*, to rhyme with "tan red bin."
From Greek: *synedrion*, "assembly."

The seventy elders, plus a patriarch or president (*nasi*),
who sat in Jerusalem, until 70 C.E., as a combination of
Supreme Court and College of Cardinals, ruling on certain
theological, ethical, civil, and political matters.

An extraordinary amount of nonsense and demagoguery has
come down through history to make the name *Sanhedrin*
appear far more mysterious than it ever was, or need be. Bigots
have exploited the myth of a supposed "international council,"
or "**Elders of Zion**,"* who allegedly rule over all Jews in secret

---

*The Protocols of the Elders of Zion, an anti-Semitic forgery created early in the
twentieth century by the secret police of the Russian Tsar, has persisted in

(Continued on page 456)

and plot dire deeds for them to perform in a worldwide conspiracy.

The *Sanhedrin* was simply a court, combining ecclesiastical and civil authority, in ancient Jerusalem. It was originally a lofty academic collegium, composed of learned men and priests who interpreted Scripture.

Many modern scholars think that there must later have been two *Sanhedrins*: one of aristocrats and priests, with jurisdiction over certain civil and criminal matters, the other a court of Pharisees who attended to matters of ritual, the calendar, rules and regulations concerning the priesthood, etc.*

When Titus destroyed the Great Temple in 70 c.e., the *Sanhedrin* lost all political powers and moved to Tiberias, there to lay the foundation for later rabbinical scholarship. Its functions were replaced by those of the *Bet Din*, or "court of law."

After Israel was founded (1948), there were requests for the revival of the *Sanhedrin*. This was not done because of legal and constitutional problems.

(Continued from page 455)

print through the decades, with various conspiracy theorists and hatemongers using it to portray the international Jewish population as a united, world-manipulating force. Auto magnate Henry Ford published and widely disseminated the *Protocols* during the 1930s; the book has been broadly distributed in the Arab world during the decades of conflict with Israel; and in the year 2000 the *Protocols* appeared for sale on the Internet bookseller Amazon.com, which fomented a good deal of protest and some boycott activity.

*"This suggestion [that there were two *Sanhedrins*] is now seen to be untenable," writes Rabbi Louis Jacobs (in *The Jewish Religion, A Companion*, Oxford University Press, 1995).
     The "Great Sanhedrin" was the ancient Jewish analogy to the Supreme Court. It had seventy-one members and met in the Temple in Jerusalem. Lesser courts were distributed throughout the land.

There is considerable contradiction, and irksome ambiguity, in the historical accounts of the ancient *Sanhedrin*. The *Mishnah*'s data do not coincide with the material in Josephus, and the New Testament varies from both.

Moses said, "Gather unto me seventy . . . elders of Israel" (Numbers 11:16). That would mean that Moses sat as the patriarch, or presiding judge, over seventy wise men. But we do not know when the first *Sanhedrin* was established. The *Talmud* says after Simon the Just died, which means (*if* Simon the Just is the same Simon who was patriarch, or high priest) in the third century B.C.E.

The *Sanhedrin* usually met in "the Hall of Hewn Stones" in the Temple. The members were seated in a semicircle, so that each could easily see, or be seen by, the others. Behind the clerks, who stood before the court, were three rows of disciples of the judges— who clearly were learned and distinguished men.

The Romans both permitted and encouraged the *Sanhedrin* to operate as the Jews' political governors and high court. In 57 B.C.E. the procurator of Judea, one Gabinius, abolished the *Sanhedrin* and set up five different councils of Jews, supported by Rome: in Jerusalem, Jericho, Hamath, Gadara, and Sepphoris. These councils were stripped of religious and ethical duties. Some historians hold that these Jewish councils served to consolidate Roman rule against rebellious, anti-Roman Jews.

When Napoleon was trying to formalize relations between the state and the Jews in his far-flung empire, he established a *Sanhedrin* of seventy-one members that included distinguished Jewish laymen as well as rabbis. It does not seem to have carved much of a niche in either French or European history.*

---

*Bonaparte convened his *Sanhedrin* in 1807, sixteen years after the French Revolution had granted Jews equal rights. The emperor posted a series of
(Continued on page 458)

schatchen
See shadkhn.

schlack
schlag
See shlock.

schlep
See shlep.

schlok
See shlock.

schloomp
schlump
See shlump.

schmaltz
See shmaltz.

(Continued from page 457)

questions to this body designed to establish an ideology of harmony between Jewish identity and French citizenship. The Napoleonic *Sanhedrin* met only once and disbanded, yet it gave fuel to the idea of Jews being equal citizens of their countries of residence—that is, Frenchmen or Germans or Britons "of the Mosaic persuasion"—an idea championed by Reform Judaism throughout the nineteenth century.

schmo
See shmo.

schmuck
See shmuck.

schneider[R]
shnayder[Y]

Pronounced SHNY-*der*, to rhyme with "wider." German: *Schnayder*, "tailor."

1. Tailor.
2. In gin rummy: To win a number of games before your opponent has won one.
3. To shut out an opponent.

The spelling with *sch-* is so well established as a family name that it is retained here, even though it is an exception to my general rule, which would dictate *shnayder*.

schnook
See shnook.

seder

Pronounced SAY-*der*, to rhyme with "nadir" or "paid her." Hebrew for "order," or "order of the service."

See Pesach.

Sefer Torah^R
Seyfer Toyre^Y

Pronounced SAY-*fer* TOE-*reh* or TOY-*rah,* to rhyme with
"wafer bow rah" or "caper Moira." Hebrew: "Book of the
Torah."

The scroll containing the Five Books of Moses that is
kept in the ark at the front of a synagogue.

The *Sefer Torah* is read from on each Sabbath and festival. The
scroll is of parchment and is hand-lettered, in Hebrew, by
specially trained scribes who must be punctilious in their copy
work. The scroll is covered with a mantle of silk or velvet and is
often adorned with a silver breastplate and crown.

See Torah.

Sefirah^R
Sfire^Y
Sefiros Haomer^R
Sfires Haomer^Y

Pronounced se-FEAR-*ah* ha-OHM-*er.* Hebrew: "counting."

The forty-nine-day period that begins with the second
day of Passover, when the *omer* (a sheaf of new barley)
was traditionally brought to the Temple in Jerusalem as
an offering, and ends on *Shevuos,* the feast of the wheat
harvest.

Beginning with the second day of Passover, the *"omer* is
counted" during daily prayers, according to a prescribed ritual, and is followed by the recitation of Psalm 67, which includes

the verse "Then shall the earth yield her increase; and God, even our own God, shall bless us."

The forty-nine days of *Sefirah* became a period of mourning in the Middle Ages, because of the many misfortunes that, tradition holds, have overtaken the Jews at this period: persecutions suffered under Roman rule, the martyrdom of saints such as Rabbi Akiba, the slaughter of Jews by the Crusaders.

The famous revolt of the Warsaw ghetto occurred during *Sefirah.*

Traditionally, Jews do not participate in festivities during this period. Weddings are not scheduled. These restrictions are lifted for *Lag Baomer,* a minor festival on the thirty-third day of the *Sefirah.*

In recent years, Israel's Independence Day, which falls during this period, has been excepted from *Sefirah* rulings and is **celebrated.***

---

* Sefirah also has a specifically cabalistic meaning, which has become widely known thanks to the breadth of contemporary interest in Jewish mysticism. The cabalists identified, graphed, and wrote extensively about the ten *sefiros* (plural), manifestations or attributes of God, seven of which were considered comprehensible by the human mind and representative of the human personality. (The astrological system of "signs" and "houses" is somewhat analogous.) Counting the *omer* was structured by the cabbalists to serve as a "count-down" of purification leading on day fifty to *Shevuos,* the holiday that celebrates the encounter with God at Mt. Sinai. Rabbi Arthur Green explains this compactly (in Michael Strassfeld's *The Jewish Holiday,* 1985): "The forty-nine days form a multiplication of seven times the seven *sefiros* . . . On each day of the counting, the cabalist seeks to restore or elevate within himself the combination of *sefiros* that belong to that day. . . . Thus the counting becomes a series of meditative and morally restorative exercises, purging the self and preparing it to stand again at Sinai." For more on Jewish mysticism, see Rosten's entries and my notes for **cabala** and **gematria.**

Sephardi [R]
Sfardi [Y]
Sephardic* (adjective)
Sephardim (plural)

*"Sephardic" is an English adaptation of *Sephardi*.

Pronounced *seh*-FAR-*dee*, to rhyme with "Bacardi." Hebrew: "Spanish." (Spain, in Hebrew, is *Sepharad*.)

Spanish and Portuguese Jews, and the descendants of the Jews of Spain and Portugal. (In modern Israel, *Sephardim* has been somewhat extended to include Jews of the Middle East.)

Spain was thought, by the rabbis of the Middle Ages, to be the *Sepharad* mentioned in the Bible (in Obadiah's prophecy), where the Jews exiled from Jerusalem found refuge. In time, all of the Jews in Spain and Portugal came to be called *Sephardim*.

Sephardic Judaism, a major force within Jewish culture from around 600 c.e. until the expulsion of the Jews from Spain at the end of the fifteenth century, was an exceptionally sophisticated blend of Talmudic thought, Greek philosophy, Aristotelianism, such science as then existed, and the ideas of Averröes, the great Islamic scholar whom medieval Christians were not permitted to read because of church prohibition. Sephardic Jews were not unacquainted with Latin, Spanish, or French. They widened Judaic thought with secular knowledge from geometry, algebra, astronomy, medicine, metaphysics, music, and mechanics.

Sephardic Jews rose to positions of eminence in Spain, Portugal, and North Africa—as physicians, philosophers, poets, financiers, advisers to kings and courts, mapmakers, astronomers, and military leaders. The Sephardic writers wrote mostly in Arabic, even when writing about *Torah* and *Talmud!* They were aristocratic; their religious services, no less than their style of living, were invested with a splendor such as Ashkenazic (eastern European) Jews did not know.

When the Sephardic Jews were expelled from the Iberian countries, they moved on to settle along the coastline of the Mediterranean and in Holland and England—and their colonies.

Until the fourth decade of the eighteenth century, the *Sephardim* (from England, Holland, and the West Indies) were the dominant Jewish group in the United States. The *Ashkenazim* began to arrive, from central and eastern Europe, after 1740 or so. There was no significant conflict in the New World between Sephardic and Ashkenazic Jews, as there clearly was, a century later, between German and Polish/Russian Jews. The *Ashkenazim* adopted some Sephardic rituals with no difficulty, and marriages between Ashkenazic and Sephardic Jews were not uncommon.

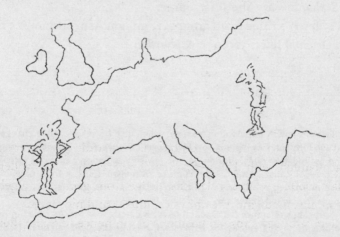

Communities of Sephardic Jews are today found throughout Asia Minor, in Israel, Turkey, Greece, England, Holland, Latin America, and, of course, the United States—where Sephardic Jews were the first Jewish immigrants. The earliest synagogues in America were Sephardic.

Sephardic Jews differ from Ashkenazic Jews in many customs, in the order and text of their prayers, in the intonation of the chants used in the synagogues. (The *Sephardim* claim that their liturgy stems from the Talmudic academies of Babylonia; *Ashkenazim* follow the Palestinian ritual.)

The vernacular used by Sephardic Jews, analogous to the Yiddish of Ashkenazic Jews, is *Ladino*. Many *Sephardim* cannot make head or tail out of Yiddish, and an *Ashkenazi* could not understand a conversation in *Ladino*.

But much more basic than these differences are the ways in which the *Sephardim* differ from the *Ashkenazim* in their style of thought and living. These I have tried to describe in several entries in this lexicon: see Ashkenazi, shtetl.*

*See also my notes to Rosten's entries for **Ashkenazi**, **Ladino**, and **Marrano**.

Sephardim are the least numerous of Jewry's three main groups: 11 million Ashkenazim; 1.5 million Oriental Jews; 500,000 *Sephardim*.†

† Rosten's Jewish population statistics, which date from 1960, have changed little in forty years owing to a very low Jewish birthrate and high intermarriage and assimilation rates. Worldwide, the Jewish population has yet to recover its pre-Holocaust status of 17 million to 18 million souls, a third of whom were murdered; 13 million to 14 million is the current estimate, with 5.6 million in the United States and 4.9 million in Israel.

Rosten's reference to "Oriental Jews" *is* dated, however. As noted in my comments on his entries for **Ashkenazi**, **mishpokhe**, and **mizrach**, Israeli Jews of Middle Eastern origin (Morocco, Yemen, etc.) are now properly referred to as *Mizrachi* Jews.

Philadelphia's National Museum of American Jewish History, which is sited in the same building as Congregation Mikveh Israel, a Spanish-Portuguese congregation founded in 1740, includes interesting exhibits about the rituals, customs, and history of Sephardic Jews in America.

seykhl ^Y
sachel ^R
seichel

Pronounced SAY-*kh'l*; rhymes with "playful." Hebrew: "understanding."

Native good sense, common sense, judgment.

The year 1048: Jerusalem was under tight Arab siege. Food and water were running low. The spirits of the Jews ran abysmally low—except for one jolly, wrinkled storekeeper who was known for his fund of stories and his inexhaustible *seykhl.* The old man hopped around with a cheerful smile, repeating the refrain "Don't worry, don't worry, everything will be all right, we'll all be saved."

"We're on the threshold of starvation, of defeat, or death!" a neighbor protested.

"So what?" came the answer. "Either we'll be saved by natural means, or we'll be saved through a miracle!"

"Explain yourself."

"It's this way: Either we'll be saved by natural means—that is, God will come to our aid, as He has done throughout history. Or, we'll be saved by a real miracle—our army will break through the siege."

PROVERB: "Many complain of their looks, but none complain of their brains."

sh-
shm-

Not words, but prefatory sounds, of mockery or dismissal, that "pooh-pooh" the word they prefix.

1. To negate or deride the meaning of a word, the word is repeated—but with *shm-* prefixed to the repetition. "The doctor says she has a serious virus? Virus-shmirus, as long as she's okay." (This is, of course, a variation of the classic "Cancer-shmancer, as long as you're healthy.") "The mayor? Mayor-shmayor, it's his wife who runs the show." "Exams-shmexams, relax!" "Girls-shmirls, *anything* to keep him from working!" "Who said that? Charley? Charley-shmarley, what does *he* know?"

2. *Sh-* is the introductory signal to a rich symphony of disesteem. A great many words of mockery and aspersion, words that jeer, sneer, and scorn (Jeer, Sneer & Scorn could be the name of a real estate firm) begin with *sh-*: *shlimazl, shlump, shmegegge, shmo, shmuck, shnook, shnorrer.*

If you eschew the *sh-* and *shm-* sounds, you rob Yinglish of two of its phonetic glories.

Mrs. Siegel confided to her neighbor that her son had gone through so miserable a phase that he was now seeing a psychoanalyst. "And the doctor says my Marvin is suffering from an Oedipus complex!"

"Oedipus-Shmoedipus," scoffed her neighbor, "so long as he loves his mother."

Shabbes[R]
Shabes[Y]
Shabbos

Pronounced SHAH-*biss*, to rhyme with "novice." Hebrew: *shabbat*, "rest" or "cessation of labor."

Sabbath.

The life of Jews was so very hard, for so very long, that the Sabbath became more than a weekly respite from servitude, from bone-wearying labor—and anxiety, if not terror. *Shabbes* is called "the Queen of the week," "the Bride," and, in however bitter a time and place, the Sabbath was the miraculous time when even the lowliest, poorest, least consequential of people could feel in communion with the Almighty, favored by God's special concern: "It is a sign between me and the children of Israel" (Exodus 31:17).

To "make *Shabbes*" means to be festive, to celebrate.

The Fourth Commandment says: "Remember the Sabbath day to keep it holy. Six days shalt thou labor, and do all thy work: But the seventh is the Sabbath of the Lord thy God."

And so, for Sabbath, down the generations, in every land, Jews have scrubbed every nook of their dwelling, bathed themselves with the utmost care, donned fresh garments, laid out (however poor) their best linens, glasses, utensils. *Shabbes* brought—each week, throughout a lifetime—a sense of personal splendor, cleanliness, devotion, and exaltation.

Mystics believed that the *Shekhinah,* or Divine Presence, descends each Friday when the sun sets.

In the *shtetl, Shabbes* was redolent with intimations of divinity, the hint of angels and arcane secrets, visions of Heaven with all the blessed seated on golden thrones under the sparkling stars. Nor was the love of *Shabbes* limited to the *shtetl.* Harry Golden, reminiscing about life on New York's Lower East Side, recaptures the feeling (in Hutchins Hapgood's *The Spirit of the Ghetto,* Funk and Wagnalls, 1966): "The Irish and Italian boys had Christmas once a year; we had exaltation every Friday. In the most populous neighborhood of the world, rent by the shouts of peddlers, the screams of children, and the myriad noises of the city, there was every Friday evening a wondrous stillness, an eloquent silence. So quiet was it that two blocks from the synagogue you could hear the muffled chant of the cantor and the murmured prayers of the congregation. Once the service was over, you came home to find your mother dressed in her wedding dress with a white silk scarf around her head. And your father told you all the sufferings throughout the centuries were dedicated for this moment, the celebration of the Sabbath."

Now, the Sabbath was a truly revolutionary concept and institution. I am astonished that neither the Greeks nor the Romans invented it. (On the contrary, Juvenal, Seneca, and Horace scorned it as superstition.) When the *Falasha* Jews were being tortured, and were goaded to name their savior, they replied: "The savior of the Jews is the Sabbath."

Shabbes begins just before sunset on Friday. The wife and mother, dressed in her very best, lights the *Shabbes* candles and offers a benediction. (Before lighting the candles, the *baleboste*, however poor, has set aside a sum for charity.) As she lights the *Shabbes* candles, she closes her eyes and passes her palms over the candles, always toward herself ("The soul is the Lord's candle," it is said in the *Talmud*), and whispers, "Blessed art Thou, O Lord our God, King of the Universe, Who has sanctified us by Thy commandments, and has commanded us to kindle the Sabbath light." Then, silently, she asks God to preserve her family: its health, its peace, its honor. (The lighting of the candles, one of the few *mitzvos* reserved to Jewish women, makes her a momentary priestess.)

Two braided loaves of bread *(challahs)* are placed at the head of the festive board, covered by an embroidered cloth. A goblet of wine stands next to the *challah:* this is the "*Kiddush* cup," with the wine that will sanctify the Sabbath.

Traditionally, the father returns from services to bless his children; then he recites the *Kiddush* (see Kiddush) and sips the wine. The entire family joins in welcoming the Sabbath angels who accompanied the father from the synagogue by singing, "Welcome to you, O ministering angels, may your coming be in peace, may you bless us with peace, and may you depart in peace."

Jewish husbands often sing a tribute to their wives on the eve of *Shabbes*, in the words of Proverbs 31:

> Strength and honor are her clothing . . .
> She openeth her mouth with wisdom . . .
> Her children arise up, and call her blessed; her husband also,
> and he praiseth her.

(The song is called "Eshes Khayil," "A Woman of Valor.")

The *Mishnah* sets forth a sizable number of Sabbath prohibitions, starting with thirty-nine activities explicitly forbidden: baking, plowing, writing, spinning, carrying, sowing, sewing, even tying a knot! (Very devout Jews would have pinned a handkerchief to their coats before *Shabbes;* a pinned object was not "carried" but was part of the clothing.)

What did the Jews do with their time on *Shabbes?* They prayed—and they studied; they read; they discussed the *Torah* and the *Talmud.* Moses had enjoined the Jews, said Philo, "[to] assemble . . . on these seventh days . . . in a respectful and orderly manner . . . [to] hear the laws read so that none should be ignorant of them." Every Sabbath, a rabbi or elder was to read the laws "and expound them point by point, until the late afternoon, when [all] depart, having gained both expert knowledge . . . and an advance in piety."

Today, every Sabbath morning a portion of the Five Books of Moses is read in the synagogue, together with an appropriate reading from the Prophets, with the entire cycle completed each year.

At home, on the six Sabbaths between Passover and *Shevuos,* fathers and grandfathers would traditionally engage the children in discussions of the *Ethics of the Fathers (Pirkey Avos)* or portions of the *Mishnah* that discuss ethical problems. I leave it to cultural historians to appraise the magnitude of the consequence of an entire people, young and old, spending one day a week, year after year, generation after generation, century after century, in a seminar on religion, morals, ethics, and **responsibility.***

*Shabbes text study and ethical discussion were generally limited, in traditional Jewish circles, to males, as few women were literate in Hebrew. Many Jewish workingmen were also less than literate in Hebrew. There did grow up, however, a literature of prayers and homilies, written in Yiddish—see my note to Rosten's entry for **mameloshn**.

For most women, *Shabbes* meant a whirlwind of shopping and household preparations—of dishes, for example, that would not require cooking during the Sabbath hours—followed by a true "day off" from domestic duties. Visiting family and neighbors, strolling, and resting were typical women's activities for *Shabbes.* Marital love on the Sabbath was also considered a *mitzva.*

Shabbes suffered greatly in the "New World," where the sweatshop economy and the majority Christian culture made it difficult to have Saturdays off from work. At the same time, *Shabbes* consciousness may have played a role in equipping Jewish immigrants for economic success. Andrew R. Heinze notes (in *Adapting to Abundance,* Columbia University Press, 1990), "For centuries, Jews had used items of luxury in the celebration of the Sabbath and holidays in order to deepen their distinction between the holy and the mundane spheres of life." Jews were therefore "quick to detect the democratic symbolism of mass-marketed luxuries in America. Their traditional culture thus helped them realize that Americans sought, in the realm of consumption, a parity with each other that was unattainable in the world of capital and labor." For more about Jewish success in mass-market industries, see my note to Rosten's entry for **luftmentsh**.

Jewish labor activists have long embraced *Shabbes* as the archetypal "day off." More recently, environmental activist Rabbi Arthur Waskow has envisioned a societywide *Shabbes* as "the cure for modernity turned cancerous. For modernity—like a cancer cell—doesn't know when to stop growing. Maybe every seven years, we should give one year off to all people who specialize in research and development. . . . When the earth itself is endangered . . . when better to reconnect the liberation of humankind with the

It is a long-honored custom for Jews to invite a stranger, a traveler, a student, or a poor man to the *Shabbes* meal. However poor a Jew might be, he sought to find someone to be his family's *oyrekh*. It is hard to overestimate how this served to make Jews everywhere feel part of one universal fellowship.

Shabbes ends at sundown, Saturday, with a home religious service called *Havdala*, which marks the "separation" of the Sabbath from the weekdays. A special braided candle is lighted, wine is poured, blessings are uttered, and the aroma of spices is inhaled—to symbolize the hope that the coming week will be sweet. See Havdala.

For a hilarious lampoon on the Sabbath guest, see the story under oyrekh.

The *Shabbes* feast is fairly standardized among Ashkenazic Jews: it includes *gefilte fish,* soup with noodles of *matzo*-ball dumplings, and chicken (boiled or roasted). Horseradish invariably accompa-

resting time of the earth?" (Quoted in my *Jews, Money and Social Responsibility,* coauthored with Jeffrey Dekro, the Shefa Fund, 1993).

The Bible itself (Leviticus 25:1–13) makes such connections by establishing every seventh year as a "sabbatical year" *(shmitah)* in which the land must lie fallow and every fiftieth year as a "jubilee" *(yovel),* in which debts are annulled and land is restored to its original owners. The biblical declaration of the jubilee, "Proclaim liberty thro' all the land . . . ," is engraved on the Liberty Bell. Neither of these biblical institutions, however, is observed in modern Jewish life.

Shabbes is when most synagogue members attend services, on Friday evenings and/or Saturday mornings. In the United States, however, only about 40 percent of the Jewish population is synagogue affiliated. Approximately the same percent also reports lighting Sabbath candles at home on Friday evenings, at least some of the time. These and other statistics of non-observance motivated Rabbi Ephraim Buchwalds to found the National Jewish Outreach Program, which since 1997 has sponsored an annual "*Shabbat* Across America and Canada" program (*Shabbat* is the Hebrew version of *Shabbes*). By 1999, some seventy thousand Jews who did not customarily observe the Sabbath were gathering in synagogues for this night of celebration.

nies the *gefilte fish,* and *tsimes* the meat. My mother always served chopped liver, celery, radishes, olives, then *gefilte fish,* then *kneydl* (dumpling) soup, then the chicken—and applesauce for either a side dish or dessert.

On Saturday, the traditional lunch (prepared by the Orthodox the day before, of course) was *cholent* (a bean stew) and *kugel* (noodle or bread pudding).

The radical idea of one labor-free day each week, even for slaves and beasts of burden, did not appeal to the Greeks and Romans. Seneca, the Stoic, abandoned his stoicism to attack the Hebrew custom that, he admitted, was spreading. ("This most outrageous people . . . lose almost a seventh part of their life in inactivity.") Juvenal jeered at the Romans, who, influenced by the Jews, "adore nothing but clouds and the divinity of heaven . . . to whom every seventh day is idle." Horace scorned, and Martial maligned, the *Shabbes.*

The historian Josephus records the fact that Roman military men knew that Jewish soldiers would fight on the Sabbath only in dire extremity (the rabbis permitted it if it was absolutely necessary—to save life or in immediate and unmistakable peril). The Romans exploited this fact in the timing of their military actions against the Jews.

Maurice Samuel wrote this marvelous poetic passage on the meaning of *Shabbes* to poor, humble Jews (from *The World of Sholem Aleichem,* Schocken, 1965):

You must make up your mind that **Tevye*** the coolie, or Tevye

*Tevye is the lead character of Sholom Aleichem's Tevye's Daughters, *upon which the Broadway hit* Fiddler on the Roof *is based; Kasrielevka is the imaginary town of many of Sholom Aleichem's works. For more on Sholom Aleichem, see* **sholem aleichem** *and my note to Rosten's entry for* **Pesach**.

the dairyman, simply will not work . . . from sundown on Friday to sundown on Saturday. No labour-leader in the world has ever been so insistent on the forty-eight or forty-hour week as Tevye on his six-day week. The Sabbath is the Lord's day; that is, it is Tevye's day for rest in the Lord. He will not work on that day, he will not carry money about, he will not touch fire or tear paper or do anything that savours of the slavery of the body. . . . You will neither bribe, bully, nor persuade him into such transgression. For the Sabbath and the festivals are all that are left to him; they are the last citadel of his freedom. On those days he will pray, meditate, and refresh his spirit with a little learning. He may be hungry; he will contrive to rise above it. He may not know where the next day's food will come from, either; he will contrive to forget that, too. . . .

There never was such obstinacy! It must not be thought, either, that Tevye, crushed under the double burden of the Jewish exile and the worker's slavery, clings to these practices merely as a grim protest. Not by any means. He enjoys them, thoroughly. He loves the Sabbath and the festivals. He loves prayer. . . .

The Sabbath siesta is not a long affair. Who wants to sleep away the loveliest of days? Half an hour passes, an hour at most. Then you hear, issuing from the dilapidated houses, and hanging over the crooked alleys, sweet, haunting melodies in a minor key; not formal songs, but vague chants, carrying not formal phrases, but half phrases, words and half words, repeated over and over again. Melancholy but not depressed, suppliant but not importunate, the voices linger over the townlet with the tenderness of bells. "Ah, Father—Father—bim—bom Father in heaven—ai—ai—look upon us—bim—bom—Thy people—Father—ai—ai—King—" The words and half words, the melodies, the grace-notes, say nothing and say everything. They are mnemonics, mysterious and meaningless to the outsider, intimate, lucid and vivid to the insider, evoking dimly a long history of homelessness, of faithfulness and hope. As the sadness of great stretches of space informs the songs of the Russian peasant, so the sadness of great stretches of time haunts the truncated words, the elisions and repetitions of these minor Jewish chants. . . . "Life is hard, God is good, a time will come, bim-bom, remember Thy people, hard, good, people, Father—ai, Father, little Father. . . ." And meanwhile the Sabbath is slipping away, the Queen is preparing her departure, the harsh world, the daily struggle, the bitterness of life, stand at the gates of the evening. Get everything you can out of this heavenly interlude, an hour or two of prayer, an hour or two of study, in the synagogue or at home. Till the moment of the Separation comes, and with incense box uplifted, his family gathered about him, the Kasrielevkite takes regretful leave of the Sabbath, and the wife sings, in homely Yiddish, the valedictory of Reb Isaac of Berditchev, Reb Levi Isaac the Compassionate. . . .

What kind of Sabbath is it, I ask you, which leaves the world around you utterly unchanged from the weekdays? The shops are open, the marketplace is filled, the horses neigh, buyers and sellers chaffer, the [streetcar] thunders past the synagogue, and the Sabbath siesta is a day-mare in a din of blaring radios and yelling children playing baseball in the street. And . . . traditionalists and modernists alike remember now and again with a nostalgic pang the far-off magic of those sacred hours, those transfigured interludes of the Sabbaths and festivals for which even progress and freedom have found no substitute.

"Tell nothing on the Sabbath which will draw tears," is written in *Sefer Hasidim* (13c, no. 625).

"Let melancholy and passion, born of spleen and bile, be banished from all hearts on the Sabbath day" (Moses Hasid, a moralist who lived in Prague; 1717).

"Who spends for the Sabbath," says the *Talmud,* "is repaid by the Sabbath."

Asher Ginzberg, better known as Ahad ha-Am, made this succinct and memorable observation: "More than the Jews have kept the Sabbath, the Sabbath has kept the Jews."

Rabbi Korshak, the young, modern rabbi in a suburban temple, greatly loved to play golf. He played as often as he could, usually with members of his congregation; but he took his pastoral duties so seriously that he could not find time to play more than four or five times a year.

One sunny Sabbath morning, after services, Rabbi Korshak saw that his calendar was clear and felt so powerful a craving to play golf, even if only for a few holes, that he begged God to forgive him for breaking the Sabbath, tossed his golf bag into the back of his car, and sped off to a golf course a good thirty miles away, where he was certain no one would recognize him.

With an apology to his Maker on his lips, and a song of sixpence in his heart, the rabbi teed off. . . .

Up in heaven, Moses, looking down to earth, observing the ways and follies of humankind, suddenly bolted upright. "Lord! My Lord!" he cried. "I beseech Thee: Gaze down. Do my eyes deceive me? There, Holy One—beyond those clouds—do you *see?*"

"Y-yes," said the Lord.

"That's Rabbi Korshak!" said Moses. "Playing *golf!* On Your Holy Sabbath!"

"Dear Me," sighed the Lord.

"Such a transgression!" said Moses. "From a rabbi yet. How will You punish him?"

"I," said the Lord, "will teach him a lesson."

And with that God cupped His hands over His mouth and—just as Rabbi Korshak teed off for the second hole—the Almighty One, King of the Universe, let out His breath in a long, mighty, cosmic *Whooooosh!* that caught the rabbi's golf ball in midair, lifted it three hundred yards, and flipped it around a tree, over a stream, and against a rock, where it ricocheted in a miraculous parabola to make—a hole in one!

Moses stared at God in bewilderment. "*That* you call a punishment, Lord?"

"Mmh," said the Lord with a smile. "Whom can he *tell*?"

Shabbes goy

Pronounced SHAH-*bes goy*, to rhyme with "Bob is boy." *Shabbes:* Sabbath; *goy:* Gentile.

1. The Gentile who is asked on the Sabbath by Orthodox Jews to light the fire, put out candles, perform a chore—all of which are forbidden the devout on the holy *Shabbes*.

Since any physical exertion, any workaday routine or activity, was held to desecrate the Sabbath, Orthodox Jews in eastern Europe would ask a Gentile to fetch wood or water, light the fire in stove or oven, put out the candles, and so on. A small tip, or a piece of *challah* or cake, was customary.

In America, the Orthodox would ask a non-Jewish neighbor, or the janitor, to press an electric light switch (just as the Amish sect in Pennsylvania, forbidden by their church to own automobiles, will ride in a car hired from, and driven by, a non-Amish).

The rabbis, following the Fourth Commandment, frowned upon the custom of using a *Shabbes goy;* they said that it "breaks the Sabbath" even to ask someone else to do so.

2. As used, on occasion, by Orthodox Jews: A
Jew who is not Orthodox or "observing."
"His father and mother—long may they
live—are good Jews, but he, I hate to tell
you, is a *Shabbes goy*."

Shabtsitvaynik

Pronounced scornfully: *shob-tzee-*TVY-*nik,* to rhyme with
"popsy rye wick." Yiddishism: adds -*nik* to the popular pronunciation of *Sabbatai Zvi,* the so-called "Messiah of
Izmir."
1. A fake religious seer, prophet, or self-proclaimed Messiah.
2. One who believes in, or follows the precepts of, a religious charlatan.
See meshiekh.

shachris^R
shakhris^Y

Pronounced SHAKH-*ris,* to rhyme with "Bach kiss."
Hebrew: "morning."
The morning prayers.

One of the three daily prayers. See mincha, mairev.

shadkhn^Y
shadchen^R

Pronounced sHOD-*khen*, to rhyme with "bodkin"—if you pronounce the *k* as a hearty *kh*. Plural: *shadkhnim* (*shod-*KHUN-*im*). From the Hebrew: *shidukh*, "marital match."

1. A professional matchmaker.
2. Anyone who brings together, introduces, or maneuvers a man and woman into a meeting that results in a wedding.

Jewish marriages were customarily arranged by the heads of two families. Rabbis were sometimes *shadkhnim*, for the task of arranging marriages was considered a sacred matter: the union of two souls, and the agreement to have children and raise them as Jews, was part of Israel's obligation in its special compact with God. (Commentaries on the Talmudic tractate *Baba Kama* deal with the role of the matchmaker in perpetuating Israel's existence; rabbinical decisions set proper fees for arranged marriages.)*

The professional *shadkhn* performed an important social function, gathering information about eligible mates, weighing family background, individual qualities, and personality factors in a

---

*Traditional Jewish marriages were often contracted by the families of children, even very young children, under condition that they agree to the arrangement upon reaching puberty. While the Jewish sages strongly discouraged betrothing a daughter to a much older or ill-tempered man, such matches were hazards that young Jewish women, particularly from households of limited means, had to face.

The American abolitionist Ernestine Rose (1810–1892) fled from Poland at age sixteen when her father, a rabbi, tried to force her into an arranged marriage. In the United States she became a prominent voice in favor of women's rights and free public schools and against slavery. Her continual agitation helped bring about passage by the New York State Legislature of the 1848 Married Women's Property Act, the first such law in the land.

matching undertaking that is today assigned to computers. (See yikhes.)

As the Jewish communities in eastern Europe grew larger, more deeply rooted, the *shadkhnim* became seedy Cupids, more commercial in their concern, more vigorous in their salesmanship, less exact in their representations. Soon the rabbis began to criticize the vulgarity and venality of *shadkhnim*. The *shadkhn* did become a suspect fellow, useful but distrusted, a magpie, too shrewd, fluttering around with his notebooks and inevitable umbrella. (A touching story about a modern rabbi's ambivalent encounter with a *shadkhn* is in Bernard Malamud's *The Magic Barrel*.)*

God is considered the supreme *shadkhn;* indeed, the sages of yore maintained that God pays as much attention to, and expends as much effort in, pairing off compatible couples as He devoted to the parting of the waters of the Red Sea. So every *shadkhn* considers himself charged with a quasi-divine mission, and almost every

---

*More recent novels that deal with Jewish arranged marriages include Anne Roiphe's *Lovingkindness* (1997) and Naomi Ragen's *Jephte's Daughter* (1996).

Jew, and surely every *yidene*, is an amateur but permanent *shadkhn*.

Our aversion to the idea of arranged marriages is, of course, a post-eighteenth-century attitude: it did not occur to earlier Jews, or to their contemporaries, that "love and marriage" go together. Romantic love is relatively new in human history.

The *shadkhn's* functions have been taken over today by a dozen institutional devices: synagogues with social programs for young men and women, "friendship clubs," and computer dating operations.*

*At this writing, the Yahoo! Internet search engine displays more than 2,100 sites devoted to Jewish computer matchmaking of every variety.

A wisecrack defines a *shadkhn* as "a marriage broker who knows the perfect girl for you—and married the wrong girl himself."

Sholem Aleichem defined a *shadkhn* as "a dealer in livestock."

A *shadkhn*, having sung the praises of a female client, brought his excited male prospect to see her. The young man took one look at the damsel to whom the *shadkhn* elaborately introduced him and recoiled.

"What's the matter?" asked the *shadkhn*.

"You said she was young," the young man whispered, "and she's forty if she's a day! You said she was beautiful, and she looks like a duck! You said she was shapely, and she's fat enough for two! You said—"

"You don't have to whisper," said the *shadkhn*. "She's also hard of hearing."

A young man, having patiently and skeptically endured the *shadkhn's* hyperbole, said, "But you left out one thing, didn't you?"

"Never! What?"

"She limps."

"Only when she walks!" cried the *shadkhn*.

The prospective groom scowled. "You lied to me."

"*I?*" said the *shadkhn*. "How? Isn't she pretty? Isn't she rich? Isn't she intelligent?"

"Yes, yes, but you told me she comes from an illustrious family. You said her father is dead—and I just learned *he's been in jail for the past six years!*"

"So?" cried the *shadkhn*. "That you call living?"

The *shadkhn* was impressing the young woman with the boundless virtues of a female and ended: "And to look at, she's a regular picture!"

The young man could not wait for his blind date.

But when he accosted the *shadkhn* the next day, his voice was frosty: "Her eyes are crossed, her nose is crooked, and when she smiles one side of her mouth goes down—"

"Just a minute," interrupted the *shadkhn*. "Is it my fault you don't like **Picasso**?"*

*Rosten delights in jokes about disappointing brides, yet the dangers of arranged marriages (and marriage in general) have probably weighed far more heavily upon Jewish women, who face incidents of domestic violence on a par with American society at large. According to Rabbi Julie Spitzer—a pioneering researcher into Jewish domestic violence who died at age forty-one in 1999—"one in five Jews have some connection to this issue." Other researchers, defining domestic violence to include threats, shoving, and thrown objects, peg the rate at over 30 percent. In Israel, approximately two hundred thousand women, 11 percent of the adult female population, have been victims of violence by their spouse at least once, according to a 1998 study by the JDC-Brookdale Institute.

Jewish women apparently stay in abusive marriages twice as long as non-Jews, perhaps because of the Jewish tradition's strong emphasis on *sholem bayis*, household peace, and a tendency within the community to turn a blind

(Continued on page 482)

shah!
sha!

Pronounced SHAH, to rhyme with "Pa," "Ma," "ha." Onomatopoetic.

    An order to be quiet; a command to "shut up." *Shah!*
Shah!†

To a group, a request or instruction to quiet down or be silent
is given as *"Zol zayn shah!"*—"Let there be quiet!"

shalom
See sholem.

shammes^R
shames^Y
shamus, shammus

Pronounced SHAH-*mes*, to rhyme with "promise."
Hebrew: *shamash*, "servant."

(Continued from page 481)

eye to the problem. In Orthodox and Conservative life, the withholding of the
get (religious divorce document) by abusive husbands can perpetuate the
trauma of domestic violence even after the household has been split apart.
See my note to Rosten's entry for **get**.

    Important strides have been made throughout the Jewish community
during the past ten years to acknowledge and address the problem with educational programs, rabbinic sensitization training, shelters for women fleeing
abusive situations, and other helpful programs.

† *Shah* is also used to mean "hush" and is heard frequently in Yiddish lul-
labyes.

1. The sexton or caretaker of the synagogue; the "servant" or attendant of a congregation of worshipers.

In the old country, and in the early decades of the twentieth century in America, a *shammes* had many duties beyond the janitorial. He was expected to keep the synagogue clean and warm; to repair minor damage; to see that prayer books and ceremonial objects were safely preserved. In the *shtetl,* he would go around waking up congregation members, calling them to prayer, announcing sunset and Sabbath times (often by trumpet). He also was used to carry messages and acted as a bailiff to the religious court. He collected synagogue dues, made funeral arrangements, and rounded up a *minyan.* He would even fill in for a cantor with a sore throat. (Jews did not stand on ceremony.)

2. In American slang: A detective, a policeman, a guard.

Shammes, in this usage, enjoys wide popularity in detective fiction and among the Irish, who spell it *shamus,* which sounds more like Gaelic than Yiddish.

Eric Partridge (in *A Dictionary of Slang and Unconventional English,* Macmillan, 1961) and others claim that *shamus* derives from the Irish name Seamus and say that since so many Irish immigrants became policemen, the name Seamus grew to be associated with police **personnel.***

3. A "private eye."
4. A functionary on a low level, an unimportant menial.

*Webster's Third New International Dictionary, Unabridged (1986) supports Rosten's assertion of Yiddish derivation for shamus by noting that the word is "probably from a jocular suggestion of similarity between the duties of a sexton and those of a house detective in a department store."

"A *shammes* in a pickle factory" is a Yiddish phrase for a low man on anyone's totem pole.

5. Sycophant; a hanger-on around someone. "Every movie producer has to have a *shammes*."
6. A "stool pigeon," an informer.
7. The ninth candle of the *Chanukah menorah,* used to light the others.

On the High Holy Days, seats in the synagogue are often sold in advance, to provide revenue for synagogue upkeep. In a small *shul* in Coney Island, a Jew without a ticket came running up to the door: "Let me in, let me in! I must see Abe Baum!"

The *shammes* barred his way. "No one gets in without a ticket!"

"It's an emergency! I'll come right out! It'll only take five seconds!"

"Okay," said the *shammes.* "But don't let me catch you **praying!**" †

---

† The synagogue membership dues system has changed only slightly since d. a. levy (1942–1968) wrote a painful poem about being kicked out of the "reserved seats" in synagogue over three decades ago:

> we left & it was thus i completed
> my external jewish education . . .
> my father with his lonely eyes
> trying to return home
> only to have the american god of money
> slapped in his face . . .

The *American Jewish Year Book, 1997* explains that "Jewish religious institutions charge membership dues, fees for seats, and tuition; by contrast, churches do not have formal dues structures." Churches, on the other hand, can take up collections at every prayer service, while Jewish injunctions against carrying or dealing with money on the Sabbath make this impossible in synagogues. Nevertheless, giving to Christian institutions is widely regarded as philanthropic, while synagogues suffer from the resentment and consumerist mentality that arise from obligatory dues. Fortunately, the alienation expressed by American Jews has begun to lead to some reform in the synagogue dues system.

The visiting rabbi stopped in the middle of his sermon and signaled to the *shammes.* "In the second row," he whispered, "is a man sound asleep. Wake him up."

"That's not fair," said the *shammes.*

"What do you mean, 'not fair'?"

"You put him to sleep; you wake him up."

sharopnikel

Pronounced *shah-*ROPP*-ni-kel,* to rhyme with "bar up, pickle." Pure Ameridish.

A small object that effectuates a shutting up—hence, a baby's pacifier; a teething ring; Linus's blanket in the comic strip *Peanuts.*

This enchanting fusion of English and Yiddish takes the English "shut up," squeezes it into *sharop* (as was the custom), adds the *−nik* to make a substantive, and tacks on the affectionate diminutive *-el.* Amazing.

NOTE: "Pacifier" comes from "pacify" and can mean anything from a Swiss diplomat to a tranquilizing pill. *Sharopnikel,* on the other hand, sternly excludes diplomacy, international relations, or pharmaceuticals.

shaytl
See sheytl.

sheeny

Vulgarism; pronounced SHEE-*nee*, to rhyme with "gleamy."

1. A thoroughly offensive name, combining contempt and disparagement, for a Jew.

C. T. Onions's *Oxford Dictionary of English Etymology* (1966) says that *sheeny* is slang and appeared in the nineteenth century, origin unknown. *The Oxford English Dictionary* calls *sheeny* slang of obscure origin, possibly from the Russian, Polish, and Czech words for Jews, emerging in the early nineteenth century. (Portuguese sailors called a Jew a *sheeny*.)

The word is branded opprobrious in *The Shorter Oxford English Dictionary*, but "inoffensive" in J. C. Hotten's *The Slang Dictionary* (1874 edition). The word may not have offended J. C. Hotten, but it would offend any Jew.

Ernest Weekley (*Etymological Dictionary of Modern English*, Dover, 1957) suggests that *sheeny* is derived from the way Jews pronounced the German word *schön* ("pretty," "beautiful") in describing the merchandise they offered for sale.

Maurice Samuel tells me he thinks *sheeny* comes from *a mise meshine* ("a weird death"), a phrase widely used by and among Jews, the *sheeny* being a Gentile remembrance and identification of the final syllable and sound.

English slang for
2. a pawnbroker.
3. a tramp.
4. in the military: a frugal, economy-minded man.
5. fraudulent.
6. base.

In such company, it is small wonder that the word raises the hackles of Jews.

Shehecheyanu ᴿ
Shekheyonu ʸ

Pronounced *sheh-heh-kheh-*YAW-*noo,* to rhyme with "fella macaw Lou." Hebrew: "that He let us live."

The main word in the *brokhe* (benediction) used for joyous events that do not occur every day.

The benediction is: "Blessed art Thou, O Lord our God, King of the Universe, who gave us life, and kept us strong, and brought us to this time."

A Jew makes *Shehecheyanu* on the three major festivals of the year: *Pesach, Succos,* and *Shevuos.* In addition, when observing Jews move into a new home, or put on new clothes, or eat the first fruits of the season, etc., they "make *Shehecheyanu.*"

shekel ᴿ
shekl ʸ

Pronounced SHEH-*kl,* to rhyme with "heckle." Hebrew: "coin," "weight." Plural: *shkolim.*

1. A coin.
2. Money.

A *shekel* was the most important silver coin in biblical times. It is mentioned in Genesis (33:12–16) as the money used by Abraham when he purchased the Cave of Machpela as a burying ground. And half a *shekel* was the tax Moses imposed upon the Israelites for the Tabernacle (Exodus 30:13).

When the first Zionist Congress was convened in Basel, Switzerland, in 1897, the nominal sum set up for membership dues was called a *shekel*.

Shakespeare used the word in *Measure for Measure* (II:2): "Not with fond shekels of tested gold. . . ."

Shekel or *shekels* is widely used, in American slang, to mean "coins" or "money." "Come on, lay out some *shekels*." "He has more *shekels* than you have hairs."

Which is more important: money or wisdom?

"Wisdom," says the philosopher.

"Ha!" scoffs the cynic. "If wisdom is more important than money, why is it that the wise wait on the rich, and not the rich on the wise?"

"Because," says the scholar, "the wise, being wise, understand the value of money; but the rich, being only rich, do not know the value of wisdom."

Shekhinah
Shechinah

Pronounced *sh'*KHEE*-neh,* to rhyme with "Salina." Use the Scottish *kh.* Hebrew: "Divine Presence." From the root, *shakhan,* "to dwell."

1. The term used to symbolize God's spirit and omni-presence, and another way of referring to God without using His Name. (See Adonai, Adoshem.)

2. The actual, dazzling, radiant, shining Presence of the Lord **Himself**.*

The *Shekhinah* was said to have appeared to Moses in the burning bush. It also descended in the pillar of smoke that guided the Israelites through the desert. It rested on Mount Sinai when the Ten Commandments were given to the children of Israel.

The *Talmud* teaches that the *Shekhinah* is everywhere. Observing Jews say that the *Shekhinah* descends each Friday at sunset to transform each Jewish home during the Sabbath.

3. When people are converted to the Jewish faith, they are said to have come "under the wings of *Shekhinah*."

---

*In the cabalistic tradition, *Shekhinah* is often identified as a feminine aspect of the Godhead, intimate and nurturing, and is associated with the *sefirah Malkhut*, "Sovereignty." See Rosten's entry and my note for **Sefirah**. *Shekhinah* is now widely used as a name for God by Jewish women and men interested in bringing more egalitarian language and attitude to Jewish liturgy.

Emperor Hadrian once approached Rabbi Joshua ben Hananiah and said, "I desire to see your God."

Rabbi Joshua asked the emperor to stand facing the sun and gaze upon it.

The emperor did so for a moment, then said, "I cannot! It is too bright. It blinds my eyes!"

Said Rabbi Joshua, "If you are not able to look upon the sun, which is only a servant of God, how much less can you gaze upon the *Shekhinah*."

Shema
Sh'ma

Rhymes with "aha." Hebrew: "hearken," "hear."

The first word of the prayer that proclaims the Jews' faith: "Hear, O Israel, the Lord our God, the Lord is One. . . . "

See Shema Yisrael.

Shema Yisrael
Sh'ma Yisrael

Pronounced *sheh*-MA *yis-roe*-AIL. Hebrew: *shema*, "hear," *Yisrael*, "Israel."

The most common of Hebrew prayers, recited three or four times a day by Orthodox Jews; it is the last prayer uttered on the deathbed.

This lyrical declaration of faith reads:

Hear, O Israel: The Lord our God, the Lord is One!—And thou shalt love the Lord thy God with all thy heart, and with all thy soul, and with all thy might. And these words, which I command thee this day, shall be upon thy heart, and thou shalt teach them diligently unto thy children, and thou shalt talk of them when thou sittest in thy house, and when thou walkest by the way, and when thou liest down, and when thou risest up. And thou shalt bind them for a sign upon thy hand, and they shall be for frontlets betweeen thine eyes. And thou shalt write them upon the doorposts of thy house and upon thy gates.

The words are found in Deuteronomy 6:4–7.

Jews who were being tortured, flogged, flayed, hanged, torn apart, burned at the stake, boiled in oil, or otherwise introduced to earnest and pious efforts to convert them would try to die with the prayer on their lips. Unlearned observers of these peculiar evangelical attempts came to think that *Shema Yisrael* meant "Long live the Jew!"—but they were wrong.

See also mezuzah and tefillin.

Shemona Esray
See daven.

shemozzl
shlemozzl

Pronounced *sheh*-MOZ-zl or *shle*-MOZ-zl, to rhyme with "den nozzle." NOTE: These words are not Yiddish, and not Yinglish, but slang used by our cousins in England

and Ireland. I include them because they are often spelled and pronounced like the Yiddish *shlimazl*, to which they bear not the slightest resemblance.

A *shemozzl* or *shlemozl* is

1. an uproar, a fight, a confusion, a "rhubarb." "The umpire's decision set off a terrific *shemozzl*." "He'll stir up a big *shemozzl*." This usage comes from the race-track touts and bookmakers of London.

2. to decamp, to abscond, to make off with something. This usage is given in Eric Partridge's *A Dictionary of Slang and Unconventional English* (Macmillan, 1961).

Shevuos [R]
Shvues[Y]
Shavuos, Shavuot, Shevuoth, Shabuot

Pronounced *sheh-*vu-*ess*, to rhyme with "the Lewis." Hebrew: *Shavuot*, "weeks."

The Festival of Weeks, or Pentecost. (It was called Pentecost by Greek Jews, meaning "the fiftieth," for *Shevuos* occurred fifty days after the second day of Passover.)

This two-day holiday (one day in Israel) falls seven weeks after the second day of Passover. It is the anniversary of the Covenant between God and Israel on Mount Sinai and is called "the season of the giving to us of our Holy Torah."

It is also "the holiday of the first fruits," for it is one of the three happy pilgrimages to Jerusalem, when the Jews in Palestine went up to the great Temple bringing offerings of the first fruits of their harvest. To commemorate this aspect of the holiday, synagogues are decorated with greens on *Shevuos.*

Many congregations hold a confirmation ceremony for teenage boys and girls at this time. This links the youths' conscious declaration of participation in Jewry with the giving of the *Torah* on Mount Sinai and extends a tradition that began in the Middle Ages, when parents enrolled their young sons in the *cheder* on *Shevuos.*

The section of Exodus dealing with Sinai and the Ten Commandments is read on *Shevuos,* as is the book of Ruth, which tells the story of a lovely Moabite woman who became converted to Judaism and accepted its laws: "Thy people shall be my people . . . and thy God my God."*

It is customary to eat dairy dishes on this holiday, especially delicacies made of cheese—cheese *blintzes,* cheese *latkes,* cheesecakes. It is also a time to forget diets.

sheygets^Y
shaygets ^R
shaygetz, shaygits

Pronounced SHEY-*gits,* to rhyme with "hay kits." Possible Hebrew origin. Plural: *shkotsim.* Feminine: *shikse.*

---

*The book of Ruth ends with a genealogy that establishes its heroine, Ruth, as the grandmother of King David. Traditionally, therefore, the messiah, who is predicted to emerge from the Davidic line, is the descendant of a Jew-by-choice, a convert. (See Rosten's entry for **meshiekh**.) Another important theme of the story is economic justice and dignity for the poor: Ruth sustains herself and her mother-in-law, Naomi, by exercising her right to "glean" in fields that are being harvested—that is, to pick up the dropped produce and to pick from the corners of the field. This right is biblically established and is one of the significant components of the *kosher* laws. For a rich and varied discussion of Ruth, see *Reading Ruth,* edited by Judith A. Kates and Gail Twersky Reimer (Ballantine Books, 1994).

1. A Gentile boy or young man. "She's going around with a *sheygets*."
2. A clever lad; a rascal; a handsome, mischievous, charming devil—Jewish or Gentile. "Oh, is he a *sheygets* with the girls!" "Who can say no to such a *sheygets*?"
3. An arrogant cock-of-the-walk. "He strutted in as boldly as a *sheygets*."
4. An uneducated boy; one who has no intellectual ambitions. "You won't study? Do you want to grow up into a *sheygets*?"

Lest you think meaning 3. condescending, let me remark that to the Jews, for untold centuries, the conduct of *shkotsim* hardly inspired affection. As to 4.: For the same centuries, when the overwhelming majority of Europeans were illiterate, it would have been hard to find a Jewish male over the age of five who could not read. Virtually every Jewish boy *had* to learn Hebrew.

See cheder, khokhem, and talmid khokhem.

The two traveling salesmen, competitors in selling notions, spied each other on the platform. "Hello, Liebowitz."

"Hello, Posner."

Silence.

"So—where are you going?" asked Liebowitz

"To Minsk," said Posner.

Silence.

"Listen, Posner," sighed Liebowitz, who was a very bright *sheygets*, "when you say you're going to Minsk, you want me to think you're going to Pinsk. But I happen to know that you *are* going to Minsk—so why are you lying?!"

sheyner Yid

Pronounced SHAY-*ner* YEED, to rhyme with "trainer deed." German: *schön*, "pretty."

Literally, *sheyner Yid* means "beautiful Jew," but the phrase is used not as a comment on physical attractiveness, but to praise personal character, rectitude, and *Yiddishkayt* ("Jewishness").

A *sheyner Yid* is a Jew of whom other Jews are proud, a man of honor, kindness, circumspection, sensitivity to others. A *sheyner Yid* can be poor as a church mouse (church mice do not discriminate; they visit synagogues, too). The butcher on our block was hailed by one and all as a *sheyner Yid* because of his singular quietness, his air of gravity and refinement, and his exemplary modesty.

Melnikoff and Spiegel were talking. The name of one Shmerl came up.

"Who's he?" asked Melnikoff.

"Shmerl. Shmerl Kaminsky," said Spiegel.

"I can't place him. What does he look like?"

"He's ugly, poor man, very short, has a huge nose, is pockmarked."

"N-no . . ."

"Shmerl's left hand is deformed, he holds it like this, and one ear is lopsided."

"I still don't place him. . . ."

"Shmerl talks through his nose," Spiegel persisted, "has a bad stutter, and he's hunchbacked!"

"Ah!" cried Melnikoff. "*That* Shmerl. Sure. A *sheyner Yid!*"

sheytl ^Y
shaytl ^Y
sheitel ^R

Pronounced SHY-*tl* *or* SHEY-*tl*, to rhyme with "title" or "fatal." Plural: *sheytlin* or *sheytlekh*, pronounced SHEYT-*lin*, SHEYT-*lekh*. German: "crown of the head."

The wig traditionally worn by Orthodox Ashkenazic Jewish women after they are married.

The *sheytl* is made either of the user's own hair, of someone else's hair, or of false—that is, manufactured—hair.

Sephardic and Oriental Jewish women never adopted the *sheytl* but instead wore a shawl, turban, or veil over their own hair after marriage.

The custom of using a *sheytl* spread slowly among the Jews of central and eastern Europe, and against opposition from the rabbis, who preferred a simple scarf.* At first, a *sheytl* was worn over the hair only on the Sabbath and holidays, the head being covered by a veil or scarf at other times. Some rabbis even protested that there was nothing in either the laws or traditions of Israel that called for a wig.

> *In the *shtetl*, the *sheytl* was a mark of prosperity, as it was only the relatively well-to-do women who could afford the purchase or manufacture of a wig.

The rabbis decreed that once married, a woman's hair, her well-known crowning beauty, should not be visible lest it distract men from prayer or study. (Jews also worried that attractive Jewish women might draw the attention of lecherous anti-Semites, so unmarried women braided their hair.) The *Mishnah* warns a married woman never to appear outside her home with her hair visible: that was ruled grounds for divorce.

Legend has it that God prettified Eve's uncombed locks before

Adam saw her—and legend will have to remain uncontested, as
far as I'm concerned, because I know of no evidence to dispute it.
See also payess.

A photograph of each of my grandmothers shows them in *sheytlin;*
and if there was any doubt in my mind about how unbecoming a
wig can be on a lady, that doubt was dispelled by the pictures.

I should think the *sheytl* must have discouraged adultery in the
shtetl.

The awesome symbolic powers people attribute to human hair are
too numerous (and too childish) to be explored properly here.
Consider the story of Samson, or the potent erotic influence a
woman's locks are presumed to exercise over helpless males.

Under Talmudic law, incidentally, if a married woman went
out of the house bareheaded, that was grounds for divorce
(*Ketubot,* 7:6).

The *Midrash* states that after God created Eve, He decided to
give her a pleasing coiffure before presenting her to Adam.

The *Talmud* reports that in the olden days brides appeared for
their nuptials with disheveled (or, at least, unbraided) hair. The
custom of unbraiding the hair (for instance, when in labor) is
affiliated with the old superstition that evil spirits cast "binding
spells" that can be avoided by loosening.

Catholic and Greek Orthodox monks wear skullcaps over their
tonsure (a shaved circle on the back-top portion of the skull).

A Catholic novitiate's hair was, originally, entirely cut; now the
tonsure is reduced to a small circle, principally as a sign of the
renunciation of sexuality. Tonsuring was performed immediately
upon the uttering of the vow of chastity.

In many Eastern countries, religious novitiates cut their hair as
a sign of virginity—and dedication to it.

Life and strength are believed to reside in the hair, by many people and in many cultures: hence the ancient fear of cutting a baby's hair during the first year of its life;* or the widely held notion that warriors gain strength from letting their hair grow long. The *Iliad*, you may recall, speaks of "long-haired Achaeans."

A bride's locks, in ancient Greece, were shorn just before she took the wedding vows, and the tresses were dedicated to a goddess.

In some societies that border the Black and Caspian Seas, the bride's hair was cut off on her wedding eve, and she wore a head shawl or turban thereafter.

shidekh^Y
shiddach^R

Pronounced SHID-*dakh*, to rhyme with "Bid, *ach!*" From Hebrew: *shidukh*, "marital match."

An arranged marriage: a "match." "She made a *shidekh* between Florence and Al."

See shadkhn.

---

*Some traditional Jewish families wait until a boy is three years old to cut his hair for the first time. This initial haircut symbolizes the inauguration of the boy's education. Three is regarded as a particularly potent number in the magical folklore of Jewish tradition: according to Ellen Frankel (in *The Encyclopedia of Jewish Symbols*, Jason Aronson, 1992), "Magical actions were performed three hours before sunrise, three days before the New Moon, or three days in a row; magical rituals required three objects; incantations were repeated three times; any experience, especially dreams, recurring three times was regarded as an omen."

In a certain town, there was a grievous shortage of marriageable young men. One of them, ugly but conceited, came to the *shadkhn* and said, "I am considering getting married. But I warn you— I'll accept nothing but a remarkable *shidekh*."

The *shadkhn* studied the young man sourly, then said, "I have just the girl for you. Her father is rich and she is beautiful, well educated, charming—"

"Wait a minute," the young man said suspiciously. "Why isn't such a girl married?"

The *shadkhn* raised his hand. "You want to know why such a girl would accept someone who is not—excuse me—the most attractive young man in the world? I will be perfectly frank. This beautiful, educated, charming girl has an affliction: once a year she goes crazy."

"She goes *crazy*?"

"But that need not disturb you. She does not cause any trouble. She just goes a little *meshuge*—for only one day. Then she's as charming and normal as ever for another year!"

"That's not so bad," said the young man, "if she's as rich and beautiful as you say. Let's go see her."

"Not now," said the *shadkhn*. "Your *shidekh* must wait."

"Until when?"

"Until the day she goes out of her mind."

shiker[Y]
shikker[R]

Pronounced SHICK-*er*, to rhyme with "stick her." From Hebrew: *shikor*, "drunkard."

1. A drunkard. "He's a *shiker*."
2. Adjective: Drunk. "She got a wee bit *shiker*."

The Jewish drunkard is almost unknown in Jewish folklore or literature, yet drinking is not foreign to Jewish culture. A Jewish child may be introduced to a sip of wine at an early age: the blessing over wine sanctifies each *Shabbes* and festival (see Kiddush).

The goodness of wine is often mentioned in the Bible: the Psalms compare Israel to a vine that has taken deep root and prospered (80:9–11); and in time of peace, every man shall sit "under his vine and under his fig tree" (1 Kings 5:5). Many biblical metaphors use wine as an allusion to prosperity and good times.

The rabbis also believed that wine possessed splendid curative properties: "Wine is the greatest of all medicine." "Where wine is lacking, drugs are necessary," Rabbi Huna said. "Wine helps to open the heart to reasoning." But the sages always stressed moderation, in drinking as in all else—except study.

Jews have a certain contempt for anyone who loses control of his faculties or acts in an uncouth, "bestial," irresponsible manner. Rabbi Abraham Joshua Heschel wrote (in *The Earth Is the Lord's*, Abelard-Schuman, 1964):

> ... drunkards were rarely seen among Jews. When night came and a man wanted to pass away time, he did not hasten to a tavern to take a drink, but went to pore over a book or joined a group which—either with or without a teacher—revered books. . . . Physically worn out by their day's toil, they sat over open volumes, playing the austere music of the Talmud . . . or the sweet melodies of . . . piety of the ancient sages.

Drinking, if not drunkenness, has clearly increased among **American Jews;*** I do *not* attribute this to the injunction (one of my

---

*The level of Jewish addiction to alcohol and chemical substances has reached a critical enough proportion to warrant the creation of the Jewish

favorites) in the *Talmud* "When a man faces his Maker, he will have to account for those pleasures of life he failed to experience."

PROVERB: "A tavern can't corrupt a good man, and a synagogue can't reform a bad one."

Shikered, to mean "drunk," is commonly used in Australia, say H. Wentworth and S. B. Flexner in *The Dictionary of American Slang* (Crowell, 1960). How the word got all the way down to the Antipodes I do not know.

By three things a man gives himself away: by his tumbler, his tipping, and his temper.

—*Talmud*†

When one man tells you you're *shiker,* hesitate; when two tell you, slow up; when three tell you—lie down!

—My version of an old saw

In the lounge of a Catskill resort, an hour before dinner, Mrs. Meckler asked Mrs. Smelkin, "How about a cocktail before dinner?"

Alcoholics, Chemically Dependent Persons and Significant Others (JACS), a network that provides Jewishly rooted "Twelve Step" programs, recovery services, and other resources in more than a dozen states to help Jews beat their addictions. (JACS can be reached at www.jacsweb.org.) Rabbi Kerry Olitzky, director of the Jewish Outreach Institute, has several books about Jewish recovery from addiction, including, most recently, *One Hundred Blessings Every Day: Daily Twelve-Step Recovery Affirmations* (Jewish Lights, 2000).

Whether Jewish alcoholism has actually increased in modern America, as Rosten states, or has simply been made visible by increased advocacy around issues of addiction, domestic violence, and so on, is debatable.

† "And some say," the passage continues (*Eruvin* 65b), "also by his laughter."

"No thanks. I never drink."

"No? Why not?"

"Well, in front of my children, I don't believe in taking a drink. And when I'm away from my children, who *needs* it?"

shiksa[R]
shikse[Y]

Pronounced SHIK-*seh*, to rhyme with "pick the." The feminine of *sheygets*. Possible Hebrew origin.

1. A non-Jewish woman, especially a young one.
2. As used, on occasion, by Orthodox Jews: A Jewish woman who is not Orthodox, pious, observing, does not keep a *kosher* household, and so on.

As the Polish servant girl carried bucket after bucket of water from the well to the house, the rabbi sat down to eat with his disciples. But he sprinkled a very few drops of water on his hands before making the traditional *brokhe*.

A disciple asked why he was so stingy about water.

The rabbi replied: "It is surely pious to wash before each meal; but one must not be pious at even a servant's—a *shiksa's*— expense."

shivah[R]
shive[Y]
shiva, shiveh

Pronounced SHI-*vah*, to rhyme with a southerner's pronunciation of "river." From the Hebrew: "seven."

The seven solemn days of mourning for the dead, beginning immediately after the funeral, when Jews "sit *shivah*" in the home of the deceased.

The traditional practice requires members of the immediate family to remove their shoes, don cloth slippers, and sit on stools or low benches, customs derived from ancient mourning rituals. Mirrors are covered. ("Vanity of vanities, all is vanity.") The mourners wear garments with a rip in the lapel. This is the age-old symbol of grief—the rending of the garments. (The tear is made just before the funeral, and the mourner has uttered the words "Blessed be the righteous Judge," signifying acceptance of the inevitability of loss.)

During the *shivah* period, mourners remain in the house and do not work or even study the *Torah* (save for certain permitted portions). A *minyan* comes to the house, morning and evening, to hold services and enable the mourners to recite the Kaddish, or mourner's prayer. Friends pay visits out of respect to the deceased and to honor the mourners. The conversation is limited to praises of the dead. The traditional expression of sympathy is "May the Almighty comfort you among the mourners for Zion and Jerusalem." The mourners do not offer or acknowledge greetings, for they must be preoccupied with their grief and the memory of the dead.

The first meal served to the mourners upon returning from the funeral is prepared by neighbors and customarily includes hard-boiled eggs, which are said to be symbolic of the need for life to go on—among the mourners.

The sages of the *Talmud* astutely instruct Jews not to mourn self-accusingly. They even prescribe the protocol and phasing of grief: three days of weeping, followed by four days of eulogy. The seven-day *shivah* period is followed by a thirty-day period (*sheloshim*) of lesser mourning and an eleven-month period during which the mourner recites the *Kaddish* twice daily. Thereafter, the deceased is remembered each year on the anniversary of his death. See yort-sayt.

The closeness and intensity of life within the Jewish community developed institutions for virtually every occasion—including a Society to Comfort Mourners, which called upon anyone struck by a death in the family and brought food to the mourners.

At the funeral of a very wealthy man, a stranger joined the funeral procession and began weeping and wailing louder than all the others.

"Are you a relative?" someone asked.

"No."

"Then why are you crying?"

"That's why."

shlemiehl
schlemiel
schlemihl

See shlemiel.

shlemiel[R]
shlemil[Y]
schlemiel, shlemiehl

Pronounced *shleh*-MEAL, to rhyme with "reveal."

1. A foolish person; a simpleton. "He has the brains of a *shlemiel.*"
2. A consistently unlucky or unfortunate person, a hard-

luck type; a "fall guy," a born loser; a submissive and uncomplaining victim. "That poor *shlemiel* always gets the short end of the stick." A Yiddish proverb goes: "The *shlemiel* falls on his back and breaks his nose."

3. A clumsy, butterfingered, all-thumbs, gauche type. "Why does a *shlemiel* like that ever try to fix anything?"

4. A social misfit, congenitally maladjusted. "Don't invite that *shlemiel* to the party."

5. A pipsqueak, a Caspar Milquetoast. "He throws as much weight as a *shlemiel*." "No one pays attention to that *shlemiel*."

6. A naive, trusting, gullible customer. This usage is common among furniture dealers, especially those who sell the gaudy, gimcrack stuff called "borax."

7. Anyone who makes a foolish bargain or wagers a foolish bet. This usage is wide in Europe; it probably comes from Chamisso's tale "Peter Schlemihl's Wunderbare Geschichte," a fable in which the protagonist sold his shadow and, like Faust, sold his soul to Satan.

It is important to observe that *shlemiel,* like *nebekh,* carries a distinctive note of pity. In fact, a *shlemiel* is often the *nebekh's* twin brother. The classic definition goes: "A *shlemiel* is always knocking things off a table; the *nebekh* picks them up."

Shlemiel is said to come from the name Shlumiel, the son of a leader of the tribe of Simeon (Numbers 2). Whereas the other generals in Zion often triumphed on the field of war, poor Shlumiel was always losing.

Another theory about the origin of *shlemiel* runs that it is a variation of *shlimazl.* (See shlimazl.) I can't quite see how *shlimazl* gave birth to *shlemiel;* the words are as different as "hard luck" is from "that jerk."

The classic attempt to discriminate between the two types runs as follows: "A *shlemiel* is a man who is always spilling hot soup—down the neck of a *shlimazl*." Or, to make a triple distinction: "The *shlemiel* trips, and knocks down the *shlimazl*; and the *nebekh* repairs the *shlimazl*'s glasses."

I suppose that *shlimiels* often are *shlemazls*—but that need not be. A *shlemiel* can make a fortune through sheer luck; a *shlimazl* can't: he loses a fortune through bad luck.

Nor is every *shlimazl* a *shlemiel*: for example, a gifted, able, talented man is no *shlemiel*, but he may run into such bad luck that he is a *shlimazl*. Thus Gregor Mendel and Thomas Alva Edison, both of whom encountered strings of perverse fortune in their experiments—one might have called them *shlimazls*, but surely never *shlemiels*.

Can a brilliant or learned man be a *shlemiel*? Of course he can; many a savant is: the absentminded professor, the impractical genius, are paradigms of *shlemielkayt* (*shlemiel*-ness).

"A *shlemiel* takes a bath, forgets to wash his face."

A *shlemiel* came to his rabbi, distraught. "Rabbi, you've got to advise me. Every year my wife brings forth a baby. I have nine children already, and barely enough money to feed them. Rabbi, what can I do?"

The sage thought not a moment. "Do nothing."

A man came home from the steambaths—minus his shirt.

"*Shlemiel!*" cried his wife. "Where's your shirt?"

"My shirt? That's right. Where can it be? Aha! Someone at the baths must have taken my shirt by mistake, instead of his."

"So where is *his* shirt?"

The *shlemiel* scratched his head. "The fellow who took my shirt—he forgot to leave his."

Two *shlemiels* were drinking tea. In time, one looked up and announced portentously: "Life! What is it? Life—is like a fountain!"

The other pondered for a few minutes, then asked, "Why?"

The first thought and thought, then sighed. "So okay: life *isn't* like a fountain."

shlep
shleper [Y] (noun)
shlepper [R]
shlepn (infinitive verb)

Pronounced SHLEP, to rhyme with "hep," and SHLEP-*per*, to rhyme with "pepper." German: *schleppen*, "to drag."

Shlepn

1. To drag, pull, or lag behind. "Don't *shlep* all those packages; let the store deliver them." "Pick up your feet; don't *shlep*." "They *shlepped* me all the way out to see their house." "He is a *shlep* if ever I saw one." (See also *shleper*.)

2. To stall, drag one's heels, delay; to move or perform slowly, lazily, inefficiently. "At the rate you're *shlepping*

along, we'll never finish." "He'll *shlep* that work out so that it takes twice as long as it should."

Shleper

1. A "drag," a drip, a jerk, a maladroit performer. "Who wants to act with a *shleper* [or *shlep*] like that?" "Ever since then, she acts like a *shleperke* [or *shlep*]."*

*The use of *shlep* to mean somebody who *shleps* is an Ameridish innovation. Classic Yiddish would refer to a man who *shleps* as a *shleper* and a woman who *shleps* as a *shleperke*.

2. Someone unkempt, untidy, run-down-at-the-heels. "Why doesn't she do her hair and stop looking like a *shleperke*?" "Hike up your slip; straighten your seams; you look like a *shleperke*."

3. A beggar or petty thief. "How does he earn a living? He's a *shleper*."

4. An underling who carries the heavy baggage; a moving man.

Shleper has become a familiar word in movie and theater argot, as have *shtik*, *cockamamy*, and *bubeleh*.

See nokhshleper, tsutshepenish.

Mrs. Hoffenstein, visiting London, went shopping at the famous confectioners Fortnum & Mason. She bought jars of marmalade, biscuits, tins of cookies, and candies to take back to her hotel.

"And where," asked the striped-trousered salesman, "shall we deliver these, madam?"

"Don't bother. I'll carry them."

"But madam, we'll be *happy* to deliver this order—"

"I know, but I don't mind, I'm from the Bronx."

"I understand, madam," said the clerk, "but still—why *shlep*?"

shlimazl
schlimazel, shlemazl

Pronounced *shli*-MOZ-*zl,* to rhyme with "thin nozzle."
From the German: *schlimm,* "bad," and the Hebrew:
mazel, "luck." (It is not unusual for a Yiddish word to
combine Hebrew with German, Hebrew with English,
Hebrew with Russian or Polish or Hungarian.)

A chronically unlucky person; someone for whom
nothing seems to go right or turn out well: a born "loser."
Let me illustrate by combining four folk sayings: "When a
shlimazl winds a clock, it stops; when he kills a chicken, it
walks; when he sells umbrellas, the sun comes out; when
he manufactures shrouds, people stop dying."

A *shlimazl* sighed wryly: "From *mazel* to *shlimazl* is but a tiny step;
but from *shlimazl* to *mazel*—*oy,* is that far!"

A world-weary Jew once said: "They say that the poor have no
mazel, which is undeniably true, for if the poor had *mazel,* would
they be poor?"

PROVERB: "Only *shlimazls* believe in *mazel.*"

The twelfth-century poet Abraham ibn Ezra, whom you encountered in high school as Browning's Rabbi ben Ezra (may his tribe
increase), limpidly described the *shlimazl's* lot when he wrote:

> If I sold lamps,
> The sun,
> In spite,
> Would shine at night.

Mintz came to his rabbi and said, "Whatever I do goes sour. My wife and children soon won't have anything to eat. What can I *do?*"

"Become a baker," said the rabbi.

"A baker? Why?"

"Because if you're a baker, even if business is bad, you and your loved ones will have bread!"

Mintz pondered. "And what if the day comes when I don't have enough money to buy flour?"

"Then you won't be a baker," said the rabbi, "but a *shlimazl.*"

"Hello, Yussel! How are things?"

"Good. Everything is good!"

"Really? I hear you've had a terrible year. How can you say everything's *good?*"

"It is," said Yussel. "Every morning, I'm good and depressed. Every evening, I'm good and tired. In the summer, I'm good and hot, and in the winter, I'm good and cold. My roof has so many leaks that I get good and wet, and my floors are so rickety that to take five steps makes me good and angry. My children are so lazy, I'm good and disgusted with them, and my wife is such a *yenta* that I'm good and sick of her. In fact, everything about my life is so good, I'm good and tired of living!"

shlock ᴿ
shlak ʸ
schlock, schlack

Rhymes with "clock." *Shlock* is both an adjective and a noun. From German: *Schlacke,* "slag" or "dross."

1. A shoddy, cheaply made article. "It's a piece of *shlock*." "Where did you buy that? In a *shlock*-house?"

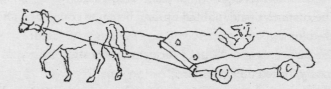

2. A defective or fake article; an object one was cheated over. "That watch will never keep time. It's *shlock* merchandise."
3. A disagreeable, peevish person.
4. A shrew, a whining wife, a *yenta*—and a slob to boot. "His beloved? There's a *shlock* of a girl."

shlock-house

A store that sells cheap, distressed, defective, "fire sale" articles. A **gyp joint.***

In the furniture business, *shlock-house* merchandise is called "borax."

---

*The common use of "gyp" (from "Gypsy") to mean "cheat or swindle" has been recognized in recent years as an ethnic slur on a par with "Indian giver" (someone who takes back a gift) or "jewing someone down" (driving a hard bargain).

Jews have been particularly sensitized to this by contemporary Holocaust scholarship showing that the Gypsy, or Roma, people suffered from genocidal persecutions under the Nazis. *O Porayimos*—the Devouring, as it is called by the Gypsies—took the lives of hundreds of thousands of them, including three-quarters of the German Gypsy population and half of the Austrian Gypsies.

The Gypsies originated in northern India and entered Europe some thousand years ago. The name derives from the false belief among the settled peoples of Europe that the nomadic Gypsies originated in Egypt.

The customer asked the tobacconist to recommend a good cigar.

"Here's the best cigar in the place. Fifty cents."

The customer paid, lighted up, and began to cough and choke. "I asked for a good cigar and you give me *this*?" he cried.

The owner sighed. "What a lucky man you are."

"*Lucky*," cried the customer. "Are you mad?"

"You own only one of those *shlock-house* cigars; I must have twenty dozen!"

shlub
See zhlob.

shlump
shloomp, shlomp

Pronounce the *u* as in "put." German: *Schlumpe,* a "slovenly female," a "slattern." Ameridish version of the Yiddish *shlumper.*

As a Noun
A drip, a "drag," a wet blanket. "That *shlump* can depress anyone." "He's half *shlump,* half *shlemiel.*" *

> *This use of *shlump* as a noun is Ameridish. In classic Yiddish, the noun would be *shlumper.*

I like to visualize a *shlump* as a *shlep* with droopy shoulders or a *shmo* who drags his feet.

As a Verb
1. To drag about, to shuffle.

2. To perform in a pro forma way; to "kiss off" with nominal effort or enthusiasm. "She *shlumps* through a role."

I once heard *shlump* from two Radcliffe girls, neither of whom knew a word of Yiddish; they also tossed off *shtus* and *nudzh* as if chatting in classical Harvardese.

Shlump seems popular on Broadway, off Broadway, in college theatricals, and among young people.

See also shmo, shlep, shmuck, shlemiel.

On a very cold day, the faithful huddled around the stove in the synagogue. One *shlump* said, "When it's bitterly cold like this—I know exactly what to do."

"What?"

"Shiver."

shmaltz ᴿ
shmalts ʸ
schmaltz

Pronounced SHMOLTS, to rhyme with "doll" plus *tz*. German: *schmaltz*, "fat," "drippings."

As a Noun

1. Cooking fat; melted or rendered fat—usually, chicken fat.

A great treat around our house was a slice of bread spread with *shmaltz*. This happened only occasionally, because my mother, whose ideas about biochemistry I thought foolish folklore (but now turn out to be sound), was convinced that all greasy things were messengers of indigestion.

If you like chopped liver, be sure to have a little *shmaltz* over, or mixed into, it.

2. "Corn," pathos; maudlin and mawkish substance, excessive sentimentality; overly emotional mush; sugary banality.

This usage is wide in theatrical circles, which are havens for aficionados of the self-dramatizing. "As an actor, he goes in for too much *shmaltz*." "Tone it down; it's as *shmaltzy* as organ music." "The way he delivered that speech, you could cut the *shmaltz* with a fork."

3. Luxury, wealth, good luck. One Yiddish saying goes, "He fell into a tub of *shmaltz*, that's how lucky he is."

As an Adjective

Shmaltzy: corny, mawkish, hackneyed emotionalism. "'Hearts and Flowers' is about as *shmaltzy* a song as I ever heard."

As a Verb

To *shmaltz* ("to *shmaltz* it up"): to add "corn," pathos, mawkishness.

shmatte^R
shmate^Y
shmotte, schmatte, shmatteh

Pronounced SHMOT-*ta*, to rhyme with "pot a." Polish: *szmata*, "rag," "piece of cloth."

1. A rag. "That you call a dress? It's a *shmatte*."

2. Cheap, shoddy, junk. "I wouldn't drive in a *shmatte* like that." "The movie? A *shmatte!*"
3. A person unworthy of respect; someone "you can wipe your feet on." "She changes her opinion to suit everyone, that *shmatte*." "They treated him like a *shmatte*." "What am I: *tate* [father] or *shmatte* [rag]?" "Stand up for your rights; don't be a *shmatte!*"
4. A woman of weak character, weak will, or wicked ways; a slattern. "She has as much self-respect as the *shmatte* she is." "As a girl, she was decent; now she's a *shmatte*."
5. A fawner, a sycophant, a toady. "Praise drips from that *shmatte* for everyone."

See the story of the shopper in Paris, under chutzpa.

shmeer [R]
shmir [Y]
shmirn (infinitive verb)

Pronounced as it is written; rhymes with "shear." German: *Shmiere*, "grease" or "bribe."

1. To paint.
2. To smear.
3. To spread. "*Shmeer* it on the bread."
4. A spread or paste. "With drinks, a caviar *shmeer* on crackers goes well." "Smoked fish, cream cheese, sour cream, and chives make a wonderful cocktail *shmeer*."
5. To bribe; a bribe. This is the most interesting usage and has long been part of American slang. It is related to "greasing the palm." "Do the officials expect to be *shmeered* there?" "Do they take a *shmeer*?" There's a saying, "*Az men shmeert nist, fort men nit.*" ("If you don't bribe, you don't ride"—or, less literally, "Without bribery, you'll get nowhere.")
6. To strike or beat. "He landed a *shmeer* between the eyes."
7. "The whole package," "the entire deal."

shmegegge
shmegege, shmegeggy

Pronounced, always with disdain, *shmeh-*GEH*-geh* or *shmeh-*GEH*-gee*, to rhyme with "the mega" or the "Peggy." Ameridish slang. Yiddish: *megege*, "dawdler," "idler."

1. An unadmirable, petty person.
2. A maladroit, untalented type.
3. A sycophant, a *shleper*, a whiner, a drip.

Also:

4. A lot of "hot air," "baloney," a *cockamamy* story. "Don't give me that *shmegegge!*" (This will be contested, but usage is usage: for the product of thinking of a *shmegegge*.)

I think of a *shmegegge* as a cross between a *shlimazl* and a *shlemiel*—or even between a *nudnik* and a *nebekh*.

The word is popular in theatrical circles, conjuring up, by its very sound, vividly unlikable characteristics.

Sophia Loren used the word with considerable brio in an interview with a *New York Times* reporter. The combination of great beauty, an Italian accent, an eloquent shrug, a tone of derisive dismissal, and an Ameridish word marked a high point in the life of this colorful epithet.

shmek tabik ^Y
shmeck tabac ^R

Pronounced *shmeck* TAH-*bic*, to rhyme with "check rob lick." German: "a taste of tobacco." In Yiddish, *shmek* means "smell." Polish Jews also use it to mean "taste."

1. A pinch of snuff.
2. Anything that is of scant value, that is worth "no more than a pinch of snuff."

A charming story is told about the three "pillars" of Judaism— *Torah* (Learning), *Avodah* (Worship), and *Gemilus Chasadim* (Deeds of Kindness)—who came before God and cried that with the dispersion of the Jewish people they would be forgotten.

"Not so," answered God. "I shall have the Jews build synagogues and they will attend services every *Shabbes*. The rabbi will teach them *Torah,* and the cantor will lead them in worship."

"But how will I be remembered?" asked Deeds of Kindness.

"Ah," said the Lord, "during the service, each Jew will turn toward his neighbor and offer his snuffbox, saying, 'Have a *shmek tabik!'"*

shmendrik
shmendrick

Pronounced SHMEN-*drik,* to rhyme with "Hendrick." From the name of a character in an operetta by Abraham Goldfaden.

1. A Caspar Milquetoast; a kind of *shlemiel*—but weak and thin. (That, at least, is how I visualize it.) A *shlemiel* can be physically impressive, but not a *shmendrik.* A *shmendrik* is small, short, weak, thin, a young *nebekh,* perhaps an apprentice *shlemiel.*
2. A pipsqueak; a no-account; the opposite of a *mentsh.* "That *shmendrik,* maybe he'll grow up to be a *mentsh.*"
3. Someone who can't succeed but thinks he can and persists in acting as though he might. "He has all the unrealistic hopes of a *shmendrik.*"
4. A boy or young man; someone "wet behind the ears." "That *shmendrik* can't be trusted with such responsibility."
5. A child (affectionately). "How's my little *shmendrik?*"
6. Penis (colloquially; rarely used by men. When used by a female, the intention is to deride by diminutizing).

A woman began to beat her *shmendrik* of a husband, who crawled under the bed.

"Come out!" she cried.

"No!" he said. "I'll show you who's boss in this house!"

shmo
schmo

Rhymes with "stow." A euphemistic neologism for *shmuck*.
This is not a Yiddish word, but an Ameridish invention.

1. A boob, a *shlemiel;* a hapless, clumsy, unlucky jerk.
2. A "butt," a fall guy, the goat of a joke.*

Al Capp,† the fertile intelligence who took L'il Abner down
several exuberant decades of hillbilly hijinks, adopted *shmo*
for the name of an egg-shaped creature that loves to be kicked and
gives milk; but *shmo* was in use long before that, as a drawing
room abbreviation for the lusty, but off-bounds, *shmuck*. Fred
Allen, on a radio program in 1947, protested: "I've been standing
here like a *shmo* for twenty minutes."

See shmuck.

---

*Shmo is also used to describe an average nobody, a man-in-the-street—"Joe
Shmo," like "Joe Blow," is a slightly more colorful way to say "John Doe."
Shmohawk takes *shmo* one step further into hipster slang and has gained
a new lease on life since the advent of the Mohawk punk hairstyle.

Shmo also serves duty as an acronym: State Hazard Mitigation Officers
(who anticipate and try to ameliorate the impact of natural disasters) are
known as SHMOs, as are Social Health Maintenance Organizations (which
combine nursing home and HMO services).

†Al Capp (born Alfred Gerald Caplin) died at age seventy in 1979, two years
after retiring from *Li'l Abner*, which he launched in 1934. At its peak, the strip
was read by more than sixty million people. The "shmo" character to whom
Rosten refers was actually named "Shmoo" (plural: *shmoon*), a highly benevolent life form "discovered" by Capp in 1948. Licensed Shmoo merchandise
sold wildly in the 1940s and early 1950s.

Stolinsky came out of the richest mansion in town and confided to his wife: "I tell you, Hinda, things aren't going too well in there!"

"*What?* I can't believe it! What makes you say a crazy thing like that?"

"I saw both of his daughters playing on one piano!"

He was a bit of a *shmo*.

shmooz [R]
shmues [Y]
shmuesn (infinitive verb)
shmooze, shmoos

Rhymes with "loose"; some pronounce it to rhyme with "ooze." Hebrew: *shmuos* (originally), "things heard"; (in time) "rumors," "idle talk," "news."

In Ameridish both a verb and noun, *shmooz* means a friendly, gossipy, prolonged, heart-to-heart talk—or to have such a talk. "They had a little *shmooz* and settled everything." "She *shmoozed* with her father until dinner." "How about a walk and a *shmooz*?" "There's nothing better, to get something off your chest, than a *shmooz* with a friend."

I have never encountered a word that conveys "heart-to-heart chitchat" as warmly as does *shmooz*.*

Gelett Burgess, who invented the word *blurb* and was the creator of the limerick about "the purple cow," once tried to smuggle

---

*In our cynical age, *shmooz* has also come to mean a more manipulative sort of banter—a kind of *shmeering* with beguiling words. "Don't try *shmoozing* me—no deal!" "I *shmoozed* her up until she was ready to believe anything."

"huzzlecoo," a word he coined, into English. "Huzzlecoo" never caught on; but it was a dead ringer for *shmooz*.

shmuck ᴿ
shmok ʸ

Rhymes with "stuck." From German, in some way or other, where *Schmuck* means "an ornament," "jewelry"; *schmuck* (adj.) means "neat," "smart," and *schmücken* (verb) means "to decorate." †

1. Obscene: Penis.

Never utter *shmuck* lightly or in polite company. Indeed, it was uneasiness about *shmuck* that led to the truncated euphemism *shmo*—and any *shmo* knows what *shmo* comes from.

Jews tend to be puritanical about public references to the pubic.

I never heard any elders, certainly not my father or mother, use *shmuck*, which was regarded as so vulgar as to be taboo. But vulgarity has its raison d'être.

2. Obscene: A dope, a jerk, a boob; a clumsy, bumbling fellow.

In this sense, *shmuck*, like its English equivalent, is widely used by males, and with gusto; few impolite words express comparable contempt. "What a *shmuck* I was to believe him!" "That *shmuck* fell for the stupidest trick you ever saw."

---

† Based on this derivation, one Yiddishist friend speculates that *shmuck* (and *putz*, derived, as Rosten notes, from the Germanic *putzen*, "to decorate") was probably coined by women as an affectionate slang word for "penis."

3. Obscene: A detestable fellow; a son of a bitch.

I suppose that in every language, the word for the male organ has been enlisted in the service of the contumelious.

NOTE: There is a Slovene word, *smok*, that also means a fool, an innocent, a gullible dolt—but I have it on the authority of Dr. Shlomo Noble of the YIVO Institute that *smok* came from *shmuck*, not the other way around.

Mr. Lefkowitz—sixty-five, a widower—was having a very lonely time in Miami Beach, and he observed a man of his age who was never without a companion; people forever streamed around him, extending invitations, swapping jokes. So Lefkowitz screwed up his courage, leaned over, and said to the popular paragon, "Mister, excuse me. What should I do to make friends?"

"Get—a camel," the other said with a sneer. "Ride up and down Collins Avenue every day, and before you know it, everyone in Miami will be asking, 'Who *is* that man?' and you'll have to hire a social secretary to handle all the invitations! Don't bother me again with such a foolish question."

So Mr. Lefkowitz bought a paper and looked through the ads, and by good fortune he read of a circus, stranded in Miami, that needed capital. Mr. Lefkowitz telephoned the circus owner and within half an hour had rented a camel.

The next morning, Mr. Lefkowitz, wearing khaki shorts and a pith helmet, mounted his camel and set forth on Collins Avenue. Everywhere people stopped, buzzed, gawked, pointed.

Every day for a week, Lefkowitz rode his trusty steed. One morning, just as he was about to get dressed, the telephone rang. "Mr. Lefkowitz! This is the parking lot! Your camel—it's gone! Stolen!"

At once, Mr. Lefkowitz phoned the police. A Sergeant O'Neill answered: "*What?* ... It sounded as though you said someone had stolen your camel."

"That's right!"

"Er—I'll fill out a form. .... How tall was the animal?"

"From the sidewalk to his back, where I sat, a good six feet."

"What color was it?"

"What color?" echoed Lefkowitz. "Camel color: a regular, camel-colored camel!"

"Male or female?"

"*Hanh?*"

"Was the animal male or female?"

"How am I supposed to know about the sex of a camel?" Lefkowitz exclaimed. "Wait! Aha! It was a male!"

"Are you sure?"

"Absolutely."

"But Mr. Lefkowitz, a moment ago you—"

"I'm *positive*, Officer, because I just remembered: Every time and every place I was riding on that camel, I could hear people yelling: 'Hey! Look at the *shmuck* on that camel!'"

shnaps
schnaps, schnapps

Rhymes with "tops." German: *Schnaps*, "intoxicating spirits."

1. Brandy.
2. Any intoxicating spirits.

Any holiday or happy event was the occasion for a little toast with *shnaps*. When I say little, I mean little. None of your long drinks. *Shnaps* was poured out in a jigger-size glass. No ice, no water, no club soda. A little drink, downed in a minute. Of course, the little glass could be refilled. . . .

The phrase used to introduce the toasting is "*Lomir makhn a shnaps*" (LAW-*mir* MAKH-*en a* SHNOPS): "Let us 'make' a *shnaps*."

Shnippishok

Pronounced SHNIP-*pi-shawk*.

Shnippishok was a Jewish suburb of Vilna, used as a name in jokes and proverbs—rather like Chelm or Hotzeplotz.

See Hotseplots.

Lupowitz returned to Warsaw, considerably miffed, and explained to the circle of listeners who crowded around him, eager to hear of his adventures: "And the most terrible thing of all happened in one town when a man came up to me and without a word or reason hit me a terrific *klop* on the head!"

"What?"

"No!"

"Imagine!"

"*Where* did that happen?"

"In *Shnippishok*," Lupowitz said.

"*Mn-yeh!*" scoffed a bystander. "*That* you call a town?"

shnook
shnuk, schnook

Pronounced to rhyme with "crook." Ameridish. Possibly from the German *Schnucke*, "a kind of small sheep," or

Schnucki, the German colloquialism for "pet," a pet dog, one's "darling," or wife; but I doubt it (see below).

1. A timid *shlemiel,* a meek patsy; a passive, unassertive, ineffectual type.
2. A Sad Sack, more to be pitied than despised. A *shnook* is pathetic but likable; if not likable, he would probably be called a *shmuck.*

Shnook is almost certainly an American-Yiddish coinage. None of my informants had ever heard it in any eastern Europe tongue, or in German, or in European Yiddish; and every person I questioned said he first heard it in America.

The word was disseminated via radio and vaudeville. Thus, Jack Benny on radio, October 9, 1951: "Don't be such an apologetic *shnook.*" (Quoted in *The Dictionary of American Slang,* Crowell, 1966.) In the movie *The Apartment,* the protagonist, played by Jack Lemmon, is characterized as "that *shnook.*"

Snuckl means a customer overcharged by a dishonest salesman, according to *The American Thesaurus of Slang* (Crowell, 1943).

shnorrer ᴿ
shnorer ʸ
shnorren ᴿ (infinitive verb)
shnorn ʸ
schnorrer

Pronounced SHNOR-*rer,* to rhyme with "snorer." German: *schnorren,* "to beg." Perhaps related to *schnarchen,* "to snore"; some energetic philologists relate the whining of beggars to snoring; but Jewish beggars do not whine—as you may read below.

As a Noun

1. A beggar, a panhandler, a moocher.
2. A cheapskate, a chiseler.
3. A bum, a drifter.
4. A compulsive bargain hunter and bargainer.
5. An impudent indigent.

As a Verb

Shnorren means to beg, to panhandle, to borrow.

Every Jewish community once had at least one *shnorrer* and often a platoon. The *shnorrer* was not a run-of-the-mill mendicant. He was no more an ordinary moocher than a *nudnik* is an ordinary bore, or a *mamzer* an ordinary child. The Jewish *shnorrer* was not apologetic; he did not fawn or whine. He regarded himself as a craftsman, a professional. He did not so much ask for alms as claim them. He expected recognition of his skill, if not encomiums for his character.

Shnorrers considered themselves respectable members of an occupational group. They were brash, cynical, quick to take offense, expert in needling prospective benefactors, and quick in repartee. Their *chutzpa* was of a rare and umbrageous order. They often baited their benefactors, haggled over the sum proffered, denounced those who underpaid or refused to cough up.

Many *shnorrers* considered they had a license from the Lord and were doing His bidding: after all, they were helping Jews discharge solemn obligations to help the poor and the unfortunate, through which noble acts a good Jew could actually accumulate *mitzvas!* Any man who served as agent for the acquisition of *mitzvas* was part of God's marvelous scheme for improving the human race.

Shnorrers seemed to know that they were both exploiting and assuaging one of the most powerful and pervasive psychological forces in the psyche of Jews everywhere: guilt. They were also expediting a symbolic and magical propitiation of fate: "I, thank God, am not a pauper. How small a coin may avert displeasure from the Compassionate One."

On the part of the Jewish community, *shnorrers* were somehow regarded as performing a social function. Exactly what this function was, I could never fathom, as a child; but everyone seemed to take it for granted—and took it for granted that no explanation was necessary. (Maybe *shnorrers* served this purpose: often excellent raconteurs, they circulated stories, jokes, and gossip.)

The *shnorrer* "recoiled from demeaning himself . . . from sheer arrogance and vanity. Since he was obliged to live by his wits," writes Nathan Ausubel (in *A Treasury of Jewish Folklore*, Crown, 1948), "he developed all the facile improvisations of an adventurer. . . . He would terrorize his prey by the sheer daring of his importunities, leaving him both speechless and wilted."

The *shnorrer* was no fool, please note, no simpleton. He often had read a good deal, could quote from the *Talmud*, and was quick on the verbal draw. *Shnorrers* were "regulars" in the synagogue and, between prayers, took part in long discussions of theology with their benefactors. The status points involved here are too delicate for Newtonian physics, or **Parsonian** sociology,* to handle. (Certain Hindu and Oriental groups recognize the beggar in the same way.)

*Named for Talcott Parsons, 1902–1979, a Harvard sociologist who founded "structural-functional" theory, which seeks to systematically classify the characteristics of societies.

Israel Zangwill's *The King of Schnorrers*, published in 1893, contains these memorable observations on London's breed: ". . . none exposed sores like the lazars of Italy or contortions like the cripples of Constantinople. Such crude methods are eschewed in the fine art of schnorring. A green shade might denote

weakness of sight, but the stone-blind man bore no braggart plac-
ard—his infirmity was an old established concern, well-known to
the public, and conferring upon the proprietor a definite status in
the community. He was no anonymous atom, such as drifts
blindly through Christendom, vagrant and apologetic. Rarest of all
sights, in this pageantry of Jewish pauperdom, was the hollow
trouser-leg or the empty sleeve, or the wooden limb fulfilling
either and pushing out a proclamatory peg."

There are enough stories about the hauteur of *shnorrers* to fill a
book ten times the size of this one. I cull but the skimpiest sample.

A *shnorrer* came to the back door on his biweekly rounds.

"I haven't a penny in the house," the *baleboste* said apologetically. "Come back tomorrow."

"Tomorrow?" said the *shnorrer* with a frown. "Lady, don't let it
happen again. I've lost a fortune, extending credit."

The blind man stood at the corner, jiggling his tin cup.

A woman stopped and dropped a quarter into the cup.

The blind man said, "God bless you. I knew you had a kind
heart the minute I laid eyes on you."

The pedestrian said to the *shnorrer:* "Give *you* a nickel? Why? Why
don't you go to work? You've got the arms and legs of a horse!"

"Ha!" cried the *shnorrer.* "For one lousy nickel, am I supposed
to cut off my limbs?"

Better strip a carcass of its hide than beg.
                                    —*Talmud, Pesakhim,* 113

Two *shnorrers* came before a wealthy man, and the first *shnorrer*
pointed to the second and announced, "Behold a man who is the

son of scholars, the grandson of saints, a scholar and a saint himself—and he is starving!"

The rich man handed the saintly *shnorrer* some money.

"And what about me?" asked the first *shnorrer*.

"You? Why should I give you anything?"

"Didn't *I* bring you this saintly scholar?"

A *shnorrer* knocked on the door of the rich man's house at six-thirty in the morning.

The rich man cried, "How dare you wake me up so early?"

"Listen," said the *shnorrer*, "I don't tell you how to run your business, so don't tell me how to run mine."

A *shnorrer* came to a rich man. "Don't think I came here to beg. I came to make a bet with you."

"You want to bet me? What about?"

"I'll bet you ten rubles I can get something that you cannot!"

The rich man, amused, put up the ten rubles. The *shnorrer* put them in his pocket. "I," said he, "can get a certificate showing I am a pauper."

The *shnorrer* stopped the *alrightnik* and asked for "maybe a quarter."

"I," said the *alrightnik*, "don't hand out money on the street!"

"So what should I do," asked the *shnorrer*, "open an office?"

shnoz
shnozzle
shnozl

Pronounced SHNOZ, to rhyme with "Pa's,"
and SHNOZ-z'l, to rhyme with "sozzle."
From German: *Schnauze,* "snout."
1. Slang: Nose.
2. A long, very large, or unattractive
nose.

shnozzola

Pronounced *shnoz*-ZOE-*la,* to rhyme with "Roz Ola."

The demotic embellishment of *shnozzle,* used mainly
by show business people to refer to the entertainer Jimmy
Durante.

In the Brown Derby Restaurant in Hollywood, where the walls
are crammed with amusing caricatures of that golden breed
known as "stars of stage and screen," the representation of Mr.
Durante occupies two separate frames—the second of which contains only the crowning end of the proboscis that the first is presumably too small to encompass.

shnuk
See shnook.

shnur
shnir

Pronounced SHNOOR, to rhyme with "spoor," or SHNEE-*er*, to rhyme with "keyer." From early High German.

Daughter-in-law.

"A good daughter makes a good daughter-in-law." (*"A gute tokhter iz a gute shnur."*) "One can talk to a daughter, but mean the daughter-in-law." (*"Tsu der tokhter ret men, ober di shnur meynt men."*)

Also: "Angry with the *shnur*, one yells at the daughter"—or vice versa.

Mrs. Botnick and Mrs. Krasnitz had not met in years. "Tell me," asked Mrs. Botnick, "what happened to your son?"

"My son—*oy*, what a misfortune!" wailed Mrs. Krasnitz. "He married a girl who doesn't lift a finger around the house. She can't cook, she can't sew a button on a shirt, all she does is sleep late. My poor boy brings her breakfast in bed, and all day long she stays there, loafing, reading, eating candy!"

"How terrible," said Mrs. Botnick. "And what about your daughter?"

"Ah, my daughter—such *mazel!*" Mrs. Krasnitz said, beaming. "She married a man, an angel! He won't let her set foot in the kitchen. He gives her a full-time maid, and a cook, and a laundress. And every morning he brings her breakfast in bed! And he makes her stay in bed all day, relaxing, reading, eating chocolate. . . ."

Et cetera.

shofar

Pronounced SHOW-*fer*, or SHOY-*fur*, to rhyme with "goiter,"
or SHAY-*fer*, like the name of the pen company. Hebrew
for "trumpet," "horn," and specifically a "ram's horn."

A ram's horn that is blown in the synagogue during
the High Holy Days of *Rosh Hashanah* and *Yom Kippur*.

The bend in the *shofar* is supposed to represent how a human
heart, in true repentance, bends before the Lord. (A conch
shell was also used centuries ago.) The ram's horn serves to
remind the pious how Abraham, offering his son, Isaac, in
sacrifice, was reprieved, when God decided that Abraham could
sacrifice a ram instead.

The person who blows the *shofar* blows blasts of different tim-
bre, some deep, some high, some quavering. The ritual is elaborate—and adds up to about one hundred *tkiyes* (Hebrew:
tekiot)—ritualized arrangements of *shofar* sounds.

See Rosh Hashanah.

Shofarim were often used in Palestine to announce holidays, to
signal danger or call for defense, as a war sign, to signalize a
peace, to usher in the new moon, to inaugurate a religious fast or
feast, to call together convocations, or as a regular watchman's
sound of reassurance.

In Israel today, the *shofar* is used on high official occasions. In
Orthodox neighborhoods, the *shofar* is sounded on Friday eve to
herald the Sabbath.

When Moses went up to Mount Sinai for the second time, a
great *shofar* sounded—to tell Israel never again to become idol-
aters.

The Bible enjoins the sounding of the *shofar* only for *Rosh
Hashanah* (Numbers 29:1) and nowhere describes the nature,

sequence, or meaning of the blasts. The rabbis developed complex rules—for instance, that the broken notes should resemble sobbing and that a long, unbroken note *(tekiah)* precede and follow broken notes of sobbing *(shevarim)* and wailing *(teruah)*.

Maimonides said that the shofar's message is this: "Awake, ye sleepers from your sleep; and ye that are in slumber, rouse yourselves. Consider your ways, remember God, turn unto Him" (Laws of Repentance, 3:4).

sholem
shalom
sholom

Shalom is Sephardic Hebrew, pronounced *sha-*LOHM; *sholem* is Ashkenazic Hebrew (Yiddish), pronounced SHO-*lem* or SHAW-*lem*. From the Hebrew root word meaning "whole," "entire"—"peace."

1. Peace.
2. Hello.
3. So long, au revoir, good-bye.

Why is *sholem* used for both "hello" and "good-bye"?

Israelis say: "Because we have so many problems that half the time we don't know whether we're coming or going."

The Israeli cabinet was discussing the endless and seemingly insoluble problems Israel confronted—even in a condition of *sholem*. Whereupon one member of the cabinet said, "I have an idea. Let's declare war on the United States!"

His colleagues looked at him incredulously. "Declare war on the United States? Israel? Are you *crazy*? A war like that would last half an hour!"

"Exactly," said the minister. "And the United States, having won, would do what it always does: rebuild the vanquished country, build roads, harbors, hospitals; lend money, give free aid, send food, remodel everything! What better fate for us than to be beaten by the United States?"

"But," said a cynic, "suppose we *win*?" *

sholem aleichem ^R
sholem aleykhem ^Y
sholom aleichem
aleichem sholem

Pronounced SHO-*lem* (or SHAW-*lem*) A-LAY-*khem*; deliver the *kh* as if clearing a bread crumb from the roof of your mouth. Hebrew: *shalom alekhem*, "peace unto you."

1. The traditional greeting or salutation of Jews; it is used for "Hello," "How do you do?," etc. The response to this greeting reverses the words; thus:

2. *"Aleichem sholem"* ("And unto you, peace") is the tra-

---

*This anecdote comprised the plot of a 1959 film starring Peter Sellers, *The Mouse That Roared*. The warmongering nation was not Israel, but an imaginary diminutive country. In fact, the United States supplies more foreign aid to Israel—over $3 billion per year—than to any other country. Since 1949, approximately $90 billion in U.S. foreign aid has gone to Israel, along with generous U.S. Defense Department funding of joint military ventures.

ditional response to *"Sholem aleichem"*; the exchange is uttered by Jews when parting as well as when meeting.

3. Ironically: "Finally we get to the heart of the matter!" "At long last!" "Hallelujah!" Thus:

    "Okay, I owe you ten dollars."

    "Sholem aleichem!"

4. The pen name of Sholom (Solomon) Rabinowitz (1859–1916), the immortal Jewish writer and humorist, often dubbed "the Jewish Mark Twain."

    It is said that when Mark Twain met Rabinowitz in New York, he said, "I am the American *Sholom Aleichem."* *

shoykhet [superscript Y]
shochet [superscript R]
shokhet

Pronounced SHOW-*khet* or SHOY-*khet* (Yiddish); render the *kh* as a MacTavish would. Rhymes respectively with "show bet" and "joy net." Hebrew: "ritual slaughterer."

The authorized slaughterer of animals, according to *kosher* requirements.

---

*Best known today for his novel *Tevye's Daughters*, from which *Fiddler on the Roof* was spun, Sholom Aleichem was by far the most beloved of the modern Yiddish writers and a master of wry humor and homey narration. "He conjures up the collective anxiety," writes one of his many translators, Ruth R. Wisse, "and then dispels it magically, laughing the danger away." At his funeral in 1916, more than one hundred thousand New Yorkers turned out for the procession. Manhattan's East 33rd Street between Fifth and Madison Avenues (where the Workmen's Circle is headquartered) was recently renamed "Sholom Aleichem Place."

The *shoykhet* was authorized by rabbis, and his work was supervised by them. A *shoykhet* had to be (1) thoroughly conversant with the many rules governing *kosher* food in the *Shulkan Arukh,* the code adopted in the sixteenth century; (2) physically healthy; (3) mentally able to undertake and execute his responsibilities; (4) of blameless character and repute.

A *shoykhet* served an apprenticeship before he could use his own initials in the branding iron used to signify approval of slaughtered animals.

shtchav^R
shtshav^Y
shchav

Pronounced *sh*-TCHOV to rhyme with "*sh*-RAHV," with the sibilant consonants, as in "fresh cheese." Polish: *szczaw,* "sorel."

1. Sorrel soup.
2. Sour-grass or cabbage soup made with chopped beets.

shtetl
shteytl

Pronounced SHTEH-*t'l,* to rhyme with "kettle," or SHTEI-*t'l,* to rhyme with "fatal." From German: *Stadt,* "a town." Plural: *shtetlakh.*

Little city, small town, village*—in particular, the Jewish communities of eastern Europe, where the culture of *Ashkenazim* flourished before World War II.

*"Village" has its own Yiddish word, *dorf.* A "hamlet" might be known as a *khuter.*

The *shtetl*, a term of special importance in the history of the Jews, evokes special meaning and memories. In many a *shtetl*, most of the inhabitants were Jews; in others, all were Jews. And it was in the *shtetlakh*—in Galicia, Poland, Lithuania, the Ukraine, Romania, Hungary, Bessarabia, Bohemia—that certain Jewish traditions and values were preserved and embellished until they achieved a character distinctly their own.

The *shtetl* was the incubator and fortress of Ashkenazic culture. The Jews of the *shtetl* were poor folk, fundamentalist in faith, often *Chasidim*, earthy, superstitious, stubbornly resisting secularism or change. They wrote in Hebrew (the elite) or, far more commonly, in Yiddish, shunning foreign tongues among themselves. They were dairymen, draymen, cobblers, tailors, butchers, fishmongers, shopkeepers, peddlers. They considered their exile temporary and dreamed of the messianic miracle that would—any day—return them, and their brethren around the world, to the shining glory of a restored Israel in the Holy Land.

We must remember that the Tsars had confined Jews to the "Pale of Settlement," twenty-five provinces of the Russian empire. To live outside, a Jew needed special permission from the authorities—and some skilled workers, professionals, and businesspeople did receive (or purchase, via bribery) such permission. But the vast majority of the Jews in the tsarist empire lived within a restricted area. They could not move without approval from the police. Entire local populations could be abruptly "resettled," forced out of their homes, with no more legality than the arbitrary impulse of an often besotted governor.

Jews were forbidden to own land. They were barred (with exceptions) from colleges and universities. They were barred from the humblest government jobs. They were not allowed to practice certain crafts, skills, and trades.

Inside the *shtetl*, life was so bound in, so shut off from the rest of Europe, so insulated from the magical world "beyond the Pale," that even the simplest amenities of city life seemed, in the words of Ruth Gay (*The Jews in America*, Basic Books, 1965), "as legendary as Babylon or Nineveh." Living in the *shtetl* was very hard. (In Galicia, some years, thousands literally starved to death.) Jews were spat upon, beaten, killed, their synagogues and cemeteries desecrated—either in "minor incidents" shrugged off by the authorities or in full-scale pogroms instigated by successive regimes. The hooliganism of drunken thugs and the ghastly bloodbaths by pious Cossacks were alike tolerated by government officials, witnessed by unprotesting Eastern Orthodox priests, openly abetted by the notoriously anti-Semitic police.

In the *shtetlakh*, the Jews produced their own people's culture, an independent style of life and thought, an original gallery of human types, fresh and rueful modes of humor, irony, lyricism, paradox—all unlike anything, I think, in history. There *Yiddishkayt* entered a golden age. According to Rabbi Abraham Joshua Heschel (in *The Earth Is the Lord's*, Abelard-Schuman, 1964):

> They apologized to no one, neither to philosophers nor theologians, nor did they ask the commendation of either prince or penman. They felt no need to compare themselves with anyone else, and they wasted no energy in refuting hostile opinions. There, in Eastern Europe, the Jewish people came into its own. . . . [They] lived without reservation and without disguise, outside their homes no less than within them. They drew their style from the homespun prose of Talmudic sayings rather than from the lofty rhetoric of the Prophets.

The world of the Jews in Germany, France, England, Holland, Italy, and Austria was vastly different from the world of *shtetl* Jews in eastern Europe. The world of the first was contemporary, the world of the second only contemporaneous. City Jews in eastern, as in western, Europe were caught up in political and libertarian movements; they were both workers and bourgeoisie; they became trade unionists, social democrats, socialists, revolutionaries. But the *shtetl* was another world . . . .*

The "Pale," established by Catherine II in 1791, ended, under severe economic and political pressures, during the First World War. The *shtetl* exists no more. Thousands of Jews left it for the factories of Odessa, Kiev, Warsaw, Lodz, Moscow, and Petrograd—and from there went on, out of unholy Russia, anywhere: to Germany, England, South America, the United States.

History will surely record the *shtetl* as a phenomenon worthy of remembrance. It was a world isolated from time, medieval in texture, living on the daily edge of fear. And it was a triumph of human endurance, a crucible from which flamed a brilliant and unexpected efflorescence of scholarship and literature.

The attitude of American Jews to the *shtetl* is torn by ambivalence. As Maurice Samuel has written (in *Little Did I Know,* Knopf, 1963):

> On the one hand [the *shtetl*] is remembered sentimentally . . . it sends up a nostalgic glow for its survivors and for those who have received the tradition from parents and grandparents. It

*To some extent, Rosten exaggerates and romanticizes the isolation and provincialism of the *shtetl*. The Jews of eastern Europe were a relatively literate people, with a lively press and an emergent Yiddish literature; some traveled for business purposes within the Pale of Settlement and observed the Jewish and non-Jewish worlds around them. Ultimately, the gulf between the larger cities and towns and the rural *shtetlakh* could not endure beyond the middle of the nineteenth century. As Lucy Dawidowicz notes in *The Golden Tradition* (Beacon Press, 1967), by the late 1800s the "proletarianization of the Jewish masses and their accelerated urbanization began to disrupt segments of traditionalist society where earlier modernist movements had not penetrated." Thus did Jewish Bundism, Zionism, and other social movements emerging from the *Haskala* (Enlightenment) find root, even in the *shtetl*, particularly among young people.

is pictured as one of the rare and happy breathing-spells of the Exile, the nearest thing to a home from home that the Jews have ever known. On the other hand, it is recalled with a grimace of distaste. The *shtetlakh!* Those forlorn little settlements in a vast and hostile wilderness, isolated alike from Jewish and non-Jewish centers of civilization, their tenure precarious, their structure ramshackle, their spirit squalid. Who would want to live in one of them? . . . [The *shtetl* offers] a pattern of the exalted and the ignominious.

The rabbi of a *shtetl* was seen talking to a pretty woman—in the public market! The elders summoned the rabbi and dressed him down for such a breach of decorum. When they finished, the rabbi sighed, "Well, my friends, I think it better to talk with a pretty woman, thinking of the Almighty's blessings, than to pray to the Almighty—while thinking of a pretty woman."

shteyger ^Y
shtayger ^Y
shteiger ^R

Pronounced SHTEY-*ger*, to rhyme with "bay girl," or SHTY-*ger*, to rhyme with "tiger." German: *Steiger*, "a climber."

Slant or style of life; ambience; mode of thought. "He may not go to a synagogue, but his whole *shteyger* is Jewish."

shtik
shtikl (diminutive)
shtikele^Y
shtikeleh^R (more diminutive)
shtiklekh (plural)
shtick

Pronounced SHTIK, to rhyme with "quick"; SHTIK'l, to rhyme with "pickle"; SHTI-k'l-leh, to rhyme with "piccolo" (with an "eh," not "o," at the end); and SHTIK-lekh, which rhymes with "wick loch" or "wick ech!" Just be sure to pronounce that final kh as a Scotsman would. German: Stück, "piece."

1. A piece. "Give him a *shtik* cake." (Never say a *shtik* "of" anything.)
2. A part, part of, bit of. "He is a *shtik nar* [fool]" means "He is a real fool."
3. A prank, a piece of clowning. "He made us laugh with his *shtik*." "You never saw a man with such *shtik* [or *shtiklekh*]."
4. A piece of misconduct. "In company, one should not perpetrate a *shtik* like that."
5. A devious trick; a bit of cheating. "How did you ever fall for a *shtik* like that?"
6. A studied, contrived, or characteristic piece of "business" employed by an actor or actress; overly used gestures, grimaces, or devices to steal attention. "Watch him use the same *shtik*." "The characterization would be better without all those *shtiklekh*." "Play it straight: no *shtiklekh*."

The last usage is spreading far beyond Broadway and Hollywood circles, where I first heard it.

Shtikl, the Diminutive of *Shtik*

1. A small piece. "She is a *shtikl* crazy." ("She is slightly 'off.'")
2. A bit of. "Oh, he is a *shtikl nar*." ("He is a bit of a fool.")

Shtiklele, a Further Diminutive of *Shtikl*

A really *small* little piece.

Shtiklekh

Plural of all the meanings cited above. *Shtiklekh und brek-lekh* ("pieces and crumbs") means "odds and ends."

A woman in a delicatessen saw some small pickles on the counter, under a sign *"Nosh."*

"How much costs today a pickle?" she asked.

"A pickle," said the man behind the counter, "is a nickel."

"A *nickel?* . . . So tell me: How much is this *shtikl?*"

"That *shtikl*—is a nickel."

"My God! . . . And this *pickele?*"

"That *pickele*," said the owner, "is a *nickele!*"

shtrayml ^Y
shtreimel ^R

Pronounced SHTRY-*m'l*, to rhyme with "primal." Derivation: unknown.

A black, broad-brimmed hat, trimmed with velvet or edged in fur, worn by religious Jewish men, especially in Galicia and Poland.

A bearded man with long *payess*, in a long, black caftan robe, wearing a high, wide-brimmed *shtrayml*, was often seen in Jewish neighborhoods in America in the earlier years of the century. Now, a *shtrayml* is worn only by the very Orthodox and by *Chasidim*.

Jews in various cultures also wore high hats, fur hats, hats of Persian lamb, silk turbans, and fezlike coverings.

shtunk

Pronounced with the short *u* of "put." From German: *stinken*, "to stink."

Vulgarism

1. A stinker, a nasty person.
2. A fool, a dope, a jerk, an unpleasant *shlemiel*.
3. An ungrateful, mean person. "What a *shtunk* he turned out to be!"
4. A scandalous mess. "He made a terrible *shtunk*." "It is such a *shtunk*, I don't know how to get out of it."
5. A slob or sloven.

shtup
shtupn (infinitive verb)
shtoop

Pronounced with the *u* of "put," not the *u* of "cup." Thus, *shtup* is pronounced like the first syllable of "Stuttgart," changing the *tt* to *p*, or like *putsch* pronounced backward.

1. To push, press, shove. "Don't *shtup*" means "Don't push"—both literally and figuratively—as in, don't be aggressive.

"*Shtup zikh nit vu men darf nit*" means "Don't push yourself into places where you shouldn't be."

A man who *shtups* himself in "*di hoykhe fenster*" ("the high windows") is a man who is a social climber.

CAUTION: *Shtup*, in vulgar vernacular, also means the following:

2. To fornicate *(shtupn)*. This usage is heard in American slang. "Did he *shtup* her?" "Does she or doesn't she *shtup*?"
3. The act of copulation. "He gave her a *shtup*."
4. A female who fornicates. "That one is a real *shtup* [or *shtupper*]."

shtus ^Y
shtuss ^R

Rhymes with "puss." Hebrew: "stupidity."
1. Nonsense. "What he says is just a lot of *shtus*."
2. A commotion. "Pipe down; don't make such a *shtus*."
3. A contretemps, a disturbance, a "rhubarb" caused by a complaint or protest. "She made such a *shtus* that they had to go to court."

   I heard this usage from a Radcliffe student.
   See also tsimes.

shul

Rhymes with "full"; sometimes edging toward "fool." From the Greek *schola*, via the German *Schule*. The Hebrew word for a house of prayer is *bet ha-knesset*, a house of assembly. Similarly, the Greek word *synagogue* means "assembly," "congregation."

Synagogue.

The *shul* was the center, the "courthouse square," the forum of Jewish communal life. Day and night men sat, read, prayed, studied, discoursed, debated in the synagogues—many of which never closed their doors. Some Jews spent more time in *shul* than at work.

Most of the study, be it noted, was in groups. "Learning is really achieved only in company" (*Berakhot* 63). Men would drift from group to group in the *shul*, between prayers, listening with one ear to catch a word from those reading aloud, reciting, or arguing. "They sang their studies," wrote Abraham Menes (in Louis Finkelstein's *The Jews: Their History, Culture and Religion*, Harper, 1960); "they sang them fervently and felt transported to a higher world. There was a certain enchantment to studying a page of the Talmud."

The synagogue seems to date from 586 B.C.E., when Nebuchadnezzar drove the Jews into exile. In Babylonia they sought to replace the great Temple of Jerusalem, which had been destroyed.* (A legend has it that some Jews preserved stones from the Temple, carried them into captivity, and used them in building a synagogue in the small town of Nehardea.)

---

*The Babylonian captivity, as the Jewish exile is known, was recalled by reggae pioneer Bob Marley in "By the Rivers of Babylon," a hit song based upon Psalm 137. See Rosten's entry for **Zion**.

The ruins of *shuls* dating back to the first few centuries C.E. have been unearthed in modern Israel, Italy, and other Mediterranean locations. The magnificent variety of synagogue architectures worldwide are modeled at Israel's Beth Hatefutsot museum.

The synagogue is never mentioned in the *Torah*;* it is often referred to in the New Testament. The early Catholics called a Jewish place of worship *schola Judaeorum*.

God Himself proceeds from synagogue to synagogue, says the *Talmud*, "and from *bet midrash* [house of study; Yiddish: *besmedresh*] to bet midrash . . . [to] give His blessings to Israel."

Before the Temple was destroyed, Jews worshiped *through* priests with animal sacrifices. In the synagogue, worshipers addressed God directly—and **individually**.†

In time it became a solemn obligation for Jews to build a *shul* as soon as a community contained ten males (a *minyan*). Synagogues were established, in time, all through Palestine, Babylonia, Arabia, Egypt, Persia, around the Crimea, Syria—in the cities of Greece, in Rome, and eventually in every country where Jews were taken, as slaves, or allowed to reside.

Philo, who was a rabbi and a Platonist, said it was the *schola* that made all Jews philosophers.

A visitor to a *shul* in a tiny village, whose inhabitants believed their *tzaddik* possessed miraculous powers, asked, "What miracle did

---

*Rules for *shul* construction and etiquette are widely discussed in the *Shulkhan Arukh*, the sixteenth-century standardization of Jewish law created by Joseph Karo and Moses Isserles: "The synagogue must be built on the high point of the city." "A person may not sleep in a synagogue—not even a short nap—though this is permitted in a *besmedresh* [study house]." "The customary way to honor synagogues is to sweep and mop their floors." "If a synagogue has two doors, a person may not go in one of them to make it a shortcut to the other." And a personal favorite: "If a house was built just as a house, and then afterwards it was dedicated as a synagogue . . . it is not considered holy until people have prayed in it." (Translations are by Danny Siegel in *Where Heaven and Earth Touch*, Jason Aronson, 1989).

†Numerous parts of the Jewish liturgy, however, require there to be a *minyan* present—a quorum of ten worshipers. See Rosten's entry, and my note, for **minyan**.

your *rebbe* perform recently?"

"Well, there are miracles and miracles. Would you think it a miracle if God did exactly what our *rebbe* asked?"

"I certainly would!"

"Well, here we think it a miracle that our rebbe does what God asks *him*."

shvartz^R (adjective)
shvarts^Y
shvartzer (masculine noun and adjective)
shvartze^Y (feminine noun and adjective)
shvartzeh^R

Pronounced to rhyme respectively with "darts," "Hartzer," "parts a." From German: schwarz, "black."

1. **Black.***
2. Unfortunate, unhappy, ill-starred. A common Yiddish curse goes: *"A shvartz yor oyf im!"* ("A black year may he have!")
3. Ominous, gloomy, boding no good. "It looks pretty *shvartz* to me."
4. Unskilled. "He's doing *shvartz* work."
5. Contraband, "black market" goods: *"Shvartze s'khoyre* [merchandise] was his downfall."

Shvartzer

1. As adjective, masculine: Black.

---

*Shvartz is occasionally used to mean "ultra-Orthodox" or "highly pious." The English equivalent is calling someone a "black hat," in reference to the clothing worn by *Chasidim*. See Rosten's entry for **Chasid** and **shtrayml**.

2. As noun: A Negro, a black man.

Shvartze
1. As adjective, feminine: Black.
2. As noun: Negress, a black woman.

Shvartzer and *shvartzeh,* to mean black man and woman, became "inside" words among Jews—cryptonyms for black servants, employees, customers, etc. After the growth of the civil rights movement, these uses **declined**.† Many Jews would not, for instance, approve of the retelling now of the following true, well-known, and (to me, at least) disarming story:

A Jewish matron dialed a number and asked, "Hello, Mrs. Weiss?" "No, ma'am," came a melodious voice. "This is the *shvartze.*"

shviger

Pronounced SHVI-*ger,* to rhyme with "trigger." From German: *Schwiegermutter,* "mother-in-law."
Mother-in-law.

---

† For years the debate raged among Jews whether the use of *shvartzer,* which is Yiddish for "black," was racist. In strictly lexigraphical terms, it is neutral—but its widespread usage as a "code word," usually disparaging or disrespectful, earned it an offensive connotation over time, particularly as used by English-speaking Jews. In an interview with *Billboard* magazine, Quincy Jones commented about how he broke the color line in the field of composing for Hollywood films: "It took me about ten years to figure out that *shvartzer* didn't mean 'arranger' or 'composer'—'Be cool, here comes the *shvartzer.*'"

Yiddish speakers use *neger* or *nyeger* (Negro) instead of *shvartzer.* To the American ear, however, *neger* uncomfortably resembles "nigger," so the problem persists.

The folk humor of Jews is as extensive and variegated as you will find in any culture on earth; but there are fewer stories about mothers-in-law, surprisingly, than one would expect. I have no idea why this is so; perhaps a Jewish husband is careful about poking fun at his *shviger* in front of his wife.

FOLK SAYING: "A daughter-in-law is always a bit of a mother-in-law."

Sholom Aleichem called Adam the luckiest man who ever lived—because he had no *shviger*.

Bessie Shatz had delivered triplets. Her *shviger* came to the hospital and said how unusual it was for a woman to have triplets. "No one on our side of the family *ever* had triplets!"

The new mother said, "My doctor told me it happens only once in a million times."

"My God, Bessie!" cried her *shviger*. "When did you have time to do the housework?"

shvitsbod ^Y
shvitzbud ^R
shvitzbad

Pronounced SHVITS-*bud*, to rhyme with "flits could," or SHVITZ-*bod*, to rhyme with "Fritz cod." German: *Schwitzbad*, "sweat bath."

Sweat bath—for instance, Turkish bath.

Men's bathhouses were a widespread and popular institution among the Jews in the old country; the Sabbath requires spotlessness of body and raiment, and few Jews could afford a bathing place of their own. (In some parts of Europe, Jews were not allowed to bathe in a stream, river, or lake—on the stern ground that the immersion of a Jew in such waters would pollute them for Christian use.)

When the Jews came to America, one of the first communal institutions they required was a *shvitsbod*.

"Turkish baths" were enormously popular on New York's Lower East Side.

See also mikve.

Mr. Toplinski was walking down Houston Street when he saw Mr. Sverdloff. "*Sholem aleichem,* Sverdloff," he said with a smile.

To which Sverdloff replied: "*Gey in drerd!*" ("Drop dead!")

Toplinski recoiled. "Sverdloff! I give you a polite hello and you answer, '*Gey in drerd!*' Why?"

Said Sverdloff, "I'll tell you why. Suppose I answer you politely, '*Aleichem sholem*'—so you ask me where I'm going. So I tell you to the Houston Street *shvitsbod*. So you say the Avenue A *shvitsbod* is better. So I tell you I don't like the Avenue A *shvitsbod*. So you tell me that a man who prefers the Houston Street *shvitsbod* to the Avenue A *shvitsbod* must have a hole in his head! So I holler that a man who chooses the Avenue A over the Houston Street is *meshuge!* So you call me a *shmuck!* So I holler, 'What? A *shmuck?!* Gey in drerd!'* Right? . . . Well, instead of going through that whole long *hoo-ha,* I answer right away, 'Drop dead,' and that ends it. *Aleichem sholem!*"

shvitser [Y]
shvitzer [R]

Pronounced SHVITS-*er*, to rhyme with "fits her." From German: *schwitzen*, "to sweat."
1. Literally: One who has overactive sweat glands.
2. A braggart, a person who blows his own horn, who shows off.

See plosher.

siddur [R]
sider [Y]

Pronounced SID-*der*, to rhyme with "kidder." Hebrew: "arrangement," "order."

The daily and Sabbath prayer book.

The *siddur* contains the three daily services, the Sabbath prayers, and (in some editions) the festival prayers, *Ethics of the Fathers (Pirkey Avos)*, and special readings.

The *siddur* as we now know it is based on a compilation of prayers made during the ninth century in an academy in Babylonia. Additions and emendations have since been inserted, and various communities have developed slightly different liturgies.

The first printed *siddur* appeared in 1486—just thirty years after the Gutenberg Bible. Its colophon reads: "Here is completed the sacred work for the special *minhag* [ritual] of the Holy Congregation of Rome, according to the order arranged by an expert." The Hebrew date given, 2 Iyar 5246, corresponds to April 7, 1486.

simcha[R]
simkhe[Y]

Pronounced sim-*kha*, with a true Scottish *kh*. Hebrew: "rejoicing."

1. A happy occasion, a celebration, a party. "Come over, we're celebrating a *simcha*—our son's graduation."
2. A great pleasure.
3. That which provides great pleasure. "May you have many more such *simchas*."

A rich brother told his poor brother, "Look, you have been living off me for three years now. Enough! Good-bye! Don't come back— except for a *simcha!*"

Off went the poor brother, and back he came in the morning, saying, "When you saw me leave, you must have felt a great *simcha*, no? I have come to share it."

The poor brother would have made a splendid *shnorrer*.

'Tis said that Hitler, disturbed by nightmares, called in a soothsayer.

The seer consulted a crystal ball and said, "Ah, mighty Führer, it is foretold that you will die on a Jewish holiday."

"Which one?" said Hitler with a scowl.

"Any day you die will be a Jewish holiday."

Simchas Torah[R]
Simkhes Toyre[Y]

Pronounced sim-*khess* toe-*rah*, or toy-*reh*, with a McGregorish *kh*. Hebrew: *Simkhat Torah*, "the day of rejoicing in the law."

A festival, observed on the ninth and final day of *Succos*, that honors the *Torah*.

*S*imchas Torah is a gay occasion, with feasting and dancing, to celebrate the yearly end and new beginning of the consecutive weekly readings of the *Torah* in the synagogue. On this day, the last chapters of Deuteronomy are read—and immediately after, the first chapter of Genesis is begun, to signal the continuing cycle of worship and show that the *Torah* has neither beginning nor end.

A learned member of the congregation is usually given the honor of reading the final verses of the *Torah*. He is called *khatan Torah* (Ashkenazic: *khosen toyre*), "the bridegroom of the *Torah*." And the man called to start the *Torah*-reading cycle anew is called *khatan bereshit* (Ashkenazic: *khosen breyshis*), "the bridegroom of Genesis." (Reform temples may honor a woman by letting her read from the Prophets; she is called, naturally, "the bride of the Scriptures.")*

*The traditional ceremonies that Rosten describes for *Simchas Torah* have been expanded in most non-Orthodox synagogues to invite the full participation of women congregants. Even in congregations that still practice gender separation during services, *Simchas Torah* is often the one time of the year when women are permitted to enter the men's section in order to have contact with the *Torah* scrolls as they circulate.

A contemporary innovation that is becoming popular during morning services on *Simchas Torah* is to unroll the entire *Torah* scroll so that it is held, from beginning to end, by all the congregants standing in a large circle. Rabbi Zalman Schachter-Shalomi urges that everyone in the circle then "read a section from where they are holding the parchment. This becomes their revelation for that year" (see Michael Strassfeld's *The Jewish Holidays: A Guide and Commentary*, Harper & Row, 1985).

For Soviet Jews, *Simchas Torah* became a particularly powerful symbol of resistance to anti-Semitism, anti-Zionism, and assimilation throughout the 1970s and 1980s. Thousands of Jews would "spontaneously" fill the streets outside major synagogues (most prominently in Moscow) and brave arrest in order to dance with the *Torah* and proclaim their Jewish identities.

The holy scrolls—adorned with silver breastplates and crowns—are removed from the synagogue's ark on the eve of *Simchas Torah,* and each male in the congregation takes a turn in conveying them around. By tradition, at least seven "turns" *(hakafot)* are made around the entire congregation. (Seven often partakes of the magical: God rested on the seventh day of making the world; the patriarchs of Israel were seven—if you include David.) During this ceremony, the congregation sings and the men honored by carrying the *Torah* scrolls "dance" with them. Chasidic congregations rise to a somewhat feverish exaltation during the celebration.

During *Simchas Torah,* children carry banners, join in the procession of the scrolls, and are rewarded with goodies. Children not yet of *b'nai mitzva* age gather around the *bema,* the platform or pulpit, and a prayer shawl is spread over their heads like a canopy; a passage from the *Torah* is read, and the rabbi blesses them as Jacob blessed his grandsons, Ephraim and Menasseh (Genesis 48:16).†

singlemon

Pronounced SING'l-mon, to rhyme with "single Khan." Yinglish, from the Lower East Side.

A man who is single—that is, not married.

A *singlemon* was highly prized, much propagandized, and widely courted, because of the intense feeling among Jews

---

† This special *aliyah,* called *ha-ne-arim* ("all the children"), is the only time in the year that pre–*bar* and *bas mitzva* children go up to the *bema* to recite the *Torah* blessings.

that everyone should marry. "He who is without a wife," says the *Talmud,* "dwells without blessing, life, joy, help, good, and peace."
See khosn, shadkhn.

skhus^Y
zchuss^R

Pronounced s'KHUSS. From Hebrew: "the legal right in possession."

1. Originally: A legal right by virtue of possession. An heir may claim a *skhus* in an estate.
2. A person's right to, or claim upon, reward for special deeds of *mitzvas.* "His *skhus* justifies such luck."
3. The special merit or consideration a person may acquire because of ancestry. "He may not be worthy, but he has the *skhus* of his ancestors." "Judge every man on the side of *skhus,*" says the *Talmud,* which means "Give a man the likelihood that he is right before condemning him"—that is, when judging, give the benefit of the doubt, with a kindly *skhus.*

A n excellent example of *skhus:*

As the rabbi walked home from the synagogue on *Tisha B'Av,* lost in sorrowful thoughts, he encountered a member of his congregation happily chewing away on a chicken.

The rabbi, shocked, exclaimed, "Have you forgotten that today is *Tisha B'Av?*"

"Not at all."

"Then you must be sick. I suppose the doctor forbade you to fast?"

"Oh, no, Rabbi. I'm not sick. I feel fine."

The rabbi promptly raised his eyes to Heaven: "O Lord, see how pious are Israel's children. This man would rather admit his sins than tell a falsehood!"

succah[R]
suke[Y]
sukkah

See Succos.

Succos[R]
Sukes[Y]
Sukkos, Sukkot, Succoth

Pronounced SUK-*kess*, to rhyme with "took us." Hebrew: *Sukkot*, "booths."

The Festival of Tabernacles, or the Feast of Booths.

This holiday starts the fifth day after *Yom Kippur,* the Day of Atonement, and is celebrated for eight days by the Orthodox, seven in Israel and among Reform Jews.* Throughout the week,

---

*"You shall dwell in huts seven days," says Leviticus 23:42, in defining the harvest festival of *Succos*. The "eighth day" that Rosten describes is *Shemini Atzeret*, the Eighth Day of Assembly, which the Talmudic rabbis described as a completely independent festival—though it was apparently established as an additional day following *Succos* on which pilgrims to Jerusalem could tarry in the holy city. The service for *Shemini Atzeret* includes a prayer for rain and *Yizkor*, the prayer memorializing the dead.

Shemini Atzeret immediately precedes *Simchas Torah* (see Rosten's entry and my note for **Simchas Torah**). The Jewish calendar therefore has virtually nonstop holiday observance from early to mid-autumn: *Rosh Hashanah, Yom Kippur, Succos, Shemini Atzeret,* and *Simchas Torah*. Combined in America with the back-to-school season, Halloween, and Thanksgiving, this can be a

an observing family eats its meals in a *succah,* or booth that is set up out of doors (the children love to help), roofed with branches (the stars must be visible from the inside), and decorated inside with flowers and fruit. The booth is intended to look temporary, or it represents the hastily-set-up dwellings Jews used in their forty years of wandering in the wilderness. In Leviticus 23:43 God says: ". . . your generations may know that I made the children of Israel to dwell in booths, when I brought them out of the land of Egypt."

Succos is a thanksgiving holiday, held at the time of the **full moon,**† when the crops had been harvested in ancient Palestine. God told Moses: "And thou shalt observe . . . the feast of ingathering at the year's end" (Exodus 34:22).

On the first two and final two days of *Succos,* special religious services are offered in the synagogue. The men carry a *lulav* (palm branch), combined with sprigs of myrtle and willow, and an *esrog* (ES-rogue), a fragrant citron. These "four species" represent particular virtues and characteristics of human beings.‡

Hoshanah Rabbah, "the great Hosanna," is observed on the

fairly overwhelming schedule; most minimally observant Jews tend to run out of energy after *Yom Kippur,* although many do build *succahs* of their own or visit a communal *succah* at their synagogue to take at least one meal under the open sky.

† *Pesach* (Passover), *Shevuos,* and *Succos* are all agriculturally linked festivals, reminders of the fact that the entirety of Jewish law and custom was developed within the context of an agricultural society. *Pesach* and *Succos* are also full-moon holidays (the Jewish calendar is a lunar calendar aligned with the solar year through the addition of seven lunar months during a nineteen-year cycle).

‡ The *lulav* is associated with the spine, the myrtle with the eye, the willow with the mouth, and the *esrog* with the heart. Louis Jacobs writes (in *The Jewish Religion, A Companion,* Oxford University Press, 1995) that "the *lulav,* which has taste (the dates) but no fragrance represents the Jew who has learning but few good deeds; the myrtle which has fragrance but no

(continued on page 558)

seventh day of *Succos* by a lengthy procession around the synagogue; the palm and willow branches are carried, and the entire congregation chants special verses in praise of God. The willow branches are beaten against the pulpit or platform, some say as a symbol of penitence. (By tradition, the fate of a Jew is sealed on *Hoshanah Rabbah* in, I suppose, a celestial Bureau of **Records**.)*

Philo considered the *succah* a democratic institution because all Jews, rich or poor, were asked to dwell in a primitive shelter. Equality of this sort, he reckoned, moved the concept out of theory into practice.

(continued from page 557)

taste the Jew who has good deeds ... but little learning; the willow the Jew with neither taste nor fragrance; and the *etrog* [*esrog*] the learned Jew rich also in good deeds. All four are combined to note that it takes all sorts to make a Jewish community. ..."

The *esrog* is strongly associated with female fertility; folkloric remedies for the pains of difficult childbirth involve use of this fruit. According to Jewish legend, an *esrog* may have been the forbidden fruit of the Garden of Eden. Ellen Frankel writes (in *The Encyclopedia of Jewish Symbols*, Jason Aronson, 1992) that the cabalistic tradition "regarded the *luluv* as a symbol of ... the sexual aspect of the Divine Spirit. Furthermore, the *lulav*, which is a phallic symbol, when joined with the *etrog*, a symbol of female generativity, represents sexual completion, a fitting symbol for the harvest festival of Sukkot [*Succos*]."

*The *Hoshanah* hymns recited on *Hoshanah Rabbah* ask for deliverance from famine and drought. Among environmentally conscious Jews, *Succos* has become a favored holiday because of its rich associations with the natural world, and the relatively obscure *Hoshanah Rabbah* ritual has been mobilized—notably by Rabbi Arthur Waskow, director of the Shalom Center in Philadelphia—as a means of protesting the pollution of rivers and waterways.

t

tachlis [R]
takhles [Y]

Pronounced TOKH-*liss*, to rhyme with "Bach Liss." From the Hebrew for "purpose," "end."

1. Achievement; that which amounts to something or establishes one's self. "If only that man would arrive at a little *tachlis*." "What *tachlis* will that produce?"
2. The point, heart, nub, or substance of the matter. "Let's talk *tachlis*" means "Let's get down to brass tacks." "What's the *tachlis*?" means "What are the real effects, the practical aspects?"

It is said that when they told Levi Yitzkhok, a famous rabbi, that one of his congregants, a man of seventy-four, had decided to become a Christian, the rabbi raised his eyes to Heaven and cried, "How loyal are Your People, O Lord! Imagine! For seventy-four years that man held fast!"

I would call Levi Yitzkhok a wizard in the discernment of *tachlis*.*

*The "Berditchever rebbe," Levi Yitzkhok (1740–1810), did indeed blend profound theology with a *tachlis* approach to leadership—but the anecdote that Rosten tells is only an elusive illustration of the *tachlis* of *tachlis*. For an in-depth meditation on the teachings of Levi Yitzkhok, see David R. Blumenthal's *God at the Center* (Harper & Row, 1988).

tallis ^R
tales^Y

Pronounced TAHLL-*iss*, to rhyme with "Hollis" or "solace."
Hebrew: *tallit*, "prayer shawl." The plural, *taleysim* (ta-LAY-sim), is Yiddish (Hebrew: *tallitot*).

Prayer shawl, used by males* at religious services.

An Orthodox bride gives her groom a *tallis*, just as his father gave him one on the occasion of his *bar mitzva*. Sometimes a *tallis* serves as a canopy during a marriage ceremony.

The Good Book tells Jewish males to wear a four-fringed garment (fringed, that is, at the corners). It serves to remind him of his bond and duty to God. At one time, the *tallis* was a gown or cloak; but because of public humiliations, the rabbis decreed it be used in the synagogue—or at home, during prayer services.

Chasidim and Orthodox Jews wear longer *taleysim;* Reform Jews wear shorter, less full ones.

Black or blue bands cross the prayer shawl—to memorialize the destruction of the Temple and mourn it forever.

A traditional Jew is buried in a shroud and with his *tallis*.

See also tsitsis.

An old rabbi, passing a door, heard a faint, faint crying from

---

*The 1986 Conservative *siddur*, *Siddur Sim Shalom*, included a prayer for putting on a *tallis* that used feminine Hebrew verb endings. This removed one of the last obstacles to women's use of the *tallis*, which today is accepted in non-Orthodox American Jewish communities. As designers and buyers of *taleysim*, women have helped to enrich the patterns, color schemes, and symbolism of the shawls themselves. Laurie Gross is a well-known contemporary fabric artist who uses the *tallis* as a motif. Another is Robert Gottlieb, who creates sculptural *taleysim* out of such materials as barbed wire, newspapers, and Israeli and Palestinian flags.

within—perhaps the muffled cry of a child. He knocked on the door. There was no answer—only that soft, sad wail. He knocked again; no one answered, so he tried the door. It was open. The rabbi entered. No one was in the front room, or in the second room, or in the kitchen—but the muffled weeping continued; and the rabbi, deeply alarmed, traced the cries to—a drawer in a bureau. He pulled it open as fast as he could.

In the drawer was nothing but a *tallis,* and to the rabbi's astonishment he heard the *tallis* sobbing.

"Little *tallis,* little *tallis,*" said the rabbi, "why are you crying?"

"Because my master," wept the *tallis,* "went off on a trip, and he took his wife and all of his children, and he left me here to cry alone."

"Ah, little *tallis,*" sighed the rabbi, "do not cry. One day soon your master will take you on a trip, only you, and leave all of them behind."

talmid khokhem^Y
talmid chachem^R

Pronounced TOL-*mid* KHAW-*khem* (both *kh*'s in the Scottish burr), to rhyme with "Sol would *'hoch!'* 'em." Hebrew: "student of a wise man." NOTE: *Talmid* should not be confused with *Talmud.* The plural of *khokhem* is *khokhamim.*

A learned scholar, an expert on *Talmud.*

The most honored figure in the life and culture of traditional Jewry was the *talmid khokhem.* He was the scholar of scholars, a sage, *and* a saint, one of the rare, entirely spiritual souls fit to be called "a disciple of the wise." He was one of those who might contribute to the vast, accumulated teachings and ruminations of savants that were known as "the sea of the *Talmud*."

The scholar was erudite, of course, but in addition he had to be immaculate in his clothes and person; indifferent to physical comforts and material rewards; gentle in manner; sensitive to others; quiet and humble (eyes ever downcast) in bearing; impeccable in conduct. He had to combine scholarship with compassion—and conspicuous rectitude.

Indeed, these virtues were assumed to go hand in hand, in the conviction that those who study are virtuous and that those who really know cannot do evil. A venal, vain, or salacious *talmid khokhem* was unthinkable—a contradiction in terms.

No formal agency, incidentally, could make a man a *talmid khokhem*. The title came via a slow accretion of recognition from his peers and colleagues. As a young scholar demonstrated greater and greater sagacity in his discussions—deeper insight, nobler humility—he began to be called a *khokhem*. By that time, of course, he would no longer be young.

The *talmid khokhem* remained a student throughout his life, be it noted; that is, he could not "finally" discover truth. The *khokhem* is forever a seeker, a student, an inquirer. He never reaches his goal: learning is endless.

The Jews exempted many a *talmid khokhem* from paying taxes (that is, Jewish communal taxes), not only because the *khokhamim* were notoriously poor, but because Jews wanted them to spend every moment in *Talmud* study. Who could foresee what benefits might accrue from their learning? The *Talmud* says, "*Talmidei khokhamim* strengthen peace in the world."

The *khokhem* studied *for* the community, as it were, and for its welfare. In return, the *Talmud* scholar was supported by the community—and by his wife, whom the community respected, because her labors enabled her husband to study without interruption.

An impudent—an *unbelievably* impudent—young Pole put both hands behind his back and challenged a rabbi in this way: "Your attention! I hold a little bird behind my back, in one of my hands. Guess which one! If you guess right, the bird will go free; but if you guess wrong, I'll smother it and its death will be on your head! . . . What does your precious *Talmud* tell Jews about a dilemma such as this?"

The *talmid khokhem* studied the young man dolorously, then sighed. "Our *Talmud* tells us that the awful choice between life and death—is in your hands."

PROVERB: "A table is not blessed if it has fed no scholars."

A famous rabbi was so wise, so great a logician, that he could answer any question his students put to him—even on the most difficult and involved points in the *Talmud*. His powers of reason seemed so great that one of his disciples cried: "Our rabbi can think his way through *any* dilemma!"

"Yes," said another, "it is true that our beloved rabbi has a mind of unparalleled powers—but I wonder what would happen if he were tired, drowsy, even a wee bit tipsy. Would his reason still prevail with all its splendor?"

And so the loving but curious acolytes decided to test the genius of their revered *talmid khokhem*. At the feast of *Succos* they gave him enough wine to make him tipsy, then, while he slept, carried him (reverently, to be sure) to the cemetery, where they laid him on the grass—and hid behind the tombstones, waiting to see what the rabbi would say when he opened his eyes and saw where he was. . . .

What he said is a triumph of Talmudic reasoning: "If I am living, then what am I doing here? . . . And if I am dead, why do I want to go to the bathroom?"

*The Jewish Publication Society's 1985 translation has it: "Good sense is a fountain of life to those who have it, And folly is the punishment of fools."

Understanding is a wellspring of life unto him that hath it; but the instruction of fools is folly.
—Proverbs 16:22.*

The great scholar, a true *talmid khokhem,* returned from lunch and repaired to his study—but could not find his glasses. He searched for them high and low, but they were nowhere to be found.

"What to do, what to do-o?" he asked himself in a singsong pattern. "This is a prob-lem, and to solve a prob-lem, one must employ reason. Very well. Hypothesis: 'May-be someone came in and stole my glasses while I was out?' N-no. Why not? Because *if* it was someone who needed glasses to read by, he would own his own; and if he *didn't* need glasses to read by, why would he steal mine? . . . Second hypothesis: 'Maybe a *thief* stole my glasses, not to use—but to sell!' Aha! But to whom can you sell a pair of reading glasses? If the thief offers them to someone who needs glasses, *that* man surely owns a pair already; and if the thief offers them to someone who *doesn't* use glasses, why should such a man buy them? No! . . . So, where does this take us? Clearly: 'The glasses must have been taken by somebody who needs glasses and has glasses, but cannot find them!' *Why* can't he find them? Perhaps he was so absorbed in his studies that, absentmindedly, he pushed his glasses up from his nose to his forehead, then, forgetting he had done so—took mine!"

The scholar hesitated. "I will even push the reasoning further!" he exclaimed. "Perhaps *I* am that man—the man who needs glasses, owns glasses, and moved his glasses up from his nose to his forehead and forgot that he had done so! If my reasoning is correct, that's where my spectacles ought to be right now!" He raised his hand to his forehead. His glasses were there, and he went back to his studies.

Talmud

Pronounced TOL-*mud*, to rhyme with "doll could." From Hebrew: *lamod*, "to study," or *lamade*, "to teach."

The *Talmud*. It is not the Bible. It is not the Old Testament. It is not "a" book. It is meant not to be read, but to be studied.

The *Talmud* is a massive and monumental compendium of sixty-three books: the learned debates, dialogues, conclusions, commentaries, commentaries upon commentaries, commentaries upon commentaries *upon* commentaries, of the scholars who for over a thousand years interpreted the *Torah* (the first five books in the Bible, also known as the Five Books of Moses) and applied its teachings to problems of law, ethics, ceremony, and traditions.

Ezra and Nehemiah (fifth century B.C.E.) established the canon of the *Torah*, the Five Books of Moses. This virtually sealed the contents against change. They initiated the custom of having an interpreter present to explain complex passages whenever the *Torah* was publicly read aloud. Since it became increasingly

difficult to interpret ancient injunctions so that they seemed relevant to contemporary problems, the interpreters began to stray
from the text, offering more pertinent or imaginative interpretations; so was born an exegesis, a "science" of analysis and interpretation called *midrash* ("exposition") and what was to become
the *Talmud.*

The first division of the *Talmud* is the *Mishnah* (from the
Hebrew *shano,* "to study," "to teach"), a collection of interpretations
of the biblical laws as they were applied to social conditions in
Palestine between the fifth century before, and the second century
of, the Common Era. (See my entry for Mishnah.) These laws,
which included court decisions, opinions, regulations, ethical teachings, etc., were transmitted orally; the *Mishnah* is therefore known
as the "Oral Law," as distinct from the "Written Law" of the *Torah.*

The *Mishnah* began, apparently independently, in both
Palestine and Babylonia. The Pharisees held *Mishnah* to be an
exalted effort to probe into and reveal God's meaning, but this was
opposed by many Saducees, who held a fundamentalist position:
The sacred text of Scripture was self-revealing and unalterable;
interpretation was not needed and, indeed, verged on blasphemy.

Whatever each faction hoped for, the masses took to *Mishnah*
with enthusiasm, for now any ordinary Jew could read the holy
books and discuss and question the sages' interpretations. New
exegetes rose from the ranks of common people; their occupations
were no bar to the once priestly privilege and monopoly of interpreting the holy books. And since the rabbis foresaw the energy
and growth that *Mishnah* would acquire, and feared that it might
in time replace—or, at least, compete with—the *Torah,* they
decreed that no one was allowed to write down any *Mishnah;* this
meant that *Mishnah* had to be memorized and could be passed on
only orally. Hence, *Mishnah* became known as "Oral Law."

But being sensible men no less than scholars, the rabbis knew that the Oral Laws would surely be changed and misinterpreted unless *some* written document served as authority; so they secretly made abbreviated notations! (These notes also helped them in the onerous task of memorizing the *Mishnah* word for word.) Little by little, the task of codifying the *Mishnah* was undertaken. Akiba (or Akiva), who died around 135 C.E., the greatest scholar of his time, to whom thousands upon thousands of students flocked, perfected his own method of biblical exegesis and collected the Oral Law, which he classified by subject matter. This great work was used by Judah ha-Nasi (the Prince), the head of the *Sanhedrin* (a great council of rabbis, sages, and scribes; a Supreme Court, so to speak), who completed the work in about 200 C.E.

The six sections containing sixty-three tractates are written in Hebrew.

The second division of the *Talmud* is known as the *Gemara* (from the Aramaic "to learn"), the vast compendium of commentaries upon the *Mishnah*. The language of the *Gemara* is Aramaic but contains a great deal of Hebrew. (See my entry for Gemara.)

The continuing colloquium that resulted in the *Gemara* took place in the great academies of Palestine and Babylonia from the second to the fifth centuries, when the *Talmud* was edited and assembled. (The first time *"Talmud"* was used as a written name for the burgeoning body of knowledge that began as far back as the fifth century B.C.E. seems to have been 1,100 years later—in the sixth century C.E.)

The Palestinian and the Babylonian academies produced separated *Talmuds*: the *Talmud Yerushalmi*, which was redacted around the fifth century; and the *Talmud Babli*, about a century later. NOTE: When we speak of the *Talmud* today, we generally refer to the Babylonian *Talmud*, because it had a much greater influence on Jewish law and life. (Besides, the Jerusalem text was not preserved in toto.)

The legal parts of the *Talmud* are called the *Halakha*. The elements that are ethical, poetic, allegorical, and anecdotal are known as *Agada*.*

The *Talmud* embraces everything from theology to contracts, cosmology to cosmetics, jurisprudence to etiquette, criminal law to diet, delusions, and drinking. It is a reservoir of rabbinical thought on every then-known subject under the sun—and moon. It roams from exegesis to aesthetics. It is crammed with anecdotes, aphorisms, thumbnail biographies, philosophical treatises, and tiresome hair-splittings. It touches upon medicine, agriculture, geography, history, astronomy.

It is majestic (and pedantic); brilliant (and dreary); insightful (and trivial); awesome—and maddeningly obscure, superstitious, and casuistic. Sophistry runs rife, abracadabras abound, and profundity often ends in mythology, astrology, numerology, and quaint nonsense: wrestlings with the Devil and his demons, revelations from shining angels and celestial messengers, mystical miasmas beyond measuring. Like Catholic scholastics, the Talmudists spend a good deal of time and intellect in dialectical taffy pulls.

The *Talmud* is not dogma. Judaism has few (the *Mishnah* has a few dogmas). The *Talmud* is not a catechism. It is a long, involved explication of a text, the *Torah*, and the commentaries on that text. It illustrates the *ways* in which biblical passages can be interpreted, argued over, and reinterpreted. For over the sprawling terrain of the *Talmud*, disagreements rage, views clash, arguments

---

*"*Halakha* wears a frown, *Agada* a smile," wrote the great Hebrew poet Hayim Nahman Bialik. "The one is pedantic, severe, unbending—all justice; the other is accommodating, lenient, pliable—all mercy. . . . *Halakha* is the crystallization, the ultimate and inevitable quintessence, of *Agada*; *Agada* is the *content* of *Halakha*." For more about Bialik's work at making *Agada* accessible, see my note to Rosten's entry for **Haggadah**.

are marshaled, advanced, withdrawn. (The effect on the young Jews who studied *Talmud* was to encourage questioning, arguing, refinements of distinction and analysis.)

Rabbinical law, by the way, is very far from being unitary or consistent; opposing views and heated—even rancorous—disagreement are set forth in the *Talmud*'s pages. The rabbis taught that "both these [words] and these [words] are the words of the living God."

For over two centuries rival schools in Jerusalem, one loyal to Hillel, the other to Shammai, wrangled and debated on religious and juridical matters, on ethics, morality, custom, observance. No fewer than 316 of these debates are preserved in the *Talmud*. Shammai was a "conservative," a strict textual adherent, a legalist. Hillel was a "liberal," a philosopher-humanist. Shammai stressed a position somewhat similar to what we would call "strict Constitutionalism"; Hillel was concerned less with "property rights" than "human rights." Hillel's disciples nearly always win the arguments—because the Hillelites were always forbearing and humble, presenting even the argument of their opponents with exemplary deference.

It was the *Talmud*—commonly read, commonly studied, a monumental body of thought and faith—that held together a people spread and dispersed throughout Europe, North Africa, the Middle East. The *Talmud* made them one intellectual commonwealth, with a common language, a common code of laws, morals, ethics, and obligations. Traditional Jews live not by biblical law, but by the rabbinical teachings and decisions based thereon.

In the eighth century, an antirabbinical movement known as *Karaism*, created by Anan, held that only the *Torah* and the words of the Prophets were valid for Israel. The Karaites attacked the Oral Law and the *Talmud* as a mare's nest of absurdities and pipe dreams. The most important Karaite leader was Benjamin ben Moses Nahavendi, who wrote the first systematic exposition of the Karaite position.

The supporters of the *Talmud* waged polemical battle against Karaism, under the leading Talmudist of his time, Saadia Gaon (892–942).*

The *Talmud* was also not recognized by sects such as the *Falashas*. These are dark-skinned Jews in Ethiopia north of Lake Tana. Probably descended from converts to Judaism, they claim to be direct descendants of the ten tribes ejected from Palestine. Romantic commentators think them descended from Solomon's son—by the queen of Sheba.

The Falashas know no Hebrew. They know only the Old Testament (in Geez), and nothing of *Talmud*. They regard Moses' story as meant explicitly for them. Very strict in morals and literal in observance, they fast every Monday and Thursday, at every new moon, and on Passover. They worship in synagogues and observe the laws of the Sabbath.†

---

*The Karaite sect remains alive today, with some 25,000 Karaites in Israel, 3,000 in Poland and the former Soviet Union, and 1,200 in the United States, mostly in San Francisco, which has the only active Karaite synagogue in North America. The great majority of Karaites are of Egyptian-Jewish extraction. Most striking about their tradition is their fixing of Jewish holidays strictly according to the cycles of the moon, as dictated in the *Torah*. Karaite observance of Jewish holidays therefore "floats" through the year and can diverge widely from the mainstream Jewish calendar.

† Nearly all of the Falasha population was airlifted to Israel during the 1980s. Rabbi Joseph Telushkin notes (in *Jewish Literacy*, William Morrow, 1991) that "the Ethiopian Jews' ignorance of Talmudic Judaism caused many Orthodox rabbis to question their Jewishness. If the Ethiopians were to be considered age-old Jews, it challenges a basic tenet of Orthodoxy: that the Oral Law of the Talmud dates back to the time of Moses." Therefore, when Israel's Sephardic chief rabbi, Ovadia Yosef, ruled in 1973 that the Ethiopians were to be regarded as Jews, many Ashkenazic rabbis opposed the decision. Never-

You would be surprised by the number of aphorisms now widespread that are found, in one form or another, in the *Talmud*.

"Give every man the benefit of the doubt."

"The ignorant cannot be pious."

"Look at the contents, not at the bottle."

"One good deed leads to another."

"Don't threaten the child: either punish or forgive him."

"Begin a lesson with a humorous illustration."

"Bad neighbors count a man's income, but not his expenses."

"Judge a man not by the words of his mother, but from the comments of his neighbors."

"When in a city—follow its customs."

"All is well that ends well." And it certainly is.

The role the *Talmud* has played in the economic life of the West has been sparsely cited by historians. True, Werner Sombart attributes much of the beginnings of capitalism itself to Europe's Jews, and W. E. H. Lecky stresses the part Jews played in organizing and injecting life into trade among nations. Other historians remark upon the part Jews played in devising a money system, a credit system, a sense of investment and capital accumulation, the idea of legitimate interest rates as against "usury," and so on.

The *Talmud* was of immense economic value to Jews. Along with its application of dialectics to *Torah,* the *Talmud* laid down

theless, Telushkin continues, "That the Ethiopians had always been Jews seems very likely, since throughout their history the community had preserved seven words in Hebrew, one of them *goy.* That in the remote villages of Ethiopia, this group divided the world into two camps, themselves and the *goyim* (the other nations), seems to be convincing proof of their Jewishness." For more historical and contemporary information about Ethiopian Jewry, see my note to Rosten's entries for **mishpokhe** and **oy.**

abiding (and remarkably intelligent) rules about property, commerce, contracts, insurance, real estate, trade, governance, equity, torts—and international law! Back in 1200 C.E., Maimonides wrote that economic life, to grow, required that money be used by being lent—and that interest, far from being usurious and wicked, served a crucial and salutary function.

The activity of "moneylending," so hated by Christian theologians (though not by kings and popes, who enlisted the aid of Jews to finance the building of cathedrals), was a sine qua non of economic growth in medieval times. But the laws governing interest and finance were as startling as they were ill advised. Roman law held that a debt was personal, that a note could not be transferred. In Germany, a man who owed money was obliged to pay it only to the original lender—hence, debts died when a creditor died. Even in enlightened England, up to the middle of the nineteenth century (!), some debts were not transferable. But the *Talmud* says a debt must be honored even if a creditor or debtor dies. The Talmudists understood the concept of the negotiable.

Christian Church fathers made the economically catastrophic error of considering any form of banking usurious, no matter how proper or modest the interest rate charged. (The *Talmud*, incidentally, forbids Jews to take "excessive" interest; the rabbis determined "proper" rates.) To buy tools, seed, or livestock, to recover from a drought, to pay taxes, to tide a man over a disastrous season or harvest, accident or disease—for any of these, loans were imperative. And for these, the kings and barons, and the clergy, too, went to the Jews. The church considered it a sin to lend money for a fee; but since Jews were not part of the Christian community and were doomed to perdition anyway, let the Jews take on one more sin.

Students of economics will not be surprised to learn that, almost invariably, when Jews were forced out of banking, investment, and moneylending activities, to be replaced by Christians (who persuaded the authorities to push the Jews out), interest rates rose.

Several popes denounced Christian moneylenders for their "heartless" rates, and Dante put them into the deepest abyss of his Inferno.

Seventeenth-century English monarchs earnestly asked Jews to lend money—so as to undercut the high interest rates being charged by Christians. (William of Orange even knighted Solomon Medina, a Jewish banker.) William Pitt also enlisted the aid of Jews against English bankers whose interest rates were strangling the treasury's efforts to raise money.

Goebbels, the Nazi minister of propaganda, came to an elderly rabbi and said, "Jew! I have heard that you Jews employ a special form of reasoning, called Talmudic, which explains your cleverness. I want you to teach it to me."

"Ahh, Herr Goebbels," the old rabbi said with a sigh. "I fear you are a little old for that."

"Nonsense! Why?"

"Well, when a Jewish boy wishes to study *Talmud*, we first give him an examination. It consists of three questions. Those lads who answer the questions correctly are admitted to the study of the *Talmud*; those who can't, are not."

"Excellent," said Goebbels. "Give me the exam!"

The old rabbi shrugged. "Very well. The first question: Two men fall down a chimney. One emerges filthy, covered with soot; the other emerges clean. Which one of them washes?"

Goebbels scoffed, "The dirty one, of course!"

"Wrong. The clean one."

"The *clean* one washes?" asked Goebbels in astonishment. "Why?"

"Because as soon as the two men emerge from the chimney, they look at each other, no? The dirty one, looking at the clean one, says to himself, 'Remarkable—to fall down a chimney and come out clean!' But the clean one, looking at the dirty one, says to himself, 'We certainly got *filthy* coming down that chimney, and I'll wash up at once.' So it is the clean one who washes, not the dirty one."

"Ah," Goebbels said with a nod. "Very clever! Let's have the second question."

"The second question," the rabbi said, "is this: Two men fall down a chimney. One emerges filthy, covered with soot; the other emerges clean. Which—"

"That's the same question!" exclaimed Goebbels.

"No, no, Herr Goebbels, excuse me. This is a different question."

"Very well. You won't fool me, Jew. The one who's *clean* washes!"

"Wrong," sighed the elder.

"But you just told me—"

"That was an entirely different problem, Herr Goebbels. In this one, the *dirty* man washes—because, as before, the two men look at each other. The one who is clean looks at the dirty one and says, 'My! How dirty *I* must be!' But he looks at his hands and he sees that he is *not* dirty. The dirty man, on the other hand, looks at the clean one and says, 'Can it be? To fall down a chimney and emerge so clean? Am *I* clean?' So he looks at his hands and sees that *he* is filthy; so he, the dirty one, washes, naturally."

Goebbels nodded. "Clever, Jew; very clever. Now, the third question?"

"Ah, the third question," said the rabbi, "is the most difficult of all. Two men fall down a chimney. One emerges clean, the other—"

"But that's the same question!"

"No, Herr Goebbels. The *words* may be the same, but the problem is an entirely new one."

'The dirty one washes!" exclaimed Goebbels.

"Wrong."

"The clean one!"

"Wrong."

"Then what *is* the answer?" Goebbels shouted.

"The answer," said the rabbi, "is that this is a silly examination. *How* can two men fall down the same chimney and one emerge dirty and the other clean? Anyone who can't see that will never be able to understand *Talmud*."*

In the *Talmud (Sanhedrin 4)* the question is raised: Why did God create only one Adam? Why did he not create an entire race?

*Rosten lightly uses Goebbels as an enemy patsy in this Talmudic story. In reality, anti-Semitic powers, in particular Catholic Church officials, burned the *Talmud* more than a dozen times during the medieval period, in hopes of cutting off the Jewish community from its heritage to leave it more vulnerable to conversion. These burnings occurred before the era of the printing press. Several Jewish communities would be dependent upon a single, *handwritten* copy of the multivolumed *Talmud*, and the loss of each was incalculable. Usually the burning would be preceded by a "disputation," in which Jewish sages would be forced into debating theology with church officials and vainly defending the Jewish community from anti-Semitic slanders. Because of the wide-ranging, uncensored nature of Talmudic discussion, these slanders might often be rooted in passages of the *Talmud* itself.

The *Talmud* is written in a cryptic, abbreviated style. In the eleventh century, the great French sage Rashi (Rabbi Sholo Ben Isaac, 1040–1105) created a running commentary on the *Talmud* that explicated and summed up its debates. This commentary became a part of the Talmudic text itself. In 1935, the Soncino Press of London published an English, word-for-word translation of the *Talmud*. In our own time, Rabbi Adin Steinsaltz translated the *Talmud* into modern Hebrew, with summary and commentary, and is proceeding to translate this monumental work into English (published by Random House), providing true access to the "Sea of *Talmud*" for modern English readers.

The discussion reaches several conclusions:

1. God created only one Adam because He wanted to show human beings that any one person is an entire world. Therefore, whoever kills a person is as guilty as if he had killed all people. And whoever saves one person's life is as noble as if he had saved all people's lives.

2. God created only one Adam to prevent people from feeling superior to one another or boasting of their ancestry. For if God had created many Adams, you may be sure some people would say, "My Adam was more distinguished than yours."

3. God thought that if He created more than one Adam, pagans would think there was more than one God. So God created only one human to show His unity.

4. God wanted to show people the beauty of diversity, for even though all people come from one Adam, no two are ever exactly alike. Therefore, every person must respect his or her uniqueness and integrity; and every person must, in effect, say: "The Lord created the world in me and for me; let me not impair my immortality for some trifling reason or foolish passion."

Talmud Torah[R]
Talmetoyre[Y]

Pronounced TOL-*m'd* TOY-*reh,* or TOE-*reh,* to rhyme with "doll mid Moira" or "doll mid Nora," or "doll mid Roma."

A Hebrew school (in America).

The *Talmud Torah* in the United States offered a two-hour Hebrew session after the public schools closed each day, and classes all Sunday morning. Many Jewish children thus spent ten to fifteen hours a week in schooling in addition to their public school attendance.

Talmud Torah schools have declined in number, partly because many of their activities were absorbed into the educational departments of **synagogues.****

*For more on Jewish education, see Rosten's entry and my note for **melamed**.

A little boy came home from the *Talmud Torah.* "What did you learn today?" asked his father.

"Oh, the teacher told us the story about General Moses, how General Moses was leading all the Jews out of Egypt, with General Pharaoh's Egyptians hot on their trail. And there was the Red Sea in front of Moses, so he dropped an atomic bomb! Bang! So the waters parted, the Jews got across, and the Egyptians were all drowned."

"Is *that* what he told you?" gasped the father.

The boy shrugged. "Nope, but if I told it to you the way he did, Pop, you'd never believe it."

tarrarom[R]
tareram[Y]
terrarom

Pronounced *teh-reh-*ROM, like "betta bomb," or *tuh-ruh-*BOM, like "but-a-bomb." Roll the *rr.*

An onomatopoetic word, meaning a "to-do," a "hulla-baloo," "a big fuss," "a big stink."

To "make a *tarrarom*" is to create a ruckus.

tate^Y
tata^R
tatte, tateh
tatele (diminutive)
tateleh

Pronounced TAH-*teh,* to rhyme with "not a," or TOT-*teh-leh*
to rhyme with "not a la." From a widespread root, found
in Semitic as well as Indo-European languages.

Dad; papa.

*T*ate is the affectionate, informal way of addressing one's
father. Jews say *tate* much more often than *futter* (father).
One's parents are often called *tate-mame,* not *elteren* (parents).

The phrase *"Oy, tate!"* or *"Oy, tate ziser!"* ("sweet father") is
often used as an evocative exclamation, as, in English, "Man oh
man!"

Interestingly enough, when one inquires of another in
Yiddish: "How is your father [or mother]?" one says, "How is *the*
father [or mother]?" So *der tate* or *di mame* can mean "the [your]
father" and "the [your] mother."

Tatele is the diminutive—often used to address a little boy (as
bobele or *mamele* is, for a little girl).

This is a carryover, no doubt, from the time when stratagems
to evade the evil eye involved magical words—in this case, loudly
attributing more years to a child, to ward off child-hating demons.

FOLK SAYINGS:

"When a father helps a son, both smile; when a son must help
a father, both cry."

"One father can support ten children, but ten children don't
seem to be enough to support one father."

Taytsh-Khumesh[Y]
Teitsh-Chumash [R]
Taytsh-Chumash, Taytsh-Chumesh,
Teitch-Chumesh

Pronounced TYTCH KHU-*mish*. Hebrew: *chumash*, "the first five books of the Bible" (the Pentateuch); *taytsh* or *teutsch* is a Yiddishization of the old German word for *Deutsch*, "German." *Taytsh*, which means "interpretation," is used loosely to mean "translation."

The popular name for the translation into Yiddish of the Five Books of Moses (in condensed form), plus selections from the writings of the Prophets, weekly prayers, the books of Ecclesiastes, Esther, Ruth, Lamentations, and the Song of Songs.

A t the beginning of the sixteenth century, translations of the Pentateuch were made to help the teachers of elementary Hebrew (the *melamdim*); these, in turn, paved the way for translations into Yiddish meant for women (Jewish girls were not usually taught Hebrew) and for all people who did not understand Hebrew.

The first popular morality book of which we know is the *Sefer Mides* (MID-*ess*, *Book on Behavior*), published in 1542. The *Brantshpigl (Burning Mirror)*, published in Basel in 1602, was aimed directly at female readers. *Lev Tov (The Good Heart)*, 1620, was deeply religious and appealed to both men and women.

One Isaac Yanover in the sixteenth century wrote the unpretentious "home book" that became immensely popular in eastern and central Europe: the *Taytsh-Khomesh*, a charming, informal array of material from Bible and *Talmud*, of course, and from the colorful reservoir of Jewish history, folklore, humor, allegories, superstitions, and legends. In its pages, the women of Israel found their devotional and instructional guide, their ethical counselor, their household reference work on every conceivable problem— from dress and dancing to prayer and proper behavior.

The *Taytsh-Khumesh* was even translated into Latin, in the mid-sixteenth century; I cannot guess why.

For more on Yiddish religious literature, see mameloshn.

tayvl^Y
teivel^R
teuvel, teufel

Pronounced TY-*v'l*, to rhyme with "rival." German: *Teufel*, "devil."

1. A devil.
2. The Devil.

A common Jewish curse is *"A tayvl zol im khopn"*—"May a devil catch him!"

tchotchke

See tsatske.

tefillin^R
tfiln^Y
t'fillin

Pronounced *te*-FILL-*in*, to rhyme with "a'willin'." Hebrew: *tefillah*, prayer.

Phylacteries.

*T*efillin are two long, thin leather straps—with a two- or three-inch square leather box on each. The boxes contain tiny parchments on which are inscribed, in Hebrew, four passages from Exodus and Deuteronomy. *Tefillin* are worn during morning prayers by Orthodox males past the age of *bar mitzva.**

The custom of donning *tefillin* is derived from the injunction in Exodus 13:9: "And it shall be for a sign unto thee upon thine hand, and for a memorial between thine eyes, that the Lord's law may be in thy mouth," and a similar commandment in Deuteronomy 6:8.

The process of putting on *tefillin* is elaborate and carefully prescribed. They are worn while standing, as a mark of reverence. One box is placed on the inner side of the left arm, just above the elbow (this places it next to the heart when the worshiper is praying); the strap is coiled around the left forearm seven times. The other box is placed in the middle of the forehead, high up, above the hairline generally, and the strap is looped around the head and knotted. The two ends of the strap are joined over the shoulder and brought forward. Then the armband strap is wound around the middle finger three times. This signifies *shin*, the Hebrew let-

---

*For many non-Orthodox Jews, their only encounter with *tefillin* may have come aboard a "*mitzva* mobile." These were vans that the Lubavitcher *Chasidim* (see Rosten's entry and my note for **Chasid**) sent into Jewish neighborhoods during the 1970s and 1980s. *Chasidim* would accost men on the street with the question "Are you Jewish?" and invite the Jews into the van to "*lay tefillin*" (wrap the *tefillin* while saying the proper blessings). The Lubavitchers are also very active in encouraging this *mitzva* at the Western Wall in Jerusalem.

During the current strong revival of ritual observance and spirituality among synagogue-affiliated Jews, more have been experimenting with *tefillin*—including women, especially those in the rabbinate.

Tefillin originated as amulets. According to Rabbi Arthur Green (in *These Are the Words: A Vocabulary of Jewish Spiritual Life*, Jewish Lights, 1999), "The Jews of late antiquity began a process that transformed a protective device into a statement of witness: The person who wears *tefillin* seeks to fulfill the divine words that are contained within them."

ter with which one of the cabalistic names for God (*Shaddai*) begins.

The entire ritual has the effect of removing mundane preoccupations from the prayer's mind and focusing attention entirely on devotions. Maimonides (twelfth century) thought the sanctitiy of *tefillin* "very great" and argued that while they were worn, a man would devote his entire mind "to truth and righteousness."

Phylacteries were not permitted to be worn on the Sabbath. The Sabbath is a day of holiness and does not need the added sanctification of phylacteries.

There is a charming old saying: "God Himself wears *tefillin*."

The rules regulating the way in which *tefillin* may be made, and the ritual by which they are put on, taken off, worn under which conditions—all this is much too voluminous to be covered here. A sixteenth-century code, the *Shulkhan Arukh*, lists 160 laws governing *tefillin*.

The Jews thought that when a Jew wears the *tefillin*, "God's radiance" falls upon him and wards off all possible harm: hence, it was forbidden to cover all of the *tefillin* with the prayer shawl. Wearing *tefillin* in the street was once the custom, but since this called the attention of anti-Semites to Jews, the custom faded away.

Josephus, the great Jewish historian, wrote that the rite of *tefillin* was an ancient one—and Josephus was writing in the first century C.E.

The word *phylacteries*, by the way, comes from the Greek word for "protection" or "fortress" (*phylakterion*) and is found in the Greek gospel, Matthew 23:5.

See daven.

timtum

Pronounced TIM-*tum*, using a short *u*, to rhyme with "rim rum." From Hebrew: *tum*, "moron."*

1. An androgynous person—that is, one who has bisexual or ambiguous characteristics; one who is hard to identify as either male or female.
2. An effeminate man.
3. A beardless youth with a high-pitched voice.

In the *Mishnah*, a *timtum* is a person whose sex is not determinable—because clothes conceal the genital areas.

The original meaning fanned out, and Jews would call a young man who was beardless, delicate, high-pitched of voice, "a *timtum*."

One authority informs me that in some circles *timtum* came to mean "a total loss," an unproductive, uncreative misfit. Thus: "He may read a lot, but he's a *timtum*" or "He can't help; he's a *timtum*."

Tisha B'Av
Tisha Bov

Pronounced TISH-*a bawv*, to rhyme with "Misha dove." Hebrew: "the ninth day of the month *Av*."

The day of fasting and mourning that commemorates

---

*Rabbi Samson Raphael Hirsch (1808–1888) noted a relationship between the Hebrew word for ritual impurity or uncleanness, *tumah*, and the word *timtum*, defined as "confused." This connection might be helpful for those disturbed by biblical texts that associate menstruation, childbirth, sex, death, and other natural processes with "uncleanness," for Hirsch's observation seems to suggest that the intensity of physical experience, rather than its innate yuckiness, is what renders a person "unclean" by virtue of his or her being emotionally overwhelmed.

both the first (586 B.C.E.) and the second (70 C.E.) destruction of the Temple in Jerusalem. (The Babylonians razed the First Temple, the Romans the Second.) Reform Jews do not observe this day of communal lamentation.†

D own the gloomy centuries, *Tisha B'Av*, known as "the blackest day in the Jewish calendar," has added disasters, catastrophes, and horrors to the destructions of the Temple: the doomed Bar Kokhba revolt in 135; the slaughter of Bar Kokhba's followers in 138; Hadrian's leveling of Jerusalem; the death of the brilliant

†The Reform movement abolished *Tisha B'Av* observances in the nineteenth century because the notion of rebuilding the Jerusalem Temple, as well as the folkloric belief that the *meshiakh* (messiah) would be born on *Tisha B'Av*, ran counter to Reform ideology. Reform Judaism endorsed a prophetic, "light unto the nations" role for Judaism in the world and replaced the messianic concept with a humanistic faith in progress toward a "messianic age." Rabbi David Einhorn, a radical in the early Reform movement (and an active antislavery abolitionist), even proposed turning *Tisha B'Av* into a feast day to mark the emergence of the Jewish people from their nation-state onto the world historical stage! Such ideology also gave impetus to Reform Judaism's early opposition to the Zionist movement, though Reform figures such as Rabbi Stephen S. Wise, Louis Brandeis, and Rabbi Abba Hillel Silver did eventually become leaders of the American Zionism.

Some contemporary Reform Jews now observe the *Tisha B'Av* fast in commemoration of the Holocaust and other historical disasters that have confronted the Jews. However, the widespread observance of *Yom HaShoah* (established by the Israeli *Knesset* in 1951) each spring has assured Holocaust commemoration in its own right and has restricted the expansion of *Tisha B'Av* into a catch-all day of mourning.

The need for the *Tisha B'Av* fast and the prayer for the "rebuilding of Jerusalem" has also been broadly debated, even among Orthodox Jews, ever since the establishment of the modern state of Israel and the worldwide celebration among Jews of *Yom HaAtzmaut* (Israel Independence Day, May 14, 1948), followed by *Yom HaZikaron*, the Day of Remembrance for Israel's war dead.

Secular Jews in some left-wing circles have associated *Tisha B'Av* with the nuclear bombing of Hiroshima and Nagasaki, the anniversaries of which (August 6 and 9) often overlap with the ninth of *Av*.

Rabbi Akiba and nine other martyrs; the Holy Crusades and their unholy massacres, rapes, and depredations; England's expulsion of Jews in 1290; the Spanish expulsion of the Jews in 1492 . . .

Tisha B'Av (which usually falls during August) climaxes nine days of mourning during which meat is not eaten and marriages are not performed. Many of the practices of the funeral *shivah* period are adopted on this day: eating, drinking, and bathing are forbidden; so are smiles, laughter, and conversation. Those who enter the synagogue do not even greet one another. They sit on the floor or on low benches, as a sign of mourning. A black curtain is draped over the ark, and only one flickering light, the Eternal Light, which burns day and night at the ark, illuminates the synagogue.

The book of Lamentations is recited by the cantor, in a low and depressing chant. (In Sephardic communities, the book of Job is also read.) Poems of suffering and dirges of immense sadness (some dating from the Middle Ages) are intoned.

But the day ends on a note of hope, with the reading of Judah ha-Levi's (1085–1145) *Zionide:*

> Zion, wilt thou not ask if the wing of peace
> Shadows the captives that ensue thy peace,
> Left lonely from thine ancient shepherding?
> Lo! West and east and north and south
> All those from far and near, without surcease,
> Salute thee: Peace and Peace from every side.

Among some Jews, *Tisha B'Av* used to include an appeal to Moses and Aaron, begging them to ask God, at long last, to help Israel—so long dispersed, despised, afflicted, tormented.

Yiddish is permitted in the *Tisha B'Av* prayers of some Conservative synagogues—to recount the Hitler catastrophe.

The prophet Zecharaiah, asked whether a Jew should weep on *Tisha B'Av*, inquired whether the mourning was for the sake of

God or for the self-consolation of the mourner. This austere, if not superhuman, standard was raised by Zechariah, who advised Jews that, however horrible their experience, and however just the cause for weeping, they should evidence true piety by showing mercy, acting justly, and displaying "compassion by every man to his brother." Zechariah bade his people "oppress not the widow nor the fatherless, the stranger, nor the poor."

T.L.

Pronounce the letters as English: "tea el." Abbreviation for *tokhes leker*. From Hebrew: *takhat*, "under part," and German, *lecken*, "to lick." Ameridish.

Vulgarism

1. Literally: *T.L.* stands for "ass licker"; or, more popularly, "ass kisser"; or, in the more palatable camouflage of euphemism, "apple polisher."
2. A sycophant, a fawner; one who shamelessly curries favor with superiors. "How do you think he got where he is? He's the worst *T.L.* you ever saw!" "He's a shameless *tokhes leker*."

tokhes[Y]
tochis[R]
tuchis
T.O.T. (abbreviation)

Pronounced TUKH-*is*, to rhyme with "duck hiss," or TAWKH-*is*, to rhyme with "caucus." Remember that guttural *kh*. Hebrew: "under," "beneath."

1. Vulgarly: The behind, rear end, posterior, buttocks. "Get off your *tokhes*" means "Get off your tail" or "Get moving." "*A patsh in tokhes*" is a spanking, a swat on the behind. This was a commonly heard warning to children—but never did I hear my puritanical mother use it! Such words made her shudder.

2. "*Tokhes afn tish*" does not mean "buttocks on the table," which is its literal translation, but "Put up or shut up," "Let's get down to brass tacks," "Lay all your cards on the table."

3. *T.O.T.* The phrase above is lusty and picturesque, but unquestionably improper, and because it is infra dig, the initials *T.O.T.* are often used as genteel shorthand: "Let's stop evading the issue: *T.O.T.*, please."

I. I. Mendelson's Ali Baba Toy Emporium was having its problems. The tots just loved to try out the tricycles and the hobbyhorses, the swings and the teeter-totters; but whenever a parent or a salesman tried to coax the little ones off these toys, they screamed and raged and dug in their little heels and threw violent temper tantrums, and the whole store sounded like a madhouse. I. I. Mendelson was sorely troubled. What to do, what to do?

One day there appeared before him a genial, cherubic, white-haired gentleman, who said: "Freibush is the name. Professor Oscar Freibush, doctor of child psychology and consultant on infant behavior. I have heard of your difficulties, which I believe I can solve for a fee of fifty dollars."

"Fifty dollars?" echoed I. I. Mendelson.

Dr. Freibush smiled. "No obligation. Satisfaction guaranteed or you don't pay a penny."

"Come with me," said Mr. Mendelson. He led Professor Freibush into the store. "Look. Listen. Did you ever hear such a *tarrarom?*"

On the hobbyhorse from which his frantic mother was trying to lift him, a little boy was screaming like a banshee. On a tricycle, a little girl was kicking and screeching at her father, who was trying to wrestle her off. On the teeter-totter, two children were caterwauling like demons at two salesmen.

Professor Freibush studied the howling scene but a moment, went over to the hobbyhorse, patted the screaming lad on the head, leaned over, and, smiling, whispered a few words into the boy's ear. At once the lad ceased screeching, slid off the little hobbyhorse, and let his mother lead him away.

Professor Freibush went to the little girl on the tricycle, stroked her locks fondly, leaned over, whispered something into her ear— and the hellion stopped screaming at once, descended from the tricycle, and meekly placed her little hand in her father's.

With the squawling pair on the teeter-totter, Professor Freibush plied his same swift, incredible magic. A fond pat, a kind smile, those mesmeric whispered words—and decorum promptly replaced hysteria.

"It's unbelievable!" cried I. I. Mendelson. "What do you say to them?"

"My fee . . . "

"Here! . . . Now, what do you say?"

"I pat their hair," said the great psychologist, smiling and folding the $50 into his wallet, "then I put my mouth close to their little ears and whisper, 'Listen, darling, get off that toy or I'll give you such a *patsh* on the *tokhes* you won't be able to sit down for a week.'"

Torah ^R
Toyre ^Y

Pronounced TOY-*ra*, to rhyme with "Moira," or TOE-*rah*, to rhyme with "Bowra," or TAW-*ra*, to rhyme with "Nora." Hebrew: "teaching," "doctrine."

1. The Pentateuch, or Five Books of Moses: Genesis, Exodus, Leviticus, Numbers, and Deuteronomy.
2. The scroll containing the Five Books of Moses, handwritten by a scribe on parchment, kept in the ark in the synagogue, and read in the synagogue on *Shabbes*, on festivals, and on Mondays and Thursdays.
3. All of Jewish law and religious studies. *Torah shebalpe* (SHEH-*bal-peh*) refers to the oral teachings of the rabbis, as contrasted with *Torah shebiksav* (SHEH-*bik-sov*), the written teachings of the Pentateuch, Prophets, and Hagiographa (Sacred Writings).*

The very essence of Judaism—as a religion, a philosophy, a commitment, a set of values—is said to lie in the historic triad "God, *Torah*, Israel."

The *Torah* has always held a cardinal and sacrosanct place in Jewish history, which bursts with tales of the martyrdom and sacrifices Jews endured in order to preserve and transmit "our holy *Torah*" from one generation to the next.

The text of the Pentateuch has been carefully preserved, and scribes were specially trained to copy the ancient scrolls (*Sefer*

Torah may also be used to compliment insightful comments by one's contemporaries. An original interpretation of a text, or an ethical insight informed by Jewish values, or some other form of Jewish teaching, might be referred to as "a piece of *Torah*."

Torah, "book of the Torah") with fidelity. A Torah scroll is considered priceless.

The highest ideal held before every Jew was the study of Torah. The Talmud is full of admonitions such as this: "A single day devoted to the Torah outweighs a thousand sacrifices."

"God weeps over one who might have occupied himself with Torah but neglected to do so."

"Not only should a person not neglect study because of the pursuit of pleasures; he should not neglect it even for his occupation."

And Maimonides taught: "How long is one required to study Torah? Till the day of his death. . . . Some of the greatest of the wise men of Israel were wood-choppers, others drawers of water, some even blind—who, nevertheless, studied Torah day and night."

In order to enable even the least educated masses to learn Torah, a section (parsha) of the Pentateuch was read in the synagogue each Monday and Thursday morning (originally, these were market days in agricultural Palestine) and each Sabbath and holiday. By the end of the year, the cycle of Torah readings was completed—and immediately begun once more!

See Simchas Torah.

The word Torah is found in many epigrams and proverbs:

"Toyre* iz di beste skhoyre"— "Learning is the best merchandise."

"Im eyn torah eyn derekh eretz:"— "Without the study of the law, there are no good manners."

> *Use of the YIVO transliteration here captures the rhyme of the epigram.

"May you live to introduce [him] to study [Torah], marriage, and good deeds." This is the expression of good wishes extended to parents at a son's bris.

"Prayer and the study of the Law," wrote Hutchins Hapgood after his singularly sensitive observation of the Lower East Side (in *The Spirit of the Ghetto,* Funk and Wagnalls, 1965), "constitute practically the whole life of the religious Jew."

Hillel, the great and saintly teacher, noblest of the Pharisees, the paradigm of modesty and grace in learning, was once baited by a heathen to condense the *Torah* into its briefest possible form. Hillel replied: "What is hateful to thee, never do to thy fellow man. That is the entire *Torah;* all else is commentary."

". . . toytn bankes" Y
". . . toyten bankes" R

Pronounced TOY-*ten* BONK-*kiss,* to rhyme with "Boyton konk hiss." *Toyten,* from German: *tod,* "dead"; *bankis,* from Russian, *banka,* a "cup" used for bleeding the sick.

The phrase "*Es vet helfn vi a toytn bankes*" means "It will help about as much as cupping can help a corpse."

It used to be customary to bleed a sick person, in an attempt to reduce fever, by drawing blood to the surface of the skin under a small heated cup, which formed a partial vacuum. The skin was then lanced to draw blood. The phrase "It will help as much as cupping will help a corpse" is about as graphic as you can get.

treyf ^Y
trayf ^R
treif

Pronounced to rhyme with "safe." From the Hebrew: *teref,* "torn to pieces."

An animal not slain according to the ritual laws and by an authorized *shoykhet;* any food that is not *kosher.* "Pork is *treyf.*" "Oysters and shrimp may taste delicious, but they are *treyf.*"

To form a noun, *treyf* becomes a *treyfne* (woman) or *treyfnyak* (man)—someone untrustworthy, malicious, tricky, of whom you should be aware.

trombenik
trombenyik

Pronounced TROM-*beh-nik,* to rhyme with "Brahma kick," or TRAUM-*beh-nik,* to rhyme with "brawn the pick." From the Polish: *tromba,* "trumpet."

1. A blowhard, a braggart, a blower of his own horn. "That *trombenik* can drive you crazy."
2. A glutton.
3. A lazy man or woman; a ne'er-do-well.
4. A parasite.
5. A fake, a phony, a four-flusher.

Any way you look at it, *trombenik* is not a word of praise. A *trombenik* is part of the raucous gallery of *nudniks, shlepers,* and *paskudnyaks.*

"I," boasted the *trombenik*, "have been to Europe three times in the past three years."

"So? I *come* from there."

tsatske
tsatskele
tchotchke
tchotchkele

Pronounced TSAHTS-*keh*, to rhyme with "Tosca"; TSAHTS-*keh-leh*, to rhyme with "Oscela;" TCHOCH-*keh*, to rhyme with "botch a"; TCHOTCH-*keh-leh*, to rhyme with "notch a la." From Polish: *tsatsko*, "a toy" or "a beautiful, useless thing."

Tsatske and the Yinglish *tchotchke* are used interchangeably. *Tsatskele* and *tchotchkele* are affectionate diminutes of *tsatske* and *tchotchke*.

A *tsatske* is

1. a toy, a little plaything. "I bought the child a *tsatske*."
2. an inexpensive, unimportant thing, a gewgaw, a trinket. "He gave her some *tsatske* or other for her trouble."
3. a bruise, a contusion, a wound. "He had a *tsatske* under each eye."
4. a nobody; no bargain. "Don't listen to that one; he's some *tsatske*."
5. a misfit, an unadjusted child, a problem and burden to one and all. "What can we do about him? Since he joined the club he's been a *tsatske*."
6. a loose or kept woman.
7. an ineffectual person, a fifth wheel, a disappointment.
8. a cute female, a pretty little number, a chick, a babe, a playgirl.

9. a sexy but brainless broad.*

> *For a comment on sexist usage, see my note to Rosten's entry for **chotchke**.

Old Mr. Gluck had finally moved to the suburbs. On a trip into New York, he met a friend who bombarded him with questions. "How do you like it? Living in the country, so far from everyone!"

"At first I had problems," said Gluck. "I thought I'd never be able to stand it! Then I listened to my neighbors, and got a paramour. From then on, everything has been fine!"

"A paramour! You? Gluck, how can you *do* such a terrible thing? What does your wife think?"

"My wife?" Gluck frowned. "Why should she care how I cut the grass?"

tsedreyt ^Y (adjective)
tsedrayt ^R
tsedreyter (masculine noun)
tsedreyte (feminine noun)
tsedreydlt (adjective)

Pronounced *tse*-DREYT, to rhyme with "de-freight." From German: *drehen*, "to turn," "to twist."

1. *Tsedreyt* (adjective) or *tsedreydelt* means mixed up, confused, wacky, demented. "I can't make heads or tails out of it; it's *tsedreyt*."

2. A *tsedreyter* is a man or boy who is all mixed up, a kook, a crank, a crackpot. "Poor man, he's a hopeless *tsedreyter*."

3. A *tsedreyte* is a woman or girl nut, a crank, a kook, a lunatic. "Who can believe her? She's a *tsedreyte*."

Someone with a *tsedreyter kop* (deranged head) is pleasantly pix-ilated—or not so pleasantly demented.

See also kopdreyenish and tsedudlt.

"If you want to live forever," a *tsedreyter* told a rich man, "come and live in our dreary little town."

"Why? Is it that healthy?"

"Listen, *never* has a rich man died there."

tsedudlt [Y]
tsedoodelt [R] (adjective)
tsedudlter (masculine noun)
tsedudlte (feminine noun)

Pronounced *tseh*-DOO-*d'lt*, to rhyme with "the zoo belt."

Confused, mixed up, pixilated, kooky, wacky.

See also tsedreyt.

A *tsedudlter* said that if he found a million dollars in the street, he would keep it—unless, of course, he discovered that it belong to some poor man, in which case he would return it at once.

tsetumlt [Y] (adjective)
tsetummelt [R]
tsetumlte (feminine noun)
tsetumlter (masculine noun)

Pronounced *tse*-TU-*m'lt*, to rhyme with "'ts tumult." See tuml.

Confused, bewildered. "I've never been so *tsetumlt* in my life."

A *tsetumlter* (*tse*-TU-*m'l-ter*) is a confused, discombobulated man. A *tsetumlte* (*tse*-TU-*m'l-teh*) is a bewildered, dotty, scatterbrained female. "*Oy*, is she a *tsetumlte*."

tshepe ^Y
tcheppeh ^R
tshepen (infinitive verb)
cheppeh

Pronounced TCHEP-*eh*, to rhyme with "Beppa," with a *ch* as in "church." From Russian: *tchupat*, "to touch," "to feel."

1. To annoy, to nag. "Stop *tsheping* me." This is primarily an American usage.
2. To bait, to try deliberately to provoke. In Yiddish, this requires a reflexive form of the verb: *zikh tshepn*.
3. To touch.

I heard *tshepen* used to describe the kind of malicious, sadistic baiting an agent provocateur would use on a Jew in order to provoke an excuse for reprisal. "An anti-Semite *tshepes* you—to give him an excuse to beat you up."

There is a saying, "*Ale tsores tshepen zikh tsu mir*"—"All troubles seem to latch on to me."

tsimes ^Y
tsimmes ^R

Pronounced TSIM-*mess*, to rhyme with "Kim less." A Yiddish contraction of *tsum esn,* "to eat."

1. A side dish of mixed cooked vegetables and fruits, slightly sweetened. The ingredients may be carrots and peas, prunes and potatoes, sweet potatoes, etc.
2. A dessert of stewed fruits.

Since making *tsimes* took time and various mixings, the word came to mean the following:

3. A prolonged procedure, an involved business, a mix-up. "Don't make a whole *tsimes* out of it." (Don't blow it up out of proportion; why make a federal case of it?) "It's no *tsimes* to me." (It doesn't bother me very much.) "Trouble? It was a regular *tsimes.*" (It was a mess, a mix-up, a real stew.)
4. Troubles, difficulties, a contretemps. A newspaper advertisement announced: "Skip the fuss. Leave the *tsimes* to us."

See also shtus.

tsitser

Pronounced TSI-*tzer,* to rhyme with "hits 'er." An onomatopoetic coinage.

1. One who is always going "Ts! Ts!" or "Tsk! Tsk!" or even "Tchk! Tchk!"
2. A habitual sympathizer and bystander, not a participant.
3. A *kibitzer* given to expressing feelings with sibilant "tchk"–ings.
   See also dopes.

tsitsis^Y
tzitzit^R

Pronounced TSI-*tsiss*, to rhyme with "kisses." Hebrew: *tzitzit*, "fringes."

The fringes at the corners of the prayer shawl (*tallis*) and the *tallis katan*—the short, jacketlike garment worn by Orthodox males under coat or vest.

T'*sitsis* are meant as reminders of one's duty to the laws of Judaism: more exactly, to the 613 specific instructions extrapolated from the *Torah*. The authority for wearing *tsitsis* comes from God—according to Numbers 15:37–39, at least: God told Moses to tell the children of Israel to make fringes "throughout their generations" in the borders of their garments and "put upon the fringe of the borders a riband of blue." (Blue died out as blue dye became scarce.)*

The cabalists performed all sorts of abracadabra with the number of knots, double knots, sections, and windings ("seven times around and made fast by a double knot") that are required in the *tsitsis*. The mystical gymnasts counted thirty-nine windings in each fringe and derived an identical "value," in a numerical sense, out of the triumphant *Adonai Echad* ("The Lord is One") that ends the great *Shma* prayer.

It is said that the four *tsitsis* stand for the "four corners" of the

*The ancient dye for the *tekhelet* (thread of blue) was apparently derived from a Mediterranean snail, but uncertainty about which species and how correctly to manufacture the dye led to its abandonment.

Some scholars speculate that the Catholic rosary, consisting of five sets of ten beads, derives from *tsitsis*, which have five knots in each bundle of eight strings.

earth. The discovery that the earth is round has not altered the
metaphor.†

See tallis.

tsores [Y]
tsuris [R]
tsouris, tsoriss, tsuriss

Pronounced TSOO-*riss,* or TSAW-*riss,* to rhyme with "juris"
or "Boris." The plural of *tsorah* or *tsureh.* From Hebrew:
tsarah, "trouble."

Troubles, woes, worries, suffering.

---

† The number four has much symbolism in Jewish life: the four-letter name of
God (or Tetragrammaton; see Rosten's entry for **Adonai**), four seasons, four
biblical matriarchs—and, at Passover, four cups of wine, four questions, and
"the four children" (traditionally, four sons). Ellen Frankel and Betsy Platkin
Teutsch note (in their *Encyclopedia of Jewish Symbols,* Jason Aronson, 1992),
"Within the daily liturgy, Jews pray that the scattered remnants of Israel be
gathered in 'from the four corners of the earth' (*arba kanfot ha-aretz*), to be
sheltered under the wings (a second meaning of *kanfot*) of the *Shekhinah* in
Jerusalem, the center of the square. 'Four' here represents dispersion contrasted to the One, i.e., God and the Holy Land."

Tsitsis can also be interpreted to represent "open borders." While
Judaism is very concerned with borders and separations—between the Sabbath and the week, kosher and *treyf,* Jew and non-Jew, etc.—the concept of a
fringed border helps prevent such concern from becoming obsessive and
dogmatic. Rabbi Arthur Waskow (in *Godwrestling—Round 2,* Jewish Lights,
1996) writes that *tsitsis* "celebrate the fact that between individuals within a
community there must be not high hard fences but soft and fading boundaries.... In biblical tradition, this was affirmed by assigning the produce of
the corners of 'my' field to the communal needs of the poor, the stranger, the
orphan.... Just as the shared communal use of the corners of the field betokened God's share in my property, so the communal fringes of the garment
betokened God's share in my identity. God's representative, in both cases,
was the community."

The singular is *tsure* (TSOO-*reh*), but trouble is rarely singular.

Tsores has gained considerable vogue in theatrical and literary circles. "Oh, have I got *tsores!*" "Her life these years has been one *tsore* after another." "All he adds up to is—*tsores.*"

The phrase "He's *oyf tsores*" means "He has real troubles," "He's sick," "He's depressed."

And when *tsores* pass beyond the cozy realm of the ordinary, they are called *gehakte* (chopped-up) *tsores*. Why troubles are worse when chopped up like chicken liver, I do not know, but the phrase certainly *sounds* authoritative.

FOLK SAYINGS:

"Troubles are partial to wetness—to tears, and whiskey."

"Don't worry about tomorrow; who knows what will befall you today?"

"From luck to *tsores* is but a step; but from *tsores* to *mazel* is a mile long."

"And how many children do *you* have?"

"None."

"No children?! So what do you do for aggravation?"

tsutshepenish Y
tsutcheppenish R

Pronounced TSOO-*chep-peh-nish*; rhymes with "too help a dish." Blend of Russian, *tchupat*, "to touch," and German, *zu*, "to."

1. Something irritating, undesirable, that "attaches itself"; an obsession. "He has a *tsutshepenish* that is driving everyone else crazy."

2. Someone who becomes a persistent, unshakable nuisance. "She turned into a *tsutshepenish* I never expected." See also nokhshleper.

tuml ^Y
tummel ^R

Pronounced TUM-*m'l*, to rhyme with "tumul(t)." German: *Tummel*, "tumult."

Noise, commotion, noisy disorder. "He can drive a person crazy; everywhere he goes he creates *tuml*."

tumler ^Y
tummler ^R

Pronounced TOOM-*ler*, with the *oo* pronounced as in *took*.
1. One who creates a lot of noise (*tuml*) but accomplishes little.
2. A funmaker, a "live wire," a clown, a prankster, the "life of the party."
3. The paid social director and entertainer in those Catskill resorts that constitute "the Borsht Belt."

It is the *tumler's* job to guarantee, to the blasé (but insatiable) patrons of a summer resort, that most dubious of vacation boons: "Never a dull moment!" The *tumler* performs—that is, entertains in a formal sense—every night: as a comic, singer, actor, master of ceremonies. He acts, writes, directs, and produces shows. He extemporizes, monologizes, and plagiarizes. He puts on vaudeville skits, minstrel shows, amateur nights, ordeals-by-dance.

But the rest of the eighteen-hour day the *tumler* is a noisemaker, a fun generator, a hilarity organizer, and an overall buffoon. He initiates endless tomfooleries—individual and en masse. He tells stories, cracks jokes, plays pranks. He wears outlandish costumes, imitates peculiar people, trips over chairs, falls off diving boards. He leads songs like "Old MacDonald Had a Farm" and games like Simon Says. He perpetrates broad hoaxes and risqué treasure hunts. He pretends to be a waiter, a doctor, a dishwasher, a cretin. He launches public and putative romances for the favor of the fattest, shortest, tallest, or least pulchritudinous females. He forever traverses the grounds, the dining room, the recreation hall, in an uninterrupted exhibition of joking, jollying, baiting, burlesquing, heckling, clowning. He makes, in short, whatever complete fool of himself is necessary to "keep the guests in stitches"—which can be as painful as it sounds. His mission is to force every paying customer to "have a ball." His guiding principle is the maxim "Have *fun!!*" And his shattering resourcefulness is put to the final, awful test on those most gruesome and challenging days: rainy. For only the *tumler* stands between the guests' incipient depression and departure.

The ideal *tumler* (if "ideal" is quite the right word) would be a cross between Milton Berle and Jerry Lewis. Both have, as a matter of fact, won signal honors in the fun-loving Catskills.

To give recognition where such is deserved, "the Borsht Belt" *did* send to the glittering world of vaudeville, stage, movies, and television an astounding number of talents—comedians, playwrights, directors, singers, producers: Danny Kaye, Moss Hart, Clifford Odets, Dore Schary, Arthur Kober, Garson Kanin, Don Hartman, John Garfield, Shelley Winters, Sid Caesar, Joey Bishop, Buddy Hackett, Phil Silvers, Jackie Mason, Jan Peerce, Robert Merrill, Red Buttons, Tony Curtis, and heaven only knows how many others.

The *tumlers* of our time may not know of the historic tradition in which they function: a professional *badkhn*, a jokester-MC, used to be engaged to make merry at Jewish weddings.

See batkhn.

tzaddik ^R
tsadek ^Y

Pronounced TZOD-*dick*, rhymes with "sod Dick." Hebrew: "a righteous man." The plural is *tzaddikim*, pronounced *tsa*-DICK-*im*.

1. A most righteous man.
2. A holy man (in particular, a Chasidic *rebbe*); a man of surpassing virtue and (possibly) supernatural powers.
3. Used ironically: An unholy, wicked, cynical man.
4. The Yiddish name for the eighteenth letter of the Hebrew alphabet.

Originally, *tzaddikim* were regarded as upright, honorable men who, by their example, brought others closer to righteousness. The medieval cabalists and, later, the *Chasidim*, attributed mirific powers to the *tzaddik*.

The famous legend of the Thirty-six Saints (*Lamed-vav Tzaddikim*) says that on earth there live thirty-six saints—who do not know it; the world continues to exist, by God's favor, only because of these nameless thirty-six and their unselfish ways and work. No one can tell who they are: one may be a pauper, one a drayman, a janitor, a shoemaker . . .

The legend holds that the *lamed-vavniks* disclose their identity only on rare occasions—especially emergencies, when Jews are in danger. Then a *tzaddik* will do God's bidding in a sudden, magical rescue mission—and vanish, for he must never have his identity revealed. (That, apparently, would deplete his supernatural powers.)

The idea of doing good secretly, without reward, fleeing from any recognition or gratitude, held great fascination for the men of the *Talmud*. The less publicly a good deed is done, the more for its own quintessential goodness, the more admirable it is. Heaven will know . . . God will remember. . . .

A famous old *tzaddik* was being extolled before a congregation, by a rabbi who waxed more eloquent by the second: ". . . our beloved *tzaddik* is a man of such wisdom that even the most learned sit at his feet; of such kindness that young and old alike flock to him for advice; of such honesty that men and women are uplifted by his example; with such keen understanding of human problems that even saints bare their innermost secrets to him; a man of such . . ."

At this point, the *tzaddik* tugged at the orator's sleeve and whispered, "Don't forget my humility."

Moishe the shoemaker was astounded to receive a letter from the leading *tzaddik* in his town, which read:

O Light of Israel, Eagle of Understanding, Ocean of Learning: Please come and fetch my shoes, which need mending.

Reb Shmuel

Moishe dropped everything and hastened to the wise man's home. "Reb Shmuel, I have come as fast as my feet could carry me. I am only a shoemaker, not versed in such matters, but please tell me: Why did you address me in such a lofty manner?"

"Eh? What 'lofty' manner?"

"As 'O Light of Israel, Eagle of Understanding, Ocean of Learning' . . ."

The *tzaddik* looked puzzled and, stroking his beard, said, "But that's exactly the way people always write to me. . . ."

"Our *tzaddik* prayed that the rich should give more to the poor— and already God answered *half* the prayer: the poor have agreed to accept."

A rabbi visited a village reputed to have a miracle-working *tzaddik* and asked: "What miracles has your *tzaddik* actually performed?"

"Our *tzaddik* has fasted every day for three whole years now!"

"Three *years?!* But that's impossible. He'd be dead by now!"

"Certainly he would! But our *tzaddik* knows that if he fasted *every* day, that demonstration of saintliness would put everyone else to shame; so he eats only to spare everyone's feelings—and conceals the fact that *privately* he's fasting."

tzedakah [R]
tsedoke [Y]
tzedaka, tsadaka, tsadakah

Pronounced *tse-DOCK-a*, to rhyme with "the Rocca."
Hebrew; the root of the word is *tzedek*, "righteousness."

The obligation to establish justice by being righteous,
upright, compassionate—and, above all, helping one's fellow human being.

J ews never separated charity from a *duty*, a moral and religious
obligation to act justly and generously. Deuteronomy 15:11
says: "For the poor shall never cease out of the land; therefore I
command thee, saying, thou shalt open thine hand wide unto thy
brother. . . ." And Proverbs 19:17 tells us: "He that hath pity upon
the poor lendeth unto the Lord."

The poor and needy must, moreover, be spared embarrassment. Every Jewish community placed great stress on helping the
poor, the sick, the handicapped—and refugees, who have always
been a saddening part of the history of the Jews. Every community
had a special fund for the needy; every holiday included philanthropic activities; and every home contained little boxes into which
coins, for variously benefited charities, were dropped. (See
pushke.) Every Jewish child was told and taught very early in life
to feel a duty to help those who needed it; children were often
given coins to give to mendicants who came to the door. And life
in any Jewish community in America is studded with "benefits,"
"memorials," "affairs," "parlor meetings," and other fund-raising
ingenuities.

The singular independence, not to say impertinence, of Jewish
shnorrers, those remarkable types, was rooted in a certain sense of
the obligations owed them by tradition and Talmudic precept.

Maimonides set down variously rated forms of *tzedakah*. The highest form of charity, he said, is to help someone to help him-self;* after that, to help anonymously and secretly—so that the benefactor does not know whom is being helped and the bene-factee does not know who has helped.

Jews are flatly forbidden to ignore or turn away anyone who asks for help.

The shabby, half-starved tramp stood before the rich man, in the rich man's parlor, and asked for help, and the rich man called in his butler and said, "*Look* at this poor unfortunate! His toes are sticking out of his shoes. His trousers are patched in a dozen places. He looks as if he hasn't been able to bathe or shave for a week. He hasn't had a decent meal in God knows how long. It breaks my heart to look at this poor, miserable creature—so throw him out!"

That man clearly lacked an understanding of *tzedakah*. "The longest road in the world," says a folk saying, "is the one that leads to the pocket."

---

*Maimonides recommended (in his *Mishneh Torah: Laws of Gifts to the Poor*) making a loan or creating a business partnership—that is, investing in the poor person and getting truly involved in his or her life. In transactions below this pinnacle, anonymity was emphasized, to minimize the power relation-ships formed by money, particularly in the intimate Jewish communities of past centuries.

During the 1970s and 1980s, several of the newly forming *chavurot* (small religious communities—see my note to Rosten's entry for **chevra**) created *tzedakah* collectives, circles that practiced group giving, often guided by inti-mate discussion about money and its anxieties. See Jeffrey Dekro and Betsy Tessler's *Building Community, Creating Justice: A Guide for Organizing Tzedakah Collectives* (Shefa Fund, 1994).

For more about the customs and rules of *tzedakah*, see my note to Ros-ten's entry for **pushke**.

A teacher, meeting her class on the first day, asked each child to stand and give his or her name and hobby.

The first child rose and said, "My name is Sally Farnsworth, I'm ten years old, and I like to roller-skate."

The second student rose. "My name is Jacob Burns, I'm nine years old, and I collect stamps."

The third student rose. "My name is Morris Wexler, I'm ten years old, and I pledge five **dollars**."*

*This and many other jokes satirize the aggressiveness with which Jewish organizations do their fund-raising. (Another joke tells of a Jewish couple who are stranded and dying in the desert, without hope, until the husband realizes: He has an unredeemed pledge with the United Jewish Appeal—they're sure to find him!) For the more genteel and egalitarian-minded baby boom generation, however, these techniques have had diminishing returns. Notwithstanding Judaism's emphasis on *tzedakah* as everyone's responsibility (even recipients of *tzedakah* are obligated to give *tzedakah*, instructs the *Shulkhan Arukh*), Jewish fund-raising has been relatively oligarchical: of the $700-plus million raised annually by the Jewish Federations/United Jewish Appeal (now the United Jewish Communities), nearly 60 percent comes from only 1 percent of the donors, according to Paul Ritterband and Barry A. Kosmin's *Contemporary Jewish Philanthropy in America* (Rowman and Littlefield, 1991). This pattern indicates underrepresentation among women, among Jews who are not wealthy, and among many other marginalized Jewish subgroups.

During the past decade, Federations and other Jewish organizations have been pursuing creative innovations in their fund-raising in order to expand their base of donors and create a culture of giving among baby boomers and younger Jews. A new generation of "alternative" Jewish nonprofits has also established itself (including the New Israel Fund, Jewish Fund for Justice, Abraham Fund, the Shefa Fund, and the American Jewish World Service) by emphasizing relationship building between funders and the projects being funded, by highlighting projects that are oriented toward peace and civil liberties in Israel, and by linking Jewish values to humanitarian goals. "In the typical [Jewish] community," writes Marshall Sklare (in *Observing America's Jews*, Brandeis University Press, 1993), "about two-thirds of [poll] respondents said that 'supporting all humanitarian causes' was essential to being a good Jew, while only one-third thought that 'supporting Jewish philanthropies' was essential to being a good Jew. What we are observing, then, is a marked shift in attitude, if not yet of practice. Many Jews speak in a nonsectarian way but continue to give in a sectarian one."

u

ungepotchket
See ongepatshket.

utz *

Pronounced to rhyme with "foots."
German: *utzen,* "to tease," "to fool."

Verb
To goad, to nag, to needle, to torment verbally. "He likes to *utz* you until you could scream." "Stop *utsing* me!"

Noun
A piece of goading, verbal needling. "He's a master of the *uts.*" "Did he give her an *utz!*"

*This word is not found in either Alexander Harkavy's or Uriel Weinreich's standard Yiddish dictionaries. Rosten is probably referring to the German verb, which, like many German words, has been incorporated into Yiddish conversation.

vitsᵞ
vitzᴿ

Pronounced as written: rhymes with "sits." German: *Witz*, "joke."

A pointed piece of humor, a witticism, a wisecrack.

My father, who had the readiest, most generous, loveliest sense of humor of anyone I knew, loved to ask me, "Well, have you heard a good *vits* lately?"

My mother once taught me this piece of folk wisdom: "He is a hero who represses a *vits*."

———————————

A very neat *vits:*

When Groucho Marx, who wanted to join a certain beach club in Santa Monica, was told by a friend to forget it because the club was known to be anti-Semitic, Mr. Marx said, "My wife isn't Jewish, so will they let my son go into the water up to his knees?"

yahrtzeit
See yortsayt.

Yahveh
See Adonai, Jehovah.

yakhne [Y]
yachne [R]
yachna

Pronounced YOKH-*neh*, to rhyme with a *kh*-guttural "Bach-na" and *not* with "botch-na." The feminine form of the Hebrew name Johanan. (There are over fifty different Johanans in the *Talmud;* the name John also comes from Johanan.)

A gossip, a yakkety-yak, a busybody, a coarse, shallow woman, a malicious, rumormongering, troublemaking female. "She has the manners of a *yakhne*."

Yakhne is blood sister to a *yenta*.
Yakhne is never used in a favorable or approving sense.
Yakhne was a respectable girl's name at one time; no one knows which bearer of this appellation propelled it into immortality via

the energy of her tongue and the indelicacy of her **manners.***

See also yenta and yidene.

Mrs. Kotchin and Mrs. Mishkin sat rocking on the porch of the Villa Lipshitz, a Catskill resort, when a young man approached.

"Gottenyu!" exclaimed Mrs. Kotchin. *"Look* at that boy! Did you ever see such a big nose? Such shifty eyes? Such a crooked mouth?"

In a freezing voice, Mrs. Mishkin replied, "It so happens you are talking about my son!"

"Well," said Mrs. Kotchin, "on *him,* it's becoming!"

yarmulke
yarmulkah[R]
yarmlke[Y]
yarmulka

Pronounced YAHR-*m'l-keh,* to rhyme with "bar culpa." Derivation **uncertain.**† The Hebrew word for skullcap is *kippah* (KEEP-*ah*).

*****Loshn hara,* "evil speech," is the Talmudic phrase for gossip, slander, and talebearing. Judaism is highly respectful of the power of speech for both creation and destruction (God creates the universe, after all, through the utterance of words). The *Talmud* therefore goes so far as to describe *loshn hara* as "more vicious than murder, unchastity, and idolatry put together." Today, many children in Jewish schools learn about *loshn hara* early in their education about Jewish values. Whether it can inoculate them against the gossip-crazed culture of television and radio talk shows, celebrity-obsessed magazines, and vituperative political partisanship is anybody's guess.

†Sholom Aleichem wrote (*Yidishes Folksblat,* 1884) that *yarmulke* derives from the Hebrew *yaray may-Elo'ah* (fear of God), according to Macy Nulman (*The Encyclopedia of the Sayings of the Jewish People,* Jason Aronson, 1997). "Others," Nulman adds, "attribute the name to a Slavic derivation."

The skullcap worn by observing Jewish **males.**†

No religious edict I can uncover directs Jews to cover their heads—though Exodus prescribes head covering for the Temple priests. During the early Middle Ages, the rabbis instructed Jewish men not to go about bareheaded. Why? Because man should cover his head as a sign of respect before God, whose glory and radiance are, as Maimonides said, "around and above [us]." Covering the head as a sign of respect and reverence is a custom not restricted to Jews, of course; it is common among the peoples of the East, from Arabia to India.

Since the *yarmulke* has become the outwardly recognizable symbol of the Jew, the rabbis who participated in civil rights marches (including Reform rabbis) often wore *yarmulkes* to serve as an identification of their **faith.***

---

† In non-Orthodox synagogues, *yarmulkes* are increasingly worn by women (including, but not limited to, women rabbis). Most Conservative and Reconstructionist rabbis wear them as a matter of course in daily life. Reform temples, which once upon a time were *yarmulke*-free, now host services with majorities wearing them. Synagogues of all denominations make *yarmulkes* available to visitors who lack them.

Large, pillbox-shaped, multicolored *yarmulkes* hailing from Yemen and Bukhara have come into fashion among regular wearers. One useful item, a strip of Velcro designed to keep the *yarmulke* from slipping off the head, is cleverly called "Kip-on" (a pun on *kippah*, Hebrew for *yarmulke*) by its manufacturer.

*Some rabbis were quite active in the civil rights movement of the 1960s, and their history is well told in Rabbi Marc Shneier's *Shared Dreams: Martin Luther King, Jr., and the Jewish Community* (Jewish Lights Publishing, 2000). Among the heroes he features are Rabbi Abraham Joshua Heschel, who walked side by side with King on the 1965 Selma-to-Montgomery march ("My feet were praying," Heschel reported); Rabbi Israel Dresner, a Freedom Rider in 1961; Rabbi Maurice Eisendrath, then head of the Reform synagogue movement, who rallied Jewish support for the Montgomery bus boycott and other campaigns; and Rabbi Joachim Prinz, who spoke after Jesse Jackson at

(Continued on page 614)

Old Hirshbein, in a *yarmulke*, appeared at Nazi police headquarters carrying a newspaper, in which he had circled an advertisement.

Exclaimed the sergeant: "*You* came about this ad?"

"That's right."

"But it reads: 'Wanted: young man, well-built, over six feet tall!' You're at least seventy, thin as a match, and not over five feet two. The ad says: 'Must have excellent eyesight.' Your glasses are so thick you can barely see! The ad says, 'Must be Aryan,' and you are a Jew! Why did you come here?"

"I just want to tell you," said Hirshbein, "that on *me*, you shouldn't depend."

A cartoon in an Israeli newspaper showed the pope, during his historic visit to Palestine in 1964, with the president of Israel. The caption read: "The Pope is the one with the yarmulke."

(Continued from page 613)

the 1963 March on Washington. (The all-male cast testifies to the fact that women were not ordained as rabbis before 1972—and to the sexism pervasive in the movement, as in the culture at large. During the entire three-hour program of the 1963 March on Washington, there was not one woman speaker.) Other key Jews in the movement were Dr. King's trusted adviser Stanley Levison; Morris Abram, a president of Brandeis University and the American Jewish Committee, who led a long campaign for voting rights in Georgia and against the Ku Klux Klan; and Allard Lowenstein, who helped develop the 1962 voter registration drive in Mississippi in which Goodman, Schwerner, and Chaney were killed.

An interesting and related bit of Yiddish cultural lore: Edward Rosewater, the great-grandfather of Kathryn Hellerstein, a prominent contemporary translator of Yiddish poetry, was the only Jewish member of the corps of telegraphers serving the Union war department and had the honor of sending the Emancipation Proclamation out over the telegraph wires on January 1, 1863.

Yekke

Pronounced YEK-*keh*, to rhyme with "Mecca." Origin: unknown.

Yekke is the slang name Ashkenazic Jews used for a German. The name suggests "Teutonic," "pedantic," "rigid"—in any case, not popular. (Some Israelis think *yekke* an acronym for three Hebrew words, meaning "a Jew of scant intelligence," but my experts call this folklore, not philology.)

yekl

Pronounced YEK-*k'l*, to rhyme with "heckle." A Yiddish diminutive of the biblical name Jacob.

1. A stupid person; a sucker.
2. A "greenhorn," a newcomer to the United States who is taken advantage of; a yokel.

A braham Cahan, author, journalist, founder and editor of the *Jewish Daily Forverts* (*Forward*), an important figure in the story of the spread of Yiddish in the United States, wrote a novel called *Yekl* that described the adventures of an innocent and often wronged immigrant in New York.*

---

*Abraham Cahan (1860–1951) was at the helm of the Yiddish *Forverts* for more than fifty years (the first issue appeared in April 1897). At its peak in the 1920s, the paper had a circulation of 250,000, which made it one of New York City's most influential papers in any language. It was socialist oriented and launched or cultivated the careers of many well-known Yiddish writers, including Sholem Asch and I. J. and I. B. Singer. The *Forverts* became the guiding light for hundreds of thousands of Jewish immigrants who were

(Continued on page 616)

yenta
yente

Pronounced YEN-*ta*, to rhyme with "bent a." *Yenta*, I am told, was a perfectly acceptable name for a woman, derived from the Italian *gentile*—until some ungracious *yenta* gave it a bad name. (So, too, the Spanish *esperanza* became the basis for the Jewish name "Shprintze," *señor* the original for "Shnaiur" or "Shneour," and "Phoebus" the origin of "Feivish.") It is also suggested that *yenta* is an ironic corruption of the French feminine for well-bred, *gentille*, but I doubt it.

1. A woman of low origins or vulgar manners; a shrew; a

(Continued from page 615)

attempting to make their way into American culture. Cahan's authority and influence within that population were beyond measure.

His impact upon the Yiddish language was also profound—but controversial. The *Forverts* gladly published and cultivated Yinglish and Ameridish words as part of its overall promotion of assimilation, "Americanization," for immigrant Jews. For language purists, the *Forverts* was viewed as a corrupting influence. (The name of the paper was itself German, not Yiddish.)

Cahan was also a significant novelist. His first novel, *Yekel, A Tale of the New York Ghetto*, was published in 1896. His best-regarded work was *The Rise of David Levinsky* (1917), a classic portrayal of American Jewish immigrants and their acculturation. *The Rise of David Levinsky* and two other books about the Lower East Side—Henry Roth's *Call It Sleep* and Anzia Yezierska's *Bread Givers*—were "rediscovered" and reissued during the 1960s and 1970s, as the baby boom generation of Jews rediscovered Jewish identity. All three of these evocative books are now regularly read in college courses dealing with immigration or the American Jewish experience.

The *Forverts* is still published as a Yiddish weekly. In 1990, the Forward Association launched an English weekly, the *Forward*, which has become a strong voice among American Jewish periodicals. In 1995, a Russian-language version of the paper was launched to appeal to the three hundred thousand–plus members of the Russian Jewish immigrant community in New York and beyond.

shallow, coarse termagant. "She is the biggest *yenta* on the block." "She has the tact of a *yenta*."

2. A gossipy woman, a scandal spreader, a rumormongerer; one unable to keep a secret or respect a confidence. In this sense, men are sometimes described as *yentas,* just as one might call a male blabbermouth "an old woman."

Yenta Telebende was a famous character in a Yiddish newspaper published in New York; she was invented by the humorous writer "B. Kovner," the pen name of **Jacob Adler.***

*Adler was a major dramatic actor on the American Yiddish stage in the late nineteenth and early twentieth centuries.

The rapid-fire comedian Jack E. Leonard once called the garrulous moderator of a television discussion program "a *yenta* with facts."

One of the more amusing buttons worn by the button-happy hippie youth read:

MARCEL PROUST

IS A

YENTA

yents^Y
yentz ^R
yentsn (infinitive verb)

Rhymes with "rents." From German: *jenes* (see below).

1. To copulate.
2. To cheat, to swindle, to defraud. In this usage, *yents* is

akin to the English slang use of "screw." Thus: "Don't trust him; he'll *yents* you."

Y*ents* is a most coarse word, an obscenity never used in the presence of people who are likely to blush.

The Yiddish equivalent for the best-known four-letter English word for sexual congress, *yents* has become part of the vernacular of the American underworld.

The origin of the word is interesting. *Yents* comes from the German demonstrative pronoun *jenes,* meaning "that," "that thing," "the other," "the other thing." The German pronunciation is YAYN-*es;* the Yiddish rendition became *yents.* But how did "the other" or "that thing" become infested with carnal content? Quite simply, as a euphemism—as in "that unmentionable thing." In the United States, in the twenties, the word *it* was used for copulation: "They did it"; "Does she—do it?"

NOTE: Standard Hebrew contains no words for the sex organs. The male member is called "that organ" (*ever* or *gid*); the female receptacle is called "that place" (*ossu mokum*).

With such a prudish tradition, it is not surprising that Jews seized upon *jenes,* which, incidentally, is how genteel ladies' maids and governesses in Germany referred to you-know-whats.

yentser ^Y
yentzer ^R

Rhymes with "rents 'er." Yiddish vernacular.

Obscenity

1. One who copulates—male or female.
2. One who is promiscuous. "She left him because he is a *yentser.*"

3. One who copulates rather more than most or who claims inordinate sexual powers. *Yentser* might have served Dr. Kinsey as a synonym for "sexual athlete."

4. A crook, a swindler; someone who takes advantage of others by guile, cunning, misrepresentation, or outright dishonesty. "He is a born *yentser*."

yeshiva^R
yeshive^Y

Pronounced *yeh*-SHEE-*va*, to rhyme with "believe a." Hebrew: *yeshiva*, "academy," from *yeshov*, "to sit." (Students sat while studying, and the places where they so sat became known as *yeshivot*.) Plural in Hebrew: *yeshivot*; in English usage, *yeshivas*. (The Hindu Upanishads are named for the Sanskrit word "to sit near"; students sat near teachers for oral instruction.)

1. A rabbinical college or seminary.
2. A college or academy for Talmudic study.*
3. In the United States: A secondary Hebrew school; an elementary school in which both religious and secular subjects are studied.

The *yeshiva* was an outgrowth of the *besmedresh*, the "house of study," the place in the Jewish community where men met to

---

*Customarily an Orthodox term, *yeshiva* is being applied nowadays to describe certain liberal institutes of adult Jewish learning. In Toronto, Kolel, the Center for Liberal Jewish Learning, is commonly referred to as a Reform *yeshiva*; in Jerusalem, Bat Kol: A Feminist House of Study is commonly referred to as a feminist *yeshiva*. Neither is a rabbinic seminary, but both seek to develop a high level of Jewish literacy among students.

study and discuss the *Torah* and the *Talmud*. The great *Mishnah*, compiled by Judah the Prince in the latter part of the second century, drew upon the vast accumulated body of knowledge, interpretations, and debates for the unending seminars in the innumerable "houses of study," where Jews carried on their unending discussions on God, faith, good, evil, and responsibility.

One of the earliest *yeshivas* was established in Palestine, at Yavneh, by Rabbi Johanan ben Zakkai. This rabbi, who was looked upon with favor by the Roman emperor Vespasian (he had predicted Vespasian would become emperor), asked Vespasian as a special favor to spare Yavneh and its scholars from the destruction Rome visited upon Jerusalem and other centers of Jewish religion and nationalism. After the destruction of Jerusalem and the great Temple, the *Sanhedrin* (council of rabbis and sages) moved to Yavneh, and the academy there attracted many scholars and became the seat of Jewish scholarship. Permitting the *yeshiva* at Yavneh to exist enabled the Jews to continue their studies, to write the *Mishnah* and the *Gemara*, to maintain their tradition of learning, to perpetuate themselves as a people—albeit without a land or political structure.

During the Talmudic period, *yeshivas* were established elsewhere in Palestine and Babylonia, and they were the creative source and critical laboratory of all Jewish theology, law, ethics, and moral guidance. Jewish schools of learning were created in Galilee, Caesarea, Tiberias (where the Babylonian *Talmud* was put together), and Babylonian centers like Sura. From the tenth century on, *yeshivas* spread wherever Jews lived or migrated—to North Africa, Spain, France, Italy, Germany, England, Holland, and especially in eastern Europe.

In the twelfth century, the *yeshiva* in Baghdad had over two thousand students, plus five hundred in graduate work. There were impressive *yeshivas* in Tunisia, in Morocco, and, of course, in Europe, in virtually every large city.

Yeshivas underwent a dynamic growth, both in number and distribution, during the Renaissance—especially in central and northern Europe.

Relatively few of the students at a *yeshiva* in eastern Europe received or wanted a rabbinical degree. The purpose of the *yeshiva* was not primarily to produce rabbis, but to produce Jews who were well versed in the *Talmud*, learned men, erudite men, men disciplined in their thinking and ascetic in their habits, men who would dedicate themselves to live according to the *Torah*, men who would spend several hours a day for the rest of their lives studying the ever-discussable tractates of the *Talmud*.

Abraham Menes writes (in Louis Ginsburg's *The Jews, Their History, Culture and Religion*):

> The cities and towns of Eastern Europe were . . . full of learned householders, who studied not only . . . to fulfill the commandment to study, but because they actually felt an urge to study. They sang their studies, they sang them fervently, and felt transported to a higher world.

In Spain, the *yeshivas* included courses in secular philosophy, astronomy, medicine, and mathematics. In eastern Europe, it was unheard of to read anything but the Bible and the *Talmud*. All secular works—philosophy, science, fiction, poetry—were strictly excluded. Religious Jews greatly feared that secularization and a falling away from piety would follow if worldly and non-Jewish influences were permitted to attract the Jewish young. In the late nineteenth century, however, the *yeshiva* of Volozhin (Poland) advocated the acquisition of secular knowledge.

The *yeshivas* of Poland came to dominate Jewish theological scholarship, especially after the expulsion of the Jews from Spain. Poland suffered less from Roman Catholic and secular interference than did most European countries.

The most distinguished *yeshiva* for a time was the one in Cracow, where the Aristotelian influence was permitted to exercise itself via the writings of Maimonides.

The traditional *Talmud*-studying-only, no-secular-courses *yeshiva* is rare in America. The first American *yeshiva*, Etz Chayim Talmudical Academy, was organized in New York City in 1886. It later merged with the Rabbi Isaac Elchanan Yeshiva and eventually grew into Yeshiva University, which in addition to a rabbinical seminary includes institutions ranging from high schools to its own medical school. The first rabbinical college for Reform Jews was established in Cincinnati in 1875: Hebrew Union College. The Jewish Theological Seminary was founded in New York in 1886, was reorganized in 1902, and is today the leading Conservative rabbinical training center.*

A great scholar, a luminary of his *yeshiva*, was taking a journey on a ship. The other passengers were tradesmen, bringing their merchandise to foreign markets.

"What kind of merchandise are you carrying?" they asked the poorly dressed scholar.

"What I carry is the most valuable merchandise," said he.

"And what is that?"

He smiled and would not answer.

The merchants searched the scholar's cabin and interrogated the crew and learned that the scholar was, in fact, escorting no merchandise whatsoever. So they laughed and made fun of him and called him a fool.

*To complete the picture, the Reconstructionist Rabbinical College opened its doors in 1968 and has been ordaining men and women since 1973.

Among Orthodox Jews, there are numerous small *yeshivas* granting *smikhe* (rabbinic ordination).

Several days later, pirates attacked the ship and robbed all of the passengers, stripping them down to their clothes. And when the ship reached port, the merchants scarcely knew what to do. They had no money. They had nothing to sell. But the scholar went to the house of study and sat down and began to discuss the law. And when the local Jews saw how learned he was, they gave him food and fine clothing and lodged him in the finest house in town.

And the merchants, begging in the street, saw him pass and said, "Yes, his merchandise *is* the most valuable in all the world: it is learning."

A young scholar at a *yeshiva* was so learned that men came from all over Poland to marvel at his erudition.

One day, a visitor asked the head of the seminary, "Rabbi, what do *you* think of this young man? One wonders how he knows so much."

The rabbi said, "I wonder about something else; this young man reads so much that I wonder when he will find the time to *know*."

yeshiva bokher
yeshive bokher ᵞ
yeshiva bucher ᴿ
yeshiva bocher

Pronounced *ye*-SHEE-*va* BOO-*kher* or BAW-*kher*, with a Scottish *kh*. Hebrew: *yeshov*, "to sit," and *bakhur*, literally "chosen," but also "young man" or "bachelor." The plural of *bokher* is *bokherim,* but in English usage may be (and often is) given as *bokhers.*

1. A young man who is a student at a *yeshiva* (college for Talmudic study).
2. A scholarly, shy, unworldly type. "He is as gentle as a *yeshiva bokher.*"
3. Used ironically: A naive, gullible type; an inexperienced and unrealistic sort. "He has about as much knowledge of girls as a *yeshiva bokher.*" "Don't ask him for an opinion; he's a *yeshiva bokher.*"

The archetypal *yeshiva bokher* was an eastern European, seventeen or eighteen years old, who studied the *Talmud* at an academy of higher studies. Study at a *yeshiva* was extremely demanding, beginning with early prayers and continuing all day, in rigorous cerebral discipline, until late at night. It took about seven years of *yeshiva* study to become a rabbi. The *Mishnah* tells the young scholar to "eat a morsel of bread with salt, drink of water a measure, sleep upon the ground—and lead a life of deprivation while you toil in *Torah.*"

Poor students were supported by the community. Those who came from far distances to a *yeshiva* were boarded and lodged with local families. It was considered an act of piety to feed and lodge a *yeshiva bokher,* many of whom went from home to home, eating and sleeping in a different place each night. (The custom of the *essen tog,* or eating day, was widespread.) Some slept on the benches in the *yeshiva* where students studied all day. The *yeshiva bokher* often lived on the edge of malnutrition, and not without humiliation.

With his wide black hat, long black caftan, uncut sidelocks *(payess),** pallid skin, soft hands, and modest ways (it was the style

*Rosten here gives a classic portrait of a young Polish *Chasid.* During the short career of the *Bal Shem Tov*—who preached for only twenty-four years, 1736–1760, in an age without telegraph, telephone, or mass transit—Chasidism spread with astounding speed in southern Poland, sweeping up well over

of scholars to walk with downcast eyes, absorbed in some Talmudic problem—never letting their eyes fall on a woman!), the *yeshiva bokher* was a familiar figure in eastern Europe. His innocence, his asceticism, and his gentleness became legendary. (Rabbi Jonah, in the *Talmud,* told Jews never to behave "frivolously" in the presence of a scholar.)

A *yeshiva bokher* was a matrimonial prize. The *Talmud (Pesakhim)* says: "If you must, sell everything and . . . marry your daughter to a scholar."

The father of the bride would settle an amount on the scholarly groom as dowry; or would provide him with support; or would guarantee to pay his bills for a year. Honor attached to any family that included a *yeshiva bokher.*

A student who dedicated himself to perpetual study—daily, lifelong study—was called a *matmid* (plural: *matmidim*).

The story is told of a *yeshiva* in Russia where all the *yeshiva bokhers* were once drafted into the Tsar's infantry. To everyone's surprise, the would-be rabbis turned out to be superlative marksmen.

Came war.

The Talmudic regiment went into the front lines. The enemy advanced.

"Fire!" shouted the Russian CO.

No shot was heard. The enemy came closer.

"Fire!" cried the officer again.

His rifles were silent, the enemy at pistol range.

"What's the *matter* with you?" cried the CO. *"Why don't you shoot?"*

half of the Jews living there. Jews in the northern provinces of Poland and in many other communities, however, remained apart from and even opposed to Chasidism, while nevertheless pursuing scholarship in *yeshivas.*

One of the *yeshiva* soldiers blurted, "But those are *men* coming toward us, sir. If we fire, someone will get hurt!"

I am told that a student at a *yeshiva*, who had become interested in Freud, was asked by one of his classmates: "Tell me, Abe, what's the difference between a psychotic and a neurotic?"

Abe scratched his chin but a moment before replying: "A psychotic thinks that two plus two makes five. A neurotic knows that two plus two makes four—he just can't *stand* it!"

YHVH
See Adonai.

Yid

Pronounced YEED, to rhyme with "deed." (If you pronounce it YID, to rhyme with "did," you will be guilty of a faux pas: "Yid" is offensive—and the way anti-Semites pronounce it.) From the German: *Jude*, "Jew." And *Jude* is a truncated form of *Yehuda*, which was the name given to the Jewish Commonwealth in the period of the Second Temple. That name, in turn, was derived from the name of one of Jacob's sons, *Yehuda* (Judah, in English), whose descendants constituted one of the tribes of Israel and who settled in that part of Canaan from Jerusalem south to Kadesh-Barnea (fifty miles south of Beersheba) and from Jericho westward to the Mediterranean.

A Jew (male or female).

Yid is a neutral term (if pronounced YEED, not YID)—but *yidene* never is. See yidene.

The Ku Klux Klan, deciding to harass Mr. Levine, who ran a tailor shop in a hamlet in Mississippi, told the schoolchildren to stand in front of the shop every afternoon and shout, *"Yid, Yid!"*

The children set to their work with enthusiasm. Out came Mr. Levine. "Thank you, thank you," he said. "If you'll come back and do that tomorrow, I'll give each of you a dime."

The next day the children came back—with reinforcements; and after the hooting began, Mr. Levine distributed dimes to each *kleyne* Klanner.

The following day—more children, more catcalls. But this time Mr. Levine distributed only nickels.

On the morrow the children returned but got not a penny. "What's the idea?" they wanted to know.

"I'm sorry, kids, but I can't afford any more advertising," sighed Mr. Levine.

The children never came back.

In the days of the Tsar, Koplinski fell off a bridge and began to drown—thrashing around and shouting for help at the top of his lungs.

Two Tsarist policemen heard his cries and ran to the rail, but when they saw it was a Jew in the water, they simply laughed.

"Help! Help!" cried Koplinski. "I'm drowning!"

"So drown, *Zhid [Yid]!"*

And just as Koplinski started under for the proverbial third time, he had an inspiration: "Down with the Tsar!" he shouted.

At once, the policemen jumped into the water, pulled Koplinski out, and arrested him for sedition.

Yiddish[R]
Yidish[Y]

Pronounced   YID-*dish*,   to
rhyme with **"mid fish."*** From
German: *jüdisch*, "Jewish."

**Just as *Yid* is pronounced YEED
so is *Yiddish* pronounced YEED-
dish* by veteran Yiddish speakers.*

The language of eastern European, or Ashkenazic,
Jews. (The vernacular of Sephardic Jews is *Ladino*.)

Jews do not speak "Jewish" any more than Methodists speak
"Methodist" or Canadians speak "Canadish." "Jewish" is an
adjective, not a noun. But because "Yiddish" means "Jewish" in
Yiddish, many Jews use the two words interchangeably and refer
to "a Jewish newspaper," for instance, when speaking about a Yiddish paper. The distinction between the adjective "Jewish" and the
noun/adjective "Yiddish" is, accordingly, widely ignored.

Yiddish is not Hebrew, which remains (with Aramaic) the
Jews' language of prayer and religious ceremonies. Hebrew is the
official language of Israel.

Yiddish uses the *letters* of the Hebrew alphabet; it is written
from right to left; its spelling, which has been standardized, is
emphatically phonetic.

Perhaps 15 to 20 percent of the vocabulary of Yiddish consists
of Hebrew words and phrases—but Yiddish and Hebrew are as
different as, say, English and Hungarian. In addition to its quotient of Hebrew words, the vocabulary of Yiddish is adapted from
German (70 to 75 percent) and from Polish, Russian, Romanian,
Ukrainian, various Slovene dialects, and, within the last century,
English.

Yiddish is not a "new" or even a "young" language, believe it or
not. It is older than modern German, which may be said to have
begun with Martin Luther's translation of the Bible, and it is older

than modern English, which dates from 1475, according to *The Random House Dictionary.*†

†Yiddish can be found in a handwritten prayer book from the Rhineland dated 1272.

Yiddish is descended from the form of German heard by Jewish settlers from northern France, about a thousand years ago. As Jews settled in towns along the Rhineland, they adopted and adapted the local vernacular.* They wrote German with their Hebrew alphabet, phonetically—just as Jews used Hebrew letters to write many other languages. They shunned Latin and its alphabet, for Latin was associated with things Christian, including pogroms.

The Germanic tongue, heavily studded with Hebrew words and phrases (names, holidays, all religious or ritualistic matters), added words from other languages as the Jews traveled. The new linguistic mélange took root and flourished in eastern Europe; it

*Jews lived in the Rhineland since the height of the Roman Empire, probably as early as the first century C.E.

Robert D. King writes (in *Reconstructing Languages and Cultures,* Edgar C. Polem and Werner Winter, ed., Mouton de Gruyter, 1992) that "Yiddish has points of similarity with two German dialects only: East Central German and Bavarian. . . . With Bavarian . . . Yiddish has a remarkable number of features in common."

Kevin Alan Brook, author of *The Jews of Khazaria* (Jason Aronson, 1999), writes (in private correspondence) that "many of today's scholars . . . [conclude] that East European Jews descend from three groups: (1) Czech Jews, (2) German Jews, and (3) Khazarian Jews." In his book, Brook notes that "the Ashkenazic ethnogenesis, having been formed by migrations from the East (Khazaria), West (e.g., Germany, Austria, Bohemia), and South (e.g., Greece, Mesopotamia, Khorasan), is more complex than previously envisioned."

Benjamin Harshav (in *The Meaning of Yiddish,* University of California Press, 1990), asserts: "The label 'Ashkenazi' does not necessarily mean that all Ashkenazi Jews came from Germany but that they adopted the cluster of Ashkenazi culture which included the specific Ashkenazi religious rite and the German-based Yiddish language. Thus, it is plausible that Slavic-speaking Jewish communities in Eastern Europe (which existed there from early times) became dominated in the sixteenth century by Ashkenazi culture and adopted the Yiddish language."

became the beloved native tongue of the *Ashkenazim*—and was never used by, or known to, the *Sephardim*.†

Since Jewish women were not taught Hebrew, the "sacred tongue," they spoke Yiddish to the children—who, in turn, spoke it to their parents and, later, to their own children. So Yiddish became known as *mameloshn*, "mother language," to distinguish it from *loshn ha-kodesh*, "the sacred language."

Indeed, Hebrew had become too emphatically "sanctified," too closely tied to the holy writings, to religious services, to theology, and to *Talmud*; had become the language of Jewish men and not Jewish women; was too deeply steeped in the arcane preoccupations of rabbis, exegeticists, casuists; was far, far removed from the sweat and tears, the homely jokes and endearing anecdotes, of daily living that Jews so cherish.

Yiddish—a lusty, pliable, eclectic tongue—was certain to exercise a profound, indeed an irresistible, attraction to Jews.

As far back as the fifteenth century, the gifted Elijah Bochur, a Hebrew scholar, wrote and published poems in Yiddish. He wrote two stories in Yiddish that were adaptations from Italian.

In 1602 there appeared the *Mayse Bukh*, a Yiddish collection of folktales, legends, and stories out of the *Talmud*, which exercised a powerful influence on Yiddish prose.

A book on morals and manners, the *Sefer Mides*, or *Book on Behavior*, meant for Jewish women, appeared in 1542.

Josephus's *Antiquities of the Jews* was adapted into Yiddish in Zurich in 1546.

The first Yiddish newspaper in the world began publication in 1686–1687 in Amsterdam.

J. C. Rich of the *Jewish Daily Forward* writes that modern Yiddish

---

† The exception to Rosten's generalization, of course, is Sephardic Jews who moved to eastern Europe over the centuries.

may be said to have begun in the year 1856, when a story by Isaac Meir Dick was published, in Yiddish, in the city of Warsaw.

Alexander Harkavy's *English-Yiddish Dictionary*, the first of its kind, was published in 1891. No authoritative English textbook of Yiddish grammar appeared until 1949 (!), when YIVO published Uriel Weinreich's *College Yiddish.**

As the *Haskala*, or Enlightenment, spread among Europe's Jews in the eighteenth century, its proponents, who were intensely conscious of their Jewishness, championed Hebrew and wanted to revive it as a modern tongue. (They were themselves resented by the Hebraicist purists who opposed making Hebrew secular.) The champions and publicists of *Haskala*, called *Maskilim*, attacked Yiddish as vulgar, as slang, as an illegitimate, déclassé, low-grade jargon. Enters a paradox: The *Maskilim* had to use Yiddish in order to reach the very people they were trying to wrench away from it! So it was that their earnest campaigns served to strengthen the attachment of the Jewish masses to that vernacular they already called "the people's tongue" or "the language of the masses." (It was not the first time that Jews became entangled in paradox.)

In the twentieth century,† Yiddish became a political football because, among other reasons, it was championed by the

---

*More recent works of scholarship about Yiddish include Joshua A. Fishman's *Never Say Die: A Thousand Years of Yiddish in Jewish Life and Letters* (Mouton de Gruyter, 1981), Benjamin Harshav's *The Meaning of Yiddish* (University of California, 1990), and Max Weinreich's *Geshikhte fun der Yidisher Shprakh* (*History of the Yiddish Language*, translated by Shlomo Noble, YIVO, 1973).

†The 1908 Czernowitz Yiddish Conference (in Bukovina) represented an unprecedented effort, led by Nathan Birnbaum, I. L. Peretz, Matisyohu Mieses, and Chaim Zhitlovsky, to establish respect for Yiddish as "a national language of the Jewish people." For a study of the Yiddish language movement, see Emanuel S. Goldsmith's *Modern Yiddish Culture* (Fordham University Press, 1976, 1997).

Bundists—in Poland, Lithuania, and Russia. The Bundists were socialists and social democrats, deeply involved in the Russian revolutions of 1905 and 1917. They were energetic exponents of a new Enlightenment, of a bold secularism, agnosticism, even atheism. They adamantly opposed the use of Hebrew and the rising credo of Zionism.

The Zionists, on the other hand, sought to revive Hebrew and make it the Jews' everyday language. Yet Orthodox Jews clung to Yiddish, paradoxically, for Hebrew was too sacred to be used outside of religious discourse! The Zionists wanted to make Hebrew a contemporary tongue; and many Hebraicists who were not Zionists ardently supported them.

To complicate even further these snarled lines of affiliation and hostility, the first Yiddish schools in America were established in 1910 by Zionists—who were also socialists! *They* supported Yiddish because it was "the language of the masses."

The Workmen's Circle, the extremely influential labor-socialist, once anti-Zionist organization, organized schools, in various cities, in which Yiddish was taught (speaking, reading, writing, literature) to the children of working-class, and largely trade-union, immigrants.* The Bundists were antireligious and antitraditional, as were most Jewish labor leaders—yet they feared

*The Jewish wing of the Communist movement, a constant and contentious rival to the left-liberal Workmen's Circle, ran its own system of Yiddish schools under the auspices of the Jewish People's Fraternal Order (JPFO). A third Yiddish supplementary school system, the Sholom Aleichem Folks Institute, has some surviving institutions today. At their height in 1950, Yiddish schools had a combined enrollment of about twenty thousand pupils.

Secular Jewish organizations also ran vibrant, Yiddish-oriented summer camps, including the now defunct Camp Boiberik (1923–1979, named after a vacation resort described by Sholom Aleichem) and Camp Hemshekh ("the future," run by the Jewish Bund)—and the still active Camp KinderRing, run by the Workmen's Circle, and Camp Kinderland, which has long outlived its founding organization, the JPFO.

that their children would "lose their Jewishness" along with their piety.

In Israel, where Hebrew became the national language, the state officially shunned Yiddish; many Israelis refused to speak Yiddish entirely. It was a shattering experience for elderly Jews, arriving in Zion, to find Yiddish derided. True enough, Hebrew was the national, the revered tongue—but Yiddish was "the language of the heart," of suffering, the encapsulated record of Jewish history and suffering for a thousand years.

In Palestine, before the founding of Israel, zealots rebuked anyone who spoke Yiddish. For more recent *sabras* (native-born Israelis), Yiddish is a language disgraced—the bastard tongue of Jews in the long Exile, and worse, the offspring of detested German, with its reminders of the Nazi nightmare.

Today, Israel has relaxed its antipathy to **Yiddish**.† But the governing attitude is still reverence and pride vis-à-vis Hebrew. The frank and affectionate recognition of Yiddish as the container and crucible of sixty generations of experience seems missing.

Generally, Yiddish uses Hebrew words for all references to the

†The Israeli campaign against Yiddish reached a true cease-fire with the establishment of a National Authority for Yiddish Culture, under the Ministry of Education, in 1996. The inaugural meeting of this Authority in 1999 was unpublicized, however—"thus," writes Gerald Stillman (in *Jewish Currents*, January 2000), "a major opportunity was lost to proclaim that the government had acknowledged Yiddish to be part of the national cultural heritage of Israel." According to Abraham Melamed, a former Knesset MK who was named president of the new Authority, "The State of Israel did not [even] allow a Yiddish newspaper to be published in the Jewish land. The idea was that all Jews in the State must speak only *Ivrit* [Sephardic Hebrew]. . . . Three generations of Israelis have been speaking *Ivrit*, so we can now afford a law in favor of Yiddish." (Melamed was interviewed in the Nov. 12, 1999, *Forverts*; Stillman translated the interview in *Jewish Currents*.)

Shortly afterward, however, Melamed resigned from the Authority and a planned Yiddish festival was canceled. At this writing, the role of the Authority in Israel is up in the air.

Bible, the *Talmud*, religious tenets, observances, rituals; for customs and ceremonies, holidays and historical events; and for certain concepts (*emes*, truth; *eytse*, advice). The words are spelled as they are in Hebrew—except in the USSR, where official pressures forced changes in the spelling!

The Hebrew alphabet consists only of consonants—twenty-two of them. In Yiddish, four of these consonants are used to represent vowel sounds: points above and below these letters indicate the pronunciation. This is less complicated than it sounds. It is as if "fame" were spelled fãm, "dawn" dan, "light" lit.

Experts differ in their estimates of the number of Hebrew words that are part of Yiddish. Yudel Mark, perhaps the world's ranking authority, has said that 10 percent of all Yiddish words are from Hebrew. Uriel Weinreich said that Hebrew constitutes over 15 percent of Yiddish. Nathan Ausubel guesses that Yiddish today contains 20 percent Hebrew, 70 percent German, and 10 percent other languages (chiefly Russian, Polish, Hungarian, and Romanian). My learned friend Maurice Samuel, who has as sensitive an expertise as one could hope for, guesses that Hebrew words account for 10 to 15 percent of the Yiddish vocabulary.

Yiddish has influenced Hebrew, much to the discomfiture of Hebraicists. For instance, the diminutive suffix, so widely employed in Yiddish to express affection, has been adopted in Hebrew. And since Hebrew contains no "four-letter" obscene words, its speakers, when driven to cursing, resort to Aramaic—or Yiddish.

Yiddish is only one of many vernaculars fashioned by Jews throughout the ages. Judeo-Greek was spoken in Byzantium, under Christian rule. Some Greek Jews still write Greek using the Hebrew alphabet, in a Judeo-Greek that contains relatively few Hebrew words or phrases and virtually no Yiddish. Persian Jews speak Judeo-Persian, which takes different forms in central Asia. Jews in the Caucasus Mountains, who date back to the time of the Second Temple, use a form of Farsi-Tat and have their own literature, rich in Hebraic, Aramaic, and biblical phrases.

The Jews of Spain wrote Spanish with the letters of the Hebrew alphabet; after they were driven out, in 1492, they brought this form to the Islamic countries where they found temporary asylum: Bulgaria, Greece, Turkey, North Africa. (See Ladino.)

In Italy, a Judeo-Latin vernacular arose that used Hebrew letters to write Italian (in prayer books and a translation of the Bible) because many Jews in Italy could not, or would not, decipher Latin letters, which were considered "monkish."

But Yiddish is the one that spread most widely, adapted itself most vigorously, and has flourished most successfully. Before World War II, approximately eleven million people throughout the world spoke Yiddish. Yiddish newspapers and journals existed all over Europe, the United States, Latin America, and Australia. A vital Yiddish theater flourished in Europe, the United States, and South America. The golden age of Yiddish literature—novels, stories, plays, social criticism, journalism—began in the middle of the nineteenth century and reached its peak in the early decades of the twentieth.

Hitler's gory harvest changed that forever.

Today, familiarity with Yiddish appears to be correlated directly with age: the older the Jew, the more can he or she be expected to understand Yiddish. I think it is safe to generalize that more Jews understand Yiddish than speak it; more can speak it than read it;* more can manage to read it than write it.

*The growth of academic programs in Yiddish at such prestigious institutions as Oxford, Columbia, and McGill Universities during the past three

(Continued on page 636)

I was long ago struck by the fact that any Jew who gives an affirmative answer to the question "Do you understand Yiddish?" does so with a sudden grin. Whatever else may be said of this

decades may have undone Rosten's generalization; there are probably now more college students who can read Yiddish than speak it. Other colleges giving instruction for credit in Yiddish include Brandeis, Brooklyn College, Duke University, George Washington, Indiana University at Bloomington, Ohio State, and the state universities of Massachusetts, Maryland, and Pennsylvania—among others.

In January 2001, the Dora Teitelboim Center for Yiddish Culture and Florida International University jointly launched the first Yiddish on-line college program in the world. Students can attend classes at the university in North Miami Beach, "attend" classes via the Internet and computer microphones, or pursue their studies on the Internet at their convenience. The program has also recruited Yiddish-speaking seniors in Florida to mentor the students (www.yiddishculture.org).

Internet Web sites are called *vebeter* in Yiddish; e-mail is *blizpost*. Some leading Yiddish-language *vebeter* include

1. the international "Mendele" listserv (mendele@lists.yale.edu), founded by Noyekh Miller in 1991 and named for Mendele Mokher Seforim, the *zeyde* (grandfather) of modern Yiddish literature. More than two thousand participants on the Mendele list trade insights and news about Yiddish, song lyrics, vocabulary, jokes, and more.
2. "A User's Guide to Yiddish on the Internet" (www.uyip.org), an excellent resource for beginners.
3. "Refoyl Finkl's *Yiddish Vebletl*" (www.cs.engr.uky.edu/~raphael/yiddish.html), which includes a Yiddish transliteration spell-check and a Yiddish song database.
4. "*Der Bay*" (www.derbay.org), established in 1991 by Philip "Fishl" Kutner in the San Francisco Bay Area and featuring a very useful FAQs guide to Yiddish resources.
5. The "Robert and Molly Freedman Jewish Music Archive" at the University of Pennsylvania (www.library.upenn.edu/friends/freed), which offers audio and video samples from the collection.
6. "Avivale's Yiddish Page" (www.starkman.com/aviva/yiddish.html), a charming and very diversified site; and
7. Ari Davidow's "Virtual Ashkenaz" (www.ivritype.com/ashkenaz/virtual.html), which features discussions of *new* Yiddish culture.

Most Yiddish *vebeter*—there are over eight thousand of them—are generously linked to others and will lead Yiddish-seeking surfers all around the globe.

gamin of a language, it inspires enormous affection.

In the technical world of linguistics, Yiddish is classified as "Judeo-German." But it also contains what philologists call Loez— which is Jewish correlates of Old French and Old Italian. *The Standard Jewish Encyclopedia* (Doubleday, 1966) offers this chronology: Initial Yiddish, 1000–1250 c.e.; Old Yiddish, 1250–1500; Medieval Yiddish, 1500–1750; Modern Yiddish, 1750 to date.

Philologists identify three main types of Yiddish: Lithuanian, Polish, south Russian (Ukrainian). (Romanian Yiddish is close to Polish Yiddish; Austrian and Hungarian versions are close to Ukrainian.) In the newspapers and journals published in the United States, Lithuanian Yiddish has predominated.

In the United States, Jewish immigrants, who were as noteworthy for their resourcefulness as for their rectitude, cheerfully borrowed English words, altered them to suit their own resilient requirements of case, mood, and inflection, arranged them in startling variations of traditional syntax ("A raise I should ask him for yet?" "Him you call a philosopher?"), negated negatives with breezy assurance ("I didn't agree and I didn't not agree"), and garnished Anglo-Saxon words with the heady spices of enthusiastic mispronunciation: *donton* (downtown), *izebox* (icebox), *svit-hot* (sweetheart), Abraham Lincohen, Judge **Vashington**.* Even as a child, I was enchanted by such blithe spirit.

Yiddish possesses an incomparable vocabulary of words to express shades of feeling; a juicy catalog of praises, expletives, and

*Such borrowings and hybrids have been a matter of great controversy among Yiddishists. One of the many bones of contention between the Yiddish *Forverts* and its Communist rival, the now defunct *Morgn Freiheit* (*Morning Freedom*, founded in 1922), was about linguistic purity, which Jews of the far Left (the *Freiheit*) tended to champion. See my note to Rosten's entry for **yekl**.

curses; and a richer array of characterization names than can be found, I think, in any other language on this globe: consider *nudnik, nebekh, shleper, shlump, shmendrik, shlemiel, tumler, kibitzer, ganef, shnook, shlump, mamzer, bren, A.K., kokhlefl, platke-makher, yenta, shtunk, yakne, alrightnik, bulbenik, plosher, boychik, khokhm, tsedudlter*—each of which holds an honored place in these pages.

The purists who sniff at Yiddish for its exuberant adoption of words from other languages should pause to reflect on the fact that of all the languages in the world, English has, from its very origins, been the most energetic borrower and lifter. "No language can show a more varied assortment of foreign 'loan-words' and foreign-inspired locutions." So say the distinguished Sir William A. Craigie and H. Kurath (in *Chambers' Encyclopedia*, Appleton-Century-Crofts, 1954).

Yiddish possesses a rich and immensely attractive literature—stories, novels, poems, essays; but much of it has not been translated.†

The reader will, I trust, forgive me for quoting myself:

---

†An enormous body of Yiddish literature has been salvaged, literally, from trash bins through the efforts of the National Yiddish Book Center, an organization founded by Aaron Lansky in 1980, when he was a graduate student studying Yiddish in Montreal. Lansky became aware that hundreds of private libraries of Yiddish books were being discarded when their elderly owners changed residences or died. With groups of young volunteers, he began saving Yiddish books from this fate. By 2000, the National Yiddish Book Center, headquartered in Amherst, Mass., had collected over 1.4 million books, including hundreds of rare and valuable volumes, and had strengthened the Yiddish collections of 437 libraries in twenty countries, including Harvard, Hebrew University, and the Library of Congress. Lansky became a MacArthur Foundation Fellow (the "genius award") for his efforts. The center is engaged in translation work—with an emphasis on women authors and other less-known writers and works not previously translated into English. The *Pakn Treger* (*Peddler with a Sack*), the center's Yiddish magazine, is a major new source of information about, and contribution to, Yiddish culture.

One thing is certain: It was in Yiddish that was created the unique and radiant culture, a triumph over excruciating adversity, of the *shtetl*. And it is in Yiddish that that civilization—so poor, so rich, so realistic, so romantic, so frightened, so brave, so raucous, so sensitive, so anxious, so gallant, so pathetic, so proud, so cynical, so sentimental, so irreverent, so pious, so resigned, so passionate and honorable and majestic—is preserved.

Yiddish incorporates the essence of a life which is distinctive and unlike any other.

—Israel Zangwill

With this cosmopolitan jargon, made of the rags of every language, he [Morris Rosenfeld, poet] created a music like that of a lamenting harp.

—Léon Bloy

To call Yiddish an offshoot of Middle High German with an admixture of Hebrew and Slavic [is entirely misleading] . . . the tone and spirit of [Yiddish] are as remote from German as the poetry of Burns is from the prose of Milton.

—Maurice Samuel

I am sure this never happened, but how I wish it had: Yuseleh Shpeisel, reporter for the *Forverts* (*Jewish Daily Forward*), dashed into a phone booth on Delancey Street, dropped his coins, dialed, barked, "Managing editor!," and cried, "Chief? Shpeisel. I've got a story that'll rip this town wide open! Hold the back page!"

Leonard and Manny, both lovers of Yiddish, were comparing its charms to those of other languages, and Lenny observed, "Do you know something remarkable? There's no word in Yiddish for 'disappointed'!"

"Really? I can't believe it. You *must* be wrong. Wait, I'll call my mother."

And to his mother, who barely spoke English, Manny said in fluent Yiddish, "*Mamele,* listen. Suppose I told you I was coming to dinner on Friday. And suppose you worked all day Friday to make me the finest meal ever—from *challah* and chopped liver and *gelfilte fish* and *kneydlakh* soup down through the chicken and *kugel* and *tsimes* and applesauce and two kinds of *strudel* for dessert. And on Friday, two minutes before I'm supposed to arrive, I telephone and say that something so important has come up that I just can't come to *Shabbes* dinner! What would you say?"

"What I would *say?*" wailed his mother. "I'd say, '*Oy, bin ikh* [am I] disappointed.'"

yidene^Y
yideneh^R

Pronounced YEED-*eh-neh,* to rhyme with "lead in a." The feminine form of *Yid.*

1. Derogatory: An elderly Jewish woman. *Yidene* is usually used in a scornful sense—to mean gossipy, interfering, stupid. *Yidene* can be a synonym for *yakne* and *yente,* and it is almost impossible to draw exact distinctions between them.

2. Any gossipy, uncultivated, shallow person, whether male or female, Jew or gentile. In this usage *yidene* is like "silly old woman," which in English is used for male fuddy-duddies.

   See yenta and yakhne.

Two *yidenes* were talking about their children. "My son?" said the first. "Who could ask for a better boy? Every Friday, rain or shine, he eats dinner at my house. Every summer, he makes me spend a month with him in Bayshore. Every winter he sends me to California!"

The second woman said, "I have a son, an angel, too. He's going to the most expensive psychiatrist in New York—every day, month in, month out, he goes there, and he talks, talks, talks each day for an hour. And do you know what he talks about, paying a hundred dollars an hour? Me!"

The ladies were having tea. As the hostess passed the cookies around, she said, "So take a cookie."

"I already had five," sighed Mrs. Bogen.

"You had, excuse me, six, but take another: who's counting?"

"My wife is so well read," said Nudelman, "and goes to so many lectures, and is so up to the minute on current events, that she can talk all night on any subject!"

"*My* wife," said Kugelman, "doesn't require a subject."

yikhes^Y
yiches^R
yichus, yihus

Pronounced YIKH-*ess*, with a strong uvular *kh* sound, in the Scottish or German manner. Hebrew: "pedigree," "genealogy."

Family status or prestige.

Y*ikhes* refers to more than pedigree or family "name," for *yikhes* must be deserved, earned as well as inherited.

The crucial ingredients of *yikhes* are learning, virtue, philanthropy, service to the community. One who does not live up to his family's past record swiftly "loses" his *yikhes*.

The highest *yikhes* attaches to the man of learning. *Yikhes* is the hallmark of the "aristocrat"—in the sense that highest deference among Jews was accorded those learned in the *Talmud*.

Yikhes does not attach itself merely to the successful or the wealthy; wealth or success never warrants or receives the respect accorded knowledge.

A *shadkhn* would enter in his record of a marriageable male or female a careful listing of the scholars, teachers, and rabbis in the family background. The greater the learning, the higher the *yikhes*.

Newly rich Jews would try to marry their daughter to a young man of illustrious background, however poor—that is, a boy with true *yikhes*. And for their son, they sought a rabbi's daughter.

A universe of *yikhes* aspiration lies in the heartfelt cry of a Jewish woman at the seashore: "Help! Help! My son the doctor is drowning!"

Yisroel
Yisrael

Pronounced *yis*-RO-*el* or *yis*-ROY-*el*, to rhyme with "this goal" or "miss royal." Hebrew: Israel. (In Hebrew the pronunciation is *yis*-*ra*-EL.)

1. The land of Israel. See Eretz Yisroel.
2. The people of Israel, the Jews. In Jewish literature, *Yisroel* is used interchangeably with "Jew" and "Hebrew."

3. The name Jacob assumed after he wrestled with the Angel of the Lord (Genesis 32:29).*
4. The collective name given the twelve tribes who left Egypt and settled in Canaan.
5. The name of the northern kingdom of Israel (933–722 B.C.E.) that was formed when the ten tribes seceded after the death of King Solomon.
6. The name of the state of Israel *(Medinat Yisroel)*.

In Tel Aviv, one dark and ominous night, 06 Dash 4 looked up and down the street, darted into the apartment building, slipped the Colt into his outer pocket, knocked on the door of 2-D twice, paused, knocked once, paused, knocked twice again.

From inside, a voice inquired, "Who is it?"

"Horowitz?" whispered 06 Dash 4.

The door opened: a bald-headed little man in pajamas said, *"Sholem aleichem."*

"The oranges," murmured 06 Dash 4, "are ripe in Valencia."

"Ha-anh?" asked Horowitz.

"The oranges," repeated 06 Dash 4, more slowly, "are ripe . . . in Valencia!"

A light entered the eyes of the bald-headed little man. "Ahh! I'm Horowitz the violin teacher. You want Horowitz the spy. Upstairs, 3-E."

---

*In the *Torah*, the Hebrews are referred to as both the "House of Jacob" and the "Children of Israel." The Talmudic rabbis interpreted the first phrase to refer to the women, the second to the men.

Yizkor ^R
Yisker ^Y

Pronounced YISS-*kor*, to rhyme with "disk oar." Hebrew:
"May [God] remember."
  Memorial service for the dead, held in a synagogue.

*Y*izkor is the shortened, popular name for the memorial service, *Hazkarat Neshamot* (Remembrance of the Souls),
which is recited on the eighth day of *Pesach*, second day of *Shevuos*,
eighth day of *Succos*, and *Yom Kippur*. (Sephardic Jews observe a
Yizkor on *Yom Kippur* eve.)

  The service opens with a reading that emphasizes the living
more than the dead, asking that those in the congregation be permitted to "complete in peace the number of our years . . . [and]
bear ourselves faithfully and blamelessly during the years of our
pilgrimage." The deceased kinfolk and parents, "the crown of our
head and glory," are recalled: "Their desire was to train us in the
good and righteous way, to teach us Thy statutes and commandments, and to instruct us to do justice and to love mercy. We
beseech Thee, O Lord, grant us strength to be faithful to their
charge while the breath of life is within us."

  Private prayers are then recited in memory of close relatives, in
which God is asked to "bind [his, her] soul in the bond of eternal
life, in the company . . . of all the righteous. . . ." Those reciting
Yizkor also pledge to perform "acts of charity and goodness" in
honor of the deceased's memory.

  The service continues with a congregational prayer, *El Mole
Rakhamim*, which petitions God to grant peace and eternal life to
the departed souls. This concept is interpreted as continuing
communion of the generations, the idea that children and grandchildren are a person's life after death—for their memory keeps

the beloved dead "alive."

Part of the *Yizkor* service is a memorial to the martyrs, of all generations, who died for the sanctification of God's name (see **Kiddush Hashem**). Many synagogues recite a special memorial prayer for the six million victims of the Nazis. In Israel, a *Yizkor* prayer is said for the men and women who fell while defending Israel in its War of Independence.

In the United States, some Jews who observe virtually no other religious service continue to observe *Yizkor*. Some close shop, or do not report to work, for the entire day, to attend a synagogue or temple.

Yizkor began long ago in the west of Germany to honor and remember the great number of Jews who had been slaughtered during the First Crusade (1096 C.E.).

yold

Pronounced YULD, to rhyme with "culled." Possibly from Hebrew: *yeled,* "child," "boy."

1. A simpleton, a fool, a boob, a yokel, a harmless dolt; one whose gullibility and naiveté get him into **trouble.***
   "Oh, is he a *yold!*" "He fooled me completely; I acted like a real *yold.*"

---

*Rosten presents several Yiddish words used to identify dim-witted people. It is worth noting that actual mental retardation, like many physical handicaps, was traditionally considered to be a disqualifying "blemish"—deaf people, for example, were excluded by Jewish law from leading public prayer, serving as witnesses, or purchasing property. However, with the advent of the disability rights movement in the 1970s and 1980s, the American Jewish community began to respond to people with "special needs" and their demands for inclusion. Today, synagogue and summer camp accessibility is

(Continued on page 646)

2. A dude, a fop.

See shlemiel.

A *yold* is a man who walks into a friend's antique shop and calls out, "Hello! What's new?"

A *melamed*, discovering that he had left his comfortable slippers back in the house, sent a student after them with a note for his wife. The note read: "Send me your slippers with this boy."

When the student asked why he had written "your" slippers, the *melamed* answered, "*Yold!* If I wrote 'my' slippers, she would read 'my' slippers and would send me her slippers. What could I do with her slippers? So I wrote 'your' slippers; she'll read 'your' slippers and send me mine."

Yom Kippur ^R
Yom Kiper ^Y

Pronounced *yum-*KIP-*per,* to rhyme with "hum dipper." Hebrew: "Day of Atonement." (Some scholars trace *kippur* to the Babylonian for "purge," "clean," "wipe off.")

The last day of the annual Ten Days of Penitence; one of the two High Holy Days of the Jewish calendar. *Yom Kippur* is, perhaps, the day that has the strongest hold on the Jewish conscience.

(Continued from page 645)

a fairly high priority in all the Jewish denominations, and autism, retardation, deafness, blindness, and other forms of handicap no longer automatically block families from celebrating life passages, including *bar* and *bat mitzva,* in synagogue settings.

Rosh Hashanah marks the first day of the Ten Days of Penitence (*Yamin Noraim*). On that day, say the Orthodox, all people stand before God for judgment; but the Lord's decision is made on the *last* of the Ten Days—and that day is *Yom Kippur*.

The *Mishnah* instructs pious Jews not to eat or drink, wash, or wear shoes on *Yom Kippur*. Maimonides gravely advises: "All people should confess their sins, and turn away from them on Yom Kippur."

Because Jews hold that offenses against other people can be forgiven only by other people (and not by God), on *Yom Kippur* eve, before *Kol Nidre,* Jews would hurry around to those they had offended or been unfriendly to during the year—and beg their pardon. The observing Jew must ask forgiveness from another three times before giving up.

Pious families would gather and ask forgiveness of each other for any slights, insensitivities, or injustices they might have committed against each other in the preceding year. Husband and wife would ask each other's forgiveness; children would ask forgiveness of each parent and of each other; each parent would ask each child for forgiveness! The custom is still observed in part or in whole, according to the degree and interpretation of religious commitment. The idea is that each mortal should enter upon *Yom Kippur* with a clear conscience.

The synagogue service begins just before nightfall the evening before *Yom Kippur.** In the synagogue, the cantor stands before the ark, flanked on either side by an honored worshiper from the congregation. Each carries a large scroll of the *Torah*. The cantor

---

*Jewish holidays all begin the "evening before" because the *Torah* counts the days of creation that way: "God called the light Day, and the darkness He called Night. And there was evening and there was morning, a first day" (Genesis 1:5). *Shabbes,* too, goes from sundown to sundown.

and two worshipers act as representatives for the congregation standing before an invisible judge and tribunal. They recite:

> By the authority of the Court on high, and by the authority of the Court below, by the permission of the Lord, blessed be He, and by the permission of this sacred congregation, we declare it lawful to pray with those who have transgressed.

This is thrice repeated; then the **cantor*** begins to intone *Kol Nidre*.

Prayers on the day of *Yom Kippur* continue, virtually without interruption, from morning until after sunset. Since purity of conscience is the leitmotif of the day, white predominates. The curtain of the ark and the *Torah* coverings are white (they may be of varied colors during the year). The rabbi and cantor wear white robes; many in the congregation where white *yarmulkes* (skull-caps) instead of the traditional black.

The primary feature of *Yom Kippur* is the Confession, repeated several times during the day. It involves a cataloging of no fewer than fifty-six categories of sin. Traditional Jews repeat the formula, "For the sin we have committed before Thee by [stating one of the fifty-six varieties], O God of forgiveness, forgive us, pardon us, grant us remission," and beat their breasts.

It is interesting to note that the confession of guilt is recited as a collective "we," not as an individual "I." On *Yom Kippur*, Jews "share" each other's transgressions—plus general responsibility for the misdeeds and shortcomings of humankind.† The ecu-

---

*Many small congregations do not have cantorial or even rabbinic leadership and rely on knowledgeable congregants to lead *Yom Kippur* services.

†Numerous other Jewish prayers are spoken in a collective voice. "The conviction that personhood is shaped, nourished and sustained in community," writes theologian Judith Plaskow (in *Standing Again at Sinai*, HarperCollins,

menical spirit is not new to Jews. In Jewish tradition, the community is responsible as long as even one sinner is left on earth: for example, the thief would not have sinned had "we" provided for him or taught him proper morals.

The morning reading from the Prophets teaches the kind of repentance God seeks of us (Isaiah 58:5–7):

> Is not this the fast that I have chosen?
> To loose the bands of wickedness,
> To undo the heavy burdens,
> And to let the oppressed go free,
> And that ye break every yoke?
> Is it not to deal thy bread to the hungry
> And that thou bring the poor that are cast out to thy house?
> When thou seest the naked, that thou cover him,
> And that thou hide not thyself from thine own flesh? ‡

During the afternoon, the reading is the book of Jonah, the theme of which is God's clemency toward those who truly repent.

The liturgical readings, which describe the atonement ritual as it was practiced in the ancient Temple, hold a prominent place in

1990), "is a central assumption [of] Judaism. . . . The covenantal history that begins with Abraham, Isaac and Jacob finds its fulfillment only at Sinai, when the whole congregation answers together. . . ."

‡ In the more modern Jewish Publication Society rendering:

> No, this is the fast I desire:
> To unlock fetters of wickedness,
> And untie the cords of the yoke
> To let the oppressed go free;
> And to break off every yoke.
> It is to share your bread with the hungry,
> And to take the wretched poor into your home;
> When you see the naked, to clothe him,
> And not to ignore your own kin.

the *Yom Kippur* service. When the cantor describes how the high priest would pronounce, on this one occasion during the entire year, the Ineffable Name of God, he follows the ancient practice, bowing and prostrating himself, and many of the pious join him.

As the long day of fasting, prayer, inner searchings, and new resolve draws to a close, the *Ne'ilah* service is held. This service begins the moment the setting sun is level with the treetops; and it is timed to end with the appearance of the first stars. The congregation makes one last profession of repentance and one last request for forgiveness.

> Lord, though every power be Thine,
> And every deed tremendous,
> Now, when heaven's gates are closing,
> Let Thy grace defend us.

Yom Kippur ends with the cantor proclaiming in a loud voice: "Hear, O Israel, the Lord our God, the Lord is One," followed by a thrice-repeated "Blessed be the Name of the One whose glorious kingdom endures forever." (These are the words with which the worshipers responded when the high priest pronounced God's Name in the Temple.) Then he repeats seven times, "The Lord is God." These are statements a pious Jew is expected to utter at the moment of death; they have indeed been the last words of many martyrs.

Yom Kippur ends with the call of the *shofar*.

Yom Kippur is sometimes called "Instant Lent."

Belinsky could scarcely believe his eyes: there, on the Day of Atonement, at a table right in the window of the Sea King Restaurant, sat his old friend Herman Hochshuler—eating oysters!

Into the Sea King dashed Belinsky. "Herman! *Gottenyu!* Eating?! Today?! And *oysters?!!*"

"So?" said the blasé Hochshuler. "Isn't there an 'r' in *'Yom Kippur'?*"*

yontif ᴿ
yontev ʸ
yontiff, yom tov
yontifdik (adjective)
yontifdig

Pronounced ʏᴜɴ-*tiff* in Yiddish, to rhyme with "bum miff."
From Hebrew: *yom*, "day," *tov*, "good."
1. Holiday. "The post office is closed; it's *yontif.*" "A good *yontif* to you!" "Happy *yontif!*"
2. A celebration, a festivity. "I felt all *yontifdik* that day."

Several odd facts about *yontif:*
The two Hebrew words *yom*
... even though there Yiddish was a Hebrew word for holiday: *chag* (pronounced ᴋʜᴀɢ).*

speakers generally used *chag* to indicate Gentile, as opposed to Jewish, holidays.

To say "Good *yontif!*" would seem redundant, like "a good good-day," except that *yontif* has been given its own meaning: "holiday."

In Israel, people use the Hebrew phraseology: "*Chag sameach*" (ᴋʜᴀɢ *sa*-ᴍᴇʏ-*yakh*), "Happy holiday."

*The punch line refers to a non-Jewish *bobe-mayse* (old wives' tale) that advises against eating oysters during months lacking r in their names—that is, the summer months, when shellfish were thought to spoil more easily.

A denizen of Flatbush, having seen the pope in one of the large, public papal audiences, felt obliged to send His Holiness a Christmas greeting. It ran: "Good *yontif*, Pontiff."

yortsayt[Y]
yortzeit[R]
yahrzeit

Pronounced either YAWR-*tzite*, to rhyme with "court site," or YAR-*tzite*, to rhyme with "dart site." The first pronunciation is Yiddish, the second German. German: *Jahrzeit*, "year's time" or "anniversary."

The anniversary of someone's death.

Many observances are incumbent on religious Jews to commemorate the death of someone in the family. (See Kaddish and Yizkor.)

On the anniversary, a memorial candle or lamp is lighted in the home, and another in the synagogue, where it burns from sunset to sunset. A burning light is comm... ity—perhaps as suggested in Proverbs 20:27: "The spirit of man is the candle of the Lord. . . . "*

Orthodox Jews fast all day at *yortsayt*.†

The *yortsayt* ceremony, by the way, is the one religious ritual of Jews that has no Hebrew name (although *Yom hashana* means

*Modern Jewish Publication Society translation: "The lifebreath of man is the lamp of the Lord."

† *Chasidim* often observe the *yortsayts* of their *tzaddikim* (holy men) with celebration rather than rituals of mourning.

"Day of the year").

The idea of an annual prayer for the dead probably was adopted when the Jews were in **Persia**.‡ The custom of lighting a candle for the dead may come from that proverb in Proverbs that compares the soul to a candle; it may also have come about after the Christians spread the ceremony so widely.§

believed to cross a bridge spanning hell, which narrowed for the wicked until they tumbled but widened for the righteous to guide them to the realm of light. Jewish candlelighting for the *yortsayt* may have been influenced by these religious concepts, which were dominant in Persia.

§According to Rabbi Louis Jacobs (*The Jewish Religion, A Companion*, Oxford University Press, 1995), *yortsayt* observances "originated among the Ashkenazim, German Jews, in the 15th century, from where they spread to other Jewries." However, "As early as Talmudic times there is a reference to people abstaining from eating meat and drinking wine on the anniversary of the death of a parent (*Nedarim* 12a)." Jacobs adds: "Even Jews not otherwise known for their strict observance of the rituals" may light a *yortsayt* candle and follow *yortsayt* customs.

A worthwhile collection of brief essays about the meaning of Jewish rituals of death and mourning is Rabbi Jack Riemer's *Jewish Reflections on Death* (Schocken, 1974).

Z

zaddik
See tzaddik.

zaftik ^Y
zaftig ^R

Pronounced ZOFF-*tik*, to rhyme with "soft wick," or ZOFF-*tig*,
to rhyme with "boff wig." From German: "juicy," "luscious."

1. Juicy. "What a *zaftik* plum!"
2. Provocative, seminal, germinal. "The book is full of
   zaftik ideas."
3. Plump, buxom, well-rounded (of a female). This is the
   most freque...

Zaftik describes in one word what it takes two hands, outlining
an hourglass figure, to do.

_____

Two *zaftik* matrons talking:
   "I think women like us should take a
greater interest in politics. . . . Tell me,
what do you think of the **Common Market**?"*
   "I still prefer the A & P."

*Predecessor to the
European Union.

zchuss
See skhus.

zets ^Y
zetz ^R

Pronounced as spelled; rhymes with "gets." From German: *setzen,* "to attack," "to fall upon."

A strong blow or punch. "He gave me a *zets* I'll never forget!"

zeyde ^Y
zayde ^R

Pronounced ZEY-*deh,* to rhyme with "fade a." From Polish: *dziad,* "grandfather," "old man."

1. Grandfather. "My *bobe* and *zeyde* came to visit yesterday."*

You may say to any old Jew, "How are ____ Frenchman or Chinese will ____ who is not his grandfa-

In Israel, an American visitor saw an elderly Jew crying, tears streaming down his face.

The American, who ____ the old man's wailing, asked, "*Zeyde* . . . please . . . why are you weeping so bitterly?"

"Because—I want to be with my people!" sobbed the old man.

"But you *are,* in Israel, the Promised Land."

"I mean with my people in Miami!" said the *zeyde.*

*Just as *Bubby* has become an Americanized nickname for grandmothers, *Zeyde* is often pronounced ZEY-*dee* and used as a nickname by non-Yiddish-speaking grandchildren.

zhlob[Y]
zhlub[R]

Pronounced ZHLUB or ZHLAWB, to rhyme with "rub" or "baub(le)." From Polish: *zhlòb*, "coarse fellow."

1. A coarse, insensitive, ill-mannered person. "He acts like a *zhlob*, that *zhlob*."
2. A clumsy, gauche, graceless person. "Vassar-Shmassar, the girl's still a *zhlob*."
3. An oaf, a yokel, a bumpkin. "What can you expect from such a *zhlob*?"

A Jew came running into a railway station, perspiration pouring down his face as he panted and cried, "Stop, train, stop!"

A *zhlob* said, "What's the matter?"

"I missed my train!" the man exclaimed. "By twenty measly seconds!"

"The way you're carrying on," said the *zhlob*, "on⸺ you had missed it by an hour!"

See also klutz, bu⸺

Zion
Tziyon

Pronounced TZEE-*yohn*, to rhyme with "see bone."
Hebrew: Zion.
The land of Israel.

Since the first exile of the Jews to Babylonia, Zion has been synonymous with the idea of a reunited Jewish people in their own, original homeland. "By the rivers of Babylon, there we sat

A denizen of Flatbush, having seen the pope in one of the large, public papal audiences, felt obliged to send His Holiness a Christmas greeting. It ran: "Good *yontif,* Pontiff."

yortsayt^Y
yortzeit^R
yahrzeit

Pronounced either YAWR-*tzite,* to rhyme with "court site," or YAR-*tzite,* to rhyme with "dart site." The first pronunciation is Yiddish, the second German. German: *Jahrzeit,* "year's time" or "anniversary."

The anniversary of someone's death.

Many observances are incumbent on religious Jews to commemorate the death of someone in the family. (See Kaddish and Yizkor.)

On the anniversary, a memorial candle or lamp is lighted in the home, and another in the synagogue, where it burns from sunset to sunset. A burning light is connected with the idea of immortality—perhaps as suggested in Proverbs 20:27: "The spirit of man is the candle of the Lord. . . ."*

Orthodox Jews fast all day at *yortsayt.*†

The *yortsayt* ceremony, by the way, is the one religious ritual of Jews that has no Hebrew name (although *Yom hashana* means

---

*Modern Jewish Publication Society translation: "The lifebreath of man is the lamp of the Lord."

† *Chasidim* often observe the *yortsayts* of their *tzaddikim* (holy men) with celebration rather than rituals of mourning.

Into the Sea King dashed Belinsky. "Herman! *Gottenyu!* Eating?! Today?! And *oysters?!!*"

"So?" said the blasé Hochshuler. "Isn't there an 'r' in 'Yom Kippur'?"*

yontif ᴿ
yontev ʸ
yontiff, yom tov
yontifdik (adjective)
yontifdig

Pronounced ʏᴜɴ-*tiff* in Yiddish, to rhyme with "bum miff." From Hebrew: *yom,* "day," *tov,* "good."

1. Holiday. "The post office is closed; it's *yontif.*" "A good *yontif* to you!" "Happy *yontif!*"
2. A celebration, a festivity. "I felt all *yontifdik* that day."

S everal odd facts about *yontif:*
    The two Hebrew words *yom tov* were joined to make a Yiddish word, even though there was a Hebrew word for holiday: *chag* (pronounced ᴋʜᴀɢ).*

> *Yiddish speakers generally used *chag* to indicate Gentile, as opposed to Jewish, holidays.

To say "Good *yontif!*" would seem redundant, like "a good good-day," except that *yontif* has been given its own meaning: "holiday."

In Israel, people use the Hebrew phraseology: "*Chag sameach*" (ᴋʜᴀɢ sa-ᴍᴇʏ-*yakh*), "Happy holiday."

---

*The punch line refers to a non-Jewish *bobe-mayse* (old wives' tale) that advises against eating oysters during months lacking r in their names—that is, the summer months, when shellfish were thought to spoil more easily.

"Day of the year").

The idea of an annual prayer for the dead probably was adopted when the Jews were in Persia.‡ The custom of lighting a candle for the dead may come from that proverb in Proverbs that compares the soul to a candle; it may also have come about after the Christians spread the ceremony so widely.§

‡Zoroastrian beliefs included a special veneration for fire. The dead were believed to cross a bridge spanning hell, which narrowed for the wicked until they tumbled but widened for the righteous to guide them to the realm of light. Jewish candlelighting for the *yortsayt* may have been influenced by these religious concepts, which were dominant in Persia.

§According to Rabbi Louis Jacobs (*The Jewish Religion, A Companion,* Oxford University Press, 1995), *yortsayt* observances "originated among the Ashkenazim, German Jews, in the 15th century, from where they spread to other Jewries." However, "As early as Talmudic times there is a reference to people abstaining from eating meat and drinking wine on the anniversary of the death of a parent (*Nedarim* 12a)." Jacobs adds: "Even Jews not otherwise known for their strict observance of the rituals" may light a *yortsayt* candle and follow *yortsayt* customs.

A worthwhile collection of brief essays about the meaning of Jewish rituals of death and mourning is Rabbi Jack Riemer's *Jewish Reflections on Death* (Schocken, 1974).

Z

zaddik
See tzaddik.

zaftik ^Y
zaftig ^R

Pronounced ZOFF-*tik*, to rhyme with "soft wick," or ZOFF-*tig*, to rhyme with "boff wig." From German: "juicy," "luscious."
1. Juicy. "What a *zaftik* plum!"
2. Provocative, seminal, germinal. "The book is full of *zaftik* ideas."
3. Plump, buxom, well-rounded (of a female). This is the most frequent American usage.

Zaftik describes in one word what it takes two hands, outlining an hourglass figure, to do.

Two *zaftik* matrons talking:
"I think women like us should take a greater interest in politics. . . . Tell me, what do you think of the **Common Market**?"*
"I still prefer the A & P."

*Predecessor to the European Union.

zchuss
See skhus.

zets^Y
zetz ^R

Pronounced as spelled; rhymes with "gets." From German: *setzen*, "to attack," "to fall upon."

A strong blow or punch. "He gave me a *zets* I'll never forget!"

zeyde ^Y
zayde ^R

Pronounced zey-*deh*, to rhyme with "fade a." From Polish: *dziad*, "grandfather," "old man."

1. Grandfather. "My *bobe* and *zeyde* came to visit yesterday."*
2. An old man. You may say to any old Jew, "How are you, *zeyde*?" just as a Frenchman or Chinese will affectionately greet an old man who is not his grandfather.

In Israel, an American visitor saw an elderly Jew praying, tears streaming down his face.

The American, who could not bear the old man's wailing, asked, "*Zeyde* . . . please . . . why are you weeping so bitterly?"

"Because—I want to be with my people!" sobbed the old man.

"But you *are*, in Israel, the Promised Land."

"I mean with my people in Miami!" said the *zeyde*.

---

*Just as *Bubby* has become an Americanized nickname for grandmothers, *Zeyde* is often pronounced zey-*dee* and used as a nickname by non-Yiddish-speaking grandchildren.

zhlob^Y
zhlub^R

Pronounced ZHLUB or ZHLAWB, to rhyme with "rub" or "baub(le)." From Polish: *zhlòb*, "coarse fellow."
1. A coarse, insensitive, ill-mannered person. "He acts like a *zhlob*, that *zhlob*."
2. A clumsy, gauche, graceless person. "Vassar-Shmassar, the girl's still a *zhlob*."
3. An oaf, a yokel, a bumpkin. "What can you expect from such a *zhlob?*"

A Jew came running into a railway station, perspiration pouring down his face as he panted and cried, "Stop, train, stop!"

A *zhlob* said, "What's the matter?"

"I missed my train!" the man exclaimed. "By twenty measly seconds!"

"The way you're carrying on," said the *zhlob*, "one would think you had missed it by an hour!"

See also klutz, bulvon, grob.

Zion
Tziyon

Pronounced TZEE-*yohn*, to rhyme with "see bone." Hebrew: *Zion*.

The land of Israel.

Since the first exile of the Jews to Babylonia, Zion has been synonymous with the idea of a reunited Jewish people in their own, original homeland. "By the rivers of Babylon, there we sat down, yea, we wept when we remembered Zion" (Psalm 137).

Wherever they have lived, traditional Jews have turned in the direction of Zion when they prayed. The great Hebrew poet of the Middle Ages, Judah ha-Levi, who was also a physician and a philosopher, wrote:

> My heart is in the East
> But I am in the farthest West,
> How then can I taste what I eat,
> And how can food to me be sweet?

Pious Jews would seek to be buried in Zion, and it became customary to bring a small sack of earth from the Holy Land to be placed in one's coffin, to provide a symbolic burial, at least, in the soil of *Zion*.*

Chaim Weizmann, who later became the first president of Israel, was an ardent Zionist. As an illustrious scientist, he had access to many important European personages. One day he visited Paul Ehrlich, the discoverer of "606," a drug used in the treatment of syphilis. Weizmann sought to convince Ehrlich of the importance of the Zionist cause and to enlist his support. He spoke earnestly and at great length, until Ehrlich broke in: "You know, Dr. Weizmann, hundreds of people come to see me each week. I never give them more than five minutes each. You have already taken up forty-five minutes of my time!"

*When the leader of the Lubavitcher *Chasidim*, Rabbi Menachem Schneerson, died without an heir in 1994, the question of whether he would be buried in Brooklyn, his lifelong home, or in Zion (Israel), to where he had never journeyed, was invested with tremendous meaning by Jewish pundits. An Israeli burial, they judged, would have meant that the wing of the Lubavitcher movement committed to the idea that Schneerson was the *meshiakh* would take over the reins of power. He ended up buried in Brooklyn, and the messianic speculation has since been fairly subdued. See Rosten's entry for **meshiakh**.

"The difference, Dr. Ehrlich," replied Weizmann, "is that they come to get an injection—and I, to give you one."

Zohar ᴿ
Zoyer ʸ

Pronounced ᴢᴏʜ-*harr*, to rhyme with "go far." From *Sefer ha Zohar*, or *Book of Splendor*. The most important book of the cabalistic movement, probably written in the thirteenth century.

The most influential book in the literature of the *cabala* is the volume called the *Zohar*, believed to have been written/assembled by the Spanish rabbi Moses or Moshe de Leon—who deliberately attributed the work to a second-century rabbi, **Simeon ben Yohai.***

The *Zohar* is an utterly fantastic compendium of superstitions, mysticism, folklore, and abracadabra used to reveal supposedly hidden meanings in the Bible. It is a hodgepodge of abstruse codes, dreams, symbols; a cryptic excursion into demonology (and angelology); it explains ways of exorcising devils; it delves into the transmigration of human souls; it is steeped in supernaturalism and astrology. The *Zohar* is especially beholden to a "science of numbers" that endows numbers with special meanings and powers in a method called *gematria* (see my entry for cabala and gematria); for example, a numerical value is assigned to each

---

*Rabbi Simeon ben Yohai, an important figure in the *Talmud*, is described as denouncing Rome and then fleeing persecution by spending thirteen years in a cave with his adult son, Rabbi Eleazar. It is during this exile that the *Zohar* was allegedly written as a revelation from the Prophet Elijah.

Hebrew letter, then a text from the Bible is analyzed, and the text is arranged in every conceivable pattern—vertically, backward, diagonally, upside down, in a triangle shape, as a hexagon, a palindrome, an acronym, an acrostic, etc., etc. One name—of a prophet, say—may be arranged in all the possible permutations of its separate letters.

The *Zohar* also contains some wonderful stories, ethical pronouncements, and moving prayers. The book exerted a significant influence on the religious thought of large groups of Jews, particularly the *Chasidim*. The rabbis often warned the laity not to court mental danger by too deep immersion in the *Zohar*'s cosmological mumbo jumbo—and I can only agree with them.*

*Readers wishing to endanger their mental state might check out Daniel C. Matt's poetic translation of *Zohar* excerpts: *Zohar, the Book of Enlightenment* (Paulist Press, 1988).

english-yiddish dictionary

alas .... *nebekh*

all vows .... *Kol Nidre*

alphabet .... *alef-beys*

amen .... *amen*

anniversary of a death ... *yortsayt*

annoy .... *tshepe*

another .... *nokh*

apostate .... *meshumed*

apostatizing .... *geshmat*

arrogance .... *chutzpa*

audacity .... *chutzpa*

aunt .... *tante, mume*

authority .... *maven*

bachelor .... *singlemon* (Yinglish)

backside .... *tokhes*

bad guy ... no-goodnik (Yinglish)

bandit .... *bandit*

bargain .... *metsieh*

bastard .... *mamzer*

bathhouse .... *mikve*

beam with pride .... *kvell*

beans; something
   worthless .... *bobkes*

beast (esp. cow) .... *beheyme*

beet soup .... *borsht*

beggar, panhandler ..... *shnorrer*

belly button, belly .... *pupik*

big-shot .... *makher, k'nocker*

birdy .... *feygele*

black *(adj.)* .... *shvartz*

black, Negro,
   African-American .... *shvartze*

bless   *bentsh*
         (infinitive: *bentshn*)

blessing .... *brokhe*

blessing over bread .... *motzi*

blessing over wine ...... *Kiddush*

boarder *(female)* ...... *boarderkeh*
   (Yinglish)

boob *shmendrik, shmo* (Ameridish)

boss .... *balebos*

braggart, blowhard *fonfer, k'nocker,*
                plosher, trombenik

brandy .... *shnaps*

bribe .... *shmeer*

bride .... *kale*

bridegroom .... *khosn*

brother .... *bruder*

brother-in-law .... *shvoger*

buckwheat .... *kashe*

bum .... *lump, oysvorf*

bum *(female)* .... *bummerkeh*
  (Yinglish)

bumpkin .... *Kuni Leml*

bundle .... *pekl*

bungalow .. *kochaleyn* (Ameridish)

burst .... *plotz*

buxom .... *zaftik*

bystander .... *dopes*

cantor .... *chazzen*

celebration .... *simcha*

charity .... *tzedakah*

charity can, "piggy" bank .. *pushke*

chat .... *shmooz*

cheater .... *fonfer, ganef*

chicken fat .... *shmaltz*

children .... *kinder, kinderlakh*

circumciser .... *moyl*

circumcision .... *bris*

clod .... *klutz, shlimazl, shmegegge*

coarse, vulgar .... *grob*

coin .... *shekel*

collective farm *(Israeli)* ... *kibbutz*

college .... *yeshiva*

comedian, entertainer .... *batkhn*

commandment .... *mitzva*

commotion .... *shtus, tsimes*

community leaders .... *balebatim*

compassion .... *rakhmones*

complain ...... *burtshen, kvetchen*

complainer .... *kvetcher*

comrade .... *chaver*

comraderie .... *chevra*

conformist .... *alrightnik*

confused ...... *fartutst, farshadet,*
             farblonzhet, tsedudlt,
               tsedreyt, tsetumlt

congratulations .... *mazel tov*

converted
  (from Judaism) .... *geshmat*

cookie .... *kichel*

cooking spoon .... *kokhlefl*

countryman .... *landsman*

cousin .... *kuzin* (m.), *kuzine* (f.),
             shvesterkind

cozy .... *heymish*

crap .... *drek, chozzerai*

crawl under the skin .. *krikh arayn*
             in di beyner

crazy .... *meshuge*

creep *(noun)* .. *parkh, paskudnyak*

cripple *(noun)* .... *kalike*

crook .... *ganef, gazlen, yentser*

dairy *(adj.)* .... *milkhedik*

darling; little
  grandmother ... *bubeleh, bubee*

daughter .... *tokhter*

daughter-in-law .... *shnur*

Day of Atonement ... *Yom Kippur*

dazed .... *fartshadet*

demon .... *dybbuk*

destroyed, ended .... *mekhule*

devil .... *tayvl*

diaspora, dispersion .... *galus*

divorce document .... *get*

dizzy .... *fartshadet*

doorpost amulet .... *mezuzah*

doubletalker .... *fonfer*

dour .... *farbisn*

downstairs neighbor .. *donstairsike*

(Yinglish)

dowry .... *nadn*

drag *(verb)* .... *shlep*

dragger .... *shlep, shleper*

dreamer .... *luftmentsh*

drunkard .... *shiker*

dude .... *yold*

dumplings (filled) .. *kreplekh, knish*

dumplings (matzo ball) . *kneydlekh*

earlocks .... *payess*

eat (quickly, noisily, overeat) .. *fress*

embittered .... *farbisn*

engagement .... *shidekh*

enlightenment .... *Haskala*

error; gaffe .... *bulba* (potato)

evil eye,

    guard against .... *keyn eynhore*

exegesis .... *midrash*

exhausted .... *oysgematert*

exile .... *galut*

expert .... *balmelokhe, maven*

fag, fairy .... *feygele*

family .... *mishpokhe*

far be it .... *kholile; khas vesholem*

father .... *tate, tata*

father-in-law .... *shver*

finagler .... *dreykop*

fireball; high-energy person .. *bren*

fit to eat .... *kosher*

five .... *fin*

flattery .... *kopdreyenish*

flunky .... *nokhshleper*

fool .. *nar, nefesh, shnook, shlemiel,*

    shlimazl, shmegegge, yold

foolishness .... *narishkayt*

forbidden (dietary) .... *treyf*

forgive .... *moykhl*

forgive the comparison ... *l'havdil*

fornicate .... *shtup, yents*

friend .... *chaver*

fringes .... *tsitsis*

funeral .... *levaye*

fuss *(verb)* ...... *potshke, potshkee*

    (Ameridish), *tarrarom*

Galician Jew .... *Galitzianer*

Garden of Eden ...... *Gan Eyden*

genius .... *gaon*

Gentile, non-Jew .... *goy*

"Gentile brains" ..... *goyisher kop*

Gentile man (young) .... *sheygets*

Gentile woman (young) ... *shiksa*

gentle .... *eydl*

gentleness .... *eydlkayt*

German .... *Yekke*

girl .... *moyd*

gnaw, grind .... *grizhen*

God .... *Gott*

God (names of) ... *Adonai, Adoshem,*

Elohim, Gott, Hashem,
Jehovah, Riboyne Shel Oylem,
Shekhinah, Yah, Yahveh, YHVH
God forbid
(no evil eye) ...... *keyn eynhore*
go-getter .... *kokhlefl*
golden land (America) ... *goldene*
medina
good deed .... *mitzva*
good for nothing ..... *oyf kapores*
gorge *(verb)* .. *fres* (infinitive: *fresn*)
gossip, busy-body .. *platke-makher,*
yakhne, yenta, yidene
grandchild .... *eynikl*
grandchildren .... *eyniklekh*
grandfather .... *zeyde*
grandmother .... *bobe*
great-grandchild .... *ur-eynikl*
great-grandchildren .. *ur-eyniklekh*
great-grandfather ...... *elter zeyde*
great-grandmother ...... *elte bobe*
groan *(noun)* .... *krekhts*
groan *(verb)* .... *krekhtsn*
groom .... *khosn*
group, circle of friends .... *chevra*
gut .... *kishke*

hairsplitting .... *pilpul*
hallelujah .... *halevay*
Hanukkah lamp .... *menorah*
hat, black with fur ...... *shtrayml*
hell .... *Gehenna*
hello .... *sholem aleichem*
hell with it .... *a kapore*
help! .... *gevalt!*
heretic .... *apikoyres*

hijinx .... *shtik*
hole in the head ...... *lokh in kop*
holiday .... *yontif*
homey .... *heymish*
honker .... *fonfer*
honor .... *koved*
house of study
(synagogue) .... *besmedresh*
hullabaloo .... *tarrarom*
human being .... *mentsh*
husband .... *man*

if only .... *halevay*
ignoramus .... *am horets*
illegitimate child .... *mamzer*
illness .... *krenk*
incubus .... *dybbuk*
in-law:
a child's father-in-law . *mekhutn*
a child's
mother-in-law .... *mekhuteneste*
insanity, wackiness ..... *mishegas*
intestines .... *kishke*
Israel .... *Yisroel, Zion*

jerk . *shnook, shmegegge, shmendrik*
Jew .... *Yid* [YEED]
Jew (pejorative) .. *kike, sheeny, yid*
|YID|
Jew, good Jew,
beautiful Jew ...... *sheyner Yid*
Jewish law .... *Halakha*
Jewish star .... *Mogen David*
Joe Shmo .... *Chaim Yankel*
joker .... *kibitzer, lets*
Judaeo-Spanish .... *Ladino*

judge . . . . *dayen*

judgment, good judgment . . *seykhl*

junk . . . . *chozzerai, shlock*

kidder . . . . *kibitzer*

King of kings . . *Melekh Ham'lokhim*

knapsack . . . . *pekl*

knot . . . . *knipl*

knowledge, understanding . *seykhl*

land . . . . *medine*

landlord . . . . *lendler* (Yinglish)

land of Israel . . . . *Eretz Yisroel*

law . . . . *Halakha*

leavened,

   unfit for Passover . . *chometzdik*

liar, deceiver *(male)* . . . . . . *bluffer*

lifestyle, outlook . . . . *shteyger*

Lithuanian Jew . . . . *Litvak*

loathesome thing . . . . . . *khaloshes*

loser . . . . *shlemiel, shlimazl*

lost . . . . *farblondzhet*

luck, good luck . . . . *mazel*

makeshift;

   slapped together . . *ongepatshket*

man . . . . *mentsh*

man of the people . . . *folks-mentsh*

Master of the

   Good Name . . . . . *Bal Shem Tov*

match . . . . *shidakh*

maybe . . . . *epes*

meat, not dairy . . . . *fleyshik*

memorial service . . . . *Yizkor*

mercy . . . . *rakhmones*

merit . . . . *skhus*

messiah . . . . *meshiakh*

messy, messed up . . . . *farpatshket*

mix-up . . . . *mish-mosh*

modest . . . . *eydl*

modesty . . . . *eydlkayt*

money, cash . . . . *gelt, mazuma*

                           (Yinglish), *shekel*

monster . . . . *golem*

more . . . . *nokh*

morsel . . . . *pitsl*

mother . . . . *mame, mama*

mother-in-law . . . . *shviger*

mother tongue . . . . . . *mameloshn*

   (Yiddish)

mourner's prayer . . . . *Kaddish*

mouth, yap . . . . *pisk*

mourning ritual . . . . *shivah*

music (dance music,

   wedding music) . . . . . . *klezmer*

musicians . . . . *klezmorim*

mysticism . . . . *cabala*

nag *(noun)* . . . . . *nudzh* (Yinglish)

nag *(verb)* . . . . *nudzhn, utsn*

navel . . . . *pupik*

nephew . . . . *plimenik*

nerve . . . . *chutzpa*

neutral (dietetically) . . . . . . *pareve*

New Year

   (Head of the Year) . . . . *Rosh

      Hashanah*

next-door neighbor . . *nexdoorekeh*

                           (Yinglish)

niece . . . . *plimenitse*

Ninth of Av . . . . *Tisha B'Av*

noodles . . . . *lokshn*

nose .... *shnoz*

numerology .... *gematria*

oaf .... *bulvon, lump, klutz, golem, zhlob*

obsession .... *aynredenish, tsutshepenish*

of blessed memory *alev ha-sholem*

old bag .... *yente, yidene*

old fart .... *alter kocker*

old wives' tale .... *bobe-mayse*

omigod .... *Gottenyu*

onion board .... *pletsl*

ornament .... *tsatske*

outcast .... *oysvorf*

outcry .... *shtus*

outlook, lifestyle .... *shteyger*

pacifier .. *sharopnikel* (Ameridish)

package .... *pekl*

pancake .... *latke*

paradise .... *Gan Eden*

party .... *simcha*

Passover .... *Pesach*

Passover ritual and meal ... *seder*

pathos, "corn" .... *shmaltz*

pauper .... *kaptsn*

peace .... *sholem*

pedigree .... *yikhes*

penis *(slang)* .... *putz, shmuck*

Pentecost .... *Shevuos*

performance "tricks"
or routines .... *shtik*

perhaps .... *epes*

person .... *nefesh*

pest .... *nudnik, nudzh* (Yinglish)

pester .... *nudzhn*

phew! .... *feh!*

phylacteries .... *tefillin*

piece .... *pitsl, shtik*

pig .... *chozzer*

pioneer .... *khalutz*

pious .... *frum*

pisser .... *pisher*

"Pitch and Patience"
(card game) ...... *pisha paysha*

pity .... *rakhmones*

plague (cholera) .... *kholerye*

plagues .... *makes*

pleasure *(noun)* .... *mekhaye*

potato .... *bulba*

pour; torrential rain ..... *khlyape*

practical aspects .... *tachlis*

pray .... *daven*

prayer of arrival ... *Shehekheyanu*

prayer of mourning ..... *Kaddish*

prayers, afternoon .... *mincha*

prayers, evening .... *mairev*

prayers, morning .... *shachris*

prayer shawl .... *tallis*

prayer wall hanging ..... *mizrach*

preacher .... *maggid*

prick *(pejorative slang)* ...... *putz*

priest (Jewish) .... *Kohen*

pride, joy .... *naches*

profanation of
God's name .... *chillul hashem*

prostitute .... *nafke, kurve*

punch *(noun)* ...... *khmalye, zets*

push, poke .... *shtup*

question .... *kashe*

quorum for prayer ...... *minyan*

rabbi .... *rebbe, rov*
rabbinical court .... *bes din*
rabbi's wife .... *rebbitsin*
reincarnation .... *gilgul*
revolting thing .... *khaloshes*
robber ...... *holdupnik* (Yinglish)
robe (for burial) .... *kitl*
robot .... *golem*

Sabbath .... *Shabbes*
Sabbath guest .... *Shabbes oyrekh*
saint .... *tzaddik*
sanctification of
  God's name .. *Kiddush Hashem*
scholar, expert ... *talmid khokhem*
school .... *cheder, Talmud Torah,*
  yeshiva (college)
scream *(noun)* .... *kvitsh*
scream *(verb)* .... *kvitshn*
screech *(noun)* .... *pisk*
scroll .... *megillah*
secret Jew .... *Marrano*
sensitive .... *eydl*
sensitivity .... *eydlkayt*
sexton, synagogue
  attendant .... *shammes*
shit .... *drek*
shroud .... *kitl*
sick .... *kronk*
sin .... *aveyre*
sister .... *shvester*
sister-in-law .... *shvegerin*
skullcap .... *yarmulke*
slap *(noun)* .... *frosk*

slaughterer,
  ritual butcher .... *shoykhet*
slip, slip-up .... *glitch*
slob .... *paskudnyak, shlump*
slobby .... *paskudne*
smack .... *patsh*
smarts, intelligence .... *seykhl*
smoked salmon .... *lox*
snack *(noun)* .... *nosh*
snack *(verb)* .... *noshn*
snuff, pinch of ...... *shmek tabik*
so? .... *nu?*
social director .... *tumler*
something, a bit .... *epes*
son .... *ben*
son .... *zun*
son-in-law .... *eydem*
soul .... *neshome, nefesh*
Spanish-Portuguese
  Jews .... *Sephardim*
spoon for cooking .... *kokhlefl*
spread .... *shmeer*
status .... *yikhes*
steambath, sweat bath .. *shvitsbod*
stew .... *tsimes*
stinky, stinking ..... *farshtinkener*
story .... *megillah*
storytelling, exegesis ...... *agada*
student of Talmud .. *yeshiva bokher*
stuffed fish .... *gefilte fish*
sucker, mark .... *yekl*
suddenly .... *in mitn drinen*
sweater, one who sweats .. *shvitser*
swindle *(verb)* .... *yentsn*
swindler .... *yentser*
synagogue .... *shul*

Tabernacles . . . . *Succos*
tailor . . . . *shneider*
Talmudic debate . . . . *pilpul*
teacher . . . . *melamed*
thief . . . . *ganef, gazlen*
thug . . . . *lump*
to life . . . . *l'chayim*
torment *(verb)* . . . . *mutshn*
town . . . . *shtetl*
treasure . . . . *oytser*
troubles . . . . *tsores*
tumult . . . . *kopdreyenish*

uncle . . . . *feter, onkl*
unemployed man . . . . *batlen,*
                                  luftmentsh
upstairs neighbor . . . . . *opstairsike*
                                  (Yinglish)

vagina *(slang)* . . . . *knish*

voluptuous . . . . *zaftik*

wasted . . . . *aroysgevorfn*
wedding . . . . *khasene*
wedding canopy . . . . *chuppa*
weird death . . . . *mise meshune*
widow . . . . *almone*
wife . . . . *vayb, froy*
wig . . . . *sheytl*
wisdom . . . . *khokhme*
wise man or woman . . . . *khokhem*
wit, wag . . . . *lets*
witticism, wisecrack . . . . *vits*
woe is me . . . *vey iz mir, Gottenyu*
woes . . . . *tsores*
woman of high energy . . . . . *berye*

yak, yammer . . . . . . *hak a tshaynik*
yesterday's day:
    not on your life . . *a nekhtiker tog*